SCHAUM'S
outlines

Quantum Mechanics

Quantum Mechanics

Second Edition

Yoav Peleg, Ph.D.

Reuven Pnini, Ph.D.

Elyahu Zaarur, M.Sc.

Eugene Hecht, Ph.D.

Schaum's Outline Series

New York   Chicago   San Francisco   Lisbon   London
Madrid   Mexico City   Milan   New Delhi   San Juan
Singapore   Sydney   Toronto

The **McGraw·Hill** Companies

YOAV PELEG, Ph.D., received his doctorate in physics from the Technion Institute of Technology in Haifa, Israel. He has published to date dozens of articles, mostly in the area of general relativity and quantum cosmology. Currently he is working as a researcher with Motorola Israel.

REUVEN PNINI, Ph.D., received his doctorate in physics from the Technion Institute of Technology in Haifa, Israel. He has published to date several articles, mostly in the area of condensed matter physics. He is currently the Chief Scientific Editor of Rakefet Publishing Ltd.

ELYAHU ZAARUR, M.Sc., received his master of science in physics from the Technion Institute of Technology in Haifa, Israel. He has published more than a dozen books on physics. He is currently the Managing Director of Rakefet Publishing Ltd.

EUGENE HECHT, Ph.D., is a full-time member of the Physics Department of Adelphi University in New York. He has authored nine books including *Optics*, 4th edition, published by Addison Wesley, which has been the leading text in the field, worldwide, for over three decades. Dr. Hecht has also written *Schaum's Outline of Optics* and *Schaum's Outline of College Physics*.

Schaum's Outline of QUANTUM MECHANICS

1 2 3 4 5 6 7 8 9 0   CUS/CUS   1 5 4 3 2 1 0

Sponsoring Editor: Charles Wall
Production Supervisor: Tama Harris McPhatter
Project Manager: Preeti Longia Sinha, Glyph International

ISBN 978-0-07-162358-2
MHID 0-07-162358-2

CIP data is available with the Library of Congress.

Preface

The main purpose of this second edition of *Quantum Mechanics* is to make an already fine book more usable for the student reader. Accordingly, a great deal of effort has been given to simplifying and standardizing the notation. For example, a number of modern QM textbooks now distinguish operators from other quantities by placing a cap (^) over the corresponding symbol for the operator. This simple emendation can nonetheless be very helpful to the student and that practice has been adopted throughout this edition. Similarly I have avoided using the same symbol to represent different quantities, inasmuch as this can be unduly confusing. Wherever necessary, discussions have been extended and the prose has been clarified. The all-but-unavoidable typographical and other minor first-edition errors have been corrected. Additionally, all of the art has been redrawn to improve visual readability, content, clarity, and accuracy. A substantial number of new introductory-level solved problems have been added to ensure that the student can gain a good grasp of the basics before approaching a more challenging range of questions. Indeed, it is my intention to add more such problems in future editions.

If you have any comments or suggestions, or favorite problems you'd like to share, send them along to Prof. E. Hecht, Physics Department, Adelphi University, Garden City, NY 11530 or if you prefer e-mail, genehecht@aol.com.

EUGENE HECHT
Freeport, NY

Contents

Contents

Quantum Mechanics

CHAPTER 1

Introduction

1.1 The Particle Nature of Electromagnetic Radiation

Isaac Newton considered light to be a beam of particles that set the pervading aether vibrating. The resulting aether waves guided the light particles along their way. During the nineteenth century, numerous experiments involving interference and diffraction demonstrated that light was some sort of wave. Optics was integrated into electromagnetic theory by James Maxwell who showed that light is electromagnetic. Nonetheless, the phenomenon of blackbody radiation, which was studied toward the end of the nineteenth century, could not be explained within the classical framework of electromagnetic theory. In 1900, Max Planck arrived at a formula that matched the blackbody radiation curves. He subsequently derived that formula by assuming that the oscillators in the walls of the emitting chamber could have only certain "quantized" energies. Planck's analysis was basically wrong but it introduced the powerful idea of energy quantization; energy can only appear in whole-number multiples of some basic amount.

In 1905, Einstein proposed a return to the particle theory of light. He asserted that a beam of light of frequency ν consists of energy quanta, or photons, each possessing energy $h\nu$, where $h = 6.62 \times 10^{-34}$ joules second (J·s) (i.e., Planck's constant). Einstein showed how the introduction of the photon could account for the unexplained characteristics of both blackbody radiation and the photoelectric effect. About 20 years later, the photon was shown to exist as a distinct entity (the Compton effect; see Problem 1.3).

The *photoelectric effect* was discovered by Heinrich Hertz in 1887. It is one of several processes by which electrons can be removed from a metal surface. A schematic drawing of the apparatus for studying the photoelectric effect is given in Fig. 1.1.

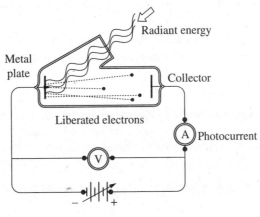

Fig. 1.1

A beam of radiant energy (usually ultraviolet) impinges on the metal plate and knocks electrons free. The electrons fly off with a range of kinetic energies (KE). By putting a negative potential (V) on the collector some of the electrons are turned back. The critical potential V_S such that $eV_S = KE_{max}$ (the maximum kinetic

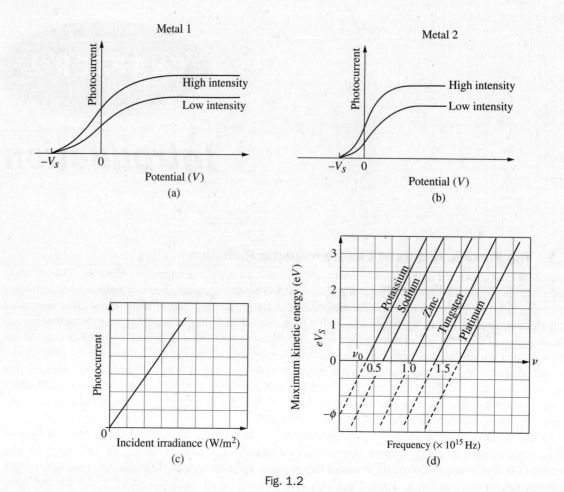

Fig. 1.2

energy of the emitted electrons) is called the *stopping potential*. The experimental results of the photoelectric effect are summarized in Fig. 1.2 and below.

(i) When radiant energy shines on a metal surface, a current flows almost instantaneously, even for a very weak incident beam.

(ii) For fixed frequency and retarding potential, the photocurrent is directly proportional to the incident intensity, or more accurately the incident irradiance (W/m^2) as shown in Fig. 1.2(c).

(iii) For constant frequency and irradiance, the photocurrent decreases with the increase of the retarding potential V, and finally reaches zero when $V = -V_S$.

(iv) For any given surface, the stopping potential V_S depends on the frequency of the light but is independent of irradiance. For each metal there is a threshold frequency ν_0 that must be exceeded for photoemission to occur; no electrons are emitted from the metal unless $\nu > \nu_0$, no matter how large the incident irradiance.

The experimental correlation between the stopping potential V_S and the frequency of radiant energy can be represented by

$$eV_S = h\nu - h\nu_0 = h\nu - \phi \tag{1.1}$$

where h is the same for all metals (Planck's constant) and ϕ is the *work function*. The work function is the minimum energy needed to liberate an electron from the surface of the metal target. It is different for each metal (see Table 1.1). In Fig. 1.2(d), each line intersects the ν axis at a value of ν_0, and the eV_S axis at a value of $-\phi$, both of which are characteristic of the particular target metal.

Table 1.1   Representative Work Function Values

Metal	Work Function (ϕ in eV)
Na	2.28
Co	3.90
Al	4.08
Pb	4.14
Zn	4.31
Fe	4.50
Cu	4.70
Ag	4.73
Pt	6.35

1.2   Quantum Particles

Quantum particles (photons, electrons, etc.) are not "particles" in our usual sense of the word; they do not behave like mini-cannonballs. Quantum particles are more like oscillating puffs of matter possessed of both wavelike and particlelike properties that defy conceptualization. The dynamic parameters of quantum particles (energy E and momentum $\mathbf{p}$) are linked to their wave parameters (frequency ν and wave or propagation vector $\mathbf{k}$) by the relations

$$\begin{cases} E = h\nu = \hbar\omega \\ \mathbf{p} = \hbar\mathbf{k} \end{cases} \tag{1.2}$$

where $\hbar = h/2\pi$.

In the second half of the 1800s, it was discovered that atoms emit or absorb electromagnetic radiation at only well-determined frequencies. This fact can be explained by assuming that the energy of an atom can take on only certain discrete values. In other words, the energy of an atom is quantized. This was one of the central assertions made by Niels Bohr in 1913 when he proposed his theory of the hydrogen atom. The existence of discrete energy levels was demonstrated in 1914 by the Frank–Hertz experiment. Bohr supposed that the electron moves in orbits restricted by the requirement that its angular momentum be an integral multiple of $h/2\pi$. For a circular orbit of radius r, the electron velocity v is given by

$$m_e v_n r_n = \frac{nh}{2\pi} \qquad n = 1, 2, \ldots \tag{1.3}$$

The relation between the Coulomb force and the centrifugal force can be written in *MKS* units as

$$k_0 \frac{e^2}{r_n^2} = \frac{m_e v_n^2}{r_n} \tag{1.4}$$

where e is the charge of the electron and k_0 is the Coulomb constant. We assume that the nuclear mass is infinite. Combining Eq. (1.3) and Eq. (1.4) we obtain

$$v_n = \frac{2\pi e^2 k_0}{nh} \tag{1.5}$$

and

$$r_n = \frac{1}{4\pi^2} \frac{n^2 h^2}{m_e e^2 k_0} \tag{1.6}$$

The orbital energy is then

$$E_n = \frac{1}{2} m_e v_n^2 - \frac{e^2}{r_n} = -\frac{2\pi^2 m_e e^4 k_0^2}{n^2 h^2} \tag{1.7}$$

Bohr postulated that electrons in these orbits do not radiate, despite their acceleration; they are in *stationary states*. Electrons can make discontinuous transitions from one allowed orbit to another. The change in energy will appear as radiation of frequency

$$\nu = \frac{E - E'}{h} \tag{1.8}$$

The physical basis of the Bohr model remained unclear until 1923, when de Broglie put forth the hypothesis that material particles have wavelike characteristics; a particle of energy E and momentum $\mathbf{p}$ is associated with a wave of angular frequency $\omega = E/\hbar$ and a wave vector $\mathbf{k} = \mathbf{p}/h$. The corresponding wavelength is therefore

$$\lambda = \frac{2\pi}{k} = \frac{h}{p} \tag{1.9}$$

This is the *de Broglie relation*.

1.3 Wave Packets and the Uncertainty Relation

The wave and particle aspects of electromagnetic radiation and matter can be united through the concept of a *wave packet*. A wave packet is a superposition of waves resulting in a sinusoidal pulse. We can construct a wave packet in which the component harmonic waves interfere with each other almost completely outside a given spatial region (Fig. 1.3). We thus obtain a localized wave packet that is a useful representation of a classical particle. A three-dimensional wave packet consisting of a superposition of plane waves may be written as

$$f(\mathbf{r}) = \frac{1}{(2\pi)^{3/2}} \int g(\mathbf{k}) e^{i\mathbf{k}\cdot\mathbf{r}} d\mathbf{k} \tag{1.10}$$

or in one dimension,

$$f(x) = \frac{1}{\sqrt{2\pi}} \int_{-\infty}^{\infty} g(k) e^{ikx} dk \tag{1.11}$$

The evolution of wave packets is determined by the *Schrödinger equation* (see Chap. 3). When a wave packet evolves according to the postulates of quantum mechanics (see Chap. 4), the widths of the curves $f(x)$ and $g(k)$ are related by

$$\Delta x \Delta k > 1 \tag{1.12}$$

Using the de Broglie relation $p = \hbar k$, we have

$$\Delta p \Delta x > \hbar \tag{1.13}$$

This is the *Heisenberg uncertainty relation*: if we try to construct a highly localized wave packet in space, then it is impossible to associate a well-defined momentum with it. In contrast, a wave packet with a defined momentum within narrow limits must be spatially very broad. Note that since $\hbar$ is very small, the notions of

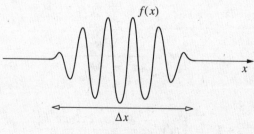

Fig. 1.3

classical physics will fail only for a microscopic system (see Problem 1.17). The uncertainty relation acts to reconcile the wave–particle duality of matter and radiation (see Problem 1.4).

Any wave pulse can be imagined to be composed of an infinite number of superimposed sinusoidal component waves. Each of these travels with a velocity known as the *phase velocity* whereas the pulse or wave packet travels with the *group velocity*. For a wave of angular temporal frequency $\omega = 2\pi\nu$ and angular spatial frequency (or propagation number) $k = 2\pi/\lambda$, the phase velocity is

$$v_p = \frac{\omega}{k} = \lambda\nu \qquad (1.14)$$

This is the rate at which a point of constant phase on any one of the constituent harmonic waves travels through space. By contrast, the pulse travels with the speed v_g which is related to the angular frequency ω and propagation number k of the component waves by the relation

$$v_g = \frac{d\omega}{dk} \qquad (1.15)$$

SOLVED PROBLEMS

1.1. Consider the experimental results of the photoelectric effect described in Sec. 1.1, i–iv. For each result discuss whether it would be expected on the basis of the classical properties of electromagnetic waves.

SOLUTION

(i) An electron in a metal will be free to leave the surface only after the incident beam provides its binding energy. Because of the continuous nature of the electromagnetic radiation, we expect the energy absorbed on the metal's surface to be proportional to the irradiance of the beam (energy per unit time per unit area), the area illuminated, and the time of illumination. A simple calculation (see Problem 1.14) shows that in the case of an irradiance of 10^{-10} W/m^2, photoemission can be expected only after 100 h. Experimentally, the delay times that were observed for the same irradiance were not longer than 10^{-9} s. Classical theory is thus unable to explain the instantaneous emission of electrons from the metal.

(ii) With the increase of radiant energy, the energy absorbed by the electrons in the metal increases. Therefore, classical theory predicts that the number of electrons emitted (and thus the current) will increase proportionally to the irradiance. Here classical theory is able to account for the experimental result.

(iii) The result described in Sec. 1.1, iii shows that there is a distribution in the energies of the emitted electrons. The distribution in itself can, within the framework of the classical theory, be attributed to the varying degrees of binding of electrons to metal, or to the varying amount of energy transferred from the beam to the electrons. But the fact that there exists a well-defined stopping potential independent of irradiance indicates that the maximum energy of released electrons does not depend on the amount of energy reaching the surface per unit time. Classical theory is unable to account for this.

(iv) According to the classical point of view, emission of electrons from the metal depends on the irradiance of the incident beam but not on its frequency. The existence of a frequency below which no emission occurs, however large the irradiance, cannot be predicted within the framework of classical theory.

In conclusion, the classical theory of electromagnetic radiation is unable to fully explain the photoelectronic effect.

1.2. Interpret the experimental results of the photoelectric effect in view of Einstein's hypothesis of the quantization of radiant energy.

SOLUTION

(i) According to the hypothesis that light consists of photons, we expect that a photon will be able to transfer its energy to an electron in a metal, and therefore it is feasible that photoemission occurs instantaneously even at a very small irradiance. This is contrary to the classical view, which proposes that the emission of electrons depends on continuous accumulation of energy absorbed from the incident beam.

(ii) According to quantum theory, irradiance is equal to the energy of each photon multiplied by the number of photons crossing a unit area per unit time. It is reasonable that the number of emitted electrons per unit time (which is equivalent to the current) will be proportional to the incident irradiance.

(iii) The frequency of the electromagnetic radiation determines the energy of the photons $h\nu$. Therefore, the energy transferred to electrons in a metal due to light absorption is well defined, and thus for any given frequency there exists a maximum kinetic energy of the photoelectrons. This explains the effect described in Fig. 1.2.

(iv) Equation (1.1) can be given a simple interpretation if we assume that the binding energy of the electrons that are least tightly bound to the metal is $\phi = h\nu_0$. The maximum kinetic energy of emitted electrons is $h\nu - \phi$. Using the definition of stopping potential, eV_S is the maximum kinetic energy; therefore, $eV_S = h\nu - h\nu_0$.

1.3. Consider the Compton effect (see Fig. 1.4). According to quantum theory, a monochromatic electromagnetic beam of frequency ν is regarded as a collection of particlelike photons, each possessing an energy $E = h\nu$ and a momentum $p = h\nu/c = h/\lambda$, where λ is the wavelength. The scattering of electromagnetic radiation becomes a problem of collision of a photon with a charged particle. Suppose that a photon moving along the x axis collides with a particle of mass m. As a result of the collision, the photon is scattered at an angle θ, and its frequency is changed. Find the increase in the photon's wavelength as a function of the scattering angle.

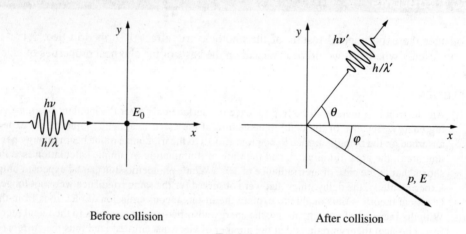

Before collision   After collision

Fig. 1.4

SOLUTION

First, since the particle may gain significant kinetic energy, we must use it by relativistic dynamics. Applying energy conservation we obtain

$$\text{(before collision)} \quad \underbrace{h\nu}_{\text{photon}} + \underbrace{E_0}_{\text{particle}} = \underbrace{h\nu'}_{\text{photon}} + \underbrace{E}_{\text{particle}} \quad \text{(after collision)} \tag{1.3.1}$$

where E_0 is the rest energy of the particle ($E_0 = mc^2$). The magnitudes of the momenta of the incident and scattered photons are, respectively,

$$p_\lambda = \frac{h\nu}{c} = \frac{h}{\lambda} \quad \text{and} \quad p_{\lambda'} = \frac{h\nu'}{c} = \frac{h}{\lambda'} \tag{1.3.2}$$

The scattering angle θ is the angle between the directions of $\mathbf{p}_\lambda$ and $\mathbf{p}_{\lambda'}$. Applying the law of cosines to the triangle in Fig. 1.5, we obtain

$$p^2 = p_\lambda^2 + p_{\lambda'}^2 - 2p_\lambda p_{\lambda'} \cos\theta \tag{1.3.3}$$

Recall that for a photon $pc = h\nu$; therefore, multiplying both sides of Eq. (1.3.3) by c^2, we obtain

$$h^2\nu^2 + h^2\nu'^2 - 2h^2\nu\nu' \cos\theta = p^2c^2 \tag{1.3.4}$$

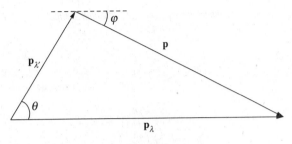

Fig. 1.5

Using Eq. (1.3.1) we have

$$h\nu - h\nu' = E - E_0 \Rightarrow h^2\nu^2 + h^2\nu'^2 - 2h^2\nu\nu' = E^2 + E_0^2 - 2EE_0 \qquad (1.3.5)$$

Relying on relativity theory, we replace E^2 with $E_0^2 + p^2c^2$. Subtracting Eq. (1.3.4) from Eq. (1.3.5), we obtain

$$-2h^2\nu\nu'(1 - \cos\theta) = 2E_0^2 - 2EE_0 \qquad (1.3.6)$$

Therefore, using Eq. (1.3.1),

$$h^2\nu\nu'(1 - \cos\theta) = E_0(E - E_0) = m_ec^2(h\nu - h\nu') \qquad (1.3.7)$$

We see that $\dfrac{h}{m_ec}(1 - \cos\theta) = \dfrac{\nu - \nu'}{\nu\nu'}c = \dfrac{c}{\nu'} - \dfrac{c}{\nu} = \lambda' - \lambda$. Therefore, the increase in the wavelength $\Delta\lambda$ is

$$\Delta\lambda = \lambda' - \lambda = \frac{h}{m_ec}(1 - \cos\theta) \qquad (1.3.8)$$

This is the basic equation of the *Compton effect.*

1.4. Consider a beam of light passing through two narrow, vertical, parallel slits that are very close together. When either one of the slits is closed, the irradiance distribution observed on a screen placed far beyond the barrier is a broad diffraction peak (see Fig. 1.6). When both slits are open, the peaks almost completely overlap and the pattern is as shown in Fig. 1.7: an interference pattern within the diffraction envelope. Note that this pattern is not the two single-slit diffraction patterns superposed. Can this phenomenon be explained in terms of classical particlelike photons? Is it possible to demonstrate particle aspects of light with this experimental setup?

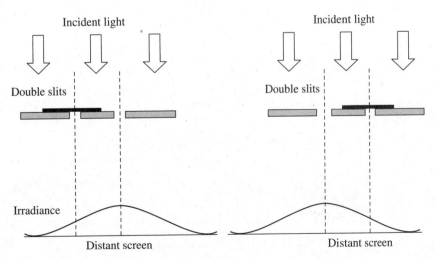

Fig. 1.6

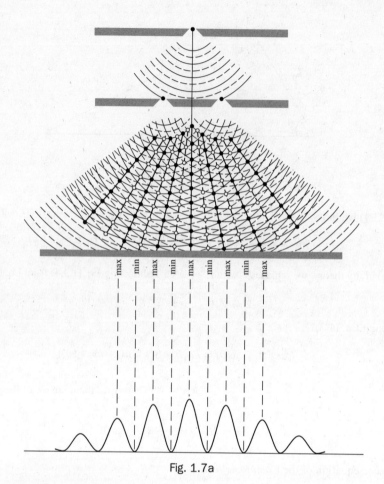

Fig. 1.7a

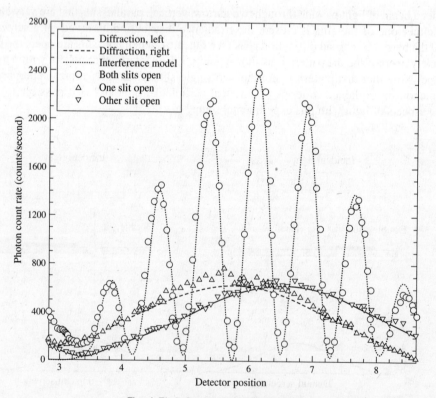

Fig. 1.7b   *Courtesy TECHSPIN Inc.*

SOLUTION

Suppose that the beam of light consisted of a stream of pointlike classical particles. If we consider each of these particles separately, we note that each one must pass through one of the slits. Therefore, the pattern obtained when the two slits are open must be the superposition of the patterns obtained when each of the slits is open separately. This is not what is observed in the experiment. The pattern actually obtained can be explained only in terms of interference of the light passing simultaneously through both of the slits (see Fig. 1.7).

However, it is possible to observe particle aspects of light in this system: if the light intensity is very weak, the photons will reach the screen at a low rate. If a photographic plate is placed at the screen, the pattern will be formed slowly, one point at a time. This indicates the arrival of separate photons on the screen. Note that it is impossible to determine which slit each of these photons passes through; such a measurement would destroy the interference pattern.

1.5. Figure 1.8 describes schematically an experimental apparatus known as Heisenberg's microscope whose purpose is to measure the position of an electron. A beam of electrons of well-defined momentum p_x moving in the positive x direction scatters light shining along the negative x axis. An electron will scatter a photon that will be detected through the microscope.

According to optics theory, the precision with which the electron can be localized is

$$\Delta x \sim \frac{\lambda}{\sin \theta} \tag{1.5.1}$$

where λ is the wavelength of the light. Show that if we minimize Δx by reducing λ, this will result in a loss of information about the x-component of the electron momentum.

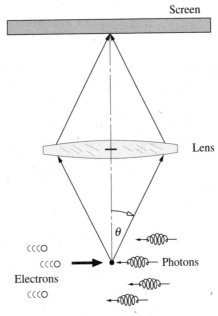

Fig. 1.8 Heisenberg microscope.

SOLUTION

According to quantum theory, recording light consists of photons, each with a momentum $h\nu/c$. The direction of the photon after scattering is undetermined within the angle subtended by the aperture, i.e., 2θ. Hence the magnitude of the x-component of the photon is uncertain by

$$\Delta p_x \sim 2 \frac{h\nu}{c} \sin \theta \tag{1.5.2}$$

Therefore,

$$\Delta x \, \Delta p_x \sim 2 \frac{h\nu}{c} \sin \theta \frac{\lambda}{\sin \theta} \sim 4\pi\hbar \tag{1.5.3}$$

We can attempt to overcome this difficulty by measuring the recoil of the screen in order to determine more precisely the x-component of the photon momentum. But we must remember that once we include the microscope as part of the observed system, we must also consider its location. The microscope itself must obey the uncertainty relations, and if its momentum is to be specified, its position will be less precisely determined. Thus, this apparatus gives us no opportunity for violating the uncertainty relation.

1.6. Prove that the Bohr hydrogen atom approaches classical conditions when n becomes very large and small quantum jumps are involved.

SOLUTION

Let us compute the frequency of a photon emitted in the transition between the adjacent states $n_k = n$ and $n_l = n - 1$ when $n \gg 1$. We define the *Rydberg constant* $R = \dfrac{2\pi^2 m_e e^4 k_0^2}{h^3 c} = 1.093 \times 10^7 \text{ m}^{-1}$. So, $E_k = \dfrac{ch}{n_k^2} R$ and $E_l = \dfrac{ch}{n_l^2} R$. Therefore, the frequency of the emitted photon is

$$\nu = \frac{n_k^2 - n_l^2}{n_k^2 n_l^2} cR = \frac{(n_k + n_l)(n_k - n_l)}{n_k^2 n_l^2} cR \tag{1.6.1}$$

$n_k - n_l = 1$, so for $n \gg 1$ we have

$$n_k + n_l \cong 2n \qquad n_k^2 n_l^2 \cong n^4 \tag{1.6.2}$$

Therefore, $\nu \cong 2cR/n^3$. According to classical electromagnetic theory a rotating charge with a frequency f will emit radiation of frequency f. On the other hand, using the Bohr hydrogen model, the orbital frequency of the electron around the nucleus is

$$f_n = \frac{v_n}{2\pi r_n} = \frac{4\pi^2 m_e e^4 k_0^2}{n^3 h^3} \tag{1.6.3}$$

or $f_n = 2cR/n^3$, which is identical to ν.

1.7. Show that the uncertainty relation $\Delta x \Delta p > \hbar$ forces us to reject the semiclassical Bohr model for the hydrogen atom.

SOLUTION

In the Bohr model we deal with the electron as a classical particle. The allowed orbits are defined by the quantization rules: the radius r of a circular orbit and the momentum $p = mv$ of the rotating electron must satisfy the quantization of angular momentum $pr = n\hbar$ ($n = 1, 2, \ldots$). To consider an electron's motion in classical terms, the uncertainties in its position and momentum must be negligible when compared to r and p; in other words, $\Delta x \ll r$ and $\Delta p \ll p$. This implies

$$\frac{\Delta x}{r} \frac{\Delta p}{p} \ll 1 \tag{1.7.1}$$

On the other hand, the uncertainty relation imposes

$$\frac{\Delta x}{r} \frac{\Delta p}{p} \geq \frac{\hbar}{rp} \Rightarrow \frac{\Delta x \Delta p}{rp} \geq \frac{1}{n} \tag{1.7.2}$$

So, Eq. (1.7.1) is incompatible with Eq. (1.7.2), unless $n \gg 1$.

1.8. (*a*) Consider a thermal neutron, that is, a neutron with speed v corresponding to the average thermal energy at the temperature $T = 300$ K. Is it possible to observe a diffraction pattern when a beam of these neutrons falls on a crystal? (*b*) In a large accelerator, an electron can be provided with an energy exceeding 1 GeV $= 10^9$ eV. What is the de Broglie wavelength corresponding to such electrons?

SOLUTION

(*a*) The average thermal energy of an absolute temperature T is $E_{av} = \dfrac{3}{2} k_B T$ where k_B is the Bolzmann constant ($k_B = 1.38 \times 10^{-23}$ J/K). Therefore, we have

$$\frac{1}{2} m_n v^2 = \frac{p^2}{2m_n} = \frac{3}{2} k_B T \tag{1.8.1}$$

According to the de Broglie relation the corresponding wavelength is

$$\lambda = \frac{h}{p} = \frac{h}{\sqrt{3m_n k_B T}} \tag{1.8.2}$$

For $T = 300$ K, we have

$$\lambda = \frac{6.63 \times 10^{-34}}{\sqrt{3 \times 1.67 \times 10^{-27} \times 1.38 \times 10^{-23} \times 300}} \cong 1.4 \text{ Å} \tag{1.8.3}$$

This is the order of magnitude of the spaces between atoms in a crystal, and therefore a diffraction phenomenon analogous to that of x-rays.

(b) We note that the electron's rest energy is $m_e c^2 \cong 0.5 \times 10^6$ eV. Therefore, if an energy of 10^9 eV is imparted to the electron, it will move with a velocity close to the speed of light, and it must be treated using relativistic dynamics. The relation $\lambda = h/p$ remains valid, but we have $E = \sqrt{p^2 c^2 + m_e^2 c^4}$. In this example, $m_e c^2$ is negligible when compared with E, and we obtain

$$\lambda \cong \frac{hc}{E} = \frac{6.6 \times 10^{-34} \times 3 \times 10^8}{1.6 \times 10^{-10}} = 1.2 \times 10^{-15} \text{ m} = 1.2 \text{ fm} \tag{1.8.4}$$

With electrons accelerated to such energies, one can explore the structure of atomic nuclei.

1.9. The wavelength and the frequency in a *wave guide* are related by

$$\lambda = \frac{c}{\sqrt{\nu^2 - \nu_0^2}} \tag{1.9.1}$$

Express the group velocity v_g in terms of c and the phase velocity $v_p = \lambda \nu$.

SOLUTION

First, we find how the angular frequency ω depends on the propagation number k. We have $\omega = 2\pi\nu$; using Eq. (1.9.1), we have

$$\omega(k) = 2\pi\sqrt{\frac{c^2}{\lambda^2} + \nu_0^2} = 2\pi\sqrt{\frac{c^2 k^2}{4\pi^2} + \nu_0^2} \tag{1.9.2}$$

Hence, the group velocity is

$$v_g = \frac{d\omega}{dk} = \frac{2\pi}{2\sqrt{\frac{c^2 k^2}{4\pi^2} + \nu_0^2}} \frac{2kc^2}{4\pi^2} = \frac{c^2 k}{2\pi\nu} = \frac{2\pi}{\lambda}\frac{c^2}{2\pi\nu} = \frac{c^2}{\lambda\nu} = \frac{c^2}{v_p} \tag{1.9.3}$$

SUPPLEMENTARY PROBLEMS

1.10. Derive an expression for the energy of a photon in eV when its wavelength is given in nanometers. Determine the energy of a 500-nm photon in eV.

Ans. $E = (1239.8 \text{ eV} \cdot \text{nm})/\lambda$, 2.48 eV

1.11. An electron crashes into the metal mask of an old color television tube operating at 20.0 kV. Find the shortest wavelength x-rays that will be emitted.

Ans. $\lambda_{min} = 0.062$ nm

1.12. Using Eq. (1.7) show that the energy levels of the hydrogen atom are given by

$$E_n = -\frac{13.6 \text{ eV}}{n^2} \tag{1.12.1}$$

1.13. How much energy would it take to raise a hydrogen atom from its ground state ($n = 1$) to its first excited state ($n = 2$)?

Ans.   10.2 eV

1.14. Refer to Problem 1.9 and find the group velocity for the following relations: (a) $v = \sqrt{\dfrac{2\pi\Upsilon}{\rho\lambda^3}}$ (water waves in shallow water; Υ is the surface tension and ρ the density). (b) $v = \sqrt{\dfrac{g}{2\pi\lambda}}$ (water waves in deep water).

Ans.   (a) $v_g = \dfrac{3}{2}v_p$;   (b) $v_g = \dfrac{1}{2}v_p$

1.15. Suppose that light of irradiance 10^{-10} W/m² usually falls normally upon a metal surface. The atoms are approximately 3 Å or 3×10^{-10} m apart and it is given that there is one free electron per atom. The binding energy of an electron at the surface is 5 eV. Assume that the light is uniformly distributed over the surface and its energy absorbed by the surface electrons. If the incident radiation is treated classically (as waves), how long must one wait after the beam is switched on until an electron gains enough energy to be released as a photoelectron?

Ans.   Approximately 2800 years.

1.16. Consider a monochromatic beam of light of irradiance I and frequency v striking a completely absorbing surface. Suppose that the light is incident along the normal to the surface. Using classical electromagnetic theory, one can show that on the surface a pressure (P) called the *radiation pressure* is acting, which is related to the irradiance by $P = I/c$. Is this relation also valid according to quantum theory?

Ans.   Yes. $P = \dfrac{h v}{c} N$, where N is the flux of the photon beam.

1.17. Suppose that monochromatic light is scattered by an electron. Use Problem 1.3 to find the shift in the wavelength when the scattering angle is 90°. What is the fractional increase in the wavelength in the visible region (say, $\lambda = 4000$ Å)? What is the fractional increase for x-ray photons of $\lambda = 1$ Å $= 0.1$ nm?

Ans. $\Delta\lambda = \dfrac{1}{m_e c}(1 - \cos\theta) = 0.0243$ Å. For $\lambda = 4000$ Å, the fractional shift is 0.006 percent. For $\lambda = 1$ Å it is 2 percent.

1.18. We wish to show that wave properties of matter are irrelevant for the macroscopic world. Take as an example a tiny particle of diameter 1 µm and mass $m = 10^{-15}$ kg. Calculate the de Broglie wavelength corresponding to this particle if its speed is 1 mm/s.

Ans. $\lambda = 6.6 \times 10^{-7}$ nm.

1.19. Consider a virus of size 1.0 nm. Suppose that its density is equal to that of water and that the virus is located in a region that is approximately equal to its size. What is minimum speed of the virus?

Ans. $v_{min} \approx 1$ m/s.

1.20. A beam of high-energy photons impinges on a target and some are backscattered by collisions with electrons that are essentially at rest. Determine the wavelength shift experienced by the scattered photons

Ans. 4.85×10^{-12} m.

1.21. If E is the energy of the incident photons in the previous problem, show that

$$E_s = \frac{m_e c^2}{m_e c^2 /E + 2} \tag{1.21.1}$$

is the energy of the scattered photons.

CHAPTER 2

Mathematical Background

2.1 The Complex Field *C*

The complex field, denoted by C, is the field generated by the complex numbers $a + bi$, where a and b are real numbers and i is the solution of the equation $x^2 + 1 = 0$, i.e., $i = \sqrt{-1}$. If $z = a + bi$, then a is called the real part of z and denoted $\mathrm{Re}(z)$; b is called the imaginary part of z and denoted $\mathrm{Im}\,(z)$. The *complex conjugate* of $z = a + bi$ is $a - bi$ and is denoted by z^*. Summation and multiplication of complex numbers is performed in the following manner:

$$(a + bi) + (c + di) = (a + c) + (b + d)i \tag{2.1}$$

$$(a + bi)(c + di) = (ac - bd) + (bc + ad)i \tag{2.2}$$

If $z \neq 0$ we define z^{-1} and division by z as

$$z^{-1} = \frac{z^*}{zz^*} = \frac{a}{a^2 + b^2} + \frac{-b}{a^2 + b^2}i \tag{2.3}$$

$$\frac{w}{z} = wz^{-1} \tag{2.4}$$

Figure 2.1 represents a geometric realization of the complex field as points in the plane.

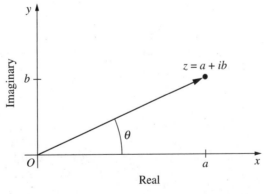

Fig. 2.1

The distance between the point z and O is denoted $|z| = \sqrt{a^2 + b^2} = \sqrt{zz^*}$ and is called the *modulus* of z. The angle θ is called the *argument* of z and denoted by $\arg(z)$. Since points in the plane can be characterized by polar coordinates, i.e., a pair (r, θ) where $r > 0$ and $0 \leq \theta \leq 2\pi$, one can write a complex number in terms of its modulus and argument. As one can easily verify,

$$a = r \cos \theta \qquad b = r \sin \theta \tag{2.5}$$

and

$$r = \sqrt{a^2 + b^2} \qquad \theta = \tan^{-1}\left(\frac{b}{a}\right) \tag{2.6}$$

and therefore $z = r(\cos\theta + i\sin\theta) = re^{i\theta}$.

2.2 Vector Spaces over *C*

A vector space over *C* is a collection of elements *V* that is closed under associative addition (+) of its elements (called *vectors*), and that satisfies the following conditions for each scalar α, β in *C* and vector *v*, *u* in *V*:

1. *V* contains a unique element denoted 0 that satisfies

$$v + 0 = 0 + v = v \tag{2.7}$$

    0 is called the *null vector*.

2. αv is also in *V*.
3. $\alpha(v + u) = \alpha v + \alpha u$.
4. $(\alpha + \beta)v = \alpha v + \beta v$.
5. $(\alpha \cdot \beta)v = \alpha(\beta v)$.
6. $0 \cdot v = 0$, $\alpha \cdot 0 = 0$, $1 \cdot v = v$.

An Important Example—*C*ⁿ

Consider elements of the form $(z_1, z_2, \ldots, z_n)$, where the z_i are complex numbers. We define addition of such elements by

$$(z_1, z_2, \ldots, z_n) + (w_1, w_2, \ldots, w_n) = (z_1 + w_1, z_2 + w_2, \ldots, z_n + w_n) \tag{2.8}$$

and we define multiplication by a scalar (a complex number *z*) by

$$z(z_1, z_2, \ldots, z_n) = (zz_1, zz_2, \ldots, zz_n) \tag{2.9}$$

It can be verified that the collection of these elements has all the properties of a vector space over *C*. This important vector space is denoted C^n.

Some Useful Definitions

A collection of vectors $u_1, \ldots, u_n$ in *V*, spans *V* if every element in *V* can be written as a *linear combination* of the *u*'s; that is,

$$v = a_1 u_1 + \cdots + a_n u_n \tag{2.10}$$

where $a_1, \ldots, a_n$ are complex numbers. The vectors $u_1, \ldots, u_n$ are called *linearly independent* if $a_1 u_1 + \cdots + a_n u_n = 0$ implies $a_1 = a_2 = \cdots = a_n = 0$. If $u_1, \ldots, u_n$ are linearly independent and span *V* they are called a *basis* of *V*. The number *n* is unique and is called the *dimension* of *V*. Suppose that *W* is a collection of vectors from a vector space *V*. *W* is a subspace of *V* if: (1) for every *v*, *w*, in *W*, *v* + *w* is also in *W*; (2) for every *w* in *W* and every scalar α, αv is also in *W*.

2.3 Linear Operators and Matrices

Linear Operators

Let *V* be a vector space over the complex field *C*. A map $\hat{T} : V \rightarrow V$ is an operator on *V* if it satisfies the following condition for every α, β in *C* and every, *u*, *v* in *V*:

$$\hat{T}(\alpha v + \beta u) = \alpha \hat{T}(v) + \beta \hat{T}(u) \tag{2.11}$$

If $\hat{T}$ and $\hat{S}$ are linear operators, their sum, the linear operator $\hat{T} + \hat{S}$, is defined by

$$(\hat{T} + \hat{S})(u) = \hat{T}(u) + \hat{S}(u) \tag{2.12}$$

for every u in V. Similarly, we define the product of two linear operators by

$$(\hat{T} \cdot \hat{S})(v) = \hat{T}[\hat{S}(v)] \tag{2.13}$$

for every v in V. The set of linear operators equipped with addition and multiplication is therefore an algebra over the complex field. For now, let us restrict ourselves to a finite dimensional vector space.

Assume $e_1, \ldots, e_n$ is a basis of V and let $\hat{T}$ be a linear operator on V. Applying $\hat{T}$ to $e_1, \ldots, e_n$ we get

$$\hat{T}(e_1) = a_{11}e_1 + \cdots + a_{1n}e_n$$
$$\vdots \tag{2.14}$$
$$\hat{T}(e_n) = a_{n1}e_1 + \cdots + a_{nn}e_n$$

where a_{ij} are complex numbers. Now we define the matrix representation of $\hat{T}$ relative to the basis e by

$$[\hat{T}]_e = (a_{ji}) = \begin{pmatrix} a_{11} & a_{21} \cdots & a_{n1} \\ a_{12} & a_{22} \cdots & a_{n2} \\ \vdots & \cdots & \vdots \\ a_{1n} & a_{2n} \cdots & a_{nn} \end{pmatrix} \tag{2.15}$$

Note that the matrix representation of an operator is dependent on the choice of basis. For infinite matrices it is possible to sum and multiply infinite matrices like finite matrices, though one must pay attention to convergence whenever infinite sums are involved. Linear operators are of great importance in quantum mechanics, since, as we shall see in the next chapters, they represent physical quantities such as energy, momentum, etc.

Inner Product

An inner product on V is a function $\langle u, v \rangle$ from $V \times V$ to the complex field (i.e., taking every pair of vectors to a complex number), that satisfies the following conditions for every u, v, u' in V and α in C:

$$\begin{aligned} &\text{(i)} \qquad \langle u, v \rangle = \langle v, u \rangle^* \\ &\text{(ii)} \ \langle u + u', v \rangle = \langle u, v \rangle + \langle u', v \rangle \\ &\text{(iii)} \qquad \langle \alpha u, v \rangle = \alpha \cdot \langle u, v \rangle \\ &\text{(iv)} \qquad \langle u, u \rangle > 0 \quad \text{if } u \neq 0 \end{aligned} \tag{2.16}$$

A vector space that has an inner product is called an *inner product space.*

We can use the inner product to specify some useful definitions. The *norm* of a vector v is

$$\| v \| = \sqrt{\langle v, v \rangle} \tag{2.17}$$

If $\| v \| = 1$, then v is called a unit vector and is said to be *normalized.*

Two vectors u and v are *orthogonal* if

$$\langle u, v \rangle = 0 \tag{2.18}$$

A set of vectors $\{u_i\}$ is orthogonal if any pair of two separate elements is orthogonal; this is, $\langle u_i, u_j \rangle = 0$ for $i \neq j$. In particular, the set is *orthonormal* if in addition each of its elements is a unit vector, or compactly,

$$\langle u_i, u_j \rangle = \delta_{ij} \tag{2.19}$$

where δ_{ij} is the *Kronecker delta function*, which is 0 for $i \neq j$ and 1 otherwise. An important result, used frequently in quantum mechanics, is the *Cauchy–Schwartz inequality*: For all vectors u and v,

$$|\langle u, v \rangle| \leq \|u\| \cdot \|v\| \tag{2.20}$$

Operators and Inner Products

Suppose $\hat{T}$ is a linear operator on V and suppose V is an inner product space. It can be shown that there is a unique linear operator denoted $\hat{T}^\dagger$ that satisfies:

$$\langle \hat{T}u, v \rangle = \langle u, \hat{T}^\dagger v \rangle \tag{2.21}$$

for every u, v in V. This operator is called the *conjugate operator* of $\hat{T}$. If $\hat{A} = (\alpha_{ij})$ is a complex matrix, $\hat{A}^\dagger$ is defined as $\hat{A}^\dagger = (\alpha_{ji})^*$, which is found by swapping indices and taking the complex conjugate. If $\hat{A}$ represents an operator $\hat{T}$, then $\hat{A}^\dagger$ represents $\hat{T}^\dagger$, which justifies the use of the same symbol $\dagger$ in each case. If $\hat{T} = \hat{T}^\dagger$, then $\hat{T}$ is called a *Hermitian operator* or *self-conjugate operator*. If $\hat{T} = -\hat{T}^\dagger$, then $\hat{T}$ is an *anti-Hermitian operator*. If $\hat{T}$ preserves the inner product, that is, $\langle \hat{T}u, \hat{T}v \rangle = \langle u, v \rangle$ for every u, v in V, then $\hat{T}$ is a *unitary operator*. If $\hat{T}\hat{T}^\dagger = \hat{T}^\dagger \hat{T}$, then $\hat{T}$ is a *normal operator*. Two vectors v and u are *orthogonal* if $\langle v, u \rangle = 0$.

2.4   Eigenvectors and Eigenvalues

Let $\hat{T}$ be a linear operator on V. A complex number λ is called an *eigenvalue* (also known as a characteristic value) of $\hat{T}$ if it satisfies $\hat{T}v = \lambda v$ for some v in V. The vector v is called the *eigenvector* of $\hat{T}$ corresponding to λ. The same definition holds for matrices. Note that if V has a basis that consists of eigenvectors of $\hat{T}$, then $\hat{T}$ is represented relative to that basis as a diagonal matrix. Diagonal matrices are not only easy to work with, but also reflect important characteristics of the physical system such as quanta of energy, and so forth.

Characteristic Polynomial

Suppose that a given linear operator $\hat{T}$ is represented in some basis by the matrix $\hat{A}$. The characteristic polynomial of $\hat{T}$ is defined by

$$\Delta(t) = \det(\lambda \hat{I} - \hat{A}) \tag{2.22}$$

where λ is the parameter (scalar) and $\hat{I}$ is the *identity* or *unit matrix*. The characteristic equation of $\hat{T}$ is defined by

$$\Delta(t) = 0 \tag{2.23}$$

These expressions are independent of the basis chosen.

The following result provides a method for finding the eigenvalues of a matrix or operator: the scalar λ is an eigenvalue of an operator $\hat{T}$ if and only if it is a root of its characteristic polynomial, that is, $\Delta(t) = 0$.

If $\hat{A}$ is a Hermitian or unitary matrix, then there exists a unitary matrix $\hat{U}$ such that $\hat{U}\hat{A}\hat{U}^{-1}$ is a diagonal matrix (this theorem will not be proved). Note also that if $\hat{A}$ and $\hat{B}$ are Hermitian matrices then a necessary and sufficient condition that they can be simultaneously diagonalized is that they commute, i.e., $\hat{A}\hat{B} = \hat{B}\hat{A}$ (see Problem 2.16). These concepts have important physical meaning and will be discussed in greater detail in Chap. 4.

2.5   Fourier Series and the Fourier Transform

Fourier Series

Consider a function $f(x)$ over the interval $0 < x < l$. The function is called *square integrable* if

$$\int_0^l |f(x)|^2 dx \tag{2.24}$$

is defined (i.e., convergent). It can be shown that the set of all such functions is an infinite dimensional vector space, denoted $L_2(0, l)$. We can define for $L_2(0, l)$ an inner product

$$\langle f, g \rangle = \int_0^l f(x)g^*(x)\,dx \tag{2.25}$$

Every function $f(x)$ in $L_2(0, l)$ can be expanded in a *Fourier series*,

$$f(x) = \sum_{n=-\infty}^{\infty} f_n e^{ik_n x} \qquad k_n = \frac{2\pi}{l} n \tag{2.26}$$

According to this relation, we can consider the functions $e_n = \frac{1}{\sqrt{l}} e^{ik_n x}$ as a "basis" of the infinite dimensional space $L_2(0, l)$: every function (vector) in this space can be expanded as a linear combination of the basis vectors. It can be shown that the $\{e_n\}$ form an orthonormal basis, that is, $\langle e_i, e_j \rangle = \delta_{ij}$. The coefficients f_n in the expansion are called *Fourier coefficients* and are derived using the relation

$$f_n = \frac{1}{l} \int_0^l f(t)e^{-ik_n t}\,dt \tag{2.27}$$

Since the functions e_n are periodic, of period l, it is not difficult to show that the Fourier expansion developed above holds also for periodic functions $f(x)$ of period l.

Fourier Transform

Now consider a function $f(x)$ defined on $(-\infty, \infty)$ that is not necessarily periodic. We can imagine $f(x)$ to be an approximation of periodic functions whose period approaches ∞. The numbers k_n become progressively denser until we have in the limit a continuous range of functions e^{ikx}. This is the intuitive basis of the following result:

$$f(x) = \frac{1}{\sqrt{2\pi}} \int_{-\infty}^{\infty} F(k)e^{ikx}\,dk \tag{2.28}$$

where $F(k)$ is given by

$$F(k) = \frac{1}{\sqrt{2\pi}} \int_{-\infty}^{\infty} f(x)e^{-ikx}\,dx \tag{2.29}$$

$F(k)$ and $f(x)$ are said to be Fourier transforms of each other. The Parseval–Plancherel formula states that a function and its Fourier transform have the same norm:

$$\int_{-\infty}^{\infty} |f(x)|^2\,dx = \int_{-\infty}^{\infty} |F(k)|^2\,dk \tag{2.30}$$

2.6   The Dirac Delta Function

In Sec. 2.3 we used the Kronecker δ_{mn} function, which returns the value 1 whenever the integers n and m are equal, and 0 otherwise. There is a continuous analogue to Kronecker's δ-function—the Dirac delta function (Dirac δ-function). Define the function $\delta_\varepsilon(x)$ as

$$\delta_\varepsilon(x) = \begin{cases} \dfrac{1}{\varepsilon} & \text{for } -\dfrac{\varepsilon}{2} < x < \dfrac{\varepsilon}{2} \\[2mm] 0 & \text{for } |x| > \dfrac{\varepsilon}{2} \end{cases} \tag{2.31}$$

Consider the arbitrary function $f(x)$, well defined for $x = 0$ with negligible variation over the interval $[-\varepsilon/2, \varepsilon/2]$. If ε is sufficiently small, then we have

$$\int_{-\infty}^{\infty} \delta_\varepsilon(x) f(x)\, dx \cong f(0) \int_{-\infty}^{\infty} \delta_\varepsilon(x)\, dx = f(0) \tag{2.32}$$

Taking the limit as $\varepsilon \to 0$ we define the δ-function by

$$\lim_{\varepsilon \to 0} \left\{ \int_{-\infty}^{\infty} \delta_\varepsilon(x) f(x)\, dx \right\} = \int_{-\infty}^{\infty} \delta(x) f(x)\, dx = f(0) \tag{2.33}$$

More generally, we can write

$$\int_{-\infty}^{\infty} \delta(x - x_0) f(x)\, dx = f(x_0) \tag{2.34}$$

One can easily show that $\int_{-\infty}^{\infty} \delta(x - y)\, dx = 1$ and that $\delta(x - y) = 0$ for $x \neq y$. Although we use the term δ-function, it is not a function in the regular sense; it is really a more complicated object called a *distribution* (it is *not* defined at the point $x = y$). That is, we only consider it when it appears inside an integral:

$$f \to \int_{-\infty}^{\infty} f(x)\, \delta(x - y)\, dy \tag{2.35}$$

As this is a linear operation that maps a *function* to a *number*, the δ-function can be viewed as a *functional*. The δ-function is often used to describe a particle located at a point $\mathbf{r}_0 = (x_0, y_0, z_0)$ in a three-dimensional Euclidian space by defining a $\delta(\mathbf{r} - \mathbf{r}_0)$:

$$\delta(\mathbf{r} - \mathbf{r}_0) = \delta(x - x_0)\delta(y - y_0)\delta(z - z_0) \tag{2.36}$$

The integral of δ over the whole space is 1, indicating the existence of the particle. On the other hand, δ vanishes when $\mathbf{r} \neq \mathbf{r}_0$.

It is straightforward to demonstrate that the following results hold for the δ-function:

1. $\delta(-x) = \delta(x)$
2. $\delta(\alpha x) = \dfrac{1}{|\alpha|}\delta(x)$
3. $x\delta(x - x_0) = x_0\delta(x - x_0)$
4. $\displaystyle\int_{-\infty}^{\infty} \delta(x - y)\, \delta(y - z)\, dy = \delta(y - z)$

The δ-function and the Fourier Transform

The Fourier transform of the δ-function is

$$\frac{1}{\sqrt{2\pi}} \int_{-\infty}^{\infty} \delta(x - y) e^{-ikx}\, dx = \frac{1}{\sqrt{2\pi}} e^{-ikx} \tag{2.37}$$

The inverse Fourier transform then yields

$$\delta(x - y) = \frac{1}{2\pi} \int_{-\infty}^{\infty} e^{-iky} e^{ikx}\, dk = \frac{1}{2\pi} \int_{-\infty}^{\infty} e^{ik(x-y)}\, dk \tag{2.38}$$

SOLVED PROBLEMS

2.1. The complex conjugate of $z = a + bi$ is $a - bi$, denoted by z^*. Show that

(a) $zz^* = |z|^2$

(b) $z + z^*$ is real

(c) $(z_1 + z_2)^* = z_1^* + z_2^*$

(d) $(z_1 z_2)^* = z_1^* z_2^*$

(e) $|z_1 z_2| = |z_1||z_2|$

SOLUTION

(a) $zz^* = (a + bi)(a - bi) = a^2 + b^2 = |z|^2$

(b) $z + z = (a + bi) + (a - bi) = 2a$, which is real

(c) $(z_1 + z_2)^* = [(a_1 + b_1 i) + (a_2 + b_2 i)]^* = [(a_1 + b_1) + (b_1 + b_2)i]^*$

$\qquad = (a_1 + a_2) - (b_1 + b_2)i = (a_1 - b_1 i) + (a_2 - b_2 i) = z_1^* + z_2^*$

(d) $(z_1 z_2)^* = [(a_1 + b_1 i)(a_2 + b_2 i)]^* = [(a_1 a_2 - b_1 b_2) + (a_1 b_2 + a_2 b_1)i]^*$

$\qquad = a_1 a_2 - b_1 b_2 - (a_1 b_2 + a_2 b_1)i = (a_1 - b_1 i)(a_2 - b_2 i) = z_1^* z_2^*$

(e) $|z_1 z_2|^2 = (z_1 z_2)(z_1 z_2)^* = z_1 z_2 z_1^* z_2^* = z_1 z_1^* z_2 z_2^* = |z_1|^2 |z_2|^2$

2.2. Calculate $\left(\dfrac{1+i}{1-i}\right)^5$.

SOLUTION

Method *a*:
$$\left(\frac{1+i}{1-i}\right)^5 = \left[\frac{(1+i)(1+i)}{(1-i)(1+i)}\right]^5 = \left[\frac{(1+i)(1+i)}{2}\right]^5 = \left(\frac{2i}{2}\right)^5 = i^5 = i \qquad (2.2.1)$$

Method *b*:
$$\left(\frac{1+i}{1-i}\right)^5 = \left[\frac{\sqrt{2}(\cos 45° + \sin 45°)}{\sqrt{2}(\cos 45° - \sin 45°)}\right]^5 = \left(\frac{e^{i\pi/4}}{e^{-i\pi/4}}\right)^5$$

$$= (e^{i\pi/2})^5 = e^{i\pi/2} = \cos 90° + i \sin 90° = i \qquad (2.2.2)$$

2.3. Here is a set of functions: $f(z) = z^2$, $g(z) = z^3$, and $h(z) = z$. Are they linearly independent on the real z axis?

SOLUTION

The condition for linear independence is that

$$a_1 f(z) + a_2 g(z) + a_3 h(z) = 0 \qquad (2.3.1)$$

implies

$$a_1 = a_2 = a_3 = 0 \qquad (2.3.2)$$

Here that is

$$a_1 z^2 + a_2 z^3 + a_3 z = 0 \qquad (2.3.3)$$

If this is to be true for all z, it must indeed be that

$$a_1 = a_2 = a_3 = 0 \qquad (2.3.4)$$

And the set of functions is linearly independent.

2.4. Consider the set of functions: $f(y) = 4y^2$, $g(y) = 2y$, and $h(y) = 10y$. Are they linearly independent on the real y axis?

SOLUTION

We need to determine if

$$a_1 f(y) + a_2 g(y) + a_3 h(y) = 0 \qquad (2.4.1)$$

can only be true if

$$a_1 = a_2 = a_3 = 0 \tag{2.4.2}$$

Here,

$$a_1 4y^2 + a_2 2y + a_3 10y = 0 \tag{2.4.3}$$

and if $a_1 = 0$, $a_2 = -5$, and $a_3 = 1$, the sum will be zero for all y. Hence these functions are not independent:

$$h(y) = 5g(y) + 0 \cdot f(y) \tag{2.4.4}$$

2.5. Consider the set of vectors in ordinary three-dimensional space: $\mathbf{A} = (6, 0, 0)$, $\mathbf{B} = (0, -4, 0)$, and $\mathbf{C} = (0, 0, 5)$ are they linearly independent?

SOLUTION

We have to examine

$$a_1 \mathbf{A} + a_2 \mathbf{B} + a_3 \mathbf{C} = 0 \tag{2.5.1}$$

and since $\mathbf{A} = 6\mathbf{i}$, $\mathbf{B} = -4\mathbf{j}$, and $\mathbf{C} = 5\mathbf{k}$, it follows that

$$a_1 6\mathbf{i} + a_2 (-4)\mathbf{j} + a_3 5\mathbf{k} = 0 \tag{2.5.2}$$

Since each term is perpendicular to the others the composite vector can only be zero if $6a_1 = 0$, $-4a_2 = 0$, and $5a_3 = 0$. That is, $a_1 = a_2 = a_3 = 0$. The vectors $\mathbf{A}$, $\mathbf{B}$, and $\mathbf{C}$ are linearly independent.

2.6. Show that the sum and product of two linear operators are linear operators.

SOLUTION

Suppose that $\hat{T}$ and $\hat{S}$ are linear operators, so

$$(\hat{T} + \hat{S})(u + \alpha v) \equiv \hat{T}(u + \alpha v) + \hat{S}(u + \alpha v)$$

$$= \hat{T}(u) + \alpha \hat{T}(v) + \hat{S}(u) + \alpha \hat{S}(v)$$

$$= (\hat{T} + \hat{S})(u) + \alpha(\hat{T} + \hat{S})(v) \tag{2.6.1}$$

and

$$(\hat{T} \cdot \hat{S})(u + \alpha v) \equiv \hat{T}[\hat{S}(u + \alpha v)] = \hat{T}[\hat{S}(u) + \alpha \hat{S}(v)]$$

$$= \hat{T}[\hat{S}(u)] + \alpha \hat{T}[\hat{S}(v)] = (\hat{T} \cdot \hat{S})(u) + \alpha(\hat{T} \cdot \hat{S})(v) \tag{2.6.2}$$

2.7. Let V be the space of infinitely differentiable functions in one variable. Prove that differentiation is a linear operator.

SOLUTION

We define the map $\dfrac{d}{dx}$ as

$$\frac{d}{dx}(f) = f'(x) \tag{2.7.1}$$

and using basic calculus we get

$$\frac{d}{dx}(f + \alpha g) = [f + \alpha g]' = f'(x) + \alpha g'(x) = \frac{d}{dx}(f) + \alpha \frac{d}{dx}(g) \tag{2.7.2}$$

2.8. Let V be C^n, i.e., the collection of n-tuples $\mathbf{a} = (a_1, \ldots, a_n)$, where the a_i are complex numbers. Show that $\langle \mathbf{a}, \mathbf{b} \rangle = \displaystyle\sum_{i=1}^{n} a_i b_i^*$ is an inner product of V.

SOLUTION

We begin by checking the four conditions that an inner product on V must satisfy:

$$\langle \mathbf{a}, \mathbf{b} \rangle = \sum_{i=1}^{n} a_i b_i^* = \left[\sum_{i=1}^{n} a_i^* b_i \right]^* = \langle \mathbf{b}, \mathbf{a} \rangle^* \tag{2.8.1}$$

$$\langle \mathbf{a} + \mathbf{a}', \mathbf{b} \rangle = \sum_{i=1}^{n} (a_i + a_i') b_i^* = \sum_{i=1}^{n} a_i \cdot b_i^* + \sum_{i=1}^{n} a_i' \cdot b_i^* = \langle \mathbf{a}, \mathbf{b} \rangle + \langle \mathbf{a}', \mathbf{b} \rangle \tag{2.8.2}$$

and

$$\langle \alpha \mathbf{a}, \mathbf{b} \rangle = \sum_{i=1}^{n} (\alpha a_i) b_i^* = \alpha \sum_{i=1}^{n} a_i b_i^* = \alpha \langle \mathbf{a}, \mathbf{b} \rangle \tag{2.8.3}$$

Finally,

$$\langle \mathbf{a}, \mathbf{a} \rangle = \sum_{i=1}^{n} a_i a_i^* = \sum_{j=1}^{n} |a_i|^2 \tag{2.8.4}$$

and is greater than zero if one of the a_i is different from zero.

2.9. If $\hat{A}$ and $\hat{B}$ are operators, prove

(*a*) that $(\hat{A}^\dagger)^\dagger = \hat{A}$

(*b*) that $(\hat{A}\hat{B})^\dagger = \hat{B}^\dagger \hat{A}^\dagger$

(*c*) that $\hat{A} + \hat{A}^\dagger$, $i(\hat{A} - \hat{A}^\dagger)$, and that $\hat{A}\hat{A}^\dagger$ are Hermitian operators.

SOLUTION

(*a*) For every u and v in V,

$$\langle \hat{A}v, u \rangle = \langle v, \hat{A}^\dagger u \rangle = \langle \hat{A}^\dagger u, v \rangle^* = \langle u, (\hat{A}^\dagger)^\dagger v \rangle^* = \langle (\hat{A}^\dagger)^\dagger v, u \rangle$$

Thus we obtain $\hat{A} = (\hat{A}^\dagger)^\dagger$.

(*b*) For every u and v in V,

$$\langle v, (\hat{A}\hat{B})^\dagger u \rangle = \langle \hat{A}\hat{B}v, u \rangle = \langle \hat{B}v, \hat{A}^\dagger u \rangle = \langle v, \hat{B}^\dagger \hat{A}^\dagger u \rangle \tag{2.9.1}$$

Hence, $\hat{B}^\dagger \hat{A}^\dagger = (\hat{A}\hat{B})^\dagger$.

(*c*) We write

$$(\hat{A} + \hat{A}^\dagger)^\dagger = \hat{A}^\dagger + (\hat{A}^\dagger)^\dagger = \hat{A}^\dagger + \hat{A} = \hat{A} + \hat{A}^\dagger \tag{2.9.2}$$

Here we use the fact that the sum of conjugates is the conjugate of the sum, $(\hat{A} + \hat{B})^\dagger = \hat{A}^\dagger + \hat{B}^\dagger$, which can be easily verified, and we also use the result of part (*a*).

$$[i(\hat{A} - \hat{A}^\dagger)]^\dagger = i^*(\hat{A} - \hat{A}^\dagger)^\dagger = -i(\hat{A}^\dagger - \hat{A}) = i(\hat{A} - \hat{A}^\dagger) \tag{2.9.3}$$

where we have used the fact that the conjugate of a complex number is the same as its conjugate as an operator. And finally,

$$(\hat{A}\hat{A}^\dagger)^\dagger = (\hat{A}^\dagger)^\dagger \hat{A}^\dagger = \hat{A}\hat{A}^\dagger \tag{2.9.4}$$

according to part (*b*).

2.10. Show that the eigenvalues of a Hermitian operator are real.

SOLUTION

Suppose λ is an eigenvalue of $\hat{T}$, and $\hat{T} = \hat{T}^\dagger$. For every $v \neq 0$ in V,

$$\lambda \langle v, v \rangle = \langle \lambda v, v \rangle = \langle \hat{T}v, v \rangle = \langle v, \hat{T}v \rangle = \langle v, \lambda v \rangle$$

$$= \langle \lambda v, v \rangle^* = \lambda^* \langle v, v \rangle \tag{2.10.1}$$

Since $\langle v, v \rangle$ is a positive real number ($v \neq 0$), it follows that $\lambda = \lambda^*$, so λ is a real number. The fact that the eigenvalues of Hermitian operators are real is of great importance, since these eigenvalues can represent physical quantities.

2.11. Show that eigenvectors that correspond to different eigenvalues of a Hermitian operator are orthogonal.

SOLUTION

Suppose $\hat{T}v = \lambda v$ and $\hat{T}u = \mu u$, where $\mu \neq \lambda$. Now,

$$\lambda\langle v, u \rangle = \langle \lambda v, u \rangle = \langle \hat{T}v, u \rangle = \langle v, \hat{T}^\dagger u \rangle = \langle v, \hat{T}u \rangle = \langle v, \mu u \rangle = \mu^*\langle v, u \rangle \tag{2.11.1}$$

so,

$$(\lambda - \mu^*)\langle v, u \rangle = (\lambda - \mu)\langle v, u \rangle = 0 \tag{2.11.2}$$

($\mu^* = \mu$, since $\hat{T}$ is Hermitian). But $\lambda - \mu \neq 0$; therefore, $\langle v, u \rangle = 0$, i.e., v and u are orthogonal.

2.12. Show that Hermitian, anti-Hermitian, and unitary operators are normal operators.

SOLUTION

If $\hat{T} = \hat{T}^\dagger$, then $\hat{T}\hat{T}^\dagger = \hat{T}^\dagger\hat{T} = \hat{T}^2$. Also, if $\hat{T} = -\hat{T}^\dagger$, then $\hat{T}\hat{T}^\dagger = \hat{T}^\dagger\hat{T} = -\hat{T}^2$. If $\hat{T}$ is unitary, then $\langle \hat{T}u, \hat{T}v \rangle = \langle u, v \rangle$ for every u, v in V. Using the definition of conjugate operator and taking $u = v$, we get

$$\langle u, u \rangle = \langle \hat{T}u, \hat{T}u \rangle = \langle u, \hat{T}\hat{T}^\dagger u \rangle \tag{2.12.1}$$

hence,

$$\langle u, (\hat{I} - \hat{T}\hat{T}^\dagger)u \rangle = 0 \tag{2.12.2}$$

for every u in V. Since $\hat{I} - \hat{T}\hat{T}^\dagger$ is a Hermitian operator, it follows that $\hat{I} - \hat{T}\hat{T}^\dagger = 0$. This also completes the proof showing $\hat{T}$ is a normal operator.

2.13. Let V be the space of nonzero square integrable continuous complex functions in one variable. For every pair of functions, define

$$\langle f, g \rangle = \int_{-\infty}^{\infty} f(x)\,g^*(x)\,dx \tag{2.13.1}$$

Show that with this definition, V is an inner product space.

SOLUTION

We must check the following conditions:

$$\langle f, g \rangle = \int_{-\infty}^{\infty} f(x)g^*(x)\,dx = \int_{-\infty}^{\infty} g(x)f^*(x)\,dx = \langle g, f \rangle^* \tag{2.13.2}$$

$$\langle f + f', g \rangle = \int_{-\infty}^{\infty} [f(x) + f'(x)]g^*(x)\,dx$$

$$= \int_{-\infty}^{\infty} f(x)g^*(x)\,dx + \int_{-\infty}^{\infty} f'(x)g^*(x)\,dx$$

$$= \langle f, g \rangle + \langle f', g \rangle \tag{2.13.3}$$

and

$$\langle \alpha f, g \rangle = \int_{-\infty}^{\infty} \alpha f(x)g^*(x)\,dx = \alpha\int_{-\infty}^{\infty} f(x)g^*(x)\,dx = \alpha\langle f, g \rangle \tag{2.13.4}$$

$$\langle f, f \rangle = \int_{-\infty}^{\infty} |f(x)|^2 dx \tag{2.13.5}$$

Since f is continuous and $f \neq 0$ in a neighborhood, its integral also differs from zero; hence $\langle f, f \rangle \neq 0$.

2.14. (*a*) Show that if $\langle v, u \rangle = \langle v, w \rangle$ for every v in V, then $u = w$.

(*b*) Show that if $\hat{T}$ and $\hat{S}$ are two linear operators in V that satisfy $\langle \hat{T}v, u \rangle = \langle \hat{S}v, u \rangle$ for every u, v in V, then $\hat{S} = \hat{T}$.

SOLUTION

(*a*) The condition $\langle v, u \rangle = \langle v, w \rangle$ implies that $\langle v, u - w \rangle = 0$ for every v in V. In particular, if $v = u - w$ we obtain

$$\langle u - w, u - w \rangle = 0 \tag{2.14.1}$$

Hence, $u - w = 0$, that is, $u = w$.

(*b*) According to part (*a*), $\langle \hat{T}v, u \rangle = \langle \hat{S}v, u \rangle$ for every v, u in V which implies that $\hat{T}v = \hat{S}v$; i.e., $\hat{T} = \hat{S}$.

2.15. Let $\hat{A}$ and $\hat{B}$ be Hermitian matrices. Show that $\hat{A}$ and $\hat{B}$ can be simultaneously diagonalized (that is, with the same matrix $\hat{U}$) if and only if $\hat{A}\hat{B} = \hat{B}\hat{A}$.

SOLUTION

Suppose $\hat{U}\hat{A}\hat{U}^{-1} = \hat{D}_1$ and $\hat{U}\hat{B}\hat{U}^{-1} = \hat{D}_2$ where $\hat{D}_1$ and $\hat{D}_2$ are diagonal matrices. Hence,

$$\hat{U}(\hat{A}\hat{B})\hat{U}^{-1} = \hat{U}\hat{A}\hat{U}^{-1}\hat{U}\hat{B}\hat{U}^{-1} = \hat{D}_1\hat{D}_2 = \hat{D}_2\hat{D}_1 = \hat{U}\hat{B}\hat{U}^{-1}\hat{U}\hat{A}\hat{U}^{-1} = \hat{U}(\hat{B}\hat{A})\hat{U}^{-1} \tag{2.15.1}$$

Multiplying on the right with $\hat{U}$ and on the left with $\hat{U}^{-1}$ we get $\hat{A}\hat{B} = \hat{B}\hat{A}$. We leave it to the reader to prove the other direction. This result is of great importance in quantum mechanics.

2.16. Show that the modulus of the eigenvalues of a unitary operator is equal to 1.

SOLUTION

Suppose $\hat{T}$ is a unitary operator, and let $v \neq 0$ be an eigenvector with an eigenvalue λ. Then,

$$\langle v, v \rangle = \langle \hat{T}v, \hat{T}v \rangle = \langle \lambda v, \lambda v \rangle = \lambda\lambda^*\langle v, v \rangle \tag{2.16.1}$$

Hence,

$$\lambda\lambda^* = |\lambda|^2 = 1 \tag{2.16.2}$$

2.17. Suppose that f is an integrable function.

(*a*) If $\lambda \neq 0$ is a real number and $g(x) = f(\lambda x + y)$, prove that

$$G(k) = \frac{1}{\lambda}e^{iky/\lambda}F\left(\frac{k}{\lambda}\right) \tag{2.17.1}$$

where F and G are the Fourier transforms of f and g, respectively.

(*b*) Prove that if xf is also integrable, then $F(k)$ is a differentiable function and

$$F[f'(x)] = F[-ixf(x)] \tag{2.17.2}$$

SOLUTION

(*a*) By definition,

$$G(k) = \int_{-\infty}^{\infty} g(x)e^{-ikx}dx = \int_{-\infty}^{\infty} f(\lambda x + y)e^{-ikx}dx$$

$$= \int_{-\infty}^{\infty} f(\lambda x + y)e^{(-ik/\lambda)(\lambda x + y)}e^{iky/\lambda}\frac{1}{\lambda}d(\lambda x + y)$$

$$= \frac{1}{\lambda}e^{iky/\lambda}\int_{-\infty}^{\infty} f(s)e^{-i(k/\lambda)s}ds = \frac{1}{\lambda}e^{iky/\lambda}F\left(\frac{k}{\lambda}\right) \tag{2.17.3}$$

(*b*) Consider the expression

$$\frac{F(k+h) - F(k)}{h} = \frac{1}{\sqrt{2\pi}}\int_{-\infty}^{\infty} f(x)e^{-ikx}\left(\frac{e^{ihx} - 1}{h}\right)dx \tag{2.17.4}$$

Taking $\lim_{h \to 0}\left(\dfrac{e^{ihx} - 1}{h}\right) = -ix$, we obtain

$$F[f'(x)] = \frac{1}{\sqrt{2\pi}}\int_{-\infty}^{\infty} -ixf(x)e^{-ikx}dx = F[-ixf(x)] \tag{2.17.5}$$

2.18. Show that

(*a*) $F[\delta(x - x_0)] = F[\delta(x)]e^{-ikx_0}$

(*b*) $F[\delta(ax)] = \dfrac{1}{a}F\left[\delta\left(\dfrac{k}{a}\right)\right]$.

SOLUTION

(*a*) By definition,

$$F[\delta(x - x_0)] = \frac{1}{\sqrt{2\pi}} \int_{-\infty}^{\infty} \delta(x - x_0)\, e^{-ikx}\, dx = \frac{1}{\sqrt{2\pi}} \int_{-\infty}^{\infty} \delta(z)\, e^{-izk} e^{-ix_0 k}\, dz = F[\delta(x)]\, e^{-ikx_0} \qquad (2.18.1)$$

(*b*)

$$F[\delta(ax)] = \frac{1}{\sqrt{2\pi}} \int_{-\infty}^{\infty} \delta(ax)\, e^{-ixk}\, dx = \frac{1}{\sqrt{2\pi}} \int_{-\infty}^{\infty} \frac{1}{a}\, \delta(z)\, e^{-ikz/a}\, dz = \frac{1}{a} F\left[\delta\left(\frac{k}{a} \right) \right] \qquad (2.18.2)$$

SUPPLEMENTARY PROBLEMS

2.19. Prove the triangle inequality for complex numbers; that is, show that $|z_1 + z_2| \le |z_1| + |z_2|$.

2.20. Are the two vectors

$\mathbf{A} = (4, -5, 0)$ and $\mathbf{B} = (-12, 15, 0)$

in ordinary three-dimensional space, linearly independent?

Ans. No, $-3a_1 = a_2$ or $-3\mathbf{A} = \mathbf{B}$.

2.21. Show that the vectors $(1, 1, 0)$, $(0, 0, \sqrt{2})$, and (i, i, i) are linearly dependent over the complex field.

2.22. Find the eigenvalues and eigenvectors of the matrix $\hat{A} = \begin{pmatrix} 0 & 1 \\ 1 & 0 \end{pmatrix}$. Hint: If λ is an eigenvalue, then $\hat{A}v = \lambda v$, or $(\hat{A} - \lambda\hat{I})v = 0$ for some $v \ne 0$; this implies that $\det(\hat{A} - \lambda\hat{I}) = 0$. Solve this equation for λ, then substitute λ and find v.

Ans. $\lambda_1 = 1,\ v_1 = \begin{pmatrix} 1 \\ 1 \end{pmatrix},\ \lambda_2 = -1, v_2 = \begin{pmatrix} 1 \\ -1 \end{pmatrix}$.

2.23. Show that the matrix

$$\hat{T} = \begin{pmatrix} \cos\theta & -\sin\theta \\ \sin\theta & \cos\theta \end{pmatrix} \qquad (2.23.1)$$

is unitary. If $u = \begin{pmatrix} x \\ y \end{pmatrix}$ is a vector in the plane, what is the geometric interpretation of $u \to \hat{T}u$?

2.24. Demonstrate that the system $\left\{ \dfrac{1}{\sqrt{2\pi}}, \dfrac{1}{\sqrt{\pi}} \sin k, \dfrac{1}{\sqrt{\pi}} \sin 2k, \dots, \dfrac{1}{\sqrt{\pi}} \cos k, \dfrac{1}{\sqrt{\pi}} \cos 2k, \dots \right\}$ is also orthonormal.

2.25. Consider the space of polynomials with degree less than or equal to n. We can think of each polynomial $p(x) = a_0 + a_1 x + \cdots + a_n x^n$ as a vector in the space C^{n+1}, $(a_0, a_1, \dots, a_n)$. In fact, this is the representation of $p(x)$ relative to the basis $\{1, x, \dots, x^n\}$. What is the matrix that represents the operator $\dfrac{d}{dx}$ relative to the basis?

Ans. $\begin{pmatrix} 0 & 1 & 0 & \cdots & 0 \\ 0 & 0 & 2 & \cdots & 0 \\ \vdots & \vdots & \vdots & \vdots & \vdots \\ 0 & 0 & \cdots & \cdots & n \\ 0 & 0 & \cdots & \cdots & 0 \end{pmatrix}$

2.26. Find the Fourier transform of $e^{-x^2/2}$.

Ans. $F(t) = e^{-k^2/2}$.

2.27. (*a*) Find the Fourier series of $f(x) = \dfrac{\pi - x}{2}$, $0 \le x \le 2\pi$.

(*b*) Using part (*a*), show that $\dfrac{\pi}{4} = \sum_{n=0}^{\infty} \dfrac{(-1)^n}{2n + 1}$.

Ans. (*a*) $\dfrac{\pi - x}{2} = \sum_{n=-\infty}^{\infty} \dfrac{-ie^{inx}}{n} = \sum_{n=0}^{\infty} \dfrac{\sin(nx)}{n}$.

CHAPTER 3

The Schrödinger Equation and Its Applications

3.1 Wavefunctions of a Single Particle

In quantum mechanics, a particle is characterized by a *wavefunction* $\Psi(\mathbf{r}, t)$, which contains information about the spatial state of the particle at time t. The wavefunction $\Psi(\mathbf{r}, t)$ is a complex function of the three coordinates x, y, z and of the time t. The interpretation of the wavefunction is as follows: the probability $dP(\mathbf{r}, t)$ of the particle being at time t in a volume element $d^3r = dx\,dy\,dz$ located at the point $\mathbf{r}$ is

$$dP(\mathbf{r}, t) = C\,|\Psi(\mathbf{r}, t)|^2\, d^3r \tag{3.1}$$

where C is a normalization constant. The *total probability* of finding the particle anywhere in space, at time t, must be equal to unity; therefore,

$$\int dP(\mathbf{r}, t) = 1 \tag{3.2}$$

According to Eqs. (3.1) and (3.2) we conclude:

(*a*) The wavefunction $\Psi(\mathbf{r}, t)$ has to be square-integrable; that is

$$\int |\Psi(\mathbf{r}, t)|^2\, d^3r \tag{3.3}$$

must be finite.

(*b*) The normalization constant is given by the relation

$$\frac{1}{C} = \int |\Psi(\mathbf{r}, t)|^2\, d^3r \tag{3.4}$$

When $C = 1$ we say that the wavefunction is *normalized*. A wavefunction $\Psi(\mathbf{r}, t)$ must be defined and continuous everywhere.

3.2 The Schrödinger Equation

Consider a particle of mass m having a potential energy $V(\mathbf{r}, t)$. The time evolution of the wavefunction is governed by the Schrödinger equation:

$$i\hbar\,\frac{\partial \Psi(\mathbf{r}, t)}{\partial t} = -\frac{\hbar^2}{2m}\nabla^2\Psi(\mathbf{r}, t) + V(\mathbf{r}, t)\Psi(\mathbf{r}, t) \tag{3.5}$$

where ∇^2 is the Laplacian operator, $\partial^2/\partial x^2 + \partial^2/\partial y^2 + \partial^2/\partial z^2$. Pay attention to two important properties of the Schrödinger equation:

(a) The Schrödinger equation is a linear homogeneous differential equation in Ψ. Consequently, the superposition principle holds; that is, if $\Psi_1(\mathbf{r}, t)$, $\Psi_2(\mathbf{r}, t)$, ..., $\Psi_n(\mathbf{r}, t)$ are solutions of the Schrödinger equation, then $\Psi = \sum_{i=n}^{n} \alpha_i \Psi_i(\mathbf{r}, t)$ is also a solution.

(b) The Schrödinger equation is a first-order equation with respect to time; therefore, the state at time t_0 determines its subsequent state at all times.

3.3 Particle in a Time-Independent Potential

The wavefunction of a particle having a time-independent potential energy $V(\mathbf{r})$ satisfies the Schrödinger equation:

$$i\hbar \frac{\partial \Psi(\mathbf{r}, t)}{\partial t} = -\frac{\hbar^2}{2m} \nabla^2 \Psi(\mathbf{r}, t) + V(\mathbf{r})\Psi(\mathbf{r}, t) \tag{3.6}$$

Performing a separation of variables $\Psi(\mathbf{r}, t) = \psi(\mathbf{r})f(t)$, we have $f(t) = Ae^{-i\omega t}$ (A and ω are constant), where $\psi(\mathbf{r})$ must satisfy the equation

$$-\frac{\hbar^2}{2m} \nabla^2 \psi(\mathbf{r}) + V(\mathbf{r})\psi(\mathbf{r}) = \hbar\omega\psi(\mathbf{r}) \tag{3.7}$$

where $\hbar\omega$ is the energy of the state E (see Problem 3.3). This is a *stationary Schrödinger equation*, where a wavefunction of the form

$$\Psi(\mathbf{r}, t) = \psi(\mathbf{r})e^{-i\omega t} = \psi(\mathbf{r})e^{-iEt/\hbar} \tag{3.8}$$

is called a *stationary solution* of the Schrödinger equation, since the probability density in this case does not depend on time [see Problem 3.3, part (b)]. Suppose that at time $t = 0$ we have

$$\Psi(\mathbf{r}, 0) = \sum_n \psi_n(\mathbf{r}) \tag{3.9}$$

where $\psi_n(\mathbf{r})$ are the spatial parts of stationary states, $\Psi_n(\mathbf{r}, t) = \psi(\mathbf{r})e^{-i\omega_n t}$. In this case, according to the superposition principle, the time evolution of $\Psi(\mathbf{r}, 0)$ is described by

$$\Psi(\mathbf{r}, t) = \sum_n \psi(\mathbf{r})e^{-i\omega_n t} \tag{3.10}$$

For a *free particle* we have $V(\mathbf{r}, t) \equiv 0$, and the Schrödinger equation is satisfied by solutions of the form

$$\Psi(\mathbf{r}, t) = Ae^{i(\mathbf{k} \cdot \mathbf{r} - \omega t)} \tag{3.11}$$

where A is a constant; k and ω satisfy the relation $\omega = \hbar\mathbf{k}^2/2m$. Solutions of this form are called *plane waves*.

Note that since the $\Psi(\mathbf{r}, t)$ are not square-integrable, they cannot rigorously represent a particle. On the other hand, a superposition of plane waves can yield an expression that is square-integrable and can therefore describe the dynamics of a particle,

$$\Psi(\mathbf{r}, t) = \frac{1}{(2\pi)^{3/2}} \int g(\mathbf{k})e^{i[\mathbf{k} \cdot \mathbf{r} - \omega(k)t]} d^3k \tag{3.12}$$

A wavefunction of this form is called a *wave packet*. We often study the case of a one-dimensional wave packet traveling in the positive x direction,

$$\Psi(x, t) = \frac{1}{\sqrt{2\pi}} \int_{-\infty}^{\infty} g(\mathbf{k}) e^{i[kx - \omega(k)t]} \, dk \tag{3.13}$$

See Sec. 1.3.

3.4   Scalar Product of Wavefunctions: Operators

With each pair of wavefunctions $\phi(\mathbf{r})$ and $\psi(\mathbf{r})$, we associate a complex number defined by

$$(\phi, \psi) = \int \phi^*(\mathbf{r}) \psi(\mathbf{r}) \, d^3r \tag{3.14}$$

where (ϕ, ψ) is the s*calar product* of $\phi(\mathbf{r})$ and $\psi(\mathbf{r})$ (see Chap. 2).

An operator $\hat{A}$ acting on a wavefunction $\psi(\mathbf{r})$ creates another wavefunction $\psi'(\mathbf{r})$. An operator is called a linear operator if this correspondence is linear, i.e., if for every complex number α_1 and α_2,

$$\hat{A}[\alpha_1 \psi_1(\mathbf{r}) + \alpha_2 \psi_2(\mathbf{r})] = \alpha_1 \hat{A} \psi_1(\mathbf{r}) + \alpha_2 \hat{A} \psi_2(\mathbf{r}) \tag{3.15}$$

There are two sets of operators that are important:

(*a*) The *spatial operators* $\hat{X}$, $\hat{Y}$, and $\hat{Z}$ are defined by

$$\begin{cases} \hat{X}\Psi(x, y, z, t) = x\Psi(x, y, z, t) \\ \hat{Y}\Psi(x, y, z, t) = y\Psi(x, y, z, t) \\ \hat{Z}\Psi(x, y, z, t) = z\Psi(x, y, z, t) \end{cases} \tag{3.16}$$

(*b*) The *momentum operators* $\hat{p}_x$, $\hat{p}_y$ and $\hat{p}_z$ are defined by

$$\begin{cases} \hat{p}_x \Psi(x, y, z, t) = \dfrac{\hbar}{i} \dfrac{\partial}{\partial x} \Psi(x, y, z, t) \\[2mm] \hat{p}_y \Psi(x, y, z, t) = \dfrac{\hbar}{i} \dfrac{\partial}{\partial y} \Psi(x, y, z, t) \\[2mm] \hat{p}_z \Psi(x, y, z, t) = \dfrac{\hbar}{i} \dfrac{\partial}{\partial z} \Psi(x, y, z, t) \end{cases} \tag{3.17}$$

The *mean value* of an operator $\hat{A}$ in the state $\psi(\mathbf{r})$ is defined by

$$\langle \hat{A} \rangle = \int \psi^*(\mathbf{r})[\hat{A}\psi(\mathbf{r})] \, d^3r \tag{3.18}$$

The *root-mean-square deviation* is defined by

$$\Delta A = \sqrt{\langle \hat{A}^2 \rangle - \langle \hat{A} \rangle^2} \tag{3.19}$$

where $\hat{A}^2$ is the operator $\hat{A} \cdot \hat{A}$.

Consider the operator called the *Hamiltonian* of the particle. It is defined by

$$\hat{H} = -\frac{\hbar^2}{2m} \nabla^2 + \hat{V}(\mathbf{r}, t) \equiv \frac{\hat{\mathbf{p}}^2}{2m} + \hat{V}(\mathbf{r}, t) \tag{3.20}$$

where $\hat{\mathbf{p}}^2$ is condensed notation for the operator $\hat{p}_x^2 + \hat{p}_y^2 + \hat{p}_z^2$. Using the operator formulation, the Schrödinger equation is written in the form

$$i\hbar \frac{\partial \Psi(\mathbf{r}, t)}{\partial t} = \hat{H}\Psi(\mathbf{r}, t) \tag{3.21}$$

If the potential energy is time-independent, a stationary solution must satisfy the equation

$$\hat{H}\psi(\mathbf{r}) = E\psi(\mathbf{r}) \tag{3.22}$$

where E is a real number called the energy of the state. Equation (3.22) is the *eigenvalue equation* of the operator $\hat{H}$; the application of $\hat{H}$ on the *eigenfunction* $\psi(\mathbf{r})$ yields the same function, multiplied by the corresponding eigenvalue E. The allowed energies are therefore the eigenvalues of the operator $\hat{H}$.

3.5 Probability Density and Probability Current

Consider a particle described by a normalized wavefunction $\Psi(\mathbf{r}, t)$. The *probability density* is defined by

$$\rho(\mathbf{r}, t) = |\Psi(\mathbf{r}, t)|^2 \tag{3.23}$$

At time t, the probability $dP(\mathbf{r}, t)$ of finding the particle in an infinitesimal volume d^3r located at $\mathbf{r}$ is equal to

$$dP(\mathbf{r}, t) = \rho(\mathbf{r}, t)d^3r \tag{3.24}$$

The integral of $\rho(\mathbf{r}, t)$ over all space remains constant at all times. Note that this does not mean that $\rho(\mathbf{r}, t)$ must be time-independent at every point $\mathbf{r}$. Nevertheless, we can express a local *conservation of probability* in the form of a *continuity equation*,

$$\frac{\partial \rho(\mathbf{r}, t)}{\partial t} + \nabla \cdot \mathbf{J}(\mathbf{r}, t) = 0 \tag{3.25}$$

where $\mathbf{J}(\mathbf{r}, t)$ is the *probability current*, defined by

$$\mathbf{J}(\mathbf{r}, t) = \frac{\hbar}{2mi}\left[\Psi^*(\nabla\Psi) - \Psi(\nabla\Psi^*)\right] = \frac{1}{m}\text{Re}\left[\Psi^*\left(\frac{\hbar}{i}\nabla\Psi\right)\right] \tag{3.26}$$

Consider two regions in a space separated by a potential energy step or barrier, see Fig. 3.1.

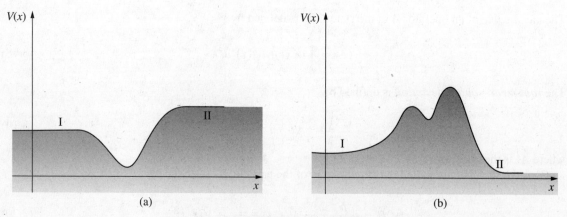

Fig. 3.1   (a) Potential step; (b) potential barrier.

We define transmission and reflection coefficients as follows. Suppose that a particle (or a stream of particles) is moving from region I through the potential energy step (or barrier) to region II. In the general case, a stationary state describing this situation will contain three parts. In region I the state is composed of the incoming wave with probability current J_I and a reflected wave of probability current J_R. In region II there is a transmitted wave of probability current J_T.

The *reflection coefficient* is defined by

$$R = \left| \frac{J_R}{J_I} \right| \tag{3.27}$$

The *transmission coefficient* is defined by

$$T = \left| \frac{J_T}{J_I} \right| \tag{3.28}$$

SOLVED PROBLEMS

3.1. Figure 3.2 depicts a plane passing through a point (x_0, y_0, z_0), perpendicular to a propagation vector $\mathbf{k}$. Using this diagram show that Eq. (3.11) represents a plane wave.

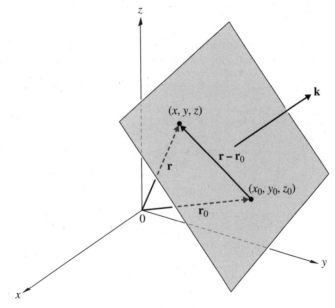

Fig. 3.2

SOLUTION

The position vector of an arbitrary point (x, y, z) is

$$\mathbf{r} = x\mathbf{i} + y\mathbf{j} + z\mathbf{k} \tag{3.1.1}$$

where $\mathbf{i}$, $\mathbf{j}$, and $\mathbf{k}$ are the usual unit basis vectors. The vector $(\mathbf{r} - \mathbf{r_0})$ goes from (x_0, y_0, z_0) to (x, y, z) and is given by

$$(\mathbf{r} - \mathbf{r_0}) = (x - x_0)\mathbf{i} + (y - y_0)\mathbf{j} + (z - z_0)\mathbf{k} \tag{3.1.2}$$

Setting

$$(\mathbf{r} - \mathbf{r_0}) \cdot \mathbf{k} = 0 \tag{3.1.3}$$

causes $(\mathbf{r} - \mathbf{r_0})$ to sweep out a plane perpendicular to the propagation vector $\mathbf{k} = k_x\mathbf{i} + k_y\mathbf{j} + k_z\mathbf{k}$.

Hence

$$k_x(x - x_0) + k_y(y - y_0) + k_z(z - z_0) = 0 \tag{3.1.4}$$

and since x_0, y_0, and z_0 are constants, as are k_x, k_y, and k_z,

$$k_x x + k_y y + k_z z = \text{constant} \tag{3.1.5}$$

Or more concisely

$$\mathbf{k} \cdot \mathbf{r} = \text{constant} \tag{3.1.6}$$

This is the equation of a plane perpendicular to $\mathbf{k}$. Hence

$$\psi(\mathbf{r}) = A\cos(\mathbf{k} \cdot \mathbf{r}) \tag{3.1.7}$$

or

$$\psi(\mathbf{r}) = A e^{i(\mathbf{k} \cdot \mathbf{r})} \tag{3.1.8}$$

is the equation for a stack of harmonically varying planes. To set the planes moving at a speed $v = \omega/k$ we need only replace $(\mathbf{k} \cdot \mathbf{r})$ by $(\mathbf{k} \cdot \mathbf{r} - \omega t)$ whereupon

$$\Psi(\mathbf{r}, t) = A\exp[i(\mathbf{k} \cdot \mathbf{r} - \omega t)] \tag{3.1.9}$$

becomes the equation of a harmonic plane wave.

3.2. Starting with the Schrödinger equation in one dimension and using a de Broglie plane wave as a solution, show that when $V = 0$ this leads to the correct nonrelativistic relationship between energy and momentum.

SOLUTION

In one dimension with $V = 0$, Eq. (3.5) becomes

$$i\hbar \frac{\partial \Psi(x, t)}{\partial t} = -\frac{\hbar^2}{2m} \frac{\partial^2 \Psi(x, t)}{\partial x^2} \tag{3.2.1}$$

In general, a plane wave has the form

$$\Psi(\mathbf{r}, t) = A\exp[i(\mathbf{k} \cdot \mathbf{r} - \omega t)] \tag{3.2.2}$$

When $\mathbf{k}$ is pointing in the positive x direction $\mathbf{k} \cdot \mathbf{r} = k_x x$ or, since $k = k_x$ under those circumstances,

$$\Psi(x, t) = A\exp[i(kx - \omega t)] \tag{3.2.3}$$

From de Broglie's hypothesis $p = h/\lambda$, and since $k = 2\pi/\lambda$, $p = \hbar k$. Similarly, $E = h\nu = \hbar\omega$. Thus

$$\Psi(x, t) = A\exp[i(px - Et)/\hbar] \tag{3.2.4}$$

Putting this into Schrödinger's equation yields

$$i\hbar A\exp[i(px - Et)/\hbar](-iE/\hbar) = -\frac{\hbar^2}{2m} \frac{\partial}{\partial x} A\exp[i(px - Et)/\hbar](ip/\hbar) \tag{3.2.5}$$

$$E\Psi(x, t) = -\frac{\hbar^2}{2m}(ip/\hbar)^2 \Psi(x, t) \tag{3.2.6}$$

and

$$E = \frac{p^2}{2m} \tag{3.2.7}$$

which is the proper nonrelativistic formula.

3.3. Consider a particle subjected to a time-independent potential $V(\mathbf{r})$. (*a*) Assume that a state of the particle is described by a wavefunction of the form $\Psi(\mathbf{r}, t) = \psi(\mathbf{r})f(t)$. Show that $f(t) = Ae^{-i\omega t}$ (A is constant) and that $\psi(\mathbf{r})$ must satisfy the equation

$$-\frac{\hbar}{2m}\nabla^2\psi(\mathbf{r}) + V(\mathbf{r})\psi(\mathbf{r}) = \hbar\omega\psi(\mathbf{r}) \tag{3.3.1}$$

where m is the mass of the particle. (*b*) Prove that the solutions of the Schrödinger equation of part (*a*) lead to a time-independent probability density.

SOLUTION

(*a*) We substitute $\Psi(\mathbf{r}, t) = \psi(\mathbf{r})f(t)$ in the Schrödinger equation:

$$i\hbar\psi(\mathbf{r})\frac{df(t)}{dt} = f(t)\left[-\frac{\hbar^2}{2m}\nabla^2\psi(\mathbf{r})\right] + f(t)V(\mathbf{r})\psi(\mathbf{r}) \tag{3.3.2}$$

In the regions in which the wavefunction $\Psi(\mathbf{r}, t)$ does not vanish, we divide both sides of Eq. (3.3.2) by $\psi(\mathbf{r})f(t)$ and obtain

$$\frac{i\hbar}{f(t)}\frac{df(t)}{dt} = \frac{1}{\psi(\mathbf{r})}\left[-\frac{\hbar^2}{2m}\nabla^2\psi(\mathbf{r})\right] + V(\mathbf{r}) \tag{3.3.3}$$

The left-hand side of Eq. (3.3.3) is a function of t only, and does not depend on $\mathbf{r}$. On the other hand, the right-hand side is a function of $\mathbf{r}$ only. Therefore, both sides of Eq. (3.3.3) depend neither on $\mathbf{r}$ nor on t, and are thus constants that we will set equal to $\hbar\omega$ for convenience. Hence,

$$i\hbar\frac{1}{f(t)}\frac{df(t)}{dt} = i\hbar\frac{d[\ln f(t)]}{dt} = \hbar\omega \tag{3.3.4}$$

Therefore,

$$\ln f(t) = \int -i\omega\,dt = -i\omega t + C = f(t) = Ae^{-i\omega t} \tag{3.3.5}$$

where A is constant. Substituting in (3.3.3), we see that $\psi(\mathbf{r})$ must satisfy the equation

$$-\frac{\hbar^2}{2m}\nabla^2\psi(\mathbf{r}) + V(\mathbf{r})\psi(\mathbf{r}) = \hbar\omega\psi(\mathbf{r}) \tag{3.3.6}$$

(*b*) For a function of the form $\Psi(\mathbf{r}, t) = \psi(\mathbf{r})e^{-i\omega t}$, the probability density is by definition

$$\rho(\mathbf{r}, t) = |\Psi(\mathbf{r}, t)|^2 = \left[\psi(\mathbf{r})e^{-i\omega t}\right]\left[\psi(\mathbf{r})e^{-i\omega t}\right]^* = \psi(\mathbf{r})e^{-i\omega t}\psi^*(\mathbf{r})e^{i\omega t} = |\psi(\mathbf{r})|^2 \tag{3.3.7}$$

We see that the probability density does not depend on time. This is why this kind of solution is called "stationary."

3.4. Consider the classical Hamiltonian for a one-dimensional system of two particles of masses m_1 and m_2 subjected to a potential that depends only on the distance between the particles $x_1 - x_2$,

$$H = \frac{p_1^2}{2m_1} + \frac{p_2^2}{2m_2} + V(x_1 - x_2) \tag{3.4.1}$$

(*a*) Write the Schrödinger equation using the new variables x and X, where

$$x = x_1 - x_2 \text{ (relative distance)} \qquad X = \frac{m_1x_1 + m_2x_2}{m_1 + m_2} \text{ (center of mass)} \tag{3.4.2}$$

(*b*) Use a separation of variables to find the equations governing the evolution of the center of mass and the relative distance of the particles. Interpret your results.

SOLUTION

(a) In terms of x_1 and x_2, the wavefunction of the two particles is governed by the Schrödinger equation:

$$i\hbar \frac{\partial \Psi(x_1, x_2, t)}{\partial t} = \hat{H} \Psi(x_1, x_2, t)$$

$$= -\frac{\hbar^2}{2m_1} \frac{\partial^2 \Psi(x_1, x_2, t)}{\partial x_1^2} - \frac{\hbar^2}{2m_2} \frac{\partial^2 \Psi(x_1, x_2, t)}{\partial x_2^2} + V(x_1 - x_2)\Psi(x_1, x_2, t) \qquad (3.4.3)$$

In order to transform to the variables x and X, we have to express the differentiations $\partial^2/\partial x_1^2$ and $\partial^2/\partial x_2^2$ in terms of these new variables. We have

$$\frac{\partial x}{\partial x_1} = 1 \qquad \frac{\partial x}{\partial x_2} = -1 \qquad \frac{\partial X}{\partial x_1} = \frac{m_1}{m_1 + m_2} \qquad \frac{\partial X}{\partial x_2} = \frac{m_2}{m_1 + m_2} \qquad (3.4.4)$$

Thus, for an arbitrary function $g(x_1, x_2)$ we obtain

$$\frac{\partial g(x_1, x_2)}{\partial x_1} = \frac{\partial g(x, X)}{\partial x} \frac{\partial x}{\partial x_1} + \frac{\partial g(x, X)}{\partial X} \frac{\partial X}{\partial x_1} = \frac{\partial g(x, X)}{\partial x} + \frac{m_1}{m_1 + m_2} \frac{\partial g(x, X)}{\partial X} \qquad (3.4.5)$$

Similarly,

$$\frac{\partial g(x_1, x_2)}{\partial x_2} = \frac{\partial g(x, X)}{\partial x} \frac{\partial x}{\partial x_2} + \frac{\partial g(x, X)}{\partial X} \frac{\partial X}{\partial x_2} = -\frac{\partial g(x, X)}{\partial x} + \frac{m_2}{m_1 + m_2} \frac{\partial g(x, X)}{\partial X} \qquad (3.4.6)$$

or

$$\frac{\partial}{\partial x_1} = \frac{\partial}{\partial x} + \frac{m_1}{m_1 + m_2} \frac{\partial}{\partial X} \qquad \frac{\partial}{\partial x_2} = -\frac{\partial}{\partial x} + \frac{m_2}{m_1 + m_2} \frac{\partial}{\partial X} \qquad (3.4.7)$$

For the second derivatives in x_1 and x_2 we have

$$\frac{\partial^2}{\partial x_1^2} = \left(\frac{\partial}{\partial x} + \frac{m_1}{m_1 + m_2} \frac{\partial}{\partial X} \right)\left(\frac{\partial}{\partial x} + \frac{m_1}{m_1 + m_2} \frac{\partial}{\partial X} \right)$$

$$= \frac{\partial^2}{\partial x^2} + \frac{m_1}{m_1 + m_2} \frac{\partial}{\partial x} \frac{\partial}{\partial X} + \frac{m_1}{m_1 + m_2} \frac{\partial}{\partial X} \frac{\partial}{\partial x} + \left(\frac{m_1}{m_1 + m_2} \right)^2 \frac{\partial^2}{\partial X^2} \qquad (3.4.8)$$

The wavefunction must be a smooth function for both x_1 and x_2; so, we can interchange the order of differentiation and obtain

$$\frac{\partial^2}{\partial x_1^2} = \frac{\partial^2}{\partial x^2} + \left(\frac{m_1}{m_1 + m_2} \right)^2 \frac{\partial^2}{\partial X^2} + \frac{2m_1}{m_1 + m_2} \frac{\partial}{\partial X} \frac{\partial}{\partial x} \qquad (3.4.9)$$

For x_2 we have

$$\frac{\partial^2}{\partial x_2^2} = \left(-\frac{\partial}{\partial x} + \frac{m_2}{m_1 + m_2} \frac{\partial}{\partial X} \right)\left(-\frac{\partial}{\partial x} + \frac{m_2}{m_1 + m_2} \frac{\partial}{\partial X} \right)$$

$$= \frac{\partial^2}{\partial x^2} + \left(\frac{m_2}{m_1 + m_2} \right)^2 \frac{\partial^2}{\partial X^2} - \frac{2m_2}{m_1 + m_2} \frac{\partial}{\partial X} \frac{\partial}{\partial x} \qquad (3.4.10)$$

Substituting Eqs. (3.4.9) and (3.4.10) in Eq. (3.4.3), we get

$$i\hbar \frac{\partial \Psi(x, X, t)}{\partial t} = -\frac{\hbar^2}{2m_1}\left[\frac{\partial^2}{\partial x^2} + \left(\frac{m_1}{m_1 + m_2}\right)^2 \frac{\partial^2}{\partial X^2} + \frac{2m_1}{m_1 + m_2}\frac{\partial}{\partial X}\frac{\partial}{\partial x}\right]\Psi(x, X, t)$$

$$-\frac{\hbar^2}{2m_2}\left[\frac{\partial^2}{\partial x^2} + \left(\frac{m_2}{m_1 + m_2}\right)^2 \frac{\partial^2}{\partial X^2} - \frac{2m_2}{m_1 + m_2}\frac{\partial}{\partial X}\frac{\partial}{\partial x}\right]\Psi(x, X, t) + V(x)\Psi(x, X, t)$$

$$= -\frac{\hbar^2}{2}\left(\frac{1}{m_1} + \frac{1}{m_2}\right)\frac{\partial^2 \Psi(x, X, t)}{\partial x^2} + V(x)\Psi(x, X, t) - \frac{\hbar^2}{2}\left(\frac{1}{m_1 + m_2}\right)\frac{\partial^2}{\partial X^2}\Psi(x, X, t)$$

$$(3.4.11)$$

(b) Since the Hamiltonian is time-independent, $\Psi(x, X, t) = \psi(x, X)f(t)$ (we separate the time and the spatial variables; see Problem 3.3). The equation governing the stationary part $\psi(x, X)$ is $\hat{H}\psi(x, X) = E_{total}\,\psi(x, X)$, where E_{total} is the total energy. Substituting in Eq. (3.2.11) we arrive at

$$-\frac{\hbar^2}{2}\left(\frac{m_1 + m_2}{m_1 m_2}\right)\frac{\partial^2 \psi(x, X)}{\partial x^2} + V(x)\psi(x, X) - \frac{\hbar^2}{2}\left(\frac{1}{m_1 + m_2}\right)\frac{\partial^2 \psi(x, X)}{\partial X^2} = E_{total}\,\psi(x, X) \quad (3.4.12)$$

Performing a separation of the variables $\psi(x, X) = \xi(x)\eta(X)$, Eq. (3.4.12) becomes

$$-\frac{\hbar^2}{2}\frac{1}{\xi(x)}\left(\frac{m_1 + m_2}{m_1 m_2}\right)\frac{\partial^2 \xi(x)}{\partial x^2} + V(x) = \frac{\hbar^2}{2}\frac{1}{\eta(X)}\frac{1}{m_1 + m_2}\frac{\partial^2 \eta(X)}{\partial X^2} + E_{total} \quad (3.4.13)$$

The left-hand side of Eq. (3.4.13) depends only on x; on the other hand, the right-hand side is a function only of X. Therefore, neither side can depend on x or X, and both are thus equal to a constant. We set

$$-\frac{\hbar^2}{2}\frac{1}{\eta(X)}\frac{1}{m_1 + m_2}\frac{\partial^2 \eta(x)}{\partial X^2} = E_{cm} \quad (3.4.14)$$

By inspection, we conclude that Eq. (3.4.14) is the equation governing the stationary wavefunction of a free particle of mass $m_1 + m_2$, i.e.,

$$-\frac{\hbar^2}{2}\frac{1}{m_1 + m_2}\frac{\partial^2 \eta(X)}{\partial X^2} = E_{cm}\eta(X) \quad (3.4.15)$$

Note that the wavefunction corresponding to the center of mass of the two particles behaves as a free particle of mass $m_1 + m_2$ and energy E_{cm}. This result is completely analogous to the classical case. Returning to Eq. (3.4.13), the equation for the relative position of the two particles is

$$-\frac{\hbar^2}{2\xi(x)}\left(\frac{m_1 + m_2}{m_1 m_2}\right)\frac{\partial^2 \xi(x)}{\partial x^2} + V(x) = E_{total} - E_{cm} \quad (3.4.16)$$

Equation (3.4.16) governs the stationary wavefunction of a particle of mass $(m_1 + m_2)/m_1 m_2$ confined by a potential energy $V(x)$ and having a total energy $E_{total} - E_{cm}$. Thus the relative position of the two particles behaves as a particle with an effective mass $(m_1 + m_2)/m_1 m_2$ and energy $E_{total} - E_{cm}$ confined by an effective potential energy $V(x)$. This is also analogous to the classical case.

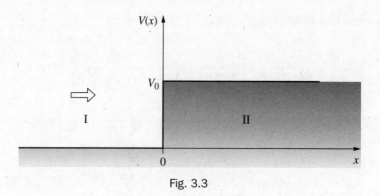

Fig. 3.3

3.5. Consider a particle of mass m confined in a finite one-dimensional "potential well" $V(x)$; see Fig. 3.3.

Prove that (a) $\dfrac{d\langle x \rangle}{dt} = \dfrac{\langle p \rangle}{m}$, and (b) $\dfrac{d\langle p \rangle}{dt} = \left\langle -\dfrac{dV}{dx} \right\rangle$ where $\langle x \rangle$ and $\langle p \rangle$ are the mean values of the

coordinate and momentum of the particle, respectively, and $\left\langle -\dfrac{dV}{dx} \right\rangle$ is the mean value of the force

acting on the particle. This result can be generalized to other kinds of operators and is called *Ehrenfest's theorem*.

SOLUTION

(a) Suppose that the wavefunction $\Psi(x, t)$ refers to a particle. The Schrödinger equation is

$$\frac{\partial \Psi(x, t)}{\partial t} = \frac{i\hbar}{2m} \frac{\partial^2 \Psi(x, t)}{\partial x^2} - \frac{i}{\hbar} V(x)\Psi(x, t) \tag{3.5.1}$$

and its conjugate equation is $\dfrac{\partial \Psi^*(x, t)}{\partial t} = -\dfrac{i\hbar}{2m} \dfrac{\partial^2 \Psi^*(x, t)}{\partial x^2} + \dfrac{i}{\hbar} V(x)\Psi^*(x, t)$. [Notice that we assume

$V(x)$ to be real.] The integral $\displaystyle\int_{-\infty}^{\infty} |\Psi(x, t)|^2 dx$ must be finite; so we get

$$\lim_{x \to \infty} |\Psi(x, t)|^2 = \lim_{x \to -\infty} |\Psi(x, t)|^2 = 0 \quad \text{and} \quad \lim_{x \to \infty} \frac{\partial \Psi(x, t)}{\partial x} = \lim_{x \to -\infty} \frac{\partial \Psi(x, t)}{\partial x} = 0 \tag{3.5.2}$$

Hence, the time derivative of $\langle x \rangle$ is

$$\frac{d\langle x \rangle}{dt} = \frac{d}{dt} \int_{-\infty}^{\infty} \Psi^*(x, t) x \Psi(x, t)\, dx = \int_{-\infty}^{\infty} \frac{\partial \Psi^*(x, t)}{\partial t} x \Psi(x, t)\, dx + \int_{-\infty}^{\infty} \Psi^*(x, t) x \frac{\partial \Psi(x, t)}{\partial t}\, dx \tag{3.5.3}$$

Substituting the Schrödinger equation and its conjugate gives

$$\frac{d\langle x \rangle}{dt} = -\frac{i\hbar}{2m} \int_{-\infty}^{\infty} \frac{\partial^2 \Psi^*(x, t)}{\partial x^2} x \Psi(x, t)\, dx + \frac{i}{\hbar} \int_{-\infty}^{\infty} \Psi^*(x, t) V(x)\Psi(x, t)\, dx$$

$$+ \frac{i\hbar}{2m} \left[\int_{-\infty}^{\infty} \Psi^*(x, t) x \frac{\partial^2 \Psi(x, t)}{\partial x^2}\, dx \right] - \frac{i}{\hbar} \int_{-\infty}^{\infty} \Psi^*(x, t) V(x)\Psi(x, t)\, dx$$

$$= -\frac{i\hbar}{2m} \lim_{\xi \to \infty} \left[\int_{-\xi}^{\xi} \frac{\partial^2 \Psi^*(x, t)}{\partial x^2} x \Psi(x, t)\, dx - \int_{-\xi}^{\xi} \Psi^*(x, t) x \frac{\partial^2 \Psi(x, t)}{\partial x^2}\, dx \right] \tag{3.5.4}$$

Integration by parts gives

$$\frac{d\langle x \rangle}{dt} = -\frac{i\hbar}{2m} \lim_{\xi \to \infty} \left\{ \left[\frac{\partial \Psi^*(x, t)}{\partial x} x \Psi(x, t) \right]_{-\xi}^{\xi} - \int_{-\xi}^{\xi} \frac{\partial \Psi^*(x, t)}{\partial x} \frac{\partial}{\partial x} [x \Psi(x, t)] dx \right.$$

$$\left. - \left[\Psi^*(x, t) x \frac{\partial \Psi(x, t)}{\partial x} \right]_{-\xi}^{\xi} + \int_{-\xi}^{\xi} \frac{\partial}{\partial x} [\Psi^*(x, t) x] \frac{\partial \Psi(x, t)}{\partial x} dx \right\} \qquad (3.5.5)$$

Using Eq. (3.5.2), the first and third terms equal zero; so we have

$$\frac{d\langle x \rangle}{dt} = -\frac{i\hbar}{2m} \lim_{\xi \to \infty} \left[-\int_{-\xi}^{\xi} \frac{\partial \Psi^*(x, t)}{\partial x} \Psi(x, t)] dx - \int_{-\xi}^{\xi} \frac{\partial \Psi^*(x, t)}{\partial x} x \frac{\partial \Psi(x, t)}{\partial x} dx \right.$$

$$\left. + \int_{-\xi}^{\xi} \frac{\partial \Psi^*(x, t)}{\partial x} x \frac{\partial \Psi(x, t)}{\partial x} dx + \int_{-\xi}^{\xi} \Psi^*(x, t) \frac{\partial \Psi(x, t)}{\partial x} dx \right] \qquad (3.5.6)$$

Eventually, integration by parts of the first term gives

$$\frac{d\langle x \rangle}{dt} = -\frac{i\hbar}{2m} \lim_{\xi \to \infty} \left[\int_{-\xi}^{\xi} -\left[\Psi^*(x, t) \Psi(x, t) \right]_{-\xi}^{\xi} + 2 \int_{-\xi}^{\xi} \Psi^*(x, t) \frac{\partial \Psi(x, t)}{\partial x} dx \right]$$

$$= \frac{1}{m} \int_{-\infty}^{\infty} \Psi^*(x, t) \frac{\hbar}{i} \frac{\partial \Psi(x, t)}{\partial x} dx = \frac{1}{m} \langle p \rangle \qquad (3.5.7)$$

(b) Consider the time derivative of $\langle p \rangle$:

$$\frac{d\langle p \rangle}{dt} = \frac{d}{dt} \int_{-\infty}^{\infty} \Psi^*(x, t) \frac{\hbar}{i} \frac{\partial \Psi(x, t)}{\partial x} dx$$

$$= \frac{\hbar}{i} \int_{-\infty}^{\infty} \frac{\partial \Psi^*(x, t)}{\partial t} \frac{\partial \Psi(x, t)}{\partial x} dx + \frac{\hbar}{i} \int_{-\infty}^{\infty} \Psi^*(x, t) \frac{\partial}{\partial t} \frac{\partial \Psi(x, t)}{\partial x} dx \qquad (3.5.8)$$

Since $\Psi(x, t)$ has smooth derivatives, we can interchange the time and spatial derivatives in the second term. Using the Schrödinger equation, Eq. (3.3.8) becomes

$$\frac{d\langle p \rangle}{dt} = -\frac{\hbar^2}{2m} \int_{-\infty}^{\infty} \frac{\partial^2 \Psi^*(x, t)}{\partial x^2} \frac{\partial \Psi(x, t)}{\partial x} dx + \int_{-\infty}^{\infty} V(x) \Psi^*(x, t) \frac{\partial \Psi(x, t)}{\partial x} dx$$

$$+ \frac{\hbar^2}{2m} \int_{-\infty}^{\infty} \Psi^*(x, t) \frac{\partial^3 \Psi(x, t)}{\partial x^3} dx - \int_{-\infty}^{\infty} \Psi^*(x, t) \frac{\partial}{\partial x} [V(x) \Psi(x, t)] dx \qquad (3.5.9)$$

Integration by parts of the first term gives

$$I \equiv \int_{-\infty}^{\infty} \frac{\partial^2 \Psi^*(x, t)}{\partial x^2} \frac{\partial \Psi(x, t)}{\partial x} dx = \lim_{\xi \to \infty} \left\{ \left[\frac{\partial \Psi^*(x, t)}{\partial x} \frac{\partial \Psi(x, t)}{\partial x} \right]_{-\xi}^{\xi} - \int_{-\xi}^{\xi} \frac{\partial \Psi^*(x, t)}{\partial x} \frac{\partial^2 \Psi(x, t)}{\partial x^2} dx \right\} \qquad (3.5.10)$$

Using Eq. (3.5.2), we arrive at

$$I = \lim_{\xi \to \infty}\left[-\int_{-\xi}^{\xi} \frac{\partial \Psi^*(x,t)}{\partial x} \frac{\partial^2 \Psi(x,t)}{\partial x^2} dx \right]$$
(3.5.11)

Again, integration by parts gives

$$I = \lim_{\xi \to \infty}\left\{ -\left[\Psi^*(x,t) \frac{\partial^2 \Psi(x,t)}{\partial x^2} \right]_{-\xi}^{\xi} + \int_{-\xi}^{\xi} \Psi^*(x,t) \frac{\partial^3 \Psi(x,t)}{\partial x^3} dx \right\}$$

$$= \int_{-\infty}^{\infty} \Psi^*(x,t) \frac{\partial^3 \Psi(x,t)}{\partial x^3} dx$$
(3.5.12)

Returning to Eq. (3.5.9), we finally have

$$\frac{d\langle p \rangle}{dp} = \int_{-\infty}^{\infty} V(x)\Psi^*(x,t) \frac{\partial \Psi(x,t)}{\partial x} dx - \int_{-\infty}^{\infty} \Psi^*(x,t) \frac{dV(x)}{dx} \Psi(x,t) dx$$

$$- \int_{-\infty}^{\infty} \Psi^*(x,t)V(x) \frac{\partial \Psi(x,t)}{\partial x} dx = \left\langle -\frac{dV}{dx} \right\rangle$$
(3.5.13)

3.6. Consider a particle described by a wavefunction $\Psi(\mathbf{r},t)$. Calculate the time-derivative $\frac{\partial \rho(\mathbf{r},t)}{\partial t}$, where $\rho(\mathbf{r},t)$ is the probability density, and show that the continuity equation $\frac{\partial \rho(\mathbf{r},t)}{\partial t} + \nabla \cdot \mathbf{J}(\mathbf{r},t) = 0$ is valid, where $\mathbf{J}(\mathbf{r},t)$ is the probability current, equal to $\frac{1}{m} \text{Re}\left[\Psi^*\left(\frac{\hbar}{i} \nabla \Psi \right) \right]$.

SOLUTION

Using the Schrödinger equation,

$$i\hbar \frac{\partial \Psi(\mathbf{r},t)}{\partial t} = -\frac{\hbar^2}{2m} \nabla^2 \Psi(\mathbf{r},t) + V(\mathbf{r},t)\Psi(\mathbf{r},t)$$
(3.6.1)

Assuming $V(x)$ is real, the conjugate expression is $-i\hbar \frac{\partial \Psi^*(\mathbf{r},t)}{\partial t} = -\frac{\hbar^2}{2m} \nabla^2 \Psi^*(\mathbf{r},t) + V(\mathbf{r},t)\Psi^*(\mathbf{r},t)$. According to the definition of $\rho(\mathbf{r},t)$ that is, Eq. (3.23), $\rho(\mathbf{r},t) = \Psi^*(\mathbf{r},t)\Psi(\mathbf{r},t)$; hence,

$$\frac{\partial \rho(\mathbf{r},t)}{\partial t} = \frac{\partial \Psi^*(\mathbf{r},t)}{\partial t}\Psi(\mathbf{r},t) + \Psi^*(\mathbf{r},t)\frac{\partial \Psi(\mathbf{r},t)}{\partial t}$$
(3.6.2)

Using Eq. (3.6.1) and its conjugate, we arrive at

$$\frac{\partial \rho(\mathbf{r},t)}{\partial t} = \left[\frac{\hbar}{2mi} \nabla^2 \Psi^*(\mathbf{r},t) \right]\Psi(\mathbf{r},t) - \frac{1}{i\hbar}V(\mathbf{r},t)\Psi^*(\mathbf{r},t)\Psi(\mathbf{r},t) - \Psi^*(\mathbf{r},t)\left[\frac{\hbar}{2mi} \nabla^2 \Psi(\mathbf{r},t) \right]$$

$$+ \frac{1}{i\hbar} \Psi^*(\mathbf{r},t)V(\mathbf{r},t)\Psi(\mathbf{r},t) = -\frac{\hbar}{2mi}[\Psi^*(\mathbf{r},t)\nabla^2 \Psi(\mathbf{r},t) - \Psi(\mathbf{r},t)\nabla^2 \Psi^*(\mathbf{r},t)]$$
(3.6.3)

We set

$$\mathbf{J}(\mathbf{r},t) = \frac{1}{m}\text{Re}\left[\Psi^*\left(\frac{\hbar}{i}\nabla \Psi \right) \right] = \frac{\hbar}{2mi}[\Psi^*(\mathbf{r},t)\nabla \Psi(\mathbf{r},t) - \Psi(\mathbf{r},t)\nabla \Psi^*(\mathbf{r},t)]$$
(3.6.4)

Using the theorem $\nabla \cdot (U\mathbf{A}) = (\nabla U) \cdot \mathbf{A} + U(\nabla \cdot \mathbf{A})$, we have

$$\nabla \cdot \mathbf{J}(\mathbf{r}, t) = \frac{\hbar}{2mi}\left[(\nabla \Psi^*) \cdot (\nabla \Psi) + \Psi^*(\nabla^2 \Psi) - (\nabla \Psi) \cdot (\nabla \Psi^*) - \psi(\nabla^2 \Psi^*)\right]$$

$$= \frac{\hbar}{2mi}\left[\Psi^* \nabla^2 \Psi - \Psi \nabla^2 \Psi^*\right] \tag{3.6.5}$$

so

$$\frac{\partial \rho(\mathbf{r}, t)}{\partial t} + \nabla \cdot \mathbf{J}(\mathbf{r}, t) = 0 \tag{3.6.6}$$

3.7. Consider the wavefunction

$$\Psi(x, t) = [Ae^{ipx/\hbar} + Be^{-ipx/\hbar}]e^{-ip^2 t/2m\hbar} \tag{3.7.1}$$

Find the probability current corresponding to this wavefunction.

SOLUTION

The probability current is by definition

$$J(x, t) = \frac{\hbar}{2mi}\left(\Psi^* \frac{\partial \Psi}{\partial x} - \frac{\partial \Psi^*}{\partial x} \Psi\right) \tag{3.7.2}$$

The complex conjugate of Ψ is $\Psi^*(x, t) = (A^* e^{-ipx/\hbar} + B^* e^{ipx/\hbar})e^{ip^2 t/2m\hbar}$; so a direct calculation yields

$$J(x, t) = \frac{\hbar}{2mi}\left[(A^* e^{-ipx/\hbar} + B^* e^{ipx/\hbar})\left(\frac{ip}{\hbar}Ae^{ipx/\hbar} - \frac{ip}{\hbar}Be^{-ipx/\hbar}\right)\right.$$

$$\left. - \left(-\frac{ip}{\hbar}A^* e^{-ipx/\hbar} + \frac{ip}{\hbar}B^* e^{ipx/\hbar}\right)(Ae^{ipx/\hbar} + Be^{-ipx/\hbar})\right]$$

$$= \frac{p}{2m}\left[(|A|^2 - A^* Be^{-2ipx/\hbar} + AB^* e^{2ipx/\hbar} - |B|^2) - (-|A|^2 - A^* Be^{-2ipx/\hbar} + AB^* e^{2ipx/\hbar} + |B|^2)\right]$$

$$= \frac{p}{m}(|A|^2 - |B|^2) \tag{3.7.3}$$

Note that the wavefunction $\Psi(x, t)$ expresses a superposition of two currents of particles moving in opposite directions. Each of the currents is constant and time-independent in its magnitude. The term $e^{-ip^2 t/2m\hbar}$ implies that the particles are of energy $p^2/2m$. The amplitudes of the currents are A and B.

3.8. Show that for a one-dimensional square-integrable wave packet,

$$\int_{-\infty}^{\infty} J(x)\,dx = \frac{\langle p \rangle}{m} \tag{3.8.1}$$

where $J(x)$ is the probability current.

SOLUTION

Consider the integral $\int_{-\infty}^{\infty} |\Psi(x, t)|^2\,dx$. This integral is finite, so we have $\lim_{x \to \pm\infty} |\Psi(x, t)|^2 = 0$. Hence,

$$\int_{-\infty}^{\infty} J(x)\,dx = \frac{\hbar}{2im}\int_{-\infty}^{\infty}\left[\Psi^*(x, t)\frac{\partial \Psi(x, t)}{\partial x} - \Psi(x, t)\frac{\partial \Psi^*(x, t)}{\partial x}\right]dx \tag{3.8.2}$$

Integration by parts gives

$$\int_{-\infty}^{\infty} \Psi(x,t)\frac{\partial \Psi^*(x,t)}{\partial x}\,dx = \lim_{\xi\to\infty}\left\{\left[\Psi(x,t)\Psi^*(x,t)\right]_{-\xi}^{\xi} - \int_{-\xi}^{\xi} \frac{\partial \Psi(x,t)}{\partial x}\Psi^*(x,t)\,dx\right\}$$

$$= -\int_{-\infty}^{\infty} \Psi^*(x,t)\frac{\partial \Psi(x,t)}{\partial x}\,dx \tag{3.8.3}$$

Therefore, we have

$$\int_{-\infty}^{\infty} J(x)\,dx = \frac{1}{m}\int_{-\infty}^{\infty} \Psi^*(x,t)\frac{\hbar}{i}\frac{\partial}{\partial x}\Psi(x,t)\,dx = \frac{\langle p \rangle}{m} \tag{3.8.4}$$

3.9. Consider a particle of mass m held in a one-dimensional potential $V(x)$. Suppose that in some region $V(x)$ is constant, $V(x) = V$. For this region, find the stationary states of the particle when (a) $E > V$, (b) $E < V$, and (c) $E = V$, where E is the energy of the particle.

SOLUTION

(a) The stationary states are the solutions of

$$-\frac{\hbar^2}{2m}\frac{\partial^2 \psi(x)}{\partial x^2} + V\psi(x) = E\psi(x) \tag{3.9.1}$$

For $E > V$, we introduce the positive constant k defined by $\hbar^2 k^2/2m = E - V$, so that

$$\frac{\partial^2 \psi(x)}{\partial x^2} + k^2\psi(x) = 0 \tag{3.9.2}$$

The solution of this equation can be written in the form

$$\psi(x) = Ae^{ikx} + A'e^{-ikx} \tag{3.9.3}$$

where A and A' are arbitrary complex constants.

(b) We introduce the positive constant ρ defined by $\hbar^2\rho^2/2m = V - E$; so Eq. (3.9.1) can be written as

$$\frac{\partial^2 \psi(x)}{\partial x^2} - \rho^2\psi(x) = 0 \tag{3.9.4}$$

The general solution of Eq. (3.9.4) is $\psi(x) = Be^{\rho x} + B'e^{-\rho x}$ where B and B' are arbitrary complex constants.

(c) When $E = V$ we have $\dfrac{\partial^2 \psi(x)}{\partial x^2} = 0$; so $\psi(x)$ is a linear function of x, $\psi(x) = Cx + C'$ where C and C' are complex constants.

3.10. Consider a particle of mass m confined in an infinite one-dimensional potential well of width a:

$$V(x) = \begin{cases} 0 & -\dfrac{a}{2} \le x \le \dfrac{a}{2} \\ \infty & \text{otherwise} \end{cases} \tag{3.10.1}$$

Find the eigenstates of the Hamiltonian (i.e., the stationary states) and the corresponding eigenenergies.

SOLUTION

For $x > a/2$ and $x < -a/2$ the potential is infinite, so there is no possibility of finding the particle outside the well. This means that

$$\psi\left(x > \frac{a}{2}\right) = 0 \qquad \psi\left(x < \frac{a}{2}\right) = 0 \tag{3.10.2}$$

Since the wavefunction must be continuous, we also have $\psi(a/2) = \psi(-a/2) = 0$. For $-a/2 \leq x \leq a/2$ the potential energy is constant, $V(x) = 0$; therefore, we can rely on the results of Problem 3.9. We distinguish between three possibilities concerning the energy E. As in Problem 3.9, part (a), for $E > 0$ we define the positive constant k, $\hbar^2 k^2/2m = E$; so we obtain $\psi(x) = Ae^{ikx} + A'e^{-ikx}$. Imposing the continuous conditions, we arrive at

$$\textbf{I} \quad Ae^{ika/2} + A'e^{-ika/2} = 0 \qquad \textbf{II} \quad Ae^{-ika/2} + A'e^{ika/2} = 0 \qquad (3.10.3)$$

Multiplying Eq. (3.10.3I) by $e^{ika/2}$ we obtain $A' = -Ae^{ika}$. Substituting A' into Eq. (3.10.3II) yields

$$Ae^{-ika/2} - Ae^{ika}e^{ika/2} = 0 \qquad (3.10.4)$$

Multiplying Eq. (3.10.4) by $e^{-ika/2}$ and dividing by A [if $A = 0$ then $\psi(x) \equiv 0$] we obtain $e^{-ika} - e^{ika} = 0$. Using the relation $e^{i\alpha} = \cos\alpha + i\sin\alpha$ we have $-2i\sin(ka) = 0$. The last relation is valid only if $ka = n\pi$, where n is an integer. Also, since k must be positive, n must also be positive. We see that the possible positive eigenenergies of the particle are

$$E_n = \frac{\hbar^2 k_n^2}{2m} = \frac{\hbar^2}{2m}\left(\frac{n\pi}{a}\right)^2 = \frac{\pi^2\hbar^2 n^2}{2ma^2} \qquad (3.10.5)$$

The corresponding eigenfunctions are

$$\psi_n(x) = Ae^{ik_n x} - Ae^{ik_n a}e^{-ik_n x} = Ae^{in\pi x/a} - e^{in\pi(a-x)/a}$$

$$= Ae^{in\pi/2}\left[e^{in\pi(x/a-1/2)} - e^{-in\pi(x/a-1/2)}\right]$$

$$= C\sin\left[n\pi\left(\frac{x}{a} - \frac{1}{2}\right)\right] \qquad (n = 1, 2, \ldots) \qquad (3.10.6)$$

where C is a normalization constant obtained by

$$\frac{1}{C^2} = \int_{-a/2}^{a/2} \sin^2\left[n\pi\left(\frac{x}{a} - \frac{1}{2}\right)\right] dx \qquad (3.10.7)$$

Defining $y = \dfrac{x}{a} - \dfrac{1}{2}$ and $dy = \dfrac{dx}{a}$, Eq. (3.8.7) becomes

$$\frac{1}{C^2} = a\int_{-1}^{0} \sin^2(n\pi y)\, dy = \frac{a}{2}\int_{-1}^{0} [1 - \cos(2\pi ny)]\, dy = \frac{a}{2}\left[y - \frac{\sin(2\pi ny)}{2\pi n}\right]_{-1}^{0} = \frac{a}{2} \qquad (3.10.8)$$

Therefore, $C = \sqrt{2/a}$. Finally,

$$\psi_n(x) = \sqrt{\frac{2}{a}}\sin\left[n\pi\left(\frac{x}{a} - \frac{1}{2}\right)\right] \qquad (3.10.9)$$

Consider now the case when $E < 0$. As in Problem 3.9, part (b), we introduce the positive constant ρ, $\hbar^2\rho^2/2m = -E$. Stationary states should be of the form $\psi(x) = Be^{\rho x} + B'e^{-\rho x}$. Imposing the boundary conditions, we obtain

$$\textbf{I} \quad Be^{\rho a/2} + B'e^{-\rho a/2} = 0 \qquad \textbf{II} \quad Be^{-\rho a/2} + B'e^{\rho a/2} = 0 \qquad (3.10.10)$$

Multiplying, Eq. (3.10.10I) by $e^{\rho a/2}$ yields $B' = -Be^{\rho a}$, so $Be^{-\rho a/2} - Be^{\rho a}e^{\rho a/2} = 0$. Multiplying by $e^{\rho a/2}$ and dividing by B, we obtain $1 - e^{2\rho a} = 0$. Therefore, $2\rho a = 0$. Since ρ must be positive, there are no states with corresponding negative energy.

Finally, we consider the case when $E = 0$. According to Problem 3.9, part (c), we have $\psi(x) = Cx + C'$. Imposing the boundary conditions yields

$$C\frac{a}{2} + C' = 0 \qquad -C\frac{a}{2} + C' = 0 \tag{3.10.11}$$

Solving these equations yields $C = C' = 0$; the conclusion is that there is no possible state with $E = 0$.

3.11. Refer to Problem 3.10. At $t = 0$ the particle is in a state described by a linear combination of the two lowest stationary states:

$$\psi(x, 0) = \alpha\psi_1(x) + \beta\psi_2(x) \qquad \left(|\alpha|^2 + |\beta|^2 = 1\right) \tag{3.11.1}$$

(a) Calculate the wavefunction $\Psi(x, t)$ and the mean value of x and p_x as a function of time.

(b) Verify the Ehrenfest theorem, $md\langle x\rangle/dt = \langle p_x\rangle$.

SOLUTION

(a) Consider part (c) of Problem 3.3. The time-evolution of the stationary states is of the form

$$\Psi_n(x, t) = \psi_n(x)\exp(-iE_n t/\hbar) \tag{3.11.2}$$

Consequently, using Eqs. (3.10.9) and (3.11.2) the superposition principle gives

$$\Psi(x, t) = \alpha\Psi_1(x, t) + \beta\Psi_2(x, t)$$

$$= \alpha\left[\sqrt{\frac{2}{a}}\sin\left[\pi\left(\frac{x}{a} - \frac{1}{2}\right)\right]\exp\left(\frac{-\pi^2 i\hbar t}{2ma^2}\right)\right] + \beta\left[\sqrt{\frac{2}{a}}\sin\left[2\pi\left(\frac{x}{a} - \frac{1}{2}\right)\right]\exp\left(\frac{-4\pi^2 i\hbar t}{2ma^2}\right)\right] \tag{3.11.3}$$

We now calculate

$$\langle x\rangle = \int_{-a/2}^{a/2}\Psi^*(x, t)\,x\,\Psi(x, t)\,dx = \int_{-a/2}^{a/2}\left[\alpha^*\Psi_1^*(x, t) + \beta^*\Psi_2^*(x, t)\right]x\left[\alpha\Psi_1(x, t) + \beta\Psi_2(x, t)\right]dx$$

$$= \alpha^2\int_{-a/2}^{a/2}x\left|\Psi_1(x, t)\right|^2 dx + \beta^2\int_{-a/2}^{a/2}x\left|\Psi_2(x, t)\right|^2 dx + 2\,\mathrm{Re}\left[\alpha^*\beta\int_{-a/2}^{a/2}x\Psi_1^*(x, t)\Psi_2(x, t)\,dx\right] \tag{3.11.4}$$

Consider each of the three elements separately:

$$I_1 \equiv \int_{-a/2}^{a/2}x\left|\Psi_1(x, t)\right|^2 dx = \frac{a}{2}\int_{-a/2}^{a/2}x\sin^2\left[\pi\left(\frac{x}{a} - \frac{1}{2}\right)\right]dx \tag{3.11.5}$$

Defining $y = \dfrac{x}{a} - \dfrac{1}{2}$, $dy = \dfrac{dx}{a}$, so

$$I_1 = a\int_{-1}^{0}(2y + 1)\sin^2(\pi y)\,dy = 2a\int_{-1}^{0}y\sin^2(\pi y)\,dy + a\int_{-1}^{0}\sin^2(\pi y)\,dy \tag{3.11.6}$$

Solving these integrals yields

$$I_1 = 2a\left[\frac{y^2}{4} - \frac{y\sin(2\pi y)}{4\pi} - \frac{\cos(2\pi y)}{8\pi^2}\right]_{-1}^{0} + a\left[\frac{y}{2} - \frac{\sin(2\pi y)}{4\pi}\right]_{-1}^{0} = -\frac{a}{2} + \frac{a}{2} = 0 \tag{3.11.7}$$

One can repeat this procedure to show that

$$I_2 \equiv \int_{-a/2}^{a/2} x \left| \Psi_2(x, t) \right|^2 dx = \frac{2}{a} \int_{-a/2}^{a/2} x \sin^2 \left[2\pi \left(\frac{x}{a} - \frac{1}{2} \right) \right] dx = 0 \tag{3.11.8}$$

Note that this result can arise from different considerations. The function $f(x) = \sin^2 \left[2\pi \left(\frac{x}{a} - \frac{1}{2} \right) \right]$ is an even function of x:

$$f(-x) = \left[\sin 2\pi \left(-\frac{x}{a} - \frac{1}{2} \right) \right]^2 = \left[-\sin 2\pi \left(\frac{x}{a} + \frac{1}{2} \right) \right]^2 = \left\{ -\sin \left[2\pi \left(\frac{x}{a} + \frac{1}{2} \right) + 2\pi \right] \right\}^2$$

$$= \left[\sin 2\pi \left(\frac{x}{a} - \frac{1}{2} \right) \right]^2 = f(x) \tag{3.11.9}$$

On the other hand, $f(x) = x$ is an odd function of x; therefore, $x \sin^2[2\pi(x/a - 1/2)]$ is an even function of x, and its integral vanishes from $-a/2$ to $a/2$. Consider now the last term in Eq. (3.11.4):

$$I_3 \equiv \int_{-a/2}^{a/2} x \Psi_1^*(x, t) \Psi_2(x, t)\, dx$$

$$= \frac{2}{a} \int_{-a/2}^{a/2} x \sin \left[\pi \left(\frac{x}{a} - \frac{1}{2} \right) \right] \sin \left[2\pi \left(\frac{x}{a} - \frac{1}{2} \right) \right] \exp \left(-\frac{3\pi^2 i \hbar t}{2ma^2} \right) dx \tag{3.11.10}$$

Defining $y = x/d - 1/2$, $dy = dx/a$, and $\omega = 3\pi^2 \hbar / 2ma^2$, we obtain

$$I_3 = ae^{-i\omega t} \int_{-1}^{0} (2y + 1) \sin(\pi y) \sin(2\pi y)\, dy = ae^{-i\omega t} \int_{-1}^{0} (2y + 1) \frac{1}{2} [\cos(\pi y) - \cos(3\pi y)]\, dy$$

$$= \frac{16a}{9\pi^2} e^{-i\omega t} \tag{3.11.11}$$

Finally, returning to Eq. (3.11.4) we obtain

$$\langle x \rangle = \frac{16a}{9\pi^2} 2\,\mathrm{Re}\,(\alpha^* \beta e^{-i\omega t}) = \frac{32a}{9\pi^2} \left[\mathrm{Re}\,(\alpha^* \beta) \cos(\omega t) + \mathrm{Re}\,(i\alpha^* \beta) \sin(\omega t) \right] \tag{3.11.12}$$

Consider the mean value of the momentum:

$$\langle p_x \rangle = \int_{-a/2}^{a/2} \Psi^* \frac{\hbar}{i} \frac{\partial}{\partial x} \Psi(x, t)\, dx$$

$$= \frac{\hbar}{t} \int_{-a/2}^{a/2} [\alpha^* \Psi_1^*(x, t) + \beta^* \Psi_2^*(x, t)] \left[\alpha \frac{\partial \Psi_1(x, t)}{\partial x} + \beta \frac{\partial \Psi_2(x, t)}{\partial x} \right] dx \tag{3.11.13}$$

We calculate separately each of the four terms in Eq. (3.11.13):

$$\int_{-a/2}^{a/2} \Psi_1^* \frac{\partial \Psi_1(x, t)}{\partial x}\, dx = \frac{2}{a} \frac{\pi}{a} \int_{-a/2}^{a/2} \sin \left[\pi \left(\frac{x}{a} - \frac{1}{2} \right) \right] \cos \left[\pi \left(\frac{x}{a} - \frac{1}{2} \right) \right] dx \tag{3.11.14}$$

$\sin\left[\pi\left(\dfrac{x}{a}-\dfrac{1}{2}\right)\right]$ is an even function of x and $\cos\left[\pi\left(\dfrac{x}{a}-\dfrac{1}{2}\right)\right]$ is an odd function, so their product is an odd function; therefore, the integral of the product between $x=-a/2$ and $x=a/2$ equals zero. Also,

$$\int_{-a/2}^{a/2}\Psi_2^*(x,t)\frac{\partial\Psi_2(x,t)}{\partial x}dx=\frac{2}{a}\frac{2\pi}{a}\int_{-a/2}^{a/2}\sin\left[2\pi\left(\frac{x}{a}-\frac{1}{2}\right)\right]\cos\left[2\pi\left(\frac{x}{a}-\frac{1}{2}\right)\right]dx \qquad (3.11.15)$$

$\sin\left[2\pi\left(\dfrac{x}{a}-\dfrac{1}{2}\right)\right]$ is an odd function of x and $\cos\left[2\pi\left(\dfrac{x}{a}-\dfrac{1}{2}\right)\right]$ is an even once; therefore, their product is an odd function, thus the integral between $x=-a/2$ and $a=2$ vanishes. We have

$$I\equiv\int_{-a/2}^{a/2}\Psi_1^*(x,t)\frac{\partial\Psi_2(x,t)}{\partial x}dx=\frac{4\pi}{a^2}\int_{-a/2}^{a/2}\sin\left[\pi\left(\frac{x}{a}-\frac{1}{2}\right)\right]\cos\left[2\pi\left(\frac{x}{a}-\frac{1}{2}\right)\right]e^{-i\omega t}dx \qquad (3.11.16)$$

Defining $y=\dfrac{x}{a}-\dfrac{1}{2}$ and $dy=\dfrac{dx}{a}$, the integral I becomes

$$I=\frac{4\pi}{a^2}e^{-i\omega t}\int_{-1}^{0}\sin(\pi y)\cos(2\pi y)\,dy=\frac{4\pi}{a}\left[\frac{\cos(\pi y)}{2\pi}-\frac{\cos(3\pi y)}{6\pi}\right]_{-1}^{0}e^{-i\omega t}=\frac{8}{3a}e^{-i\omega t} \qquad (3.11.17)$$

Finally,

$$\Gamma\equiv\int_{-a/2}^{a/2}\Psi_2^*(x,t)\frac{\partial\Psi_1(x,t)}{\partial x}dx=\frac{2\pi}{a}\int_{-a/2}^{a/2}\sin\left[2\pi\left(\frac{x}{a}-\frac{1}{2}\right)\right]\cos\left[\pi\left(\frac{x}{a}-\frac{1}{2}\right)\right]e^{i\omega t}dx \qquad (3.11.18)$$

Using the same definitions used above, we arrive at

$$\Gamma=\frac{2\pi}{a}e^{i\omega t}\int_{-1}^{0}\sin(2\pi y)\cos(\pi y)\,dy=\frac{2\pi}{a}e^{i\omega t}\left[-\frac{\cos(\pi y)}{2\pi}-\frac{\cos(3\pi y)}{6\pi}\right]_{-1}^{0}=-\frac{8}{3a}e^{i\omega t} \qquad (3.11.19)$$

Substituting the results in equation Eq. (3.11.13), we finally reach

$$\langle p_x\rangle=\frac{8\hbar}{3ia}\left[\alpha^*\beta e^{-i\omega t}-\alpha\beta^* e^{i\omega t}\right] \qquad (3.11.20)$$

(b) From Eq. (3.11.12),

$$\langle x(t)\rangle=\frac{16a}{9\pi^2}\left[\alpha^*\beta\exp\left(-\frac{3i\pi^2\hbar}{2ma^2}t\right)+\alpha\beta^*\exp\left(\frac{3i\pi^2\hbar}{2ma^2}t\right)\right] \qquad (3.11.21)$$

Therefore, we have

$$m\frac{d\langle x\rangle}{dt}=m\frac{16a}{9\pi^2}\frac{3i\pi^2\hbar}{2ma^2}\left[-\alpha^*\beta\exp\left(-\frac{3\pi^2 i\hbar}{2ma^2}t\right)+\alpha\beta^*\exp\left(\frac{3\pi^2 i\hbar}{2ma^2}t\right)\right]$$

$$=\frac{8\hbar}{3ia}\left[\alpha^*\beta e^{-i\omega t}-\alpha\beta^* e^{i\omega t}\right] \qquad (3.11.22)$$

By inspection, the last expression is identical to $\langle p_x\rangle$. Thus, for this particular case Ehrenfest's theorem is verified.

3.12. Refer again to Problem 3.10. Now suppose that the potential energy well is located between $x = 0$ and $x = a$:

$$V(x) = \begin{cases} 0 & 0 \le x \le a \\ \infty & \text{otherwise} \end{cases} \tag{3.12.1}$$

Find the stationary eigenstates and the corresponding eigenenergies.

SOLUTION

We begin by performing a formal shift of the potential energy well, $\tilde{x} = x - a/2$, so the problem becomes identical to Problem 3.10:

$$V(\tilde{x}) = \begin{cases} 0 & -a/2 \le \tilde{x} \le a/2 \\ \infty & \text{otherwise} \end{cases} \tag{3.12.2}$$

Using the solution of Problem 3.10, namely Eq. (3.10.5), the possible energies are

$$E_n = \frac{\pi^2 \hbar^2 n^2}{2ma^2} \tag{3.12.3}$$

where n is a positive integer. The corresponding eigenstates are given by Eq. (3.10.9)

$$\psi_n(\tilde{x}) = \sqrt{\frac{2}{a}} \sin\left[n\pi \left(\frac{\tilde{x}}{a} - \frac{1}{2} \right) \right] \tag{3.12.4}$$

Or, in terms of the original coordinate, we have

$$\psi_n(x) = \sqrt{\frac{2}{a}} \sin\left(\frac{n\pi x}{a} - n\pi \right) \tag{3.12.5}$$

3.13. Consider the step potential (Fig. 3.4):

$$V(x) = \begin{cases} V_0 & x > 0 \\ 0 & x < 0 \end{cases} \tag{3.13.1}$$

Consider a current of particles of energy $E > V_0$ moving from $x = -\infty$ to the right. (*a*) Write the stationary solutions for each of the regions. (*b*) Express the fact that there is no current coming back from $x = +\infty$ to the left. (*c*) Use the matching conditions to express the reflected and transmitted amplitudes in terms of the incident amplitude. Note that since the potential is bounded, it can be shown that the derivative of the wavefunction is continuous for all x.

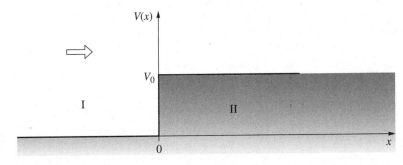

Fig. 3.4

SOLUTION

(*a*) Referring to Problem 3.9 part (*a*), we define

$$k_1 = \sqrt{\frac{2mE}{\hbar^2}} \qquad k_2 = \sqrt{\frac{2m(E - V)}{\hbar^2}} \tag{3.13.2}$$

Then the general solutions for the regions I ($x < 0$) and II ($x > 0$) are

$$\psi_{\mathrm{I}}(x) = A_1 e^{ik_1 x} + A_1' e^{-ik_1 x} \qquad \psi_{\mathrm{II}}(x) = A_2 e^{ik_2 x} + A_2' e^{-ik_2 x} \tag{3.13.3}$$

(b) The wavefunction of form e^{ikx} represents particles coming from $x = -\infty$ to the right, and e^{-ikx} represents particles moving from $x = +\infty$ to the left. $\psi_1(x)$ is the superposition of two waves. The first one is of incident particles propagating from left to right and is of amplitude A_1; the second wave is of amplitude A_1' and represents reflected particles moving from right to left. Since we consider incident particles coming from $x = -\infty$ to the right, it is not possible to find in II a current that moves from $x = +\infty$ to the left. Therefore, we set $A_2' = 0$. Thus, $\psi_{II}(x)$ represents the current of transmitted particles with corresponding amplitude A_2.

(c) First, we apply the continuity condition of $\psi(x)$ at $x = 0$, $\psi_I(0) = \psi_{II}(0)$. Substituting in Eq. (3.13.3) gives

$$A_1 + A_1' = A_2 \tag{3.13.4}$$

Secondly, $\dfrac{\partial \psi(x)}{\partial x}$ should also be continuous at $x = 0$; we have

$$\frac{\partial \psi_I(x)}{\partial x} = ik_1 A_1 e^{ik_1 x} - ik_1 A_1' e^{ik_1 x} \qquad \frac{\partial \psi_{II}(x)}{\partial x} = ik_2 A_2 e^{ik_2 x} \tag{3.13.5}$$

Applying, $\dfrac{\partial \psi_I(0)}{\partial x} = \dfrac{\partial \psi_{II}(0)}{\partial x}$, we obtain

$$ik_1 (A_1 - A_1') = ik_2 A_2 \tag{3.13.6}$$

Substituting A_2 gives $A_1 + A_1' = (A_1 - A_1')k_1/k_2$, which yields

$$\frac{A_1'}{A_1} = \frac{k_1 - k_2}{k_1 + k_2} \tag{3.13.7}$$

Eventually, substituting Eq. (3.13.7) in Eq. (3.13.4) yields $A_1\left(1 + \dfrac{k_1 - k_2}{k_1 + k_2}\right) = A_2$; therefore,

$$\frac{A_2}{A_1} = \frac{2k_1}{k_1 + k_2} \tag{3.13.8}$$

3.14. Refer to Problem 3.13. (a) Compute the probability current in the regions I and II and interpret each term. (b) Find the reflection and transmission coefficients.

SOLUTION

(a) For a stationary state $\psi(x)$, the probability current is time-independent and, as in Eq. (3.7.2), is equal to

$$J(x) = \frac{\hbar}{2mi}\left[\psi^*(x)\frac{\partial \psi(x)}{\partial x} - \psi(x)\frac{\partial \psi^*(x)}{\partial x}\right] \tag{3.14.1}$$

Using Eq. (3.13.3) for region I, we have

$$J_I(x) = \frac{\hbar}{2mi}\left[\left(A_1^* e^{-ik_1 x} + A_1'^* e^{ik_1 x}\right)\left(ik_1 A_1 e^{ik_1 x} - ik_1 A_1' e^{-ik_1 x}\right) - \left(A_1 e^{ik_1 x} + A_1' e^{-ik_1 x}\right)\left(-ik_1 A_1^* e^{-ik_1 x} + ik_1 A_1'^* e^{ik_1 x}\right)\right]$$

$$= \frac{\hbar k_1}{m}\left(|A_1|^2 - |A_1'|^2\right) \tag{3.14.2}$$

Similarly, for region II we have

$$J_{II}(x) = \frac{\hbar}{2mi}\left[A_2^* e^{-ik_2 x}(ik_2)e^{ik_2 x} - A_2 e^{ik_2 x}(-ik_2)e^{-ik_2 x}\right] = \frac{\hbar k_2}{m}|A_2|^2 \tag{3.14.3}$$

The probability current in region I is the sum of two terms: $\hbar k_1 |A_1|^2/m$ corresponds to the incoming current moving from left to right, and $-\hbar k_1 |A_1'|^2/m$ corresponds to the reflected current (moving from right to left). Note that the probability current in region II represents the transmitted wave.

(b) Using the definition of the *reflection coefficient* [refer to Eq. (3.27)], we have

$$R = \frac{|A_1'|^2 \hbar k_1/m}{|A_1|^2 \hbar k_1/m} = \left|\frac{A_1'}{A_1}\right|^2 \tag{3.14.4}$$

Substituting Eq. (3.13.7), we arrive at

$$R = \frac{(k_1 - k_2)^2}{(k_1 + k_2)^2} = 1 - \frac{4k_1 k_2}{(k_1 + k_2)^2} \qquad (3.14.5)$$

The *transmission coefficient* is

$$T = \frac{|A_2|^2 \, \hbar k_2 / m}{|A_1|^2 \, \hbar k_1 / m} = \frac{k_2}{k_1} \left| \frac{A_2}{A_1} \right|^2 \qquad (3.14.6)$$

Substituting Eq. (3.13.8), we arrive at

$$T = \frac{k_2}{k_1} \left(\frac{2k_1}{k_1 + k_2} \right)^2 = \frac{4k_1 k_2}{(k_1 + k_2)^2} \qquad (3.14.7)$$

3.15. Consider a free particle of mass m whose wavefunction at time $t = 0$ is given by

$$\Psi(x, 0) = \frac{\sqrt{a}}{(2\pi)^{3/4}} \int_{-\infty}^{\infty} e^{-a^2 (k - k_0)^2 / 4} e^{ikx} \, dk \qquad (3.15.1)$$

Calculate the time evolution of the wave packet $\Psi(x, t)$ and the probability density $|\Psi(x, t)|^2$. Sketch qualitatively the probability density for $t < 0$, $t = 0$, and $t > 0$. You may use the following identity: For complex numbers α and β such that $-\pi/4 < \arg(\alpha) < \pi/4$,

$$\int_{-\infty}^{\infty} e^{-\alpha^2 (y + \beta)^2} \, dy = \frac{\sqrt{\pi}}{\alpha} \qquad (3.15.2)$$

SOLUTION

The wave packet at $t = 0$ is a superposition of plane waves e^{ikx} with coefficients $\dfrac{\sqrt{a}}{(2\pi)^{3/4}} e^{-a^2 (k - k_0)^2 / 4}$; this is a

Gaussian curve centered at $k = k_0$. The time evolution of a plane wave e^{ikx} has the form $e^{ikx} e^{-iE(k)t/\hbar} = e^{ikx} e^{-i\hbar k^2 t / 2m}$. We set $\omega(k) = \hbar k^2 / 2m$. Using the superposition principle, the time evolution of the wave packet $\Psi(x, 0)$ is

$$\Psi(x, t) = \frac{\sqrt{a}}{(2\pi)^{3/4}} \int_{-\infty}^{\infty} e^{-a^2 (k - k_0)^2 / 4} e^{i[kx - \omega(k)t]} \, dk \qquad (3.15.3)$$

Our aim is to transform this integral into the form of Eq. (3.15.2). Therefore, we rearrange the terms in the exponent:

$$-\frac{a^2}{4}(k - k_0)^2 + i[kx - \omega(k)t] = -\left(\frac{a^2}{4} + \frac{i\hbar t}{2m} \right) k^2 + \left(\frac{a^2}{2} k_0 + ix \right) k - \frac{a^2}{4} k_0^2$$

$$= -\left(\frac{a^2}{4} + \frac{i\hbar t}{2m} \right) \left[k - \frac{\frac{a^2}{2} k_0 + ix}{2\left(\frac{a^2}{4} + \frac{i\hbar t}{2m} \right)} \right]^2 + \frac{\left(\frac{a^2}{2} k_0 + ix \right)^2}{4\left(\frac{a^2}{4} + \frac{i\hbar t}{2m} \right)} - \frac{a^2}{4} k_0^2 \qquad (3.15.4)$$

Substituting in Eq. (3.15.4) and using Eq. (3.15.2) yields

$$\Psi(x, t) = \frac{\sqrt{a}}{2^{3/4} \pi^{1/4}} \frac{\exp\left(-\dfrac{a^2 k_0^2}{4} \right)}{\sqrt{\dfrac{a^2}{4} + \dfrac{i\hbar t}{2m}}} \exp\left[\frac{\left(\dfrac{a^2}{2} k_0 + ix \right)^2}{a^2 + \dfrac{2i\hbar t}{m}} \right] \qquad (3.15.5)$$

The conjugate complex of Eq. (3.15.5) is

$$\Psi^*(x, t) = \frac{\sqrt{a}}{2^{3/4}\pi^{1/4}} \frac{\exp\left(-\dfrac{a^2 k_0^2}{4}\right)}{\sqrt{\dfrac{a^2}{4} - \dfrac{i\hbar t}{2m}}} \exp\left[\frac{\left(\dfrac{a^2}{2}k_0 - ix\right)^2}{a^2 - \dfrac{2i\hbar t}{m}}\right] \tag{3.15.6}$$

Hence,

$$|\Psi(x,t)|^2 = \frac{a}{2^{3/2}\sqrt{\pi}} \frac{\exp\left(-\dfrac{a^2 k_0^2}{2}\right)}{\sqrt{\left(\dfrac{a^2}{4} + \dfrac{i\hbar t}{2m}\right)\left(\dfrac{a^2}{4} - \dfrac{i\hbar t}{2m}\right)}} \exp\left[\frac{\left(\dfrac{a^2 k_0}{2}\right)^2 - x^2 + ia^2 k_0 x}{a^2 + 2i\hbar t/m} + \frac{\left(\dfrac{a^2 k_0}{2}\right)^2 - x^2 - ia^2 k_0 x}{a^2 - 2i\hbar t/m}\right]$$

$$= \sqrt{\frac{2}{\pi a^2}}\frac{1}{\sqrt{1 + 4\hbar^2 t^2/m^2 a^4}}\exp\left[-\frac{\dfrac{a^2 k_0^2}{2}\left(a^4 + \dfrac{4\hbar^2 t^2}{m^2}\right) + 2a^2\left(\dfrac{a^4 k_0^2}{2} - x^2\right) + \dfrac{4\hbar k_0 a^2}{m}xt}{a^4 + 4\hbar^2 t^2/m}\right]$$

$$= \sqrt{\frac{2}{\pi a^2}}\frac{1}{\sqrt{1 + 4\hbar^2 t^2/m^2 a^4}}\exp\left[-\frac{2a^2(x - \hbar k_0 t/m)^2}{a^4 + 4\hbar^2 t^2/m^2}\right] \tag{3.15.7}$$

The probability density is a Gaussian curve for every time t entered at $x_C = (\hbar k_0/m)t$. (That is, the wave packet moves with a speed $v = \hbar k_0/m$.) The value of $|\Psi(x, t)|^2$ is maximal for $t = 0$ and tends to zero when $t \to \infty$. The width of the wave packet is minimal for $t = 0$ and tends to ∞ when $t \to \infty$; see Fig. 3.5.

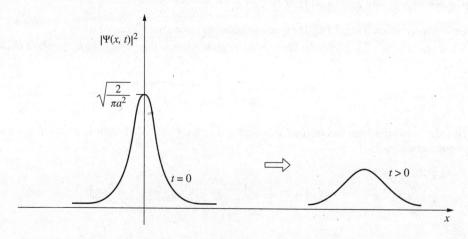

Fig. 3.5

3.16. Consider a square potential barrier (Fig. 3.6):

$$V(x) = \begin{cases} 0 & x < 0 \\ V_0 & 0 < x < l \\ 0 & l < x \end{cases} \tag{3.16.1}$$

(*a*) Assume that incident particles of energy $E > V_0$ are coming from $x = -\infty$. (*a*) Find the stationary states. Apply the matching conditions at $x = 0$ and $x = l$. (*b*) Find the transmission and reflection coefficients. Sketch the transmission coefficient as a function of the barrier's width l, and discuss the results.

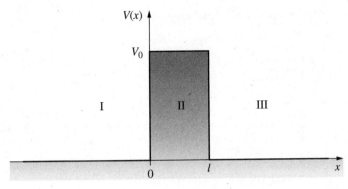

Fig. 3.6

SOLUTION

(a) Similar to Problem 3.9, part (a), we define

$$k_1 = \sqrt{\frac{2mE}{\hbar^2}} \qquad k_2 = \sqrt{\frac{2m(E - V_0)}{\hbar^2}} \qquad (3.16.2)$$

Thus, the stationary solutions for the three regions I $(x < 0)$, II $(0 < x < l)$, and III $(x > l)$ are:

$$\begin{cases} \psi_{\mathrm{I}}(x) = A_1 e^{ik_1 x} + A_1' e^{-ik_1 x} \\ \psi_{\mathrm{II}}(x) = A_2 e^{ik_2 x} + A_2' e^{-ik_2 x} \\ \psi_{\mathrm{III}}(x) = A_3 e^{ik_1 x} + A_3' e^{-ik_1 x} \end{cases} \qquad (3.16.3)$$

Each of the solutions describes a sum of terms representing movement from left to right, and from right to left. We consider incident particles from $x = -\infty$, so there should be no particles in region III moving from $x = \infty$ to the left. Therefore, we set $A_3' = 0$. The matching conditions at $x = l$ enable us to express A_2 and A_2' in terms of A_3. The continuity of $\psi(x)$ at $x = l$ yields $\psi_{\mathrm{II}}(l) = \psi_{\mathrm{III}}(l)$, so

$$A_2 e^{ik_2 l} + A_2' e^{-ik_2 l} = A_3 e^{ik_1 l} \qquad (3.16.4)$$

The continuity of $\psi'(x)$ yields

$$ik_2 A_2 e^{ik_2 l} - ik_2 A_2' e^{-ik_2 l} = ik_1 A_3 e^{ik_1 l} \qquad (3.16.5)$$

Equations (3.16.4) and (3.16.5) give

$$\begin{cases} A_2 = \left[\dfrac{k_2 + k_1}{2k_2} e^{i(k_1 - k_2)l} \right] A_3 \\ A_2' = \left[\dfrac{k_2 - k_1}{2k_2} e^{i(k_1 + k_2)l} \right] A_3 \end{cases} \qquad (3.16.6)$$

The matching conditions at $x = 0$ yield

$$\psi_{\mathrm{I}}(0) = \psi_{\mathrm{II}}(0) \Rightarrow A_1 + A_1' = A_2 + A_2' \qquad (3.16.7)$$

and

$$\psi_{\mathrm{I}}'(0) = \psi_{\mathrm{II}}'(0) \Rightarrow ik_1 A_1 - ik_1 A_1' = ik_2 A_2 - ik_2 A_2' \qquad (3.16.8)$$

so we obtain

$$A_1 = \frac{k_1 + k_2}{2k_1} A_2 + \frac{k_1 - k_2}{2k_1} A_2' \qquad (3.16.9)$$

Using (3.16.6), we can express A_1 in terms of A_3:

$$A_1 = \left[\frac{(k_1 + k_2)^2}{4k_1 k_2} e^{i(k_1 - k_2)l} - \frac{(k_1 - k_2)^2}{4k_1 k_2} e^{i(k_1 + k_2)l} \right] A_3$$

$$= \left[\frac{(k_1 + k_2)^2 - (k_1 - k_2)^2}{4k_1 k_2} \cos(k_2 l) - i \frac{(k_1 + k_2)^2 + (k_1 - k_2)^2}{4k_1 k_2} \sin(k_2 l) \right] e^{ik_1 l} A_3$$

$$= \left[\cos(k_2 l) - i \frac{k_1^2 + k_2^2}{2k_1 k_2} \sin(k_2 l) \right] e^{ik_1 l} A_3 \tag{3.16.10}$$

Similarly, we express A_1' in terms of A_3:

$$A_1' = \frac{k_1 - k_2}{2k_1} A_2 + \frac{k_1 + k_2}{2k_1} A_2' = \left[\frac{(k_1 + k_2)(k_1 - k_2)}{4k_1 k_2} e^{i(k_1 - k_2)l} + \frac{(k_1 + k_2)(k_2 - k_1)}{4k_2} e^{i(k_1 + k_2)l} \right] A_3$$

$$= \left[\frac{(k_1^2 - k_2^2) + (k_2^2 - k_1^2)}{4k_1 k_2} \cos(k_2 l) + i \frac{(k_2^2 - k_1^2) - (k_1^2 - k_2^2)}{4k_1 k_2} \sin(k_2 l) \right] A_3$$

$$= i \frac{k_2^2 - k_1^2}{2k_1 k_2} \sin(k_2 l) e^{ik_1 l} A_3 \tag{3.16.11}$$

(*b*) The reflection coefficient is the ratio of squares of the amplitudes corresponding to the incident and reflection waves (compare to Problem 3.14):

$$R = \left| \frac{A_1'}{A_1} \right|^2 \tag{3.16.12}$$

Using the results of part (*a*), we obtain

$$R = \frac{\left[\dfrac{k_2^2 - k_1^2}{2k_1 k_2} \sin(k_2 l) \right]^2}{\cos^2(k_2 l) + \left[\dfrac{k_1^2 + k_2^2}{2k_1 k_2} \sin(k_2 l) \right]^2} = \frac{(k_2^2 - k_1^2)^2 \sin^2(k_2 l)}{4k_1^2 k_2^2 + (k_1^2 - k_2^2)^2 \sin^2(k_2 l)} \tag{3.16.13}$$

Finally, the transmission coefficient is

$$T = \left| \frac{A_3}{A_1} \right|^2 = \frac{1}{\cos^2(k_2 l) + \left(\dfrac{k_1^2 + k_2^2}{2k_1 k_2} \right)^2 \sin^2(k_2 l)} = \frac{4k_1^2 k_2^2}{4k_1^2 k_2^2 + (k_1^2 - k_2^2)^2 \sin^2(k_2 l)} \tag{3.16.14}$$

The dimensionless transmission coefficient oscillates periodically as a function of l (see Fig. 3.7) between its maximum value (one) and its minimum value $[1 + V_0^2 / 4E(E - V_0)]^{-1}$. When l is an integral multiple of π/k_2, there is no reflection from the barrier; this is called *resonance scattering* (see Chap. 15).

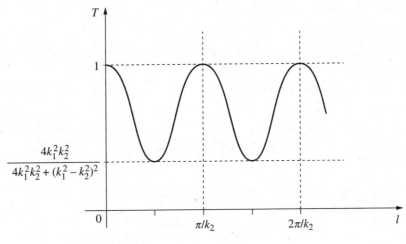

Fig. 3.7

3.17. Consider the square potential barrier of Problem 3.16. Find the stationary states describing incident particles of energy $E < V_0$. Compute the transmission coefficient and discuss the results.

SOLUTION

The method of solution is analogous to that of Problem 3.16. Referring to Problem 3-9, we define

$$k_1 = \sqrt{\frac{2mE}{\hbar^2}} \qquad \rho = \sqrt{\frac{2m(V_0 - E)}{\hbar^2}} \tag{3.17.1}$$

The stationary solutions for the three regions I ($x < 0$), II ($0 < x < l$), and III ($x > l$) are

$$\begin{cases} \psi_{\mathrm{I}}(x) = A_1 e^{ik_1 x} + A_1' e^{-ik_1 x} \\[2mm] \psi_{\mathrm{II}}(x) = A_2 e^{\rho x} + A_2' e^{-\rho x} \\[2mm] \psi_{\mathrm{III}}(x) = A_3 e^{ik_1 x} + A_3' e^{-ik_1 x} \end{cases} \tag{3.17.2}$$

We describe incident particles coming from $x = -\infty$, so we set $A_3' = 0$. Applying the matching conditions in $x = l$ gives

$$\psi_{\mathrm{II}}(l) = \psi_{\mathrm{III}}(l) \Rightarrow A_2 e^{\rho l} + A_2' e^{-\rho l} = A_3 e^{ik_1 x} \tag{3.17.3}$$

$$\psi_{\mathrm{II}}'(l) = \psi_{\mathrm{III}}'(l) \Rightarrow A_2 \rho e^{\rho l} - A_2' e^{-\rho l} = ik_1 A_3 e^{ik_1 l} \tag{3.17.4}$$

From Eqs. (3.17.3) and (3.17.4) we obtain

$$A_2 = \left[\frac{\rho + ik_1}{2\rho} e^{(ik_1 - \rho)l} \right] A_3 \qquad A_2' = \left[\frac{\rho - ik_1}{2\rho} e^{(ik_1 + \rho)l} \right] A_3 \tag{3.17.5}$$

The matching conditions at $x = 0$ yield

$$\psi_{\mathrm{I}}(0) = \psi_{\mathrm{II}}(0) \Rightarrow A_1 + A_1' = A_2 + A_2' \tag{3.17.6}$$

$$\psi_{\mathrm{I}}'(0) = \psi_{\mathrm{II}}'(0) \Rightarrow ik_1 A_1 - ik_1 A_1' = \rho A_2 - \rho A_2' \tag{3.17.7}$$

From Eqs. (3.17.6) and (3.17.7) we obtain

$$A_1 = \frac{ik_1 + \rho}{2ik_1} A_2 + \frac{ik_1 - \rho}{2ik_1} A_2' \tag{3.17.8}$$

Using Eq. (3.17.5), we arrive at

$$A_1 = \left[\frac{(ik_1 + \rho)^2}{4ik_1\rho} e^{(ik_1 - \rho)l} - \frac{(ik_1 - \rho)^2}{4ik_1\rho} e^{(ik_1 + \rho)l} \right] A_3 = \left[-i\frac{k_1^2 - \rho^2}{2k_1\rho} \sinh(\rho l) + \cosh(\rho l) \right] e^{ik_1 l} A_3 \quad (3.17.9)$$

Finally, consider the transmission coefficient:

$$T = \left| \frac{A_3}{A_1} \right|^2 = \frac{1}{\cosh^2(\rho l) + \left(\dfrac{k_1^2 - \rho^2}{2k_1\rho} \right)^2 \sinh^2(\rho l)} = \frac{1}{1 + \left(\dfrac{k_1^2 + \rho^2}{2k_1\rho} \right)^2 \sinh^2(\rho l)} \quad (3.17.10)$$

where we used the identity $\cosh^2 \alpha - \sinh^2 \alpha = 1$. Hence,

$$T = \frac{4E(V_0 - E)}{4E(V_0 - E) + V_0^2 \sinh^2\left[\dfrac{\sqrt{2m(V_0 - E)}}{\hbar} l \right]} \quad (3.17.11)$$

We see that in contrast to the classical predictions, particles of energy $E < V_0$ have a nonzero probability of crossing the potential barrier. This phenomenon is called the *tunnel effect*.

3.18. In this problem we study the bound states for a finite square potential well (see Fig. 3.8). Consider the one-dimensional potential defined by

$$V(x) = \begin{cases} 0 & (x < -a/2 \\ -V_0 & -a/2 < x < a/2 \\ 0 & (a/2 < x) \end{cases} \quad (3.18.1)$$

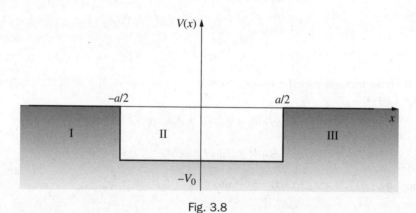

Fig. 3.8

(*a*) Write the stationary solutions for a particle of mass m and energy $-V_0 < E < 0$ for each of the regions I ($x < -a/2$), II ($-a/2 < x < a/2$), and III ($a/2 < x$). (*b*) Apply the matching conditions at $x = -a/2$ and $x = a/2$. Obtain an equation for the possible energies. Draw a graphic representation of the equation in order to obtain qualitative properties of the solution.

SOLUTION

(*a*) Referring to Problem 3.9, we define

$$\rho = \sqrt{\frac{-2mE}{\hbar^2}} \qquad k = \sqrt{\frac{2m(E + V_0)}{\hbar^2}} \quad (3.18.2)$$

Then the stationary solutions for each of the regions are

$$
\begin{cases}
\psi_{\mathrm{I}}(x) = Ae^{\rho x} + A'e^{-\rho x} \\
\psi_{\mathrm{II}}(x) = Be^{ikx} + B'e^{-ikx} \\
\psi_{\mathrm{III}}(x) = C'e^{\rho x} + Ce^{-\rho x}
\end{cases}
\tag{3.18.3}
$$

Since $\psi(x)$ must be bounded in regions I and III, we set $A' = C' = 0$; therefore,

$$
\begin{cases}
\psi_{\mathrm{I}}(x) = Ae^{\rho x} \\
\psi_{\mathrm{II}}(x) = Be^{ikx} + B'e^{-ikx} \\
\psi_{\mathrm{III}}(x) = Ce^{-\rho x}
\end{cases}
\tag{3.18.4}
$$

(*b*) The continuity of $\psi(x)$ and $\psi'(x)$ at $x = -a/2$ yields

$$
\begin{cases}
Ae^{-\rho a/2} = Be^{-ika/2} + B'e^{ika/2} \\
\rho Ae^{-\rho a/2} = ikBe^{-ika/2} - ikB'e^{ika/2}
\end{cases}
\tag{3.18.5}
$$

Similarly, the matching conditions at $x = a/2$ yield

$$
\begin{cases}
Ce^{-\rho a/2} = Be^{ika/2} + B'e^{-ika/2} \\
-\rho Ce^{-\rho a/2} = ikBe^{ika/2} - ikB'e^{-ika/2}
\end{cases}
\tag{3.18.6}
$$

Hence, we can express B and B' in terms of A:

$$
B = \left(\frac{\rho + ik}{2ik} e^{(-\rho+ik)a/2} \right) A
\qquad
B' = \left(-\frac{\rho - ik}{2ik} e^{(-\rho+ik)a/2} \right) A
\tag{3.18.7}
$$

We substitute Eq. (3.18.7) in Eq. (3.18.6) to obtain

$$
\begin{cases}
C = \left(\dfrac{\rho + ik}{2ik} e^{ika} - \dfrac{\rho - ik}{2ik} e^{-ika} \right) A \\
-\dfrac{\rho}{ik} C = \left(\dfrac{\rho + ik}{2ik} e^{ika} - \dfrac{\rho - ik}{2ik} e^{-ika} \right) A
\end{cases}
\tag{3.18.8}
$$

To obtain a nonvanishing solution of Eq. (3.18.8), we must have

$$
-\frac{\rho}{ik} \left(\frac{\rho + ik}{2ik} e^{ika} - \frac{\rho - ik}{2ik} e^{-ika} \right) = \left(\frac{\rho + ik}{2ik} e^{ika} + \frac{\rho - ik}{2ik} e^{-ika} \right)
\tag{3.18.9}
$$

which is equivalent to

$$
\left(\frac{\rho - ik}{\rho + ik} \right)^2 = e^{2ika}
\tag{3.18.10}
$$

Equation (3.18.10) is an equation for E, since ρ and k depend only on E and on the constants of the problem. The solutions of Eq. (3.18.10) in terms of E are the energies corresponding to bound states of the well.

We shall transform Eq. (3.18.10) to express it in terms of k only. There are two possible cases. The first one is

I.
$$
\left(\frac{\rho - ik}{\rho + ik} \right)^2 = -e^{ika}
\tag{3.18.11}
$$

The left-hand side of Eq. (3.18.11) is a complex number of modulus 1 and phase $-2 \tan^{-1} (k/\rho)$. Note that $\rho + ik$ is the complex conjugate of $\rho - ik$. The right-hand side of Eq. (3.18.11) is also a complex number of modulus 1, and its phase is $\pi + ka$; $-e^{ika} = e^{i\pi} e^{ika} = e^{i(\pi+ka)}$. Therefore, we have

$$\tan^{-1}\left(\frac{k}{\rho}\right) = -\left(\frac{\pi}{2} + \frac{ka}{2}\right) \Rightarrow \frac{k}{\rho} = \tan\left[-\left(\frac{\pi}{2} + \frac{ka}{2}\right)\right] = -\tan\left(\frac{\pi}{2} + \frac{ka}{2}\right)$$

$$= \cot\left(\frac{ka}{2}\right) = \frac{1}{\tan(ka/2)} \tag{3.18.12}$$

and

$$\tan\left(\frac{ka}{2}\right) = \frac{\rho}{k} \tag{3.18.13}$$

We define $k_0 = \sqrt{\dfrac{2mV_0}{\hbar^2}} = \sqrt{k^2 + \rho^2}$, where the parameter k_0 is E-independent. Consider

$$\frac{1}{\cos^2(ka/2)} = 1 + \tan^2\left(\frac{ka}{2}\right) = \frac{k^2 + \rho^2}{k^2} = \left(\frac{k_0}{k}\right)^2 \tag{3.18.14}$$

Equation (3.18.11) is thus equivalent to the following system of equations:

$$\begin{cases} \left|\cos\left(\dfrac{ka}{2}\right)\right| = \dfrac{k}{k_0} \\[2ex] \tan\left(\dfrac{ka}{2}\right) > 0 \end{cases} \tag{3.18.15}$$

where we used Eqs. (3.18.13) and (3.18.14) together with the fact that both ρ and k are positive.
    We turn to the second possible case, i.e.,

$$\textbf{II.} \qquad\qquad \left(\frac{\rho - ik}{\rho + ik}\right)^2 = e^{ika} \tag{3.18.16}$$

Similar arguments, as in case I, lead us to

$$-2\tan^{-1}\left(\frac{k}{\rho}\right) = ka \Rightarrow \tan\frac{ka}{2} = -\frac{k}{\rho} \tag{3.18.17}$$

Consider

$$\sin^2\left(\frac{ka}{2}\right) = \frac{\tan^2(ka/2)}{1 + \tan^2(ka/2)} = \frac{k^2}{k^2 + \rho^2} \tag{3.18.18}$$

Thus,

$$\begin{cases} \left|\sin\left(\dfrac{ka}{2}\right)\right| = \dfrac{k}{k_0} \\[2ex] \tan\left(\dfrac{ka}{2}\right) < 0 \end{cases} \tag{3.18.19}$$

In Fig. 3.9 we represent Eqs. (3.18.15) and (3.18.19) graphically. The straight line represents the function k/k_0, and the sinusoidal arcs represent the functions $\left|\sin\left(\dfrac{ka}{2}\right)\right|$ and $\left|\cos\left(\dfrac{ka}{2}\right)\right|$. The dotted parts are the regions where the condition on $\tan\left(\dfrac{ka}{2}\right)$ is not fulfilled.

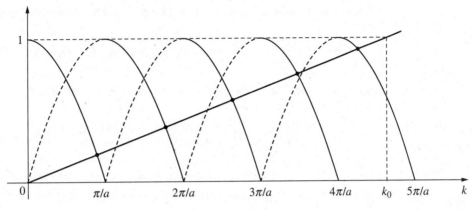

Fig. 3.9

The intersections marked with a point represent the solutions in terms of k. From these solutions it is possible to determine the possible energies. From Fig. 3.9 we see that if $k_0 \leq \pi/a$, that is, if

$$V_0 \leq V_1 \equiv \frac{\pi^2 \hbar^2}{2ma^2} \qquad (3.18.20)$$

then there exists only one bound state of the particle. Then, if $V_1 \leq V_0 < 4V_1$ there are two bound states, and so on. If $V_0 \gg V_1$, the slope $1/k_0$ of the line is very small. For the lowest energy levels we have approximately

$$k = \frac{n\pi}{a} \qquad (n = 1, 2, 3, \ldots) \qquad (3.18.21)$$

and consequently,

$$E = \frac{\pi^2 \hbar^2 n^2}{2ma^2} - V_0 \qquad (3.18.22)$$

3.19. Consider a particle of mass m and energy $E > 0$ held in the one-dimensional potential $-V_0\,\delta(x-a)$. (*a*) Integrate the stationary Schrödinger equation between $a - \varepsilon$ and $a + \varepsilon$. Taking the limit $\varepsilon \to 0$, show that the derivative of the eigenfunction $\psi(x)$ presents a discontinuity at $x = a$ and determine it. (*b*) Relying on Problem 3.9, part (*a*), $\psi(x)$ can be written

$$\begin{cases} \psi(x) = A_1 e^{ikx} + A_1' e^{-ikx} & x < a \\ \psi(x) = A_2 e^{ikx} + A_2' e^{-ikx} & x > a \end{cases} \qquad (3.19.1)$$

where $k = \sqrt{2mE/\hbar^2}$. Calculate the matrix M defined by

$$\begin{pmatrix} A_2 \\ A_2' \end{pmatrix} = M \begin{pmatrix} A_1 \\ A_1' \end{pmatrix} \qquad (3.19.2)$$

SOLUTION

(*a*) Using the Schrödinger equation,

$$-\frac{\hbar^2}{2m}\frac{d^2\psi(x)}{dx^2} + V_0\delta(x-a)\psi(x) = E\psi(x) \qquad (3.19.3)$$

Integrating between $a - \varepsilon$ and $a + \varepsilon$ yields

$$-\frac{\hbar^2}{2m}\int_{a-\varepsilon}^{a+\varepsilon}\frac{d^2\psi(x)}{dx^2}\,dx + V_0\int_{a-\varepsilon}^{a+\varepsilon}\delta(x-a)\psi(x)\,dx = E\int_{a-\varepsilon}^{a+\varepsilon}\psi(x)\,dx \qquad (3.19.4)$$

According to the definition of the δ-function (see the Mathematical Appendix), the integration gives

$$-\frac{\hbar^2}{2m}\left(\frac{d\psi(x)}{dx}\bigg|_{x=a+\varepsilon} - \frac{d\psi(x)}{dx}\bigg|_{x=a-\varepsilon}\right) + V_0\psi(a) = E\int_{a-\varepsilon}^{a+\varepsilon}\psi(x)\,dx \qquad (3.19.5)$$

Since $\psi(x)$ is continuous and finite in the interval $[a - \varepsilon, a + \varepsilon]$, in the limit $\varepsilon \to 0$,

$$-\frac{\hbar^2}{2m}\left[\lim_{\substack{x\to a \\ x>a}}\frac{d\psi(x)}{dx} - \lim_{\substack{x\to a \\ x<a}}\frac{d\psi(x)}{dx}\right] + V_0\psi(x) = 0 \qquad (3.19.6)$$

We see that the derivative of $\psi(x)$ presents a discontinuity at $x = a$ that equals $2mV_0\psi(a)/\hbar^2$.

(b) We have two matching conditions at $x = a$. The continuity of $\psi(x)$ at $x = a$ yields

$$A_1e^{ika} + A_1'e^{-ika} = A_2e^{ika} + A_2'e^{-ika} \qquad (3.19.7)$$

where the second matching condition is given in relation to Eq. (3.19.6) and yields

$$\frac{\hbar^2}{2m}\left(A_1ike^{ika} - A_1'ike^{-ika} - A_2ike^{ika} + A_2'ike^{-ika}\right) = -V_0\left(A_1e^{ika} + A_1'e^{-ika}\right) \qquad (3.19.8)$$

Equations (3.19.6) and (3.19.7) enable us to express A_2 and A_2' in terms of A_1 and A_1':

$$\begin{cases} A_2 = \left(1 + \dfrac{mV_0}{ik\hbar^2}\right)A_1 + \dfrac{mV_0}{ik\hbar^2}e^{-2ika}A_1' \\[3mm] A_2' = -\dfrac{mV_0}{ik\hbar^2}e^{2ika}A_1 + \left(1 - \dfrac{mV_0}{ik\hbar^2}\right)A_1' \end{cases} \qquad (3.19.9)$$

We therefore have

$$\begin{pmatrix} A_2 \\ A_2' \end{pmatrix} = M\begin{pmatrix} A_1 \\ A_1' \end{pmatrix} \qquad (3.19.10)$$

where

$$M = \begin{pmatrix} 1 + \dfrac{mV_0}{ik\hbar^2} & +\dfrac{mV_0}{ik\hbar^2}e^{-2ika} \\[3mm] -\dfrac{mV_0}{ik\hbar^2}e^{2ika} & 1 - \dfrac{mV_0}{ik\hbar^2} \end{pmatrix} \qquad (3.19.11)$$

3.20. In this problem we study the possible energies ($E > 0$) of a particle of mass m held in a δ-function periodic potential (see Fig. 3.10). We define a one-dimensional potential by

$$V(x) = \frac{\hbar^2\lambda}{2ma}\sum_{n=-\infty}^{\infty}\delta(x - na) \qquad (3.20.1)$$

Referring to Problem 3.9, part (a), for each of the regions Ω_n [$na < x < (n + 1)\,a$], the stationary solution can be written in the form

$$\psi_n(x) = B_ne^{ik(x-na)} + C_ne^{-ik(x-na)} \qquad (3.20.2)$$

(a) Use Problem 3.19 to find the matrix $\hat{T}$ relating the regions Ω_{n+1} and Ω_n:

$$\begin{pmatrix} B_{n+1} \\ C_{n+1} \end{pmatrix} = \hat{T}\begin{pmatrix} B_n \\ C_n \end{pmatrix} \qquad (3.20.3)$$

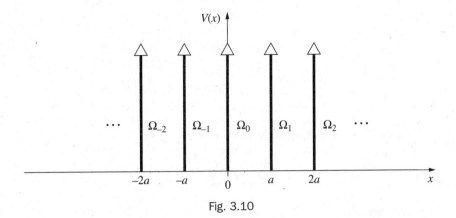

Fig. 3.10

Prove that $\hat{T}$ is not a singular matrix. (b) Since $\hat{T}$ is a nonsingular matrix, we can find a basis $(\mathbf{b}_1, \mathbf{b}_2)$ of C^2 consisting of eigenvectors of the matrix $\hat{T}$. We write

$$\begin{pmatrix} B_0 \\ C_0 \end{pmatrix} = \beta_1 \mathbf{b}_1 + \beta_2 \mathbf{b}_2 \tag{3.20.4}$$

where β_1, β_2 are complex numbers. Impose the condition that $|B_n|^2 + |C_n|^2$ does not diverge for $n \to \pm\infty$ to obtain a restriction on the eigenvalues of $\hat{T}$. Express this restriction in terms of the possible energies E.

SOLUTION

(a) We compare the definitions of $\psi_n(x)$ and $\psi_{n+1}(x)$ according to Eq. (3.20.2) and the definition of $\psi(x)$ in Problem 3.19, part (b). The analogy is depicted in Table 3.1.

Table 3.1

Problem 3.19	Problem 3.20
A_1	$B_n e^{-ikna}$
A_1'	$C_n e^{ikna}$
A_2	$B_{n+1} e^{-ik(n+1)a}$
A_2'	$C_{n+1} e^{ik(n+1)a}$
V_0	$\dfrac{\hbar^2}{2m}\dfrac{\lambda}{a}$

Also, the boundary between the two regions Ω_n and Ω_{n+1} is set in $x = (n+1)a$, whereas in Problem 3.19 the boundary condition is imposed at $x = a$. Using this analogy we have

$$\begin{cases} B_{n+1} e^{-ik(n+1)a} = B_n e^{-ikna}\left(1 - \dfrac{i\lambda}{2ka}\right) - C_n e^{ikna}\left(\dfrac{i\lambda}{2ka}\right) e^{-2ik(n+1)a} \\[2mm] C_{n+1} e^{ik(n+1)a} = B_n e^{-ikna}\left(\dfrac{i\lambda}{2ka}\right) e^{2ik(n+1)a} + C_n e^{ikna}\left(1 + \dfrac{i\lambda}{2ka}\right) \end{cases} \tag{3.20.5}$$

We therefore have

$$\begin{pmatrix} B_{n+1} \\ C_{n+1} \end{pmatrix} = \hat{T}\begin{pmatrix} B_n \\ C_n \end{pmatrix} \tag{3.20.6}$$

where

$$\hat{T} = \begin{pmatrix} \left(1 - \dfrac{i\lambda}{2ka}\right) e^{ika} & -\dfrac{i\lambda}{2ka} e^{-ika} \\ +\dfrac{i\lambda}{2ka} e^{ika} & \left(1 + \dfrac{i\lambda}{2ka}\right) e^{-ika} \end{pmatrix} \tag{3.20.7}$$

We see that $\hat{T}$ is not a singular matrix, since

$$\det \hat{T} = \left(1 + \frac{i\lambda}{2ka}\right)\left(1 - \frac{i\lambda}{2ka}\right) + \left(\frac{i\lambda}{2ka}\right)^2 = 1 \tag{3.20.8}$$

and therefore $\det \hat{T} = 0$.

(b) Since $\hat{T}$ is a nonsingular matrix, we can find a basis $(\mathbf{b}_1, \mathbf{b}_2)$ of C^2 consisting of eigenvectors of $\hat{T}$ with corresponding eigenvalues α_1 and α_2; these eigenvalues are the solutions of the cubic equation $\det(\hat{T} - \alpha \hat{I}) = 0$. By definition,

$$\begin{cases} \hat{T}\mathbf{b}_1 = \alpha_1 \mathbf{b}_1 \\ \hat{T}\mathbf{b}_2 = \alpha_2 \mathbf{b}_2 \end{cases} \tag{3.20.9}$$

Using Eq. (3.20.4), we have (for $n = 1, 2, \ldots$)

$$\begin{pmatrix} B_n \\ C_n \end{pmatrix} = \underbrace{\hat{T}\hat{T}\cdots\hat{T}}_{n \text{ times}} \begin{pmatrix} B_0 \\ C_0 \end{pmatrix} = \hat{T}^n (\beta_1 \mathbf{b}_1 + \beta_2 \mathbf{b}_2) = \beta_1 \alpha_1^n \mathbf{b}_1 + \beta_2 \alpha_2^n \mathbf{b}_2 \tag{3.20.10}$$

Consider

$$\left| B_n \right|^2 + \left| C_n \right|^2 = \left\| \begin{pmatrix} B_n \\ C_n \end{pmatrix} \right\|^2 \geq \left| \beta_1 \alpha_1^n \right|^2 \left\| \mathbf{b}_1 \right\|^2 \tag{3.20.11}$$

Therefore, $\left| \alpha_1 \right| \leq 1$; otherwise $\lim\limits_{n \to \infty}\left(\left| B_n \right|^2 + \left| C_n \right|^2 \right) = \infty$. Similarly, we must have $\left| \alpha_2 \right| \leq 1$. We apply a similar consideration for $n \to -\infty$:

$$\begin{pmatrix} B_0 \\ C_0 \end{pmatrix} = \hat{T}^n \begin{pmatrix} B_{-n} \\ C_{-n} \end{pmatrix} \qquad \text{for } n = 1, 2 \ldots \tag{3.20.12}$$

Hence,

$$\begin{pmatrix} B_{-n} \\ C_{-n} \end{pmatrix} = \hat{T}^{-n} \begin{pmatrix} B_0 \\ C_0 \end{pmatrix} = \hat{T}^{-n} (\beta_1 \mathbf{b}_1 + \beta_2 \mathbf{b}_2) = \frac{\beta_1}{\alpha_1^n}\left[\hat{T}^{-n}\left(a_1^n \mathbf{b}_1\right)\right] + \frac{\beta_2}{\alpha_2^n}\left[\hat{T}^{-n}\left(\alpha_2^n \mathbf{b_2}\right)\right]$$

$$= \frac{\beta_1}{\alpha_1^n}\left[\hat{T}^{-n}(\hat{T}^n \mathbf{b}_1')\right] + \frac{\beta_2}{\alpha_2^n}[\hat{T}^{-n}(\hat{T}^n \mathbf{b}_2)] = \frac{\beta_n}{\alpha_1^n} \mathbf{b}_1 + \frac{\beta_2}{\alpha_2^n} \mathbf{b}_2^n \tag{3.20.13}$$

Therefore,

$$\left| B_{-n} \right|^2 + \left| C_{-n} \right|^2 = \left\| \begin{pmatrix} B_{-n} \\ C_{-n} \end{pmatrix} \right\|^2 \geq \left| \frac{\beta_1}{\alpha_1^n} \right|^2 \left\| \mathbf{b}_1 \right\|^2 \tag{3.20.14}$$

so $\left| \alpha_1 \right| \geq 1$; otherwise $\left| \psi_n(x) \right|^2$ diverges for $n \to -\infty$, and similarly we must have $\left| \alpha_2 \right| \geq 1$. Summing our results, we must have $\left| \alpha_1 \right| = \left| \alpha_2 \right| = 1$, i.e., the eigenvalues of $\hat{T}$ must be of modulus 1. Therefore, we can write

$$\det(\hat{T} - e^{i\phi} \hat{I}) = 0 \tag{3.20.15}$$

where ϕ is a real constant. So,

$$\left[\left(1-\frac{i\lambda}{2ka}\right)e^{ika}-e^{i\phi}\right]\left[\left(1+\frac{i\lambda}{2ka}\right)e^{-ika}-e^{i\phi}\right]-\frac{\lambda^2}{(2ka)^2}=0 \qquad (3.20.16)$$

A rearrangement of (3.20.16) gives

$$\left(1+\frac{\lambda^2}{4k^2a^2}\right)-\left[\left(1-\frac{i\lambda}{2ka}\right)e^{ika}+\left(1+\frac{i\lambda}{2ka}\right)e^{-ika}\right]e^{i\phi}+e^{2i\phi}-\frac{\lambda^2}{(2ka)^2}=0 \qquad (3.20.17)$$

or

$$1-2\left[\cos(ka)+\frac{\lambda}{2ka}\sin(ka)\right]e^{i\phi}+e^{2i\phi}=0 \qquad (3.20.18)$$

Consider the real part of (3.20.18):

$$1-2\left[\cos(ka)+\frac{\lambda}{2ka}\sin(ka)\right]\cos\phi+\cos(2\phi)=0 \qquad (3.20.19)$$

Using the relation $\cos(2\phi)=2\cos^2\phi-1$, we arrive at

$$\cos\phi=\cos(ka)+\frac{\lambda}{2ka}\sin(ka) \qquad (3.20.20)$$

Note that since $k=\sqrt{2mE/\hbar^2}$, Eq. (3.20.20) is a constraint on the possible energies E:

$$\left|\cos(ka)+\frac{\lambda}{2ka}\sin(ka)\right|\le 1 \qquad (3.20.21)$$

We can represent this inequality schematically in the following manner. The function

$$f(k)=\cos(ka)+\frac{\lambda}{2ka}\sin(ka) \qquad (3.20.22)$$

behaves for $k\to\infty$ as $\cos(ka)$ approximately. The schematic behavior of $f(k)$ is depicted in Fig. 3.11.

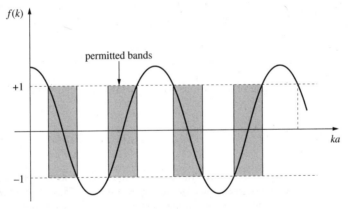

Fig. 3.11

We see that there are permitted bands of possible energies separated by domains where $|f(k)|\ge 1$, and therefore the corresponding energy E does not correspond to a possible state. For $E\to\infty$ the forbidden bands become very narrow, and the spectrum of the energy is almost continuous.

3.21. Consider a particle of mass m held in a three-dimensional potential written in the form

$$\tilde{V}(x,y,z)=V(x)+U(y)+W(z) \qquad (3.21.1)$$

Derive the stationary Schrödinger equation for this case, and use a separation of variables in order to obtain three independent one-dimensional problems. Relate the energy of the three-dimensional state to the effective energies of the one-dimensional problem.

SOLUTION

In our case the stationary Schrödinger equation is

$$-\frac{\hbar^2}{2m}\nabla^2\Psi(\mathbf{r}) + [V(x) + U(y) + W(z)]\Psi(\mathbf{r}) = E\Psi(\mathbf{r}) \qquad (3.21.2)$$

where, $\Psi(\mathbf{r})$ is the stationary three-dimensional state and E is the energy of the state. We assume that $\Psi(\mathbf{r})$ can be written in the form $\Psi(\mathbf{r}) = \phi(x)\chi(y)\psi(z)$, so substituting in Eq. (3.21.2) gives

$$-\frac{\hbar^2}{2m}\left[\left(\frac{d^2\phi(x)}{dx^2}\right)\chi(y)\psi(z) + \phi(x)\left(\frac{d^2\chi(y)}{dy^2}\right)\psi(z) + \phi(x)\chi(y)\left(\frac{d^2\psi(z)}{dz^2}\right)\right]$$

$$+ [V(x) + U(y) + W(z)]\phi(x)\chi(y)\psi(z) = E\phi(x)\chi(y)\psi(z) \qquad (3.21.3)$$

Dividing Eq. (3.21.4) by $\Psi(\mathbf{r})$ and separating the x-dependent part, we get

$$-\frac{\hbar^2}{2m}\frac{1}{\phi(x)}\frac{d^2\phi(x)}{dx^2} + V(x) = E - \left[U(y) + W(z) - \frac{\hbar^2}{2m}\left(\frac{1}{\chi(y)}\frac{d^2\chi(y)}{dy^2} + \frac{1}{\psi(z)}\frac{d^2\psi(z)}{dz^2}\right)\right] \qquad (3.21.4)$$

The left-hand side of Eq. (3.21.4) is a function of x only, while the right-hand side is a function of y and z, but does not depend on x. Therefore, both sides cannot depend on x; thus they equal a constant, which we will denote by E_x. We have

$$-\frac{\hbar^2}{2m}\frac{d^2\phi(x)}{dx^2} + V(x)\phi(x) = E_x\phi(x) \qquad (3.21.5)$$

We see that $\phi(x)$ is governed by the equation describing a particle of mass m held in the one-dimensional potential $V(x)$. Returning to Eq. (3.21.4), we can write

$$-\frac{\hbar^2}{2m}\frac{1}{\chi(y)}\frac{d^2\chi(y)}{dy^2} + U(y) = E - E_x - \left[W(z) - \frac{\hbar^2}{2m}\frac{1}{\psi(z)}\frac{d^2\psi(z)}{dz^2}\right] \qquad (3.21.6.)$$

In Eq. (3.21.6) the left-hand side depends only on y, while the right-hand side depends only on z. Again, both sides must equal a constant, which we will denote by E_y. We have

$$-\frac{\hbar^2}{2m}\frac{d^2\chi(y)}{dy^2} + U(y)\chi(y) = E_y\chi(y) \qquad (3.21.7)$$

Thus, $\chi(y)$ is a stationary state of a fictitious particle held in the one-dimensional potential $U(y)$. Finally, we have

$$-\frac{\hbar^2}{2m}\frac{d^2\psi(z)}{dz^2} + W(z)\psi(z) = E_z\psi(z) \qquad (3.21.8)$$

where we set $E_z = E - E_x - E_y$. Hence, the three-dimensional wavefunction $\Psi(\mathbf{r})$ is divided into three parts. Each part is governed by a one-dimensional Schrödinger equation. The energy of the three-dimensional state equals the sum of energies corresponding to the three one-dimensional problems, $E = E_x + E_y + E_z$.

SUPPLEMENTARY PROBLEMS

3.22. Solve Problems 3.13 and 3.14 for the case of particles with energy $0 < E < V_0$.

Ans. $R = 1$ and $T = 0$.

3.23. Consider the wavefunction

$$\Psi = e^{i(kz - \omega t)} \qquad (3.23.1)$$

The real part of Ψ corresponds to a harmonic plane wave traveling in the positive z direction. Determine the valve of the probability current.

Ans. $p/m = v$.

3.24. Consider a particle held in a one-dimensional *complex* potential $V(x)(1 + i\xi)$ where $V(x)$ is a real function and ξ is a real parameter. Use the Schrödinger equation to show that the probability current $J = \dfrac{\hbar}{2mi}\left(\psi^* \dfrac{\partial \psi}{\partial x} - \psi \dfrac{\partial \psi^*}{\partial x}\right)$

and the probability density $\rho = \psi^* \psi$ satisfy the *corrected* continuity equation $\dfrac{\partial J}{\partial x} + \dfrac{\partial \rho}{\partial t} = \dfrac{2\xi V(x)\rho}{\hbar}$. (Hint: Compare with Problem 3.6.)

3.25. Consider a particle of mass m held in a one-dimensional infinite potential energy well:

$$V(x) = \begin{cases} V_0 & 0 \le x \le a \\ \infty & \text{otherwise} \end{cases} \tag{3.25.1}$$

Find the stationary states and the corresponding energies.

Ans. $E_n = \dfrac{\pi^2 \hbar^2 n^2}{2ma^2} + V_0$ $(n = 1, 2, 3, \ldots)$. The corresponding states are the same as in Problem 3.12.

3.26. Consider an electron of energy 1 eV that encounters a potential barrier of width 0.1 nm and of energy-height 2 eV. What is the probability of the electron crossing the barrier? Repeat the same calculation for a proton.

Ans. For an electron $T \cong 0.78$; for a proton $T \cong 4 \times 10^{-19}$.

3.27. (*a*) A particle of mass m and energy $E > 0$ encounters a potential energy well of width l and depth V_0:

$$V(x) = \begin{cases} 0 & x < 0 \\ -V_0 & 0 < x < l \\ 0 & l < x \end{cases}$$

Find the transmission coefficient. (Hint: Compare with Problem 3.16.) (*b*) For which values of l will the transmission be complete if the particle is an electron of energy 1 eV and $V_0 = 4$ eV?

Ans. (*a*) $T = \dfrac{1}{1 + \dfrac{V_0^2}{4E(E + V_0)}\sin^2\left[\dfrac{\sqrt{2m(E + V_0)}}{\hbar}l\right]}$ (*b*) $l \cong n(2.7 \times 10^{-10}\,m)$, where n is an integer.

3.28. An electron is held in a finite square potential energy well of width 1.0×10^{-10} m. For which values of the well's depth V_0 are there exactly two possible bound stationary states for the electron?

Ans. $V_1 \le V_0 \le 4V_1$, where $V_1 = \dfrac{\pi^2 \hbar^2}{2ma^2} = 37.6$ eV.

3.29. Consider the wavefunction $\psi(x) = \dfrac{N}{x^2 + \alpha^2}$. (*a*) Calculate the normalization constant N where α is a real constant. (*b*) Find the uncertainty $\Delta x\,\Delta p$ (be careful calculating Δp!).

Ans. (*a*) $N = \sqrt{\dfrac{2\alpha^3}{\pi}}$; (*b*) $\Delta x\,\Delta p = \dfrac{\hbar}{\sqrt{2}}$.

3.30. Consider a particle of energy $E > 0$ confined in the potential energy well (Fig. 3.12)

$$V(x) = \begin{cases} \infty & x < -a \\ 0 & -a < x < -b \\ V_0 & -b < x < b \\ 0 & b < x < a \\ \infty & a < x \end{cases}$$

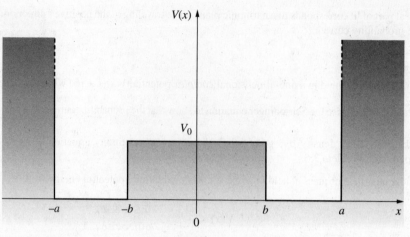

Fig. 3.12

Show that for a stationary state with a nonvanishing probability of finding the particle to the right of the barrier (i.e., at $b < x < a$), there is also a nonvanishing probability of finding it to the left of the barrier (i.e., $-a < x < -b$). Note: For $E < V_0$, this is another example of the tunnel effect of Problem 3.17.

3.31. Consider a particle of mass m confined in a one-dimensional infinite potential energy well:

$$V(x) = \begin{cases} 0 & 0 < x < L \\ \infty & \text{otherwise} \end{cases}$$

Suppose that the particle is in the stationary state, $\psi_n(x) = \sqrt{\dfrac{2}{L}} \sin\left(\dfrac{n\pi x}{L}\right)$ of energy $E_n = \dfrac{\pi^2 \hbar^2 n^2}{2mL^2}$. Calculate (a) $\langle x \rangle$ and $\langle p \rangle$; (b) $\langle x^2 \rangle$ and $\langle p^2 \rangle$; (c) $\Delta x \, \Delta p$.

Ans. (a) $\langle x \rangle = \dfrac{L}{2}$, $\langle p \rangle = 0$; (b) $\langle x^2 \rangle = L^2\left(\dfrac{1}{3} - \dfrac{1}{2\pi^2 n^2}\right)$, $\langle p^2 \rangle = \dfrac{\pi^2 \hbar^2 n^2}{L^2}$; (c) $\Delta x \, \Delta p = n\pi\hbar \sqrt{\dfrac{1}{12} - \dfrac{1}{2\pi^2 n^2}}$.

3.32. Consider a particle of mass m held in the potential

$$V(x) = -V_0[\delta(x) + \delta(x - l)]$$

where l is a constant. Find the bound states of the particles. Show that the energies are given by the relation

$$e^{-\rho l} = \pm\left(1 - \frac{2\rho}{\alpha}\right)$$

where $E = -\hbar^2 \rho^2 / 2m$ and $\alpha = 2mV_0 / \hbar^2$.

CHAPTER 4

The Foundations of Quantum Mechanics

4.1   Introduction

The State Space

In classical mechanics, the position of a particle is described by a vector having three real number elements. Though an analogous description exists in quantum mechanics, there are many significant differences. The state of a quantum mechanical system is described by an element of an abstract vector space called the *state space* and denoted as ε. In Dirac notation, an element of this space is called a **ket** and is represented by the symbol $|\ \rangle$. A ket is a vector.

Observables

In Chapter 2, the concept of a linear operator was introduced. The Hermitian operator is a linear operator that is equal to its adjoint (see Sec. 4.6). A fundamental concept of quantum mechanics is the *observable*. *An observable is a Hermitian operator for which one can find an orthonormal basis of the state space that consists of the eigenvectors of the operator (e.g., linear momentum, mass, energy, angular momentum)*. If the state space is finite-dimensional, then any Hermitian operator is an observable. In Dirac notation, an operator is represented by a letter. Since the action of an operator on a vector yields another vector, an expression of the form $\hat{A}|\psi\rangle$ also represents a ket.

The Dual Space

Recall that a functional is a mapping from a vector space to the complex field. The dual space of the state space ε consists of all linear functionals acting on ε. It is designated by ε^{*}. In Dirac notation an element of ε^{*} is called a **bra**, and is designated by the symbol $\langle\ |$. We can associate with any ket $|\phi\rangle$ of ε an element of ε^{*}, denoted by $\langle\phi|$. In other words, for every ket $|\psi\rangle$ there is a bra $\langle\psi|$ such that $(|\psi\rangle)^{*} = \langle\psi|$ and $(a|\psi\rangle)^{*} = a^{*}\langle\psi|$ where a is a complex number. Moreover, $|a\psi\rangle = a|\psi\rangle$ and so $\langle a\psi| = a^{*}\langle\psi|$. The action of a bra $\langle\psi|$ on a ket $|\chi\rangle$ is expressed by juxtaposing the two symbols, $\langle\psi|\chi\rangle$. By definition, this expression is a complex number. (The terms *bra* and *ket* come from "bracket.") The correspondence between ε and ε^{*} is closely related to the existence of a scalar product in ε.

Scalar Product

The basic properties of the scalar product are summarized below:

(a) $$\langle\phi|\psi\rangle = \langle\psi|\phi\rangle^{*}$$ (4.1)

(b) $$\langle\psi|\lambda_1\phi_1 + \lambda_2\phi_2\rangle = \lambda_1\langle\psi|\phi_1\rangle + \lambda_2\langle\phi_2|\psi\rangle$$ (4.2)

(c) $$\langle\lambda_1\phi_1 + \lambda_2\phi_2|\psi\rangle = \lambda_1^{*}\langle\phi_1|\psi\rangle + \lambda_2^{*}\langle\phi_2|\psi\rangle$$ (4.3)

(d) $\langle\psi|\psi\rangle$ is real and positive; it is zero if and only if $|\psi\rangle = 0$ (4.4)

Projector onto a Subspace of ε

Let $|\phi_1\rangle, |\phi_2\rangle, \ldots, |\phi_m\rangle$ be m normalized pairwise orthogonal vectors;

$$\langle \phi_i | \phi_j \rangle = \delta_{ij} \qquad i, j = 1, 2, \ldots, m \tag{4.5}$$

We denote by ε_m the subspace of ε spanned by these m vectors. The projector into the subspace ε_m is defined by the linear *projection operator*

$$\hat{P}_m = \sum_{i=1}^{m} |\phi_i\rangle\langle\phi_i| \tag{4.6}$$

The operator $\hat{P} = |\phi\rangle\langle\phi|$ establishes the component of any other vector that lies in the direction of the vector $|\phi\rangle$. Accordingly, $\hat{P}|\psi\rangle = \langle \phi | \psi \rangle |\phi\rangle$. Figure 4.1 presents a simple example of this concept. The set $\{|\phi_1\rangle, |\phi_2\rangle, |\phi_3\rangle\}$ is an orthonormal set of vectors. The projection of an arbitrary vector $|\psi\rangle$ into the plane spanned by $|\phi_1\rangle$ and $|\phi_2\rangle$ is given by $\hat{P}_2|\psi\rangle = (\langle\phi_1|\psi\rangle)|\phi_1\rangle + (\langle\phi_2|\psi\rangle)|\phi_2\rangle$.

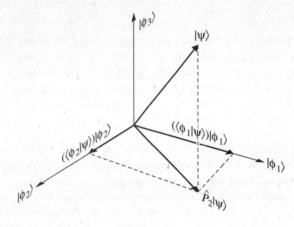

Fig. 4.1

4.2   Postulates in Quantum Mechanics

Postulate I The state of a physical system at time t_0 is defined by specifying a ket $|\psi(t_0)\rangle$ belonging to the state space ε.

Postulate II A measurable physical quantity A is described by an operator $\hat{A}$ acting on ε.

Measurement of Physical Quantities: The validity of a physical theory is continuously investigated by comparing results calculated by the theory with measurements obtained in experiments. In the context of quantum mechanics the measurement of a physical quantity involves three principal questions:

(*a*) What are the possible results of the measurement?

(*b*) What is the probability of obtaining each of the possible results?

(*c*) What is the state of the system after the measurement?

The answers to these questions in the context of quantum mechanics are found in the following three postulates.

Postulate III The possible results of the measurement of a physical quantity are the eigenvalues of the corresponding observable A.

We can now answer the second question for the case of a discrete spectrum. The generalization to the case of a continuous spectrum is treated in Prob. 4.5.

Postulate IV Let A be a physical quantity with a corresponding observable A. Suppose that the system is in a normalized state $|\psi\rangle$, so $\langle\psi|\psi\rangle = 1$. When A is measured, the probability $P(a_n)$ of obtaining the eigenvalue a_n of A is

$$P(a_n) = \sum_{i=1}^{g_n} \left|\langle u_n^i|\psi\rangle\right|^2 \tag{4.7}$$

where g_n is the degeneracy of a_n and $|u_n^1\rangle, |u_n^2\rangle, \ldots, |u_n^{g_n}\rangle$ form an orthonormal basis of the subspace ε_n that consists of eigenvectors of A with eigenvalues a_n.

In Prob. 4.3, we introduce a different (though equivalent) formulation of postulate IV. The subspace ε_n of the state space defined in postulate IV is also called the *eigenspace* associated with a_n. The following postulate describes the state of the system after a measurement.

Postulate V If the measurement of a quantity A on a physical system in the state $|\psi\rangle$ gives the result a_n, then immediately after the measurement, the state is given by the normalized projection of $|\psi\rangle$ onto the eigenspace ε_n associated with a_n; that is $\dfrac{1}{\sqrt{\langle\psi|\hat{P}_n|\psi\rangle}}\hat{P}_n|\psi\rangle$, where $\hat{P}_n$ is the projector onto ε_n.

4.3 Mean Value and Root-Mean-Square Deviation

Consider a state described by a normalized ket, $\langle\psi|\psi\rangle = 1$. The *mean value* of an observable A in the state $|\psi\rangle$ is defined by

$$\langle\hat{A}\rangle_\psi = \langle\psi|\hat{A}|\psi\rangle \tag{4.8}$$

The mean value of an observable has a clear physical meaning. Suppose the physical quantity represented by the operator $\hat{A}$ is measured a large number of times when the system is in the state $|\psi\rangle$. Then $\langle\hat{A}\rangle_\psi$ expresses the average of the results of the measurements (that is, the sum of each result multiplied by the probability of obtaining it). The derivation of this property is given in Problem 4.8.

The *root-mean-square deviation* of the observable A is defined by

$$\Delta A = \sqrt{\langle\hat{A}^2\rangle_\psi - \langle\hat{A}\rangle_\psi^2} \tag{4.9}$$

The root-mean-square deviation has a direct physical interpretation. It characterizes the dispersion of the measurement results about $\langle\hat{A}\rangle_\psi$ (see Problem 4.9).

4.4 Commuting Observables

Consider two operators, $\hat{A}$ and $\hat{B}$. In general, the expressions $\hat{A}\hat{B}$ and $\hat{B}\hat{A}$ are not identical—multiplication of operators is not commutative. An important concept in quantum mechanics is the commutator $[\hat{A}, \hat{B}]$ of two operators defined by

$$[\hat{A}, \hat{B}] = \hat{A}\hat{B} - \hat{B}\hat{A} \tag{4.10}$$

Some useful properties of a commutator are given in Problems 4.10, 4.11, and 4.12. If $[\hat{A}, \hat{B}] = 0$, then $\hat{A}$ and $\hat{B}$ are called commuting operators. Given two observables A and B, they are said to be *compatible* when their associated operators $\hat{A}$ and $\hat{B}$ commute; $[\hat{A}, \hat{B}] = 0$. If A and B are not compatible they cannot be measured simultaneously. Consider the following theorem.

Theorem: Operator observables $\hat{A}$ and $\hat{B}$ commute if and only if there exists a basis of eigenvalues common to both.

A set of operators $\hat{A}, \hat{B}, \hat{C}, \ldots$ is called a *complete set of commuting operator observables* if all subpairs commute, and there exists a unique orthonormal basis of common eigenvectors. The uniqueness is within a multiplicative factor.

4.5 Function of an Operator

Assume that in a certain domain the function F of variable x can be expanded in a power series in x:

$$F(x) = \sum_{n=0}^{\infty} a_n x^n \tag{4.11}$$

The corresponding function of the operator $\hat{A}$ is the operator $\hat{F}(\hat{A})$ defined by a series that has the same coefficients a_n:

$$\hat{F}(\hat{A}) = \sum_{n=0}^{\infty} a_n \hat{A}^n \tag{4.12}$$

4.6 Hermitian Conjugation

The adjoint (or conjugate) of an operator $\hat{A}$ is denoted by $\hat{A}^{\dagger}$. For every $|\phi\rangle$ and $|\psi\rangle$ we have

$$\langle \psi | \hat{A}^{\dagger} | \phi \rangle = \langle \phi | \hat{A} | \psi \rangle^{*} \tag{4.13}$$

The basic properties of the adjoint of an operator are derived in Problems 4.13 and 4.17. An operator $\hat{A}$ is Hermitian if it is identical to its adjoint:

$$\hat{A} \text{ is Hermitian} \Leftrightarrow \hat{A} = \hat{A}^{\dagger} \tag{4.14}$$

An inspection of Eq. (4.13) shows that in order to obtain the Hermitian (or the adjoint) of any expression, it suffices to apply the following procedure:

Replace the constants by their complex conjugates.

Replace the kets by the bras associated with them.

Replace the bras with the kets associated with them.

Replace the operators by their adjoint operators.

Reverse the order of the factors (the position of the constants is of no importance). For example,

$$\lambda \langle \phi | \hat{A}\hat{B} | \psi \rangle \rightarrow \lambda^{*} \langle \psi | \hat{B}^{\dagger}\hat{A}^{\dagger} | \phi \rangle \tag{4.15}$$

4.7 Discrete and Continuous State Spaces

A discrete set of kets $\{|u_i\rangle, \, i = 1, 2, \dots \}$ is orthonormal if it satisfies the following relation:

$$\langle u_i | u_j \rangle = \delta_{ij} \tag{4.16}$$

For a continuous set of kets $\{|w_\alpha\rangle, \, l_1 \leq \alpha \leq l_2\}$, the orthonormalization relation is written as

$$\langle w_\alpha | w_{\alpha'} \rangle = \delta(\alpha - \alpha') \tag{4.17}$$

A set of kets constitutes a basis of the state space ε if every ket $|\psi\rangle$ belonging to ε has a unique expansion on these kets:

$$|\psi\rangle = \sum_i C_i |u_i\rangle \tag{4.18}$$

and for the continuous case:

$$|\psi\rangle = \int C(\alpha)|w_\alpha\rangle d\alpha \qquad (4.19)$$

It can be proved that an orthonormal set of kets constitutes a basis if and only if it satisfies the *closure relation* (see Problems 4.19 and 4.20):

$$\sum_i |u_i\rangle\langle u_i| = \hat{I} \qquad \left(\text{for the continuous case, } \int |w_\alpha\rangle\langle w_\alpha| d\alpha = \hat{I}\right) \qquad (4.20)$$

where $\hat{I}$ denotes the identity operator in ε. Using the notion of the projector onto the space spanned by the set of kets, we can write these relations in an equivalent form:

$$P\{u_i\} = \hat{I} \qquad (\text{or } P\{w_\alpha\} = \hat{I}) \qquad (4.21)$$

4.8   Representations

The validity of a physical theory is established by comparing experimentally obtained data with the calculated results of the theory. When a basis is chosen in the abstract state space, each ket, bra, and operator can be characterized by specifying its coordinates for that basis. We say that the abstract object is represented by the corresponding set of numbers. Using these numbers, the theory-prescribed calculations are performed. Choosing a representation means choosing an orthonormal basis in the state space.

Representations of Kets and Bras

In a discrete basis $\{|u_i\rangle\}$, a ket $|\psi\rangle$ is represented by the set of numbers $C_i = \langle u_i|\psi\rangle$. These numbers can be arranged vertically to form a column matrix:

$$(C_i) = \begin{pmatrix} C_1 \\ C_2 \\ \vdots \end{pmatrix} \qquad (4.22)$$

A bra $\langle\phi|$ is represented by the sets of numbers $b_i^* = \langle\phi|u_i\rangle$, which are the complex conjugates of the components of the ket $|\phi\rangle$ associated with $\langle\phi|$. These numbers can be arranged horizontally to form a row matrix, $(b_1^*, b_2^*, \ldots)$. In a continuous basis $\{|w_\alpha\rangle\}$, kets and bras are represented by a continuous infinity of numbers, that is, by a function of α. A ket $|\psi\rangle$ is represented by the set of numbers $C(\alpha) = \langle w_\alpha|\psi\rangle$, and a bra $\langle\phi|$ is represented by $b^*(\alpha) = \langle\phi|w_\alpha\rangle$. Once a representation is chosen, we can use the components of the ket and the bra to calculate their scalar product. In the discrete case,

$$\langle\phi|\psi\rangle = \sum_i b_i^* C_i \qquad \left[\text{in the continuous case, } \langle\phi|\psi\rangle = \int b^*(\alpha)C(\alpha)d\alpha\right] \qquad (4.23)$$

Representations of Operators

In a discrete basis $\{|u_i\rangle\}$, an operator is represented by the numbers

$$A_{ij} = \langle u_i|\hat{A}|u_j\rangle \qquad (4.24)$$

These numbers can be arranged in a square matrix,

$$[A_{ij}] = \begin{pmatrix} A_{11} & A_{12} & \cdots & A_{1j} & \cdots \\ A_{21} & A_{22} & \cdots & A_{2j} & \cdots \\ \vdots & & & & \\ A_{i1} & A_{i2} & \cdots & A_{ij} & \cdots \\ \vdots & & & & \end{pmatrix} \qquad (4.25)$$

For a continuous basis $\{|w_\alpha\rangle\}$, we associate with $\hat{A}$ a continuous function of two variables:

$$\langle \alpha, \alpha' \rangle = \langle w_\alpha | \hat{A} | w_{\alpha'} \rangle \tag{4.26}$$

As a consequence of Eq. (4.13),

$$(\hat{A}^\dagger)_{ij} = A^*_{ij} \tag{4.27}$$

or

$$\hat{A}^\dagger(\alpha', \alpha) = \hat{A}^*(\alpha', \alpha) \tag{4.28}$$

If $\hat{A}$ is an Hermitian operator $(\hat{A}^\dagger = \hat{A})$, we have $\hat{A}(\alpha', \alpha) = \hat{A}^*(\alpha', \alpha)$. (Note that for the discrete case $A_{ij} = A^*_{ji}$.) In particular, the diagonal elements of a Hermitian matrix are always real numbers.

Change of Representation

We provide a simple method to obtain the representation of a bra, ket, or operator in a given basis when its representation in another basis is known. For simplicity, assume that we perform a transformation from one discrete orthonormal basis $\{|u_i\rangle\}$ to another, $\{|v_i\rangle\}$. Define the transformation matrix

$$S_{ik} = \langle u_i | v_k \rangle \tag{4.29}$$

The Hermitian conjugate of S_{ik} is given by

$$(\hat{S}^\dagger)_{ki} = (S_{ik})^* = \langle v_k | u_i \rangle \tag{4.30}$$

To pass from the components of a ket $|\psi\rangle$ represented in one basis to another, one applies the relation

$$\langle v_k | \psi \rangle = \sum_i (\hat{S}^\dagger)_{ki} \langle u_i | \psi \rangle \tag{4.31}$$

or the inverse relation, $\langle u_i | \psi \rangle = \sum_k S_{ik} \langle v_k | \psi \rangle$. For a bra $\langle \phi |$ we have

$$\langle \phi | v_k \rangle = \sum_i \langle \phi | u_i \rangle S_{ik} \qquad \left[\langle \phi | u_i \rangle = \sum_k \langle \phi | v_k \rangle (\hat{S}^\dagger)_{ki} \right] \tag{4.32}$$

Finally, the matrix elements of an operator $\hat{A}$ transform as

$$\langle v_k | \hat{A} | v_l \rangle = \sum_{i,j} (\hat{S}^\dagger)_{ki} \langle u_i | \hat{A} | u_j \rangle S_{jl} \qquad \langle u_i | \hat{A} | u_j \rangle = \sum_{k,l} S_{ik} \langle v_k | \hat{A} | v_l \rangle (\hat{S}^\dagger)_{lj} \tag{4.33}$$

$|r\rangle$- and $|p\rangle$-Representations

In Sec. 4.1 we noted that to every ket $|\phi\rangle$ there corresponds a bra $\langle\phi|$. The converse is not necessarily true; there are bras with no corresponding kets. Nevertheless, in addition to the vectors belonging to ε, we shall use generalized kets whose norm is not finite. At the same time, however, the scalar product of those kets with every ket is finite. The generalized kets do not represent physical states; they serve to help us analyze and interpret physical states represented by kets belonging to ε.

Consider the physical system of a single particle. Together with the state space of the system we introduce another vector space, called the *wavefuction space*, denoted by F. This space consists of complex functions of the coordinates (x, y, z) having the following properties:

(*a*) The functions $\psi(\mathbf{r})$ are defined everywhere as continuous and infinitely differentiable.

(*b*) The integral $\int |\psi(\mathbf{r})|^2 \, d^3r$ must be finite; i.e., $\psi(\mathbf{r})$ must be square integrable.

To every function $\psi(\mathbf{r})$ belonging to F there corresponds a ket $|\psi\rangle$ belonging to ε. Using the wavefunctions $\phi(\mathbf{r})$ and $\psi(\mathbf{r})$ corresponding to $\langle\phi|$ and $|\psi\rangle$, we define the scalar product of $\langle\phi|$ and $|\psi\rangle$:

$$\langle\phi|\psi\rangle = \int \phi^*(\mathbf{r})\psi(\mathbf{r})\,d^3r \tag{4.34}$$

Consider two particular bases of F denoted $\{\xi_{\mathbf{r}_0}(\mathbf{r})\}$ and $\{\nu_{\mathbf{p}_0}(\mathbf{r})\}$. These bases are not composed of functions belonging to F:

$$\xi_{\mathbf{r}_0}(\mathbf{r}) = \delta(\mathbf{r} - \mathbf{r}_0) \tag{4.35}$$

and

$$\nu_{\mathbf{p}_0}(\mathbf{r}) = \frac{1}{(2\pi\hbar)^{3/2}} e^{i\mathbf{p}_0\cdot\mathbf{r}/\hbar} \tag{4.36}$$

To each $\xi_{\mathbf{r}_0}(\mathbf{r})$ we associate a generalized ket denoted by $|\mathbf{r}_0\rangle$, and similarly for $\nu_{\mathbf{p}_0}(\mathbf{r})$ we associate a generalized ket $|\mathbf{p}_0\rangle$. The sets $\{|\mathbf{r}_0\rangle\}$ and $\{|\mathbf{p}_0\rangle\}$ constitute orthonormal bases in ε:

$$\langle r_0|r_0'\rangle = \delta(r_0 - r_0') \qquad \int |r_0\rangle\langle r_0|\,d^3r = \hat{I} \tag{4.37}$$

where we also have the following relations:

$$\langle p_0|p_0'\rangle = \delta(p_0 - p_0') \qquad \int |p_0\rangle\langle p_0|\,d^3p = \hat{I} \tag{4.38}$$

We obtain two representations in the state space of a (spinless) particle: the $\{|r_0\rangle\}$- and $\{|p_0\rangle\}$-representations. The correspondence between the ket $|\psi\rangle$ and the wavefunction associated with it is given by

$$\psi(\mathbf{r}_0) = \langle\mathbf{r}_0|\psi\rangle \tag{4.39}$$

$$\tilde{\psi}(\mathbf{p}_0) = \langle\mathbf{p}_0|\psi\rangle \tag{4.40}$$

where $\tilde{\psi}(\mathbf{p})$ is the Fourier transform of $\psi(\mathbf{r})$. The value $\psi(\mathbf{r})'$ of the wavefunction at the point $\mathbf{r}$ is the component of the ket $|\psi\rangle$ on the basis vector $|\mathbf{r}\rangle$ of the $|\mathbf{r}\rangle$-representation. Also, the value $\tilde{\psi}(\mathbf{p})$ of the wavefunction in the momentum space at $\mathbf{p}$ is the component of the ket $|\psi\rangle$ on the basis vector $|\mathbf{p}\rangle$ of the $|\mathbf{p}\rangle$-representation.

Exchanging between the $|\mathbf{r}\rangle$-representation and the $|\mathbf{p}\rangle$-representation is accomplished analogously to the case of continuous bases. Note that

$$\langle\mathbf{r}|\mathbf{p}\rangle = \langle\mathbf{p}|\mathbf{r}\rangle^* = \frac{1}{(2\pi\hbar)^{3/2}} e^{i\mathbf{p}\cdot\mathbf{r}/\hbar} \tag{4.41}$$

Now, we have

$$\mathbf{r}|\psi\rangle = \int \langle r|p\rangle\langle p|\psi\rangle\,d^3p \tag{4.42}$$

and inversely,

$$\langle\mathbf{p}|\psi\rangle = \int \langle p|r\rangle\langle r|\psi\rangle\,d^3r \tag{4.43}$$

Therefore, using Eq. (4.41), we obtain

$$\psi(\mathbf{r}) = \frac{1}{(2\pi\hbar)^{3/2}} \int e^{i\mathbf{p}\cdot\mathbf{r}/\hbar}\tilde{\psi}(\mathbf{p})\,d^3p \tag{4.44}$$

and

$$\tilde{\psi}(\mathbf{p}) = \frac{1}{(2\pi\hbar)^{3/2}} \int e^{-i\mathbf{p}\cdot\mathbf{r}/\hbar} \psi(\mathbf{r}) \, d^3 r \tag{4.45}$$

The Operators $\hat{\mathbf{R}}$ and $\hat{\mathbf{P}}$

Let $|\psi\rangle$ be a ket belonging to the state space and let $\psi(x, y, z) = \langle\mathbf{r}|\psi\rangle = \psi(\mathbf{r})$ be its corresponding wavefunction. The three operators $\hat{X}$, $\hat{Y}$, and $\hat{Z}$ are defined by their action in the $|\mathbf{r}\rangle$-representation:

$$\langle\mathbf{r}|\hat{X}|\psi\rangle = x\langle\mathbf{r}|\psi\rangle \qquad \langle\mathbf{r}|\hat{Y}|\psi\rangle = y\langle\mathbf{r}|\psi\rangle \qquad \langle\mathbf{r}|\hat{Z}|\psi\rangle = z\langle\mathbf{r}|\psi\rangle \tag{4.46}$$

The operator $\hat{X}$ acting on $|\psi\rangle$ yields the ket $|\psi'\rangle$, which corresponds to the wavefunction $\psi'(x, y, z) = x\,\psi(x, y, z)$, and similarly for $\hat{Y}$ and $\hat{Z}$. The operators $\hat{X}, \hat{Y}$, and $\hat{Z}$ are considered to be the components of a *vector operator* $\hat{\mathbf{R}}$. Similarly, the operators $\hat{P}_x, \hat{P}_y$, and $\hat{P}_z$ are defined by their action in the $|\mathbf{p}\rangle$-representation:

$$\langle\mathbf{p}|\hat{P}_x|\psi\rangle = p_x\langle\mathbf{p}|\psi\rangle \qquad \langle\mathbf{p}|\hat{P}_y|\psi\rangle = p_y\langle\mathbf{p}|\psi\rangle \qquad \langle\mathbf{p}|\hat{P}_z|\psi\rangle = p_z\langle\mathbf{p}|\psi\rangle \tag{4.47}$$

$\hat{P}_x, \hat{P}_y$, and $\hat{P}_z$ are the components of the vector operator $\hat{\mathbf{P}}$. The operator observables $\hat{\mathbf{R}}$ and $\hat{\mathbf{P}}$ are of fundamental importance in quantum mechanics. Their commutation relations are called *the canonical commutation relations*:

$$[\hat{R}_i, \hat{P}_j] = i\hbar\delta_{ij} \qquad [\hat{R}_i, \hat{R}_j] = 0 \qquad [\hat{P}_i, \hat{P}_j] = 0 \tag{4.48}$$

Quantization Rules

By *quantization rules* we mean the method for obtaining the quantum-mechanics analog of a classical quantity. Consider a system of a single particle. The operators $(\hat{X}, \hat{Y}, \hat{Z})$ are associated with the coordinates (x, y, z) of the particle, while $(\hat{P}_x, \hat{P}_y, \hat{P}_z)$ are associated with the momentum (p_x, p_y, p_z). We shall often use the notation $\hat{\mathbf{R}}$ for $(\hat{X}, \hat{Y}, \hat{Z})$ and $\hat{\mathbf{P}}$ for $(\hat{P}_x, \hat{P}_y, \hat{P}_z)$. In classical mechanics, a physical quantity A related to a particle is expressed in terms of the particle's position vector $\mathbf{r}$ and the momentum $\mathbf{p}$. To obtain the corresponding quantum-mechanics observable, replace $\mathbf{r} \to \hat{\mathbf{R}}$ and $\mathbf{p} \to \hat{\mathbf{P}}$. Since the expression obtained is not always Hermitian, we apply a *symmetrization* between $\hat{\mathbf{R}}$ and $\hat{\mathbf{P}}$ to obtain a Hermitian operator. In Problem 4.35 we demonstrate this method. Note that there exist quantum mechanical physical variables which have no classical equivalent (such as spin). These quantities are defined by the corresponding observables.

4.9   The Time Evolution

In the previous sections we paid no attention to the time evolution of a system but rather considered a definite static state. We shall now present methods for treating the time evolution of a system. Consider the following postulate:

   Postulate VI The time evolution of the state vector $|\psi(t)\rangle$ of a physical system is governed by the Schrödinger equation:

$$i\hbar\frac{d\,|\psi(t)\rangle}{dt} = \hat{H}(t)|\psi(t)\rangle \tag{4.49}$$

where $\hat{H}(t)$ is the observable corresponding to the classical Hamiltonian of the system.

   Some important implications of the Schrödinger equation must be noted:

(a)   Since the Schrödinger equation is a first-order differential equation in t, it follows that if an initial state $|\psi(t_0)\rangle$ is given, the state $|\psi(t)\rangle$ is determined; therefore, the time evolution is deterministic. Note that indeterminacy appears only when a physical quantity is *measured*.

(b)   Let $|\psi_1(t)\rangle$ and $|\psi_2(t)\rangle$ be two different solutions of the Schrödinger equation. If the initial state is $|\psi(t_0)\rangle = a_1|\psi_1(t_0)\rangle + a_2|\psi_2(t_0)\rangle$, where a_1 and a_2 complex numbers, then at time t the system is in the state $|\psi(t)\rangle = a_1|\psi_1(t)\rangle + a_2|\psi_2(t)\rangle$.

(c) At time t, the norm of the state vector remains constant:

$$\frac{d}{dt}\langle \psi(t) \mid \psi(t)\rangle = 0 \tag{4.50}$$

This means that the total probability of finding the particle is conserved (see Problem 4.40).

Time Evolution for a Conservative System

A physical system is *conservative* if its Hamiltonian does not depend explicitly on time. In classical mechanics, the most important consequence of such an observation is the conservation of energy. Similarly, in quantum mechanics, a conservative system possesses important properties. Most of the problems in this book concern conservative systems.

The time evolution of a conservative system can be found rather simply. Suppose the Hamiltonian $\hat{H}$ does not depend explicitly on time. The time evolution of the system that was initially in the state $\mid \psi(t_0)\rangle$ is found using the following procedure:

(a) Expand $\mid \psi(t_0)\rangle$ in the basis of eigenvectors of $\hat{H}$:

$$\mid \psi(t_0)\rangle = \sum_n \sum_k a_{nk}(t_0)\mid \phi_{nk}\rangle \tag{4.51}$$

where $a_{nk}(t_0) = \langle \phi_{n,k}\mid \psi(t_0)\rangle$.

(b) To obtain $\mid \psi(t)\rangle$ for $t > t_0$, multiply each coefficient $a_{nk}(t_0)$ by $e^{-iE_n(t-t_0)/\hbar}$ where E_n is the eigenvalue of $\hat{H}$ associated with the state $\mid \phi_{n,k}\rangle$:

$$\mid \psi(t)\rangle = \sum_n \sum_k a_{nk}(t_0) e^{-iE_n(t-t_0)/\hbar}\mid \phi_{n,k}\rangle \tag{4.52}$$

This procedure can be generalized to the case of the continuous spectrum of $\hat{H}$. So,

$$\mid \psi(t)\rangle = \sum_k \int a_k(E, t_0) e^{-iE_n(t-t_0)/\hbar}\mid \phi_{E,k}\rangle dE \tag{4.53}$$

The eigenstates of $\hat{H}$ are called *stationary states*.

Time Evolution of the Mean Value

Let $\mid \psi(t)\rangle$ be the normalized ket describing the time evolution of a physical system. The time evolution of the mean value of an observable A is governed by the equation

$$\frac{d\langle \hat{A}\rangle}{dt} = \frac{1}{i\hbar}\langle [\hat{A}, \hat{H}(t)]\rangle\left\langle \frac{\partial \hat{A}}{\partial t}\right\rangle \tag{4.54}$$

If A does not depend explicitly on time, we have

$$\frac{d\langle \hat{A}\rangle}{dt} = \frac{1}{i\hbar}\langle [\hat{A}, \hat{H}(t)]\rangle \tag{4.55}$$

By definition, a constant of motion is an observable $\hat{A}$ that does not depend explicitly on time and commutes with the Hamiltonian $\hat{H}$. In this case,

$$\frac{d\langle \hat{A}\rangle}{dt} = 0 \tag{4.56}$$

4.10 Uncertainty Relations

As we have seen in previous sections, the position or momentum of a particle in quantum mechanics is not characterized by a single number but rather by a continuous function. By the uncertainty of the position (or momentum) of a particle, we mean the degree of dispersion of the wavefunction relative to a central value. This quantity can be given a rigorous definition; however, that is beyond the scope of this volume.

The Heisenberg uncertainty relations give a lower limit for the product of the uncertainties of the position and the momentum of a particle:

$$\Delta x \Delta p_x \geq \hbar/2 \qquad \Delta y \Delta p_y \geq \hbar/2 \qquad \Delta z \Delta p_z \geq \hbar/2 \tag{4.57}$$

Momentum and position are said to be *conjugate variables*. For the case of a conservative system, there is also a relation between the uncertainty of time Δt at which the system evolves to an appreciable extent, and the uncertainty of energy ΔE:

$$\Delta t \, \Delta E \geq \hbar/2 \tag{4.58}$$

Energy and time are conjugate variables; they are linked in a fundamental way.

4.11 The Schrödinger and Heisenberg Pictures

In the formalism described in the previous sections, we considered the time-independent operators that correspond to the observables of the system. The time evolution is entirely contained in the state vector $|\psi(t)\rangle$. This approach is called the *Schrödinger picture*. Nevertheless, since the physical predictions in quantum mechanics are expressed by scalar products of bras and kets of matrix elements of operators, it is possible to introduce a different formalism for the time evolution. This formalism is called the *Heisenberg picture*. Here the state of the system is described by a ket that does not vary over time, $|\psi_H(t)\rangle = |\psi(t_0)\rangle$. The observables corresponding to physical quantities evolve over time as

$$\hat{A}_H(t) = \hat{U}^\dagger(t, t_0)\hat{A}_s\hat{U}(t, t_0) \tag{4.59}$$

where $\hat{A}_s$ is the observable in the Schrödinger picture and

$$\hat{U}(t, t_0) = \exp\left[\frac{-i\hat{H}_s(t - t_0)}{\hbar}\right] \tag{4.60}$$

The operator $\hat{U}(t, t_0)$ is called the *time evolution operator*, and is a unitary operator. Note that this operator describes the time evolution of the state vector in the Schrödinger picture:

$$|\psi_s(t)\rangle = \hat{U}(t, t_0)|\psi_s(t_0)\rangle \tag{4.61}$$

SOLVED PROBLEMS

4.1. Two states of a physical system are given by

$$|\psi_1\rangle = (4i\,|\phi_1\rangle - 12i\,|\phi_2\rangle) \quad \text{and} \quad |\psi_2\rangle = (|\phi_1\rangle - 6i\,|\phi_2\rangle) \tag{4.1.1}$$

Here $|\phi_1\rangle$ and $|\phi_2\rangle$ are orthonormal vectors. Determine both $|\psi_1 + \psi_2\rangle$ and $\langle\psi_1 + \psi_2|$.

SOLUTION

$$|\psi_1 + \psi_2\rangle = (4i\,|\phi_1\rangle - 12i\,|\phi_2\rangle) + (|\phi_1\rangle - 6i\,|\phi_2\rangle) \tag{4.1.2}$$

and

$$|\psi_1 + \psi_2\rangle = (1 + 4i)|\phi_1\rangle - 18i|\phi_2\rangle \qquad (4.1.3)$$

Taking the complex conjugate of this leads to

$$(|\psi_1 + \psi_2\rangle)^* = \langle\psi_1 + \psi_2| = (1 + 4i)^*\langle\phi_1| - (18i)^*\langle\phi_2| \qquad (4.1.4)$$

and so

$$\langle\psi_1 + \psi_2| = (1 - 4i)\langle\phi_1| + 18i\langle\phi_2| \qquad (4.1.5)$$

4.2. Two states of a physical system are represented by

$$|\psi_1\rangle = (6i|\phi_1\rangle - 3i|\phi_2\rangle) \quad \text{and} \quad |\psi_2\rangle = (-2|\phi_1\rangle + 4i|\phi_2\rangle) \qquad (4.2.1)$$

Moreover, $|\phi_1\rangle$ and $|\phi_2\rangle$ are orthonormal. Determine the salar product $\langle\psi_1|\psi_2\rangle$.

SOLUTION

We first find the bra $\langle\psi_1|$ corresponding to the ket $|\psi_1\rangle = (6i|\phi_1\rangle - 3i|\phi_2\rangle)$ using the fact that $(|\psi\rangle)^* = \langle\psi|$. Hence,

$$\langle\psi_1| = (6i|\phi_1\rangle)^* - (3i|\phi_2\rangle)^*$$
$$= -6i(|\phi_1\rangle)^* + 3i(|\phi_2\rangle)^* \qquad (4.2.2)$$

and

$$\langle\psi_1| = -6i\langle\phi_1| + 3i\langle\phi_2| \qquad (4.2.3)$$

The scalar product is

$$\langle\psi_1|\psi_2\rangle = (-6i\langle\phi_1| + 3i\langle\phi_2|)(-2|\phi_1\rangle + 4i|\phi_2\rangle) \qquad (4.2.4)$$

Recall that $|\phi_1\rangle$ and $|\phi_2\rangle$ are orthonormal, which means that $\langle\phi_1|\phi_1\rangle = \langle\phi_2|\phi_2\rangle = 1$ and $\langle\phi_1|\phi_2\rangle = \langle\phi_2|\phi_1\rangle = 0$. We will use this after we multiply the scalar product,

$$\langle\psi_1|\psi_2\rangle = (-6i\langle\phi_1|)(-2|\phi_1\rangle) + (-6i\langle\phi_1|)(4i|\phi_2\rangle) + (3i\langle\phi_2|)(-2|\phi_1\rangle) + (3i\langle\phi_2|)(4i|\phi_2\rangle)$$
$$= 12i\langle\phi_1|\phi_1\rangle + 24\langle\phi_1|\phi_2\rangle - 6i\langle\phi_2|\phi_1\rangle - 12\langle\phi_2|\phi_2\rangle \qquad (4.2.5)$$

Using the orthonormality of $|\phi_1\rangle$ and $|\phi_2\rangle$,

$$\langle\psi_1|\psi_2\rangle = 12i - 12 \qquad (4.2.6)$$

4.3. With the previous problem in mind, determine the scalar product $\langle\psi_2|\psi_1\rangle$. Verify that $\langle\psi_1|\psi_2\rangle^* = \langle\psi_2|\psi_1\rangle$, which is the equivalent of Eq. (4.1).

SOLUTION

Now find the bra $\langle\psi_2|$ corresponding to the ket $|\psi_2\rangle = (-2|\phi_1\rangle + 4i|\phi_2\rangle)$ using the fact that $(|\psi\rangle)^* = \langle\psi|$. Accordingly,

$$\langle\psi_2| = -2(|\phi_1\rangle)^* + (4i)^*(|\phi_2\rangle)^* \qquad (4.3.1)$$

and

$$\langle\psi_2| = -2\langle\phi_1| - 4i\langle\phi_2| \qquad (4.3.2)$$

The scalar product is

$$\langle\psi_2|\psi_1\rangle = (-2\langle\phi_1| - 4i\langle\phi_2|)(6i|\phi_1\rangle - 3i|\phi_2\rangle)$$
$$= -12i\langle\phi_1|\phi_1\rangle + 6i\langle\phi_1|\phi_2\rangle + 24\langle\phi_2|\phi_1\rangle - 12\langle\phi_2|\phi_2\rangle \qquad (4.3.3)$$

and so,

$$\langle \psi_2 | \psi_1 \rangle = -12i - 12 \qquad (4.3.4)$$

Since $\langle \psi_1 | \psi_2 \rangle = 12i - 12$, we see that

$$\langle \psi_1 | \psi_2 \rangle^* = -12i - 2 = \langle \psi_2 | \psi_1 \rangle \qquad (4.3.5)$$

4.4. Let $|\psi_1\rangle$ and $|\psi_2\rangle$ be two orthogonal normalized states of a physical system:

$$\langle \psi_1 | \psi_2 \rangle = 0 \quad \text{and} \quad \langle \psi_1 | \psi_1 \rangle = \langle \psi_2 | \psi_2 \rangle = 1 \qquad (4.4.1)$$

and let A be an observable of the system. Consider a nondegenerate eigenvalue of $\hat{A}_2$ denoted by α_n to which the normalized state $|\phi_n\rangle$ corresponds. We define $P_1(\alpha_n) = |\langle \phi_n | \psi_1 \rangle|^2$ and $P_2(\alpha_n) = |\langle \phi_n | \psi_2 \rangle|^2$. (*a*) What is the interpretation of $P_1(\alpha_n)$ and $P_2(\alpha_n)$? (*b*) A given particle is in the state $3|\psi_1\rangle - 4i|\psi_2\rangle$. What is the probability of getting α_n when A is measured?

SOLUTION

(*a*) According to the postulates of quantum mechanics, $P_1(\alpha_n)$ is the probability of obtaining α_n when A is measured while the system is in the state $|\psi_1\rangle$. The same is the case with $P_2(\alpha_n)$ in the state $|\psi_2\rangle$.

(*b*) The normalized state of the particle is

$$|\psi\rangle = \frac{3|\psi_1\rangle - 4i|\psi_2\rangle}{\sqrt{(3\langle\psi_1| + 4i\langle\psi_2|)(3|\psi_1\rangle - 4i|\psi_2\rangle)}} = \frac{3|\psi_1\rangle - 4i|\psi_2\rangle}{\sqrt{9+16}} = \frac{1}{5}(3|\psi_1\rangle - 4i|\psi_2\rangle)) \qquad (4.4.2)$$

Using the postulates of quantum mechanics (for a summary of the theory, see Sec. 4.2), the probability of measuring α_n is

$$P(\alpha_n) = |\langle \phi_n | \psi \rangle|^2 = \frac{1}{25} | 3\langle\phi_n|\psi_1\rangle - 4i\langle\phi_n|\psi_2\rangle |^2$$

$$= \frac{1}{25} (3\langle\phi_n|\psi_1\rangle - 4i\langle\phi_n|\psi_2\rangle)(3\langle\phi_n|\psi_1\rangle^* + 4i\langle\phi_n|\psi_2\rangle^*)$$

$$= \frac{1}{25} [9|\langle\phi_n|\psi_1\rangle|^2 + 16|\langle\phi_n|\psi_2\rangle|^2 + 12i\langle\phi_n|\psi_1\rangle\langle\phi_n|\psi_2\rangle^* - 12i\langle\phi_n|\psi_2\rangle\langle\phi_n|\psi_1\rangle^*]$$

$$= \frac{1}{25} \{9P_1(\alpha_n) + 16P_2(\alpha_n) + 2Re[12i\langle\phi_n|\psi_1\rangle\langle\phi_n|\psi_2\rangle^*]\} \qquad (4.4.3)$$

4.5. Consider postulate IV in Sec. 4.2, and generalize for the case of a continuous spectrum.

SOLUTION

Consider a physical observable A. Suppose that the system is in a normalized state $|\psi\rangle$; $\langle\psi|\psi\rangle = 1$. Let $|v_\alpha^\beta\rangle$ form an orthonormal basis of the state space consisting of eigenvectors of $\hat{A}$:

$$\hat{A}|v_\alpha^\beta\rangle = \alpha|v_\alpha^\beta\rangle \qquad (4.5.1)$$

The index β distinguishes between eigenvectors corresponding to the same degenerate eigenvalue α of $\hat{A}$. This index can be either discrete or continuous, and we assume that it is continuous and varies in the domain $B(\alpha)$. Since the spectrum of $\hat{A}$ is continuous, it is meaningless to speak about the probability of obtaining an eigenvalue α. Alternatively, we should speak about the differential probability $dP(\alpha)$ of obtaining a result between α and $\alpha + d\alpha$. We then have an analogy to postulate IV for the discrete case,

$$dP(\alpha) = \left\{ \int_{B(\alpha)} |\langle v_\alpha^\beta | \psi \rangle|^2 \, d\beta \right\} d\alpha \qquad (4.5.2)$$

4.6. Consider postulate IV for the case of a discrete spectrum. Show that an equivalent form for the probability of obtaining the eigenvalue a_n of the operator $\hat{A}$ is

$$P(a_n) = \langle \psi | \hat{P}_n^\dagger \hat{P}_n | \psi \rangle \tag{4.6.1}$$

where $\hat{P}_n$ is the projector onto the eigensubspace of $\hat{A}$ associated with a_n.

SOLUTION
Assume that $| u_n^1 \rangle, | u_n^2 \rangle, \ldots,$ and $| u_n^{g_n} \rangle$ form an orthonormal basis of the eigensubspace associated with a_n. By definition, Eq. (4.6) becomes,

$$\hat{P}_n = \sum_{i=1}^{g_n} | u_n^i \rangle \langle u_n^i | \tag{4.6.2}$$

Therefore,

$$\langle \psi | \hat{P}_n^\dagger \hat{P}_n | \psi \rangle = \sum_{i=1}^{g_n}\sum_{j=1}^{g_n} \langle \psi | u_n^i \rangle \langle u_n^i | u_n^j \rangle \langle u_n^j | \psi \rangle = \sum_{i=1}^{g_n}\sum_{j=1}^{g_n} \langle \psi | u_n^i \rangle \langle u_n^j | \psi \rangle \delta_{ij}$$

$$= \sum_{j=1}^{g_n} \left| \langle u_n^i | \psi \rangle \right|^2 \tag{4.6.3}$$

The two formulations are equivalent.

4.7. Consider two kets $| \psi \rangle$ and $| \psi' \rangle$ such that $| \psi' \rangle = e^{i\theta} | \psi \rangle$ where θ is a real number. (*a*) Prove that if $| \psi \rangle$ is normalized, then so is $| \psi' \rangle$. (*b*) Demonstrate that the predicted probabilities for an arbitrary measurement are the same for $| \psi \rangle$ and $| \psi' \rangle$; therefore, $| \psi \rangle$ and $| \psi' \rangle$ represent the same physical state.

SOLUTION
(*a*) We assume that $| \psi \rangle$ is normalized, or $\langle \psi | \psi \rangle = 1$. Then

$$\langle \psi' | \psi' \rangle = \langle \psi | e^{-i\theta} e^{i\theta} | \psi \rangle = \langle \psi | \psi \rangle = 1 \tag{4.7.1}$$

(*b*) According to postulate IV (see Sec. 4.2), the probabilities predicted for a measurement depend on terms of the form $| \langle u_n^i | \psi \rangle |^2$ or $| \langle u_n^i | \psi' \rangle |^2$. We have

$$| \langle u_n^i | \psi' \rangle |^2 = \langle u_n^i | \psi' \rangle \langle u_n^i | \psi' \rangle^* = e^{i\theta} \langle u_n^i | \psi \rangle e^{-i\theta} \langle u_n^i | \psi \rangle^* = | \langle u_n^i | \psi \rangle |^2 \tag{4.7.2}$$

Therefore, the predicted probabilities for the states $| \psi \rangle$ and $| \psi' \rangle$ are the same.

4.8. Consider a large number of measurements of an observable performed on the system. Show that the mean value of an observable expresses the average of the results. Assume that the spectrum of the operator consists of both a discrete and a continuous part, but for simplicity, assume it to be nondegenerate.

SOLUTION
Consider first an eigenvalue a_n belonging to the discrete part of the spectrum. From a quantity of N measurements of A (the system being in the normalized state $| \psi \rangle$) the eigenvalue a_n will be obtained $N(a_n)$ times with

$$\left(\frac{N(a_n)}{N} \right)_{n \to \infty} \to P(a_n) \tag{4.8.1}$$

where $P(a_n)$ is the probability of obtaining a_n in a measurement. Similarly, if $dN(\alpha)$ expresses the number of experiments that yield a result between α and $\alpha + d\alpha$ in the continuous part of the spectrum, we have

$$\left(\frac{dN(\alpha)}{N}\right)_{n \to \infty} \to dP(\alpha) \tag{4.8.2}$$

The average of the results of the N measurements is the sum of the values divided by N. It is therefore equal to

$$\text{Average }(N) = \frac{1}{N}\sum_n a_n N(a_n) + \frac{1}{N}\int \alpha\, dN(\alpha) \tag{4.8.3}$$

For $N \to \infty$, we obtain

$$\text{Average }(N \to \infty) = \sum_n a_n P(a_n) + \int \alpha\, dP(\alpha) \tag{4.8.4}$$

Suppose now that $|u_n\rangle$ for $n = 1, 2, \ldots$, together with $|v_\alpha\rangle$, where α is a continuous index, form an orthonormal basis of the state space consisting of eigenvalues of $\hat{A}$:

$$\hat{A}|u_n\rangle = a_n|u_n\rangle \qquad \hat{A}|v_\alpha\rangle = \alpha|v_\alpha\rangle \tag{4.8.5}$$

The closure relation of this basis is

$$\sum_n |u_n\rangle\langle u_n| + \int |v_\alpha\rangle\langle v_\alpha|\, d\alpha = \hat{I} \tag{4.8.6}$$

So, using Eq. (4.8.4), we arrive at

$$\text{Average }(N \to \infty) = \sum_n a_n |\langle\psi|u_n\rangle|^2 + \int \alpha |\langle\psi|v_\alpha\rangle|^2 d\alpha$$

$$= \sum_n a_n \langle\psi|u_n\rangle\langle u_n|\psi\rangle + \int \alpha\langle\psi|v_\alpha\rangle\langle v_\alpha|\psi\rangle d\alpha$$

Using Eq. (4.8.5), we obtain

$$\text{Average }(N \to \infty) = \sum_n \langle\psi|\hat{A}|u_n\rangle\langle u_n|\psi\rangle + \int \langle\psi|\hat{A}|v_\alpha\rangle\langle v_\alpha|\psi\rangle d\alpha$$

$$= \langle\psi|\hat{A}\left[\sum_n |u_n\rangle\langle u_n| + \int |v_\alpha\rangle\langle v_\alpha|\, d\alpha\right]|\psi\rangle$$

Substituting the closure relation, we finally get

$$\text{Average }(N \to \infty) = \langle\psi|\hat{A}|\psi\rangle$$

4.9. Consider another formulation for the root-mean-square deviation of the operator $\hat{A}$ (in the normalized state $|\psi\rangle$):

$$\Delta A = \sqrt{\langle(\hat{A} - \langle\hat{A}\rangle)^2\rangle} \tag{4.9.1}$$

(a) Show that this definition is equivalent to that given in Eq. (4.9). (b) Use the formulation Eq. (4.9.1) to interpret the term *root-mean-square deviation*.

SOLUTION

(a) By the given definition we have

$$\langle(\hat{A} - \langle\hat{A}\rangle)^2\rangle = \langle\psi|(\hat{A} - \langle\hat{A}\rangle)^2|\psi\rangle \tag{4.9.2}$$

Note that in this equation the term $\langle \hat{A} \rangle$ is actually a shortened form of $\langle \hat{A} \rangle \hat{I}$, where $\hat{I}$ is the identity operator; $\langle \hat{A} \rangle$ is a scalar. Hence,

$$\langle \psi | (\hat{A} - \langle \hat{A} \rangle)^2 | \psi \rangle = \langle \psi | (\hat{A}^2 - 2\langle \hat{A} \rangle \hat{A} + \langle \hat{A} \rangle^2) | \psi \rangle$$

$$= \langle \psi | \hat{A}^2 | \psi \rangle - 2\langle \hat{A} \rangle \langle \psi | \hat{A} | \psi \rangle + \langle \hat{A} \rangle^2 \langle \psi | \psi \rangle \qquad (4.9.3)$$

Using the known definition of mean value, we have

$$\langle \hat{A}^2 \rangle - 2\langle \hat{A} \rangle \langle \hat{A} \rangle + \langle \hat{A} \rangle^2 = \langle \hat{A}^2 \rangle - \langle \hat{A} \rangle^2 \qquad (4.9.4)$$

So, the two definitions coincide.

(b) The root-mean-square deviation expresses the average of the square of the deviations of $\hat{A}$ from its mean value $\langle \hat{A} \rangle$. It therefore characterizes the dispersion of the measurement results about $\langle \hat{A} \rangle$. For example, if the spectrum of $\hat{A}$ is continuous and the probability has a Gaussian shape, then $\langle \hat{A} \rangle$ characterizes the peak of the curve (the value of maximal probability), and ΔA characterizes the width of the Gaussian curve.

4.10. Prove that for the operators $\hat{A}$, $\hat{B}$, and $\hat{C}$, the following identities are valid:

(a) $[\hat{B}, \hat{A}] = -[\hat{A}, \hat{B}]$

(b) $[\hat{A} + \hat{B}, \hat{C}] = [\hat{A}, \hat{C}] + [\hat{B}, \hat{C}]$

(c) $[\hat{A}, \hat{B}\hat{C}] = [\hat{A}, \hat{B}]\hat{C} + \hat{B}[\hat{A}, \hat{C}]$

SOLUTION

(a) By definition,

$$[\hat{B}, \hat{A}] = \hat{B}\hat{A} - \hat{A}\hat{B} = -(\hat{A}\hat{B} - \hat{B}\hat{A}) = -[\hat{A}, \hat{B}] \qquad (4.10.1)$$

(b) By definition,

$$[\hat{A} + \hat{B}, \hat{C}] = (\hat{A} + \hat{B})\hat{C} - \hat{C}(\hat{A} + \hat{B}) = \hat{A}\hat{C} + \hat{B}\hat{C} - \hat{C}\hat{A} - \hat{C}\hat{B}$$

$$= (\hat{A}\hat{C} - \hat{C}\hat{A}) + (\hat{B}\hat{C} - \hat{C}\hat{B}) = [\hat{A}, \hat{C}] + [\hat{B}, \hat{C}] \qquad (4.10.2)$$

(c) We write

$$[\hat{A}, \hat{B}\hat{C}] = \hat{A}(\hat{B}\hat{C}) - (\hat{B}\hat{C})\hat{A} = (\hat{A}\hat{B}\hat{C} - \hat{B}\hat{A}\hat{C}) + (\hat{B}\hat{A}\hat{C} - \hat{B}\hat{C}\hat{A}) = [\hat{A}, \hat{B}]\hat{C} + \hat{B}[\hat{A}, \hat{C}] \qquad (4.10.3)$$

4.11. Suppose the operators $\hat{A}$ and $\hat{B}$ commute with their commutator, i.e., $[\hat{B},[\hat{A}, \hat{B}]] = [\hat{A},[\hat{A}, \hat{B}]] = 0$. Show that (a) $[\hat{A}, \hat{B}^n] = n\hat{B}^{n-1}[\hat{A}, \hat{B}]$; (b) $[\hat{A}^n, \hat{B}] = n\hat{A}^{n-1}[\hat{A}, \hat{B}]$.

SOLUTION

(a) Consider the following procedure:

$$[\hat{A}, \hat{B}^n] = \hat{A}\hat{B}^n + \hat{B}^n\hat{A} = \hat{A}\hat{B}\hat{B}^{n-1} - \hat{B}\hat{A}\hat{B}^{n-1} + \hat{B}(\hat{A}\hat{B})\hat{B}^{n-2} - \hat{B}(\hat{B}\hat{A})\hat{B}^{n-3} + \cdots + \hat{B}^{n-1}\hat{A}\hat{B} - \hat{B}^{n-1}\hat{B}\hat{A}$$

$$= [\hat{A}, \hat{B}]\hat{B}^{n-1} + \hat{B}[\hat{A}, \hat{B}]\hat{B}^{n-2} + \cdots + \hat{B}^{n-1}[\hat{A}, \hat{B}] \qquad (4.11.1)$$

Using the fact that $\hat{B}$ commutes with $[\hat{A}, \hat{B}]$, we obtain

$$[\hat{A}, \hat{B}^n] = \hat{B}^{n-1}[\hat{A}, \hat{B}] + \hat{B}^{n-1}[\hat{A}, \hat{B}] + \cdots + \hat{B}^{n-1}[\hat{A}, \hat{B}] = n\hat{B}^{n-1}[\hat{A}, \hat{B}] \qquad (4.11.2)$$

(b) According to Problem 4.10, part (a), $[\hat{A}^n, \hat{B}] = -[\hat{B}, \hat{A}^n]$. Using part (a) of the solution, we obtain

$$[\hat{A}^n, \hat{B}] = -n\hat{A}^{n-1}[\hat{B}, \hat{A}] = n\hat{A}^{n-1}[\hat{A}, \hat{B}] \qquad (4.11.3)$$

4.12. Consider the operators $\hat{A}$ and $\hat{B}$ presented in Problem 4.11. Prove that (*a*) for every analytic function $F(x)$ we have $[\hat{A}, F(\hat{B})] = [\hat{A}, \hat{B}]F'(\hat{B})$, where $F'(x)$ denotes the derivative of $F(x)$. (*b*) $e^{\hat{A}}e^{\hat{B}} = e^{\hat{A}+\hat{B}}e^{[\hat{A},\hat{B}]/2}$.

SOLUTION

(*a*) First we prove, using induction, that for every $n = 1, 2, \ldots$ we have

$$[\hat{A}, \hat{B}^n] = n[\hat{A}, \hat{B}]\hat{B}^{n-1} \tag{4.12.1}$$

Proof: For $n = 1$, Eq. (4.12.1) is clearly true. Suppose that this equation is verified for n. Then, using part (*c*) in Problem 4.10 for $n + 1$, we have

$$[\hat{A}, \hat{B}^{n+1}] = [\hat{A}, \hat{B}\hat{B}^n] = [\hat{A}, \hat{B}]\hat{B}^n + \hat{B}[\hat{A}, \hat{B}^n] = [\hat{A}, \hat{B}]\hat{B}^n + \hat{B}n[\hat{A}, \hat{B}]\hat{B}^{n-1} \tag{4.12.2}$$

$\hat{B}$ and $[\hat{A}, \hat{B}]$ commute, so we finally have

$$[\hat{A}, \hat{B}^{n+1}] = [\hat{A}, \hat{B}]\hat{B}^n + n[\hat{A}, \hat{B}]\hat{B}^n = (n+1)[\hat{A}, \hat{B}]\hat{B}^n \tag{4.12.3}$$

Equation (4.12.1) is therefore established. Consider now the expansion of the function $F(x)$ in a power series, $F(x) = \sum_n a_n x^n$. Using (4.12.1) we obtain

$$[\hat{A}, F(\hat{B})] = \left[\hat{A}, \sum_n a_n \hat{B}^n\right] = \sum_n a_n[\hat{A}, \hat{B}^n] = [\hat{A}, \hat{B}]\sum_n na_n \hat{B}^{n-1} \tag{4.12.4}$$

The power series expansion of the derivative of $F(x)$ is $F'(x) = \sum_n na_n x^{n-1}$. Therefore, by inspection we can conclude that

$$[\hat{A}, F(\hat{B})] = [\hat{A}, \hat{B}]F'(\hat{B}) \tag{4.12.5}$$

(*b*) Consider an operator $\hat{F}(s)$ depending on the real parameter s:

$$\hat{F}(s) = e^{\hat{A}s}e^{\hat{B}s} \tag{4.12.6}$$

The derivative of $\hat{F}$ with respect to s is

$$\frac{d\hat{F}}{ds} = \left(\frac{d}{ds}e^{\hat{A}s}\right)e^{\hat{B}s} + e^{\hat{A}s}\left(\frac{d}{ds}e^{\hat{B}s}\right) = \hat{A}e^{\hat{A}s}e^{\hat{B}s} + e^{\hat{A}s}\hat{B}e^{\hat{B}s}$$

$$= \hat{A}e^{\hat{A}s}e^{\hat{B}s} + e^{\hat{A}s}\hat{B}e^{-\hat{A}s}e^{\hat{A}s}e^{\hat{B}s} = (\hat{A} + e^{\hat{A}s}\hat{B}e^{-\hat{A}s})\hat{F}(s) \tag{4.12.7}$$

Using part (*a*), we can write

$$[e^{\hat{A}s}, \hat{B}] = -[\hat{B}, e^{\hat{A}s}] = -s[\hat{B}, \hat{A}]e^{\hat{A}s} = s[\hat{A}, \hat{B}]e^{\hat{A}s} \tag{4.12.8}$$

Therefore, $e^{\hat{A}s}\hat{B} = \hat{B}e^{\hat{A}s} + s[\hat{A}, \hat{B}]e^{\hat{A}s}$ and $e^{\hat{A}s}\hat{B}e^{-\hat{A}s} = \hat{B} + s[\hat{A}, \hat{B}]$. Substituting in Eq. (4.12.7) we obtain

$$\frac{d\hat{F}}{ds} = (\hat{A} + \hat{B} + s[\hat{A}, \hat{B}])\hat{F}(s) \tag{4.12.9}$$

Since $\hat{A} + \hat{B}$ and $[\hat{A}, \hat{B}]$ commute, we can integrate this differential equation. This yields

$$\hat{F}(s) + \hat{F}(0)e^{(\hat{A}+\hat{B})s+[\hat{A},\hat{B}]s^2/2} \tag{4.12.10}$$

Setting $s = 0$, we obtain $F(0) = e^{\hat{A} \cdot 0}e^{\hat{B} \cdot 0} = \hat{I} \cdot \hat{I} = \hat{I}$. Finally, substituting $\hat{F}(0)$ and $s = 1$ in Eq. (4.12.10), we obtain $e^{\hat{A}}e^{\hat{B}} = e^{\hat{A}+\hat{B}}e^{[\hat{A},\hat{B}]/2}$.

4.13. Let $\langle\psi|$ be the corresponding bra of the ket $|\psi\rangle$. We designate by $|\psi'\rangle$ the result of the action of the operator $\hat{A}$ on $|\psi\rangle$, so $|\psi'\rangle = \hat{A}|\psi\rangle$. Let $\langle\psi'|$ be the bra corresponding to $|\psi'\rangle$. Prove that

$$\langle\psi'| = \langle\psi|\hat{A}^\dagger \tag{4.13.1}$$

SOLUTION

Recall the basic definition of a bra as a functional acting on the state space. The two functionals $\langle\psi'|$ and $\langle\psi|\hat{A}^\dagger$ are identical if their action on an arbitrary ket $|\phi\rangle$ yields the same result; i.e., we have to show that

$$\langle\psi'|\phi\rangle = \langle\psi|\hat{A}^\dagger|\phi\rangle \tag{4.13.2}$$

Now, using Eq. (4.13) we have

$$\langle\psi|\hat{A}^\dagger|\phi\rangle = \langle\phi|\hat{A}|\psi\rangle^* = \langle\phi|\psi'\rangle^* \tag{4.13.3}$$

and according to the basic property of the scalar product [see Eq. (4.1)], we have

$$\langle\psi|\hat{A}^\dagger|\phi\rangle = \langle\psi'|\phi\rangle \tag{4.13.4}$$

4.14. Given that $(a\hat{A})^\dagger = a^*\hat{A}^\dagger$ and $(\hat{A}^\dagger)^\dagger = \hat{A}$ and $(\hat{A} + \hat{B})^\dagger = \hat{A}^\dagger + \hat{B}^\dagger$ and $(\hat{A}\hat{B}\hat{C})^\dagger = \hat{C}^\dagger\hat{B}^\dagger\hat{A}^\dagger$, where a is a complex number and $\hat{A}$, $\hat{B}$, and $\hat{C}$ are operators, determine the Hermitian conjugate of $(4 + 2i\hat{A} + 6\hat{B}^2)$. Once you finish this problem go on to study Problem 4.17.

SOLUTION

Call $(4 + 2i\hat{A} + 6\hat{B}^2)$ the operator $\hat{C}$. Then

$$\hat{C}^\dagger = (4 + 2i\hat{A} + 6\hat{B}^2)^\dagger = (4)^\dagger + (2i\hat{A})^\dagger + (6\hat{B}^2)^\dagger \tag{4.14.1}$$

Since $(4)^\dagger = 4$ and $(2i\,\hat{A})^\dagger = -2i\hat{A}^\dagger$ and $(6\hat{B}^2)^\dagger = 6(\hat{B}^2)^\dagger = 6\hat{B}^\dagger\hat{B}^\dagger = 6(\hat{B}^\dagger)^2$, it follows that

$$\hat{C}^\dagger = 4 - 2i\hat{A}^\dagger + 6(\hat{B}^\dagger)^2 \tag{4.14.2}$$

4.15. Given operators $\hat{A}$ and $\hat{B}$ where $\hat{A} = \hat{B}^\dagger + \hat{B}$. Show that $\hat{A}$ is Hermitian, independent of whether $\hat{B}$ is or is not Hermitian.

SOLUTION

$$\hat{A} = \hat{A}^\dagger = (\hat{B}^\dagger + \hat{B})^\dagger = (\hat{B}^\dagger)^\dagger + \hat{B}^\dagger \tag{4.15.1}$$

From Problem 2.6 $(\hat{B}^\dagger)^\dagger = \hat{A}$, hence $\hat{A}^\dagger = \hat{B} + \hat{B}^\dagger = \hat{A}$ regardless of whether $\hat{B}$ is Hermitian or not.

4.16. An operator $\hat{A}$ is said to be *skew-Hermitian* or *anti-Hermitian* if $\hat{A}^\dagger = -\hat{A}$. Show that the operator $i(\hat{B} + \hat{B}^\dagger)$ is anti-Hermitian. See Sec. 2.3.

SOLUTION

$\hat{A} = i(\hat{B} + \hat{B}^\dagger)$, hence $\hat{A}^\dagger = [i(\hat{B} + \hat{B}^\dagger)]^\dagger$ but in general, $(b\hat{B})^\dagger = b^*\hat{B}^\dagger$ where b is a complex number. Therefore,

$$\hat{A}^\dagger = (i)^*(\hat{B}^\dagger + \hat{B}) = -i(\hat{B}^\dagger + \hat{B}) \tag{4.16.1}$$

and

$$\hat{A}^\dagger = -\hat{A}$$

4.17. Derive the following properties of the adjoint of an operator:

(a) $(\hat{A}^\dagger)^\dagger = \hat{A}$

(b) $(\lambda\hat{A})^\dagger = \lambda^*\hat{A}^\dagger$, where λ is a complex number

(c) $(\hat{A} + \hat{B})^{\dagger} = \hat{A}^{\dagger} + \hat{B}^{\dagger}$

(d) $(\hat{A}\hat{B})^{\dagger} = \hat{B}^{\dagger}\hat{A}^{\dagger}$

SOLUTION

First, recall that two operators are identical if their matrix elements in a basis of the state space are the same. Therefore, if for arbitrary $|\phi\rangle$ and $|\psi\rangle$ we have $\langle\phi|\hat{A}_1|\psi\rangle = \langle\phi|\hat{A}_2|\psi\rangle$, then $\hat{A}_1$ and $\hat{A}_2$ are identical. In the following derivations we also use some of the basic properties of conjugation of complex numbers that were given in Chap. 2.

(a) Using Eq. (4.13) we have

$$\langle\psi|(\hat{A}^{\dagger})^{\dagger}|\phi\rangle = \langle\phi|\hat{A}^{\dagger}|\psi\rangle^* \tag{4.17.1}$$

and using Eq. (4.13) again, we have

$$\langle\phi|\hat{A}^{\dagger}|\psi\rangle = \langle\psi|\hat{A}|\phi\rangle^* \tag{4.17.2}$$

Therefore,

$$\langle\psi|(\hat{A}^{\dagger})^{\dagger}|\phi\rangle = \langle\phi|\hat{A}^{\dagger}|\psi\rangle^* = (\langle\psi|\hat{A}|\phi\rangle^*)^* = \langle\psi|\hat{A}|\phi\rangle \tag{4.17.3}$$

(b) We write

$$\langle\psi|(\lambda\hat{A})^{\dagger}|\phi\rangle = \langle\phi|\lambda\hat{A}|\psi\rangle^* = [\lambda\langle\phi|\hat{A}|\psi\rangle]^*$$

$$= \lambda^*\langle\phi|\hat{A}|\psi\rangle^* = \lambda^*\langle\psi|\hat{A}^{\dagger}|\phi\rangle = \langle\psi|\lambda^*\hat{A}^{\dagger}|\phi\rangle \tag{4.17.4}$$

(c) We write

$$\langle\psi|(\hat{A}+\hat{B})^{\dagger}|\phi\rangle = \langle\phi|\hat{A}+\hat{B})|\psi\rangle^* = [\langle\phi|\hat{A}|\psi\rangle + \langle\phi|\hat{B}|\psi\rangle]^*$$

$$= \langle\phi|\hat{A}|\psi\rangle^* + \langle\phi|\hat{B}|\psi\rangle^* = \langle\psi|\hat{A}^{\dagger}|\phi\rangle + \langle\psi|\hat{B}^{\dagger}|\phi\rangle = \langle\psi|(\hat{A}^{\dagger}+\hat{B}^{\dagger})|\phi\rangle \tag{4.17.5}$$

(d) Let us define $|\chi\rangle = \hat{B}|\psi\rangle$. Using the results of Problem 4.13, we have $\langle\chi| = \langle\psi|\hat{B}^{\dagger}$. Now,

$$\langle\psi|(\hat{A}\hat{B})^{\dagger}|\phi\rangle = \langle\phi|\hat{A}\hat{B}|\psi\rangle^* \equiv \langle\phi|\hat{A}|\chi\rangle^* = \langle\chi|\hat{A}^{\dagger}|\phi\rangle = \langle\psi|\hat{B}^{\dagger}\hat{A}^{\dagger}|\phi\rangle \tag{4.17.6}$$

4.18. Consider a Hermitian operator $\hat{A}$ that has the property $\hat{A}^3 = \hat{I}$. Show that $\hat{A} = \hat{I}$.

SOLUTION

First we find the possible eigenvalues of $\hat{A}$. Suppose $\hat{A}|\psi\rangle = \alpha|\psi\rangle$, so we have

$$|\psi\rangle = \hat{A}^3|\psi\rangle = \hat{A}^2(\alpha|\psi\rangle) = \alpha\hat{A}^2|\psi\rangle = \alpha^2 A|\psi\rangle = \alpha^3|\psi\rangle \tag{4.18.1}$$

Therefore, $\alpha^3 = 1$. The possible values of α are then

$$\alpha = -\frac{1}{2} + \frac{\sqrt{3}}{2}i, \quad -\frac{1}{2} - \frac{\sqrt{3}}{2}i, \quad 1 \tag{4.18.2}$$

Since $\hat{A}$ is Hermitian its eigenvalues are real; therefore, the only possible eigenvalue of $\hat{A}$ is $\alpha = 1$. We can choose an orthonormal basis of the state space consisting of eigenvalues of $\hat{A}$, so $\hat{A}|u_i\rangle = |u_i\rangle$. Every state $|\phi\rangle$ can be expanded as

$$|\phi\rangle = \sum_i |u_i\rangle \qquad \left(\text{or } |\phi\rangle = \int |u_s\rangle \, ds \text{ if the basis has a continuous index}\right) \tag{4.18.3}$$

Finally,

$$\hat{A}|\phi\rangle = \hat{A}\sum_i |u_i\rangle = \sum_i \hat{A}|u_i\rangle = \sum_i |u_i\rangle = |\phi\rangle \tag{4.18.4}$$

which implies $\hat{A} = \hat{I}$.

4.19. Prove that if an orthonormal discrete set of kets $\{|u_i\rangle, i = 1, 2, \ldots\}$ constitutes a basis, then it follows that

$$\sum_i |u_i\rangle\langle u_i| = \hat{I} \qquad (4.19.1)$$

SOLUTION

Let $|\psi\rangle$ be an arbitrary ket belonging to the state space. Since $\{|u_i\rangle\}$ is a basis, there exists, by definition, a unique expansion $|\psi\rangle = \sum_i C_i |u_i\rangle$. We use the orthonormalization relation Eq. (4.16) to obtain

$$\langle u_j | \psi\rangle = \sum_j C_i\langle u_j | u_i\rangle = \sum_j C_i\delta_{ij} = C_j \qquad (4.19.2)$$

So,

$$|\psi\rangle = \sum_i C_i |u_i\rangle = \sum_i \langle u_i | \psi\rangle |u_i\rangle = \left[\sum_i |u_i\rangle\langle u_i|\right]|\psi\rangle \qquad (4.19.3)$$

Note that since $\langle u_i | \psi\rangle$ is a scalar we could change the place of this expression. We see that for any ket $|\psi\rangle$ the action of the operator $\hat{P}(\{|u_i\rangle\}) = \sum_i |u_i\rangle\langle u_i|$ on that ket yields the same ket $|\psi\rangle$. Therefore, it is, by definition, the identity operator, $\hat{P}(\{|u_i\rangle\}) = \hat{I}$.

4.20. Show that if the closure relation is valid for an orthonormal continuous set $\{|w_\alpha\rangle\}$, then this set constitutes a basis.

Let $|\psi\rangle$ be an arbitrary ket belonging to the state space. Using the closure relation we have

$$|\psi\rangle = \hat{I} | \psi\rangle = \int |w_\alpha\rangle\langle w_\alpha | \psi\rangle d\alpha \qquad (4.20.1)$$

SOLUTION

Defining $C(\alpha) = \langle w_\alpha | \psi\rangle$ we have $|\psi\rangle = \int C(\alpha)|w_\alpha\rangle d\alpha$. We see that any ket $|\psi\rangle$ has an expansion on the $|w_\alpha\rangle$. To show that this expansion is unique we assume that we have two expansions:

$$|\psi\rangle = \int C(\alpha)|w_\alpha\rangle d\alpha \qquad |\psi\rangle = \int C'(\alpha)|w_\alpha\rangle d\alpha \qquad (4.20.2)$$

Subtracting we obtain

$$\int [C(\alpha) - C'(\alpha)] | w_\alpha\rangle d\alpha = 0 \qquad (4.20.3)$$

Applying $\langle w_{\alpha'}|$ on this ket, $\int [C(\alpha) - C'(\alpha)] \langle w_{\alpha'} | w_\alpha\rangle d\alpha = 0$ and using the orthonormalization relation we obtain

$$\int [C(\alpha) - C'(\alpha)]\delta(\alpha' - \alpha) d\alpha = 0 \qquad (4.20.4)$$

Equation (4.20.4) is valid only if $C(\alpha') - C'(\alpha') = 0$. Therefore, for any α' we have $C(\alpha') = C'(\alpha')$, and the expansion of any ket $|\psi\rangle$ on $\{|w_\alpha\rangle\}$ is unique.

4.21. Suppose that in a certain basis $\{|u_i\rangle\}$, the operators $\hat{A}$ and $\hat{B}$ are represented by the matrices (A_{ij}) and (B_{ij}), respectively; the ket $|\psi\rangle$ is represented by c_i; and the bra $\langle\phi|$ by b_i^*.

(*a*) Obtain the matrix representation of the operator $\hat{A}\hat{B}$.

(*b*) Find the representation of the ket $\hat{A} | \psi\rangle$.

(*c*) Obtain an expression for the scalar $\langle\phi | \hat{A} | \psi\rangle$ in terms of the various representations.

SOLUTION

(*a*) Consider the matrix element of $\hat{A}\hat{B}$:

$$(\hat{A}\hat{B})_{ij} = \langle u_i \mid \hat{A}\hat{B} \mid u_j \rangle = \langle u_i \mid \hat{A}\hat{I}\hat{B} \mid u_j \rangle \tag{4.21.1}$$

Using the closure relation we obtain

$$(\hat{A}\hat{B})_{ij} = \sum_k \langle u_i \mid \hat{A} \mid u_k \rangle \langle u_k \mid \hat{B} \mid u_j \rangle = \sum_k A_{ik} B_{kj} \tag{4.21.2}$$

(*b*) By definition, the ket $\hat{A} \mid \psi \rangle$ is represented by the numbers $c_i' = \langle u_i \mid \hat{A} \mid \psi \rangle$. Using the closure relation between $\hat{A}$ and $\mid \psi \rangle$, we can write

$$c_i' = \langle u_i \mid \hat{A}\hat{I} \mid \psi \rangle = \sum_j \langle u_i \mid \hat{A} \mid u_j \rangle \langle u_j \mid \psi \rangle = \sum_j A_{ij} c_j \tag{4.21.3}$$

and in matrix form,

$$\begin{pmatrix} c_1' \\ c_2' \\ \vdots \\ \vdots \end{pmatrix} = \begin{pmatrix} A_{11} & A_{12} & \cdots \\ A_{21} & A_{22} & \cdots \\ \vdots & \vdots & \\ \vdots & \vdots & \end{pmatrix} \begin{pmatrix} c_1 \\ c_2 \\ \vdots \\ \vdots \end{pmatrix} \tag{4.21.4}$$

(*c*) We write

$$\langle \phi \mid \hat{A} \mid \psi \rangle = \sum_{i,j} \langle \phi \mid u_i \rangle \langle u_i \mid \hat{A} \mid u_j \rangle \langle u_j \mid \psi \rangle = \sum_{i,j} b_i^* A_{ij} c_j \tag{4.21.5}$$

or in matrix form,

$$\langle \phi \mid \hat{A} \mid \psi \rangle = (b_1^* \, b_2^* \ldots b_i^* \ldots) \begin{pmatrix} A_{11} & A_{12} & \cdots & A_{1j} & \cdots \\ A_{21} & A_{22} & & & \\ \vdots & & & & \\ A_{i1} & A_{i2} & \cdots & A_{ij} & \\ \vdots & & & & \end{pmatrix} \begin{pmatrix} c_i \\ c_2 \\ \vdots \\ c_j \end{pmatrix} \tag{4.21.6}$$

4.22. Suppose that $\mid \phi_n \rangle$, where $n = 1, 2, \ldots$, form an orthonormal basis for the state space of a physical system. Let $\hat{A}$ be an operator with matrix elements $A_{mn} = \langle \phi_m \mid \hat{A} \mid \phi_n \rangle$. Show that the operator $\hat{A}$ can be written as

$$\hat{A} = \sum_{m,n=1}^{\infty} A_{mn} \mid \phi_m \rangle \langle \phi_n \mid \tag{4.22.1}$$

SOLUTION

Recall that two operators are identical if and only if their matrix elements in a certain basis are identical. Therefore, we write the matrix elements of the expression in Eq. (4.22.1) as

$$\langle \phi_k \mid \left[\sum_{m,n=1}^{\infty} A_{mn} \mid \phi_m \rangle \langle \phi_n \mid \right] \mid \phi_l \rangle = \sum_{m,n=1}^{\infty} \langle \phi_k \mid \phi_m \rangle \langle \phi_m \mid \hat{A} \mid \phi_n \rangle \langle \phi_n \mid \phi_l \rangle$$

$$= \sum_{m,n=1}^{\infty} \delta_{km} \langle \phi_m \mid \hat{A} \mid \phi_n \rangle \delta_{nl} = \langle \phi_k \mid \hat{A} \mid \phi_l \rangle \tag{4.22.2}$$

where we used the orthonormalization relations $\langle \phi_i \mid \phi_j \rangle = \delta_{ij}$.

4.23. Consider a two-dimensional physical system. The kets $|\psi_1\rangle$ and $|\psi_2\rangle$ form an orthonormal basis of the state space. We define a new basis $|\phi_1\rangle$ and $|\phi_2\rangle$ by

$$|\phi_1\rangle = \frac{1}{\sqrt{2}}(|\psi_1\rangle + |\psi_2\rangle) \qquad |\phi_2\rangle = \frac{1}{\sqrt{2}}(|\psi_1\rangle - |\psi_2\rangle) \tag{4.23.1}$$

An operator $\hat{P}$ is represented in the $|\psi_i\rangle$-basis by the matrix

$$(a_{ij}) = \begin{pmatrix} 1 & \varepsilon \\ \varepsilon & 1 \end{pmatrix}$$

Find the representation of $\hat{P}$ in the basis $|\phi_i\rangle$, i.e., find the matrix $\tilde{a}_{ij} = \langle\phi_i|\hat{P}|\phi_j\rangle$.

SOLUTION

Method 1: We define the transformation matrix $T_{ij} = \langle\psi_i|\varphi_j\rangle$. We calculate its elements; for example,

$$T_{11} = \langle\psi_1|\phi_1\rangle = \frac{1}{\sqrt{2}}\langle\psi_1|(|\psi_1\rangle + |\psi_2\rangle) = \frac{1}{\sqrt{2}}(1 + 0) = \frac{1}{\sqrt{2}}$$

and

$$T_{22} = \langle\psi_2|\phi_2\rangle = \frac{1}{\sqrt{2}}\langle\psi_2|(|\psi_1\rangle - |\psi_2\rangle) = \frac{1}{\sqrt{2}}(0 - 1) = -\frac{1}{\sqrt{2}}$$

and so on. Then we find

$$\hat{T} = \frac{1}{\sqrt{2}}\begin{pmatrix} 1 & 1 \\ 1 & -1 \end{pmatrix} \tag{4.23.2}$$

The adjoint matrix is $\hat{T}^\dagger = \frac{1}{\sqrt{2}}\begin{pmatrix} 1 & 1 \\ 1 & -1 \end{pmatrix}$. Using the closure relation $\sum_{i=1}^{2}|\psi_i\rangle\langle\psi_i| = \hat{I}$, we obtain

$$\tilde{a}_{kl} = \langle\phi_k|\hat{P}|\phi_l\rangle = \sum_{i,j=1}^{2}\langle\phi_k|\psi_i\rangle\langle\psi_i|\hat{P}|\psi_j\rangle\langle\psi_j|\phi_l\rangle = \sum_{i,j=1}^{2}\hat{T}^\dagger_{ki}a_{ij}\hat{T}_{jl}$$

We can accomplish the calculation in matrix form:

$$(\tilde{a}_{kl}) = \frac{1}{\sqrt{2}}\begin{pmatrix} 1 & 1 \\ 1 & -1 \end{pmatrix}\begin{pmatrix} 1 & \varepsilon \\ \varepsilon & 1 \end{pmatrix}\frac{1}{\sqrt{2}}\begin{pmatrix} 1 & 1 \\ 1 & -1 \end{pmatrix} = \frac{1}{2}\begin{pmatrix} 1 & 1 \\ 1 & -1 \end{pmatrix}\begin{pmatrix} 1+\varepsilon & 1-\varepsilon \\ 1+\varepsilon & -1+\varepsilon \end{pmatrix}$$

$$= \frac{1}{2}\begin{pmatrix} 2+2\varepsilon & 0 \\ 0 & 2+2\varepsilon \end{pmatrix} = \begin{pmatrix} 1+\varepsilon & 0 \\ 0 & 1-\varepsilon \end{pmatrix} \tag{4.23.3}$$

Method 2: Observing that $|\phi_i\rangle$ are actually eigenvectors of P,

$$\begin{pmatrix} 1 & \varepsilon \\ \varepsilon & 1 \end{pmatrix}\frac{1}{\sqrt{2}}\begin{pmatrix} 1 \\ 1 \end{pmatrix} = \frac{1}{\sqrt{2}}\begin{pmatrix} 1+\varepsilon \\ 1+\varepsilon \end{pmatrix} = (1+\varepsilon)\frac{1}{\sqrt{2}}\begin{pmatrix} 1 \\ 1 \end{pmatrix}$$

and

$$\begin{pmatrix} 1 & \varepsilon \\ \varepsilon & 1 \end{pmatrix}\frac{1}{\sqrt{2}}\begin{pmatrix} 1 \\ -1 \end{pmatrix} = \frac{1}{\sqrt{2}}\begin{pmatrix} 1-\varepsilon \\ -1+\varepsilon \end{pmatrix} = (1-\varepsilon)\frac{1}{\sqrt{2}}\begin{pmatrix} 1 \\ -1 \end{pmatrix}$$

Therefore,

$$\hat{P}|\phi_1\rangle = (1+\varepsilon)|\phi_1\rangle \qquad \hat{P}|\phi_2\rangle = (1-\varepsilon)|\phi_2\rangle$$

This implies that in the $|\phi_i\rangle$-representation $\hat{P}$ is diagonal:

$$(a_{ij}) = \begin{pmatrix} 1+\varepsilon & 0 \\ 0 & 1-\varepsilon \end{pmatrix} \tag{4.23.4}$$

4.24. Refer to Problem 4.23 and obtain the representation of the ket $e^{\hat{P}}|\psi_1\rangle$ in the $|\psi_i\rangle$-basis.

SOLUTION

Since $\hat{P}$ is diagonal in the basis, it is easier to work in this basis. Hence,

$$e^{\hat{P}}|\phi_1\rangle = e^{1+\varepsilon}|\phi_1\rangle \qquad e^{\hat{P}}|\phi_2\rangle = e^{1-\varepsilon}|\phi_2\rangle$$

so we obtain

$$e^{\hat{P}}|\psi_1\rangle = e^{\hat{P}}\left(\frac{1}{\sqrt{2}}|\phi_1\rangle + \frac{1}{\sqrt{2}}|\phi_2\rangle\right) = \frac{1}{2}\left[e^{1+\varepsilon}|\psi_1\rangle + e^{1+\varepsilon}|\psi_2\rangle + e^{1-\varepsilon}|\psi_1\rangle - e^{1-\varepsilon}|\psi_2\rangle\right]$$

$$= \frac{1}{2}\left[(e^{1+\varepsilon} + e^{1-\varepsilon})|\psi_1\rangle + (e^{1+\varepsilon} - e^{1-\varepsilon})|\psi_2\rangle\right]$$

Therefore, $e^{\hat{P}}|\psi_1\rangle$ is represented in the $|\psi_i\rangle$-basis as

$$e^{\hat{P}}|\psi_1\rangle = \frac{e}{2}\begin{pmatrix} e^{\varepsilon} + e^{-\varepsilon} \\ e^{\varepsilon} - e^{-\varepsilon} \end{pmatrix} \tag{4.24.1}$$

4.25. (*a*) Show that the ket $|\mathbf{r}\rangle$, where $\mathbf{r} = (x, y, z)$, is an eigenvector of the operator observable $\hat{X}$ with an eigenvalue x. (*b*) Show that $|\mathbf{p}\rangle$, where $\mathbf{p} = (p_x, p_y, p_z)$, is an eigenvector of $\hat{P}_x$ with an eigenvalue p_x.

SOLUTION

(*a*) Using the r-representation we have $\langle \mathbf{r}'|\hat{X}|\mathbf{r}\rangle = x'\langle \mathbf{r}'|\mathbf{r}\rangle$. Substituting the representation for $\langle \mathbf{r}'|\mathbf{r}\rangle$ we obtain

$$\langle \mathbf{r}'|\hat{X}|\mathbf{r}\rangle = x'\delta(\mathbf{r}' - \mathbf{r}) = x\delta(\mathbf{r}' - \mathbf{r}) \tag{4.25.1}$$

where $\mathbf{r}' = (x', y', z')$. Therefore, we have $\langle \mathbf{r}'|\hat{X}|\mathbf{r}\rangle = x\langle \mathbf{r}'|\mathbf{r}\rangle$. Since this holds for all $\mathbf{r}'$ we have

$$\hat{X}|\mathbf{r}\rangle = x|\mathbf{r}\rangle \tag{4.25.2}$$

(*b*) In the p-representation, we apply the same method as in part (*a*), so

$$\langle \mathbf{p}'|\hat{P}|\mathbf{p}\rangle = p_x'\langle \mathbf{p}'|\mathbf{p}\rangle = p_x'\delta(\mathbf{p}' - \mathbf{p}) = p_x\delta(\mathbf{p}' - \mathbf{p}) = p_x\langle \mathbf{p}'|\mathbf{p}\rangle \tag{4.25.3}$$

Therefore, $\hat{P}|\mathbf{p}\rangle = p_x|\mathbf{p}\rangle$. In conclusion, since analogous arguments can be applied to the y- and z-components, one can write

$$\begin{cases} \hat{X}|\mathbf{r}\rangle = x|\mathbf{r}\rangle \\ \hat{Y}|\mathbf{r}\rangle = y|\mathbf{r}\rangle \\ \hat{Z}|\mathbf{r}\rangle = z|\mathbf{r}\rangle \end{cases} \qquad \begin{cases} \hat{P}_x|\mathbf{r}\rangle = p_x|\mathbf{r}\rangle \\ \hat{P}_y|\mathbf{r}\rangle = p_y|\mathbf{r}\rangle \\ \hat{P}_z|\mathbf{r}\rangle = p_z|\mathbf{r}\rangle \end{cases} \tag{4.25.4}$$

4.26. Prove that $\langle \mathbf{r}|\hat{\mathbf{P}}|\psi\rangle = \frac{\hbar}{i}\nabla\langle \mathbf{r}|\psi\rangle$. (*b*) Write an expression for $\langle \phi|\hat{p}_x|\psi\rangle$ using the wavefunctions corresponding to $|\phi\rangle$ and $|\psi\rangle$.

SOLUTION

(*a*) Consider, for example, the x-component (the y- and z-components can be treated in a completely analogous manner). We have

$$\langle \mathbf{r}|\hat{P}_x|\psi\rangle = \int \langle \mathbf{r}|\mathbf{p}\rangle\langle \mathbf{p}|\hat{p}_x|\psi\rangle\, d^3p \tag{4.26.1}$$

where we use the closure relation of the *p*-representation. Using Eqs. (4.41) and (4.47) in Sec. 4.8 we obtain

$$\langle \mathbf{r} | \hat{P}_x | \psi \rangle = \frac{1}{(2\pi\hbar)^{3/2}} \int e^{i\,\mathbf{p}\cdot\mathbf{r}/\hbar} \hat{p}_x \tilde{\psi}(\mathbf{p}) d^3 p \qquad (4.26.2)$$

This expression is the Fourier transform of $\hat{p}_x \tilde{\psi}(\mathbf{p})$, which is $\dfrac{\hbar}{i} \dfrac{\partial \psi(\mathbf{r})}{\partial x}$. We therefore have

$$\langle \mathbf{r} | \hat{p}_x | \psi \rangle = \frac{\hbar}{i} \frac{\partial}{\partial x} \psi(\mathbf{r}) \qquad (4.26.3)$$

(*b*) Suppose that $\phi(\mathbf{r})$ and $\psi(\mathbf{r})$ are the wavefunctions corresponding, respectively, to $|\phi\rangle$ and $|\psi\rangle$; so,

$$\phi(\mathbf{r}) = \langle \mathbf{r} | \phi \rangle \qquad \psi(\mathbf{r}) = \langle \mathbf{r} | \psi \rangle \qquad (4.26.4)$$

Using the closure relation of the *r*-representation together with the result of part (*a*) we obtain

$$\langle \phi | \hat{p}_x | \psi \rangle = \int \langle \phi | \mathbf{r} \rangle \langle \mathbf{r} | \hat{p}_x | \psi \rangle d^3 r = \int \phi^*(\mathbf{r}) \frac{\hbar}{i} \frac{\partial \psi(\mathbf{r})}{\partial x} d^3 r \qquad (4.26.5)$$

4.27. Show

(*a*) that $[\hat{x}, \hat{y}] = 0$
(*b*) that $[\hat{p}_x, \hat{p}_y] = 0$
(*c*) that $[\hat{x}, \hat{p}_x] = i\hbar$
(*d*) that $[\hat{x}, \hat{p}_y] = 0$

SOLUTION

(*a*) Using the *r*-representation we obtain the action of $[\hat{x}, \hat{y}]$ on an arbitrary ket $|\psi\rangle$:

$$\langle \mathbf{r} | [\hat{x}, \hat{y}] | \psi \rangle = \langle \mathbf{r} | \hat{x}\hat{y} | \psi \rangle - \langle \mathbf{r} | \hat{y}\hat{x} | \psi \rangle$$

Using Eq. (4.46) in Sec. 4.8, we arrive at $\langle \mathbf{r} | [\hat{x}, \hat{y}] | \psi \rangle = x \langle \mathbf{r} | \hat{y} | \psi \rangle - y \langle \mathbf{r} | \hat{x} | \psi \rangle$. So,

$$\langle \mathbf{r} | \hat{x}, \hat{y} | \psi \rangle = xy \langle \mathbf{r} | \psi \rangle - yx \langle \mathbf{r} | \psi \rangle = 0 \qquad (4.27.1)$$

Since this is valid for any $\langle \mathbf{r} |$ and arbitrary $|\psi\rangle$, we have $[\hat{x}, \hat{y}] = 0$.

(*b*) We apply the same method in the *p*-representation:

$$\langle \mathbf{p} | [\hat{p}_x, \hat{p}_y] | \psi \rangle = \langle \mathbf{p} | \hat{p}_x \hat{p}_y | \psi \rangle - \langle \mathbf{p} | \hat{p}_y \hat{p}_x | \psi \rangle$$

$$= p_x \langle \mathbf{p} | \hat{p}_y | \psi \rangle - p_y \langle \mathbf{p} | \hat{p}_x | \psi \rangle = p_x p_y \langle \mathbf{p} | \psi \rangle - p_y p_x \langle \mathbf{p} | \psi \rangle = 0 \qquad (4.27.2)$$

(*c*) We write $\langle \mathbf{r} | [\hat{x}, \hat{p}_x] | \psi \rangle = \langle \mathbf{r} | \hat{x}\hat{p}_x | \psi \rangle - \langle \mathbf{r} | \hat{p}_x \hat{x} | \psi \rangle$; so,

$$\langle \mathbf{r} | [\hat{x}, \hat{p}_x] | \psi \rangle = x \langle \mathbf{r} | \hat{p}_x | \psi \rangle - \frac{\hbar}{i} \frac{\partial}{\partial x} \langle \mathbf{r} | \hat{x} | \psi \rangle = \frac{\hbar}{i} x \frac{\partial}{\partial x} \langle \mathbf{r} | \psi \rangle - \frac{\hbar}{i} \frac{\partial}{\partial x} (x \langle \mathbf{r} | \psi \rangle) \qquad (4.27.3)$$

If $\psi(\mathbf{r})$ is the wavefunction corresponding to $|\psi\rangle$, we have

$$\langle \mathbf{r} | [\hat{x}, \hat{p}_x] | \psi \rangle = \frac{\hbar}{i} \left[x \frac{\partial \psi(\mathbf{r})}{\partial x} - \frac{\partial (x \psi(\mathbf{r}))}{\partial x} \right] = \frac{\hbar}{i} \left[x \frac{\partial \psi(\mathbf{r})}{\partial x} - \psi(\mathbf{r}) - x \frac{\partial \psi(\mathbf{r})}{\partial x} \right] = i\hbar \psi(\mathbf{r}) = i\hbar \langle \mathbf{r} | \psi \rangle$$

Since the calculation is valid for all $|\psi\rangle$ and for any $|\mathbf{r}\rangle$, we obtain $[\hat{x}, \hat{p}_x] = i\hbar$.

(*d*) Again applying the method used in part (*c*), we obtain

$$\langle \mathbf{r} | [\hat{x}, \hat{p}_y] | \psi \rangle = x \langle \mathbf{r} | \hat{p}_y | \psi \rangle - \frac{\hbar}{i} \frac{\partial}{\partial y} \langle \mathbf{r} | \hat{x} | \psi \rangle$$

$$= \frac{\hbar}{i} x \frac{\partial}{\partial y} \psi(\mathbf{r}) - \frac{\hbar}{i} \frac{\partial \psi(\mathbf{r})}{\partial y} x \psi(\mathbf{r}) = \frac{\hbar}{i} \left[x \frac{\partial \psi(\mathbf{r})}{\partial y} - x \frac{\partial \psi(\mathbf{r})}{\partial y} \right] = 0 \qquad (4.27.4)$$

4.28. Consider the following operators:

$$\hat{O}_1 \psi(x) = x^3 \psi(x) \qquad \hat{O}_2 \psi(x) = x \frac{d\psi(x)}{dx} \qquad (4.28.1)$$

Find the commutation relation $[\hat{O}_1, \hat{O}_2]$.

SOLUTION

Method 1: Substituting the operators $\hat{O}_1$ and $\hat{O}_2$ in the commutation relation we obtain

$$[\hat{O}_1, \hat{O}_2] \psi = \hat{O}_1(\hat{O}_2 \psi(x)) - \hat{O}_2(\hat{O}_1 \psi(x)) = x^3 \left[x \frac{d\psi(x)}{dx} \right] - x \frac{d}{dx} [x^3 \psi(x)]$$

$$= x^4 \frac{d\psi(x)}{dx} - x \left[3x^2 \psi(x) + x^3 \frac{d\psi(x)}{dx} \right] = -3x^3 \psi(x) \qquad (4.28.2)$$

Method 2: According to the action of $\hat{x}$ and $\hat{p}$ in the x-representation, we have $\hat{O}_1 = \hat{x}^3$ and $\hat{O}_2 = i\hat{x}\hat{p}/\hbar$. Therefore,

$$[\hat{O}_1, \hat{O}_2] = \frac{i}{\hbar} [\hat{x}^3, \hat{x}\hat{p}] \qquad (4.28.3)$$

and using Problem 4.12

$$[\hat{O}_1, \hat{O}_2] = \frac{3i}{\hbar} x^2 [\hat{x}, \hat{x}\hat{p}] = \frac{3i}{\hbar} x^2 ([\hat{x}, \hat{x}]p + x[\hat{x}, \hat{p}]) = -3x^3 \qquad (4.28.4)$$

Or equivalently, $[\hat{O}_1, \hat{O}_2] \psi(x) = -3x^3 \psi(x)$.

4.29. The angular momentum is defined by $\mathbf{L} = \mathbf{r} \times \mathbf{p}$ (for example, $L_x = yp_z - zp_y$). Use the commutation relations between $\hat{\mathbf{R}}$ and $\hat{\mathbf{P}}$ and the properties of the commutator derived in Problem 4.10 to find the following commutation relations: (*a*) $[\hat{L}_x, \hat{L}_y]$; (*b*) $[\hat{L}_y^2, \hat{L}_x]$ and $[\hat{L}_z^2, \hat{L}_x]$; (*c*) $[\hat{L}^2, \hat{L}_x]$.

SOLUTION

(*a*) By definition,

$$[L_x, L_y] = [\hat{Y}\hat{P}_z - \hat{Z}\hat{P}_y, \hat{Z}\hat{P}_x - \hat{X}\hat{P}_z] = [\hat{Y}\hat{P}_z, \hat{Z}\hat{P}_x] + [\hat{Z}\hat{P}_y, \hat{X}\hat{P}_z] \qquad (4.29.1)$$

where we used the fact that $\hat{Y}\hat{P}_z$ commutes with $\hat{X}\hat{P}_z$ and $\hat{Z}\hat{P}_y$ commutes with $\hat{Z}\hat{P}_x$. Using the relation derived in Problem 4.4, part (*c*), we then have

$$\hat{Y}[\hat{P}_z, \hat{Z}]\hat{P}_x + \hat{X}[\hat{Z}, \hat{P}_z]\hat{P}_y = -i\hbar\hat{Y}\hat{P}_x + i\hbar\hat{X}\hat{P}_y = i\hbar\hat{L}_z \qquad (4.29.2)$$

(*b*) We write

$$[\hat{L}_y^2, \hat{L}_x] = \hat{L}_y[\hat{L}_y, \hat{L}_x] + [\hat{L}_y, \hat{L}_x]\hat{L}_y = -i\hbar\hat{L}_y\hat{L}_z - i\hbar\hat{L}_z\hat{L}_y \qquad (4.29.3)$$

Similarly,

$$[\hat{L}_z^2, \hat{L}_x] = \hat{L}_z[\hat{L}_z, \hat{L}_x] + [\hat{L}_z, \hat{L}_x]\hat{L}_z = i\hbar\hat{L}_z\hat{L}_y + i\hbar\hat{L}_y\hat{L}_z \qquad (4.29.4)$$

(c) We write

$$[\hat{L}^2, \hat{L}_x] = [\hat{L}_x^2, \hat{L}_x] + [\hat{L}_y^2, \hat{L}_x] + [\hat{L}_z^2, \hat{L}_x]$$

$$= 0 - i\hbar\hat{L}_y\hat{L}_z - i\hbar\hat{L}_z\hat{L}_y + i\hbar\hat{L}_z\hat{L}_y + i\hbar\hat{L}_y\hat{L}_z = 0 \qquad (4.29.5)$$

This result also holds for $[\hat{L}^2, \hat{L}_y]$ and $[\hat{L}^2, \hat{L}_z]$.

4.30. A particle is described by the wavefunction

$$\psi(x) = \left(\frac{\pi}{a}\right)^{-1/4} e^{-ax^2/2} \qquad (4.30.1)$$

Calculate Δx and Δp, and verify the uncertainty relation.

SOLUTION

We begin by considering the matrix element of x:

$$\langle x \rangle = \langle \psi | x | \psi \rangle = \int_{-\infty}^{\infty} x | \psi(x) |^2 dx = \sqrt{\frac{a}{\pi}} \int_{-\infty}^{\infty} x e^{-ax^2} dx = 0 \qquad (4.30.2)$$

where we used the fact that $x e^{-ax^2}$ is an odd function. Also,

$$\langle x^2 \rangle = \int_{-\infty}^{\infty} x^2 | \psi(x) |^2 dx = \sqrt{\frac{a}{\pi}} \int_{-\infty}^{\infty} x^2 e^{-ax^2} dx = 2\sqrt{\frac{a}{\pi}} \int_{0}^{\infty} x^2 e^{-ax^2} dx = 2\sqrt{\frac{a}{\pi}} \frac{\Gamma(1/2)}{2a^{3/2}} = \frac{1}{2a} \qquad (4.30.3)$$

so,

$$\Delta x = \sqrt{\langle x^2 \rangle - \langle x \rangle^2} = \sqrt{\frac{1}{2a}} \qquad (4.30.4)$$

In order to find Δp we calculate the wavefunction in the momentum representation:

$$\tilde{\psi}(p) = \frac{1}{\sqrt{2\pi\hbar}} \int_{-\infty}^{\infty} e^{-ipx/\hbar} \psi(x) dx = \frac{1}{\sqrt{2\pi\hbar}} \left(\frac{\pi}{a}\right)^{-1/4} \int_{-\infty}^{\infty} e^{-ipx/\hbar} e^{-ax^2/2} dx$$

$$= \frac{1}{\sqrt{2\pi\hbar}} \left(\frac{\pi}{a}\right)^{-1/4} \sqrt{\frac{2\pi}{a}} e^{-p^2/2a\hbar^2} = \frac{1}{\sqrt{\hbar}} \left(\frac{1}{\pi a}\right)^{1/4} e^{-p^2/2a\hbar^2} \qquad (4.30.5)$$

Since $\tilde{\psi}(p)$ is an odd function, we obtain $\langle p \rangle = 0$, and

$$\langle p^2 \rangle = \frac{1}{\hbar} \frac{1}{\sqrt{\pi a}} \int_{-\infty}^{\infty} p^2 e^{-p^2/a\hbar^2} dp = \frac{2}{\hbar\sqrt{a\pi}} \int_{0}^{\infty} p^2 e^{-p^2/a\hbar^2} dp = \frac{2}{\hbar\sqrt{\pi a}} \frac{\sqrt{\pi}/2}{2(1/a\hbar^2)^{3/2}} = \frac{a\hbar^2}{2}$$

so, we obtain

$$\Delta p = \sqrt{\langle p^2 \rangle - \langle p \rangle^2} = \sqrt{\frac{a}{2}} \hbar \qquad (4.30.6)$$

Eventually, the uncertainty relation will be $\Delta x \Delta p = \hbar/2$.

This example demonstrates the basic nature of the uncertainty relation. If we choose a wavefunction with smaller dispersion around the central position $\langle x \rangle$, we obtain a higher dispersion of the momentum around $\langle x \rangle$.

4.31. A particle is in the state $| \psi \rangle$ and its wavefunction is $\psi(\mathbf{r}) = \langle \mathbf{r} | \psi \rangle$. (a) Find the mean value of the operator $\hat{A} = | \mathbf{r} \rangle \langle \mathbf{r} |$. (b) Calculate $\langle \mathbf{r} | \hat{\mathbf{p}} | \psi \rangle$. (c) Find the mean value of the operator $\hat{k}_\mathbf{r} = [| \mathbf{r} \rangle \langle \mathbf{r} | \hat{\mathbf{p}} + \hat{\mathbf{p}} | \mathbf{r} \rangle \langle \mathbf{r} |]/2m$, where $\hat{\mathbf{p}}$ is the momentum operator and m is the mass of the particle.

SOLUTION

(*a*) By definition,

$$\langle \hat{A} \rangle = \langle \psi \mid \hat{A} \mid \psi \rangle = \langle \psi \mid \mathbf{r} \rangle \langle \mathbf{r} \mid \psi \rangle = \psi^*(\mathbf{r})\psi(\mathbf{r}) = |\psi(\mathbf{r})|^2 \tag{4.31.1}$$

(*b*) The *x*-component of $\langle \mathbf{r} \mid \hat{\mathbf{p}} \mid \psi \rangle$ equals

$$\langle \mathbf{r} \mid \hat{\mathbf{p}} \mid \psi \rangle_x = \langle \mathbf{r} \mid \hat{p}_x \mid \psi \rangle = \frac{\hbar}{i} \frac{\partial \psi(\mathbf{r})}{\partial x} \tag{4.31.2}$$

Therefore, $\langle \mathbf{r} \mid \hat{\mathbf{p}} \mid \psi \rangle_x = \left[\dfrac{\hbar}{i} \nabla \psi(\mathbf{r}) \right]_x$. Similarly for *y* and *z*, we obtain $\langle \mathbf{r} \mid \hat{\mathbf{p}} \mid \psi \rangle = \dfrac{\hbar}{i} \nabla \psi$.

(*c*) By definition,

$$\langle \psi \mid \hat{k}_\mathbf{r} \mid \psi \rangle = \frac{1}{2m} [\langle \psi \mid \mathbf{r} \rangle \langle \mathbf{r} \mid \hat{\mathbf{p}} \mid \psi \rangle + \langle \psi \mid \hat{\mathbf{p}} \mid \mathbf{r} \rangle \langle \mathbf{r} \mid \psi \rangle] = \frac{1}{2m} \left[\psi^*(\mathbf{r}) \frac{\hbar}{i} \nabla \psi(\mathbf{r}) + \frac{\hbar}{i} \nabla \psi^*(\mathbf{r}) \psi(\mathbf{r}) \right]$$

$$= \frac{1}{m} \mathrm{Re} \left[\psi^* \left(\frac{\hbar}{i} \nabla \psi \right) \right]$$

This example demonstrates the basic nature of the uncertainty relation: If we choose a wavefunction with smaller dispersion around the central position $\langle x \rangle$, we get a higher dispersion of the momentum around $\langle p \rangle$.

4.32. The *parity operator* $\hat{\Pi}$ is defined by

$$\hat{\Pi} \mid \mathbf{r} \rangle = \mid -\mathbf{r} \rangle \tag{4.32.1}$$

(*a*) Let $\mid \psi \rangle$ be an arbitrary ket with corresponding wavefunction $\psi(\mathbf{r})$. Find the wavefunction corresponding to $\hat{\Pi} \mid \psi \rangle$.

(*b*) Show that $\hat{\Pi}$ is a Hermitian operator.

(*c*) Find the operator $\hat{\Pi}^2$. What are the possible eigenvalues of $\hat{\Pi}$?

(*d*) We define the operators

$$\hat{p}_+ = \frac{1}{2}(\hat{I} + \hat{\Pi}) \qquad \hat{p}_- = \frac{1}{2}(\hat{I} - \hat{\Pi}) \tag{4.32.2}$$

For an arbitrary ket $\mid \psi \rangle$ we also define

$$\mid \psi_+ \rangle = \hat{p}_+ \mid \psi \rangle \qquad \mid \psi_- \rangle = \hat{p}_- \mid \psi \rangle \tag{4.32.3}$$

Show that $\mid \psi_+ \rangle$ and $\mid \psi_- \rangle$ are eigenvectors of $\hat{\Pi}$.

(*e*) Prove that the wavefunctions corresponding to $\mid \psi_+ \rangle$ and $\mid \psi_- \rangle$ are even and odd functions, respectively.

SOLUTION

(*a*) We begin by considering the ket $\mid \psi \rangle = \displaystyle\int \psi(\mathbf{r}) \mid \mathbf{r} \rangle d^3 r$, hence

$$\hat{\Pi} \mid \psi \rangle = \int \psi(\mathbf{r}) [\hat{\Pi} \mid \mathbf{r} \rangle] d^3 r = \int \psi(\mathbf{r}) \mid -\mathbf{r} \rangle d^3 r \tag{4.32.4}$$

Changing the integration variable to $\mathbf{r}' = -\mathbf{r}$, the wavefunction corresponding to $\hat{\Pi} \mid \psi \rangle$ is

$$\langle \mathbf{r} \mid \hat{\Pi} \mid \psi \rangle = \int \psi(-\mathbf{r}') \langle \mathbf{r} \mid \mathbf{r}' \rangle d^3 r' = \int \delta(\mathbf{r} - \mathbf{r}') \psi(-\mathbf{r}') d^3 r' = \psi(-\mathbf{r}) \tag{4.32.5}$$

(*b*) Using part (*a*) we have $\langle \mathbf{r} \mid \hat{\Pi} \mid \psi \rangle = \langle -\mathbf{r} \mid \psi \rangle$. Therefore, $\langle \mathbf{r} \mid \hat{\Pi} = \langle -\mathbf{r} \mid$. On the other hand, taking the Hermitian conjugate of Eq. (4.32.1) yields $\langle \mathbf{r} \mid \hat{\Pi}^\dagger = \langle -\mathbf{r} \mid$. Since this is valid for any $\langle \mathbf{r} \mid$ it follows that $\hat{\Pi} = \hat{\Pi}^\dagger$.

(c) We have

$$\hat{\Pi}^2 \,|\, \mathbf{r}\rangle = \hat{\Pi}\hat{\Pi}\,|\, \mathbf{r}\rangle = \hat{\Pi}\,|-\mathbf{r}\rangle = |\, \mathbf{r}\rangle \tag{4.32.6}$$

Since this is valid for any $|\, \mathbf{r}\rangle$, we have $\hat{\Pi}^2 = \hat{I}$. Suppose that $|\phi\rangle$ is an eigenvector of $\hat{\Pi}$ with an eigenvalue p, $\hat{\Pi}\,|\phi\rangle = p\,|\phi\rangle$. So, on the one hand we have

$$\hat{\Pi}^2 \,|\phi\rangle = \hat{I}\,|\phi\rangle = |\phi\rangle \tag{4.32.7}$$

and, on the other hand, we have,

$$\Pi^2\,|\phi\rangle = \hat{\Pi}(p\,|\phi\rangle) = p\hat{\Pi}\,|\phi\rangle = p^2\,|\phi\rangle \tag{4.32.8}$$

Therefore, $p^2 = 1$. But since $\hat{\Pi}$ is a Hermitian operator, its eigenvalues must be real. Therefore, the possible eigenvalues are $+1$ and -1.

(d) We have

$$\hat{\Pi}\,|\psi_+\rangle = \hat{\Pi}p_+\,|\psi\rangle = \frac{1}{2}\hat{\Pi}(\hat{I}+\hat{\Pi})\,|\psi\rangle = \frac{1}{2}(\hat{\Pi}+\hat{\Pi}^2)\,|\psi\rangle \tag{4.32.9}$$

Using part (c) we arrive at

$$\hat{\Pi}\,|\psi_+\rangle = \frac{1}{2}(\hat{\Pi}+\hat{I})\,|\psi\rangle = \hat{p}_+\,|\psi\rangle = |\psi_+\rangle \tag{4.32.10}$$

Hence, $|\psi_+\rangle$ is an eigenvector of $\hat{\Pi}$ with an eivenvalue $+1$. Similarly, we can conclude that $|\psi_-\rangle$ is an eigenvector of $\hat{\Pi}$ with eigenvalue -1.

(e) Using part (a) we have $\langle \mathbf{r}\,|\,\hat{\Pi}\,|\psi_+\rangle = \psi_+(-\mathbf{r})$. On the other hand, relying on part (d),

$$\langle \mathbf{r}\,|\,\hat{\Pi}\,|\psi_+\rangle = \langle \mathbf{r}\,|\psi_+\rangle = \psi_+(+\mathbf{r}) \tag{4.32.11}$$

Therefore, $\psi_+(-\mathbf{r}) = \psi_+(+\mathbf{r})$, and ψ_+ is an even function. Similarly, $\langle \mathbf{r}\,|\,\hat{\Pi}\,|\psi_-\rangle = \psi_-(-\mathbf{r})$ and

$$\langle \mathbf{r}\,|\,\hat{\Pi}\,|\psi_-\rangle = -\langle \mathbf{r}\,|\psi_-\rangle = -\psi_-(\mathbf{r}) \tag{4.32.12}$$

Therefore $\psi_-(\mathbf{r}) = -\psi_-(\mathbf{r})$, and ψ_- is an odd function. Note that we can write any $|\psi\rangle$ as $|\psi\rangle = |\psi_+\rangle + |\psi_-\rangle$. Thus we have obtained a method for separating a wavefunction into even and odd parts.

4.33. Consider a one-dimensional physical system described by the classical Hamiltonian

$$H = \frac{p^2}{2m} + V(x) \tag{4.33.1}$$

(a) Show that $[\hat{H}, \hat{x}] = -i\hbar\hat{p}/m$. (b) For a stationary state find $\langle p\rangle$ (consider only square integrable states).

SOLUTION

(a) Using Eq. (4.11.3) and considering the commutation relation,

$$[\hat{H}, \hat{x}] = \frac{1}{2m}[\hat{p}^2, \hat{x}] + [\hat{V}(x), \hat{x}] = \frac{1}{2m}2\hat{p}[\hat{p}, \hat{x}] + 0 = -\frac{i\hbar}{m}\hat{p} \tag{4.33.2}$$

(b) In a stationary state we have $\hat{H}\,|\psi\rangle = \lambda\,|\psi\rangle$, where λ is the eigenvalue. Since $\hat{H}$ is a Hermitian operator, we also have $\langle \psi|\,\hat{H} = \lambda\,|\psi\rangle$. Using part (a) we finally obtain

$$\langle \hat{p}\rangle = \langle \psi\,|\,\hat{p}\,|\psi\rangle = \frac{im}{\hbar}\langle \psi\,|\,\hat{H}\hat{x} - \hat{x}\hat{H}\,|\psi\rangle = \frac{im}{\hbar}[\lambda\langle \psi\,|\,\hat{x}\,|\psi\rangle - \lambda\langle \psi\,|\,\hat{x}\,|\psi\rangle] = 0 \tag{4.33.3}$$

4.34. Consider a free particle in one dimension whose wavefunction at $t = 0$ is given by

$$\psi(x, 0) = N\int_{-\infty}^{\infty} e^{-|k|/k_0}e^{ikx}dk \tag{4.34.1}$$

where N is a normalization constant and k_0 is a real number. In a measurement of the momentum at time t, find the probability $P(p, t)$ of getting a result between $-p_1$ and p_1.

SOLUTION

First note that the relation between the wavefunction of the particle $\psi(x, t)$ and its wavefunction in the momentum representation $\tilde{\psi}(p, t)$ is

$$\psi(x, t) = \frac{1}{\sqrt{2\pi\hbar}} \int_{-\infty}^{\infty} e^{-ipx/\hbar} \, \tilde{\psi}(p, t) \, dp \tag{4.34.2}$$

(This is a Fourier transform.) Substituting $k = p/\hbar$ in $\psi(x, 0)$ we obtain

$$\psi(x, 0) = \frac{N}{\hbar} \int_{-\infty}^{\infty} e^{-|p|/\hbar k_0} e^{ipx/\hbar} \, dp \tag{4.34.3}$$

Therefore,

$$\tilde{\psi}(p, 0) = \frac{N}{\hbar} \sqrt{2\pi\hbar} \, e^{-|p|/\hbar k_0} \tag{4.34.4}$$

From the normalization condition of $\tilde{\psi}(p, 0)$ we can find the constant N:

$$\int_{-\infty}^{\infty} |\tilde{\psi}(p, 0)|^2 dp = \frac{2\pi N^2}{\hbar} \int_{-\infty}^{\infty} e^{-2|p|/\hbar k_0} dp = \frac{2\pi N^2}{\hbar} \left[2\left(-\frac{\hbar k_0}{2}\right) e^{-2p/\hbar k_0} \Big|_0^{\infty} \right] = 2\pi k_0 N^2 = 1 \tag{4.34.5}$$

Therefore, $N = \dfrac{1}{\sqrt{2\pi k_0}}$, and

$$\tilde{\psi}(p, 0) = \frac{1}{\sqrt{\hbar k_0}} e^{-2|p|/\hbar k_0} \tag{4.34.6}$$

The Hamiltonian of a free particle is $H = p^2/2m$. The basis $|p\rangle$ of the state space consists of eigenvectors of $\hat{H}$:

$$\hat{H} |p\rangle = \frac{\hat{p}^2}{2m} |p\rangle = E_p |p\rangle \tag{4.34.7}$$

Note that for every p, $\tilde{\psi}(p, t)$ is actually the coefficient of $|p\rangle$ in the expansion of the state of the particle $|\psi(t)\rangle$ in the basis $|p\rangle$:

$$|\psi(t)\rangle = \int_{-\infty}^{\infty} \tilde{\psi}(p, t) |p\rangle \, dp \tag{4.34.8}$$

where $\tilde{\psi}(p, t) = \langle p | \psi \rangle$. The time evolution of $|\psi(t)\rangle$ is described by

$$|\psi(t)\rangle = \int_{-\infty}^{\infty} \tilde{\psi}(p, 0) \, e^{-iE_p t/\hbar} |p\rangle \, dp = \frac{1}{\sqrt{\hbar k_0}} \int_{-\infty}^{\infty} e^{-|p|/\hbar k_0} e^{-ip^2 t/2m\hbar} |p\rangle \, dp \tag{4.34.9}$$

Or equivalently,

$$\tilde{\psi}(p, t) = \frac{1}{\sqrt{\hbar k_0}} e^{-|p|/\hbar k_0} e^{-ip^2 t/2m\hbar} \tag{4.34.10}$$

So finally we obtain

$$P(p_1, t) = \int_{-p_1}^{p_1} |\tilde{\psi}(p, t)|^2 dp = \frac{1}{\hbar k_0} \int_{-p_1}^{p_1} \exp\left[2\left(\frac{p^2}{2m\hbar} t - \frac{|p|}{\hbar k_0}\right)\right] dp = \frac{2}{\hbar k_0} \int_0^{p_1} \exp\left(\frac{tp^2}{m\hbar} - \frac{2|p|}{\hbar k_0}\right) dp$$

4.35. Consider a classical quantity f expressed in terms of the dynamic variables $\mathbf{r}$ and $\mathbf{p}$, so that $f(\mathbf{r}, \mathbf{p})$. Suppose that in $f(\mathbf{r}, \mathbf{p})$ there appears a term of the form $\mathbf{r} \cdot \mathbf{p}$. Using the quantization rules, find the quantum mechanical operator corresponding to the term $\mathbf{r} \cdot \mathbf{p}$.

SOLUTION

Let the operator $\hat{\mathbf{R}}$ correspond to the classical coordinate $\mathbf{r}$, and the operator $\hat{\mathbf{P}}$ correspond to the classical momentum $\mathbf{p}$. Note that $\hat{\mathbf{R}} \cdot \hat{\mathbf{P}}$ is not a Hermitian operator:

$$(\hat{\mathbf{R}} \cdot \hat{\mathbf{P}})^{\dagger} = (\hat{X}\hat{P}_x + \hat{Y}\hat{P}_y + \hat{Z}\hat{P}_z)^{\dagger} = \hat{P}_x\hat{X} + \hat{P}_y\hat{Y} + \hat{P}_z\hat{Z} = \hat{\mathbf{P}} \cdot \hat{\mathbf{R}} \qquad (4.35.1)$$

In order to obtain the Hermitian operator corresponding to $\mathbf{r} \cdot \mathbf{p}$, we must perform a symmetrization of the operator $\hat{\mathbf{R}} \cdot \hat{\mathbf{P}}$:

$$\frac{1}{2}[\hat{\mathbf{R}} \cdot \hat{\mathbf{P}} + (\hat{\mathbf{R}} \cdot \hat{\mathbf{P}})^{\dagger}] = \frac{1}{2}(\hat{\mathbf{R}} \cdot \hat{\mathbf{P}} + \hat{\mathbf{P}} \cdot \hat{\mathbf{R}}) \qquad (4.35.2)$$

As an exercise, prove that this operator is indeed a Hermitian operator.

4.36. Consider a physical system with a three-dimensional state space. An orthonormal basis of the state space is chosen; in this basis the Hamiltonian is represented by the matrix

$$\hat{H} = \begin{pmatrix} 2 & 1 & 0 \\ 1 & 2 & 0 \\ 0 & 0 & 3 \end{pmatrix} \qquad (4.36.1)$$

(a) What are the possible results when the energy of the system is measured? (b) A particle is in the state $|\psi\rangle$, represented in this basis as $\dfrac{1}{\sqrt{3}}\begin{pmatrix} i \\ -i \\ i \end{pmatrix}$. Find $\langle \hat{H} \rangle$, $\langle \hat{H}^2 \rangle$, and ΔH.

SOLUTION

(a) The possible energies are the eigenvalues of $\hat{H}$ that are found by solving the equation $\det(\hat{H} - \lambda\hat{I}) = 0$, or

$$\begin{vmatrix} 2-\lambda & 1 & 0 \\ 1 & 2-\lambda & 0 \\ 0 & 0 & 3-\lambda \end{vmatrix} = [(2-\lambda)^2 - 1](3-\lambda) = (\lambda^2 - 4\lambda + 3)(3-\lambda)$$

$$= (3-\lambda)^2(1-\lambda) \qquad (4.36.2)$$

Therefore, $E_1 = 1$ and $E_2 = 3$. Note that E_1 is a nondegenerate eigenvalue where E_2 is degenerate, so a two-dimensional subspace corresponds to it.

(b) **Method 1:** We write

$$\langle \psi | \hat{H} | \psi \rangle = \frac{1}{\sqrt{3}}\frac{1}{\sqrt{3}}(-i \quad i \quad -i)\begin{pmatrix} 2 & 1 & 0 \\ 1 & 2 & 0 \\ 0 & 0 & 3 \end{pmatrix}\begin{pmatrix} i \\ -i \\ i \end{pmatrix} = \frac{1}{3}(-i \quad i \quad -i)\begin{pmatrix} i \\ -i \\ 3i \end{pmatrix} = \frac{1}{3}(1+1+3) = \frac{5}{3} \qquad (4.36.3)$$

Also,

$$\langle \hat{H}^2 \rangle = \langle \psi | \hat{H}^2 | \psi \rangle = \frac{1}{3}(-i \quad i \quad -i)\begin{pmatrix} 2 & 1 & 0 \\ 1 & 2 & 0 \\ 0 & 0 & 3 \end{pmatrix}^2\begin{pmatrix} i \\ -i \\ i \end{pmatrix}$$

$$= \frac{1}{3}(-i \quad i \quad -i)\begin{pmatrix} 2 & 1 & 0 \\ 1 & 2 & 0 \\ 0 & 0 & 3 \end{pmatrix}\begin{pmatrix} i \\ -i \\ 3i \end{pmatrix} = \frac{1}{3}(-i \quad i \quad -i)\begin{pmatrix} i \\ -i \\ 9i \end{pmatrix} = \frac{1}{3}(1+1+9) = \frac{11}{3} \qquad (4.36.4)$$

and

$$\Delta H = \sqrt{\langle \hat{H}^2 \rangle - \langle \hat{H} \rangle^2} = \sqrt{\frac{11}{3} - \frac{25}{9}} = \frac{2\sqrt{2}}{3} \qquad (4.36.5)$$

Method 2: We define

$$|u_1\rangle = \frac{1}{\sqrt{2}}\begin{pmatrix} i \\ -i \\ 0 \end{pmatrix} \qquad |u_2\rangle = \begin{pmatrix} 0 \\ 0 \\ i \end{pmatrix} \tag{4.36.6}$$

Thus, $|\psi\rangle = \sqrt{\frac{2}{3}}|u_1\rangle + \sqrt{\frac{1}{3}}|u_2\rangle$. Note that $|u_1\rangle$ and $|u_2\rangle$ are eigenvectors of H:

$$\hat{H}|u_1\rangle = \frac{1}{\sqrt{2}}\begin{pmatrix} 2 & 1 & 0 \\ 1 & 2 & 0 \\ 0 & 0 & 3 \end{pmatrix}\begin{pmatrix} i \\ -i \\ 0 \end{pmatrix} = \frac{1}{\sqrt{2}}\begin{pmatrix} i \\ -i \\ 0 \end{pmatrix} = |u_1\rangle = E_1|u_1\rangle \tag{4.36.7}$$

Similarly, $\hat{H}|u_2\rangle = 3|u_2\rangle = E_2|u_2\rangle$. The eigenvectors $|u_1\rangle$ and $|u_2\rangle$ are orthogonal since they correspond to different eigenvalues of H. So we obtain

$$\langle\hat{H}\rangle = \left(\sqrt{\frac{2}{3}}\langle u_1| + \sqrt{\frac{1}{3}}\langle u_2|\right)\hat{H}\left(\sqrt{\frac{2}{3}}|u_1\rangle + \sqrt{\frac{1}{3}}|u_2\rangle\right) = \frac{2}{3}E_1\langle u_1|u_1\rangle + \frac{2}{3}E_2\langle u_2|u_2\rangle = \frac{2}{3} + 1 = \frac{5}{3} \tag{4.36.8}$$

Also,

$$\langle\hat{H}^2\rangle = \langle\psi|H^2|\psi\rangle = \left(\sqrt{\frac{2}{3}}\langle u_1| + \sqrt{\frac{1}{3}}\langle u_2|\right)\hat{H}\left(\sqrt{\frac{2}{3}}E_1|u_1\rangle + \sqrt{\frac{1}{3}}E_2|u_2\rangle\right) = \frac{2}{3}E_1^2 + \frac{1}{3}E_2^2 = \frac{11}{3} \tag{4.36.9}$$

and $\Delta H = \sqrt{\langle\hat{H}^2\rangle - \langle\hat{H}\rangle^2} = 2\sqrt{2}/3$.

4.37. Refer to Problem 4.36. Suppose that the energy of the system was measured and a value of $E = 1$ was found. Subsequently we perform a measurement of a variable A described in the same basis by

$$\hat{A} = \begin{pmatrix} 5 & 0 & 0 \\ 0 & 2 & i \\ 0 & -i & 2 \end{pmatrix} \tag{4.37.1}$$

(*a*) Find the possible results of $\hat{A}$. (*b*) What are the probabilities of obtaining each of the results found in part (*a*)?

SOLUTION

(*a*) The possible results are the eigenvalues of $\hat{A}$ obtained by solving the secular equation

$$\det(\hat{A} - \lambda\hat{I}) = (5 - \lambda)[(2 - \lambda)^2 - 1] = (5 - \lambda)(3 - \lambda)(1 - \lambda) \tag{4.37.2}$$

Therefore, $a_1 = 1$, $a_2 = 3$, and $a_3 = 5$.

(*b*) The energy $E = 1$ is a nondegenerate eigenvalue of the Hamiltonian, so after the energy measurement the state of the system is well defined by the eigenvector

$$\psi = \frac{1}{\sqrt{2}}\begin{pmatrix} 1 \\ -1 \\ 0 \end{pmatrix} \tag{4.37.3}$$

Now we can find the eigenvectors of A corresponding to each of the eigenvalues obtained in part (*a*). This can be accomplished directly by solving the equation

$$\begin{pmatrix} 5 & 0 & 0 \\ 0 & 2 & i \\ 0 & -i & 2 \end{pmatrix}\begin{pmatrix} \alpha \\ \beta \\ \gamma \end{pmatrix} = a_j\begin{pmatrix} \alpha \\ \beta \\ \gamma \end{pmatrix} \tag{4.37.4}$$

for each j. For example, for a_1 we have

$$\begin{cases} 5\alpha = \alpha \\ 2\beta + i\gamma = \beta \\ -i\beta + 2\gamma = \gamma \end{cases} \tag{4.37.5}$$

Therefore, $\alpha = 0$. Choosing arbitrarily $\beta = 1$ we obtain $\gamma = i$, so after normalization we get

$$\xi_1 = \frac{1}{\sqrt{2}}\begin{pmatrix}0\\1\\i\end{pmatrix} \qquad (4.37.6)$$

In the same manner, we obtain the eigenvectors of A corresponding to a_2 and a_3:

$$\xi_2 = \frac{1}{\sqrt{2}}\begin{pmatrix}0\\i\\1\end{pmatrix} \qquad \xi_3 = \frac{1}{\sqrt{2}}\begin{pmatrix}1\\0\\0\end{pmatrix} \qquad (4.37.7)$$

Finally, the probability $P(a_j)$ of a measurement yielding a_j is $P(a_j) = |\langle \xi_1 | \psi \rangle|^2$. Thus,

$$P(a_1) = \left| \frac{1}{\sqrt{2}}(0 \quad 1 \quad -i)\frac{1}{\sqrt{2}}\begin{pmatrix}1\\-1\\0\end{pmatrix} \right|^2 = \frac{1}{4}|-1|^2 = \frac{1}{4} \qquad (4.37.8)$$

Similarly, we obtain

$$P(a_2) = \frac{1}{4}\left| (0 \quad -i \quad 1)\begin{pmatrix}1\\-1\\0\end{pmatrix} \right|^2 = \frac{1}{4} \qquad (4.37.9)$$

and

$$P(a_3) = \frac{1}{2}\left| (1 \quad 0 \quad 0)\begin{pmatrix}1\\-1\\0\end{pmatrix} \right|^2 = \frac{1}{2} \qquad (4.37.10)$$

4.38. A particle of mass m is confined within an infinite one-dimensional well, between $x = 0$ and $x = L$. The stationary states $|\phi_n\rangle$ of the particle correspond to the energies

$$E_n = \frac{\pi^2\hbar^2 n^2}{2mL^2} \qquad n = 1, 2, \ldots \qquad (4.38.1)$$

and to the wavefunctions $\phi_n(x) = \sqrt{\frac{2}{L}}\sin\left(\frac{\pi n x}{L}\right)$. Consider the case in which at time $t = 0$ the particle is in the state $|\psi(0)\rangle = [|\phi_1\rangle + |\phi_2\rangle]/\sqrt{2}$. (a) Find the time-dependent $|\psi(t)\rangle$. (b) Calculate the wavefunction $\psi(x, t)$.

SOLUTION
(a) Since $E_1 = \pi^2\hbar^2/2mL^2$ and $E_2 = 2\pi^2\hbar^2/mL^2$, we have,

$$|\psi(t)\rangle = \frac{1}{\sqrt{2}}\left[e^{-iE_1 t/\hbar}|\phi_1\rangle + e^{-iE_2 t/\hbar}|\phi_2\rangle \right] = \frac{1}{\sqrt{2}}\left[e^{-i\pi^2\hbar t/2mL^2}|\phi_1\rangle + e^{-2i\pi^2\hbar t/mL^2}|\phi_2\rangle \right] \qquad (4.38.2)$$

(b) The wavefunction $\psi(x, t)$ is obtained by $\langle x | \psi(t)\rangle$; that is

$$\psi(x, t) = \langle x | \psi(t)\rangle = \frac{1}{\sqrt{2}}\left[\langle x | \phi_1\rangle \exp\left(-\frac{i\pi^2\hbar}{2mL^2}t\right) + \langle x | \phi_2\rangle \exp\left(-\frac{i\pi^2\hbar}{mL^2}t\right) \right]$$

$$= \frac{1}{\sqrt{L}}\exp\left(-\frac{i\pi^2\hbar t}{2mL^2}\right)\sin\left(\frac{\pi x}{L}\right) + \frac{1}{\sqrt{L}}\exp\left(-\frac{2i\pi^2\hbar t}{mL^2}\right)\sin\left(\frac{2\pi x}{L}\right) \qquad (4.38.3)$$

4.39. Show that the norm of the state vector evolving from the Schrödinger equation remains constant.

SOLUTION

Consider the Schrödinger equation:

$$\frac{d}{dt}|\psi(t)\rangle = \frac{1}{i\hbar}\hat{H}(t)|\psi(t)\rangle \tag{4.39.1}$$

Taking the Hermitian conjugates of both sides of Eq. (4.39.1) we obtain

$$\frac{d}{dt}\langle\psi(t)| = -\frac{1}{i\hbar}\langle\psi(t)|\hat{H}^{\dagger}(t) = -\frac{1}{i\hbar}\langle\psi(t)|\hat{H}(t) \tag{4.39.2}$$

since $H(t)$ is an observable and it must therefore be a Hermitian operator. So we get

$$\frac{d}{dt}\langle\psi(t)|\psi(t)\rangle = \frac{d\langle\psi(t)\rangle}{dt}|\psi(t)\rangle + \langle\psi(t)|\frac{d|\psi(t)\rangle}{dt}$$

$$= \left[-\frac{1}{i\hbar}\langle\psi(t)|\hat{H}(t)\right]|\psi(t)\rangle + \langle\psi(t)|\left[\frac{1}{i\hbar}\hat{H}(t)|\psi(t)\rangle\right] = 0 \tag{4.39.3}$$

4.40. The Hamiltonian of a particle in a potential $V(\mathbf{r})$ is

$$\hat{H} = \frac{1}{2m}\hat{\mathbf{P}}^2 + \hat{V}(\hat{\mathbf{R}}) \tag{4.40.1}$$

(*a*) Write the Schrödinger equation in the *r*-representation. (*b*) Repeat part (*a*) in the *p*-representation.

SOLUTION

(*a*) Consider the Schrödinger equation:

$$i\hbar\frac{d}{dt}|\psi(t)\rangle = \hat{H}|\psi(t)\rangle \tag{4.40.2}$$

Projecting this equation into the *r*-basis, we obtain

$$i\hbar\frac{\partial}{\partial t}\langle\mathbf{r}|\psi(t)\rangle = \frac{1}{2m}\langle\mathbf{r}|\hat{\mathbf{P}}^2|\psi(t)\rangle + \langle\mathbf{r}|\hat{V}(\hat{\mathbf{R}})|\psi(t)\rangle \tag{4.40.3}$$

The wavefunction corresponding to $|\psi(t)\rangle$ is $\psi(\mathbf{r},t) = \langle\mathbf{r}|\psi(t)\rangle$. We also have

$$\langle\mathbf{r}|\hat{\mathbf{P}}^2|\psi(t)\rangle = \langle\mathbf{r}|(\hat{P}_x^2 + \hat{P}_y^2 + \hat{P}_z^2)|\psi(t)\rangle$$

$$= -\hbar^2\left(\frac{\partial^2}{\partial x^2} + \frac{\partial}{\partial y^2} + \frac{\partial^2}{\partial z^2}\right)\psi(x,y,z,t) = -\hbar^2\nabla^2\psi(\mathbf{r},t) \tag{4.40.4}$$

and we have $\langle\mathbf{r}|\hat{V}(\hat{\mathbf{R}})|\psi(t)\rangle = \hat{V}(\mathbf{r})\psi(\mathbf{r},t)$. Therefore,

$$i\hbar\frac{\partial}{\partial t}\psi(\mathbf{r},t) = \left[-\frac{\hbar^2}{2m}\nabla^2 + V(\mathbf{r})\right]\psi(\mathbf{r},t) \tag{4.40.5}$$

(*b*) We begin by projecting the Schrödinger equation onto the *p*-basis:

$$i\hbar\frac{\partial}{\partial t}\langle\mathbf{p}|\psi(t)\rangle = \frac{1}{2m}\langle\mathbf{p}|\hat{\mathbf{P}}^2|\psi(t)\rangle + \langle\mathbf{p}|\hat{V}(\hat{\mathbf{R}})|\psi(t)\rangle \tag{4.40.6}$$

The wavefunction in the momentum representation is defined by $\tilde{\psi}(\mathbf{p},t) = \langle\mathbf{p}|\psi(t)\rangle$. So we have

$$\langle\mathbf{p}|\hat{\mathbf{P}}^2|\psi(t)\rangle = p^2\tilde{\psi}(\mathbf{p},t) \tag{4.40.7}$$

In order to calculate the term $\langle \mathbf{p} | \hat{V}(\hat{\mathbf{R}}) | \psi(t) \rangle$ in Eq. (4.40.6), we insert the closure relation in the p-basis between $\hat{V}(\hat{\mathbf{R}})$ and $|\psi(t)\rangle$, and obtain

$$\langle \mathbf{p} | \hat{V}(\hat{\mathbf{R}}) | \psi(t) \rangle = \int \langle \mathbf{p} | \hat{V}(\hat{\mathbf{R}}) | \mathbf{p}' \rangle \langle \mathbf{p}' | \psi(t) \rangle d^3 p' \tag{4.40.8}$$

Using the closure relation in the r-basis we have

$$\langle \mathbf{p} | \hat{V}(\hat{\mathbf{R}}) | \mathbf{p}' \rangle = \int \langle \mathbf{p} | \mathbf{r} \rangle \langle \mathbf{r} | \hat{V}(\hat{\mathbf{R}}) | \mathbf{p}' \rangle d^3 r = \frac{1}{(2\pi\hbar)^{3/2}} \int e^{-i\mathbf{r}\cdot\mathbf{p}/\hbar} \langle \mathbf{r} | \hat{V}(\hat{\mathbf{R}}) | \mathbf{p}' \rangle d^3 r \tag{4.40.9}$$

We also have

$$\langle \mathbf{r} | \hat{V}(\hat{\mathbf{R}}) | \mathbf{p}' \rangle = V(\mathbf{r}) \langle \mathbf{r} | \mathbf{p}' \rangle = V(\mathbf{r}) e^{i\mathbf{r}\cdot\mathbf{p}'/\hbar} \tag{4.40.10}$$

So, using Eqs. (4.40.8) to (4.40.10) we see that

$$\langle \mathbf{p} | \hat{V}(\hat{\mathbf{R}}) | \psi(t) \rangle = \frac{1}{(2\pi\hbar)^{3/2}} \int \tilde{V}(\mathbf{p} - \mathbf{p}') \tilde{\psi}(\mathbf{p}', t^3) d^3 p' \tag{4.40.11}$$

where

$$\tilde{V}(\mathbf{p} - \mathbf{p}') = \frac{1}{(2\pi\hbar)^{3/2}} \int V(\mathbf{r}) e^{-i\mathbf{r}\cdot(\mathbf{p}-\mathbf{p}')/\hbar} d^3 r \tag{4.40.12}$$

Note that $\tilde{V}(\mathbf{p})$ is the Fourier transform of $V(\mathbf{r})$. Finally, we have

$$i\hbar \frac{\partial \tilde{\psi}(\mathbf{p}, t)}{\partial t} = \frac{p^2}{2m} \tilde{\psi}(\mathbf{p}, t) + \frac{1}{(2\pi\hbar)^{3/2}} \int \tilde{V}(\mathbf{p} - \mathbf{p}') \tilde{\psi}(\mathbf{p}', t) d^3 p' \tag{4.40.13}$$

4.41. Show that the operator $\exp(-il\hat{p}_x/\hbar)$ describes a displacement of a distance l along the x-direction.

SOLUTION

Consider the problem in the x-representation. We search for an operator $\hat{A}$ acting on a wavefunction $\psi(x)$, with

$$\hat{A}\psi(x) = \psi(x - l) \tag{4.41.1}$$

Using the Taylor expansion, we can write

$$\psi(x - l) = \psi(x) - l\psi'(x) + \frac{l^2}{2!}\psi''(x) + \cdots + \frac{(-l)^n}{n!}\psi^{(n)}(x) + \cdots \tag{4.41.2}$$

In the x-representation, the momentum operator acts as $\hat{p}_x \psi(x) = -i\hbar\partial\psi(x)/\partial x$. Therefore,

$$\psi(x - l) = \psi(x) - \frac{il}{\hbar}\hat{p}_x\psi(x) + \frac{1}{2!}\left(\frac{il}{\hbar}\right)^2 \hat{p}_x^2\psi(x) + \cdots + \frac{1}{n!}\left(\frac{-il}{\hbar}\right)^n \hat{p}_x^n\psi(x) + \cdots$$

$$= \exp\left(-\frac{il\hat{p}_x}{\hbar}\right)\psi(x) \tag{4.41.3}$$

4.42. Assume the validity of all the postulates given in Sec. 4.2 except postulate II; i.e., we introduce a system whose Hamiltonian is not Hermitian. Consider a system whose state space is two-dimensional. Suppose $|\phi_1\rangle$ and $|\phi\rangle_2$ form an orthonormal basis of the state space and are eigenvectors of the Hamiltonian with eigenvalues $E_1 = 5\hbar$ and $E_2 = (4 - i)\hbar$, respectively. (a) Suppose that at time $t = 0$ the system is in the state $|\phi_1\rangle$. What is the probability of finding the system at time t in the state $|\phi_1\rangle$? (b) Repeat part (a) for $|\phi_2\rangle$. (c) Interpret the results of parts (a) and (b).

SOLUTION

(a) Using the postulates of quantum mechanics, the state vector at time t is

$$|\psi(t)\rangle = e^{-iE_1 t/\hbar} |\phi_1\rangle = e^{-5it} |\phi_1\rangle \tag{4.42.1}$$

The probability of finding the system in the state $|\phi_1\rangle$ at time t is, then, $P_1(t) = |e^{-5it}|^2 = 1$.

(b) In this case, we have

$$|\psi(t)\rangle = e^{-iE_2 t/\hbar}|\phi_2\rangle = e^{-i(4-2i)t}|\phi_2\rangle \tag{4.42.2}$$

The probability of finding the system in $|\phi_2\rangle$ is $P_2(t) = |e^{-i(4-2i)t}|^2 = e^{-2it}$.

(c) By inspection, we see that the state $|\phi_2\rangle$ is unstable. The probability of finding the system in this state decreases exponentially. This is not the case for the state $|\phi_1\rangle$, which is stable and remains in the initial state permanently. This means that the Hamiltonian is not a Hermitian, and therefore cannot represent rigorously an independent physical system. Nevertheless, the system could have been a part of a larger system, and then, phenomenologically, the notion of complex energies proves to be useful for taking into account the instability of states.

4.43. Consider a particle in a stationary potential $V(r)$. Show that

$$\text{(a)} \quad \frac{d\langle \hat{\mathbf{R}}\rangle}{dt} = \frac{\langle \hat{\mathbf{P}}\rangle}{m} \qquad \text{(b)} \quad \frac{d\langle \hat{\mathbf{P}}\rangle}{dt} = -\langle \nabla \hat{V}(\hat{\mathbf{R}})\rangle \tag{4.43.1}$$

(a) and (b) are known as the *Ehrenfest equations* and are analogous to the classical *Hamilton-Jacobi equations*.

SOLUTION

We begin by considering the Hamiltonian of the system:

$$\hat{H} = \frac{\hat{\mathbf{P}}^2}{2m} + \hat{V}(\hat{\mathbf{R}}) \tag{4.43.2}$$

Since the observables $\mathbf{p}$ and $V(\hat{\mathbf{R}})$ do not depend explicitly on time, we have, according to Eq. (4.55),

$$\frac{d\langle \hat{\mathbf{R}}\rangle}{dt} = \frac{1}{i\hbar}\langle [\hat{\mathbf{R}}, \hat{H}]\rangle = \frac{1}{i\hbar}\left\langle \left[\hat{\mathbf{R}}, \frac{\hat{\mathbf{P}}^2}{2m}\right]\right\rangle \tag{4.43.3}$$

where we used the fact that $\hat{\mathbf{R}}$ and $V(\hat{\mathbf{R}})$ commute. Using the canonical commutation relations we can obtain

$$\left[\hat{\mathbf{R}}, \frac{\hat{\mathbf{P}}^2}{2m}\right] = \frac{i\hbar}{m}\langle \hat{\mathbf{P}}\rangle \tag{4.43.4}$$

Hence, $d\langle \hat{\mathbf{R}}\rangle/dt = \langle \hat{\mathbf{P}}\rangle/m$. Also, using Eq. (4.55) for $\hat{\mathbf{P}}$ and Problem 4.12,

$$\frac{d\langle \hat{\mathbf{P}}\rangle}{dt} = \frac{1}{i\hbar}\langle [\hat{\mathbf{P}}, \hat{H}]\rangle = \frac{1}{i\hbar}\langle [\hat{\mathbf{P}}, \hat{V}(\hat{\mathbf{R}})]\rangle = \frac{1}{i\hbar}\langle [-i\hbar \nabla \hat{V}(\hat{\mathbf{R}})]\rangle = -\langle \nabla \hat{V}(\hat{\mathbf{R}})\rangle \tag{4.43.5}$$

Compare with Problem 3.5.

4.44. Assume that in the Schrödinger picture all the operators are time-independent. (a) Work in the Heisenberg picture and derive an equation expressing the time evolution of an operator $\hat{A}_H(t)$. (b) Show that Eq. (4.55) is also valid in the Heisenberg picture.

SOLUTION

(a) In the Schrödinger picture, combining the Schrödinger equation and Eq. (4.61), we have

$$i\hbar \frac{\partial}{\partial t}\hat{U}(t, t_0)|\psi_s(t_0)\rangle = \hat{H}_s \hat{U}(t, t_0)|\psi_s(t_0)\rangle \tag{4.44.1}$$

Since this is valid for any $|\psi_s(t_0)\rangle$, we obtain $i\hbar \partial \hat{U}(t, t_0)/\partial t = \hat{H}_s \hat{U}(t, t_0)$. $\hat{H}_s$ is a Hermitian operator, so we also have $-i\hbar \frac{\partial}{\partial t}\hat{U}^\dagger(t, t_0) = \hat{H}_s \hat{U}^\dagger(t, t_0)$. We differentiate Eq. (4.59) with respect to time and obtain

$$\frac{d\hat{A}_H(t)}{dt} = \left[\frac{\partial}{\partial t}\hat{U}^\dagger(t, t_0)\right]\hat{A}_s \hat{U}(t, t_0) + \hat{U}^\dagger(t, t_0)\hat{A}_s\left[\frac{\partial}{\partial t}\hat{U}(t, t_0)\right] \tag{4.44.2}$$

Substituting the time derivatives we arrive at

$$\frac{d\hat{A}_H(t)}{dt} = -\frac{1}{i\hbar}[\hat{U}^\dagger(t, t_0)\hat{H}_s]\hat{A}_s\hat{U}(t, t_0) + \frac{1}{i\hbar}\hat{U}^\dagger(t, t_0)\hat{A}_s\hat{H}_s\hat{U}(t, t_0) \qquad (4.44.3)$$

Since $\hat{U}(t, t_0)\hat{U}^\dagger(t, t_0)$ is equal to the identity operator, we insert this product between $\hat{A}_s$ and $\hat{H}_s$ and obtain

$$\frac{d\hat{A}_H(t)}{dt} = -\frac{1}{i\hbar}[\hat{U}^\dagger(t, t_0)\hat{H}_s\hat{U}(t, t_0)][\hat{U}^\dagger(t, t_0)\hat{A}_s\hat{U}(t, t_0)]$$

$$+ \frac{1}{i\hbar}[\hat{U}^\dagger(t, t_0)\hat{A}_s\hat{U}(t, t_0)][\hat{U}^\dagger(t, t_0)\hat{H}_s\hat{U}(t, t_0)]$$

Using Eq. (4.59) we finally obtain $i\hbar \dfrac{d\hat{A}_H(t)}{dt} = [\hat{A}_H(t), \hat{H}_H(t)]$.

(*b*) The mean value of an operator in the Heisenberg picture is

$$\langle \hat{A}(t)\rangle = \langle \psi_H | \hat{A}_H(t) | \psi_H \rangle \qquad (4.44.4)$$

On the right-hand side of Eq. (4.44.4), only $\hat{A}_H(t)$ depends on time. Therefore,

$$\frac{d\langle \hat{A}\rangle}{dt} = \langle \psi_H \left| \left[\frac{d\hat{A}_H(t)}{dt} \right] \right| \psi_H \rangle \qquad (4.44.5)$$

We assume that A is time-independent in the Schrödinger equation, so using the result of part (*a*) we obtain

$$\frac{d\langle \hat{A}_H(t)\rangle}{dt} = \frac{1}{i\hbar}\langle [\hat{A}_H, \hat{H}_H(t)]\rangle \qquad (4.44.6)$$

4.45. In this problem we show that for a conservative system the greater the energy's uncertainty, the faster the time evolution. Consider a Hamiltonian with a continuous spectrum, and assume that the spectrum is nondegenerate. Consider a state $|\psi(t_0)\rangle$ with an uncertainty energy ΔE and show that if Δt is the time interval at the end of which the system evolves to an appreciable extent, then

$$\Delta t \, \Delta E \gtrsim \hbar \qquad (4.45.1)$$

SOLUTION

A state $|\psi(t_0)\rangle$ can be written in the form

$$|\psi(t_0)\rangle = \int \alpha(E) | \phi_E \rangle \, dE \qquad (4.45.2)$$

where $|\phi_E\rangle$ is an eigenstate of H with an eigenvalue E. We define a state for which $|\alpha(E)|^2$ has the form depicted in Fig. 4.2.

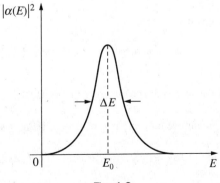

Fig. 4.2

In this case, ΔE represents the uncertainty of the energy of the system. Using Eq. (4.53), the state $|\psi(t_0)\rangle$ evolves to

$$|\psi(t)\rangle = \int \alpha(E) e^{-iE(t-t_0)/\hbar} |\phi_E\rangle dE \qquad (4.45.3)$$

In order to estimate the time interval during which the system evolves to an appreciable extent, we calculate the probability of finding the system in a state $|\chi\rangle$. This probability is

$$P(\chi, t) = |\langle \chi | \psi(t)\rangle|^2 = \left| \int \alpha(E) e^{-iE(t-t_0)/\hbar} \langle \chi | \phi_E \rangle dE \right|^2 \qquad (4.45.4)$$

If ΔE is sufficiently small, we can neglect the variation of $\langle \chi | \phi_E \rangle$ relative to the variation of $\alpha(E)$; therefore, replacing $\langle \chi | \phi_E \rangle$ by $\langle \chi | \phi_{E_0} \rangle$, we obtain

$$P(\chi, t) \cong |\langle \chi | \phi_{E_0} \rangle|^2 \left| \int \alpha(E) e^{-iE(t-t_0)/\hbar} dE \right|^2 \qquad (4.45.5)$$

Thus, $P(\chi, t)$ is approximately the square of the modulus of the Fourier transform of $\alpha(E)$ and using the properties of the Fourier transform, the width Δt of $P(\chi, t)$ is related to ΔE by

$$\frac{\Delta t}{\hbar} \Delta E \gtrsim 1 \qquad (4.45.6)$$

where Δt is the time period during which there is an appreciable probability of finding the system in $|\chi\rangle$, and therefore it can serve as an estimation of the time during which the system evolves to an appreciable extent.

SUPPLEMENTARY PROBLEMS

4.46. Consider the projector onto a subspace ε_m of ε (see Sec. 4.1). Verify that $\hat{P}_m^2 = \hat{P}_m$.

4.47. Repeat Problem 4.19 for the case of a continuous set of kets.

4.48. Repeat Problem 4.20 for the case of a discrete set of kets.

4.49. Consider the following four expressions ($\hat{A}$ is an operator):

    (i) $\langle \psi | \hat{A} | \phi \rangle \langle \psi | \phi \rangle$ (ii) $\langle \psi | \phi \rangle \langle \psi | \hat{A}$ (iii) $\langle \psi | \phi \rangle \hat{A} | \phi \rangle \langle \psi |$ (iv) $\hat{A} | \psi \rangle \langle \phi | \hat{A} | \psi \rangle$

    (*a*) For each of the expressions, find whether it is a scalar, operator, ket, or bra.
    (*b*) Obtain the Hermitian conjugate of each expression.

    Ans.   (*a*) (i) scalar; (ii) bra; (iii) operator; (iv) ket.
            (*b*) (i) $\langle \phi | \hat{A}^\dagger | \psi \rangle \langle \phi | \psi \rangle$ or $\langle \psi | \hat{A} | \phi \rangle^* \langle \psi | \phi \rangle^*$; (ii) $\langle \psi | \phi \rangle^* \hat{A}^\dagger | \psi \rangle$; (iii) $\langle \psi | \phi \rangle^* | \psi \rangle \langle \phi | \hat{A}^\dagger$;
            (iv) $\langle \phi | \hat{A} | \psi \rangle^* \langle \psi | \hat{A}^\dagger$.

4.50. Derive the expression of the scalar product

$$\langle \phi | \psi \rangle = \sum_i b_i^* C_i \quad \text{and} \quad \langle \phi | \psi \rangle = \int b^*(\alpha) C(\alpha) d\alpha \qquad (4.50.1)$$

in terms of components of the ket and the bra in a given representation. (Hint: Use the closure relations.)

4.51. Show that $e^{2\pi i x/a}$ and $e^{iap/\hbar}$ commute for every real number a. [Hint: Use Problem 4.12, part (*b*).]

4.52. Show that the transformation matrix between two orthonormal bases [Eq. (4.29)] is a unitary transformation, i.e., $\hat{S}\hat{S}^\dagger = \hat{S}^\dagger\hat{S} = \hat{I}$.

4.53. Derive Eqs. (4.31), (4.32), and (4.33) using the orthonormality and closure relations for the two bases $\{|\,u_i\rangle\}$ and $\{|\,v_k\rangle\}$.

4.54. Refer to Problem 4.34. (*a*) What is the form of the wave packet at time $t = 0$? (*b*) Calculate the product $\Delta x \Delta p$ at $t = 0$.

Ans. (*a*) $\psi(x, 0) = \sqrt{\dfrac{2k_0}{\pi}}\,\dfrac{1}{k_0^2 x^2 + 1}$; (*b*) $\Delta x \Delta p = \hbar/\sqrt{2}$.

4.55. Using the Schrödinger equation, derive Eq. (4.54).

4.56. Derive Eqs. (4.52) and (4.53) of postulate VI. [Hint: First find the time evolution of an eigenvector of the Hamiltonian and then use property (*b*) of the Schrödinger equation; see Sec. 4.9.]

4.57. Find the operator describing a shift of p_0 in the *x*-direction momentum. (Hint: Compare to Problem 4.42.)

Ans. $e^{ip_0 x/\hbar}$.

CHAPTER 5

Harmonic Oscillator

5.1 Introduction

In this chapter we consider a particle moving as a harmonic oscillator with a potential energy of

$$V(x) = \frac{1}{2}kx^2 \qquad (k = \text{constant}) \tag{5.1}$$

The general differential equation for the oscillator potential can be solved using a technique that is frequently exploited in solving quantum mechanics problems. Many problems in physics can be reduced to a harmonic oscillator with appropriate conditions. In classical mechanics, for example, when expanding potentials around a classical equilibrium point, to the second order, we obtain the harmonic potential $kx^2/2$.

Schrödinger Equation

The classical Hamiltonian for the one-dimensional harmonic oscillator is

$$H = \frac{p^2}{2m} + \frac{kx^2}{2} \tag{5.2}$$

where $k = m\omega^2$. The variables ω and m are, respectively, the angular frequency and the mass of the oscillator. We have

$$\hat{H} = \frac{\hat{P}^2}{2m} + \frac{m\omega^2 \hat{X}^2}{2} = -\frac{\hbar^2}{2m}\frac{d^2}{dx^2} + \frac{m\omega^2}{2}\hat{X}^2 \tag{5.3}$$

Thus, the stationary Schrödinger equation is

$$-\frac{\hbar^2}{2m}\frac{d^2\psi(x)}{dx^2} + \frac{m\omega^2}{2}x^2\psi(x) = E\psi(x) \tag{5.4}$$

The eigenfunctions that are the solutions of the Schrödinger equation are

$$\psi_n(x) = \left(\frac{1}{\pi\lambda^2}\right)^{1/4}\frac{1}{\sqrt{2^n n!}}H_n\left(\frac{x}{\lambda}\right)e^{-x^2/2\lambda^2} \tag{5.5}$$

where $\lambda = \sqrt{\hbar/m\omega}$ and $H_n(\varsigma)$ are the *Hermite polynomials*. The eigenvalues of the harmonic oscillator that are the eigenenergies are

$$E_n = \left(n + \frac{1}{2}\right)\hbar\omega \qquad n = 0, 1, 2, \dots \tag{5.6}$$

5.2 The Hermite Polynomials

The Hermite polynomial $H_n(\varsigma)$ is a polynomial of degree n that is symmetric for even n and antisymmetric for odd n. The Hermite polynomial is a solution of the differential equation

$$\frac{d^2 H_n(\varsigma)}{d\varsigma^2} + 2\varsigma \frac{dH_n(\varsigma)}{d\varsigma} - \left(\frac{2E_n}{\hbar\omega} - 1\right) H_n(\varsigma) = 0 \tag{5.7}$$

This equation can be reduced to

$$\frac{d^2 H_n(\varsigma)}{d\varsigma^2} - 2\varsigma \frac{dH_n(\varsigma)}{d\varsigma} + 2nH_n(\varsigma) = 0 \tag{5.8}$$

The Hermite polynomials also satisfy the following relations:

$$\frac{dH_n(\varsigma)}{d\varsigma} = 2nH_{n-1}(\varsigma) \tag{5.9}$$

and

$$H_{n+1}(\varsigma) = 2\varsigma H_n(\varsigma) - 2nH_{n-1}(\varsigma) \tag{5.10}$$

The generating function of the Hermite polynomials is

$$S(\varsigma, t) = e^{-t^2 + 2t\varsigma} = \sum_{n=0}^{\infty} \frac{H_n(\varsigma)}{n!} t^n \tag{5.11}$$

where

$$H_n(\varsigma) = \frac{d^n}{dt^n} [S(\varsigma, t)]\big|_{t=0} \tag{5.12}$$

More information on Hermite polynomials is given in the Mathematical Appendix.

5.3 Two- and Three-Dimensional Harmonic Oscillators

Similar to the one-dimensional case, the classical Hamiltonian in the two-dimensional case is

$$H_2 = \frac{p_x^2 + p_y^2}{2m} + \frac{m\omega_x^2 x^2}{2} + \frac{m\omega_y^2 y^2}{2} \tag{5.13}$$

In this case the Hamiltonian is separable in x and y, so the problem is reduced to two one-dimensional harmonic oscillators, one in x and the other in y. The eigenfunctions in this case are

$$\psi_{n_x n_y}(x, y) = \psi_{n_x}(x) \psi_{n_y}(y) \tag{5.14}$$

where $\psi_{n_i}(x_i)$ is the eigenfunction of the one-dimensional harmonic oscillator. The eigenvalue corresponding to $\psi_{n_x n_y}(x, y)$ is

$$E_{n_x n_y} = \hbar\omega_x\left(n_x + \frac{1}{2}\right) + \hbar\omega_y\left(n_y + \frac{1}{2}\right) \tag{5.15}$$

The generalization to the three-dimensional case is straightforward.

5.4 Operator Methods for a Harmonic Oscillator

Eigenfunctions can be thought of as an orthonormal basis of unit vectors in an n-dimensional vector space that is obtained by solving the Schrödinger equation. Here we will go a step further. We will find the eigenvalue spectrum and eigenfunctions using operators alone. The *lowering* and *raising* or *annihilation* and *creation* operators, $\hat{a}$ and $\hat{a}^\dagger$, are defined by

$$\hat{a} = \sqrt{\frac{m\omega}{2\hbar}}\left(\hat{X} + \frac{i\hat{P}}{m\omega}\right) \qquad \hat{a}^\dagger = \sqrt{\frac{m\omega}{2\hbar}}\left(\hat{X} + \frac{i\hat{P}}{m\omega}\right) \tag{5.16}$$

These operators are very useful tools for representing the eigenfunctions of the harmonic oscillator. Note that the Hamiltonian of the harmonic oscillator can be written as

$$\hat{H} = \hbar\omega\left(\hat{a}^\dagger\hat{a} + \frac{1}{2}\right) \tag{5.17}$$

or

$$\hat{H} = \hbar\omega\left(\hat{a}\hat{a}^\dagger - \frac{1}{2}\right) \tag{5.18}$$

It can be proved that the commutation relations for these operators are

$$[\hat{a}, \hat{a}^\dagger] = 1 \qquad [\hat{H}, \hat{a}] = -\hbar\omega\hat{a} \qquad [\hat{H}, \hat{a}^\dagger] = \hbar\omega\hat{a}^\dagger \tag{5.19}$$

Let us denote the *n*th state of the harmonic oscillator $\psi_n(x)$ as $|n\rangle$, so a and $\hat{a}^\dagger$ satisfy (see Problem 5.10)

$$\begin{cases} \hat{a}\,|\,n\rangle = \sqrt{n}\,|\,n-1\rangle \\ \hat{a}^\dagger|\,n\rangle = \sqrt{n+1}\,|\,n+1\rangle \end{cases} \tag{5.20}$$

Now we can justify the names *lowering* and *raising operators* for $\hat{a}$ and $\hat{a}^\dagger$, respectively. Thus, one can build the state $|n\rangle$ as

$$|\,n\rangle = \frac{1}{\sqrt{n!}}\,(\hat{a}^\dagger)^n\,|\,0\rangle \tag{5.21}$$

where $|0\rangle$ is the vacuum state ($n = 0$).

SOLVED PROBLEMS

5.1. A one-dimensional harmonic oscillator is characterized by the potential

$$V(x) = \frac{1}{2}kx^2 \tag{5.1.1}$$

where k is a real positive constant. It can be shown that the angular frequency is $\omega = \sqrt{k/m}$, where m is the mass of the oscillator. (*a*) Solve the stationary Schrödinger equation for this potential and find the stationary eigenstates for this system. (*b*) Refer to part (*a*), and find the energy eigenvalues of the oscillator. What is the minimal energy eigenvalue? Explain.

SOLUTION

(*a*) The Hamiltonian of this system can be written as

$$H = \frac{p^2}{2m} + \frac{1}{2}kx^2 \tag{5.1.2}$$

or

$$\hat{H} = -\frac{\hbar^2}{2m}\frac{d^2}{dx^2} + \frac{m\omega^2}{2}x^2 \tag{5.1.3}$$

Thus, the eigenvalue equation is

$$-\frac{\hbar^2}{2m}\frac{d^2\psi(x)}{dx^2} + \frac{m\omega^2}{2}x^2\psi(x) = E\psi(x) \tag{5.1.4}$$

We define $\varepsilon = \frac{2E}{\hbar\omega}$, and we change the variable to $\zeta = \sqrt{\frac{m\omega}{\hbar}}x$; hence, we have

$$\frac{d^2\psi}{dx^2} = \frac{d}{dx}\left(\frac{d\psi}{d\zeta}\frac{d\zeta}{dx}\right) = \frac{d^2\psi}{d\zeta^2}\left(\frac{d\zeta}{dx}\right)^2 = \frac{m\omega}{\hbar}\frac{d^2\psi}{d\zeta^2} \tag{5.1.5}$$

Therefore,

$$\frac{\hbar\omega}{2}\frac{d^2\psi(\zeta)}{d\zeta^2} + E\psi(\zeta) - \frac{\hbar\omega}{2}\zeta^2\psi(\zeta) = 0 \tag{5.1.6}$$

or

$$\frac{d^2\psi}{d\zeta^2} + (\varepsilon - \zeta^2)\psi = 0 \tag{5.1.7}$$

For large ζ (large x), the dominant part of the differential equation, Eq. (5.1.7), is

$$\frac{d^2\psi}{d\zeta^2} - \zeta^2\psi = 0 \tag{5.1.8}$$

The solution for this equation points to the asymptotic behavior of the wavefunction for large ζ:

$$\psi(\zeta) \sim e^{-\zeta^2/2} \tag{5.1.9}$$

So, we can assume

$$\psi(\zeta) = H(\zeta)e^{-\zeta^2/2} \tag{5.1.10}$$

Substituting into Eq. (5.1.8) yields

$$\frac{d^2\psi}{d\zeta^2} = \frac{d}{d\zeta}[H'(\zeta)e^{-\zeta^2/2} - \zeta H(\zeta)e^{-\zeta^2/2}]$$

$$= H''(\zeta)e^{-\zeta^2/2} - 2\zeta H'(\zeta)e^{-\zeta^2/2} - H(\zeta)e^{-\zeta^2/2} + \zeta^2 H(\zeta)e^{-\zeta^2/2} \tag{5.1.11}$$

or

$$\frac{d^2\psi}{d\zeta^2} = [H'' - 2\zeta H' + (\zeta^2 - 1)H]e^{-\zeta^2/2} \tag{5.1.12}$$

Thus, we have

$$[H'' - 2\zeta H' + (\zeta^2 - 1)H]e^{-\zeta^2/2} + (\varepsilon - \zeta^2)He^{-\zeta^2/2} = 0 \tag{5.1.13}$$

We obtain the *Hermite polynomials differential equation*,

$$\frac{d^2H(\zeta)}{d\zeta^2} - 2\zeta\frac{dH(\zeta)}{d\zeta} + (\varepsilon - 1)H(\zeta) = 0 \tag{5.1.14}$$

The wavefunction's behavior around $\zeta = 0$ ($x = 0$) is accounted for by these polynomials. In order to solve this equation we substitute $H(\zeta) = \sum_{n=0}^{\infty} a_n\zeta^n$, so that

$$\frac{d^2H}{d\zeta^2} = \sum_{n=0}^{\infty} a_n n(n-1)\zeta^{n-2} = \sum_{n=0}^{\infty} a_{n+2}(n+2)(n+1)\zeta^n \tag{5.1.15}$$

and

$$-2\zeta \frac{dH}{d\zeta} = -\sum_{n=0}^{\infty} 2na_n \zeta^n \tag{5.1.16}$$

Hence,

$$\sum_{n=0}^{\infty} [a_{n+2}(n+2)(n+1) - 2na_n + (\varepsilon - 1)a_n]\zeta^n = 0 \tag{5.1.17}$$

Therefore, all the coefficients of this series must vanish:

$$a_{n+2}(n+2)(n+1) + (\varepsilon - 2n - 1)a_n = 0 \tag{5.1.18}$$

or

$$a_{n+2} = \frac{2n+1-\varepsilon}{(n+2)(n+1)} a_n \tag{5.1.19}$$

We set $a_0 \neq 0$ and $a_1 = 0$ to obtain the value of $a_2, a_4, \ldots a_{2m}$ (m = positive integer); similarly, we set $a_0 \neq 0$ and $a_1 = 0$ to obtain the values of $a_3, a_5, \ldots, a_{2m-1}$ (m = positive integer). The a_0 or a_1 values are computed using a normalization condition for the wavefunction.

(b) As in part (a), we wish the wavefunction to asymptotically approach $e^{-\zeta^2/2}$ for large ζ. To begin, set the values of the coefficients of $H(\zeta)$ to zero for some value n. For that n, we obtain

$$2n + 1 - \varepsilon = 0 \tag{5.1.20}$$

That is, $\varepsilon = 2n + 1$, or

$$E_n = \left(n + \frac{1}{2}\right)\hbar\omega \tag{5.1.21}$$

Hence, we obtain the quantization condition for the energy eigenvalues. Without an energy source, the system reaches its minimal energy eigenvalue $E_0 = \hbar\omega/2$ at the temperature $T = 0$ K. This value is imposed by the uncertainty relation

$$\Delta x \, \Delta p = \frac{\hbar}{2} \tag{5.1.22}$$

and is the minimal energy eigenvalue the system can have.

5.2. A particle with energy $E = \hbar\omega/2$ moves under the potential of a harmonic oscillator. Compute the probability that the particle is found in the classically forbidden region. Compare this result to the probability of finding the particle in higher energy levels.

SOLUTION

For the classical harmonic oscillator, we have

$$x = A_n \cos(\omega t) \qquad p = -mA_n \omega \sin(\omega t) \tag{5.2.1}$$

Hence, the energy is

$$E_n = \frac{p^2}{2m} + \frac{1}{2}m\omega^2 x^2 = \frac{m\omega^2 A_n^2}{2} \tag{5.2.2}$$

which yields $A_n = \sqrt{\dfrac{2E_n}{m\omega^2}}$. The classically forbidden region is $|x| > A_n$ or $|x| > \sqrt{\dfrac{2E_n}{m\omega^2}}$. Thus, the probability of finding the particle in the classically forbidden region is

$$P_n = \int_{-\infty}^{-A_n} \psi_n^*(x)\,\psi_n(x)\,dx + \int_{A_n}^{\infty} \psi_n^*(x)\,\psi_n(x)\,dx = 2\int_{A_n}^{\infty} \psi_n^*(x)\,\psi_n(x)\,dx$$

$$= 1 - 2\int_{\infty}^{A_n} \psi_n^*(x)\,\psi_n(x)\,dx \tag{5.2.3}$$

Considering the ground state, we have

$$P_0 = 2\int_{A_0}^{\infty} \psi_0^*(x)\psi_0(x)\,dx = 2\sqrt{\frac{1}{\pi\lambda^2}}\int_{A_0}^{\infty} e^{-x^2/\lambda^2}\,dx \tag{5.2.4}$$

Changing integration variables $\eta = x/\lambda$, we obtain

$$P_0 = \frac{2}{\sqrt{\pi}}\int_{A_0/\lambda}^{\infty} e^{-\eta^2}\,d\eta = 1 - \frac{2}{\sqrt{\pi}}\int_{0}^{A_0/\lambda} e^{-\eta^2}\,d\eta \tag{5.2.5}$$

We have $A_0/\lambda = 1$; hence,

$$P_0 = 1 - \frac{2}{\sqrt{\pi}}\int_{0}^{1} e^{-\eta^2}\,d\eta \tag{5.2.6}$$

Solving this numerically, we obtain $P_0 = 0.157\,8$ (see Problem 12.8).

For excited states the probability for being in the classically forbidden region is

$$P_n = 1 - 2\int_{0}^{A_n} \frac{1}{\sqrt{\pi\lambda^2}\,2^n n!}\,H_n^2\!\left(\frac{x}{\lambda}\right) e^{-x^2/\lambda^2}\,dx = 1 - \frac{1}{\sqrt{\pi}\,2^{n-1}n!}\int_{0}^{A_n} H_n^2\!\left(\frac{x}{\lambda}\right) e^{-x^2/\lambda^2}\,d\!\left(\frac{x}{\lambda}\right) \tag{5.2.7}$$

Putting $\eta = x/\lambda$, we arrive at

$$P_n = 1 - \frac{1}{\sqrt{\pi}\,2^{n-1}n!}\int_{0}^{A_n/\lambda} H_n^2(\eta)\,e^{-\eta^2}\,d\eta \tag{5.2.8}$$

Using the known Hermite polynomials $H_0(\eta) = 1$, $H_1(\eta) = 2\eta$, $H_2(\eta) = 4\eta^2 - 2$, and $A_1/\lambda = \sqrt{3}$, we obtain:

$$P_1 = 1 - \frac{4}{\sqrt{\pi}}\int_{0}^{\sqrt{3}} \eta^2 e^{-\eta^2}\,d\eta \tag{5.2.9}$$

The numerical solution is $P_1 = 0.111\,6$. We also find

$$P_2 = 1 - \frac{1}{4\sqrt{\pi}}\int_{0}^{\sqrt{5}} (16\eta^4 - 16\eta^2 + 4)\,e^{-\eta^2}\,d\eta$$

$$= 1 - \frac{1}{\sqrt{\pi}}\int_{0}^{\sqrt{5}} (4\eta^4 - 4\eta^2 + 1)e^{-\eta^2}\,d\eta = 0.095\,1 \tag{5.2.10}$$

Thus, we have seen that $P_0 = 0.157\,3$, $P_1 = 0.111\,6$, and $P_2 = 0.095\,1$. Note that the value of P_n is smaller for higher energy levels. The reason for this is that particles with high energy are "more classical" than those with lower energies, and hence the probability for particles in higher energy levels to be in the classically forbidden region is less.

5.3. Using the uncertainty relation $\Delta p \Delta x \geq \hbar/2$, estimate the energy ground state of the harmonic oscillator.

SOLUTION

The classical Hamiltonian of the harmonic oscillator is

$$H = \frac{p^2}{2m} + \frac{m\omega^2}{2} x^2 \tag{5.3.1}$$

The expectation value of the energy is

$$\langle \hat{H} \rangle = E = \frac{\langle \hat{p}^2 \rangle}{2m} + \frac{m\omega^2}{2} \langle \hat{x}^2 \rangle \tag{5.3.2}$$

We can write

$$\Delta p^2 = \langle \hat{p}^2 \rangle - \langle \hat{p} \rangle^2 \qquad \Delta x^2 = \langle \hat{x}^2 \rangle - \langle \hat{x} \rangle^2 \tag{5.3.3}$$

for the harmonic oscillator $\langle \hat{p} \rangle = \langle \hat{x} \rangle = 0$. The proof for these results is as follows:

$$\langle \hat{x} \rangle = \int_{-\infty}^{\infty} \psi_n^*(x) \, \hat{x} \, \psi_n(x) \, dx = \int_{-\infty}^{\infty} \left| \hat{x} \, \psi_n(x) \right|^2 dx \tag{5.3.4}$$

The integral of the antisymmetric function $x \left| \psi_n(x) \right|^2$ over a symmetric interval is zero; hence, $\langle \hat{x} \rangle = 0$. Similarly,

$$\langle \hat{p} \rangle = -i\hbar \int_{-\infty}^{\infty} \psi_n^*(x) \frac{\partial \psi_n(x)}{\partial x} dx \tag{5.3.5}$$

Changing the variables to $\zeta = \frac{x}{\lambda}$ and $\lambda = \sqrt{\frac{\hbar}{m\omega}}$, we have

$$\langle \hat{p} \rangle = -i\hbar \int_{-\infty}^{\infty} \psi_n^*(\zeta) \frac{\partial \psi_n(\zeta)}{\partial \zeta} d\zeta \tag{5.3.6}$$

so,

$$\frac{\partial \psi_n(\zeta)}{\partial \zeta} = \frac{\partial H_n(\zeta)}{\partial \zeta} \frac{e^{-\zeta^2/2}}{\sqrt{\pi \lambda 2^n n!}} + \zeta \psi_n(\zeta) \tag{5.3.7}$$

Thus, we obtain

$$\langle \hat{p} \rangle = -\frac{i\hbar}{\sqrt{\pi \lambda 2^n n!}} \int_{-\infty}^{\infty} \psi_n^*(\zeta) \frac{\partial H_n}{\partial \zeta} e^{-\zeta^2/2} d\zeta - i\hbar \int_{-\infty}^{\infty} \psi^*(\zeta) \psi(\zeta) \zeta \, d\zeta \tag{5.3.8}$$

Notice that

$$\langle \hat{x} \rangle \sim \int \psi^*(\zeta) \psi(\zeta) \zeta \, d\zeta = 0 \tag{5.3.9}$$

As the Hermite polynomials are either symmetric or antisymmetric, the multiple $H_n(\zeta) \dfrac{\partial H_n(\tau)}{\partial \zeta}$ is always antisymmetric, and for the same reason that $\langle \hat{x} \rangle$ vanishes, $\langle \hat{p} \rangle$ also vanishes. Thus,

$$E = \frac{\Delta p^2}{2m} + \frac{m\omega^2}{2} \Delta x^2 \tag{5.3.10}$$

According to the uncertainty relation, the minimal value of Δp is $\Delta p = \dfrac{\hbar}{2\Delta x}$; hence,

$$E = \frac{\hbar^2}{8m \Delta x^2} + \frac{m\omega^2}{2} \Delta x^2 \tag{5.3.11}$$

Finally, the minimal value of $E(\Delta x)$ is obtained by

$$\frac{dE}{d(\Delta x)} = -\frac{\hbar^2}{4m(\Delta x)^3} + m\omega^2 \Delta x = 0 \qquad (5.3.12)$$

So, $\Delta x_0 = \sqrt{\dfrac{\hbar}{2m\omega}}$. Also,

$$\left.\frac{d^2 E}{d(\Delta x)^2}\right|_{\Delta x = \Delta x_0} = \frac{3\hbar^2}{4m(\Delta x)^4} + m\omega^2 > 0 \qquad (5.3.13)$$

Hence, the minimal value is

$$E_{min} = \frac{\hbar^2}{4m(\Delta x_0)^2} + \frac{m\omega^2}{2}(\Delta x_0)^2 = \frac{\hbar\omega}{4} + \frac{\hbar\omega}{4} = \frac{\hbar\omega}{2} \qquad (5.3.14)$$

as we expected. Here we obtained the exact solution by relying on the lower bound of the uncertainty relation $\Delta x \Delta p = \hbar/2$. This follows from the result that in the ground state, we have a Gaussian form of the eigenfunction:

$$\psi(x) = (2\pi\sigma)^{1/4} e^{-ipx/\hbar} e^{-(x-x_0)^2/4\sigma^2} \qquad (5.3.15)$$

Though the uncertainty relation is normally used to estimate the ground state energy eigenvalue, for the case given above we can evaluate it exactly.

5.4. Find the eigenfunctions and eigenvalues of a two-dimensional isotropic harmonic oscillator; find the degeneracy of the energy levels. The classical Hamiltonian of this system is

$$H = \frac{p_x^2}{2m} + \frac{p_y^2}{2m} + \frac{1}{2}m\omega^2(x^2 + y^2) \qquad (5.4.1)$$

SOLUTION

The Hamiltonian of the system can be separated into two parts, $H = H_x + H_y$, where

$$H_x = \frac{p_x^2}{2m} + \frac{m\omega^2 x^2}{2} \qquad H_y = \frac{p_y^2}{2m} + \frac{m\omega^2 y^2}{2} \qquad (5.4.2)$$

Thus, the wavefunction can be written as a multiple of two functions, $\psi_x(x)$ (the eigenfunction of $\hat{H}_x$) and $\psi_y(y)$ (the eigenfunction of $\hat{H}_y$) with eigenvalues $E_x = \hbar\omega(n_x + 1/2)$ and $E_y = \hbar\omega(n_y + 1/2)$, respectively. So, we have $\hat{H}\psi = E\psi$, where $\psi(x, y) = \psi_x(x)\psi_y(y)$; hence,

$$\hat{H}\psi(x, y) = (\hat{H}_x + \hat{H}_y)\,\psi_x(x)\,\psi_y(y) = \hat{H}_x\psi_x(x)\,\psi_y(y) + \psi_x(x)\hat{H}_y\psi_y(y)$$

$$= E_x\psi_x\psi_y + E_y\psi_x\psi_y = (E_x + E_y)\,\psi_x\psi_y \qquad (5.4.3)$$

Therefore,

$$E = E_x + E_y = (n_x + n_y + 1)\hbar\omega \equiv (n + 1)\hbar\omega \qquad (5.4.4)$$

The degeneracy of each state $E(n_x, n_y)$ is computed as follows: $(n + 1)$ is an integer that assumes all values from 0 to ∞. We can see from Fig. 5.1 that $(n + 1) = $ constant, defines a line in the $n_x n_y$ space. One can also see that the degeneracy of the state n is $n + 1$.

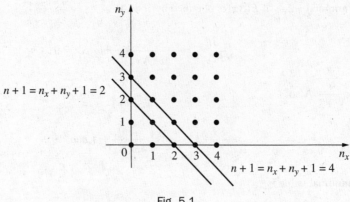

Fig. 5.1

5.5. Consider a particle with charge $+e$ moving under a three-dimensional isotropic harmonic potential:

$$V(r) = \frac{1}{2}m\omega^2 r^2 \tag{5.5.1}$$

in an electric field $\mathbf{E} = E_0\mathbf{i}$. Find the eigenstates and the energy eigenvalues of the particle.

SOLUTION

The classical Hamiltonian of the system is

$$H = \frac{\mathbf{p}^2}{2m} + \frac{m\omega^2}{2}\mathbf{r}^2 - eE_0 x \tag{5.5.2}$$

We separate the Hamiltonian into three parts: $H = H_x + H_y + H_z$, where

$$\begin{cases} H_x = \dfrac{p_x^2}{2m} + \dfrac{m\omega^2}{2}x^2 - eE_0 x \\[2mm] H_y = \dfrac{p_y^2}{2m} + \dfrac{m\omega^2}{2}y^2 \\[2mm] H_z = \dfrac{p_z^2}{2m} + \dfrac{m\omega^2}{2}z^2 \end{cases} \tag{5.5.3}$$

Notice that H_y and H_z are identical to the Hamiltonian of the one-dimensional harmonic oscillator, so we can write the wavefunction as $\psi(x, y, z) = \psi_1(x)\psi_2(y)\psi_3(z)$, where $\psi_2(y)$ and $\psi_3(z)$ are the wavefunctions of the one-dimensional harmonic oscillator:

$$\begin{cases} \psi_2(y) = \dfrac{1}{\sqrt{\pi\lambda 2^{n_2} n_2!}} H_{n_2}(y)\, e^{-y^2/2\lambda^2} \\[3mm] \psi_3(z) = \dfrac{1}{\sqrt{\pi\lambda 2^{n_3} n_3!}} H_{n_3}(z)\, e^{-z^2/2\lambda^2} \end{cases} \tag{5.5.4}$$

with $\lambda = \sqrt{\dfrac{\hbar}{m\omega}}$. The equation for $\psi_1(x)$ is

$$\hat{H}_x \psi_1(x) = -\frac{\hbar^2}{2m}\frac{\partial^2 \psi_1}{\partial x^2} + \frac{m\omega^2}{2}x^2\psi_1 - eE_0 x\psi_1 = E_1\psi_1 \tag{5.5.5}$$

Changing the variables to $\zeta = \dfrac{x}{\lambda} - \dfrac{eE_0}{\sqrt{\hbar m \omega}}$ yields

$$\frac{d^2 \psi_1}{d\zeta^2} + \left(\frac{2E_1}{\hbar \omega} + \frac{(eE_0)^2}{\sqrt{\hbar m \omega^3}} \right) \psi_1 - \zeta^2 \psi_1 = 0 \qquad (5.5.6)$$

We obtain the differential equation for a one-dimensional harmonic oscillator with the solution

$$\psi_1(\zeta) = \frac{1}{\sqrt{\pi \lambda 2^{n_1} n_1!}} H_{n_1}(\zeta) e^{-\zeta^2/2} \qquad (5.5.7)$$

or

$$\psi_1(x) = \frac{1}{\sqrt{\pi \lambda 2^{n_1} n_1!}} H_{n_1}(x) \exp\left[-\frac{1}{2}\left(\frac{x}{\lambda} - \frac{eE_0}{\sqrt{\hbar m \omega^3}} \right)^2 \right] \qquad (5.5.8)$$

The quantization condition in this case is

$$\frac{2E_1}{\hbar \omega} + \frac{(eE_0)^2}{\hbar m \omega^3} = 2n_1 + 1 \qquad (5.5.9)$$

so the energy eigenvalues are

$$(E_1)_{n_1} = \left(n_1 + \frac{1}{2} \right)\hbar \omega - \frac{(eE_0)^2}{2m \omega^2} \qquad (5.5.10)$$

In conclusion, the wavefunctions are

$$\psi(x,\, y,\, z) = \psi_1(x)\, \psi_2(y)\, \psi_3(z) \qquad (5.5.11)$$

and the energy eigenvalues are

$$E_{n_1 n_2 n_3} = E_{n_1} + E_{n_2} + E_{n_3} = \left(n_1 + n_2 + n_3 + \frac{3}{2} \right)\hbar \omega - \frac{(eE_0)^2}{2m \omega^2} \qquad (5.5.12)$$

5.6. Consider a particle with mass m in a one-dimensional harmonic potential. At $t = 0$ the normalized wavefunction is

$$\psi(x) = \left(\frac{1}{\pi \sigma^2} \right)^{1/4} e^{-x^2/2\sigma^2} \qquad (5.6.1)$$

where $\sigma^2 \neq \dfrac{\hbar}{m\omega}$ is a constant. Find the probability that the momentum of the particle at $t > 0$ is positive.

SOLUTION

We denote by $\tilde{\psi}(p, t)$ the wavefunction of the particle in the momentum space at time t. The probability P for a positive momentum is

$$P = \int_0^\infty |\tilde{\psi}(p, t)|^2 \, dp \qquad (5.6.2)$$

We can write $\tilde{\psi}(p, t)$ as a linear combination of the eigenfunctions in the momentum space:

$$\tilde{\psi}(p, t) = \sum_{n=0}^\infty C_n \tilde{\phi}_n(p) e^{-i(n+1/2)\omega t} \qquad (5.6.3)$$

where $\tilde{\phi}_n(p)$ are the stationary eigenfunctions in the momentum space and the coefficients are $C_n = \langle \phi_n(x) | \psi(x) \rangle$. Note that, here, $\phi_n(x)$ are the eigenfunctions in the coordinate space. $\psi(x, t)$ can also be written as

$$\psi(x, t) = \sum_n C_n \phi_n(x) e^{-i(n+1/2)\omega t} \tag{5.6.4}$$

The functions $\phi_n(x)$ are either symmetric or antisymmetric, as are their Fourier transforms $\tilde{\phi}_n(p)$. This attribute is conserved for every t; thus $\psi(p, 0)$ is symmetric, $\tilde{\psi}(p, 0) = \tilde{\psi}(-p, 0)$, as is $\tilde{\psi}(p, t) = \tilde{\psi}(-p, t)$. Hence,

$$\int_0^\infty |\tilde{\psi}(p, t)|^2 dp = \int_0^\infty |\tilde{\psi}(-p, t)|^2 dp = -\int_0^{-\infty} |\tilde{\psi}(+p, t)|^2 dp = \int_{-\infty}^0 |\tilde{\psi}(p, t)|^2 dp \tag{5.6.5}$$

Using the fact that $\tilde{\psi}(p, t)$ is normalized, that is,

$$\int_{-\infty}^\infty |\tilde{\psi}(p, t)|^2 dp = \int_0^\infty |\tilde{\psi}(p, t)|^2 dp + \int_{-\infty}^0 |\tilde{\psi}(p, t)|^2 dp = 1 \tag{5.6.6}$$

we obtain

$$P = \int_0^\infty |\tilde{\psi}(p, t)|^2 dp = \int_{-\infty}^0 |\tilde{\psi}(p, t)|^2 dp = \frac{1}{2} \tag{5.6.7}$$

5.7. (a) Refer to the initial condition in Problem 5.6 and calculate $\psi(x, t)$. (b) Given that at $t = 0$ the particle is in state

$$\psi(x) = \frac{1}{\sqrt{2}}[\phi_0(x) + \phi_1(x)] \tag{5.7.1}$$

where $\phi_n(x)$ are the eigenfunctions of a one-dimensional harmonic oscillator. Compute the expectation value of x at $t > 0$.

SOLUTION

(a) First, note that the given $\psi(x)$ is *not* $\psi_0(x)$ (the eigenfunction) since $\sigma^2 \neq \dfrac{\hbar}{m\omega}$, so to find $\psi(x, t)$ we must write $\psi(x)$ as a linear combination of the eigenfunctions $\phi_n(x)$:

$$\psi(x) = \sum_{n=0}^\infty C_n \phi_n(x) \tag{5.7.2}$$

and

$$\psi(x, t) = \sum_n C_n \phi_n(x) e^{-i(n+1/2)\omega t} \tag{5.7.3}$$

where

$$C_n = \langle \phi_n(x) | \psi(x) \rangle = \int_{-\infty}^\infty \phi_n^*(x) \psi(x) \, dx \tag{5.7.4}$$

Now, writing $\lambda^2 = \dfrac{\hbar}{m\omega}$, we have

$$\phi_n(x) = \frac{1}{\sqrt{\pi^{1/2} \lambda 2^n n!}} H_n\left(\frac{x}{\lambda}\right) \exp\left[-\frac{1}{2}\left(\frac{x}{\lambda}\right)^2\right] \tag{5.7.5}$$

So,

$$C_n = \frac{1}{(\sqrt{\pi} 2^n \lambda n!)^{1/2}} \frac{1}{(\sqrt{\pi}\sigma)^{1/2}} \int_{-\infty}^\infty H_n\left(\frac{x}{\lambda}\right) \exp\left[-\frac{1}{2}x^2\left(\frac{1}{\lambda^2} + \frac{1}{\sigma^2}\right)\right] dx \tag{5.7.6}$$

Recall that $H_n(x/\lambda)$ are either symmetric (for even n) or antisymmetric (for odd n); hence, since $H_n(x/\lambda)$ is antisymmetric and $\exp\left[-\frac{1}{2}x^2\left(\frac{1}{\lambda}+\frac{1}{\lambda^2}\right)\right]$ is symmetric, C_n vanishes for odd n. Thus we need only compute

$$C_{2m} = \frac{1}{[\pi 4^m (2m)! \sigma \lambda]^{1/2}} \int_{-\infty}^{\infty} H_{2m}\left(\frac{x}{\lambda}\right) \exp\left[-\frac{1}{2}x^2\left(\frac{\sigma^2+\lambda^2}{\lambda^2\sigma^2}\right)\right] dx \tag{5.7.7}$$

Substituting variables $\eta = \sqrt{\dfrac{\sigma^2+\lambda^2}{2\lambda^2\sigma^2}}$ and $x = \sqrt{\dfrac{2\lambda^2\sigma^2}{\lambda^2+\sigma^2}}\eta$ we obtain,

$$C_{2m} = \frac{1}{\sqrt{\pi 4^m (2m)! \lambda \sigma}} \int_{-\infty}^{\infty} H_{2m}\left(\sqrt{\frac{2\sigma^2}{\lambda^2+\sigma^2}}\eta\right) e^{-\eta^2} \sqrt{\frac{2\lambda^2\sigma^2}{\lambda^2+\sigma^2}} \, d\eta$$

$$= \sqrt{\frac{2\lambda\sigma}{\pi 4^m (2m)! (\lambda^2+\sigma^2)}} \int_{-\infty}^{\infty} H_{2m}\left(\sqrt{\frac{2\sigma^2}{\lambda^2+\sigma^2}}\eta\right) e^{-\eta^2} \, d\eta \tag{5.7.8}$$

Using the identity

$$\int_{-\infty}^{\infty} H_{2m}(ax) e^{-x^2} dx = \sqrt{\pi} \, \frac{(2m)!}{m!}(a^2-1)^m \tag{5.7.9}$$

we get

$$C_{2n} = \sqrt{\frac{2\lambda\sigma(2m)!}{4^m (m!)^2(\lambda^2+\sigma^2)}}\left(\frac{\sigma^2-\lambda^2}{\sigma^2+\lambda^2}\right)^m \tag{5.7.10}$$

or

$$\psi(x,t) = \sum_{n=0}^{\infty} \sigma_{2n} \Psi_{2n}(x) e^{-(2n+1/2)\omega t} \tag{5.7.11}$$

(*b*) It is given that at $t=0$ we have

$$\psi(x,0) = \frac{1}{\sqrt{2}}[\phi_0(x) + \phi_1(x)] \tag{5.7.12}$$

Thus, for $t > 0$,

$$\psi(x,t) = \frac{1}{\sqrt{2}}\left[\phi_0(x) e^{-i\omega t/2} + \phi_1(x) e^{-3i\omega t/2}\right] \tag{5.7.13}$$

By definition, the expectation value of x is

$$\langle \hat{x} \rangle = \langle \psi(x,t) | \hat{x} | \psi(x,t) \rangle = \frac{1}{2}\Big[\langle \phi_0(x) | \hat{x} | \phi_0(x) \rangle + \langle \phi_1(x) | \hat{x} | \phi_1(x) \rangle$$

$$+ e^{-i\omega t}\langle \phi_0(x) | \hat{x} | \phi_1(x) \rangle + e^{i\omega t}\langle \phi_1(x) | \hat{x} | \phi_0(x) \rangle \Big] \tag{5.7.14}$$

Let us compute each part separately:

$$\langle \phi_0(x) | \hat{x} | \phi_0(x) \rangle = \int_{-\infty}^{\infty} \phi_0^*(x) \phi_0(x) \, dx = \int_{-\infty}^{\infty} |\phi_0(x)|^2 \, dx \tag{5.7.15}$$

Since $\left|\phi_0(x)\right|^2$ is symmetric and x is an antisymmetric function, the integration vanishes on a symmetric interval, $\langle\phi_0(x)|\hat{x}|\phi_0(x)\rangle = 0$, and also on $\langle\phi_n(x)|\hat{x}|\phi_n(x)\rangle = 0$. We turn now to compute

$$\langle\phi_0(x)|\hat{x}|\phi_1(x)\rangle = \int_{-\infty}^{\infty}\phi_0^*(x)\,\phi_1(x)\,dx$$

$$= \frac{1}{\sqrt{\pi^{1/2}\lambda}}\,\frac{1}{\sqrt{2\pi^{1/2}\lambda}}\int_{-\infty}^{\infty}H_0\left(\frac{x}{\lambda}\right)H_1\left(\frac{x}{\lambda}\right)xe^{-x^2/\lambda^2}\,dx \qquad (5.7.16)$$

We have $H_0(x/\lambda) = 1$ and $H_1(x/\lambda) = 2x/\lambda$ (see the Mathematical Appendix). Therefore,

$$\langle\phi_0(x)|\hat{x}|\phi_1(x)\rangle = \sqrt{\frac{2}{\pi}}\,\frac{1}{\lambda^2}\int_{-\infty}^{\infty}x^2 e^{-x^2/\lambda^2}\,dx = \sqrt{\frac{1}{2\lambda^2}} \qquad (5.7.17)$$

or $\langle\phi_0(x)|\hat{x}|\phi_1(x)\rangle = \sqrt{\dfrac{\hbar}{2m\omega}}$ and

$$\langle\phi_1(x)|\hat{x}|\phi_0(x)\rangle = \langle\phi_0(x)|\hat{x}|\phi_1(x)\rangle^* = \sqrt{\frac{\hbar}{2m\omega}} \qquad (5.7.18)$$

So, we finally obtain

$$\langle\hat{x}\rangle = \sqrt{\frac{\hbar}{2m\omega}}\cos(\omega t) \qquad (5.7.19)$$

5.8. Consider the one-dimensional harmonic oscillator with the Hamiltonian

$$H = \frac{p^2}{2m} + \frac{1}{2}m\omega^2 x^2 \qquad (5.8.1)$$

We define new operators

$$\hat{p} = \frac{\hat{P}}{\sqrt{m\omega\hbar}} \quad \text{and} \quad \hat{q} = \hat{X}\sqrt{\frac{m\omega}{\hbar}} \qquad (5.8.2)$$

so $\hat{H} = \dfrac{\hbar\omega}{2}\left(\hat{q}^2 + \hat{p}^2\right)$. (a) compute the commutation relation $[\hat{p}, \hat{q}]$. (b) For the operators $\hat{a}$ and $\hat{a}^\dagger$ defined as

$$\hat{a} = \frac{1}{\sqrt{2}}(\hat{q} + i\hat{p}) = \sqrt{\frac{m\omega}{2\hbar}}\hat{X} + \frac{i}{m\omega}\hat{P} \qquad (5.8.3)$$

$$\hat{a}^\dagger = \frac{1}{\sqrt{2}}(\hat{q} - i\hat{p}) = \sqrt{\frac{m\omega}{2\hbar}}\hat{X} - \frac{i}{m\omega}\hat{P} \qquad (5.8.4)$$

compute $\hat{a}|n\rangle$ and $\hat{a}^\dagger|n\rangle$, where $|n\rangle$ is the eigenfunction of the oscillator for the nth energy state.

SOLUTION

(a) We use the known commutation relation $[\hat{X}, \hat{P}] = i\hbar$, so

$$[\hat{p}, \hat{q}] = \left[\frac{\hat{P}}{\sqrt{m\omega\hbar}}, \hat{X}\sqrt{\frac{m\omega}{\hbar}}\right] = \frac{1}{\hbar}[\hat{P}, \hat{X}] = -i \qquad (5.8.5)$$

(b) Using the result obtained in part (a), we can write

$$\hat{a}^\dagger\hat{a} = \frac{1}{2}(\hat{q} - i\hat{p})(\hat{q} + i\hat{p}) = \frac{1}{2}[\hat{q}^2 + \hat{p}^2 - i(\hat{p}\hat{q} - \hat{q}\hat{p})]$$

$$= \frac{1}{2}(\hat{q}^2 + \hat{p}^2 - i[\hat{p}, \hat{q}]) = \frac{1}{2}(\hat{q}^2 + \hat{p}^2 - 1) \qquad (5.8.6)$$

So, substituting in Eq. (5.8.1), we have

$$\hat{H} = \hbar\omega\left(\hat{a}^\dagger\hat{a} + \frac{1}{2}\right)$$ (5.8.7)

Now we turn to compute the commutation relation $\hat{a}$ and $\hat{a}^\dagger$:

$$[\hat{a}^\dagger, \hat{a}] = \frac{1}{2}[\hat{q} - i\hat{p}, \hat{q} + i\hat{p}] = i[\hat{q}, \hat{p}] = -1$$ (5.8.8)

Thus, $\hat{a}^\dagger\hat{a} - \hat{a}\hat{a}^\dagger = -1$. Therefore, we obtain

$$\hat{H} = \hbar\omega\left(\hat{a}\hat{a}^\dagger - \frac{1}{2}\right)$$ (5.8.9)

We also need to compute the commutation relation of $\hat{a}$ and $\hat{a}^\dagger$ with $\hat{H}$,

$$[\hat{a}, \hat{H}] = \hbar\omega[\hat{a}, \hat{a}^\dagger\hat{a}] = \hbar\omega[\hat{a}, \hat{a}^\dagger]\hat{a} = \hbar\omega\hat{a}$$ (5.8.10)

Similarly,

$$[\hat{a}^\dagger, \hat{H}] = \hbar\omega[\hat{a}^\dagger, \hat{a}\hat{a}^\dagger] = \hbar\omega[\hat{a}^\dagger, \hat{a}]\hat{a}^\dagger = -\hbar\omega\hat{a}^\dagger$$ (5.8.11)

Thus, using the eigenvalue equation of the energy $\hat{H}|n\rangle = \hbar\omega(n + 1/2)|n\rangle$, we can write

$$\hat{H}|n\rangle = \hbar\omega\left(\hat{a}^\dagger\hat{a} + \frac{1}{2}\right)|n\rangle$$ (5.8.12)

Therefore, $\hat{a}^\dagger\hat{a}|n\rangle = n|n\rangle$. Similarly,

$$\hat{H}|n\rangle = \hbar\omega\left(\hat{a}\hat{a}^\dagger - \frac{1}{2}\right)|n\rangle$$ (5.8.13)

so $\hat{a}\hat{a}^\dagger|n\rangle = (n + 1)|n\rangle$. We apply $\hat{a}^\dagger = -\frac{1}{\hbar\omega}[\hat{a}^\dagger, \hat{H}]$ on the state $|n\rangle$, so

$$\hat{a}^\dagger|n\rangle = -\frac{\hat{a}^\dagger\hat{H}}{\hbar\omega}|n\rangle + \frac{\hat{H}\hat{a}^\dagger}{\hbar\omega}|n\rangle = -\left(n + \frac{1}{2}\right)\hat{a}^\dagger|n\rangle + \frac{\hat{H}\hat{a}^\dagger}{\hbar\omega}|n\rangle$$ (5.8.14)

or

$$\hat{H}(\hat{a}^\dagger|n\rangle) = \hbar\omega\left(n + \frac{3}{2}\right)(\hat{a}^\dagger|n\rangle)$$ (5.8.15)

Hence, we conclude that $\hat{a}^\dagger|n\rangle$ is a state that is proportional to $|n + 1\rangle$, i.e.,

$$|\psi_+\rangle \equiv \hat{a}^\dagger|n\rangle = \alpha_+|n + 1\rangle$$ (5.8.16)

where α_+ is a constant given by

$$\alpha_+^2 = \langle\psi_+|\psi_+\rangle = \langle n|\hat{a}\hat{a}^\dagger|n\rangle$$ (5.8.17)

We have already seen that $\hat{a}\hat{a}^\dagger|n\rangle = (n + 1)|n\rangle$; thus $\alpha_+^2 = (n + 1)$. Choosing $\alpha_+ = \sqrt{n + 1}$, we finally get

$$\hat{a}^\dagger|n\rangle = \sqrt{n + 1}|n + 1\rangle$$ (5.8.18)

Similarly, we apply $\hat{a} = \frac{1}{\hbar\omega}[\hat{a}, \hat{H}]$ on the state $|n\rangle$ and find

$$\hat{a}|n\rangle = \frac{\hat{a}\hat{H}}{\hbar\omega}|n\rangle - \frac{\hat{H}\hat{a}}{\omega\hbar}|n\rangle = \left(n + \frac{1}{2}\right)(\hat{a}|n\rangle) - \frac{\hat{H}}{\omega\hbar}(\hat{a}|n\rangle)$$ (5.8.19)

or

$$H(a|n\rangle) = \hbar\omega\left(n - \frac{1}{2}\right)(a|n\rangle)$$ (5.8.20)

So, we conclude that $\hat{a}\,|\,n\rangle$ is a state that is proportional to $|\,n-1\rangle$, i.e.,

$$|\,\psi_-\rangle \equiv \hat{a}\,|\,n\rangle = \alpha_-\,|\,n-1\rangle \tag{5.8.21}$$

where α_- is also a constant

$$\alpha_-^2 = \langle\psi_-\,|\,\psi_-\rangle = \langle n\,|\,\hat{a}^\dagger\hat{a}\,|\,n\rangle \tag{5.8.22}$$

We have seen that $\hat{a}^\dagger\hat{a}\,|\,n\rangle = n\,|\,n\rangle$; therefore $\alpha_-^2 = n$. Choosing $\alpha_- = \sqrt{n}$, we get

$$\hat{a}\,|\,n\rangle = \sqrt{n}\,|\,n-1\rangle \tag{5.8.23}$$

Note that if we apply $\hat{a}$ to the ground state $|\,0\rangle$, we get

$$\hat{a}\,|\,0\rangle = 0 \tag{5.8.24}$$

Thus, we introduce the lowering and raising operators $\hat{a}$ and $\hat{a}^\dagger$, defined above, that satisfy

$$\begin{cases} \hat{a}\,|\,n\rangle = \sqrt{n}\,|\,n-1\rangle \\ \hat{a}^\dagger\,|\,n\rangle = \sqrt{n+1}\,|\,n+1\rangle \end{cases} \tag{5.8.25}$$

5.9. Compute the matrix elements of the operators $\hat{X}$ and $\hat{P}$ for the one-dimensional harmonic oscillator,

$$X_{nk} = \langle n\,|\,\hat{X}\,|\,k\rangle = \int_{-\infty}^{\infty} \phi_n^*(x)\,\hat{X}\,\phi_k(x)\,dx \tag{5.9.1}$$

$$P_{nk} = \langle n\,|\,\hat{P}\,|\,k\rangle = \int_{-\infty}^{\infty} \phi_n^*(x)\,\hat{P}\,\phi_k(x)\,dx \tag{5.9.2}$$

where $\phi_n(x)$ are the eigenfunctions of the harmonic oscillator.

SOLUTION

Let us write $\hat{X}$ and $\hat{P}$ using the lowering and raising operators $\hat{a}$ and $\hat{a}^\dagger$ (see Problem 5.8):

$$\hat{X} = \frac{1}{2}\sqrt{\frac{2\hbar}{m\omega}}(\hat{a} + \hat{a}^\dagger) = \sqrt{\frac{\hbar}{2m\omega}}(\hat{a} + \hat{a}^\dagger) \tag{5.9.3}$$

Similarly,

$$\hat{P} = \frac{m\omega}{2i}\sqrt{\frac{2\hbar}{m\omega}}(\hat{a} - \hat{a}^\dagger) = i\sqrt{\frac{m\omega\hbar}{2}}(\hat{a}^\dagger - \hat{a}) \tag{5.9.4}$$

from which we can now compute

$$\langle n\,|\,\hat{X}\,|\,k\rangle = \sqrt{\frac{\hbar}{2m\omega}}\langle n\,|\,(\hat{a} + \hat{a}^\dagger)\,|\,k\rangle = \sqrt{\frac{\hbar}{2m\omega}}(\langle n\,|\,\hat{a}\,|\,k\rangle + \langle n\,|\,\hat{a}^\dagger\,|\,k\rangle) \tag{5.9.5}$$

We have seen that

$$\begin{cases} \hat{a}\,|\,k\rangle = \sqrt{k}\,|\,k-1\rangle \\ \hat{a}^\dagger\,|\,k\rangle = \sqrt{k+1}\,|\,k+1\rangle \end{cases} \tag{5.9.6}$$

Therefore, we have

$$\langle n\,|\,\hat{X}\,|\,k\rangle = \sqrt{\frac{\hbar}{2m\omega}}\left(\sqrt{k}\langle n\,|\,k-1\rangle + \sqrt{k+1}\langle n\,|\,k+1\rangle\right) = \sqrt{\frac{\hbar}{2m\omega}}\left(\sqrt{k}\delta_{n,\,k-1} + \sqrt{k+1}\delta_{n,\,k+1}\right) \tag{5.9.7}$$

where

$$\delta_{nm} = \begin{cases} 1 & n = m \\ 0 & n \neq m \end{cases} \tag{5.9.8}$$

Hence,

$$\langle n \,|\, \hat{X} \,|\, k \rangle = \begin{cases} \sqrt{\dfrac{\hbar(n+1)}{2m\omega}} & k = n+1 \\[2ex] \sqrt{\dfrac{\hbar n}{2m\omega}} & k = n-1 \\[2ex] 0 & \text{otherwise} \end{cases} \tag{5.9.9}$$

In the same way, we can compute

$$\langle n \,|\, \hat{P} \,|\, k \rangle = i\sqrt{\frac{m\omega\hbar}{2}}\langle n \,|\, (\hat{a}^\dagger - \hat{a}) \,|\, k \rangle = i\sqrt{\frac{m\omega\hbar}{2}}\left(\langle n \,|\, \hat{a}^\dagger \,|\, k \rangle - \langle n \,|\, \hat{a} \,|\, k \rangle\right) \tag{5.9.10}$$

Now, using the relation in Eq. (5.9.6), we have

$$\langle n \,|\, \hat{P} \,|\, k \rangle = i\sqrt{\frac{m\omega\hbar}{2}}\left(\sqrt{k+1}\langle n \,|\, k+1 \rangle - \sqrt{k}\langle n \,|\, k-1 \rangle\right)$$

$$= i\sqrt{\frac{m\omega\hbar}{2}}\left(\sqrt{k+1}\,\delta_{n,k+1} - \sqrt{k}\,\delta_{n,k-1}\right) \tag{5.9.11}$$

So, we obtain

$$\langle n \,|\, \hat{P} \,|\, k \rangle = \begin{cases} i\sqrt{\dfrac{m\omega\hbar n}{2}} & k = n-1 \\[2ex] -i\sqrt{\dfrac{m\omega\hbar(n+1)}{2}} & k = n+1 \\[2ex] 0 & \text{otherwise} \end{cases} \tag{5.9.12}$$

We can express $\langle n \,|\, \hat{X} \,|\, k \rangle$ and $\langle n \,|\, \hat{P} \,|\, k \rangle$ in a matrix form as

$$\langle n \,|\, \hat{X} \,|\, k \rangle = \sqrt{\frac{\hbar}{2m\omega}} \begin{pmatrix} 0 & 1 & 0 & \cdots \\ 1 & 0 & \sqrt{2} & \cdots \\ 0 & \sqrt{2} & 0 & \sqrt{3} \cdots \\ 0 & 0 & \sqrt{3} & 0 \cdots \\ \vdots & \vdots & & \end{pmatrix} \tag{5.9.13}$$

and

$$\langle n \,|\, \hat{P} \,|\, k \rangle = i\sqrt{\frac{m\omega\hbar}{2}} \begin{pmatrix} 0 & -1 & 0 & \cdots \\ 1 & 0 & -\sqrt{2} & \cdots \\ 0 & \sqrt{2} & 0 & -\sqrt{3} \cdots \\ 0 & 0 & \sqrt{3} & 0 \cdots \\ \vdots & \vdots & & \end{pmatrix} \tag{5.9.14}$$

As expected, $\hat{X}$ and $\hat{P}$ are represented by Hermitian matrices.

5.10. Consider a one-dimensional oscillator in the nth energy level. Compute the expectation values

$$\langle \hat{X}^2 \rangle, \quad \langle \hat{X} \rangle, \quad \langle \hat{P}^2 \rangle, \quad \langle \hat{P} \rangle$$

What can you say about the uncertainty relation $\Delta x \Delta p$?

SOLUTION

Using the operators $\hat{a}$ and $\hat{a}^\dagger$, one can find that

$$\langle \hat{X}^2 \rangle = \frac{\hbar}{2m\omega}(2n+1) \tag{5.10.1}$$

$$\langle \hat{P}^2 \rangle = \frac{m\omega\hbar}{2}(2n+1) \tag{5.10.2}$$

and $\langle \hat{P} \rangle = 0$, $\langle \hat{X} \rangle = 0$. Therefore,

$$\Delta P = \sqrt{\langle \hat{P}^2 \rangle - \langle \hat{P} \rangle^2} = \sqrt{\frac{m\omega\hbar}{2}(2n+1)}$$

$$\Delta X = \sqrt{\langle \hat{X}^2 \rangle - \langle \hat{X} \rangle^2} = \sqrt{\frac{\hbar}{2m\omega}(2n+1)}$$

so

$$\Delta x \, \Delta p = \frac{\hbar}{2}(2n+1) \tag{5.10.3}$$

Hence, the ground state satisfies the minimum of the uncertainty relation:

$$\Delta x \, \Delta p = \frac{\hbar}{2} \tag{5.10.4}$$

5.11. The simplest molecular crystals are formed from noble gasses such as neon, argon, krypton, and xenon. The interaction between the ions in such a molecular crystal is approximated by the Lennard–Jones potential:

$$V(r) = 4V_0 \left[\left(\frac{\sigma}{r} \right)^{12} - \left(\frac{\sigma}{r} \right)^6 \right] \tag{5.11.1}$$

The values of V_0 and σ for the noble gasses are listed in Table 5.1.

Table 5.1

	Ne	Ar	Kr	Xe
V_0(eV)	0.003 1	0.010 4	0.014 0	0.020 0
σ(Å)	2.74	3.40	3.65	3.98

Find the approximate ground state energy of a single ion in such a crystal. Hint: The ion near the minimal value of $V(r)$ can be treated as a harmonic oscillator.

SOLUTION

We begin by approximating the potential $V(r)$ near the minima by a polynomial of the form

$$V(r) \approx V_m + \frac{k}{2}(r - r_m)^2 + O[(r - r_m)^3] \tag{5.11.2}$$

where V_m is the value of $V(r_m)$ and r_m are the minima. Hence,

$$\frac{dV(r)}{dr}\bigg|_{r=r_m} = 4V_0 \left(-12\frac{\sigma^{12}}{r_m^{13}} + 6\frac{\sigma^6}{r_m^7} \right) = 0 \Rightarrow r_m = 2^{1/6}\sigma \tag{5.11.3}$$

and thus $V(r_m) = -V_0$. Similarly,

$$k = \frac{d^2V(r)}{dr^2}\bigg|_{r=r_m} = 4V_0 \left(156\frac{\sigma^{12}}{r^{14}} - 42\frac{\sigma^6}{r^8} \right) = 36 \cdot 2^{2/3}\frac{V_0}{\sigma^2} \tag{5.11.4}$$

Now we can approximate the behavior of an ion in the crystal to the behavior of a harmonic oscillator. The ground state of a harmonic oscillator with potential $V(r) = U_0 + \left(\frac{k}{2} \right)(r - r_0)^2$ is

$$E_0 = \frac{\hbar\omega}{2} + U_0 = \frac{\hbar}{2}\sqrt{\frac{k}{m}} + U_0 \tag{5.11.5}$$

where m is the mass of the ion. Therefore,

$$E_0 \approx V_m + \frac{\hbar}{2}\sqrt{\frac{k}{m}} = \frac{3\hbar \cdot 2^{1/3}}{\sigma}\sqrt{\frac{V_0}{m}} - V_0 \tag{5.11.6}$$

SUPPLEMENTARY PROBLEMS

5.12. Show that the eigenfunctions of the harmonic oscillator in the ground state and in the first excited state have inflection points wherever the condition $V(x) = E$ is satisfied, i.e.,

$$\frac{m\omega^2}{2}x^2 = \hbar\omega\left(n + \frac{1}{2}\right) \tag{5.12.1}$$

5.13. Find the eigenenergies and eigenfunctions for a particle moving under the potential

$$V(x) = \begin{cases} \dfrac{m\omega^2}{2}x^2 & x > 0 \\[2mm] \infty & x \le 0 \end{cases} \tag{5.13.1}$$

Hint: It is easy to solve the Schrödinger equation for $x > 0$ and for $x < 0$ separately, and then demand that the eigenfunction for all values of x will be continuous.

Ans. The eigenfunctions are ϕ_n for n odd where ϕ_n are the eigenfunctions of the harmonic oscillator. The

corresponding eigenenergies are $E_n = \hbar\omega\left(n + \dfrac{1}{2}\right)$.

5.14. Consider an isotropic three-dimensional harmonic oscillator. (*a*) Perform a separation of variables and find the eigenstates of the system. (*b*) Find the eigenenergies and determine the degeneracy of the levels.

Ans. (*a*) $\psi(x, y, z) = \dfrac{1}{(\pi\lambda)^{3/2}}\dfrac{H_{n_1}(x)\,H_{n_2}(y)\,H_{n_3}(z)}{\sqrt{2^{(n_1+n_2+n_3)}n_1!\,n_2!\,n_3!}}\,e^{-(x^2+y^2+z^2)/2\lambda^2}$

(*b*) $g_n = \dfrac{(3-1+n)!}{n!(3-1)!} = \dfrac{(n+1)(n+2)}{2}$

5.15. The wavefunction of a harmonic oscillator at time $t = 0$ is

$$\psi(x, 0) = \sqrt{2}A\phi_1 + \frac{1}{\sqrt{2}}A\phi_2 + A\phi_3 \tag{5.15.1}$$

where ϕ_n is the stationary eigenfunction of the oscillator for the nth state and A is a normalization constant. (*a*) Compute the constant A. (*b*) Compute the eigenfunciton $\psi(x, t)$ for all values of t. (*c*) Calculate the average $\langle E \rangle$ at times $t = 0$, $t = \pi/\omega$, and $t = 2\pi/\omega$.

Ans. (*a*) $A = \sqrt{\dfrac{2}{7}}$; (*b*) $\psi(x, t) = \sqrt{\dfrac{2}{7}}\left(\sqrt{2}\phi_1 e^{-3i\omega t/2} + \dfrac{1}{\sqrt{2}}\phi_2 e^{-5i\omega t/2} + \phi_3 e^{-7i\omega t/2}\right)$;

(*c*) $\langle E \rangle\big|_{t=0} = \langle E \rangle\big|_{t=\frac{\pi}{\omega}} = \langle E \rangle\big|_{t=\frac{2\pi}{\omega}} = \dfrac{31}{14}\hbar\omega$

5.16. Consider an isotropic two-dimensional harmonic oscillator. (*a*) Write the stationary Schrödinger equation for the oscillator. Solve the equation in cartesian coordinates. (*b*) Write the stationary Schrödinger equation in polar coordinates and solve it for the ground state. Is this state degenerate?

Ans. (*a*) Schrödinger equation:

$$\frac{1}{2m}\left(\frac{\partial^2}{\partial x^2} + \frac{\partial^2}{\partial y^2}\right)\psi(x, y) + \frac{m\omega^2}{2}(x^2 + y^2)\psi(x, y) = E\psi(x, y) \tag{5.16.1}$$

$$\psi_{00}(x, y) = \sqrt{\frac{m\omega}{\pi\hbar}}\exp\left[-\frac{m\omega}{4}(x^2 + y^2)\right] \tag{5.16.2}$$

(*b*) Schrödinger equation:

$$\frac{1}{2m}\frac{1}{r}\frac{\partial}{\partial r}r\psi(r,\theta) + \frac{1}{r^2}\frac{\partial^2\psi(r,\theta)}{\partial\theta^2} + \frac{m\omega^2}{2}r^2\psi(r,\theta) = E\psi(r,\theta) \tag{5.16.3}$$

$$\psi_{00}(r,\theta) = \sqrt{\frac{m\omega}{\pi\hbar}}\exp\left(-\frac{m\omega}{4}r^2\right) \tag{5.16.4}$$

and the state is not degenerate (ground state).

5.17. Compute the matrix elements $\langle n|\hat{X}^2|m\rangle$ and $\langle n|\hat{P}^2|m\rangle$ for the one-dimensional harmonic oscillator.

Ans. $\langle n|\hat{X}^2|m\rangle = \frac{\hbar}{2m\omega}\begin{cases} \sqrt{m(m-1)} & n = m-2 \\ (2m+1) & n = m \\ \sqrt{(m+1)(m+2)} & n = m+2 \\ 0 & \text{otherwise} \end{cases}$ (5.17.1)

$\langle n|\hat{P}^2|m\rangle = -\frac{m\hbar\omega}{2}\begin{cases} \sqrt{m(m-1)} & n = m-2 \\ -(2m+1) & n = m \\ \sqrt{(m+1)(m+2)} & n = m+2 \\ 0 & \text{otherwise} \end{cases}$ (5.17.2)

5.18. Compute $\langle n|\hat{P}\hat{X}|m\rangle$ for the one-dimensional harmonic oscillator.

Ans. $\langle n|\hat{P}\hat{X}|m\rangle = \begin{cases} \dfrac{i\hbar}{2} & m = n \\ \dfrac{i\hbar}{2}\sqrt{(n-1)n} & m = n-2 \\ \dfrac{i\hbar}{2}\sqrt{(n+2)(n+1)} & m = n+2 \end{cases}$ (5.18.1)

5.19. Compute the matrix elements $\langle n|\hat{X}^3|m\rangle$ and $\langle n|\hat{X}^4|m\rangle$ for the one-dimensional harmonic oscillator.

Ans. $\langle n|\hat{X}^3|m\rangle = \begin{cases} \left(\dfrac{\hbar}{2m\omega}\right)^{3/2}\sqrt{(n+3)(n+2)(n+1)} & m = n+3 \\ 3\left(\dfrac{\hbar(n+1)}{2m\omega}\right)^{3/2} & m = n+1 \\ 3\left(\dfrac{\hbar n}{2m\omega}\right)^{3/2} & m = n-1 \\ \left(\dfrac{\hbar}{2m\omega}\right)^{3/2}\sqrt{n(n-1)(n-2)} & m = n-3 \end{cases}$ (5.19.1)

$\langle n|\hat{X}^4|m\rangle = \begin{cases} \left(\dfrac{\hbar}{2m\omega}\right)^2\sqrt{(n+1)(n+2)(n+3)(n+4)} & m = n+4 \\ 4\left(\dfrac{\hbar}{2m\omega}\right)^2 n\sqrt{(n+1)(n+2)} & m = n+2 \\ 2\left(\dfrac{\hbar}{2m\omega}\right)^2(3n^2+2n+1) & m = n \\ (4n-2)\left(\dfrac{\hbar}{2m\omega}\right)^2\sqrt{(n-1)n} & m = n-2 \\ \left(\dfrac{\hbar}{2m\omega}\right)^2\sqrt{n(n-1)(n-2)(n-3)} & m = n-4 \end{cases}$ (5.19.2)

CHAPTER 6

Angular Momentum

6.1 Introduction

In classical mechanics the angular momentum of a particle with linear momentum **p** and position **r** is defined as

$$\mathbf{L} = \mathbf{r} \times \mathbf{p} \tag{6.1}$$

where, in cartesian coordinates,

$$\mathbf{L} = (L_x, L_y, L_z) \qquad \mathbf{p} = (p_x, p_y, p_z) \qquad \mathbf{r} = (x, y, z) \tag{6.2}$$

By contrast, in quantum mechanics these observables are replaced by their corresponding quantum operators. Nowadays, there are three different notational schemes in common use. For example, the linear momentum operator is often written as $\hat{\mathbf{P}}$, **p**, or $\hat{\mathbf{p}}$. Here we will use the latter representation, which is slightly less prone to misinterpretation. Thus, the angular momentum operator is

$$\begin{cases} \hat{L}_x = \hat{y}\hat{p}_z - \hat{z}\hat{p}_y = -i\hbar \left(y\dfrac{\partial}{\partial z} - z\dfrac{\partial}{\partial y} \right) \\[3mm] \hat{L}_y = \hat{z}\hat{p}_x - \hat{x}\hat{p}_z = -i\hbar \left(z\dfrac{\partial}{\partial x} - x\dfrac{\partial}{\partial z} \right) \\[3mm] \hat{L}_z = \hat{x}\hat{p}_y - \hat{y}\hat{p}_x = -i\hbar \left(x\dfrac{\partial}{\partial y} - y\dfrac{\partial}{\partial x} \right) \end{cases} \tag{6.3}$$

and

$$\hat{L}^2 = \hat{L}_x^2 + \hat{L}_y^2 + \hat{L}_z^2 \tag{6.4}$$

In cartesian coordinates, the commutation relations between $\hat{L}_j (j = x, y, z)$ are

$$[\hat{L}_x, \hat{L}_y] = i\hbar\hat{L}_z \tag{6.5}$$

$$[\hat{L}_y, \hat{L}_z] = i\hbar\hat{L}_x \tag{6.6}$$

$$[\hat{L}_z, \hat{L}_x] = i\hbar\hat{L}_y \tag{6.7}$$

6.2 Commutation Relations

Using the commutation relations in Sec. 6.1, one can also find another useful commutation relation:

$$[\hat{L}^2, \hat{\mathbf{L}}] = 0 \Rightarrow [\hat{L}^2, \hat{L}_z] = [\hat{L}^2, \hat{L}_x] = [\hat{L}^2, \hat{L}_y] = 0 \tag{6.8}$$

$$[\hat{L}_i, \hat{r}_j] = i\hbar \sum_k \varepsilon_{ijk} \hat{L}_k \tag{6.9}$$

$$[\hat{L}_i, \hat{p}_j] = i\hbar \sum_k \varepsilon_{ijk} \hat{p}_k \tag{6.10}$$

$$[\hat{L}_i, \hat{p}^2] = [\hat{L}_i, \hat{r}^2] = [\hat{L}_i, \hat{\mathbf{r}} \cdot \hat{\mathbf{p}}] = 0 \tag{6.11}$$

where

$$\varepsilon_{ijk} = \begin{cases} 1 & ijk \text{ have cyclic permutation} \\ -1 & ijk \text{ have anticyclic permutation} \\ 0 & \text{otherwise} \end{cases}$$

6.3 Lowering and Raising Operators

We define the *raising operator* as

$$\hat{L}_+ = \hat{L}_x + i\hat{L}_y \tag{6.12}$$

Similarly, the *lowering operator* is defined as

$$\hat{L}_- = \hat{L}_x - i\hat{L}_y \tag{6.13}$$

so we can write

$$\hat{L}_x = \frac{\hat{L}_+ + \hat{L}_-}{2} \qquad \hat{L}_y = \frac{\hat{L}_+ - \hat{L}_-}{2i} \tag{6.14}$$

$\hat{L}_+$ and $\hat{L}_-$ are not Hermitian operators since it can be proved that

$$\hat{L}_+ = \hat{L}_-^\dagger \tag{6.15}$$

Moreover,

$$\hat{L}^2 = \hat{L}_z^2 + \frac{1}{2}(\hat{L}_+\hat{L}_- + \hat{L}_-\hat{L}_+) \tag{6.16}$$

and

$$\hat{L}_+\hat{L}_- = \hat{L}^2 - \hat{L}_z^2 + \hbar\hat{L}_z \tag{6.17}$$

$$\hat{L}_-\hat{L}_+ = \hat{L}^2 - \hat{L}_z^2 + \hbar\hat{L}_z \tag{6.18}$$

Thus, we have the commutation relations:

$$[\hat{L}^2, \hat{L}_\pm] = 0 \tag{6.19}$$

$$[\hat{L}_z, \hat{L}_\pm] = \pm\hbar\hat{L}_\pm \tag{6.20}$$

$$[\hat{L}_+, \hat{L}_-] = 2\hbar\hat{L}_z \tag{6.21}$$

The operators $\hat{L}_-$ and $\hat{L}_+$ enable us to represent all the eigenfunctions of $\hat{L}^2$ and $\hat{L}_z$ using only one eigenfunction and the operators $\hat{L}_+$ and $\hat{L}_-$.

6.4 Algebra of Angular Momentum

The operators $\hat{L}^2$ and $\hat{L}_z$ describe physical quantities and therefore, they must be Hermitian operators; that is,

$$(\hat{L}_i)^\dagger = \hat{L}_i \Rightarrow (\hat{L}^2)^\dagger = \hat{L}^2 \tag{6.22}$$

One can verify that $\hat{L}^2$ and $\hat{L}_z$ are commutative operators, $[\hat{L}^2, \hat{L}_z] = 0$ [see Problem 6.2, part (*a*)]; it is thus possible to find the simulation eigenfunctions of both $\hat{L}^2$ and $\hat{L}_z(|lm\rangle)$, which constitute a complete orthonormal basis:

$$\hat{L}^2 \,|\, lm\rangle = l(l+1)\hbar^2 \,|\, lm\rangle \tag{6.23}$$

$$\hat{L}_z \,|\, lm\rangle = m\hbar \,|\, lm\rangle \tag{6.24}$$

Applying the raising and lowering operators to $|\, lm\rangle$ gives

$$\hat{L}_+ \,|\, lm\rangle = \sqrt{l(l+1) - m(m+1)}\,\hbar \,|\, l, m+1\rangle = \sqrt{(l-m)(l+m+1)}\,\hbar \,|\, l, m+1\rangle \tag{6.25}$$

$$\hat{L}_- \,|\, lm\rangle = \sqrt{l(l+1) - m(m-1)}\,\hbar \,|\, l, m-1\rangle = \sqrt{(l+m)(l-m+1)}\,\hbar \,|\, l, m-1\rangle \tag{6.26}$$

Note that if $|\, lm\rangle$ is an eigenvector of $\hat{L}^2$ with eigenvalue $l(l+1)$, then for a fixed l there are $(2l+1)$ possible eigenvalues for $\hat{L}_z$:

$$m = -l, -l+1, \ldots, 0, \ldots, l-1, l \tag{6.27}$$

Thus,

$$\hat{L}_+ \,|\, l, l\rangle = 0 \tag{6.28}$$

$$\hat{L}_- \,|\, l, -l\rangle = 0 \tag{6.29}$$

The basis $|\, lm\rangle$ is orthonormal, i.e,

$$\langle l_1 m_1 \,|\, l_2 m_2\rangle = \delta_{l_1 l_2}\delta_{m_1 m_2} \tag{6.30}$$

This basis is called the *standard basis*. The closure relation for the standard basis is

$$\sum_{l=0}^{\infty}\sum_{m=-l}^{l} |\, lm\rangle\langle lm \,| = \hat{I} \tag{6.31}$$

6.5 Differential Representations

The representation of eigenvectors and eigenvalues is often more convenient using spherical coordinates:

$$x = r\sin\theta\cos\varphi \qquad y = r\sin\theta\sin\varphi \qquad z = r\cos\theta \tag{6.32}$$

The representation of the angular momentum operators in spherical coordinates is

$$\begin{cases} \hat{L}_x = i\hbar\left(\sin\varphi\dfrac{\partial}{\partial\theta} + \dfrac{\cos\varphi}{\tan\theta}\dfrac{\partial}{\partial\varphi}\right) \\[2mm] \hat{L}_y = i\hbar\left(-\cos\varphi\dfrac{\partial}{\partial\theta} + \dfrac{\sin\varphi}{\tan\theta}\dfrac{\partial}{\partial\varphi}\right) \\[2mm] \hat{L}_z = -i\hbar\dfrac{\partial}{\partial\varphi} \end{cases} \tag{6.33}$$

which yields

$$\hat{L}^2 = -\hbar^2\left(\frac{\partial^2}{\partial\theta^2} + \frac{1}{\tan\theta}\frac{\partial}{\partial\theta} + \frac{1}{\sin^2\theta}\frac{\partial^2}{\partial\varphi^2}\right) \tag{6.34}$$

$$\hat{L}_+ = \hbar e^{i\varphi}\left(\frac{\partial}{\partial\theta} + i\cot\theta\frac{\partial}{\partial\varphi}\right) \tag{6.35}$$

$$\hat{L}_- = \hbar e^{-i\varphi}\left(-\frac{\partial}{\partial\theta} + i\cot\theta\frac{\partial}{\partial\varphi}\right) \tag{6.36}$$

Thus, the eigenvectors of $\hat{L}^2$ and $\hat{L}_z$ are functions that depend on the angles θ and φ only; hence, we can represent the wavefunction as

$$\psi(r, \theta, \varphi) = R(r)Y_l^m(\theta, \varphi) \tag{6.37}$$

For a central potential $V(\mathbf{r}) = V(r)$, we find that $Y_l^m(\theta, \varphi)$ are the *spherical harmonics*, where

$$|lm\rangle = Y_l^m(\theta, \varphi) \tag{6.38}$$

The algebraic representation of $Y_l^m(\theta, \varphi)$ for $m > 0$ is

$$Y_l^m(\theta, \varphi) = (-1)^m\sqrt{\frac{2l+1}{4\pi}\frac{(l-m)!}{(l+m)!}}\,P_l^m(\cos\theta)e^{im\varphi} \tag{6.39}$$

and for $m < 0$,

$$Y_l^m(\theta, \varphi) = (-1)^{|m|}\sqrt{\frac{2l+1}{4\pi}\frac{(l-|m|)!}{(l+m)!}}\,P_l^{|m|}(\cos\theta)e^{im\varphi} \tag{6.40}$$

$P_l^m(x)$ are the associated Legendre functions defined by

$$P_l^m(x) = \sqrt{(1-x^2)^m}\,\frac{d^m}{dx^m}P_l(x) \tag{6.41}$$

where $P_l(x)$ are the Legendre polynomials,

$$P_l(x) = \frac{(-1)^l}{2^l l!}\frac{d^l}{dx^l}(x^2-1)^l \tag{6.42}$$

This is known as the *Rodrigues formula*.

Note that the $Y_l^m(\theta, \varphi)$ are uniquely defined except for sign, which is changeable. The spherical harmonic functions, the associated Legendre functions, and Legendre polynomials are described in detail in the Mathematical Appendix.

6.6 Matrix Representation of an Angular Momentum

We have already mentioned in Chap. 4 that an operator can be represented in matrix form; this representation depends on the basis vectors (eigenvectors) that we choose. For an angular momentum operator, we usually use the standard basis $|lm\rangle$, so every matrix element A_{ij} that represents the operator $\hat{A}$ satisfies

$$A_{ij} = \langle li | \hat{A} | lj \rangle \tag{6.43}$$

Thus, for every l = constant, we can write a $(2l + 1) \times (2l + 1)$ matrix for $\hat{L}^2$, $\hat{L}_x$, $\hat{L}_y$, and $\hat{L}_z$; that is,

$$(\hat{L}^2)_{ij} = \langle li | \hat{L}^2 | lj \rangle = l(l + 1)\hbar^2 \delta_{ij} \tag{6.44}$$

$$(\hat{L}_z)_{ij} = \langle li | \hat{L}_z | lj \rangle = j\hbar \delta_{ij} \tag{6.45}$$

$$(\hat{L}_x)_{ij} = \langle li | \hat{L}_x | lj \rangle = \frac{\hbar}{2}\left[\sqrt{(l - m)(l + m + 1)}\,\delta_{i,j+1} + \sqrt{(l + m)(l - m + 1)}\,\delta_{i,j-1}\right] \tag{6.46}$$

$$(\hat{L}_y)_{ij} = \langle li | \hat{L}_y | lj \rangle = \frac{\hbar}{2}\left[\sqrt{(l - m)(l + m + 1)}\,\delta_{i,j+1} - \sqrt{(l + m)(l - m + 1)}\,\delta_{i,j-1}\right] \tag{6.47}$$

For the case when $l = 1$, we have

$$\hat{L}^2 = 2\hbar^2 \begin{matrix} & \begin{matrix} |11\rangle & |10\rangle & |1-1\rangle \end{matrix} & \\ \begin{pmatrix} 1 & 0 & 0 \\ 0 & 1 & 0 \\ 0 & 0 & 1 \end{pmatrix} & \begin{matrix} |11\rangle \\ |10\rangle \\ |1-1\rangle \end{matrix} \end{matrix} \tag{6.48}$$

and

$$\hat{L}_x = \frac{\hbar}{\sqrt{2}}\begin{pmatrix} 0 & 1 & 0 \\ 1 & 0 & 1 \\ 0 & 1 & 0 \end{pmatrix} \qquad \hat{L}_y = \frac{\hbar}{\sqrt{2}}\begin{pmatrix} 0 & -i & 0 \\ i & 0 & -i \\ 0 & i & 0 \end{pmatrix}$$

$$\hat{L}_z = \hbar \begin{pmatrix} 1 & 0 & 0 \\ 0 & 0 & 0 \\ 0 & 0 & -1 \end{pmatrix} \tag{6.49}$$

6.7 Spherical Symmetry Potentials

From classical mechanics we know that when a spherical symmetry potential $V(x, y, z) = V(r)$ acts on a particle, its angular momentum is a constant of motion. In terms of quantum mechanics, this means that the angular momentum operator $\hat{L}^2$ commutes with the Hamiltonian:

$$\hat{H} = \frac{\hat{p}^2}{2m} + \hat{V}(r) = -\frac{\hbar^2}{2m}\frac{1}{r^2}\frac{\partial}{\partial r}\left(r^2 \frac{\partial}{\partial r}\right) + \frac{\hat{L}^2}{2mr^2} + \hat{V}(r) \tag{6.50}$$

where the angular dependence of the Hamiltonian is found only in $\hat{L}^2$. We can thus split the wavefunction in two: an angular part depending only on θ and φ, and a radial part depending only on r (see Problems 6.16 and 6.18).

6.8 Angular Momentum and Rotations

Let $|\psi\rangle$ be a state vector of a system in a certain coordinate system O. To represent the state vector in another coordinate system O' we define the *rotation operator* $\hat{U}_R$, such that the state vector in O' is given by

$$|\psi'\rangle = \hat{U}_R |\psi\rangle \tag{6.51}$$

For a system O' obtained by the rotation of O around an axis in the direction of the unit vector **n** through an angle θ, $\hat{U}_R$ is given as

$$\hat{U}_R(\theta, \mathbf{n}) = \exp\left(-\frac{i}{\hbar}\theta\,\mathbf{n}\cdot\hat{\mathbf{L}}\right) \tag{6.52}$$

where $\hat{\mathbf{L}}$ is the angular momentum operator. $\hat{\mathbf{L}}$ is said to be a *generator of rotation*. One can conclude from the definition that

$$\langle\psi'| = \langle\psi|\hat{U}_R^{\dagger} \tag{6.53}$$

Note that to obtain $\hat{U}_R$ we usually use the infinitesimal rotation operator:

$$\hat{U}_R(d\theta, \mathbf{n}) = 1 - \frac{i}{\hbar}d\theta\,\hat{\mathbf{L}}\cdot\mathbf{n} \tag{6.54}$$

Also note that

$$\hat{U}_R(2\pi, \mathbf{n}) = \hat{U}_R(0, \mathbf{n}) = \hat{I} \tag{6.55}$$

$\hat{U}_R$ can be used as a rotation operator not only for state vectors, but also for other operators or observables. Thus, an observable $\hat{A}$ in the system O is transformed to $\hat{A}$ in the system O' such that

$$\hat{A}' = \hat{U}_R\hat{A}\hat{U}_R^{\dagger} \tag{6.56}$$

Or similarly,

$$\hat{A} = \hat{U}_R^{\dagger}\hat{A}'\hat{U}_R \tag{6.57}$$

SOLVED PROBLEMS

6.1. Using the definition of angular momentum, $\mathbf{L} = \mathbf{r} \times \mathbf{p}$, prove the following commutation relations: $(a)\,[\hat{L}_i, \hat{r}_j] = i\hbar\sum_k \varepsilon_{ijk}\hat{r}_k; (b)\,[\hat{L}_i, \hat{L}_j] = i\hbar\sum_k \varepsilon_{ijk}\hat{L}_k\,(i, j, k = x, y, z)$. Note that if $\hat{\mathbf{A}}$ and $\hat{\mathbf{B}}$ are vector operators, then the kth component of the vector operator $\hat{\mathbf{A}} \times \hat{\mathbf{B}}$ is

$$(\hat{\mathbf{A}} \times \hat{\mathbf{B}})_k = \sum_{ij} \varepsilon_{ijk}\hat{A}_i\hat{B}_j \tag{6.1.1}$$

Also use the identity $\sum_k \varepsilon_{ijk}\varepsilon_{mnk} = \delta_{im}\delta_{jn} - \delta_{in}\delta_{jm}$.

SOLUTION

(a) Using the definition $\mathbf{L} = \mathbf{r} \times \mathbf{p}$ we obtain $\hat{L}_i = \sum_{kl}\varepsilon_{kli}\hat{r}_k\hat{p}_l$; thus,

$$[\hat{L}_i, \hat{r}_j] = \sum_{kl}\varepsilon_{kli}[\hat{r}_k\hat{p}_l, \hat{r}_j] = \sum_{kl}\varepsilon_{kli}(\hat{r}_k[\hat{p}_l, \hat{r}_j] + [\hat{r}_k, \hat{r}_j]\hat{p}_l) \tag{6.1.2}$$

Using the commutation relations $[\hat{r}_k, \hat{r}_j] = 0$ and $[\hat{p}_l, \hat{r}_j] = -i\hbar\delta_{lj}$, where

$$\delta_{lj} = \begin{cases} 1 & l = j \\ 0 & \text{otherwise} \end{cases} \tag{6.1.3}$$

we obtain

$$[\hat{L}_i, \hat{r}_j] = \sum_{kl} \varepsilon_{kji}(-i\hbar)\delta_{lj}\hat{r}_k = -i\hbar\sum_k \varepsilon_{kji}\hat{r}_k = -i\hbar\sum_k \varepsilon_{ikj}\hat{r}_k = i\hbar\sum_k \varepsilon_{ijk}\hat{r}_k \tag{6.1.4}$$

(b) We decompose the commutation relation $[\hat{L}_i, \hat{L}_j] = i\hbar\sum_k \varepsilon_{ijk}\hat{L}_k$ into the following three commutation

relations: $[\hat{L}_x, \hat{L}_y] = i\hbar\hat{L}_z$; $[\hat{L}_y, \hat{L}_z] = i\hbar\hat{L}_x$; and $[\hat{L}_z, \hat{L}_x] = i\hbar\hat{L}_y$. Note that

$$\hat{L}_x = (\hat{\mathbf{r}} \times \hat{\mathbf{p}})_x = \hat{r}_y\hat{p}_z - \hat{r}_z\hat{p}_y \qquad \hat{L}_y = (\hat{\mathbf{r}} \times \hat{\mathbf{p}})_y = \hat{r}_z\hat{p}_x - \hat{r}_x\hat{p}_z \tag{6.1.5}$$

Thus,

$$\begin{aligned}[\hat{L}_x, \hat{L}_y] &= [\hat{r}_y\hat{p}_z - \hat{r}_z\hat{p}_y, \hat{r}_z\hat{p}_x - \hat{r}_x\hat{p}_z] \\ &= [\hat{r}_y\hat{p}_z, \hat{r}_z\hat{p}_x] - [\hat{r}_y\hat{p}_z, \hat{r}_x\hat{p}_z] - [\hat{r}_z\hat{p}_y, \hat{r}_z\hat{p}_x] + [\hat{r}_z\hat{p}_y, \hat{r}_x\hat{p}_y] \end{aligned} \tag{6.1.6}$$

We compute each part separately:

$$\begin{aligned}[\hat{r}_y\hat{p}_z, \hat{r}_z\hat{p}_x] &= \hat{r}_y[\hat{p}_z, \hat{r}_z\hat{p}_x] + [\hat{r}_y, \hat{r}_z\hat{p}_x]\hat{p}_z \\ &= \hat{r}_y(\hat{r}_z[\hat{p}_z, \hat{p}_x] + [\hat{p}_z, \hat{r}_z]\hat{p}_x) + (\hat{r}_z[\hat{r}_y, \hat{p}_x] + [\hat{r}_y, \hat{r}_z]\hat{p}_x)\hat{p}_z \end{aligned} \tag{6.1.7}$$

Now, using the known relations

$$[\hat{p}_z, \hat{p}_x] = 0 \qquad [\hat{p}_z, \hat{r}_z] = -i\hbar \qquad [\hat{r}_y, \hat{p}_x] = 0 \qquad [\hat{r}_y, \hat{r}_z] = 0 \tag{6.1.8}$$

we obtain $[\hat{r}_y\hat{p}_z, \hat{r}_z\hat{p}_x] = -i\hbar\hat{r}_y\hat{p}_x$. Similarly,

$$\begin{aligned}[\hat{r}_y\hat{p}_z, \hat{r}_x\hat{p}_z] &= \hat{r}_y[\hat{p}_z, \hat{r}_x\hat{p}_z] + [\hat{r}_y, \hat{r}_x\hat{p}_z]\hat{p}_z \\ &= \hat{r}_y(\hat{r}_x[\hat{p}_z, \hat{p}_z] + [\hat{p}_z, \hat{r}_x]\hat{p}_z) + ([\hat{r}_y, \hat{r}_x]\hat{p}_z + \hat{r}_x[\hat{r}_y, \hat{p}_z])\hat{p}_z = 0 \end{aligned} \tag{6.1.9}$$

and

$$\begin{aligned}[\hat{r}_z\hat{p}_y, \hat{r}_z\hat{p}_x] &= \hat{r}_z[\hat{p}_y, \hat{r}_z\hat{p}_x] + [\hat{r}_z, \hat{r}_z\hat{p}_x]\hat{p}_y \\ &= \hat{r}_z([\hat{p}_y, \hat{r}_z]\hat{p}_x + \hat{r}_z[\hat{p}_y, \hat{p}_x]) + ([\hat{r}_z, \hat{r}_z]\hat{p}_x + \hat{r}_z[\hat{r}_z, \hat{p}_x])\hat{p}_y = 0 \end{aligned} \tag{6.1.10}$$

Also,

$$\begin{aligned}[\hat{r}_z\hat{p}_y, \hat{r}_x\hat{p}_z] &= \hat{r}_z[\hat{p}_y, \hat{r}_x\hat{p}_z] + [\hat{r}_z, \hat{r}_x\hat{p}_z]\hat{p}_y \\ &= \hat{r}_z([\hat{p}_y, \hat{r}_x]\hat{p}_z + \hat{r}_x[\hat{p}_y, \hat{p}_z]) + ([\hat{r}_z, \hat{r}_x]\hat{p}_z + \hat{r}_x[\hat{r}_z, \hat{p}_z])\hat{p}_y = i\hbar\hat{r}_x\hat{p}_y \end{aligned} \tag{6.1.11}$$

Thus, we obtain

$$[\hat{L}_x, \hat{L}_y] = i\hbar(\hat{r}_x\hat{p}_y - \hat{r}_y\hat{p}_x) = i\hbar(\hat{\mathbf{r}} \times \hat{\mathbf{p}})_z = i\hbar\hat{L}_z \tag{6.1.12}$$

We leave it to the reader to prove the other two relations.

6.2. Prove the following relations for the angular momentum operator: (a) $[\hat{L}^2, \hat{L}_z] = 0$; (b) $\hat{\mathbf{L}} \times \hat{\mathbf{L}} = i\hbar\hat{\mathbf{L}}$.

SOLUTION

(a) The operator $\hat{L}^2$ can be written as $\hat{L}^2 = \hat{L}_x^2 + \hat{L}_y^2 + \hat{L}_z^2$, and hence

$$[\hat{L}^2, \hat{L}_z] = [\hat{L}_x^2 + \hat{L}_y^2 + \hat{L}_z^2, \hat{L}_z] = [\hat{L}_x^2, \hat{L}_z] + [\hat{L}_y^2, \hat{L}_z] + [\hat{L}_z^2, \hat{L}_z] \tag{6.2.1}$$

SOLUTION

(*a*) Consider the operators $\hat{L}^2$ and $\hat{L}_z$. They operate only on the part of the function that depends on the angles φ and θ. Note that we can write ψ as

$$\psi(r, t = 0) = -\sqrt{\frac{8\pi}{3}} Nr \exp\left(\frac{-r^2}{2r_0^2}\right) Y_1^1(x, y, z) \tag{6.13.3}$$

Hence, we see that the possible values in a measurement of $\hat{L}^2$ and $\hat{L}_z$ are $2\hbar^2$ and $\hbar$, respectively, with a probability of 100 percent (since $\hat{L}^2$ and $\hat{L}_z$ operate only on $Y_1^1(x, y, z)$, which is an eigenfunction of these operators with these eigenvalues).

(*b*) Consider a system K' in which the x', y', and z' axes are parallel to the x, y, and z axes of our system. In this system the operator $\hat{L}_{z'}$ is similar to $\hat{L}_x$ in K; thus the eigenfunction of $\hat{L}_{z'}$ is also the eigenfunction of $\hat{L}_x$ with the following substitutions: $x' \to y$; $y' \to z$; $z' \to x$. The eigenfunction of $\hat{L}_{z'}$ is

$$(Y_1^1(x', y', z'))_{L_{z'}} = -\sqrt{\frac{3}{8\pi}} \frac{\xi'}{r'} = -\sqrt{\frac{3}{8\pi}} \frac{x' + iy'}{\sqrt{x'^2 + y'^2 + z'^2}} \tag{6.13.4}$$

Therefore, the eigenfunction of $\hat{L}_x$ is

$$(Y_1^1(x, y, z))_{L_x} = -\sqrt{\frac{3}{8\pi}} \frac{y + iz}{\sqrt{x^2 + y^2 + z^2}} = -\sqrt{\frac{3}{8\pi}} \frac{y + iz}{r} \tag{6.13.5}$$

Since $\hat{L}^2$ commutes with $\hat{L}_z$ and $\hat{L}_x$, $(Y_1^1)_{L_x}$ is an eigenfunction of $\hat{L}_x$; it is also an eigenfunction of $\hat{L}^2$. Similarly,

$$(Y_0^1)_{L_x} = \sqrt{\frac{3}{4\pi}} \frac{x}{r} \qquad (Y_1^{-1})_{L_x} = \sqrt{\frac{3}{8\pi}} \frac{y - iz}{r} \tag{6.13.6}$$

(*c*) Following parts (*a*) and (*b*), we use the expansion theorem to write (see Chap. 4)

$$\psi(r, t = 0) = Nr \exp\left(-\frac{r^2}{2r_0^2}\right) \sqrt{\frac{4\pi}{3}} \left((Y_0^1)_{L_x} + \frac{i}{\sqrt{2}}\left[(Y_1^{-1})_{L_x} + (Y_1^1)_{L_x}\right]\right) \tag{6.13.7}$$

Consider only the part of ψ that is an eigenfunction of $\hat{L}_x$ and $\hat{L}^2$:

$$P(x, y, z) = \alpha\left((Y_0^1)_{L_x} + \frac{i}{\sqrt{2}}\left[(Y_1^{-1})_{L_x} - (Y_1^1)_{L_x}\right]\right) \tag{6.13.8}$$

where α is a normalization constant, $\langle P | P \rangle = \alpha^2\left(1 + \frac{1}{2} + \frac{1}{2}\right) = 1 \Rightarrow \alpha = \frac{1}{\sqrt{2}}$. Therefore,

$$P(x, y, z) = \frac{1}{\sqrt{2}}\left((Y_0^1)_{L_x} + \frac{i}{\sqrt{2}}\left[(Y_1^{-1})_{L_x} - (Y_1^1)_{L_x}\right]\right) \tag{6.13.9}$$

The values expected from the measurements of $\hat{L}_x$ and $\hat{L}^2$ are therefore as follows: For $\hat{L}^2 = 2\hbar^2$ and $\hat{L}_x = 0$, the probability is $\left|\langle (Y_0^1)_{L_x} | P \rangle\right|^2 = \frac{1}{2}$. For $\hat{L}^2 = 2\hbar^2$ and $\hat{L}_x = \hbar$, the probability is $\left|\langle (Y_1^1)_{L_x} | P \rangle\right|^2 = \frac{1}{4}$. Finally, for $\hat{L}^2 = 2\hbar^2$ and $\hat{L}_x = -\hbar$, the probability is $\left|\langle (Y_1^{-1})_{L_x} | P \rangle\right|^2 = \frac{1}{4}$.

6.14. Consider a particle in a spherical and infinite potential energy well:

$$V(r) = \begin{cases} 0 & 0 \leq r \leq a \\ \infty & a < r \end{cases} \tag{6.14.1}$$

(*a*) Write the differential equations of the radial and angular parts, and solve the angular equation.
(*b*) Compute the energy levels and the stationary wave equation for $l = 0$.

SOLUTION

(*a*) We begin by writing the Hamiltonian of the system:

$$\hat{H} = \frac{\hat{p}^2}{2m} + V(r) = -\frac{\hbar^2}{2m}\nabla^2 + V(r) \tag{6.14.2}$$

where ∇^2 in spherical coordinates is

$$\nabla^2 = \frac{1}{r}\frac{\partial^2}{\partial r^2}(r) + \frac{1}{r^2}\left[\frac{1}{\sin\theta}\frac{\partial}{\partial\theta}\left(\sin\theta\frac{\partial}{\partial\theta}\right) + \frac{1}{\sin^2\theta}\frac{\partial^2}{\partial\varphi^2}\right] = \frac{1}{r}\frac{\partial^2}{\partial r^2}(r) - \frac{\hat{L}^2}{\hbar^2 r^2} \tag{6.14.3}$$

Thus,

$$\hat{H} = -\frac{\hbar^2}{2m}\frac{1}{r}\frac{\partial^2}{\partial r^2}(r) + \frac{\hat{L}^2}{2mr^2} + V(r) \tag{6.14.4}$$

The differential equation for the stationary wavefunction $\psi(r,\theta,\varphi)$ is

$$\hat{H}\psi = -\frac{\hbar^2}{2m}\frac{1}{r}\frac{\partial^2}{\partial r^2}(r\psi) + \frac{\hat{L}^2\psi}{2mr^2} + V(r)\psi = E\psi \tag{6.14.5}$$

It is evident that $[\hat{H}, \hat{L}^2] = 0$; hence, we write $\psi(r,\theta,\varphi) = R_{nl}(r)Y_l^m(\theta,\varphi)$ and obtain

$$-\frac{\hbar^2}{2m}\frac{Y_l^m(\theta,\varphi)}{r}\frac{\partial^2}{\partial r^2}[rR_{nl}(r)] + \frac{R_{nl}(r)\hat{L}^2 Y_l^m(\theta,\varphi)}{2mr^2} + R_{nl}(r)V(r)Y_l^m(\theta,\varphi) = ER_{nl}(r)Y_l^m(\theta,\varphi) \tag{6.14.6}$$

Since $Y_l^m(\theta,\varphi)$ is the eigenfunction of $\hat{L}^2$,

$$\hat{L}^2 Y_l^m(\theta,\varphi) = \hbar^2 l(l+1)Y_l^m(\theta,\varphi)$$

Hence, the radial equation is

$$-\frac{\hbar^2}{2m}\frac{1}{r}\frac{\partial^2}{\partial r^2}[rR_{nl}(r)] + \left[\frac{\hbar^2}{2mr^2}l(l+1) + V(r)\right]R_{nl}(r) = ER_{nl}(r) \tag{6.14.7}$$

(*b*) For $l = 0$, we have

$$-\frac{\hbar^2}{2m}\frac{1}{r}\frac{\partial^2}{\partial r^2}[rR_{n0}(r)] + V(r)R_{n0}(r) = ER_{n0}(r) \tag{6.14.8}$$

We denote $R_{n0}(r) = R(r)$. For $r > a$, the function must vanish [because $V(r)$ is infinite]; therefore, we have for $0 \le r \le a$:

$$-\frac{\hbar^2}{2m}\frac{1}{r}\frac{\partial^2}{\partial r^2}(rR(r)) = ER(r) \tag{6.14.9}$$

We substitute $U(r) = rR(r)$; hence, $-\frac{\hbar^2}{2m}\frac{\partial^2 U}{\partial r^2} = EU(r)$, or

$$\frac{\partial^2 U}{\partial r^2} + \frac{2mE}{\hbar^2}U(r) = 0 \tag{6.14.10}$$

The solution of Eq. (6.14.10) is

$$U(r) = A\cos(kr) + B\sin(kr) \tag{6.14.11}$$

where $k = \sqrt{2mE/\hbar^2}$. A and B are constants that can be determined using the boundary conditions:

1. The value of U vanishes on $r = 0$: $U(r=0) = [rR(r)]\big|_{r=0} = 0$.
2. The value of U vanishes on $r = a$: $U(r=a) = [rR(r)]\big|_{r=a} = 0$.

Thus, from the first condition we have $U(0) = A = 0$, and using the second condition,

$$U(a) = B\sin(ka) = 0 \Rightarrow ka = n\pi \tag{6.14.12}$$

we obtain

$$E_n = \frac{\pi^2 \hbar^2}{2ma^2} n^2 \tag{6.14.13}$$

Finally, to compute the value of B we use the normalization condition of the wavefunction $R(r)$:

$$R(r) = \frac{U(r)}{r} = \begin{cases} B \dfrac{\sin(kr)}{r} & 0 \le r \le a \\ 0 & \text{otherwise} \end{cases} \tag{6.14.14}$$

Hence,

$$\int_0^\infty |R(r)|^2 4\pi r^2 \, dr = \int_0^a 4\pi B^2 \frac{\sin^2(kr)}{r^2} r^2 \, dr = 4\pi B^2 \int_0^a \sin(kr)\, dr$$

$$= \frac{4\pi B^2}{k} \left[-\frac{1}{2} \cos x \sin x + \frac{1}{2} x \right]_0^{\left|\begin{array}{c} ka=n\pi \end{array}\right.} = \frac{2n\pi^2 B^2}{n\pi/a} = 1 \tag{6.14.15}$$

so $B = \dfrac{1}{\sqrt{2\pi a}}$. Thus, for $l = 0$ we have

$$\psi(r, \theta, \varphi) = R(r) = \frac{1}{\sqrt{2\pi a}} \frac{1}{r} \sin\left(\sqrt{\frac{2mE}{\hbar^2}} r \right) \tag{6.14.16}$$

6.15. Consider the classical Hamiltonian of a three-dimensional isotropic harmonic oscillator:

$$H = \frac{1}{2m}(p_x^2 + p_y^2 + p_z^2) + \frac{m\omega^2}{2}(x^2 + y^2 + z^2) \tag{6.15.1}$$

(*a*) Write the Hamiltonian in spherical coordinates. (*b*) Find the eigenfunctions of the Hamiltonian in spherical coordinates. (*c*) Find the energy eigenvalues.

SOLUTION

(*a*) We begin by writing

$$\hat{p}_x^2 + \hat{p}_x^2 + \hat{p}_x^2 = -\hbar^2 \left(\frac{\partial^2}{\partial x^2} + \frac{\partial^2}{\partial y^2} + \frac{\partial^2}{\partial z^2} \right) = -\hbar^2 \nabla^2 \tag{6.15.2}$$

which, in spherical coordinates, becomes

$$-\hbar^2 \nabla^2 = -\hbar^2 \left[\frac{1}{r} \frac{\partial^2 (r)}{\partial r^2} + \frac{1}{r^2 \sin\theta} \frac{\partial}{\partial \theta}\left(\sin\theta \frac{\partial}{\partial \theta} \right) + \frac{1}{r^2 \sin^2\theta} \frac{\partial^2}{\partial \varphi^2} \right] \tag{6.15.3}$$

Using $\hat{L}^2 = -\hbar^2 \left[\dfrac{1}{\sin\theta} \dfrac{\partial}{\partial\theta}\left(\sin\theta \dfrac{\partial}{\partial\theta} \right) + \dfrac{1}{\sin^2\theta} \dfrac{\partial^2}{\partial\varphi^2} \right]$, we arrive at

$$-\hbar^2 \nabla^2 = -\frac{\hbar^2}{r} \frac{\partial^2 (r)}{\partial r^2} + \frac{\hat{L}^2}{r^2} \tag{6.15.4}$$

In spherical coordinates, the Hamiltonian is therefore

$$\hat{H} = -\frac{\hbar^2}{2m} \frac{1}{r} \frac{\partial^2 (r)}{\partial r^2} + \frac{\hat{L}^2}{2mr^2} + \frac{m\omega^2}{2} r^2 \tag{6.15.5}$$

(*b*) The angular dependence of the Hamiltonian comes only from $\hat{L}^2$; therefore, writing the eigenfunction in the form $\psi(r, \theta, \varphi) = R(r)Y_l^m(\theta, \varphi)$, we have

$$\hat{H}\psi = -\frac{\hbar^2}{2m}\frac{Y_l^m(\theta, \varphi)}{r}\frac{d^2}{dr^2}(rR(r)) + \frac{R(r)}{2mr^2}\hat{L}^2 Y_l^m(\theta, \varphi) + \frac{m\omega^2}{2}r^2 R(r)Y_l^m = E\psi \qquad (6.15.6)$$

or

$$\hat{H}R(r)Y_l^m = -\frac{\hbar^2}{2m}\frac{Y_l^m}{r}\frac{d^2}{dr^2}(rR(r)) + \frac{\hbar^2 l(l+1)}{2mr^2}R(r)Y_l^m + \frac{m\omega^2}{2}R(r)Y_l^m + \frac{m\omega^2}{2}r^2 R(r)Y_l^m$$

$$= ER(r)Y_l^m \qquad (6.15.7)$$

We get the radial equation

$$-\frac{\hbar^2}{2m}\frac{1}{r}\frac{d^2}{dr^2}(rR(r)) + \left[\frac{\hbar^2 l(l+1)}{2mr^2} + \frac{m\omega^2}{2}r^2\right]R(r) = ER(r) \qquad (6.15.8)$$

By substituting $u(r) = rR(r)$, Eq. (6.15.8) becomes

$$-\frac{\hbar^2}{2m}\frac{1}{r}\frac{d^2 u}{dr^2} + \left(\frac{\hbar^2 l(l+1)}{2mr^3} + \frac{m\omega^2}{2}r\right)u(r) = E\frac{u(r)}{r}$$

or

$$\left[\frac{d^2}{dr^2} - \frac{l(l+1)}{r^2} - \frac{m^2\omega^2}{\hbar^2}r^2 + \frac{2mE}{\hbar^2}\right]u(r) = 0 \qquad (6.15.9)$$

We denote $\beta^2 \equiv \dfrac{m^2\omega^2}{\hbar^2}$ and $\varepsilon \equiv \dfrac{2mE}{\hbar^2}$; so, we obtain

$$\left[\frac{d^2}{dr^2} - \frac{l(l+1)}{r^2} - \beta^2 r^2 + \varepsilon\right]u(r) = 0 \qquad (6.15.10)$$

Note that for large r, the dominant part of Eq. (6.15.10) is $\left(\dfrac{d^2}{dr^2} - \beta^2 r^2\right)u(r) = 0$. Therefore, for larger r,

$$u(r) \sim g(r)e^{-\beta r^2/2} \qquad (6.15.11)$$

Let us compute

$$\frac{d^2 u}{dr^2} = \frac{d}{dr}(g'e^{-\beta r^2/2} - \beta r g e^{-\beta r^2/2})$$

$$= (g''e^{-\beta r^2/2} - \beta g e^{-\beta r^2/2} - 2\beta r g' e^{-\beta r^2/2} + \beta^2 r^2 g e^{-\beta r^2/2})$$

$$= (g'' - \beta g - \beta r g' + \beta^2 r^2 g)e^{-\beta r^2/2} \qquad (6.15.12)$$

Hence, we have

$$\left[g'' - \beta g - 2\beta r g' + \beta^2 r^2 g - \frac{l(l+1)g}{r^2} - \beta^2 r^2 g - \varepsilon g\right]e^{-\beta r^2/2} = 0 \qquad (6.15.13)$$

The differential equation for $g(r)$ is

$$g'' - 2\beta r g' + (\varepsilon - \beta)g - \frac{l(l+1)}{r^2}g = 0 \qquad (6.15.14)$$

We substitute $g(r) = r^s \sum_{n=0}^{\infty} a_n r^n$ (for $a_0 \neq 0$), so $g' = \sum_{n=0}^{\infty} a_n (n+s) r^{s+n-1}$, and

$$g'' = \sum_{n=0}^{\infty} a_n (n+s)(n+s-1) r^{s+n-2} = \sum_{n=-2}^{\infty} a_{n+2}(n+s+2)(n+s+1) r^{s+n} \tag{6.15.15}$$

Note that $\dfrac{g}{r^2} = \sum_{n=0}^{\infty} a_n r^{s+n-2} = \sum_{n=-2}^{\infty} a_{n+2} r^{s+n}$, so Eq. (6.15.4) becomes

$$\sum_{n=-2}^{\infty} a_{n+2}[(n+s+2)(n+s+1) - l(l+1)] r^{s+n} + \sum_{n=0}^{\infty} a_n[-2\beta(n+s) + \varepsilon - \beta] r^{s+n} = 0 \tag{6.15.16}$$

For $n = -2$, we have $[s(s-1) - l(l+1)] a_0 = 0$. Since $a_0 \neq 0$, it follows that $s = l+1$. For $n = -1$, we have $[(s+1) s - l(l+1)] a_1 = 0$. Since $s = l+1$, we obtain $a_1 = 0$; so,

$$a_{n+2} = \frac{\varepsilon - 3\beta - 2\beta(n+l)}{(n+l+3)(n+l+2) - l(l+1)} a_n \tag{6.15.17}$$

(c) The eigenfunction must be bounded for large r, so we must demand that $g(r)$ be a polynomial of a finite degree; i.e., we set $a_{n_0} = 0$ for a certain n_0:

$$\frac{\varepsilon - 3\beta - 2\beta(n_0 + l)}{(n_0 + l + 3)(n_0 + l + 2) - l(l+1)} = 0 \tag{6.15.18}$$

or $\varepsilon = 3\beta + 2\beta(n_0 + l) = 2mE_{n_0}/\hbar^2$. Thus, the energy eigenvalues are

$$E_{n'l} = \frac{\hbar^2}{2m}[3\beta + 2\beta(n'+l)] = \frac{\hbar^2}{2m}\frac{m\omega}{\hbar}[3 + 2(n'+l)] = \left(\frac{3}{2} + n' + l\right)\hbar\omega \tag{6.15.19}$$

6.16. Consider the infinitesimal rotation operator:

$$\hat{U}_R(d\theta, \mathbf{n}) = \hat{I} - d\theta \hat{\mathbf{L}} \cdot \mathbf{n} \tag{6.16.1}$$

where $\mathbf{n}$ is a unit vector. Find the rotation operator for a finite angle θ. Hint: Define $d\theta = \theta/N$ for $N \to \infty$.

SOLUTION

Let $|\psi\rangle$ be a state vector in a coordinate system O. The state vector in coordinate system O' that rotates around $\mathbf{n}$ by an angle θ (relative to O) is

$$|\psi'\rangle = [\hat{U}_R(d\theta, \mathbf{n})]^N |\psi\rangle \tag{6.16.2}$$

Hence, the rotation operator for a finite angle θ is $\hat{U}_R(\theta, \mathbf{n}) = [\hat{U}_R(d\theta, \mathbf{n})]^N$. Defining $d\theta = \theta/N$, we arrive at

$$\hat{U}_R(\theta, \mathbf{n}) = \lim_{N \to \infty} \left(\hat{I} - \frac{i}{\hbar}\hat{\mathbf{L}} \cdot \mathbf{n} \frac{\theta}{N}\right)^N \tag{6.16.3}$$

Recall that $\lim_{N \to \infty} \left(1 + \dfrac{\alpha}{N}\right)^N = e^\alpha$; using this identity we finally obtain

$$\hat{U}_R(\theta, \mathbf{n}) = \lim_{N \to \infty} \left[\hat{I} + \frac{1}{N}\left(\frac{-i\hat{\mathbf{L}} \cdot \mathbf{n}}{\hbar}\theta\right)\right]^N = \exp\left(-\frac{i}{\hbar}\theta \hat{\mathbf{L}} \cdot \mathbf{n}\right) \tag{6.16.4}$$

6.17. (*a*) Refer to Problem 6.16 and compute the rotation operator around **n** = **j**, which is a unit vector in the *y*-direction, for $l = 1$. (*b*) Use the rotation operator obtained in part (*a*), and find the representation of the eigenvectors of $\hat{L}_x$ in the standard basis of $\hat{L}_z$.

SOLUTION

(*a*) Consider the rotation operator $\hat{U}_R = \exp\left(-\dfrac{i\theta}{\hbar}\hat{\mathbf{L}}\cdot\mathbf{n}\right)$. For **n** = **j**, we obtain

$$\hat{U}_R = \exp\left(-\frac{i}{\hbar}\theta\hat{L}_y\right) = \sum_{n=0}^{\infty}\frac{1}{n!}\left(-\frac{1}{\hbar}\theta\hat{L}_y\right)^n \tag{6.17.1}$$

Let us compute

$$\frac{\hat{L}_y}{\hbar} = \frac{1}{\sqrt{2}}\begin{pmatrix}0 & -i & 0\\ i & 0 & -i\\ 0 & i & 0\end{pmatrix} = \frac{i}{\sqrt{2}}\begin{pmatrix}0 & -1 & 0\\ 1 & 0 & -1\\ 0 & 1 & 0\end{pmatrix} \tag{6.17.2}$$

$$\left(\frac{\hat{L}_y}{\hbar}\right)^2 = -\frac{1}{2}\begin{pmatrix}-1 & 0 & 1\\ 0 & -2 & 0\\ 1 & 0 & -1\end{pmatrix} \tag{6.17.3}$$

and

$$\left(\frac{\hat{L}_y}{\hbar}\right)^3 = -\frac{i}{\sqrt{8}}\begin{pmatrix}0 & 2 & 0\\ -2 & 0 & 2\\ 0 & -2 & 0\end{pmatrix} = \frac{i}{\sqrt{2}}\begin{pmatrix}0 & -1 & 0\\ 1 & 0 & -1\\ 0 & 1 & 0\end{pmatrix} = \frac{\hat{L}_y}{\hbar} \tag{6.17.4}$$

so we obtain

$$\hat{U}_R = \hat{I} + \sum_{n=0}^{\infty}\frac{(-i\theta)^{2n+1}}{(2n+1)!}\left(\frac{\hat{L}_y}{\hbar}\right) + \sum_{n=1}^{\infty}\frac{(-i\theta)^{2n}}{(2n)!}\left(\frac{\hat{L}_y}{\hbar}\right)^2$$

$$= \hat{I} - i\frac{\hat{L}_y}{\hbar}\sum_{n=0}^{\infty}\frac{(-1)^n\theta^{2n+1}}{(2n+1)!} + \left(\frac{\hat{L}_y}{\hbar}\right)^2\sum_{n=1}^{\infty}\frac{(-1)^n\theta^{2n}}{(2n)!} \tag{6.17.5}$$

Note that

$$\sin\theta = \sum_{n=0}^{\infty}\frac{(-1)^n\theta^{2n+1}}{(2n+1)!} \qquad \cos\theta - 1 = \sum_{n=1}^{\infty}\frac{(-1)^n\theta^{2n}}{(2n)!} \tag{6.17.6}$$

therefore,

$$\hat{U}_R = \hat{I} - i\sin\theta\frac{\hat{L}_y}{\hbar} + (\cos\theta - 1)\left(\frac{\hat{L}_y}{\hbar}\right)^2 \tag{6.17.7}$$

or

$$\hat{U}_R = \begin{pmatrix}1 & 0 & 0\\ 0 & 1 & 0\\ 0 & 0 & 1\end{pmatrix} + \frac{\sin\theta}{\sqrt{2}}\begin{pmatrix}0 & -1 & 0\\ 1 & 0 & -1\\ 0 & 1 & 0\end{pmatrix} - (\cos\theta - 1)\begin{pmatrix}-1 & 0 & 1\\ 0 & -2 & 0\\ 1 & 0 & -1\end{pmatrix}$$

$$= \begin{pmatrix}\dfrac{1+\cos\theta}{2} & -\dfrac{\sin\theta}{\sqrt{2}} & \dfrac{1-\cos\theta}{2}\\[2mm] \dfrac{\sin\theta}{\sqrt{2}} & \cos\theta & -\dfrac{\sin\theta}{\sqrt{2}}\\[2mm] \dfrac{1-\cos\theta}{2} & \dfrac{\sin\theta}{\sqrt{2}} & \dfrac{1+\cos\theta}{2}\end{pmatrix} \tag{6.17.8}$$

(b) To obtain the eigenvectors of $\hat{L}_x$ by using the eigenvectors of $\hat{L}_z$, we must rotate the eigenvectors of $\hat{L}_z$ by $\theta = \pi/2$; hence, in this case, where **j** is a unit vector in the y direction, we have

$$\hat{U}_R(\pi/2, \mathbf{j}) = \begin{pmatrix} 1/2 & -1/\sqrt{2} & 1/2 \\ 1/\sqrt{2} & 0 & -1/\sqrt{2} \\ 1/2 & 1/\sqrt{2} & 1/2 \end{pmatrix} \tag{6.17.9}$$

Thus,

$$|1\rangle_x = \hat{U}_R\left(\frac{\pi}{2}, \mathbf{j}\right)|1\rangle \qquad |0\rangle_x = \hat{U}_R\left(\frac{\pi}{2}, \mathbf{j}\right)|0\rangle \qquad |-1\rangle_x = \hat{U}_R\left(\frac{\pi}{2}, \mathbf{j}\right)|-1\rangle \tag{6.17.10}$$

where

$$|1\rangle = \begin{pmatrix} 1 \\ 0 \\ 0 \end{pmatrix} \qquad |0\rangle = \begin{pmatrix} 0 \\ 1 \\ 0 \end{pmatrix} \qquad |-1\rangle = \begin{pmatrix} 0 \\ 0 \\ 1 \end{pmatrix} \tag{6.17.11}$$

are the standard basis. Therefore,

$$|1\rangle_x = \begin{pmatrix} 1/2 \\ 1/\sqrt{2} \\ 1/2 \end{pmatrix} = \frac{1}{2}|1\rangle + \frac{1}{\sqrt{2}}|0\rangle + \frac{1}{2}|-1\rangle \tag{6.17.12}$$

$$|0\rangle_x = \begin{pmatrix} -1/\sqrt{2} \\ 0 \\ 1/\sqrt{2} \end{pmatrix} = -\frac{1}{\sqrt{2}}(|1\rangle - |-1\rangle) \tag{6.17.13}$$

and

$$|-1\rangle_x = \begin{pmatrix} 1/2 \\ -1/\sqrt{2} \\ 1/2 \end{pmatrix} = \frac{1}{2}|1\rangle - \frac{1}{\sqrt{2}}|0\rangle + \frac{1}{2}|-1\rangle \tag{6.17.14}$$

SUPPLEMENTARY PROBLEMS

6.18. Prove the following relations: (a) $[\hat{L}_i, \hat{p}_j] = i\hbar \sum_k \varepsilon_{ijk}\hat{p}_k$. (b) $[\hat{L}_i, \hat{p}^2] = [\hat{L}_i, \hat{r}^2] = [\hat{L}_i, \hat{\mathbf{r}} \cdot \hat{\mathbf{p}}] = 0$.

Recall that i, j, and k can assume the values x, y, and z, and that ε_{ijk} is

$$\varepsilon_{ijk} = \begin{cases} 1 & ijk \text{ cyclic permutation of } xyz \\ -1 & ijk \text{ anticyclic permutation of } xyz \\ 0 & \text{otherwise} \end{cases} \tag{6.18.1}$$

Hint: By definition, $\mathbf{L} = \mathbf{r} \times \mathbf{p}$ and use $\hat{L}_k = (\hat{\mathbf{r}} \times \hat{\mathbf{p}})_k = \sum_{i,j} \varepsilon_{ijk}\hat{r}_i\hat{p}_j$.

6.19. Prove the following relations for the angular momentum operator: (a) $\hat{L}^2 = \hat{L}_+\hat{L}_-\hat{p} - \hbar\hat{L}_z + \hat{L}_z^2$; (b) $[\hat{L}_z, \hat{L}_\pm] = \pm\hbar\hat{L}_\pm$.

6.20. Show that if the matrices of $\hat{L}_x$ and $\hat{L}_y$ are real, i.e.,

$$\langle lm|\hat{L}_x|l'm'\rangle^* = \langle lm|\hat{L}_x|l'm'\rangle \qquad \langle lm|\hat{L}_y|l'm'\rangle^* = \langle lm|\hat{L}_y|l'm'\rangle \tag{6.20.1}$$

then the matrix of $\hat{L}_z$ is imaginary, $\langle lm|\hat{L}_z|l'm'\rangle^* = \langle lm|\hat{L}_z|l'm'\rangle$. Hint: Recall that $[\hat{L}_x, \hat{L}_y] = i\hbar\hat{L}_z$.

6.21. For a system with an angular momentum $l = 1$, find the eigenvalues and eigenvectors of $\hat{L}_x\hat{L}_y + \hat{L}_y\hat{L}_x$.

Ans. $|v_1\rangle = |1, 0\rangle; |v_2\rangle = \frac{1}{\sqrt{2}}(i|1, 1\rangle + |1, -1\rangle); |v_3\rangle = \frac{1}{\sqrt{2}}(-i|1, 1\rangle + |1, -1\rangle)$

6.22. In a system with an angular momentum $l = 1$, the eigenvalues of $\hat{L}_z$ are given by $|+1\rangle$, $|0\rangle$, and $|-1\rangle$, where

$$\hat{L}_z\,|+1\rangle = \hbar\,|+1\rangle \qquad \hat{L}_z\,|-1\rangle = -\hbar\,|-1\rangle \qquad \hat{L}_z = |0\rangle \tag{6.22.1}$$

The Hamiltonian is $\hat{H} = \dfrac{\omega_0}{\hbar}(\hat{L}_x^2 - \hat{L}_y^2)$, where ω_0 is a constant. Find (*a*) The matrix representation of $\hat{H}$ in the basis $|+1\rangle$, $|0\rangle$, and $|-1\rangle$; (*b*) the eigenvalues and the eigenvectors.

Ans.   (*a*) $\quad |+1\rangle \; |0\rangle \; |-1\rangle$

$$\hat{H} = \hbar\omega_0 \begin{pmatrix} 1 & 0 & 0 \\ 0 & 2 & 0 \\ 0 & 0 & 1 \end{pmatrix} \begin{matrix} |+1\rangle \\ |0\rangle \\ |-1\rangle \end{matrix}$$

     (*b*) The eigenvalues and eigenstates are $\omega_0\hbar$ ($|+1\rangle$), $2\omega_0\hbar$ ($|0\rangle$), and $\omega_0\hbar(|-1\rangle)$.

6.23. Prove that, in spherical coordinates, the operators $\hat{L}_x$, $\hat{L}_y$, and $\hat{L}_z$ are written as

$$\begin{cases} \hat{L}_x = -\dfrac{\hbar}{i}\left(\sin\varphi\,\dfrac{\partial}{\partial\varphi} + \cos\varphi\,\cot\theta\,\dfrac{\partial}{\partial\varphi} \right) \\[2mm] \hat{L}_y = \dfrac{\hbar}{i}\left(\cos\varphi\,\dfrac{\partial}{\partial\theta} - \sin\varphi\,\cot\theta\,\dfrac{\partial}{\partial\varphi} \right) \\[2mm] \hat{L}_z = \dfrac{\hbar}{i}\,\dfrac{\partial}{\partial\varphi} \end{cases} \tag{6.23.1}$$

6.24. The Hamiltonian of a three-dimensional isotropic harmonic oscillator is

$$H = \frac{1}{2m}(p_x^2 + p_y^2 + p_z^2) + \frac{1}{2}m\omega^2(x^2 + y^2 + z^2) \tag{6.24.1}$$

Calculate the following commutation relations: (*a*) $[\hat{H}, \hat{L}_z]$; (*b*) $[\hat{H}, \hat{H}_z]$; (*c*) $[\hat{L}, \hat{H}_z]$, where $\hat{H}_z = \dfrac{1}{2m}\hat{p}_z^2 + \dfrac{1}{2}m\omega^2 z^2$.

Ans.   (*a*) $[\hat{H}, \hat{L}_z] = 0$; (*b*) $[\hat{H}, \hat{H}_z] = 0$; (*c*) $[\hat{L}, \hat{H}_z] = 0$.

6.25. Prove that the time derivative of the mean value of the angular momentum operator $\hat{\mathbf{L}}$ is given by

$$\frac{d\langle\hat{\mathbf{L}}\rangle}{dt} = -\langle\hat{\mathbf{r}} \times \nabla V\rangle \tag{6.25.1}$$

where V is the potential. What can you say about the time derivative of $\hat{\mathbf{L}}$ for a central potential?

Ans.   For a central potential, $\nabla V \propto \hat{\mathbf{r}} \Rightarrow \hat{\mathbf{r}} \times \nabla V = 0$, and the time derivative of $\hat{\mathbf{L}}$ vanishes; thus, the eigenvalues of $\hat{L}^2$ are time-independent.

6.26. Use the following data to compute $P_4(x)$: (*a*) $P_4(x)$ is a polynomial of the fourth degree; (*b*) $P_4(1) = 1$; (*c*) $P_4(x)$ is orthogonal to $1, x, x^2$, and x^3; i.e., $\displaystyle\int_{-1}^{1} x^k P_4(x)\,dx = 0$ for $k = 0, 1, 2, 3$. Hint: Choose $P_4(x)$ to be of the form $P_4(x) = \displaystyle\sum_{k=0}^{4} C_k x^k$.

Ans. $P_4(x) = \dfrac{1}{8}(35x^4 + 30x^2 + 3)$.

6.27. Let $|\psi\rangle$ be a state function of a certain system and $\hat{U}_R(\theta, \mathbf{n})$ be a rotation operator with angle θ around $\mathbf{n}$ ($\mathbf{n}$ is a unit vector), so that $|\psi'\rangle = \hat{U}_R|\psi\rangle$ is the state function rotated by angle θ about $\mathbf{n}$. Using a matrix representation, show that for $l = 1$, $\hat{U}_R(\theta, \mathbf{n}) = \exp\left(-\dfrac{i}{\hbar}\theta\mathbf{n}\cdot\hat{\mathbf{L}}\right)$ (this operator is the rotation operator for all values of l).

CHAPTER 7

Spin

7.1 Definitions

Spin is an intrinsic property of particles. This property was deduced from the Stern-Gerlach experiment. The formal definition of the spin operator $\hat{\mathbf{S}}$ is analogous to the angular momentum operator (see Chap. 6),

$$\hat{S}^2 |\alpha\rangle = s(s+1)\hbar^2 |\alpha\rangle \tag{7.1}$$

$|\alpha\rangle$ being an eigenfunction of $\hat{S}^2$ and $s(s+1)$ the corresponding eigenvalues. We also define

$$\hat{S}^2 = \hat{S}_x^2 + \hat{S}_y^2 + \hat{S}_z^2 \tag{7.2}$$

where $\hat{S}_x$, $\hat{S}_y$, and $\hat{S}_z$ obey the following commutation relations:

$$[\hat{S}_x, \hat{S}_y] = i\hbar \hat{S}_z \qquad [\hat{S}_y, \hat{S}_z] = i\hbar \hat{S}_x \qquad [\hat{S}_z, \hat{S}_x] = i\hbar \hat{S}_y \tag{7.3}$$

Analogous to angular momentum, the quantum number of spin in the z direction is $m_s = -s, -s+1, \ldots, +s$, and

$$\hat{S}_z |\alpha\rangle = m_s \hbar |\alpha\rangle \tag{7.4}$$

7.2 Spin 1/2

For particles (an electron, for example) with spin 1/2 we have $m_s = \pm 1/2$ and two distinct eigenvectors of $\hat{S}^2$ and $\hat{S}_z$ denoted by $\left|+\frac{1}{2}\right\rangle$ and $\left|-\frac{1}{2}\right\rangle$. These eigenvectors are called the *standard basis*, where

$$\hat{S}^2 \left|\pm\tfrac{1}{2}\right\rangle = \frac{3}{4}\hbar^2 \left|\pm\tfrac{1}{2}\right\rangle \qquad \hat{S}_z \left|\pm\tfrac{1}{2}\right\rangle = \pm\frac{\hbar}{2}\left|\pm\tfrac{1}{2}\right\rangle \tag{7.5}$$

As its name implies, it is this basis that is usually used, though alternative bases are available. Any wavefunction in the spin space can be written as a linear combination of the standard basis.

7.3 Pauli Matrices

The Pauli matrices $\hat{\sigma} = (\hat{\sigma}_x, \hat{\sigma}_y, \hat{\sigma}_z)$ are defined using

$$\hat{\mathbf{S}} = \frac{\hbar}{2}\hat{\sigma} \tag{7.6}$$

where

$$\hat{\sigma}_x = \begin{pmatrix} 0 & 1 \\ 1 & 0 \end{pmatrix} \qquad \hat{\sigma}_y = \begin{pmatrix} 0 & -i \\ i & 0 \end{pmatrix} \qquad \hat{\sigma}_z = \begin{pmatrix} 1 & 0 \\ 0 & -1 \end{pmatrix} \tag{7.7}$$

S is written in the standard basis. The commutation relations of the Pauli matrices are

$$[\hat{\sigma}_x, \hat{\sigma}_y] = 2i\hat{\sigma}_z \qquad [\hat{\sigma}_y, \hat{\sigma}_z] = 2i\hat{\sigma}_x \qquad [\hat{\sigma}_z, \hat{\sigma}_x] = 2i\hat{\sigma}_y \tag{7.8}$$

Other useful relations for the Pauli matrices are

$$\hat{\sigma}_x^2 = \hat{\sigma}_y^2 = \hat{\sigma}_z^2 = \hat{I} \tag{7.9}$$

and also

$$(\hat{\sigma} \cdot \mathbf{A})(\hat{\sigma} \cdot \mathbf{B}) = (\mathbf{A} \cdot \mathbf{B})\hat{I} + i\hat{\sigma} \cdot (\mathbf{A} \times \mathbf{B}) \tag{7.10}$$

where **A** and **B** are two spatial vectors.

7.4 Lowering and Raising Operators

Analogously to the angular momentum, we define the raising and lowering spin operators:

$$\hat{S}_+ = \hat{S}_x + i\hat{S}_y \qquad \hat{S}_- = \hat{S}_x - i\hat{S}_y \tag{7.11}$$

where

$$\hat{S}_+\left|+\tfrac{1}{2}\right\rangle = 0 \qquad \hat{S}_-\left|+\tfrac{1}{2}\right\rangle = \hbar\left|-\tfrac{1}{2}\right\rangle \tag{7.12}$$

$$\hat{S}_+\left|-\tfrac{1}{2}\right\rangle = \hbar\left|+\tfrac{1}{2}\right\rangle \qquad \hat{S}_-\left|-\tfrac{1}{2}\right\rangle = 0 \tag{7.13}$$

7.5 Rotations in the Spin Space

To find the representation of a state $|\alpha\rangle$ in a given coordinate system that is rotated by an angle θ around an axis in the direction of the unit vector **u** (see Fig. 7.1), we compute

$$|\alpha\rangle' = \exp\left(-\frac{i}{\hbar}\theta\mathbf{u} \cdot \hat{\mathbf{S}}\right)|\alpha\rangle \tag{7.14}$$

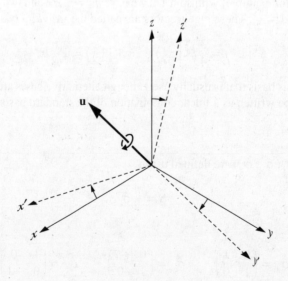

Fig. 7.1

Thus, the rotation matrix is

$$\hat{U}_R = \exp\left(-\frac{i}{\hbar}\theta\mathbf{u}\cdot\hat{\mathbf{S}}\right) = \begin{pmatrix} \cos(\theta/2) & -\sin(\theta/2)e^{-i\varphi} \\ \sin(\theta/2)e^{i\varphi} & \cos(\theta/2) \end{pmatrix} \tag{7.15}$$

Notice that for $\varphi = 0$ (rotation around the z axis) we have

$$\hat{U}_R = \begin{pmatrix} \cos(\theta/2) & -\sin(\theta/2) \\ \sin(\theta/2) & \cos(\theta/2) \end{pmatrix} \tag{7.16}$$

which is a rotation of $\theta/2$ around the z axis. The rotation of a *spin vector* differs from that of a spatial vector. This result is unique to the spin vector and can thus be used to define a spin vector. A spin vector is called a *spinor*.

7.6   Interaction with a Magnetic Field

Consider a system consisting of particles with a spin $\hat{\mathbf{S}}$. Applying a magnetic field $\mathcal{B}$ will introduce an additional term to the free Hamiltonian $\hat{H}_0$, so that

$$\hat{H} = \hat{H}_0 + \hat{H}_{\text{int}} = \hat{H}_0 + \frac{e\mathcal{B}}{mc}\cdot\hat{\mathbf{S}} \tag{7.17}$$

SOLVED PROBLEMS

7.1. Calculate the commutation relation $[\hat{\sigma}_i, \hat{\sigma}_j]$, where $j = x, y, z$ and $\hat{\sigma}_i$ are the Pauli matrices.

SOLUTION

We begin by considering the Pauli matrices:

$$\hat{\sigma}_x = \begin{pmatrix} 0 & 1 \\ 1 & 0 \end{pmatrix} \qquad \hat{\sigma}_y = \begin{pmatrix} 0 & -i \\ i & 0 \end{pmatrix} \qquad \hat{\sigma}_z = \begin{pmatrix} 1 & 0 \\ 0 & -1 \end{pmatrix}$$

Therefore, we see that

$$[\hat{\sigma}_x, \hat{\sigma}_y] = \hat{\sigma}_x\hat{\sigma}_y - \hat{\sigma}_y\hat{\sigma}_x = \begin{pmatrix} 0 & 1 \\ 1 & 0 \end{pmatrix}\begin{pmatrix} 0 & -i \\ i & 0 \end{pmatrix} - \begin{pmatrix} 0 & -i \\ i & 0 \end{pmatrix}\begin{pmatrix} 0 & 1 \\ 1 & 0 \end{pmatrix}$$

$$= \begin{pmatrix} i & 0 \\ 0 & -i \end{pmatrix} - \begin{pmatrix} -i & 0 \\ 0 & i \end{pmatrix} = 2i\begin{pmatrix} 1 & 0 \\ 0 & -1 \end{pmatrix} = 2i\hat{\sigma}_z \tag{7.1.1}$$

Also,

$$[\hat{\sigma}_y, \hat{\sigma}_z] = \hat{\sigma}_y\hat{\sigma}_z - \hat{\sigma}_z\hat{\sigma}_y = \begin{pmatrix} 0 & -i \\ i & 0 \end{pmatrix}\begin{pmatrix} 1 & 0 \\ 0 & -1 \end{pmatrix} - \begin{pmatrix} 1 & 0 \\ 0 & -1 \end{pmatrix}\begin{pmatrix} 0 & -i \\ i & 0 \end{pmatrix}$$

$$= \begin{pmatrix} 0 & i \\ i & 0 \end{pmatrix} - \begin{pmatrix} 0 & -i \\ -i & 0 \end{pmatrix} = 2i\hat{\sigma}_x \tag{7.1.2}$$

and, finally,

$$[\hat{\sigma}_z, \hat{\sigma}_x] = \hat{\sigma}_z\hat{\sigma}_x - \hat{\sigma}_x\hat{\sigma}_z = \begin{pmatrix} 1 & 0 \\ 0 & -1 \end{pmatrix}\begin{pmatrix} 0 & 1 \\ 1 & 0 \end{pmatrix} - \begin{pmatrix} 0 & 1 \\ 1 & 0 \end{pmatrix}\begin{pmatrix} 1 & 0 \\ 0 & -1 \end{pmatrix}$$

$$= \begin{pmatrix} 0 & 1 \\ -1 & 0 \end{pmatrix} - \begin{pmatrix} 0 & -1 \\ 1 & 0 \end{pmatrix} = 2i\hat{\sigma}_y \tag{7.1.3}$$

So, we conclude that

$$[\hat{\sigma}_i, \hat{\sigma}_j] = 2i\varepsilon_{ijk}\hat{\sigma}_k \tag{7.1.4}$$

where

$$\varepsilon_{ijk} = \begin{cases} 1 & ijk \text{ have cyclic permutation} \\ -1 & ijk \text{ have anticyclic permutation} \\ 0 & \text{otherwise} \end{cases} \tag{7.1.5}$$

7.2. Using the basis vectors of $\hat{S}_z$ eigenvectors, calculate $\hat{S}_i|+\frac{1}{2}\rangle$ and $\hat{S}_i|-\frac{1}{2}\rangle$ $(i = x, y, z)$, where $|+\frac{1}{2}\rangle$ and $|-\frac{1}{2}\rangle$ are the eigenvectors of $\hat{S}_z$ with eigenvalues $+\hbar/2$ and $-\hbar/2$, respectively.

SOLUTION

The basis vectors of $\hat{S}_z$ eigenvectors are (see Sec. 4.2)

$$\hat{S}_x = \frac{\hbar}{2}\begin{pmatrix} 0 & 1 \\ 1 & 0 \end{pmatrix} \qquad \hat{S}_y = \frac{\hbar}{2}\begin{pmatrix} 0 & -i \\ i & 0 \end{pmatrix} \qquad \hat{S}_z = \frac{\hbar}{2}\begin{pmatrix} 1 & 0 \\ 0 & -1 \end{pmatrix} \tag{7.2.1}$$

and $\hat{\mathbf{S}} = \dfrac{\hbar}{2}\hat{\sigma}$. Denoting $|+\frac{1}{2}\rangle \equiv \begin{pmatrix} 1 \\ 0 \end{pmatrix}$, $|-\frac{1}{2}\rangle \equiv \begin{pmatrix} 0 \\ 1 \end{pmatrix}$, we write

$$\hat{S}_x|+\tfrac{1}{2}\rangle = \frac{\hbar}{2}\begin{pmatrix} 0 & 1 \\ 1 & 0 \end{pmatrix}\begin{pmatrix} 1 \\ 0 \end{pmatrix} = \frac{\hbar}{2}\begin{pmatrix} 0 \\ 1 \end{pmatrix} = \frac{\hbar}{2}|-\tfrac{1}{2}\rangle \tag{7.2.2}$$

$$\hat{S}_x|-\tfrac{1}{2}\rangle = \frac{\hbar}{2}\begin{pmatrix} 0 & 1 \\ 1 & 0 \end{pmatrix}\begin{pmatrix} 0 \\ 1 \end{pmatrix} = \frac{\hbar}{2}\begin{pmatrix} 1 \\ 0 \end{pmatrix} = \frac{\hbar}{2}|+\tfrac{1}{2}\rangle \tag{7.2.3}$$

Note that $\hat{S}_x$ produces a transition between the eigenstates of $\hat{S}_z$, so that when $\hat{S}_x$ operates on one eigenstate it produces a multiple of the other. Similarly, for $\hat{S}_y$:

$$\hat{S}_y|+\tfrac{1}{2}\rangle = \frac{\hbar}{2}\begin{pmatrix} 0 & -i \\ i & 0 \end{pmatrix}\begin{pmatrix} 1 \\ 0 \end{pmatrix} = \frac{\hbar}{2}\begin{pmatrix} 0 \\ i \end{pmatrix} = \frac{\hbar i}{2}|-\tfrac{1}{2}\rangle \tag{7.2.4}$$

$$\hat{S}_y|-\tfrac{1}{2}\rangle = \frac{\hbar}{2}\begin{pmatrix} 0 & -i \\ i & 0 \end{pmatrix}\begin{pmatrix} 0 \\ 1 \end{pmatrix} = \frac{\hbar}{2}\begin{pmatrix} -i \\ 0 \end{pmatrix} = -\frac{\hbar}{2}|+\tfrac{1}{2}\rangle \tag{7.2.5}$$

And so, as expected,

$$\hat{S}_z|+\tfrac{1}{2}\rangle = \frac{\hbar}{2}\begin{pmatrix} 1 & 0 \\ 0 & -1 \end{pmatrix}\begin{pmatrix} 1 \\ 0 \end{pmatrix} = \frac{\hbar}{2}\begin{pmatrix} 1 \\ 0 \end{pmatrix} = \frac{\hbar}{2}|+\tfrac{1}{2}\rangle \tag{7.2.6}$$

$$\hat{S}_z|-\tfrac{1}{2}\rangle = \frac{\hbar}{2}\begin{pmatrix} 0 & 1 \\ 1 & 0 \end{pmatrix}\begin{pmatrix} 0 \\ 1 \end{pmatrix} = -\frac{\hbar}{2}\begin{pmatrix} 0 \\ 1 \end{pmatrix} = -\frac{\hbar}{2}|-\tfrac{1}{2}\rangle \tag{7.2.7}$$

7.3. (a) If the z component of an electron spin is $+\hbar/2$, what is the probability that its component along a direction z' that forms an angle θ with the z axis equals $+\hbar/2$ or $-\hbar/2$ (see Fig. 7.2)? (b) What is the average value of the spin along z'?

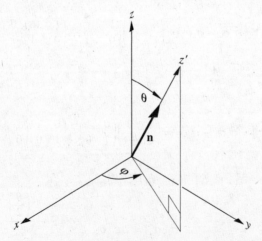

Fig. 7.2

SOLUTION

(*a*) The present state of the electron is $\left|+\frac{1}{2}\right\rangle$; the spin operator component along z' is

$$\hat{S}_{z'} = \hat{\mathbf{S}} \cdot \mathbf{n} = \frac{\hbar}{2} \hat{\sigma} \cdot \mathbf{n} \tag{7.3.1}$$

where $\mathbf{n}$ is a unit vector along z'. In our case $\mathbf{n} = \mathbf{i}\sin\theta\cos\varphi + \mathbf{j}\sin\theta\sin\varphi + \mathbf{k}\cos\theta$ and therefore,

$$\hat{S}_{z'} = \hat{S}_x \sin\theta\cos\varphi + \hat{S}_y \sin\theta\sin\varphi + \hat{S}_z \cos\theta \tag{7.3.2}$$

The eigenvalues of $\hat{S}_{z'}$ are $+\hbar/2$ or $-\hbar/2$, and the eigenvectors of $\hat{S}_{z'}$ with the basis eigenvectors of S_z are

$$\left|+\tfrac{1}{2}\right\rangle' = a\left|+\tfrac{1}{2}\right\rangle + b\left|-\tfrac{1}{2}\right\rangle \tag{7.3.3}$$

$$\hat{S}_{z'}\left|+\tfrac{1}{2}\right\rangle' = +\frac{\hbar}{2}\left|+\tfrac{1}{2}\right\rangle' \tag{7.3.4}$$

and

$$\left|-\tfrac{1}{2}\right\rangle' = c\left|+\tfrac{1}{2}\right\rangle + d\left|-\tfrac{1}{2}\right\rangle \tag{7.3.5}$$

$$\hat{S}_{z'}\left|-\tfrac{1}{2}\right\rangle' = -\frac{\hbar}{2}\left|-\tfrac{1}{2}\right\rangle' \tag{7.3.6}$$

where a, b, c, and d are complex constants. By substituting Eq. (7.3.2) and Eq. (7.3.3) into Eq. (7.3.4) we obtain

$$(\hat{S}_x \sin\theta\cos\varphi + \hat{S}_y \sin\theta\sin\varphi + \hat{S}_z \cos\theta)\left(a\left|+\tfrac{1}{2}\right\rangle + b\left|-\tfrac{1}{2}\right\rangle\right) = \frac{\hbar}{2}\left(a\left|+\tfrac{1}{2}\right\rangle + b\left|-\tfrac{1}{2}\right\rangle\right) \tag{7.3.7}$$

Using the known relations

$$\begin{cases} \hat{S}_x\left|+\tfrac{1}{2}\right\rangle = \dfrac{\hbar}{2}\left|-\tfrac{1}{2}\right\rangle \\[2mm] \hat{S}_y\left|+\tfrac{1}{2}\right\rangle = \dfrac{i\hbar}{2}\left|-\tfrac{1}{2}\right\rangle \\[2mm] \hat{S}_z\left|+\tfrac{1}{2}\right\rangle = \dfrac{\hbar}{2}\left|+\tfrac{1}{2}\right\rangle \end{cases} \qquad \begin{cases} \hat{S}_x\left|-\tfrac{1}{2}\right\rangle = \dfrac{\hbar}{2}\left|+\tfrac{1}{2}\right\rangle \\[2mm] \hat{S}_y\left|-\tfrac{1}{2}\right\rangle = -\dfrac{i\hbar}{2}\left|-\tfrac{1}{2}\right\rangle \\[2mm] \hat{S}_z\left|-\tfrac{1}{2}\right\rangle = -\dfrac{\hbar}{2}\left|-\tfrac{1}{2}\right\rangle \end{cases} \tag{7.3.8}$$

Eq. (7.3.7) turns into the form

$$\frac{\hbar a}{2}\left\{\sin\theta\cos\varphi\left|-\tfrac{1}{2}\right\rangle + i\sin\theta\sin\varphi\left|-\tfrac{1}{2}\right\rangle + \cos\theta\left|+\tfrac{1}{2}\right\rangle\right\}$$

$$+ \frac{\hbar b}{2}\left\{\sin\theta\cos\varphi\left|+\tfrac{1}{2}\right\rangle - i\sin\theta\sin\varphi\left|+\tfrac{1}{2}\right\rangle - \cos\theta\left|-\tfrac{1}{2}\right\rangle\right\} = \frac{\hbar}{2}\left(a\left|+\tfrac{1}{2}\right\rangle + b\left|-\tfrac{1}{2}\right\rangle\right) \tag{7.3.9}$$

Hence, we obtain

$$\begin{cases} a\sin\theta\cos\varphi + ia\sin\theta\sin\varphi - b\cos\theta = b \\ a\cos\theta + b\sin\theta\cos\varphi - ib\sin\theta\sin\varphi = a \end{cases} \tag{7.3.10}$$

or $a = \dfrac{(1+\cos\theta)b}{\sin\theta(\cos\varphi + i\sin\varphi)}\left|+\tfrac{1}{2}\right\rangle$ must be a unit vector; thus, $|a|^2 + |b|^2 = 1$ and $|b|^2\left(1 + \dfrac{(1+\cos\theta)^2}{\sin^2\theta}\right) = 1$, so

$$|b|^2 = \frac{\sin^2\theta}{2 + 2\cos\theta} = \frac{\sin^2\theta}{4\cos^2\left(\dfrac{\theta}{2}\right)} = \frac{4\sin^2\left(\dfrac{\theta}{2}\right)\cos^2\left(\dfrac{\theta}{2}\right)}{4\cos^2\left(\dfrac{\theta}{2}\right)} = \sin^2\left(\frac{\theta}{2}\right) \tag{7.3.11}$$

We choose $b = e^{i\varphi} \sin(\theta/2)$; hence,

$$a = \frac{(1 + \cos\theta)}{\sin\theta\, e^{i\varphi}} \sin\left(\frac{\theta}{2}\right) e^{i\varphi} = \frac{2\cos^2\left(\dfrac{\theta}{2}\right)\sin\left(\dfrac{\theta}{2}\right)}{\sin\theta} = \cos\left(\frac{\theta}{2}\right) \qquad (7.3.12)$$

so we obtain

$$\left|+\tfrac{1}{2}\right\rangle' = \cos\left(\frac{\theta}{2}\right)\left|+\tfrac{1}{2}\right\rangle + \sin\left(\frac{\theta}{2}\right)e^{i\varphi}\left|-\tfrac{1}{2}\right\rangle \qquad (7.3.13)$$

Since $\left|-\tfrac{1}{2}\right\rangle'$ is orthogonal to $\left|+\tfrac{1}{2}\right\rangle'$ we have

$$\left\langle+\tfrac{1}{2}\middle|-\tfrac{1}{2}\right\rangle = c\cos\left(\frac{\theta}{2}\right) + d\sin\left(\frac{\theta}{2}\right)e^{-i\varphi} = 0 \Rightarrow c = -\tan\left(\frac{\theta}{2}\right)e^{-i\varphi}d \qquad (7.3.14)$$

Note that $\left|-\tfrac{1}{2}\right\rangle'$ is also a unit vector, so $|c|^2 + |d|^2 = 1$. Substituting c, we obtain $[\tan^2(\theta/2) + 1]\,|d|^2 = 1$, or $|d|^2 = \cos^2(\theta/2)$. We choose $d = -\cos(\theta/2)$, and so $c = -e^{-i\varphi}\sin(\theta/2)$. Therefore,

$$\left|-\tfrac{1}{2}\right\rangle' = -\sin\left(\frac{\theta}{2}\right)e^{-i\varphi}\left|+\tfrac{1}{2}\right\rangle + \cos\left(\frac{\theta}{2}\right)\left|-\tfrac{1}{2}\right\rangle \qquad (7.3.15)$$

The present state of the electron represented by the basis eigenvectors of $S_{z'}$ is

$$\left|+\tfrac{1}{2}\right\rangle = {}'\!\left\langle+\tfrac{1}{2}\middle|+\tfrac{1}{2}\right\rangle\left|+\tfrac{1}{2}\right\rangle' + {}'\!\left\langle+\tfrac{1}{2}\middle|-\tfrac{1}{2}\right\rangle\left|-\tfrac{1}{2}\right\rangle' = \cos\left(\frac{\theta}{2}\right)\left|+\tfrac{1}{2}\right\rangle' + \sin\left(\frac{\theta}{2}\right)e^{-i\varphi}\left|-\tfrac{1}{2}\right\rangle' \qquad (7.3.16)$$

Therefore, the probability that the spin component along z' is $+\hbar/2$:

$$P\left(\frac{+\hbar}{2}\right) = \left|{}'\!\left\langle+\tfrac{1}{2}\middle|+\tfrac{1}{2}\right\rangle\right|^2 = \cos^2\left(\frac{\theta}{2}\right) \qquad (7.3.17)$$

and the probability that it is $-\hbar/2$:

$$P\left(-\frac{\hbar}{2}\right) = \left|{}'\!\left\langle-\tfrac{1}{2}\middle|+\tfrac{1}{2}\right\rangle\right|^2 = \sin^2\left(\frac{\theta}{2}\right) \qquad (7.3.18)$$

(*b*) The average value of the spin along z' is $\left\langle\hat{S}_{z'}\right\rangle = \left\langle+\tfrac{1}{2}\middle|\hat{S}_{z'}\middle|+\tfrac{1}{2}\right\rangle$. Using the relation

$$\hat{S}_{z'}\left|+\tfrac{1}{2}\right\rangle = \hat{S}_{z'}\left(\cos\left(\frac{\theta}{2}\right)\left|+\tfrac{1}{2}\right\rangle' + \sin\left(\frac{\theta}{2}\right)e^{-i\varphi}\left|-\tfrac{1}{2}\right\rangle'\right) = \frac{\hbar}{2}\left(\cos\left(\frac{\theta}{2}\right)\left|+\tfrac{1}{2}\right\rangle' - \sin\left(\frac{\theta}{2}\right)e^{-i\varphi}\left|-\tfrac{1}{2}\right\rangle'\right) \qquad (7.3.19)$$

we obtain

$$\begin{aligned}
\left\langle\hat{S}_{z'}\right\rangle &= \left\langle+\tfrac{1}{2}\middle|\hat{S}_{z'}\middle|+\tfrac{1}{2}\right\rangle = \left\langle+\tfrac{1}{2}\middle|\frac{\hbar}{2}\left(\cos\left(\frac{\theta}{2}\right)\left|+\tfrac{1}{2}\right\rangle' - \sin\left(\frac{\theta}{2}\right)e^{-i\varphi}\left|-\tfrac{1}{2}\right\rangle'\right)\right. \\
&= \frac{\hbar}{2}\left[\cos\left(\frac{\theta}{2}\right)\left\langle+\tfrac{1}{2}\middle|+\tfrac{1}{2}\right\rangle' - \sin\left(\frac{\theta}{2}\right)e^{-i\varphi}\left\langle+\tfrac{1}{2}\middle|-\tfrac{1}{2}\right\rangle'\right] \\
&= \frac{\hbar}{2}\left[\cos\left(\frac{\theta}{2}\right)\cos\left(\frac{\theta}{2}\right) - \sin\left(\frac{\theta}{2}\right)e^{i\varphi}\sin\left(\frac{\theta}{2}\right)e^{-i\varphi}\right] \\
&= \frac{\hbar}{2}\left[\cos^2\left(\frac{\theta}{2}\right) - \sin^2\left(\frac{\theta}{2}\right)\right] = \frac{\hbar\cos\theta}{2} \qquad (7.3.20)
\end{aligned}$$

7.4. Consider a particle with spin 1/2. (*a*) Find the eigenvalues and eigenfunctions of the operator $\hat{S}_x + \hat{S}_y$ where $\hat{S}_i$ is the spin operator in the *i* direction ($i = x, y, z$). (*b*) Assume that $|\alpha\rangle$ designates the eigenfunction of $\hat{S}_x + \hat{S}_y$ that belongs to the maximal eigenvalue, and that the particle is in state $|\alpha\rangle$. If we measure the spin in the z direction, what are the values and their probabilities? (*c*) The particle is in state $|\alpha\rangle$. Find, if possible, the direction **n** in which the spin measurement will, with certainty, yield the value $\hat{S}_n = \hbar/2$.

SOLUTION

(*a*) We begin by writing the matrices

$$\hat{S}_x = \frac{\hbar}{2}\begin{pmatrix} 0 & 1 \\ 1 & 0 \end{pmatrix} \qquad \hat{S}_y = \frac{\hbar}{2}\begin{pmatrix} 0 & -i \\ i & 0 \end{pmatrix} \qquad \hat{S}_z = \frac{\hbar}{2}\begin{pmatrix} 1 & 0 \\ 0 & -1 \end{pmatrix} \tag{7.4.1}$$

thus,

$$\hat{A} = \hat{S}_x + \hat{S}_y = \frac{\hbar}{2}\begin{pmatrix} 0 & i-1 \\ i+1 & 0 \end{pmatrix} \tag{7.4.2}$$

To find the eigenvalues of this operator ($\lambda\hbar/2$), we must solve the equation $\det[\hat{A} - (\lambda\hbar/2)\hat{I}] = 0$; that is,

$$\det\left\{\frac{\hbar}{2}\begin{pmatrix} -\lambda & 1-i \\ 1+i & -\lambda \end{pmatrix}\right\} = 0 \Rightarrow \left(\frac{\hbar}{2}\right)^4 [\lambda^2 - (1-i)(1+i)] = 0 \tag{7.4.3}$$

So, $\lambda^2 - 2 = 0$, which yields $\lambda = \pm\sqrt{2}$, and the eigenvalues of $\hat{A}$ are $\pm\hbar/\sqrt{2}$. Recall that the kernel of a matrix $\hat{A}$ is the set of vectors **u** for which $\hat{A}\mathbf{u} = \mathbf{0}$. The eigenfunction of $\hat{A}$ corresponding to the eigenvalue $+\hbar/\sqrt{2}$ is

$$\ker\left\{\frac{\hbar}{2}\begin{pmatrix} -\sqrt{2} & 1-i \\ 1+i & -\sqrt{2} \end{pmatrix}\right\} = \ker\begin{pmatrix} -\sqrt{2} & 1-i \\ 1+i & -\sqrt{2} \end{pmatrix} \tag{7.4.4}$$

That is the state $a\left|+\frac{1}{2}\right\rangle + b\left|-\frac{1}{2}\right\rangle$, where

$$\begin{pmatrix} -\sqrt{2} & 1-i \\ 1+i & -\sqrt{2} \end{pmatrix}\begin{pmatrix} a \\ b \end{pmatrix} = \begin{pmatrix} 0 \\ 0 \end{pmatrix} \Rightarrow \begin{cases} -\sqrt{2}a + (1-i)b = 0 \\ (1+i)a - \sqrt{2}b = 0 \end{cases} \tag{7.4.5}$$

Thus, $a = \frac{\sqrt{2}}{1+i}b$. For $a\left|+\frac{1}{2}\right\rangle + b\left|-\frac{1}{2}\right\rangle$ to be normalized we must satisfy the condition $|a|^2 + |b|^2 = 1$; hence,

$$\left(\left|\frac{\sqrt{2}}{1+i}\right| + 1\right)|b|^2 = 1 \tag{7.4.6}$$

which yields $b = 1/\sqrt{2}$ and $a = \frac{1}{i+1} = \frac{1-i}{2} = \frac{e^{-i\pi/4}}{\sqrt{2}}$. Therefore, the first eigenstate $|v_1\rangle = a\left|+\frac{1}{2}\right\rangle + b\left|-\frac{1}{2}\right\rangle$ is found to be $|v_1\rangle = \frac{e^{-i\pi/4}}{\sqrt{2}}\left|+\frac{1}{2}\right\rangle + \frac{1}{\sqrt{2}}\left|-\frac{1}{2}\right\rangle$. Simiarly, for the second eigenfunction of $\hat{A}$ corresponding to the eigenvalue $-\hbar/\sqrt{2}$ we obtain

$$\ker\left\{\frac{\hbar}{2}\begin{pmatrix} \sqrt{2} & 1-i \\ 1+i & \sqrt{2} \end{pmatrix}\right\} = \ker\begin{pmatrix} \sqrt{2} & 1-i \\ 1+i & \sqrt{2} \end{pmatrix} \tag{7.4.7}$$

Or $|v_2\rangle = c\left|+\frac{1}{2}\right\rangle + d\left|-\frac{1}{2}\right\rangle$, where

$$\begin{pmatrix} \sqrt{2} & 1-i \\ 1+i & \sqrt{2} \end{pmatrix}\begin{pmatrix} c \\ d \end{pmatrix} = \begin{pmatrix} 0 \\ 0 \end{pmatrix} \Rightarrow \begin{cases} \sqrt{2}c + (1-i)d = 0 \\ (1+i)c + \sqrt{2}d = 0 \end{cases} \tag{7.4.8}$$

so $c = -\dfrac{\sqrt{2}}{1+i} d$. The normalization condition of $|v_2\rangle$ yields $d = 1/\sqrt{2}$ and $c = -\dfrac{1}{i+1} = e^{3\pi/4}/\sqrt{2}$, and therefore, $|v_2\rangle = \dfrac{e^{3\pi/4}}{\sqrt{2}}|+\tfrac{1}{2}\rangle + \dfrac{1}{\sqrt{2}}|-\tfrac{1}{2}\rangle$; so, finally

$$(\hat{S}_x + \hat{S}_y)|v_1\rangle = -\frac{\hbar}{\sqrt{2}}|v_1\rangle \qquad (\hat{S}_x + \hat{S}_y)|v_2\rangle = \frac{\hbar}{\sqrt{2}}|v_2\rangle \tag{7.4.9}$$

(b) The maximal eigenvalue of $\hat{S}_x + \hat{S}_y$ is $+\hbar/\sqrt{2}$; thus,

$$|\alpha\rangle = |v_1\rangle = \frac{e^{-i\pi/4}}{\sqrt{2}}|+\tfrac{1}{2}\rangle + \frac{1}{\sqrt{2}}|-\tfrac{1}{2}\rangle \tag{7.4.10}$$

The values that can be obtained from a measurement of $\hat{S}_z$ are $\pm\hbar/2$. The probability for $\hat{S}_z = \hbar/2$ is

$$P\left(\frac{\hbar}{2}\right) = \left|\langle+\tfrac{1}{2}|\alpha\rangle\right|^2 = \left|\frac{e^{-\pi i/4}}{\sqrt{2}}\right|^2 = \frac{1}{2} \tag{7.4.11}$$

Therefore the probability for $\hat{S}_z = -\hbar/2$ is

$$P\left(-\frac{\hbar}{2}\right) = 1 - P\left(\frac{\hbar}{2}\right) = \frac{1}{2} \tag{7.4.12}$$

(c) If the measurement of an observable gives only one result, then the state of the system is an eigenstate of that observable; thus, the state $|\alpha\rangle$ is the eigenstate of a spin operator in a certain direction (the one we wish to find). As we have seen in part (a),

$$|\alpha\rangle = |v_1\rangle = \frac{e^{-i\pi/4}}{\sqrt{2}}|+\tfrac{1}{2}\rangle + \frac{1}{\sqrt{2}}|-\tfrac{1}{2}\rangle \tag{7.4.13}$$

$|v_1\rangle$ is also an eigenstate of $\hat{S}_x + \hat{S}_y$ with the eigenvalue $\hbar/\sqrt{2}$, that is,

$$(\hat{S}_x + \hat{S}_y)|\alpha\rangle = \frac{\hbar}{\sqrt{2}}|\alpha\rangle \Rightarrow \frac{1}{\sqrt{2}}(\hat{S}_x + \hat{S}_y)|\alpha\rangle = \frac{\hbar}{2}|\alpha\rangle \tag{7.4.14}$$

Hence, $|\alpha\rangle$ is the eigenstate of $(\hat{S}_x + \hat{S}_y)/\sqrt{2}$ and the measurement of $(\hat{S}_x + \hat{S}_y)/\sqrt{2}$ always yields the result $\hbar/2$. Note that $(\hat{S}_x + \hat{S}_y)/\sqrt{2}$ is the spin operator in the direction of the spatial unit vector $\mathbf{n} = \mathbf{i} + \mathbf{j}$ where $\mathbf{i}$ and $\mathbf{j}$ are unit vectors in the x and y directions, respectively.

7.5. Consider a particle with spin 1/2. (a) What are the eigenvalues and eigenvectors of $\hat{S}_x$, $\hat{S}_y$, and $\hat{S}_z$? (b) Consider a particle in eigenstate $\hat{S}_x$. What are the possible results and their probabilities if we measure the z component of the spin? (c) At $t = 0$, the particle is in the eigenstate $\hat{S}_x$, which corresponds to the eigenvalue $-\hbar/2$. The particle is in a magnetic field and its Hamiltonian is $\hat{H} = \dfrac{eB}{mc}\hat{S}_z$. Find the state at $t > 0$. (d) If we measure $\hat{S}_x$ at $t = t_1$, what is the result? What is the result for a measurement of $\hat{S}_z$ at $t = t_1$? Explain the difference in t_1-dependence. (e) Calculate the expectation values of $\hat{S}_x$ and $\hat{S}_z$ at $t = t_1$.

SOLUTION

(a) Consider the matrices $\hat{S}_x$, $\hat{S}_y$, and $\hat{S}_z$ written in the basis eigenvectors of $\hat{S}_z$,

$$\hat{S}_x = \frac{\hbar}{2}\begin{pmatrix} 0 & 1 \\ 1 & 0 \end{pmatrix} \qquad \hat{S}_y = \frac{\hbar}{2}\begin{pmatrix} 0 & -i \\ i & 0 \end{pmatrix} \qquad \hat{S}_z = \frac{\hbar}{2}\begin{pmatrix} 1 & 0 \\ 0 & -1 \end{pmatrix} \tag{7.5.1}$$

First, we shall determine the eigenvectors of $\hat{S}_z$. For eigenvalue $+\hbar/2$ we have $|+\tfrac{1}{2}\rangle_z = \begin{pmatrix} 1 \\ 0 \end{pmatrix}$ and for eigenvalue $-\hbar/2$ we have $|-\tfrac{1}{2}\rangle_z = \begin{pmatrix} 0 \\ 1 \end{pmatrix}$. The eigenvalues of $\hat{S}_x$ are $\hbar\lambda/2$, where $\det(\hat{S}_x - (\hbar\lambda/2)\hat{I}) = 0$; that is,

$$\det\left\{\frac{\hbar}{2}\begin{pmatrix} 0 & 1 \\ 1 & 0 \end{pmatrix} - \frac{\hbar}{2}\begin{pmatrix} \lambda & 0 \\ 0 & \lambda \end{pmatrix}\right\} = \left(\frac{\hbar}{2}\right)^2 \begin{vmatrix} -\lambda & 1 \\ 1 & -\lambda \end{vmatrix} = 0 \tag{7.5.2}$$

or $\lambda^2 - 1 = 0$. Therefore, we obtain the eigenvalues $\pm\hbar/2$. The eigenvector corresponding to the eigenvalue $+\hbar/2$ is $\left|+\frac{1}{2}\right\rangle_x = a\left|+\frac{1}{2}\right\rangle_z + b\left|-\frac{1}{2}\right\rangle_z \equiv \begin{pmatrix} a \\ b \end{pmatrix}$, hence

$$\hat{S}_x\left|+\tfrac{1}{2}\right\rangle_x = \frac{\hbar}{2}\left|+\tfrac{1}{2}\right\rangle_x \Rightarrow \frac{\hbar}{2}\begin{pmatrix} 0 & 1 \\ 1 & 0 \end{pmatrix}\begin{pmatrix} a \\ b \end{pmatrix} = \frac{\hbar}{2}\begin{pmatrix} a \\ b \end{pmatrix} \tag{7.5.3}$$

Solving Eq. (7.5.3), we obtain $b = a$. Now, $\left|+\frac{1}{2}\right\rangle_x$ must be normalized, so we set the condition $|a|^2 + |b|^2 = 1$. Substituting for a, we obtain

$$2|b|^2 = 1 \Rightarrow a = b = \frac{1}{\sqrt{2}} \tag{7.5.4}$$

Thus, the eigenvector of $\hat{S}_x$ with eigenvalue $+\hbar/2$ is

$$\left|+\tfrac{1}{2}\right\rangle_x = \frac{1}{\sqrt{2}}\begin{pmatrix} 1 \\ 1 \end{pmatrix} = \frac{1}{\sqrt{2}}\left(\left|+\tfrac{1}{2}\right\rangle_z + \left|-\tfrac{1}{2}\right\rangle_z\right) \tag{7.5.5}$$

The other eigenvector $\left|-\frac{1}{2}\right\rangle_x$ (with eigenvalue $-\hbar/2$) is obtained either from orthogonality and normalization conditions (since the two eigenvectors belong to different eigenvalues), or in the same manner in which the first eigenvector was obtained. We will follow the former course:

$$\left|-\tfrac{1}{2}\right\rangle_x = c\left|+\tfrac{1}{2}\right\rangle_z + b\left|-\tfrac{1}{2}\right\rangle_z \equiv \begin{pmatrix} c \\ d \end{pmatrix} \tag{7.5.6}$$

and

$$_x\left\langle-\tfrac{1}{2}\middle|+\tfrac{1}{2}\right\rangle_x = (c \quad d)\begin{pmatrix} 1/\sqrt{2} \\ 1/\sqrt{2} \end{pmatrix} = \frac{c}{\sqrt{2}} + \frac{d}{\sqrt{2}} = 0 \tag{7.5.7}$$

giving $c = -d$. Using the normalization condition $|c|^2 + |d|^2 = 1$, we can choose $c = -d = 1/\sqrt{2}$ and obtain

$$\left|-\tfrac{1}{2}\right\rangle_x = \frac{1}{\sqrt{2}}\begin{pmatrix} 1 \\ -1 \end{pmatrix} = \frac{1}{\sqrt{2}}\left(\left|+\tfrac{1}{2}\right\rangle_z - \left|-\tfrac{1}{2}\right\rangle_z\right) \tag{7.5.8}$$

Similarly, the eigenvalues of $\hat{S}_y$ are $(\hbar/2)\lambda$, where

$$\det\left(\hat{S}_y - \frac{\hbar}{2}\lambda\hat{I}\right) = \left(\frac{\hbar}{2}\right)^2\begin{pmatrix} -\lambda & -i \\ i & -\lambda \end{pmatrix} = 0 \tag{7.5.9}$$

or $\lambda^2 - 1 = 0$; the eigenvalues of $\hat{S}_y$ are also $\pm\hbar/2$, and the eigenvector corresponding to the eigenvalue, $+\hbar/2$ is

$$\left|+\tfrac{1}{2}\right\rangle_y = a\left|+\tfrac{1}{2}\right\rangle_z + b\left|-\tfrac{1}{2}\right\rangle_z \equiv \begin{pmatrix} a \\ b \end{pmatrix} \tag{7.5.10}$$

where

$$\hat{S}_y\left|+\tfrac{1}{2}\right\rangle_y = \frac{\hbar}{2}\begin{pmatrix} 0 & -i \\ i & 0 \end{pmatrix}\begin{pmatrix} a \\ b \end{pmatrix} = \frac{\hbar}{2}\begin{pmatrix} a \\ b \end{pmatrix} = \frac{\hbar}{2}\left|+\tfrac{1}{2}\right\rangle_y \tag{7.5.11}$$

and $ia = b$. Using the normalization condition $|a|^2 + |b|^2 = 1$, we obtain $2|b|^2 = 1$, so we can choose $b = 1/\sqrt{2}$ and $a = -i/\sqrt{2}$. And finally, we obtain

$$\left|+\tfrac{1}{2}\right\rangle_y = \frac{1}{\sqrt{2}}\left(-i\left|+\tfrac{1}{2}\right\rangle_z + \left|-\tfrac{1}{2}\right\rangle_z\right) \tag{7.5.12}$$

Using the orthogonality relation of $\left|-\frac{1}{2}\right\rangle_y$ to $\left|+\frac{1}{2}\right\rangle_y$, we have $\left|-\frac{1}{2}\right\rangle_y = c\left|+\frac{1}{2}\right\rangle_z + d\left|-\frac{1}{2}\right\rangle_z$ and

$$_y\left\langle-\tfrac{1}{2}\middle|+\tfrac{1}{2}\right\rangle_y = (c \quad d)\begin{pmatrix} -i/\sqrt{2} \\ 1/\sqrt{2} \end{pmatrix} = -\frac{ic}{\sqrt{2}} + \frac{d}{\sqrt{2}} = 0 \tag{7.5.13}$$

so $d = ic$, and from the normalization condition we get $|c|^2 + |d|^2 = 2|c|^2 = 1$. Thus, $c = 1/\sqrt{2}$ and $d = i/\sqrt{2}$; therefore,

$$\left|-\tfrac{1}{2}\right\rangle_y = \frac{1}{\sqrt{2}}\left(\left|+\tfrac{1}{2}\right\rangle_z + i\left|-\tfrac{1}{2}\right\rangle_z\right) \tag{7.5.14}$$

(b) As we found in part (a), the eigenstates of S_x are

$$\left|+\tfrac{1}{2}\right\rangle_x = \frac{1}{\sqrt{2}}\left(\left|+\tfrac{1}{2}\right\rangle_z + \left|-\tfrac{1}{2}\right\rangle_z\right) \qquad \left|-\tfrac{1}{2}\right\rangle_x = \frac{1}{\sqrt{2}}\left(\left|+\tfrac{1}{2}\right\rangle_z - \left|-\tfrac{1}{2}\right\rangle_z\right) \tag{7.5.15}$$

If we measure the spin component in the z direction, the state of the particle will be either $\left|+\tfrac{1}{2}\right\rangle_z$, resulting in $\hat{S}_z = \hbar/2$, or $\left|-\tfrac{1}{2}\right\rangle_z$, resulting in $\hat{S}_z = -\hbar/2$. The probability for $\hat{S}_z = \hbar/2$ is

$$P\left(\frac{\hbar}{2}\right) = \left|{}_z\langle+\tfrac{1}{2}|\pm\tfrac{1}{2}\rangle_x\right|^2 = \frac{1}{2} \tag{7.5.16}$$

and for $\hat{S}_z = -\hbar/2$ is

$$P\left(-\frac{\hbar}{2}\right) = \left|{}_z\langle+\tfrac{1}{2}|\pm\tfrac{1}{2}\rangle_x\right|^2 = \frac{1}{2} \tag{7.5.17}$$

Note that if the initial state is either $\left|+\tfrac{1}{2}\right\rangle_x$ or $\left|-\tfrac{1}{2}\right\rangle_x$, we obtain the same results.

(c) At $t = 0$, the particle is in initial state:

$$\left|+\tfrac{1}{2}\right\rangle_x = \frac{1}{\sqrt{2}}\left(\left|+\tfrac{1}{2}\right\rangle_z + \left|-\tfrac{1}{2}\right\rangle_z\right) \tag{7.5.18}$$

We want to find the time evolution of this state, therefore we use the Schrödinger equation, $i\hbar\dfrac{\partial\psi}{\partial t} = \hat{H}\psi$. In as much as the Hamiltonian is time-independent, we write $\psi(\mathbf{r}, \mathbf{s}, t) = \phi_1(\mathbf{r}, \mathbf{s})\phi_2(t)$; substituting in the Schrödinger equation gives

$$\phi_1(\mathbf{r}, \mathbf{s})\frac{\partial\phi_2(t)}{\partial t} = \phi_2(t)\hat{H}\phi_1(\mathbf{r}, \mathbf{s}) \tag{7.5.19}$$

Assuming that $\phi_2(t)$ is of the form $\phi_2(t) = e^{-iEt/\hbar}$, where E is a constant, we obtain

$$E\phi_1(\mathbf{r}, \mathbf{s})\,e^{-iEt/\hbar} = \phi_2(t)\hat{H}\phi_1(\mathbf{r}, \mathbf{s}) \Rightarrow E\phi_1(\mathbf{r}, \mathbf{s})\phi_2(t) = \phi_2(t)\hat{H}\phi_1(\mathbf{r}, \mathbf{s}) \tag{7.5.20}$$

and we must require that $\phi_1(\mathbf{r}, \mathbf{s}) = E\phi_1(\mathbf{r}, \mathbf{s})$. In other words, $\phi_1(\mathbf{r}, \mathbf{s})$ must be an eigenfunction of the Hamiltonian $\hat{H}$. Note that

$$\hat{H} = \frac{eB}{mc}\hat{S}_z = (\text{const.})\,\hat{S}_z \tag{7.5.21}$$

Thus, the eigenstates of $\hat{H}$ are similar to the eigenstates of $\hat{S}_z$, where the eigenvalues of $\hat{H}$ are the eigenvalues of $\hat{S}_z$ multiplied by the constant eB/mc. Therefore,

$$\left|\psi_1(\mathbf{r}, \mathbf{s})\right\rangle = \left|+\tfrac{1}{2}\right\rangle_z \qquad E = \frac{eB\hbar}{2mc} \tag{7.5.22}$$

and

$$\left|\psi_1(\mathbf{r}, \mathbf{s}, t)\right\rangle = e^{-ieBt/2mc}\left|+\tfrac{1}{2}\right\rangle_z \tag{7.5.23}$$

Also,

$$\left|\psi_1(\mathbf{r}, \mathbf{s})\right\rangle = \left|-\tfrac{1}{2}\right\rangle_z \qquad E = -\frac{eB\hbar}{2mc} \tag{7.5.24}$$

which gives

$$\left|\psi_1(\mathbf{r}, \mathbf{s}, t)\right\rangle = e^{ieBt/2mc}\left|-\tfrac{1}{2}\right\rangle_z \tag{7.5.25}$$

Therefore, each state of the particle can be written as

$$|\psi(\mathbf{r}, \mathbf{s}, t)\rangle = \alpha|\psi_1(\mathbf{r}, \mathbf{s}, t)\rangle + \beta|\psi_2(\mathbf{r}, \mathbf{s}, t)\rangle = \alpha e^{-ieBt/2mc}\left|+\tfrac{1}{2}\right\rangle_z + \beta e^{i/2mc}\left|-\tfrac{1}{2}\right\rangle_z \quad (7.5.26)$$

For our system, the initial condition is

$$|\psi(\mathbf{r}, \mathbf{s}, t = 0)\rangle = \frac{1}{\sqrt{2}}\left(\left|+\tfrac{1}{2}\right\rangle_z + \left|-\tfrac{1}{2}\right\rangle_z\right) = \alpha\left|+\tfrac{1}{2}\right\rangle_z + \beta\left|-\tfrac{1}{2}\right\rangle_z \quad (7.5.27)$$

Hence, $\alpha = \beta = 1/\sqrt{2}$, giving

$$|\psi(\mathbf{r}, \mathbf{s}, t)\rangle = \frac{1}{\sqrt{2}}\left(e^{-ieBt/2mc}\left|+\tfrac{1}{2}\right\rangle_z + e^{ieBt/2mc}\left|-\tfrac{1}{2}\right\rangle_z\right) \quad (7.5.28)$$

(d) A measurement of $\hat{S}_x$ or $\hat{S}_z$ will give either $+\hbar/2$ or $-\hbar/2$. The probability for a measurement $\hat{S}_x = +\hbar/2$ is

$$P_x\left(+\frac{\hbar}{2}\right) = \left|_x\langle+\tfrac{1}{2}|\psi(\mathbf{r}, \mathbf{s}, t_1)\rangle\right|^2 = \left|\tfrac{1}{2}(e^{-ieBt_1/2mc} - e^{ieBt_1/2mc})\right|^2 = \cos^2\left(\frac{eBt_1}{2mc}\right) \quad (7.5.29)$$

and for $\hat{S}_x = -\hbar/2$ we have

$$P_x\left(-\frac{\hbar}{2}\right) = \left|_x\langle-\tfrac{1}{2}|\psi(\mathbf{r}, \mathbf{s}, t_1)\rangle\right|^2 = \left|\tfrac{1}{2}(e^{-ieBt_1/2mc} - e^{ieBt_1/2mc})\right|^2 = \sin^2\left(\frac{eBt_1}{2mc}\right) \quad (7.5.30)$$

Similarly, the probability for $\hat{S}_z = +\hbar/2$ is

$$P_z\left(+\frac{\hbar}{2}\right) = \left|_z\langle+\tfrac{1}{2}|\psi(\mathbf{r}, \mathbf{s}, t_1)\rangle\right|^2 = \left|\frac{1}{\sqrt{2}}e^{-ieBt_1/2mc}\right|^2 = \frac{1}{2} \quad (7.5.31)$$

and for $\hat{S}_z = -\hbar/2$,

$$P_z\left(-\frac{\hbar}{2}\right) = \left|_z\langle-\tfrac{1}{2}|\psi(\mathbf{r}, \mathbf{s}, t_1)\rangle\right|^2 = \left|\frac{1}{\sqrt{2}}e^{ieBt_1/2mc}\right|^2 = \frac{1}{2} \quad (7.5.32)$$

(e) We can calculate the expectation value of $\hat{S}_i$ in two ways: the first by calculating $\langle\psi(\mathbf{r}, \mathbf{s}, t_1)|\hat{S}_i|\psi(\mathbf{r}, \mathbf{s}, t_1)\rangle$ and the second by summing over the products of the possible values multiplied by their probability. Using the second method,

$$\langle\hat{S}_x\rangle = +\frac{\hbar}{2}P_x\left(+\frac{\hbar}{2}\right) - \frac{\hbar}{2}P_x\left(-\frac{\hbar}{2}\right) = \frac{\hbar}{2}\left[\cos^2\left(\frac{eBt_1}{2mc}\right) - \sin^2\left(\frac{eBt_1}{2mc}\right)\right] = \frac{\hbar}{2}\cos\left(\frac{eBt_1}{mc}\right) \quad (7.5.33)$$

Similarly,

$$\langle\hat{S}_z\rangle = +\frac{\hbar}{2}P_z\left(+\frac{\hbar}{2}\right) - \frac{\hbar}{2}P_z\left(-\frac{\hbar}{2}\right) = \frac{\hbar}{2}\left(\frac{1}{2} - \frac{1}{2}\right) = 0 \quad (7.5.34)$$

Note that $\langle\hat{S}_x\rangle$ is not conserved in time; this is because $[\hat{H}, \hat{S}_x] = \frac{eB}{mc}[\hat{S}_z, \hat{S}_x] \neq 0$, while $\langle\hat{S}_z\rangle$ is conserved since

$$[\hat{H}, \hat{S}_z] = \frac{eB}{mc}[\hat{S}_z, \hat{S}_z] = 0 \quad (7.5.35)$$

7.6. (a) Prove that $[\hat{S}^2, \hat{S}_z] = 0$ where $\hat{S}^2 = \hat{S}_x^2 + \hat{S}_y^2 + \hat{S}_z^2$. (b) Show that the eigenvectors' basis of $\hat{S}_z$ diagonalizes $\hat{S}^2$. Find the eigenvalues of $\hat{S}^2$.

SOLUTION

(a) In Problem 7.1, we found that $[\hat{\sigma}_x, \hat{\sigma}_y] = 2i\hat{\sigma}_z$; $[\hat{\sigma}_y, \hat{\sigma}_z] = 2i\hat{\sigma}_x$; and $[\hat{\sigma}_z, \hat{\sigma}_x] = 2i\hat{\sigma}_y$. Therefore, recalling that $\hat{S} = \hbar\hat{\sigma}/2$ we write

$$[\hat{S}_x, \hat{S}_y] = i\hbar\hat{S}_z \qquad [\hat{S}_y, \hat{S}_z] = i\hbar\hat{S}_x \qquad [\hat{S}_z, \hat{S}_x] = i\hbar\hat{S}_y \quad (7.6.1)$$

Hence,

$$[\hat{S}^2, \hat{S}_z] = [\hat{S}_x^2 + \hat{S}_y^2 + \hat{S}_z^2, \hat{S}_z] = \sum_i [\hat{S}_i^2, \hat{S}_z] \tag{7.6.2}$$

where $i = x, y, z$. We see that

$$[\hat{S}_i^2, \hat{S}_z] = \hat{S}_i^2 \hat{S}_z - \hat{S}_z \hat{S}_i^2 + \hat{S}_i \hat{S}_z \hat{S}_i - \hat{S}_i \hat{S}_z \hat{S}_i$$

$$= \hat{S}_i(\hat{S}_i \hat{S}_z - \hat{S}_z \hat{S}_i) + (\hat{S}_i \hat{S}_z - \hat{S}_z \hat{S}_i)\hat{S}_i = \hat{S}_i [\hat{S}_i, \hat{S}_z] + [\hat{S}_i, \hat{S}_z]\hat{S}_i \tag{7.6.3}$$

so $[\hat{S}_z^2, \hat{S}_z] = 0$. Also,

$$[\hat{S}_x^2, \hat{S}_z] = \hat{S}_x [\hat{S}_x, \hat{S}_z] + [\hat{S}_x, \hat{S}_z]\hat{S}_x = -i\hbar [\hat{S}_x \hat{S}_y + \hat{S}_y \hat{S}_x] \tag{7.6.4}$$

and

$$[\hat{S}_y^2, \hat{S}_z] = \hat{S}_y [\hat{S}_y, \hat{S}_z] + [\hat{S}_y, \hat{S}_z]\hat{S}_y = -i\hbar (\hat{S}_y \hat{S}_x + \hat{S}_x \hat{S}_y) \tag{7.6.5}$$

Finally,

$$[\hat{S}^2, \hat{S}_z^2] = \sum_i [\hat{S}_i^2, \hat{S}_z] = i\hbar(\hat{S}_y \hat{S}_x + \hat{S}_x \hat{S}_y) - i\hbar(\hat{S}_x \hat{S}_y + \hat{S}_y \hat{S}_x) = 0 \tag{7.6.6}$$

(*b*) To obtain the matrix representation of S^2 we calculate it using the matrices of $\hat{S}_x$, $\hat{S}_y$, and $\hat{S}_z$ in the basis of the eigenvectors of $\hat{S}_z$; that is,

$$\hat{S}_x = \frac{\hbar}{2}\begin{pmatrix} 0 & 1 \\ 1 & 0 \end{pmatrix} \qquad \hat{S}_y = \frac{\hbar}{2}\begin{pmatrix} 0 & -i \\ i & 0 \end{pmatrix} \qquad \hat{S}_z = \frac{\hbar}{2}\begin{pmatrix} 1 & 0 \\ 0 & -1 \end{pmatrix} \tag{7.6.7}$$

Hence,

$$\hat{S}^2 = \hat{S}_x^2 + \hat{S}_y^2 + \hat{S}_z^2 = \left(\frac{\hbar}{2}\right)^2 (\hat{\sigma}_x^2 + \hat{\sigma}_y^2 + \hat{\sigma}_z^2) \tag{7.6.8}$$

Using the known result that $\hat{\sigma}_i^2 = \hat{I}$, we obtain

$$\hat{S}^2 = 3\left(\frac{\hbar}{2}\right)^2 \hat{I} = \frac{3\hbar^2}{4}\begin{pmatrix} 1 & 0 \\ 0 & 1 \end{pmatrix} \tag{7.6.9}$$

We see that the $\hat{S}^2$ is diagonalized (in the basis of the eigenvectors of $\hat{S}_z$). From linear algebra, we know that if a vector basis diagonalizes the matrix of an operator, then the basis is comprised of the operator's eigenvectors, i.e., $\left|+\frac{1}{2}\right\rangle$ and $\left|-\frac{1}{2}\right\rangle$ are also the eigenvectors of $\hat{S}^2$. In other words, we conclude that if the commutation relation of two operators is zero, then we can find similar eigenvectors for both of them. To find the eigenvalue of $\hat{S}^2$ for the eigenvector $\left|+\frac{1}{2}\right\rangle$ we calculate

$$\hat{S}^2 \left|+\tfrac{1}{2}\right\rangle = \frac{3\hbar^2}{4}\begin{pmatrix} 1 & 0 \\ 0 & 1 \end{pmatrix}\begin{pmatrix} 1 \\ 0 \end{pmatrix} = \frac{3\hbar^2}{4}\begin{pmatrix} 1 \\ 0 \end{pmatrix} = \frac{3\hbar^2}{4}\left|+\tfrac{1}{2}\right\rangle \tag{7.6.10}$$

So, the eigenvalue of $\left|+\frac{1}{2}\right\rangle$ is $3\hbar^2/4$, and the eigenvalue of $\left|-\frac{1}{2}\right\rangle$ is

$$\hat{S}^2 \left|-\tfrac{1}{2}\right\rangle = \frac{3\hbar^2}{4}\begin{pmatrix} 1 & 0 \\ 0 & 1 \end{pmatrix}\begin{pmatrix} 0 \\ 1 \end{pmatrix} = \frac{3\hbar^2}{4}\begin{pmatrix} 0 \\ 1 \end{pmatrix} = \frac{3\hbar^2}{4}\left|-\tfrac{1}{2}\right\rangle \tag{7.6.11}$$

Thus the eigenvalue of $\left|-\frac{1}{2}\right\rangle$ is also $3\hbar^2/4$. Note that if we set $s = 1/2$ to be the quantum number of the total spin, then (like the angular momentum theory) the eigenvalue $3\hbar^2/4$ can be written as $\hbar^2 s(s+1)$.

7.7. Find the result of applying the operators $\hat{S}_x + i\hat{S}_y$ and $\hat{S}_x - i\hat{S}_y$ on the eigenvectors $\left|+\frac{1}{2}\right\rangle$ and $\left|-\frac{1}{2}\right\rangle$ of $\hat{S}_z$. What is the importance of these operators?

SOLUTION

We begin with the operator $\hat{S}_x + i\hat{S}_y$ and calculate

$$(\hat{S}_x + i\hat{S}_y)\left|+\tfrac{1}{2}\right\rangle = \hat{S}_x\left|+\tfrac{1}{2}\right\rangle + i\hat{S}_y\left|+\tfrac{1}{2}\right\rangle = \frac{\hbar}{2}\left|-\tfrac{1}{2}\right\rangle + \left(i\frac{\hbar}{2}\right)i\left|-\tfrac{1}{2}\right\rangle = 0 \tag{7.7.1}$$

and

$$(\hat{S}_x + i\hat{S}_y)\left|-\tfrac{1}{2}\right\rangle = \hat{S}_x\left|-\tfrac{1}{2}\right\rangle + i\hat{S}_y\left|-\tfrac{1}{2}\right\rangle = \frac{\hbar}{2}\left|+\tfrac{1}{2}\right\rangle + \left(i\frac{\hbar}{2}\right)i\left|+\tfrac{1}{2}\right\rangle = \hbar\left|+\tfrac{1}{2}\right\rangle \tag{7.7.2}$$

For the operator $\hat{S}_x - i\hat{S}_y$, we have

$$(\hat{S}_x - i\hat{S}_y)\left|+\tfrac{1}{2}\right\rangle = \hat{S}_x\left|+\tfrac{1}{2}\right\rangle - i\hat{S}_y\left|+\tfrac{1}{2}\right\rangle = \frac{\hbar}{2}\left|-\tfrac{1}{2}\right\rangle - \left(i\frac{\hbar}{2}\right)i\left|-\tfrac{1}{2}\right\rangle = \hbar\left|-\tfrac{1}{2}\right\rangle \tag{7.7.3}$$

and

$$(\hat{S}_x - i\hat{S}_y)\left|-\tfrac{1}{2}\right\rangle = \hat{S}_x\left|-\tfrac{1}{2}\right\rangle - i\hat{S}_y\left|-\tfrac{1}{2}\right\rangle = \frac{\hbar}{2}\left|+\tfrac{1}{2}\right\rangle - \left(i\frac{\hbar}{2}\right)(-i)\left|+\tfrac{1}{2}\right\rangle = 0 \tag{7.7.4}$$

To conclude, we have

$$\hat{S}_+\left|+\tfrac{1}{2}\right\rangle = 0 \qquad \hat{S}_-\left|+\tfrac{1}{2}\right\rangle = \hbar\left|-\tfrac{1}{2}\right\rangle \qquad \hat{S}_+\left|-\tfrac{1}{2}\right\rangle = \hbar\left|+\tfrac{1}{2}\right\rangle \qquad \hat{S}_-\left|-\tfrac{1}{2}\right\rangle = 0 \tag{7.7.5}$$

where, from Eq. (7.11), $\hat{S}_+ \equiv \hat{S}_x + i\hat{S}_y$ and $\hat{S}_- \equiv \hat{S}_x - i\hat{S}_y$. The latter relations justify calling $\hat{S}_+$ a *spin-raising* operator, since it increases the spin in z direction from $-\hbar/2$ to $+\hbar/2$. Similarly, we call $\hat{S}_-$ a *spin-lowering* operator, since it lowers the z component of the spin from $+\hbar/2$ to $-\hbar/2$. $\hat{S}_+$ and $\hat{S}_-$ allow us to jump from one eigenstate of $\hat{S}_z$ to the other. These operators are very useful in spin calculations.

7.8. Using the operators $\hat{S}_+$ and $\hat{S}_-$, compute the matrices $\hat{S}_x$ and $\hat{S}_y$; show that $\hat{S}^2 = \hat{S}_x^2 + \hat{S}_y^2 + \hat{S}_z^2$ is diagonalized in the basis of eigenvectors of $\hat{S}_z$.

SOLUTION

The spin-raising $\hat{S}_+$ operator and the spin-lowering $\hat{S}_-$ operator are defined as

$$\hat{S}_+ = \hat{S}_x + i\hat{S}_y \qquad \hat{S}_- = \hat{S}_x - i\hat{S}_y \tag{7.8.1}$$

Hence, we can write

$$\hat{S}_x = \frac{1}{2}(\hat{S}_+ + \hat{S}_-) \qquad \hat{S}_y = \frac{1}{2i}(\hat{S}_+ - \hat{S}_-) \tag{7.8.2}$$

Therefore,

$$\begin{aligned} \hat{S}^2 &= \hat{S}_z^2 + \hat{S}_x^2 + \hat{S}_y^2 = \hat{S}_z^2 + \frac{1}{4}(\hat{S}_+ + \hat{S}_-)^2 - \frac{1}{4}(\hat{S}_+ - \hat{S}_-)^2 \\ &= \hat{S}_z^2 + \frac{1}{4}(\hat{S}_+^2 + \hat{S}_+\hat{S}_- + \hat{S}_-\hat{S}_+ + \hat{S}_-^2) - \frac{1}{4}(\hat{S}_+^2 - \hat{S}_+\hat{S}_- - \hat{S}_-\hat{S}_+ + \hat{S}_-^2) \\ &= \hat{S}_z^2 + \frac{1}{2}(\hat{S}_+\hat{S}_- + \hat{S}_-\hat{S}_+) \end{aligned} \tag{7.8.3}$$

To find the matrix representation of $\hat{S}^2$ we compute

$$\hat{S}^2\left|+\tfrac{1}{2}\right\rangle = \left(\hat{S}_z^2 + \frac{1}{2}(\hat{S}_+\hat{S}_- + \hat{S}_-\hat{S}_+)\right)\left|+\tfrac{1}{2}\right\rangle = \hat{S}_z^2\left|+\tfrac{1}{2}\right\rangle + \frac{1}{2}\hat{S}_+\hat{S}_-\left|+\tfrac{1}{2}\right\rangle + \frac{1}{2}\hat{S}_-\hat{S}_+\left|+\tfrac{1}{2}\right\rangle$$

$$= \left(\frac{\hbar}{2}\right)^2\left|+\tfrac{1}{2}\right\rangle + \frac{\hbar}{2}\hat{S}_+\left|-\tfrac{1}{2}\right\rangle + 0 = \left(\frac{\hbar^2}{4} + \frac{\hbar^2}{2}\right)\left|+\tfrac{1}{2}\right\rangle = \frac{3\hbar^2}{4}\left|+\tfrac{1}{2}\right\rangle \tag{7.8.4}$$

And also

$$\hat{S}^2\left|-\tfrac{1}{2}\right\rangle = \left(\hat{S}_z^2 + \frac{1}{2}(\hat{S}_+\hat{S}_- + \hat{S}_-\hat{S}_+)\right)\left|-\tfrac{1}{2}\right\rangle = \hat{S}_z^2\left|-\tfrac{1}{2}\right\rangle + \frac{1}{2}\hat{S}_+\hat{S}_-\left|-\tfrac{1}{2}\right\rangle + \frac{1}{2}\hat{S}_-\hat{S}_+\left|-\tfrac{1}{2}\right\rangle$$

$$= \left(\frac{\hbar}{2}\right)^2\left|-\tfrac{1}{2}\right\rangle + \frac{\hbar}{2}\hat{S}_-\left|+\tfrac{1}{2}\right\rangle + 0 = \left(\frac{\hbar^2}{4} + \frac{\hbar^2}{2}\right)\left|-\tfrac{1}{2}\right\rangle = \frac{3\hbar^2}{4} \tag{7.8.5}$$

Therefore,

$$|+\tfrac{1}{2}\rangle \quad |-\tfrac{1}{2}\rangle$$

$$[\hat{S}^2] = \begin{array}{c} |+\tfrac{1}{2}\rangle \\ |-\tfrac{1}{2}\rangle \end{array} \begin{pmatrix} \dfrac{3\hbar^2}{4} & 0 \\ 0 & \dfrac{3\hbar^2}{4} \end{pmatrix} = \frac{3\hbar^2}{4}\begin{pmatrix} 1 & 0 \\ 0 & 1 \end{pmatrix} \tag{7.8.6}$$

which is diagonalized.

7.9. For a particle with spin 1/2, compute, in two ways, the expectation value of $i\hat{S}_x\hat{S}_y\hat{S}_x$, where the particle wavefunction is $\dfrac{1}{\sqrt{2}}\left(|+\tfrac{1}{2}\rangle + |-\tfrac{1}{2}\rangle\right)$: (a) using $\hat{S}_+$ and $\hat{S}_-$ operators, where $\hat{S}_+ = \hat{S}_x + i\hat{S}_y$ and $\hat{S}_- = \hat{S}_x - i\hat{S}_y$; (b) in a direct way.

SOLUTION

(a) Consider the matrices $\hat{S}_+$ and $\hat{S}_-$:

$$\hat{S}_x = \frac{1}{2}(\hat{S}_+ + \hat{S}_-) \qquad \hat{S}_y = \frac{1}{2i}(\hat{S}_+ + \hat{S}_-) \tag{7.9.1}$$

Therefore,

$$\hat{A} \equiv i\hat{S}_x\hat{S}_y\hat{S}_x = \frac{i}{8i}(\hat{S}_+ + \hat{S}_-)(\hat{S}_+ - \hat{S}_-)(\hat{S}_+ + \hat{S}_-) = \frac{1}{8}(\hat{S}_+^2 - \hat{S}_+\hat{S}_- + \hat{S}_-\hat{S}_+ - \hat{S}_-^2)(\hat{S}_+ + \hat{S}_-)$$

$$= \frac{1}{8}(\hat{S}_+^3 - \hat{S}_+\hat{S}_-\hat{S}_+ + \hat{S}_-\hat{S}_+^2 - \hat{S}_-^2\hat{S}_+ + \hat{S}_+\hat{S}_-^2 - \hat{S}_+\hat{S}_-^2 + \hat{S}_-\hat{S}_+\hat{S}_- - \hat{S}_-^3) \tag{7.9.2}$$

Recall that

$$\hat{S}_+|+\tfrac{1}{2}\rangle = 0 \qquad \hat{S}_+|-\tfrac{1}{2}\rangle = \hbar|+\tfrac{1}{2}\rangle \qquad \hat{S}_-|+\tfrac{1}{2}\rangle = \hbar|-\tfrac{1}{2}\rangle \qquad \hat{S}_-|-\tfrac{1}{2}\rangle = 0 \tag{7.9.3}$$

Hence,

$$\hat{S}_+^2|-\tfrac{1}{2}\rangle = 0 \qquad \hat{S}_-^2|+\tfrac{1}{2}\rangle = 0 \tag{7.9.4}$$

Therefore, all the expressions in $\hat{A}$ that contain $\hat{S}_+^2$ or $\hat{S}_-^2$ do not contribute to the expectation value, that is,

$$\langle\hat{A}\rangle = \frac{1}{2}\left[\left(\langle+\tfrac{1}{2}| + \langle-\tfrac{1}{2}|\right)i\hat{S}_x\hat{S}_y\hat{S}_x\left(|+\tfrac{1}{2}\rangle + |-\tfrac{1}{2}\rangle\right)\right]$$

$$= \frac{1}{16}\left[\left(\langle+\tfrac{1}{2}| + \langle-\tfrac{1}{2}|\right)\hat{S}_-\hat{S}_+\hat{S}_- + \hat{S}_+\hat{S}_-\hat{S}_+\left(|+\tfrac{1}{2}\rangle + |-\tfrac{1}{2}\rangle\right)\right] \tag{7.9.5}$$

It can be seen that

$$\hat{S}_-\hat{S}_+\hat{S}_-|+\tfrac{1}{2}\rangle = \hbar^3|-\tfrac{1}{2}\rangle \qquad \hat{S}_-\hat{S}_+\hat{S}_-|-\tfrac{1}{2}\rangle = 0 \tag{7.9.6}$$

and also,

$$\hat{S}_+\hat{S}_-\hat{S}_+|+\tfrac{1}{2}\rangle = 0 \qquad \hat{S}_+\hat{S}_-\hat{S}_+|+\tfrac{1}{2}\rangle = \hbar^3|+\tfrac{1}{2}\rangle \tag{7.9.7}$$

Substituting into Eq. (7.9.5), we obtain

$$\langle\hat{A}\rangle = \frac{\hbar^3}{16}\left\{\left(\langle+\tfrac{1}{2}| + \langle-\tfrac{1}{2}|\right)\left(|+\tfrac{1}{2}\rangle + |-\tfrac{1}{2}\rangle\right) - \left(\langle+\tfrac{1}{2}| + \langle-\tfrac{1}{2}|\right)\left(|-\tfrac{1}{2}\rangle + |+\tfrac{1}{2}\rangle\right)\right\} = 0 \tag{7.9.8}$$

(b) The matrix representation of $i\hat{S}_x\hat{S}_y\hat{S}_x$ in the standard basis is

$$\hat{A} = i\hat{S}_x\hat{S}_y\hat{S}_x = \frac{\hbar^3 i}{8}\begin{pmatrix} 0 & 1 \\ 1 & 0 \end{pmatrix}\begin{pmatrix} 0 & -i \\ i & 0 \end{pmatrix}\begin{pmatrix} 0 & 1 \\ 1 & 0 \end{pmatrix} = \frac{i\hbar^3}{8}\begin{pmatrix} 0 & 1 \\ 1 & 0 \end{pmatrix}\begin{pmatrix} 0 & 1 \\ -1 & 0 \end{pmatrix}\begin{pmatrix} 0 & 1 \\ 1 & 0 \end{pmatrix}$$

$$= \begin{pmatrix} 0 & 1 \\ 1 & 0 \end{pmatrix}\begin{pmatrix} 0 & 1 \\ -1 & 0 \end{pmatrix} = \frac{i\hbar^3}{8}\begin{pmatrix} 0 & 1 \\ -1 & 0 \end{pmatrix} \tag{7.9.9}$$

The particle wavefunction in the standard basis is $\frac{1}{\sqrt{2}}\left(\left|+\frac{1}{2}\right\rangle + \left|-\frac{1}{2}\right\rangle\right) \equiv \frac{1}{\sqrt{2}}\begin{pmatrix}1\\1\end{pmatrix}$ and, therefore,

$$\langle \hat{A} \rangle = \frac{i\hbar^3}{16}(1 \quad 1)\begin{pmatrix}0 & -1\\1 & 0\end{pmatrix}\begin{pmatrix}1\\1\end{pmatrix} = \frac{i\hbar^3}{16}(1 \quad 1)\begin{pmatrix}-1\\1\end{pmatrix} = 0 \tag{7.9.10}$$

7.10. Consider the commutation relations:

$$[\hat{S}_x, \hat{S}_y] = i\hbar\hat{S}_z \tag{7.10.1}$$

$$[\hat{S}_z, \hat{S}_y] = i\hbar\hat{S}_x \tag{7.10.2}$$

$$[\hat{S}_z, \hat{S}_x] = i\hbar\hat{S}_y \tag{7.10.3}$$

Given that $\hat{S}_x$, $\hat{S}_y$, and $\hat{S}_z$ are Hermitian operators with eigenvalues $\pm\hbar/2$, find the matrix representation of $\hat{S}_x$, $\hat{S}_y$, and $\hat{S}_z$ in a basis where $\hat{S}_z$ is diagonalized.

SOLUTION

Note that $\hat{S}_x$, $\hat{S}_y$, and $\hat{S}_z$ each have two eigenvectors and that they are Hermitian operators; thus, we conclude that their matrix representation is 2×2. So,

$$\hat{S}_x = \begin{pmatrix}a_1 & b_1\\c_1 & d_1\end{pmatrix} \qquad \hat{S}_y = \begin{pmatrix}a_2 & b_2\\c_2 & d_2\end{pmatrix} \qquad \hat{S}_z = \begin{pmatrix}a_3 & b_3\\c_3 & d_3\end{pmatrix} \tag{7.10.4}$$

We want to express the matrices in a basis in which $\hat{S}_z$ is diagonalized; thus, we write

$$\hat{S}_z = \begin{pmatrix}\hbar/2 & 0\\0 & -\hbar/2\end{pmatrix} = \frac{\hbar}{2}\begin{pmatrix}1 & 0\\0 & -1\end{pmatrix} \tag{7.10.5}$$

Substituting $\hat{S}_x$ and $\hat{S}_z$ in Eq. (7.10.3) gives

$$\frac{\hbar}{2}\begin{pmatrix}1 & 0\\0 & -1\end{pmatrix}\begin{pmatrix}a_1 & b_1\\c_1 & d_1\end{pmatrix} - \frac{\hbar}{2}\begin{pmatrix}a_1 & b_1\\c_1 & d_1\end{pmatrix}\begin{pmatrix}1 & 0\\0 & (-1)\end{pmatrix} = i\hbar\begin{pmatrix}a_2 & b_2\\c_2 & d_2\end{pmatrix} \tag{7.10.6}$$

or

$$\frac{\hbar}{2}\left\{\begin{pmatrix}a_1 & b_1\\-c_1 & -d_1\end{pmatrix} - \begin{pmatrix}a_1 & -b_1\\c_1 & -d_1\end{pmatrix}\right\} = i\hbar\begin{pmatrix}a_2 & b_2\\c_2 & d_2\end{pmatrix} \tag{7.10.7}$$

Thus, we obtain

$$\begin{pmatrix}0 & -ib_1\\ic_1 & 0\end{pmatrix} = \begin{pmatrix}a_2 & b_2\\c_2 & d_2\end{pmatrix} = \hat{S}_y \tag{7.10.8}$$

$\hat{S}_y$ is a Hermitian matrix; i.e., $\hat{S}_y^\dagger = \hat{S}_y$, or $\begin{pmatrix}0 & -ib_1\\ic_1 & 0\end{pmatrix} = \begin{pmatrix}0 & -ic_1^*\\-ib_1^* & 0\end{pmatrix}$. Therefore, $b_1 = c_1 \equiv \alpha$. Hence,

$$\hat{S}_y = \begin{pmatrix}0 & -i\alpha\\i\alpha^* & 0\end{pmatrix} \qquad \hat{S}_x = \begin{pmatrix}a_1 & \alpha\\\alpha^* & d_1\end{pmatrix} \tag{7.10.9}$$

Substituting $\hat{S}_z$ and $\hat{S}_y$ in Eq. (7.10.2) gives

$$\frac{\hbar}{2}\left\{\begin{pmatrix}0 & -i\alpha\\i\alpha^* & 0\end{pmatrix}\begin{pmatrix}1 & 0\\0 & -1\end{pmatrix} - \begin{pmatrix}1 & 0\\0 & -1\end{pmatrix}\begin{pmatrix}0 & -i\alpha\\i\alpha^* & 0\end{pmatrix}\right\} = i\hbar\begin{pmatrix}a_1 & \alpha\\\alpha^* & d_1\end{pmatrix} \tag{7.10.10}$$

or

$$\frac{1}{2i}\left\{\begin{pmatrix}0 & i\alpha\\i\alpha^* & 0\end{pmatrix} - \begin{pmatrix}0 & -i\alpha\\-i\alpha^* & 0\end{pmatrix}\right\} = \begin{pmatrix}a_1 & \alpha\\\alpha^* & d_1\end{pmatrix} \qquad \begin{pmatrix}0 & \alpha\\\alpha^* & 0\end{pmatrix} = \begin{pmatrix}a_1 & \alpha\\\alpha^* & d_1\end{pmatrix} \tag{7.10.11}$$

Thus, we obtain

$$\hat{S}_y = \begin{pmatrix}0 & -i\alpha\\i\alpha^* & 0\end{pmatrix} \qquad \hat{S}_x = \begin{pmatrix}0 & \alpha\\\alpha^* & 0\end{pmatrix} \tag{7.10.12}$$

Finally, we substitute $\hat{S}_x$ and $\hat{S}_y$ in Eq. (7.10.1) and obtain

$$\left\{\begin{pmatrix} 0 & \alpha \\ \alpha^* & 0 \end{pmatrix}\begin{pmatrix} 0 & -i\alpha \\ i\alpha^* & 0 \end{pmatrix} - \begin{pmatrix} 0 & -i\alpha \\ i\alpha^* & 0 \end{pmatrix}\begin{pmatrix} 0 & \alpha \\ \alpha^* & 0 \end{pmatrix}\right\} = \frac{i\hbar^2}{2}\begin{pmatrix} 1 & 0 \\ 0 & -1 \end{pmatrix} \tag{7.10.13}$$

or

$$\begin{pmatrix} -i|\alpha|^2 & 0 \\ 0 & -i|\alpha|^2 \end{pmatrix} - \begin{pmatrix} -i|\alpha|^2 & 0 \\ 0 & i|\alpha|^2 \end{pmatrix} = \frac{i\hbar^2}{2}\begin{pmatrix} 1 & 0 \\ 0 & -1 \end{pmatrix} \Rightarrow \begin{pmatrix} |\alpha|^2 & 0 \\ 0 & -|\alpha|^2 \end{pmatrix} = \frac{\hbar^2}{4}\begin{pmatrix} 1 & 0 \\ 0 & -1 \end{pmatrix} \tag{7.10.14}$$

Thus, $|\alpha|^2 = \hbar^2/4$. If we choose α to be a real positive number ($\alpha = \hbar/2$), we obtain the standard representation of $\hat{S}_x$, $\hat{S}_y$, and $\hat{S}_z$:

$$\hat{S}_x = \frac{\hbar}{2}\begin{pmatrix} 0 & 1 \\ 1 & 0 \end{pmatrix} \qquad \hat{S}_y = \frac{\hbar}{2}\begin{pmatrix} 0 & -i \\ i & 0 \end{pmatrix} \qquad \hat{S}_z = \frac{\hbar}{2}\begin{pmatrix} 1 & 0 \\ 0 & -1 \end{pmatrix} \tag{7.10.15}$$

7.11. Using the Pauli matrices, prove: $(a)\,(\hat{\sigma}\cdot\hat{\mathbf{A}})(\hat{\sigma}\cdot\hat{\mathbf{B}}) = (\hat{\mathbf{A}}\cdot\hat{\mathbf{B}})\hat{I} + i\hat{\sigma}\cdot(\hat{\mathbf{A}}\times\hat{\mathbf{B}})$, where $\hat{\sigma} = (\hat{\sigma}_x, \hat{\sigma}_y, \hat{\sigma}_z)$ and $\hat{I}$ is a 2×2 matrix, $\hat{\mathbf{A}} = (\hat{A}_x, \hat{A}_y, \hat{A}_z)$, $\hat{\mathbf{B}} = (\hat{B}_x, \hat{B}_y, \hat{B}_z)$; $(b)\,\exp\left(\dfrac{-i\theta}{2}\mathbf{n}\cdot\hat{\sigma}\right) = \cos(\theta/2)\hat{I} - i\mathbf{n}\cdot\hat{\sigma}\sin(\theta/2)$.

Recall that we can expand an operator $\hat{A}$ in a Taylor series, $e^{\hat{A}} = \displaystyle\sum_n \frac{1}{n!}(\hat{A})^n$ (see Chap. 4).

SOLUTION

(a) We begin by considering the Pauli matrices:

$$\hat{\sigma}_x = \begin{pmatrix} 0 & 1 \\ 1 & 0 \end{pmatrix} \qquad \hat{\sigma}_y = \begin{pmatrix} 0 & -i \\ i & 0 \end{pmatrix} \qquad \hat{\sigma}_z = \begin{pmatrix} 1 & 0 \\ 0 & -1 \end{pmatrix} \tag{7.11.1}$$

so

$$\hat{\sigma}\cdot\hat{\mathbf{A}} = \hat{\sigma}_x\hat{A}_x + \hat{\sigma}_y\hat{A}_y + \hat{\sigma}_z\hat{A}_z = \begin{pmatrix} 0 & \hat{A}_x \\ \hat{A}_x & 0 \end{pmatrix} + \begin{pmatrix} 0 & -i\hat{A}_y \\ i\hat{A}_y & 0 \end{pmatrix} + \begin{pmatrix} \hat{A}_z & 0 \\ 0 & -\hat{A}_z \end{pmatrix}$$

$$= \begin{pmatrix} \hat{A}_z & \hat{A}_x - i\hat{A}_y \\ \hat{A}_x + i\hat{A}_y & -\hat{A}_z \end{pmatrix} \tag{7.11.2}$$

Similarly, $\hat{\sigma}\cdot\hat{\mathbf{B}} = \begin{pmatrix} \hat{B}_z & \hat{B}_x - i\hat{B}_y \\ \hat{B}_x + i\hat{B}_y & -\hat{B}_z \end{pmatrix}$. Thus, we obtain

$$(\hat{\sigma}\cdot\hat{\mathbf{A}})(\hat{\sigma}\cdot\hat{\mathbf{B}}) = \begin{pmatrix} \hat{A}_z & \hat{A}_x - i\hat{A}_y \\ \hat{A}_x + i\hat{A}_y & -\hat{A}_z \end{pmatrix}\begin{pmatrix} \hat{B}_z & \hat{B}_x - i\hat{B}_y \\ \hat{B}_x + i\hat{B}_y & -\hat{B}_z \end{pmatrix}$$

$$= \begin{pmatrix} \hat{A}_z\hat{B}_z + \hat{A}_x\hat{B}_x + \hat{A}_y\hat{B}_y + i\hat{A}_x\hat{B}_y - i\hat{A}_y\hat{B}_x & \hat{A}_z\hat{B}_x - i\hat{A}_z\hat{B}_y - \hat{A}_x\hat{B}_z + i\hat{A}_y\hat{B}_z \\ \hat{A}_x\hat{B}_z + i\hat{A}_y\hat{B}_z - \hat{A}_z\hat{B}_x - i\hat{A}_z\hat{B}_y & \hat{A}_x\hat{B}_x + \hat{A}_z\hat{B}_z + i\hat{A}_y\hat{B}_x - i\hat{A}_x\hat{B}_y + \hat{A}_y\hat{B}_y \end{pmatrix}$$

$$= (\hat{\mathbf{A}}\cdot\hat{\mathbf{B}})\hat{I} + \begin{pmatrix} i(\hat{A}_x\hat{B}_y - \hat{A}_y\hat{B}_x) & (\hat{A}_z\hat{B}_x - \hat{A}_x\hat{B}_z) + i(\hat{A}_y\hat{B}_z - \hat{A}_z\hat{B}_y) \\ (\hat{A}_x\hat{B}_z - \hat{A}_z\hat{B}_x) + i(\hat{A}_y\hat{B}_z - \hat{A}_z\hat{B}_y) & i(\hat{A}_y\hat{B}_x - \hat{A}_x\hat{B}_y) \end{pmatrix}$$

$$= (\hat{\mathbf{A}}\cdot\hat{\mathbf{B}})\hat{I} + (\hat{A}_x\hat{B}_y - \hat{A}_y\hat{B}_x)\begin{pmatrix} i & 0 \\ 0 & -i \end{pmatrix} + (\hat{A}_z\hat{B}_x - \hat{A}_x\hat{B}_z)\begin{pmatrix} 0 & 1 \\ -1 & 0 \end{pmatrix} + (\hat{A}_y\hat{B}_z - \hat{A}_z\hat{B}_y)\begin{pmatrix} 0 & i \\ i & 0 \end{pmatrix}$$

$$\tag{7.11.3}$$

Note that

$$\hat{\mathbf{A}} \times \hat{\mathbf{B}} = \begin{vmatrix} \mathbf{i} & \mathbf{j} & \mathbf{k} \\ \hat{A}_x & \hat{A}_y & \hat{A}_z \\ \hat{B}_x & \hat{B}_y & \hat{B}_z \end{vmatrix} = (\hat{A}_y\hat{B}_z - \hat{A}_z\hat{B}_y)\mathbf{i} + (\hat{A}_z\hat{B}_x - \hat{A}_x\hat{B}_z)\mathbf{j} + (\hat{A}_x\hat{B}_y - \hat{A}_y\hat{B}_x)\mathbf{k} \qquad (7.11.4)$$

so that

$$(\hat{\sigma} \cdot \hat{\mathbf{A}})(\hat{\sigma} \cdot \hat{\mathbf{B}}) = (\hat{\mathbf{A}} \cdot \hat{\mathbf{B}})\hat{I} + (\hat{\mathbf{A}} \times \hat{\mathbf{B}})_z i\hat{\sigma}_z + (\hat{\mathbf{A}} \times \hat{\mathbf{B}})_y i\hat{\sigma}_y + (\hat{\mathbf{A}} \times \hat{\mathbf{B}})_x i\hat{\sigma}_x$$

$$= (\hat{\mathbf{A}} \cdot \hat{\mathbf{B}})\hat{I} + i\hat{\sigma} \cdot (\hat{\mathbf{A}} \times \hat{\mathbf{B}}) \qquad (7.11.5)$$

(*b*) We expand the exponent as

$$\exp\left(-i\frac{\theta}{2}\mathbf{n}\cdot\hat{\sigma}\right) = \sum_{n=0}^{\infty} \frac{1}{n!}\left(-i\frac{\theta}{2}\mathbf{n}\cdot\hat{\sigma}\right)^n \qquad (7.11.6)$$

Note that

$$(\mathbf{n}\cdot\hat{\sigma})^n = \begin{cases} \hat{I} & \text{for even } n \\ \mathbf{n}\cdot\hat{\sigma} & \text{for odd } n \end{cases} \qquad (-i)^n = \begin{cases} 1 & \text{for even } n \\ (-i)(-1)^{(n-1)/2} & \text{for odd } n \end{cases}$$

Thus, we obtain

$$\exp\left(i\frac{\theta}{2}\mathbf{n}\cdot\hat{\sigma}\right) = \sum_{n=0}^{\infty}\left[\frac{1}{(2n)!}\left(\frac{\theta}{2}\right)^{2n}\hat{I}\right] - \sum_{n=0}^{\infty}\left[\frac{1}{(2n+1)!}\left(\frac{\theta}{2}\right)^{2n+1}(\mathbf{n}\cdot\hat{\sigma})\right]$$

$$= \hat{I}\sum_{n=0}^{\infty}\frac{1}{(2n)!}\left(\frac{\theta}{2}\right)^{2n} - i\mathbf{n}\cdot\hat{\sigma}\sum_{n=0}^{\infty}\frac{(-1)^n}{(2n+1)!}\left(\frac{\theta}{2}\right)^{2n+1} \qquad (7.11.7)$$

Using the known expansions of

$$\cos\alpha = \sum_{n=0}^{\infty}\frac{\alpha^{2n}}{(2n)!} \qquad \sin\alpha = \sum_{n=0}^{\infty}\frac{(-1)^n}{(2n+1)!}\alpha^{2n+1}$$

we eventually obtain

$$\exp\left(-\frac{i\theta}{2}\mathbf{n}\cdot\hat{\sigma}\right) = \cos\left(\frac{\theta}{2}\right)\hat{I} - i\mathbf{n}\cdot\hat{\sigma}\sin\left(\frac{\theta}{2}\right) \qquad (7.11.8)$$

7.12. Consider the eigenvectors of $\hat{S}_n$, the spin component in the $\mathbf{n}$ direction, where $\mathbf{n}$ is a unit vector:

$$\mathbf{n} = \mathbf{i}\sin\theta\cos\varphi + \mathbf{j}\sin\theta\sin\varphi + \mathbf{k}\cos\theta \qquad (7.12.1)$$

Find the rotation operator $\hat{U}_R$, where

$$\hat{U}_R\left|+\tfrac{1}{2}\right\rangle = \left|+\tfrac{1}{2}\right\rangle' \qquad \hat{U}_R\left|-\tfrac{1}{2}\right\rangle = \left|-\tfrac{1}{2}\right\rangle' \qquad (7.12.2)$$

$\left|+\tfrac{1}{2}\right\rangle$ and $\left|-\tfrac{1}{2}\right\rangle$ are the standard bases of $\hat{S}_z$ eigenvectors; $\left|+\tfrac{1}{2}\right\rangle'$ and $\left|-\tfrac{1}{2}\right\rangle'$ are the eigenvectors of $\hat{S}_\mathbf{n}$ with eigenvalues $+\hbar/2$ and $-\hbar/2$, respectively. Recall that

$$\begin{cases} \left|+\tfrac{1}{2}\right\rangle' = \cos\left(\frac{\theta}{2}\right)\left|+\tfrac{1}{2}\right\rangle + \sin\left(\frac{\theta}{2}\right)e^{i\varphi}\left|-\tfrac{1}{2}\right\rangle \\ \left|-\tfrac{1}{2}\right\rangle' = -\sin\left(\frac{\theta}{2}\right)e^{-i\varphi}\left|+\tfrac{1}{2}\right\rangle + \cos\left(\frac{\theta}{2}\right)\left|-\tfrac{1}{2}\right\rangle \end{cases} \qquad (7.12.3)$$

SOLUTION

We choose $\left|+\frac{1}{2}\right\rangle = \begin{pmatrix} 1 \\ 0 \end{pmatrix}$ and $\left|-\frac{1}{2}\right\rangle = \begin{pmatrix} 0 \\ 1 \end{pmatrix}$, so that

$$\left|+\tfrac{1}{2}\right\rangle' = \begin{pmatrix} \cos(\theta/2) \\ \sin(\theta/2)\,e^{i\varphi} \end{pmatrix} \qquad \left|-\tfrac{1}{2}\right\rangle' = \begin{pmatrix} -\sin(\theta/2)\,e^{-i\varphi} \\ \cos(\theta/2) \end{pmatrix} \tag{7.12.4}$$

Assume that the matrix representation of $\hat{U}_R$ is $\hat{U}_R = \begin{pmatrix} a & b \\ c & d \end{pmatrix}$; then the condition from Eq. (7.12.2) $\hat{U}_R\left|-\frac{1}{2}\right\rangle = \left|-\frac{1}{2}\right\rangle'$ can be written as

$$\begin{pmatrix} a & b \\ c & d \end{pmatrix}\begin{pmatrix} 1 \\ 0 \end{pmatrix} = \begin{pmatrix} \cos(\theta/2) \\ \sin(\theta/2)\,e^{i\varphi} \end{pmatrix} \Rightarrow \begin{pmatrix} a \\ b \end{pmatrix} = \begin{pmatrix} \cos(\theta/2) \\ \sin(\theta/2)\,e^{i\varphi} \end{pmatrix} \tag{7.12.5}$$

Similarly, for $U_R\left|-\frac{1}{2}\right\rangle = \left|-\frac{1}{2}\right\rangle'$ we obtain $\begin{pmatrix} b \\ d \end{pmatrix} = \begin{pmatrix} -\sin(\theta/2)\,e^{-i\varphi} \\ \cos(\theta/2) \end{pmatrix}$; so finally, we get

$$\hat{U}_R = \begin{pmatrix} a & b \\ c & d \end{pmatrix} = \begin{pmatrix} \cos(\theta/2) & -\sin(\theta/2)\,e^{-i\varphi} \\ \sin(\theta/2)\,e^{i\varphi} & \cos(\theta/2) \end{pmatrix}$$

$$= \begin{pmatrix} \cos(\theta/2) & 0 \\ 0 & \cos(\theta/2) \end{pmatrix} + \begin{pmatrix} 0 & -\sin(\theta/2)\cos\varphi \\ \sin(\theta/2)\cos\varphi & 0 \end{pmatrix} + \begin{pmatrix} 0 & +\sin(\theta/2)\sin\varphi \\ \sin(\theta/2)\sin\varphi & 0 \end{pmatrix}$$

$$= \cos\left(\frac{\theta}{2}\right)\hat{I} - i\sin\left(\frac{\theta}{2}\right)(\cos\varphi)\,\hat{\sigma}_y - i\sin\left(\frac{\theta}{2}\right)(-\sin\varphi)\,\hat{\sigma}_x$$

$$= \cos\left(\frac{\theta}{2}\right)\hat{I} - i\sin\left(\frac{\theta}{2}\right)(\mathbf{u}\cdot\hat{\sigma}) \tag{7.12.6}$$

where $\mathbf{u} = -\mathbf{i}\sin\varphi + \mathbf{j}\cos\varphi$ is a unit vector (see Fig. 7.3). Note that $\mathbf{u} = \dfrac{\mathbf{k}\times\mathbf{n}}{|\mathbf{k}\times\mathbf{n}|}$, so

$$\mathbf{k}\times\mathbf{n} = \begin{vmatrix} \mathbf{i} & \mathbf{j} & \mathbf{k} \\ 0 & 0 & 1 \\ \sin\theta\cos\varphi & \sin\theta\sin\varphi & \cos\theta \end{vmatrix} = -\mathbf{i}\sin\theta\sin\varphi + \mathbf{j}\sin\theta\cos\varphi \Rightarrow |\mathbf{k}\times\mathbf{n}| = \sin\theta \tag{7.12.7}$$

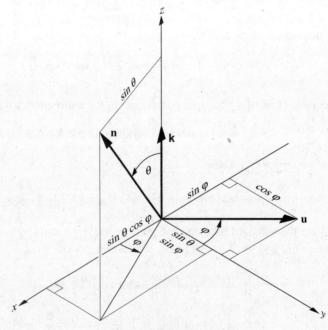

Fig. 7.3

In Prob. 7.11, part (*b*), we obtain the result

$$\cos\left(\frac{\theta}{2}\right)\hat{I} - i\sin\left(\frac{\theta}{2}\right)(\mathbf{u}\cdot\hat{\mathbf{S}}) = \exp\left(-\frac{i\theta}{\hbar}\mathbf{u}\cdot\hat{\mathbf{S}}\right) \tag{7.12.8}$$

In conclusion, the rotation operator is

$$\hat{U}_R = \exp\left(-\frac{i\theta}{\hbar}\mathbf{u}\cdot\hat{\mathbf{S}}\right) \tag{7.12.9}$$

where **u** is a unit vector in the direction of the axis around which we want to rotate the system, $\mathbf{u} = \dfrac{\mathbf{k}\times\mathbf{n}}{|\mathbf{k}\times\mathbf{n}|}$.

Furthermore, **n** is a unit vector in the direction of the new *z* axis, and θ is the angle between the new and old *z* axes.

SUPPLEMENTARY PROBLEMS

7.13. Prove that $\hat{\sigma}_x^2 = \hat{\sigma}_y^2 = \hat{\sigma}_z^2 = \hat{I}$, where $\hat{I}$ is a 2×2 unit matrix.

7.14. Calculate the anticommutation relation $[\hat{\sigma}_i, \hat{\sigma}_j]_+$ where we defined $[\hat{A}, \hat{B}]_+ = \hat{A}\hat{B} + \hat{B}\hat{A}$.

Ans. $[\hat{\sigma}_i, \hat{\sigma}_j]_+ = 0$.

7.15. Show that the matrix of $\hat{S}^2 = \hat{S}_x^2 + \hat{S}_y^2 + \hat{S}_z^2$ is diagonalized in the basis of eigenvectors of both $\hat{S}_x$ and $\hat{S}_y$.

7.16. Calculate the value of $\langle\hat{S}_i\rangle$ and ΔS_i $(i=x, y, z)$ for the spinor $\frac{1}{\sqrt{2}}\left(e^{i\varphi/2}\left|+\frac{1}{2}\right\rangle + e^{-i\varphi/2}\left|-\frac{1}{2}\right\rangle\right)$.

Ans. $\langle\hat{S}_x\rangle = \frac{\hbar}{2}\cos\varphi$, $\Delta S_x = \frac{\hbar}{2}\sin\varphi$; $\langle\hat{S}_y\rangle = -\frac{\hbar}{2}\cos\varphi$, $\Delta S_y = \frac{\hbar}{2}\cos\varphi$; $\langle\hat{S}_z\rangle = 0$, $\Delta S_z = \frac{\hbar}{2}$.

7.17. The matrix representation of $\hat{S}_x$ in a certain basis is $\hat{S}_x = \frac{\hbar}{2}\begin{pmatrix}1 & 0\\0 & -1\end{pmatrix}$. Find the basis and the matrix representation of $\hat{S}_y$ and $\hat{S}_z$.

Ans. $\left|+\frac{1}{2}\right\rangle_x = \frac{1}{\sqrt{2}}\left(\left|+\frac{1}{2}\right\rangle_x + \left|-\frac{1}{2}\right\rangle_x\right)$; $\left|-\frac{1}{2}\right\rangle_x = \frac{1}{\sqrt{2}}\left(\left|+\frac{1}{2}\right\rangle_x - \left|-\frac{1}{2}\right\rangle_x\right)$; $\hat{S}_y = \frac{\hbar}{2}\begin{pmatrix}0 & 1\\1 & 0\end{pmatrix}$; $\hat{S}_z = \frac{\hbar}{2}\begin{pmatrix}0 & -i\\i & 0\end{pmatrix}$.

7.18. Consider the rotation operator

$$\hat{U}_R(\theta, \mathbf{u}) = \exp\left(\frac{i\theta}{\hbar}\mathbf{u}\cdot\hat{\mathbf{S}}\right) = \exp\left(\frac{i\theta}{2}\mathbf{u}\cdot\hat{\sigma}\right) \tag{7.18.1}$$

By rotating the eigenvectors of $\hat{S}_z$, find the eigenvectors of $\hat{S}_x$ and $\hat{S}_y$ in the standard basis.

Ans. $\left|+\frac{1}{2}\right\rangle_x = \hat{U}_R\left(\theta=\frac{\pi}{2}, \mathbf{u}=\mathbf{j}\right)\left|+\frac{1}{2}\right\rangle_z = \frac{1}{\sqrt{2}}\left(\left|+\frac{1}{2}\right\rangle_z + \left|-\frac{1}{2}\right\rangle_z\right)$

$\left|-\frac{1}{2}\right\rangle_x = \hat{U}_R\left(\theta=\frac{\pi}{2}, \mathbf{u}=\mathbf{j}\right)\left|-\frac{1}{2}\right\rangle_z = \frac{1}{\sqrt{2}}\left(\left|+\frac{1}{2}\right\rangle_z - \left|-\frac{1}{2}\right\rangle_z\right)$

$\left|+\frac{1}{2}\right\rangle_y = \hat{U}_R\left(\theta=\frac{\pi}{2}, \mathbf{u}=-\mathbf{i}\right)\left|+\frac{1}{2}\right\rangle_z = \frac{1}{\sqrt{2}}\left(-i\left|+\frac{1}{2}\right\rangle_z + \left|-\frac{1}{2}\right\rangle_z\right)$

$\left|-\frac{1}{2}\right\rangle_y = \hat{U}_R\left(\theta=\frac{\pi}{2}, \mathbf{u}=-\mathbf{i}\right)\left|-\frac{1}{2}\right\rangle_z = \frac{1}{\sqrt{2}}\left(\left|+\frac{1}{2}\right\rangle_z + i\left|-\frac{1}{2}\right\rangle_z\right)$

Hydrogen-like Atoms

8.1   A Particle in a Central Potential

The Hamiltonian of a particle of mass M placed in a central potential $V(r)$ is

$$\hat{H} = \frac{\hat{\mathbf{p}}^2}{2M} + \hat{V}(r) = -\frac{\hbar^2}{2M}\nabla^2 + \hat{V}(r) \tag{8.1}$$

where the Laplacian ∇^2 in spherical coordinates is

$$\nabla^2 = \frac{1}{r}\frac{\partial^2}{\partial r^2} + \frac{1}{r^2}\left(\frac{\partial^2}{\partial\theta^2} + \frac{1}{\tan\theta}\frac{\partial}{\partial\theta} + \frac{1}{\sin^2\theta}\frac{\partial^2}{\partial\varphi^2}\right) \tag{8.2}$$

Comparing Eq. (8.2) with the expression for the operator $\hat{\mathbf{L}}^2$ obtained in Chap. 6, we see that $\hat{H}$ can be written as

$$\hat{H} = -\frac{\hbar^2}{2M}\frac{1}{r}\frac{\partial^2}{\partial r^2}r + \frac{1}{2Mr^2}\hat{\mathbf{L}}^2 + \hat{V}(r) \tag{8.3}$$

The three components of $\hat{\mathbf{L}}$ commute with $\hat{\mathbf{L}}^2$, and therefore, according to Eq. (8.3), they also commute with $\hat{H}$:

$$[\hat{H}, \hat{L}_x] = [\hat{H}, \hat{L}_y] = [\hat{H}, \hat{L}_z] = 0 \tag{8.4}$$

We can now solve the three eigenvalue equations:

$$\hat{H}\psi(r, \theta, \varphi) = E\psi(r, \theta, \varphi) \tag{8.5}$$

$$\hat{\mathbf{L}}^2\psi(r, \theta, \varphi) = l(l+1)\hbar^2\psi(r, \theta, \varphi) \tag{8.6}$$

$$\hat{L}_z\psi(r, \theta, \varphi) = m\hbar\psi(r, \theta, \varphi) \tag{8.7}$$

to determine those states that are eigenfunctions of $\hat{H}$, $\hat{\mathbf{L}}^2$, and $\hat{L}_z$ (we used the notations of Chap. 6). Using separation of variables (see Problem 8.1), we get

$$\psi(r, \theta, \varphi) = R_{nl}(r)Y_l^m(\theta, \varphi) \tag{8.8}$$

where Y_l^m is the spherical harmonic function and $R_{nl}(r)$ is the radial function (which does not depend on the quantum number m). Since the $Y_l^m(\theta, \varphi)$ are normalized, by definition,

$$\int_0^{2\pi} \int_0^{\pi} (Y_l^{m'})^* (Y_l^m) \sin\theta \, d\theta \, d\varphi = \delta_{ll'} \delta_{mm'} \tag{8.9}$$

The normalization condition is

$$\int_0^\infty r^2 |R(r)|^2 \, dr = 1 \tag{8.10}$$

According to Problem 8.1, the radial equation for $R_{nl}(r)$ is

$$\left[-\frac{\hbar^2}{2M} \frac{1}{r} \frac{d^2}{dr^2} r + \frac{l(l+1)\hbar^2}{2Mr^2} + V(r) \right] R_{nl}(r) = E R_{nl}(r) \tag{8.11}$$

We can simplify this equation by writing

$$R_{nl}(r) = \frac{1}{r} U_{nl}(r) \tag{8.12}$$

from which we have

$$\left[-\frac{\hbar^2}{2M} \frac{d^2}{dr^2} r + \frac{l(l+1)\hbar^2}{2Mr^2} + V(r) \right] U_{nl}(r) = E U_{nl}(r) \tag{8.13}$$

Equation (8.13) is analogous to the one-dimensional problem of a particle of mass M moving in an effective potential $V_{eff}(r)$, where

$$V_{eff}(r) = V(r) + \frac{l(l+1)\hbar^2}{2Mr^2} \tag{8.14}$$

For the angular part, we have the equations:

$$-i\frac{\partial}{\partial\varphi} Y_l^m(\theta, \varphi) = m Y_l^m(\theta, \varphi) \tag{8.15}$$

$$-\left[\frac{1}{\sin\theta} \frac{\partial}{\partial\theta} \left(\sin\theta \frac{\partial}{\partial\theta} \right) + \frac{1}{\sin^2\theta} \frac{\partial^2}{\partial\varphi^2} \right] Y_l^m(\theta, \varphi) = l(l+1) Y_l^m(\theta, \varphi) \tag{8.16}$$

8.2 Two Interacting Particles

Consider a system of two spinless particles of mass m_1 and m_2 and positions $\mathbf{r}_1$ and $\mathbf{r}_2$. We assume that the potential energy depends only on the distance between the particles, $V(\mathbf{r}_1 - \mathbf{r}_2)$. The study of the motion of the two particles is simplified if we adopt the coordinates of the center of mass:

$$\mathbf{r}_{cm} = \frac{m_1 \mathbf{r}_1 + m_2 \mathbf{r}_2}{m_1 + m_2} \tag{8.17}$$

and the relative coordinates:

$$\mathbf{r} = \mathbf{r}_1 - \mathbf{r}_2 \tag{8.18}$$

We can then derive the equations (see Problem 8.2):

$$-\frac{\hbar^2}{2(m_1 + m_2)} \nabla^2 \phi(\mathbf{r}_{cm}) = E_{cm} \phi(\mathbf{r}_{cm}) \tag{8.19}$$

and

$$\left[-\frac{\hbar^2}{2\mu}\nabla^2 + V(\mathbf{r})\right]\chi(\mathbf{r}) = E_{cm}\chi(\mathbf{r})$$ (8.20)

where μ is the *reduced mass* of the two particles:

$$\mu = \frac{m_1 m_2}{m_1 + m_2}$$ (8.21)

From Eq. (8.19) we conclude that the center of mass behaves like a free particle of mass $m_1 + m_2$ and energy E_{cm}. The relative motion of the two particles is determined by Eq. (8.20) and is analogous to the motion of a particle of mass μ placed in a potential $V(\mathbf{r})$.

8.3   The Hydrogen Atom

The hydrogen atom consists of a proton of mass $m_p = 1.67 \times 10^{-27}$ kg and charge $e = 1.6 \times 10^{-19}$ C, and an electron of mass $m_e = 0.91 \times 10^{-30}$ kg and charge $-e$. The interaction between these two particles is essentially electrostatic, and the potential energy in MKS units is

$$V(r) = -\frac{k_0 e^2}{r}$$

Some authors still use CGS, or Gaussian, units when dealing with atoms in which case

$$V(r) = -\frac{e^2}{r}$$ (8.22)

where r is the distance between the two particles. Since m_p is much greater than m_e, the reduced mass μ of the system is very close to m_e:

$$\mu = \frac{m_e m_p}{m_e + m_p} \cong m_e\left(1 - \frac{m_e}{m_p}\right)$$ (8.23)

This means that the center of mass of the system is practically in the same place as the proton; the relative motion can be identified, to a good approximation, with the electron.

According to Eqs. (8.8) and (8.12), we may write the states of the system in the form

$$\psi_{nlm}(r, \theta, \varphi) = \frac{1}{r}U_{nl}(r)Y_l^m(\theta, \varphi)$$ (8.24)

We introduce the *Bohr radius* a_0, which characterizes atomic dimensions:

$$a_0 = \frac{\hbar^2}{\mu e^2} \cong 0.52 \text{ Å}$$ (8.25)

and the *ionization energy* of the hydrogen atom:

$$E_1 = \frac{\mu e^4}{2\hbar^2} \cong 13.6 \text{ eV}$$ (8.26)

To solve the radial equation for the hydrogen atom, we define $\rho = r/a_0$ and $\lambda_{kl} = \sqrt{-E_{kl}/E_1}$. The radial equation, Eq. (8.13), then becomes

$$\left[\frac{d^2}{d\rho^2} - \frac{l(l+1)}{\rho^2} + \frac{2}{\rho} - \lambda_{kl}^2\right]U_{kl}(\rho) = 0$$ (8.27)

where we use the index k instead of n; $n = k + l$. The radial equation is solved by performing a change of function (see Problem 8.1):

$$U_{kl}(\rho) = e^{-\rho\lambda_{kl}}\xi_{kl}(\rho) \tag{8.28}$$

and expanding ξ_{kl} in powers of ρ:

$$\xi_{kl}(\rho) = \rho^s \sum_{q=0}^{\infty} C_q \rho^q \tag{8.29}$$

The coefficients C_q can be obtained from the recursion relation (see Problem 8.1):

$$C_q = (-1)^q \left(\frac{2}{k+1}\right)^q \frac{(k-1)!}{(k-q-1)!}\frac{(2l+1)!}{q!(q+2l+1)}C_0 \tag{8.30}$$

The solution for $R_{nl}(\rho)$ can be written in the form

$$R_{nl}(\rho) = -\sqrt{\left(\frac{2}{na_0}\right)^3 \frac{(n-l-1)!}{2n[(n+1)!]^3}}\, e^{-\rho/2}\rho^l L_{n+l}^{2l+1}(\rho) \tag{8.31}$$

where $L_p^q(\rho)$ are the associated Laguerre polynomials (for detailed information, see the Mathematical Appendix). Some examples of the radial functions are

$$R_{n=1, l=0}(r) = 2(a_0)^{-3/2}e^{-r/a_0} \tag{8.32}$$

$$R_{n=2, l=0}(r) = 2(2a_0)^{-3/2}\left(1 - \frac{r}{2a_0}\right)e^{-r/2a_0} \tag{8.33}$$

$$R_{n=2, l=1}(r) = (2a_0)^{-3/2}\frac{1}{\sqrt{3}}\frac{r}{a_0}e^{-r/2a_0} \tag{8.34}$$

8.4 Energy Levels of the Hydrogen Atom

For fixed l, there exists an infinite number of possible energy values:

$$E_{kl} = -\frac{E_n}{(k+l)^2} \qquad k = 1, 2, 3, \ldots \tag{8.35}$$

Each of them is *at least* $(2l + 1)$-fold degenerate. This *essential degeneracy* results from the radial equation being independent of the quantum number m. Some of the energy values manifest *accidental degeneracy*. Here the E_{kl} do not depend on k and l separately but only on their sum. We set $n = k + l$, and then

$$E_n = -\frac{1}{n^2}E_1 = -\frac{\mu e^4}{2\hbar^2 n^2} = -\frac{1}{n^2} \times 13.6 \text{ eV} \tag{8.36}$$

The shell characterized by n is said to contain n subshells, each corresponding to one of the values of l:

$$l = 0, 1, 2, \ldots, n-1 \tag{8.37}$$

Each subshell contains $2l + 1$ distinct states corresponding to the possible values of m,

$$m = -l, -l + 1, \ldots, l - 1, l \tag{8.38}$$

The total degeneracy of the energy level E_n is

$$g_n = \sum_{l=0}^{n-1} (2l + 1) = \frac{2(n-1)n}{2} + n = n^2 \tag{8.39}$$

If one takes into account the electron's spin (which can be in one of two possible orientations) then the number g_n should be multiplied by 2.

For historical reasons (from the period in which the study of atomic spectra resulted in empirical classification of the lines observed), the various values of l are associated with letters of the Latin alphabet, as follows:

$$(l = 0) \leftrightarrow s$$

$$(l = 1) \leftrightarrow p$$

$$(l = 2) \leftrightarrow d$$

$$(l = 3) \leftrightarrow f \tag{8.40}$$

$$(l = 4) \leftrightarrow g$$

$$\vdots \qquad \vdots$$

in alphabetical order

8.5 Mean Value Expressions

The following list includes some mean value expressions of r^k that are useful in many problems:

$$\langle r^k \rangle \equiv \int_0^\infty r^{k+2} [R_{nl}(r)]^2 \, dr \tag{8.41}$$

$$\langle r \rangle = \frac{a_0}{2} [3n^2 - l(l+1)] \tag{8.42}$$

$$\langle r^2 \rangle = \frac{a_0^2 n^2}{2} [5n^2 + 1 - 3l(l+1)] \tag{8.43}$$

$$\left\langle \frac{1}{r} \right\rangle = \frac{1}{a_0 n^2} \tag{8.44}$$

and

$$\left\langle \frac{1}{r^2} \right\rangle = \frac{1}{a_0^2 n^3 (l + 1/2)} \tag{8.45}$$

8.6 Hydrogen-like Atoms

The results obtained in Sec. 8.5 originate in calculations for systems of two particles with mutual attraction energy inversely proportional to the distance between them. There are many physical systems that satisfy this condition: deuterium, tritium, ions that contain only one electron, muonic atoms, positronium, etc. The results are applicable to these systems, provided that we properly select the constants introduced in the calculations. For example, if the charge of a nucleus is Z, then $e^2 \to Ze^2$ in all the calculations.

SOLVED PROBLEMS

8.1. (*a*) Write the eigenvalue equation for a particle in a central potential $V(r)$, and perform the separation of variables in the wavefunction. Obtain the radial equation and the two angular equations. (*b*) Solve the radial equation for the potential of the hydrogen atom $V(r) = -e^2/r$.

SOLUTION

(*a*) Consider the Hamiltonian of the system:

$$\hat{H} = -\frac{\hbar^2}{2\mu}\frac{1}{r}\frac{\partial}{\partial r^2}(r) + \frac{\hat{L}^2}{2\mu r^2} + V(r) \tag{8.1.1}$$

We have the following eigenvalue equation:

$$\left[-\frac{\hbar^2}{2\mu}\frac{1}{r}\frac{\partial^2}{\partial r^2}(r) + \frac{\hat{L}^2}{2\mu r^2} + V(r)\right]\psi(r,\theta,\varphi) = E\psi(r,\theta,\varphi) \tag{8.1.2}$$

The three observables $\hat{H}$, $\hat{L}^2$, and $\hat{L}_z$ commute. Thus, we can look for functions $\psi(r,\theta,\varphi)$ that are eigenfunctions of $\hat{L}^2$ and $\hat{L}_z$. We have the following system of differential equations:

$$\hat{H}\psi(r,\theta,\varphi) = E\psi(r,\theta,\varphi) \tag{8.1.3}$$

$$\hat{L}^2\psi(r,\theta,\varphi) = l(l+1)\hbar^2\psi(r,\theta,\varphi) \tag{8.1.4}$$

and

$$\hat{L}_z\psi(r,\theta,\varphi) = m\hbar\psi(r,\theta,\varphi) \tag{8.1.5}$$

Note that we have three differential equations for $\psi(r,\theta,\varphi)$, which is a function of three variables. Since

$$\hat{L}^2 = -\hbar^2\left(\frac{\partial}{\partial\theta^2} + \frac{1}{\tan\theta}\frac{\partial}{\partial\theta} + \frac{1}{\sin^2\theta}\frac{\partial^2}{\partial\varphi^2}\right) \tag{8.1.6}$$

and $\hat{L}_z = -i\hbar\dfrac{\partial}{\partial\varphi}$ (see Chap. 6), Eqs. (8.1.4) and (8.1.5) can be replaced by

$$-\left(\frac{\partial}{\partial\theta^2} + \frac{1}{\tan\theta}\frac{\partial}{\partial\theta} + \frac{1}{\sin^2\theta}\frac{\partial^2}{\partial\varphi^2}\right)\psi(r,\theta,\varphi) = l(l+1)\psi(r,\theta,\varphi) \tag{8.1.7}$$

and

$$-i\frac{\partial\psi(r,\theta,\varphi)}{\partial\varphi} = m\psi(r,\theta,\varphi) \tag{8.1.8}$$

The solutions $\psi(r,\theta,\varphi)$ to these equations corresponding to fixed values of l and m must be products of a function of r and the spherical harmonic $Y_l^m(\theta,\varphi)$:

$$\psi(r,\theta,\varphi) = R(r)Y_l^m(\theta,\varphi) \tag{8.1.9}$$

Substituting Eq. (8.1.9) in Eqs. (8.1.2), (8.1.8), and (8.1.9), we obtain

$$\left[-\frac{\hbar^2}{2\mu}\frac{1}{r}\frac{d^2}{dr^2}(r) + \frac{l(l+1)\hbar^2}{2\mu r^2} + V(r)\right]R(r) = ER(r) \tag{8.1.10}$$

$$\left[-\frac{\partial}{\partial\theta^2} + \frac{1}{\tan\theta}\frac{\partial}{\partial\theta} + \frac{1}{\sin^2\theta}\frac{\partial}{\partial\varphi^2}\right]Y_l^m(\theta,\varphi) = l(l+1)Y_l^m(\theta,\varphi) \tag{8.1.11}$$

and

$$-i\frac{\partial}{\partial\phi}Y_l^m(\theta,\varphi) = mY_l^m(\theta,\varphi) \tag{8.1.12}$$

Equation (8.1.10) is the radial equation; Eqs. (8.1.11) and (8.1.12) are the angular equations. From Eq. (8.1.12) we can conclude that the φ-dependence of $Y_l^m(\theta,\varphi)$ is of the form $e^{im\varphi}$. Thus, $Y_l^m(\theta,\varphi) = G_l^m(\theta)e^{im\varphi}$, where $G_l^m(\theta)$ is a function of θ only.

(b) We write the radial equation in the form

$$\left[-\frac{\hbar^2}{2\mu}\frac{1}{r}\frac{d^2}{dr^2}(r) + \frac{l(l+1)\hbar^2}{2\mu r^2} + V(r)\right]R_{kl}(r) = E_{kl}R_{kl}(r) \tag{8.1.13}$$

Introducing the function $u_{kl}(r) = rR_{kl}(r)$ we arrive at

$$\left[-\frac{\hbar^2}{2\mu}\frac{d^2}{dr^2} + \frac{l(l+1)\hbar^2}{2\mu r^2} + V(r)\right]u_{kl}(r) = E_{kl}u_{kl}(r) \tag{8.1.14}$$

We define an effective potential:

$$V_{\text{eff}} = V(r) + \frac{l(l+1)\hbar^2}{2\mu r^2} \tag{8.1.15}$$

We may view Eq. (8.1.14) as a one-dimensional problem, i.e., a particle of mass μ moving in the effective potential V_{eff}, the one difference being that r assumes nonnegative values only. To express Eq. (8.1.14) in dimensionless form, we define

$$E_I = \frac{\mu e^4}{2\hbar^2} \qquad a_0 = \frac{\hbar^2}{\mu e^2} \qquad \lambda_{kl} = \sqrt{\frac{-E_{kl}}{E_I}} \qquad \rho = \frac{r}{a_0} \tag{8.1.16}$$

Equation (8.1.14) becomes

$$\left[\frac{d^2}{d\rho^2} - \frac{l(l+1)}{\rho^2} + \frac{2}{\rho} - \lambda_{kl}^2\right]u_{kl}(\rho) = 0 \tag{8.1.17}$$

Let us define $u_{kl}(\rho) = e^{-\rho\lambda_{kl}}\xi_{kl}(\rho)$; we now obtain

$$\left[\frac{d^2}{d\rho^2} - 2\lambda_{kl}\frac{d}{d\rho} + \left(\frac{2}{\rho} - \frac{l(l+1)}{\rho^2}\right)\right]\xi_{kl}(\rho) = 0 \tag{8.1.18}$$

with the boundary condition $\xi_{kl}(0) = 0$. An expansion of $\xi_{kl}(\rho)$ in a power series of ρ yields $\xi_{kl}(\rho) = \rho^s\sum_{q=0}^{\infty}C_q\rho^q$, where C_0 is the first nonzero coefficient. Thus,

$$\frac{d\xi_{kl}(\rho)}{d\rho} = \sum_{q=0}^{\infty}(q+s)C_q\rho^{q+s-1} \tag{8.1.19}$$

and

$$\frac{d^2\xi_{kl}(\rho)}{d\rho^2} = \sum_{q=0}^{\infty}(q+s)(q+s-1)C_q\rho^{q+s-2} \tag{8.1.20}$$

Substituting Eqs. (8.1.19) and (8.1.20) into Eq. (8.1.18), we obtain a power series on the left-hand side and zero on the right-hand side; thus, the coefficients of the powers of ρ equal zero. We assume that the solution of Eq. (8.1.13) behaves at the origin as r^s:

$$R_{kl}(r) \underset{r\to 0}{\sim} Cr^s \tag{8.1.21}$$

Substituting Eq. (8.1.21) in to Eq. (8.1.13) we obtain

$$l(l+1) - s(s+1) = 0 \tag{8.1.22}$$

which is satisfied if $s = l$ or $s = -(l+1)$. Therefore, for a given value of E_{kl}, there are two linearly independent solutions of Eq. (8.1.13). The solutions behave at the origin as r^l and $1/r^{l+1}$, respectively. The latter solution must be rejected, as it can be shown that $(1/r^{l+1})Y_l^m(\theta,\varphi)$ is not a solution of the eigenvalue equation, Eq. (8.1.2), for $r=0$. It follows that the solutions of Eq. (8.1.13) go to zero at the origin for all l, since $u_{kl}(r) \underset{r\to 0}{\sim} Cr^{l+1}$. Therefore, the condition $u_{kl}(0) = 0$ should be added to Eq. (8.1.13). In the power series that we obtain we now take the lowest term and equate its coefficient to zero. It follows that

$$[-l(l+1) + s(s-1)]C_0 = 0 \tag{8.1.23}$$

Since $C_0 \neq 0$, we have $s = -l$ or $s = l+1$. Next, we set the coefficient of the general term ρ^{q+s-2} equal to zero (for $s = l+1$) and obtain the following recurrence relation:

$$q(q+2l+1)C_q = 2[(q+l)\lambda_{kl} - 1]C_{q-1} \tag{8.1.24}$$

Hence, assuming that C_0 is known, we can calculate $C_1, C_2, \ldots$. Since $C_q/C_{q-1} \to 0$ when $q \to \infty$, the series is convergent for all ρ. One can show that

$$C_q = (-1)^q \left(\frac{2}{k+l}\right)^q \frac{(k-1)!}{(k-q-1)!}\frac{(2l+1)!}{(q+2l+1)!}C_0 \tag{8.1.25}$$

where C_0 can be determined from the normalization condition:

$$\int_0^\infty r^2 |R_{kl}(r)|^2 dr = \int_0^\infty |u_{kl}(r)|^2 dr \tag{8.1.26}$$

8.2. A hydrogen atom can be viewed as two point-charged particles—a proton and an electron with Coulomb's interacting potential between them. Write the Schrödinger equation for such a system and separate it into two parts: one describing the motion of the center of mass, and another describing the relative motion of the proton and the electron.

SOLUTION

The Schrödinger equation for the proton and the electron is

$$\left(-\frac{\hbar}{2}\left[\frac{\nabla_1^2}{m_p} + \frac{\nabla_2^2}{m_e}\right] + V(r)\right)\psi = E\psi \tag{8.2.1}$$

where m_e and m_p denote the mass of the proton and the electron, respectively. The indices 1 and 2 refer to the proton and the electron, respectively. The potential between the particles is

$$V(r) = V(r_1 - r_2) = -Ze^2 \frac{1}{\sqrt{(x_1-x_2)^2 + (y_1-y_2)^2 + (z_1-z_2)^2}} = -\frac{Ze^2}{r} \tag{8.2.2}$$

Define the relative coordinates:

$$x_r = x_2 - x_1 \qquad y_r = y_2 - y_1 \qquad z_r = z_2 - z_1 \tag{8.2.3}$$

and the center of mass coordinates $r_{cm} = \dfrac{m_p r_1 + m_e r_2}{m_p + m_e}$. For the differential operators we have

$$\frac{\partial^2}{\partial x_1^2} = \left(\frac{m_p}{m_p+m_e}\right)^2 \frac{\partial^2}{\partial x_{cm}^2} - \frac{2m_p}{m_p+m_e}\frac{\partial^2}{\partial x_{cm}\partial x_r} + \frac{\partial^2}{\partial x_r^2} \tag{8.2.4}$$

and

$$\frac{\partial^2}{\partial x_2^2} = \left(\frac{m_e}{m_p + m_e}\right)^2 \frac{\partial^2}{\partial x_{cm}^2} + \frac{2m_e}{m_p + m_e}\frac{\partial^2}{\partial x_r \partial x_{cm}} + \frac{\partial^2}{\partial x_r^2} \tag{8.2.5}$$

Similar relations hold for the operators $\frac{\partial^2}{\partial y_1^2}, \frac{\partial^2}{\partial y_2^2}, \frac{\partial^2}{\partial z_1^2}$, and $\frac{\partial^2}{\partial z_2^2}$. Substituting the operators into Eq. (8.2.1), we obtain

$$-\frac{\hbar^2}{2}\left[\frac{1}{m_p + m_e}\left(\frac{\partial^2}{\partial x_{cm}^2} + \frac{\partial^2}{\partial y_{cm}^2} + \frac{\partial^2}{\partial z_{cm}^2}\right) + \frac{1}{\mu}\left(\frac{\partial^2}{\partial x_r^2} + \frac{\partial^2}{\partial y_r^2} + \frac{\partial^2}{\partial z_r^2}\right)\right] - \frac{Ze^2}{r}\right)\psi = E\psi \tag{8.2.6}$$

where μ is the reduced mass, $\mu = \frac{m_p m_e}{m_p + m_e}$. We separate the wavefunction ψ into two parts. The first part depends only on the center-of-mass coordinates, while the second part depends only on the relative coordinates, $\psi = \phi(r_{cm})\chi(r_r)$. Substituting into Eq. (8.2.6) We arrive at

$$-\frac{\hbar^2}{2\phi(r_{cm})}\left[\frac{1}{m_p + m_e}\nabla_{cm}^2\phi(r_{cm})\right] = \frac{\hbar^2}{2\chi(r_r)}\left[\frac{1}{\mu}\nabla_r^2 + \frac{Ze^2}{r} + E\right]\chi(r_r) \tag{8.2.7}$$

For Eq. (8.2.7) to be valid for all values of r_{cm} and r_r, each side of the equation must be equal to a constant. Therefore we obtain two separate equations:

$$\left[\frac{\hbar^2}{2(m_p + m_e)}\nabla_{cm}^2 + E_{cm}\right]\phi(r_{cm}) = 0 \tag{8.2.8}$$

and

$$\left(\frac{\hbar^2}{2\mu}\nabla_r^2 + \frac{Ze^2}{r} + E_r\right)\chi(r_r) = 0 \tag{8.2.9}$$

E_{cm} is the translational kinetic energy of the center-of-mass frame and E_r is the relative energy. Clearly, we have $E = E_{cm} + E_r$. To obtain the wavefunction of a hydrogen atom's electron one must solve Eq. (8.2.9) (see Problem 8.1).

8.3. The wavefunction of an electron in a hydrogen-like atom is $\psi(r) = Ce^{-r/a}$, where $a = a_0/Z$; $a_0 \approx 0.5$ Å is the Bohr radius (the nucleus charge is Ze and the atom contains only one electron). (*a*) Compute the normalization constant. (*b*) If the nucleus number is $A = 173$ and $Z = 70$, what is the probability that the electron is in the nucleus? Assume that the radius of the nucleus is $1.2 \times A^{1/3}$ fm. (*c*) What is the probability that the electron is in the region $x, y, z > 0$?

SOLUTION

(*a*) The normalization condition is $\int\int\int \psi^*\psi \, d^3r = 1$. Substituting for ψ we have

$$C^2\int_0^\infty r^2 e^{-2r/a}dr \int_0^{2\pi} d\varphi \int_0^\pi \sin\theta \, d\theta = 4\pi C^2 \int_0^\infty r^2 e^{-2r/a} \, dr = 1 \tag{8.3.1}$$

The integral in Eq. (8.3.1) is

$$\int_0^\infty r^2 e^{-2r/a} \, dr = \left(\frac{a}{2}\right)^3 \Gamma(3) = \left(\frac{a}{2}\right)^3 2! = \frac{a^3}{4} \tag{8.3.2}$$

Therefore, $C = \left(\frac{1}{4\pi}\frac{4}{a^3}\right)^{1/2} = \frac{1}{\sqrt{\pi a^3}}$.

(b) Denoting by R the radius of the nucleus, the probability that the electron is found in the nucleus is

$$P = \int_0^R r^2 |\psi(r)|^2 \, dr \int_0^{2\pi} d\varphi \int_0^\pi \sin\theta \, d\theta = 4\pi C^2 \int_0^R r^2 e^{-2r/a} \, dr \tag{8.3.3}$$

Since R is small compared to a ($R \sim 1$ fm $= 10^{-5}$ Å and $a \sim 1$ Å), we can consider $|\psi|^2$ as a constant in the nucleus, i.e., $e^{-2r/a} \sim e^{-2R/a} \sim 1$. Thus, we have

$$P = \frac{4}{a^3} \int_0^R r^2 \, dr = \frac{4}{3}\left(\frac{R}{a}\right)^3 = \frac{4}{3}\left(\frac{Zr_0}{a_0}\right)^3 A = 1.1 \times 10^{-6} \qquad (r_0 = 1.2 \text{ fm}) \tag{8.3.4}$$

(c) The wavefunction is independent of both θ and φ (it is a symmetrical function). Thus the probability that the electron is found in 1/8 of the space (i.e., in $x, y, z > 0$) is simply 1/8.

8.4. Compute the normalized momentum distribution of a hydrogen atom electron in states $1s$, $2s$, and $2p$.

SOLUTION

The normalized momentum distribution is $|\psi(\mathbf{p})|^2$, where $\psi(\mathbf{p})$ is the wavefunction in the momentum representation. In order to find $\psi(\mathbf{p})$, we perform a Fourier transform of the wavefunction $\psi(\mathbf{r})$.

$$\psi(\mathbf{p}) = \frac{1}{\sqrt{(2\pi\hbar)^3}} \int e^{-i\mathbf{p}\cdot\mathbf{r}/\hbar} \psi(\mathbf{r}) \, d^3r \tag{8.4.1}$$

We then substitute into Eq. (8.4.1) the explicit forms of $\psi_{1s}(\mathbf{r})$, $\psi_{2s}(\mathbf{r})$, and $\psi_{2p}(\mathbf{r})$, and obtain

$$\begin{cases} \psi_{1s}(p) = \frac{1}{\pi}\left(\frac{2a}{\hbar}\right)^{3/2} \frac{1}{[(p^2 a^2/\hbar^2 + 1)]^2} \\ |\psi_{1s}(p)|^2 = \frac{1}{\pi^2}\left(\frac{2a}{\hbar}\right) \frac{1}{[(p^2 a^2/\hbar^2 + 1)]^4} \end{cases} \tag{8.4.2}$$

and

$$\begin{cases} \psi_{2s}(p) = \frac{1}{2\pi}\left(\frac{2a}{\hbar}\right)^{3/2} \frac{1}{[(p^2 a^2/\hbar^2 + 1/4)]^3}\left(\frac{p^2 a^2}{\hbar^2} - \frac{1}{4}\right) \\ |\psi_{2s}(p)|^2 = \frac{1}{(2\pi)^2}\left(\frac{2a}{\hbar}\right)^3 \frac{1}{[(p^2 a^2/\hbar^2 + 1/4)]^6}\left(\frac{p^2 a^2}{\hbar^2} - \frac{1}{4}\right)^2 \end{cases} \tag{8.4.3}$$

There are three different eigenfunctions for the state $2p$: $m = -1, 0, 1$. Thus,

$$m = 0: \quad \begin{cases} \psi_{2p}(p) = -i\frac{1}{\pi}\left(\frac{a}{\hbar}\right)^{3/2} a\frac{ap_z}{\hbar[(p^2 a^2/\hbar^2 + 1/4)]^3} \\ |\psi_{2p}(p)|^2 = \frac{1}{\pi^2}\left(\frac{a}{\hbar}\right)^3 \frac{(ap_z)^2}{\hbar^2[(p^2 a^2/\hbar^2 + 1/4)]^6} \end{cases} \tag{8.4.4}$$

and

$$m = \pm 1: \quad \begin{cases} \psi_{2p}(p) = -i\frac{1}{\pi\sqrt{2}}\left(\frac{a}{\hbar}\right)^{3/2} \frac{a(p_x \pm ip_y)}{\hbar[(p^2 a^2/\hbar^2 + 1/4)]^3} \\ |\psi_{2p}(p)|^2 = \frac{1}{2\pi^2}\left(\frac{a}{\hbar}\right)^3 \frac{a^2(p_x \pm ip_y)^2}{\hbar^2[(p^2 a^2/\hbar^2 + 1/4)]^6} \end{cases} \tag{8.4.5}$$

8.5. Consider a wavefunction for a hydrogen-like atom:

$$\psi(r,\theta) = \frac{1}{81}\sqrt{\frac{2}{\pi}}Z^{3/2}(6 - Zr)Zre^{-Zr/3}\cos\theta \tag{8.5.1}$$

where r is expressed in units of a_0. (a) Find the corresponding values of the quantum numbers n, l, and m. (b) Construct from $\psi(r, \theta)$ another wavefunction with the same values of n and l, but with a different magnetic quantum number, $m + 1$. (c) Calculate the most probable value of r for an electron in the state corresponding to ψ and with $Z = 1$.

SOLUTION

(a) Consider the exponential factor in $\psi(r, \theta)$; it has the form $\exp(-\sqrt{-E}r)$. Since $E = -Z^2/n^2$, we conclude that $n = 3$. The angular quantum number l can be determined either by exploiting the factor r^l, which multiplies the Laguerre polynomial in hydrogen-like wavefunctions, or by carrying out the following operation:

$$\hat{L}^2\psi(r, \theta) = \hat{L}^2 f(r)\cos\theta = f(r)\left[-\frac{1}{\sin\theta}\frac{\partial}{\partial\theta}\left(\sin\theta\frac{\partial}{\partial\theta}\cos\theta\right)\right]$$

$$= f(r)\left[\frac{1}{\sin\theta}\frac{d}{d\theta}(\sin\theta)^2\right] = 2f(r)\cos\theta = l(l+1)\psi(r, \theta) \quad (8.5.2)$$

Thus, $l = 1$. To find the magnetic quantum number, we use the operator $\hat{L}_z$:

$$\hat{L}_z\psi(r, \theta) = -i\frac{\partial}{\partial\varphi}[f(r)\cos\theta] = 0 = m\psi(r, \theta) \quad (8.5.3)$$

It follows then that $m = 0$.

(b) In order to generate a new hydrogen-like wavefunction with a magnetic quantum number $m + 1$, we use the raising operator $\hat{L}_+$ (see Chap. 6). Since $l = 1$ and $m = 0$, we have

$$\hat{L}_+\psi_m = \sqrt{(l-m)(l+m+1)}\,\psi_{m+1} = \sqrt{2}\,\psi_{m+1} \quad (8.5.4)$$

We use the differential representation of $\hat{L}_+$:

$$\hat{L}_+ = \hat{L}_x + i\hat{L}_y = i(\sin\varphi - i\cos\varphi)\frac{\partial}{\partial\theta} + i(\cos\varphi + i\sin\varphi)\cot\theta\frac{\partial}{\partial\varphi} \quad (8.5.5)$$

and obtain

$$\hat{L}_+\psi_{m=0} = e^{i\varphi}\frac{\partial}{\partial\theta}f(r)\cos\theta = -e^{+i\varphi}f(r)\sin\theta \quad (8.5.6)$$

Combining Eqs. (8.5.4) and (8.5.6) we obtain

$$\psi_{m+1} = -\frac{1}{\sqrt{2}}f(r)\sin\theta\,e^{i\varphi} = -\frac{1}{81\sqrt{\pi}}Z^{3/2}(6-Zr)Zr\,e^{-Zr/3}\sin\theta\,e^{i\varphi} \quad (8.5.7)$$

(c) The most probable value of r occurs when $(r\psi)^2$ assumes its maximum value. For $Z = 1$ we have

$$\frac{\partial(r\psi)}{\partial r} = 0 = \frac{\partial}{\partial r}(6-r)r^2e^{-r/3} = e^{-r/3}\left(\frac{r^3}{3} - 5r^2 + 12r\right) \quad (8.5.8)$$

We obtain the quadratic equation $r^2 - 15r + 36 = 0$; its roots are $r = 12$ and $r = 3$. Evaluating $|r\psi|$ we find that it is maximal for $r = 12$. Therefore, the most probable value of r is $12a_0$.

8.6. Consider a particle in a central field and assume that the system has a discrete spectrum. Each orbital quantum number l has a minimum energy value. Show that this minimum value increases as l increases.

SOLUTION

We begin by writing the Hamiltonian of the system:

$$\hat{H} = \frac{\hbar^2}{2mr^2}\frac{\partial}{\partial r}\left(r^2\frac{\partial}{\partial r}\right) + \frac{\hbar^2}{2m}\frac{l(l+1)}{r^2} + V(r) \quad (8.6.1)$$

Using $\hat{H}_1 = -\dfrac{\hbar^2}{2mr^2}\dfrac{\partial}{\partial r}\left(r^2\dfrac{\partial}{\partial r}\right) + V(r)$, we have

$$\hat{H} = \hat{H}_1 + \frac{\hbar^2}{2m}\frac{l(l+1)}{r^2} \tag{8.6.2}$$

The minimum value of the energy in the state l is

$$E_{min}^l = \int \psi_l^*\left[\hat{H}_1 + \frac{\hbar^2}{2m}\frac{l(l+1)}{r^2}\right]\psi_l\, d^3r \tag{8.6.3}$$

The minimum value of the energy in the state $l+1$ is given by

$$E_{min}^{l+1} = \int \psi_{l+1}^*\left[\hat{H}_1 + \frac{\hbar^2}{2m}\frac{l(l+1)(l+2)}{r^2}\right]\psi_{l+1}\, d^3r \tag{8.6.4}$$

Equation (8.6.4) can be written in the form

$$E_{min}^{l+1} = \int \psi_{l+1}^*\frac{\hbar^2}{m}\frac{l+1}{r^2}\psi_{l+1}\, d^3r + \int \psi_{l+1}^*\left[\hat{H}_1 + \frac{\hbar^2}{2m}\frac{l(l+1)}{r^2}\right]\psi_{l+1}\, d^3r \tag{8.6.5}$$

Since $|\psi_{l+1}|^2$ and $\dfrac{\hbar^2}{m}\dfrac{l+1}{r^2}$ are positive, the second term in Eq. (8.6.5) is always positive. Consider now the first term of Eq. (8.6.5). The minimum eigenvalue of the Hamiltonian $\hat{H} = \hat{H}_1 + \dfrac{\hbar^2}{2m}\dfrac{l(l+1)}{r^2}$ corresponds to the eigenfunction ψ_l. Thus,

$$\int \psi_i^*\left[\hat{H}_0 + \frac{\hbar^2}{2m}\frac{l(l+1)}{r^2}\right]\psi_l\, d^3r < \int \psi_{l+1}^*\left[\hat{H}_0 + \frac{\hbar^2}{2m}\frac{l(l+1)}{r^2}\right]\psi_{l+1}\, d^3r \tag{8.6.6}$$

This proves that $E_{min}^l < E_{min}^{l+1}$.

8.7. Write the Schrödinger equation for a two-dimensional hydrogen atom. Suppose that the potential energy is $-e^2/r$, where $r = \sqrt{x^2 + y^2}$. Using separation of variables, find the radial and the angular equations. Solve the angular equation. Describe the quantum numbers that characterize the bound states and the degeneracies of the system.

SOLUTION

Consider the Schrödinger equation in two dimensions:

$$-\frac{\hbar^2}{2m}\left[\frac{1}{r}\frac{\partial}{\partial r}\left(r\frac{\partial\psi}{\partial r}\right) + \frac{1}{r^2}\frac{\partial^2\psi}{\partial\varphi^2}\right] - \frac{e^2}{r}\psi = E\psi \tag{8.7.1}$$

Performing a separation of variables $\psi = R(r)\Phi(\varphi)$, we obtain the angular equation

$$\frac{\partial^2\Phi(\varphi)}{\partial\varphi^2} = -m^2\Phi(\varphi) \tag{8.7.2}$$

The constant m must be an integer number, so the solution of Eq. (8.7.2) is

$$\Phi_m(\varphi) = \frac{1}{\sqrt{2\pi}}e^{im\varphi} \tag{8.7.3}$$

Consider the radial equation:

$$-\frac{\hbar^2}{2m}\left(\frac{d^2R}{dr^2} + \frac{1}{r}\frac{dR}{dr}\right) + \frac{\hbar^2 m^2}{2mr^2}R(r) - \frac{e^2}{r}R(r) = ER(r) \tag{8.7.4}$$

Every state $R_{n|m|}(r)$ is characterized by the principal quantum numbers n and the absolute value of the angular quantum number m. The energies of the system are $E_{n|m|}$. Every state with $m \neq 0$ is twofold degenerate, and the states with $m = 0$ are not degenerate.

8.8. The muon is a particle with fundamental properties similar to those of the electron, with the exception of mass.

$$m_\mu = 207 m_e \tag{8.8.1}$$

The physical system formed by a μ^+ and an electron is called *muonium*. Muonium behaves like a light isotope of hydrogen, and its electrostatic attraction is the same as that of a proton and an electron. Determine the ionization energy and Bohr radius of muonium.

SOLUTION

The reduced mass of muonium is

$$\mu_\mu = \frac{m_e m_\mu}{m_e + m_\mu} = \frac{207}{208} m_e = \left(1 - \frac{1}{208}\right) m_e \tag{8.8.2}$$

The Bohr radius is

$$a_0(\text{muonium}) = \frac{\hbar^2}{\mu e^2} \cong a_0(\text{H})\left(1 + \frac{1}{200}\right) \tag{8.8.3}$$

where $a_0(\text{H})$ is the Bohr radius of the hydrogen atom. The ionization energy is

$$E_1(\text{muonium}) = \frac{\mu e^4}{2\hbar^2} \cong E_1(\text{H})\left(1 - \frac{1}{200}\right) \tag{8.8.4}$$

where $E_1(\text{H}) = 13.6$ eV is the ionization energy of the hydrogen atom. The study of the muon is of great interest. The two particles that comprise muonium are not subject to strong nuclear interactions, thus enabling energy levels to be calculated with great precision.

8.9. Prove the following relation between the spherical harmonic functions:

$$\sum_{m=-l}^{m=+l} Y_{lm}^*(\theta, \varphi) Y_{lm}(\theta, \varphi) = \text{const.} \tag{8.9.1}$$

Use the expansion of the Legendre polynomials (see the Mathematical Appendix):

$$P_l(\cos\gamma) = \sum_{m=-l}^{m=+l} \frac{(l - |m|)!}{(l + |m|)!} P_l^{|m|}(\cos\theta_1) P_l^{|m|}(\cos\theta_2) e^{im(\varphi_1 - \varphi_2)} \tag{8.9.2}$$

where γ is the angle between two directions given by θ_1, φ_1 and θ_2, φ_2.

SOLUTION

We write the spherical harmonic functions in the form

$$Y_{lm}(\theta, \varphi) = \frac{(-1)^{(m+|m|)/2}}{\sqrt{4\pi}} \sqrt{\frac{(2l + 1)(l - |m|)!}{(l + |m|)!}} P_l^{|m|}(\cos\theta) e^{im\varphi} \tag{8.9.3}$$

Then,

$$\sum_{m=-l}^{m=+l} Y_{lm}^*(\theta, \varphi) Y_{lm}(\theta, \varphi) = \frac{2l + 1}{4\pi} \sum_{m=-l}^{m=+l} \frac{(l - |m|)!}{(l + |m|)!} \left| P_l^{|m|}(\cos\theta) \right|^2 \tag{8.9.4}$$

We substitute $\theta_1 = \theta_2 = \theta$, and $\varphi_1 = \varphi_2 = \varphi$ into Eq. (8.9.2) and obtain

$$P_l(\cos\gamma) = \sum_{m=-l}^{m=+l} \frac{(l - |m|)!}{(l + |m|)!} \left| P_l^{|m|}(\cos\theta) \right|^2 = P_l(0) = 1 \tag{8.9.5}$$

Substituting Eq. (8.9.5) into Eq. (8.9.4) we arrive at

$$\sum_{m=-l}^{m=+l} Y_{lm}^*(\theta, \varphi) Y_{lm}(\theta, \varphi) = \frac{2l + 1}{4\pi} \tag{8.9.6}$$

Since $(2l + 1)/4\pi$ is a constant, we have established the proof.

8.10. The *parity operator* is defined by the replacement $\mathbf{r} \to -\mathbf{r}$ (see Chap. 4). How does the parity operator affect the electron's wavefunction in a hydrogen atom?

SOLUTION

In a hydrogen atom we can express the wavefunctions using the spherical coordinates (r, θ, φ); we determine how the parity operation affects these coordinates (see Fig. 8.1).

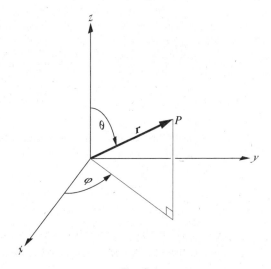

Fig. 8.1

We see that under the parity operator $r \to r$, $\theta \to \pi - \theta$ and $\phi \to \pi + \varphi$. Since the radial part of the hydrogen atom's eigenfunctions depends only on r, we conclude that the parity operator affects only the spherical harmonics part. For spherical harmonics, we have $Y_l^l(\theta, \varphi) = a_l(\sin\theta)^l e^{il\varphi}$; thus,

$$Y_l^l(\pi - \theta, \pi + \varphi) = (-1)^l Y_l^l(\theta, \varphi) \tag{8.10.1}$$

Therefore, under the parity operator,

$$Y_l^l(\theta, \varphi) \to (-1)^l Y_l^l(\theta, \varphi) \tag{8.10.2}$$

Moreover, since $\frac{\partial}{\partial\theta} \to -\frac{\partial}{\partial\theta}$ and $\frac{\partial}{\partial\varphi} \to \frac{\partial}{\partial\varphi}$, it follows that the operators $\hat{L}_\pm$ are not affected by the parity operation. Since we have obtained the explicit form of $Y_l^m(\theta, \varphi)$ by applying the operator $\hat{L}_-$ on Y_l^l, we can conclude, without any further calculation, that

$$Y_l^m(\pi - \theta, \pi + \varphi) = (-1)^l Y_l^m(\theta, \varphi) \tag{8.10.3}$$

In other words, under the parity operation

$$Y_l^m(\theta, \varphi) \to (-1)^l Y_l^m(\theta, \varphi) \tag{8.10.4}$$

SUPPLEMENTARY PROBLEMS

8.11. Consider a hydrogen atom in a state $n = 2$, $l = 0$, and $m = 0$. Find the probability that an electron has a value r that is smaller than the Bohr radius.

Ans. 0.176.

8.12. For an electron in the state n and $l = n - 1$ in a hydrogen-like atom, find the most probable value of r.

Ans. $r = n^2/Z$ in units of a_0.

8.13. Show that the degeneracy of the nth shell in a hydrogen atom equals $2n^2$. Take into account the spin of the electron but not the spin of the proton.

8.14. The six wavefunctions of the state $2p$ for the hydrogen atom are

$$m_l = +1, \quad m_s = \pm\frac{1}{2}, \quad \psi_{+1} = A\frac{re^{-r/2a_0}}{a_0}\sin\theta\, e^{i\varphi}$$

$$m_l = 0, \quad m_s = \pm\frac{1}{2}, \quad \psi_0 = B\frac{re^{-r/2a_0}}{a_0}\cos\theta \qquad (8.14.1)$$

$$m_l = -1, \quad m_s = \pm\frac{1}{2}, \quad \psi_{-1} = C\frac{re^{-r/2a_0}}{a_0}\sin\theta\, e^{-i\varphi}$$

where a_0 is the Bohr radius and A, B, and C are the normalization constants. (a) Compute the constants A, B, and C. (b) Show that the sum $\left|\psi_{m_l}\right|^2$ is a function of r only. (c) Compute $\langle r \rangle$ for $m_l = 0$.

Ans. (a) $A = -\dfrac{1}{8\sqrt{\pi a_0^3}}$, $B = \dfrac{1}{4\sqrt{2\pi a_0^3}}$, $C = \dfrac{1}{8\sqrt{\pi a_0^3}}$; (c) $\langle r \rangle = 5a_0$.

8.15. Consider a hydrogen atom in the state with the quantum numbers n and l. Calculate the dispersion of the distance of the electron from the nucleus. Note that the dispersion is defined by $\sqrt{\langle r^2 \rangle - \langle r \rangle^2}$.

Ans. $\dfrac{\sqrt{n^2(n^2 + 2) - l^2(l + 1)^2}}{2}$.

8.16. In a hydrogen atom the wavefunction $\psi(\mathbf{r})$ describes the relative motion of a proton and an electron. If the coordinates of the center of mass of this system are $x = 0$, $y = 0$, and $z = 0$, show that the probability density of the proton equals $\left(\dfrac{m + M}{m}\right)^3\left|\psi\left(\dfrac{m + M}{m}\mathbf{r}\right)\right|^2$.

8.17. For a two-dimensional hydrogen-like atom, the Schrödinger equation is $(-\nabla^2 - 2Z/r)\psi = E\psi$ (in atomic units). Use cylindrical coordinates to find the equations for $R(r)$ and $\Phi(\varphi)$.

Ans. $\dfrac{d^2\Phi}{d\varphi^2} = -m^2\Phi(\varphi)$ and $\dfrac{1}{r}\dfrac{d}{dr}\left(r\dfrac{dR}{dr}\right) + \left(\dfrac{2Z}{r} - \dfrac{m^2}{r^2} + E\right)R(r) = 0$.

8.18. Consider a particle in a spherical well, $V(r) = \begin{cases} -V_0 & r < a \\ 0 & r > a \end{cases}$. Assuming that the angular momentum is zero, find the particle's energy spectrums.

Ans. The energy spectrums are given by $ka = n\pi - \arcsin\left(\dfrac{\hbar k}{\sqrt{2mV_0}}\right)$ and $E = \dfrac{\hbar^2 k^2}{2m}$. These equations can be solved either graphically or numerically (see Chap. 12).

CHAPTER 9

Particle Motion in an Electromagnetic Field

9.1 The Electromagnetic Field and Its Associated Potentials

Consider an electromagnetic field, characterized by the values of the electric field $\mathcal{E}(\mathbf{r}, t)$ and of the magnetic field $\mathcal{B}(\mathbf{r}, t)$. The fields $\mathcal{E}(\mathbf{r}, t)$ and $\mathcal{B}(\mathbf{r}, t)$ are not independent; they must satisfy *Maxwell's equations*. It is possible to introduce a *scalar potential* $\phi(\mathbf{r}, t)$ and a *vector potential* $\mathbf{A}(\mathbf{r}, t)$ such that

$$\mathcal{E} = -\nabla\phi - \frac{1}{c}\frac{\partial \mathbf{A}}{\partial t} \tag{9.1}$$

and

$$\mathcal{B} = \nabla \times \mathbf{A} \tag{9.2}$$

Using Maxwell's equations, it can be shown that ϕ and $\mathbf{A}$ can always be found. However, when $\mathcal{E}$ and $\mathcal{B}$ are given, ϕ and $\mathbf{A}$ are not uniquely determined. When we choose a particular set of potentials, we say that we choose a *gauge*. From one set of potentials $(\phi, \mathbf{A})$ we can obtain another set, $(\phi', \mathbf{A}')$ by performing a *gauge transformation*:

$$\phi' = \phi - \frac{1}{c}\frac{\partial f(\mathbf{r}, t)}{\partial t} \tag{9.3}$$

and

$$\mathbf{A}' = \mathbf{A} + \nabla f(\mathbf{r}, t) \tag{9.4}$$

where $f(\mathbf{r}, t)$ is an arbitrary function of $\mathbf{r}$ and t (see Problem 9.2). The equations describing the physical system involve the potentials ϕ and $\mathbf{A}$, but we shall see that in quantum mechanics, as in classical physics, the predictions of the theory do not depend on the gauge chosen (that is, the particular set of ϕ and $\mathbf{A}$ describing the electromagnetic field). This important property is called the *gauge invariance* (see Problem 9.5).

Let us consider two examples of gauges describing a constant magnetic field in the z direction, $\mathcal{B} = \mathcal{B}_0\mathbf{k}$. First we have the symmetric gauge,

$$\mathbf{A} = -\frac{1}{2}\mathbf{r} \times \mathcal{B} = -\frac{1}{2}\begin{vmatrix} \mathbf{i} & \mathbf{j} & \mathbf{k} \\ x & y & z \\ 0 & 0 & \mathcal{B}_0 \end{vmatrix} \tag{9.5}$$

or $\mathbf{A} = \dfrac{\mathcal{B}_0}{2}(-y, x, 0)$. Another gauge is the Landau gauge:

$$\mathbf{A} = (-\mathcal{B}_0 y, 0, 0) \tag{9.6}$$

9.2   The Hamiltonian of a Particle in the Electromagnetic Field

Consider a particle of mass m and charge q. The classical equation of motion (in CGS units) in the presence of electric and magnetic fields $\mathcal{E}$ and $\mathcal{B}$ is

$$m\frac{d^2\mathbf{r}}{dt^2} = q\mathcal{E} + \frac{q}{c}\mathbf{v}\times\mathcal{B} \tag{9.7}$$

The classical Hamiltonian that leads to this equation of motion is

$$H = \frac{1}{2m}\left(\mathbf{p}-\frac{q}{c}\mathbf{A}\right)\cdot\left(\mathbf{p}-\frac{q}{c}\mathbf{A}\right) + q\phi \tag{9.8}$$

where ϕ and $\mathbf{A}$ are the potentials relating to $\mathcal{E}$ and $\mathcal{B}$ according to Eqs. (9.1) and (9.2) (see Problem 9.1).

In this chapter we use a semiclassical theory for particle motion in an electromagnetic field. In this theory the field is analogous to a classical field, while the system is treated according to the postulates of quantum mechanics. Thus, the particle is described by a wavefunction $\Psi(\mathbf{r}, t)$, and the Hamiltonian is written as in Eq. (9.8), but now $\hat{\mathbf{p}}$, $\hat{\mathbf{A}}$, and $\hat{\phi}$ represent the corresponding operators (see Problem 9.3).

When we perform a gauge transformation according to Eqs. (9.3) and (9.4), the wavefunction describing the particle transforms (see Problem 9.4) as

$$\tilde{\Psi}'(\mathbf{r}, t) = \exp\left[\frac{iq}{c\hbar}f(\mathbf{r}, t)\right]\Psi(\mathbf{r}, t) \tag{9.9}$$

9.3   Probability Density and Probability Current

Given a wavefunction $\Psi(\mathbf{r}, t)$, the probability density is

$$\rho = \left|\Psi(\mathbf{r}_0, t)\right|^2 \tag{9.10}$$

where ρ expresses the probability of finding the particle at time t at the point $\mathbf{r}_0$. For particles with mass m and charge q (without a magnetic moment), the probability current density is

$$\mathbf{j} = \frac{1}{2m}\left[\frac{\hbar}{i}(\Psi^*\nabla\Psi - \Psi\nabla\Psi^*) - \frac{2q}{c}\mathbf{A}\Psi^*\Psi\right] \tag{9.11}$$

If we consider a particle with spin s and a magnetic moment μ_s, we have

$$\mathbf{j} = \frac{1}{2m}\left[\frac{\hbar}{i}(\Psi^*\nabla\Psi - \Psi\nabla\Psi^*) - \frac{2q}{c}\mathbf{A}\Psi^*\Psi\right] + \frac{\mu_s c}{s}\nabla\times(\Psi^*\mathbf{S}\Psi) \tag{9.12}$$

The continuity equation

$$\frac{\partial\rho}{\partial t} + \nabla\cdot\mathbf{j} = 0 \tag{9.13}$$

relates the probability density and the probability current (see Problem 9.3). Both ρ and $\mathbf{j}$ do not depend on the gauge chosen, and they are said to be gauge-invariant; see Problem 9.5. The "real" current corresponding to a particle of charge q is defined by

$$\mathbf{I} = q\mathbf{j} \tag{9.14}$$

9.4 The Magnetic Moment

For a particle with a magnetic moment μ_s in a magnetic field B, the interaction Hamiltonian is

$$H_{\text{int}} = -\mu_s \cdot B \tag{9.15}$$

This term should be added to the Hamiltonian. An electron of spin S has a magnetic moment

$$\mu = -\frac{eg}{2mc} S \tag{9.16}$$

where g, the gyromagnetic relation constant is very close to 2:

$$g = 2\left(1 + \frac{\alpha}{2\pi} + \cdots\right) = 2.002\,319 \tag{9.17}$$

9.5 Units

In discussing electromagnetic phenomena, it is customary to adopt one of the many possible systems of units. The MKS system is popular in solving practical or engineering problems. In the study of the interaction of electromagnetic radiation with the fundamental constituents of matter, it is sometimes more convenient to adopt the Gaussian system of units. Here we will use the latter system.

SOLVED PROBLEMS

9.1. The classical equation of motion for a particle with mass m and charge q in the presence of electric and magnetic fields $\mathcal{E}$ and B is

$$m\mathbf{a} = q\mathcal{E} + \frac{q}{c}\mathbf{v} \times B \tag{9.1.1}$$

where $\mathbf{a}$ is the acceleration of the particle and $\mathbf{v}$ is its velocity $\left(\mathbf{v} = \frac{d\mathbf{r}}{dt} \equiv \dot{\mathbf{r}} \text{ and } \mathbf{a} = \frac{d\mathbf{v}}{dt} \equiv \ddot{\mathbf{r}}\right)$. $\mathcal{E}$ and B must satisfy Maxwell's equations, so it is possible to define the vector potential $\mathbf{A}(\mathbf{r}, t)$ and the scalar potential $\phi(\mathbf{r}, t)$ such that

$$\mathcal{E} = -\nabla\phi - \frac{1}{c}\frac{\partial \mathbf{A}}{\partial t} \tag{9.1.2}$$

and

$$B = \nabla \times \mathbf{A} \tag{9.1.3}$$

Show that the Hamiltonian

$$H = \frac{1}{2m}\left(\mathbf{p} - \frac{q}{c}\mathbf{A}\right) \cdot \left(\mathbf{p} - \frac{q}{c}\mathbf{A}\right) + q\phi \tag{9.1.4}$$

leads to the equation of motion. Use the Hamilton equations:

$$\dot{\mathbf{r}} = \frac{\partial H}{\partial \mathbf{p}} \tag{9.1.5}$$

and

$$\dot{\mathbf{p}} = -\frac{\partial H}{\partial \mathbf{r}} \tag{9.1.6}$$

Proceed with the following steps: (*a*) Write $\dot{\mathbf{r}}$ as a function of $\dot{\mathbf{p}}$ and $\mathbf{A}$. (*b*) Write $\ddot{\mathbf{r}}$ as a function of $\mathbf{p}$ and $\mathbf{A}$. (*c*) Use Eq. (9.1.6) to write $\dot{\mathbf{p}}$ as a function of $\mathbf{v}$ and $\mathbf{A}$. (*d*) Use the vector "chain rule,"

$$\frac{d\mathbf{A}}{dt} = \frac{\partial \mathbf{A}}{\partial t} + \left(\frac{d\mathbf{r}}{dt} \cdot \nabla \right) \mathbf{A} = \frac{\partial \mathbf{A}}{\partial t} + (\mathbf{v} \cdot \nabla)\mathbf{A} \tag{9.1.7}$$

and the vector identity

$$(\mathbf{v} \cdot \nabla)\mathbf{A} = -\mathbf{v} \times (\nabla \times \mathbf{A}) + \nabla(\mathbf{v} \cdot \mathbf{A}) \tag{9.1.8}$$

to find $\dfrac{d\mathbf{A}}{dt}$. (*e*) Combine parts (*a*) to (*d*) to get the equation of motion.

SOLUTION

(*a*) Using Eqs. (9.1.5) and (9.1.4) we get

$$\dot{\mathbf{r}} = \frac{\partial}{\partial \mathbf{p}} \left[\frac{1}{2m} \left(\mathbf{p} - \frac{q}{c}\mathbf{A} \right) \cdot \left(\mathbf{p} - \frac{q}{c}\mathbf{A} \right) + q\phi \right] = \frac{1}{m} \left(\mathbf{p} - \frac{q}{c}\mathbf{A} \right) = \mathbf{v} \tag{9.1.9}$$

(*b*) As in part (*a*) we obtain

$$\ddot{\mathbf{r}} = \frac{d\dot{\mathbf{r}}}{dt} = \frac{d}{dt} \left[\frac{1}{m} \left(\mathbf{p} - \frac{q}{c}\mathbf{A} \right) \right] = \frac{1}{m} \left[\frac{d\mathbf{p}}{dt} - \frac{q}{c}\frac{d\mathbf{A}}{dt} \right] = \frac{1}{m} \left[\ddot{\mathbf{p}} - \frac{q}{c}\dot{\mathbf{A}} \right] \tag{9.1.10}$$

(*c*) From Eqs. (9.1.6) and (9.1.4) we arrive at

$$\dot{\mathbf{p}} = -\frac{\partial H}{\partial \mathbf{r}} = -\nabla H = -\nabla \left[\frac{1}{2m} \left(\mathbf{p} - \frac{q}{c}\mathbf{A} \right) \cdot \left(\mathbf{p} - \frac{q}{c}\mathbf{A} \right) + q\phi \right] \tag{9.1.11}$$

Recall that $\mathbf{r}$ and $\mathbf{p}$ are independent phase space variables in Hamilton's approach, so $\nabla \cdot \mathbf{p} = 0$. Using $\nabla(\mathbf{p} \cdot \mathbf{p}) = 0$, we write Eq. (9.1.11) as

$$\dot{\mathbf{p}} = \frac{1}{m} \nabla \left[\left(\mathbf{p} - \frac{q}{c}\mathbf{A} \right) \cdot \left(\frac{q}{c}\mathbf{A} \right) \right] - q\nabla\phi \tag{9.1.12}$$

From Eq. (9.1.9) and from Eq. (9.1.12) we have

$$\dot{\mathbf{p}} = \frac{q}{c} \nabla(\mathbf{v} \cdot \mathbf{A}) - q\nabla\phi \tag{9.1.13}$$

(*d*) From Eqs. (9.1.7) and (9.1.8) we obtain

$$\frac{d\mathbf{A}}{dt} = \frac{\partial \mathbf{A}}{\partial t} - \mathbf{v} \times (\nabla \times \mathbf{A}) + \nabla(\mathbf{v} \cdot \mathbf{A}) \tag{9.1.14}$$

Finally, using Eq. (9.1.3) we have

$$\dot{\mathbf{A}} = \frac{d\mathbf{A}}{dt} = \frac{\partial \mathbf{A}}{\partial t} - \mathbf{v} \times \mathcal{B} + \nabla(\mathbf{v} \cdot \mathbf{A}) \tag{9.1.15}$$

(*e*) Combining Eqs. (9.1.10), (9.1.13), and (9.1.15) we obtain

$$\ddot{\mathbf{r}} = \frac{1}{m} \left[\frac{q}{c}(\mathbf{v} \times \mathcal{B}) - q \left(\frac{1}{c}\frac{\partial \mathbf{A}}{\partial t} + \nabla\phi \right) \right] \tag{9.1.16}$$

Multiplying Eq. (9.1.16) by m and using Eq. (9.1.2) we arrive at

$$m\ddot{\mathbf{r}} = \frac{q}{c}(\mathbf{v} \times \mathcal{B}) + q\mathcal{E} \tag{9.1.17}$$

which is the equation of motion.

9.2. Let A $(\mathbf{r}, t)$ and ϕ $(\mathbf{r}, t)$ satisfy Eqs. (9.1.2) and (9.1.3). For electric and magnetic fields, $\mathcal{E}$ and $\mathcal{B}$, are the potentials A and ϕ determined uniquely? If not, explain.

SOLUTION

Assume that $\mathbf{A}_1$ and $\mathbf{A}_2$, ϕ_1 and ϕ_2 satisfy Eqs. (9.1.2) and (9.1.3) with the same $\mathcal{E}$ and $\mathcal{B}$, namely,

$$\mathcal{E} = -\nabla\phi_1 - \frac{1}{c}\frac{\partial\mathbf{A}_1}{\partial t} = -\left(\nabla\phi_2 + \frac{1}{c}\frac{\partial\mathbf{A}_2}{\partial t}\right) \tag{9.2.1}$$

and

$$\mathcal{B} = \nabla \times \mathbf{A}_1 = \nabla \times \mathbf{A}_2 \tag{9.2.2}$$

Now, if $\mathbf{A}$ and ϕ are determined uniquely, then we must have $\mathbf{A}_1 = \mathbf{A}_2$ and $\phi_1 = \phi_2$. We define $\mathbf{a} \equiv \mathbf{A}_1 - \mathbf{A}_2$ and $\phi = \phi_1 - \phi_2$ and investigate whether $\mathbf{a} = 0$ and $\phi = 0$. From Eq. (9.2.2) we obtain

$$\nabla \times \mathbf{a} = 0 \tag{9.2.3}$$

Since the gradient of *any* function $f(\mathbf{r}, t)$ satisfies $\nabla \times (\nabla f) = 0$, one can show that $\mathbf{a} = \nabla f$ for some function $f(\mathbf{r}, t)$. If we use Eq. (9.2.1), we obtain

$$\nabla\phi + \frac{1}{c}\frac{\partial\mathbf{a}}{\partial t} = 0 \tag{9.2.4}$$

From Eq. (9.2.4) we get $\nabla\phi + \frac{1}{c}\nabla\left(\frac{\partial f}{\partial t}\right) = 0$ or

$$\phi = -\frac{1}{c}\frac{\partial f}{\partial t} + C(t) \tag{9.2.5}$$

where $C(t)$ is a function of t. Without loss of generality, choose $C = 0$, since this corresponds to shifting the energy by a constant. From Eq. (9.2.5) we therefore obtain

$$\mathbf{a} = \nabla f \qquad \phi = -\frac{1}{c}\frac{\partial f}{\partial t} \tag{9.2.6}$$

where $f(\mathbf{r}, t)$ is *any* function of $\mathbf{r}$ and t. We see that $\mathbf{a}$ and ϕ are not necessarily zero. The potentials A and ϕ are not determined uniquely since f is arbitrary. The nonuniqueness in Eq. (9.2.6) is called *gauge freedom*. This means that if $\mathbf{A}$ and ϕ satisfy Eqs. (9.1.2) and (9.1.3), then $\mathbf{A}'$ and ϕ' obtained by the transformation equations

$$\mathbf{A}' = \mathbf{A} + \nabla f \qquad \phi' = \phi - \frac{1}{c}\frac{\partial f}{\partial t} \tag{9.2.7}$$

are also potentials.

9.3. (a) Write the quantum Hamiltonian for a particle with mass m and charge q in the presence of an electromagnetic field. (b) What is the probability density for finding the particle in $\mathbf{r} = \mathbf{r}_0$ at $t = t_0$? (c) Obtain the equation of conservation of probability and find the probability current density.

SOLUTION

(a) From the classical Hamiltonian (9.1.4) we reach the quantum Hamiltonian by replacing $\mathbf{r}$ and $\mathbf{p}$ with the operators $\hat{\mathbf{r}}$ and $\hat{\mathbf{p}}$. Remember, however, that $\mathbf{A}(\mathbf{r}, t)$ and ϕ $(\mathbf{r}, t)$ are functions of $\mathbf{r}$, so we must also replace $\mathbf{r}$ with $\hat{\mathbf{r}}$ in these functions. Thus, we obtain

$$\hat{H} = \frac{1}{2m}\left(\hat{\mathbf{p}} - \frac{q}{c}\hat{\mathbf{A}}(\hat{\mathbf{r}}, t)\right)^2 + q\hat{\phi}(\hat{\mathbf{r}}, t) \tag{9.3.1}$$

(b) Let $\Psi(\mathbf{r}, t)$ be the wavefunction of the particle. Then the probability density of finding the particle in $\mathbf{r} = \mathbf{r}_0$ at $t = t_0$ is

$$\rho\,(\mathbf{r}_0, t_0) = \left|\Psi\,(\mathbf{r}_0, t_0)\right|^2 = \Psi^*(\mathbf{r}_0, t_0)\,\Psi\,(\mathbf{r}_0, t_0) \tag{9.3.2}$$

(c) First calculate $\frac{\partial\rho}{\partial t}$:

$$\frac{\partial\rho}{\partial t} = \frac{\partial}{\partial t}(\Psi^*\Psi) = \frac{\partial\Psi^*}{\partial t}\Psi + \Psi^*\frac{\partial\Psi}{\partial t} \tag{9.3.3}$$

Using the Schrödinger equation and its complex conjugate $-i\hbar \dfrac{\partial \Psi^*}{\partial t} = (\hat{H}\Psi)^*$

$$\frac{\partial \rho}{\partial t} = -\frac{1}{i\hbar}[(\hat{H}\Psi^*)\Psi - \Psi^*(\hat{H}\Psi)] \tag{9.3.4}$$

Use the representations

$$\hat{\mathbf{r}} = \mathbf{r} \qquad \hat{\mathbf{p}} = -i\hbar\nabla \tag{9.3.5}$$

In a coordinate representation, $\hat{\mathbf{A}}(\hat{\mathbf{r}}, t)$ becomes a vector function, so

$$\hat{\mathbf{A}}(\hat{\mathbf{r}}, t) = \mathbf{A}(\mathbf{r}, t) \tag{9.3.6}$$

and the quantum Hamiltonian is

$$\hat{H} = \frac{1}{2m}\left(i\hbar\nabla + \frac{q}{c}\mathbf{A}\right) \cdot \left(i\hbar\nabla + \frac{q}{c}\mathbf{A}\right) + q\phi \tag{9.3.7}$$

Equation (9.3.4) then gives

$$\frac{\partial \rho}{\partial t} = -\frac{1}{i\hbar}\left\{ \Psi \frac{1}{2m}\left[\left(-i\hbar\nabla + \frac{q}{c}\mathbf{A}\right) \cdot \left(-i\hbar\nabla + \frac{q}{c}\mathbf{A}\right)\Psi^*\right] \right.$$
$$\left. - \Psi^* \frac{1}{2m}\left[\left(-i\hbar\nabla + \frac{q}{c}\mathbf{A}\right) \cdot \left(i\hbar\nabla + \frac{q}{c}\mathbf{A}\right)\Psi\right]\right\} \tag{9.3.8}$$

which can be written as

$$\frac{\partial \rho}{\partial t} = -\nabla\left\{\frac{1}{2m}\left[\frac{\hbar}{i}(\Psi^*\nabla\Psi - \Psi\nabla\Psi) - \frac{2q}{c}\mathbf{A}\Psi^*\Psi\right]\right\} \tag{9.3.9}$$

The equation describing probability conservation is

$$\frac{\partial \rho}{\partial t} + \nabla \cdot \mathbf{j} = 0 \tag{9.3.10}$$

where $\mathbf{j}$ is the probability current density. From Eqs. (9.3.9) and (9.3.10) we conclude

$$\mathbf{j} = \frac{1}{2m}\left[\frac{\hbar}{i}(\Psi^*\nabla\Psi - \Psi\nabla\Psi^*) - \frac{2q}{c}\hat{\mathbf{A}}\Psi^*\Psi\right] \tag{9.3.11}$$

which is the probability current density for a particle moving in a region with an electromagnetic field. In a vacuum in which there is no electromagnetic field, $\mathbf{A} = 0$, and Eq. (9.3.11) is reduced to the known probability current density described in Chap. 3.

9.4. According to the postulates of quantum mechanics, a given physical system is characterized by a state vector $|\Psi\rangle$. Consider a particle of mass m and charge q influenced by an electric field $\mathcal{E}$ and a magnetic field $\mathcal{B}$. In Problem 9.2 we have shown how different pairs of potentials $\mathbf{A}$ and ϕ can describe the same $\mathcal{E}$ and $\mathcal{B}$. In this problem, we study how the state vector $|\Psi\rangle$ depends on the choice of gauge ($\mathbf{A}$ and ϕ). Follow these steps: (*a*) Write the Hamiltonian with $\mathbf{A}$ and ϕ; then with $\mathbf{A}'$ and ϕ' relate $\mathbf{A}$ and ϕ by Eq. (9.2.7). (*b*) Write the Schrödinger equation for the two cases. (*c*) Show that if Ψ is the solution of the first Schrödinger equation, then

$$\tilde{\Psi}(\mathbf{r}, t) = e^{iqf(\mathbf{r}, t)/c\hbar}\Psi(\mathbf{r}, t) \tag{9.4.1}$$

is the solution of the second equation [where f is the same as in Eq. (9.2.7)]. (*d*) Discuss the results.

SOLUTION

(*a*) According to Eq. (9.1.4), the classical Hamiltonian for **A** and φ is

$$H = \frac{1}{2m}\left(\mathbf{p} - \frac{q}{c}\mathbf{A}\right)\cdot\left(\mathbf{p} - \frac{q}{c}\mathbf{A}\right) + q\phi \tag{9.4.2}$$

Similarly, for **A′** and φ′ we have

$$\tilde{H} = \frac{1}{2m}\left(\mathbf{p} - \frac{q}{c}\mathbf{A}'\right)\cdot\left(\mathbf{p} - \frac{q}{c}\mathbf{A}'\right) + q\phi' \tag{9.4.3}$$

Using Eq. (9.2.7) we obtain

$$\tilde{H} = \frac{1}{2m}\left(\mathbf{p} - \frac{q}{c}\mathbf{A} - \frac{q}{c}\nabla f\right)\cdot\left(\mathbf{p} - \frac{q}{c}\mathbf{A} - \frac{q}{c}\nabla f\right) + q\phi - \frac{q}{c}\frac{\partial f}{\partial t} \tag{9.4.4}$$

(*b*) The Schrödinger equation for the first case is

$$\hat{H}|\Psi\rangle = i\hbar\frac{d|\Psi\rangle}{dt} \tag{9.4.5}$$

We can use Eq. (9.4.2) to write the Schrödinger equation, in the coordinates representation, by replacing **p** with $-i\hbar\nabla$, and obtain

$$\left[\frac{1}{2m}\left(-i\hbar\nabla - \frac{q}{c}\hat{\mathbf{A}}\right)^2 + q\phi\right]\Psi(\mathbf{r}, t) = i\hbar\frac{\partial\Psi(\mathbf{r}, t)}{\partial t} \tag{9.4.6}$$

For the second case we have

$$\hat{H}|\tilde{\Psi}\rangle = i\hbar\frac{d|\Psi\rangle}{dt} \tag{9.4.7}$$

Using Eq. (9.4.4) we have, in the coordinates representation,

$$\left[\frac{1}{2m}\left(-i\hbar\nabla - \frac{q}{c}\hat{\mathbf{A}} - \frac{q}{c}\nabla f\right)^2 + q\phi - \frac{q}{c}\frac{\partial f}{\partial t}\right]\tilde{\Psi}(\mathbf{r}, t) = i\hbar\frac{\partial\tilde{\Psi}(\mathbf{r}, t)}{\partial t} \tag{9.4.8}$$

(*c*) Suppose that $\Psi(\mathbf{r}, t)$ is a solution of Eq. (9.4.6). Define

$$\tilde{\Psi}(\mathbf{r}, t) = e^{iqf(\mathbf{r}, t)/c\hbar}\Psi(\mathbf{r}, t) \tag{9.4.9}$$

We wish to show that $\tilde{\Psi}$ is the solution of Eq. (9.4.8). Using Eqs. (9.4.6) and (9.4.9)

$$i\hbar\frac{\partial\tilde{\Psi}(\mathbf{r}, t)}{\partial t} = -\frac{q}{c}\frac{\partial f(\mathbf{r}, t)}{\partial t}e^{iqf(\mathbf{r},t)/c\hbar}\Psi(\mathbf{r}, t) + e^{iqf(\mathbf{r},t)/c\hbar}\left(i\hbar\frac{\partial\Psi(\mathbf{r}, t)}{\partial t}\right)$$

$$= -\frac{q}{c}\frac{\partial f(\mathbf{r}, t)}{\partial t}\tilde{\Psi}(\mathbf{r}, t) + e^{iqf(\mathbf{r},t)/c\hbar}\left[\frac{1}{2m}\left(-i\hbar\nabla - \frac{q}{c}\hat{\mathbf{A}}\right)^2 + q\phi\right]e^{iqf(\mathbf{r},t)/c\hbar}\tilde{\Psi}(\mathbf{r}, t) \tag{9.4.10}$$

So,

$$i\hbar\frac{\partial\tilde{\Psi}(\mathbf{r}, t)}{\partial t} = \left[-\frac{q}{c}\frac{\partial f(\mathbf{r}, t)}{\partial t} + q\phi\right]\tilde{\Psi}(\mathbf{r}, t) + e^{iqf(\mathbf{r},t)/c\hbar}\left[\frac{1}{2m}\left(-i\hbar\nabla - \frac{q}{c}\hat{\mathbf{A}}\right)^2\right]e^{-iqf(\mathbf{r},t)/c\hbar}\tilde{\Psi}(\mathbf{r}, t) \tag{9.4.11}$$

We calculate the last term in the right-hand side of Eq. (9.4.11):

$$\left[\left(-i\hbar\nabla - \frac{q}{c}\hat{\mathbf{A}}\right)\cdot\left(-i\hbar\nabla - \frac{q}{c}\hat{\mathbf{A}}\right)\right]e^{-iqf(\mathbf{r},t)/c\hbar}\,\tilde{\Psi}(\mathbf{r},t)$$

$$= \left(-i\hbar\nabla - \frac{q}{c}\hat{\mathbf{A}}\right)\cdot\left[e^{-iqf(\mathbf{r},t)/c\hbar}\left(-\frac{q}{c}\nabla f(\mathbf{r},t) - i\hbar\nabla - \frac{q}{c}\hat{\mathbf{A}}\right)\right]\tilde{\Psi}(\mathbf{r},t)$$

$$= e^{-iqf(\mathbf{r},t)/c\hbar}\left(-\frac{q}{c}\nabla f - i\hbar\nabla - \frac{q}{c}\hat{\mathbf{A}}\right)\cdot\left(-\frac{q}{c}\nabla f - i\hbar\nabla - \frac{q}{c}\hat{\mathbf{A}}\right)\tilde{\Psi}(\mathbf{r},t) \qquad (9.4.12)$$

hence,

$$i\hbar\frac{\partial\tilde{\Psi}(\mathbf{r},t)}{\partial t} = \left[-\frac{q}{c}\frac{\partial f(\mathbf{r},t)}{\partial t} + q\phi + \frac{1}{2m}\left(-\frac{q}{c}\nabla f - i\hbar\nabla - \frac{q}{c}\hat{\mathbf{A}}\right)^2\right]\tilde{\Psi}(\mathbf{r},t) \qquad (9.4.13)$$

So, $\tilde{\Psi}(\mathbf{r},t)$ is indeed the solution of the Schrödinger equation (9.4.8).

(d) When we pass from one gauge to another, the state vector describing the system is transformed by the unitary transformation $e^{-iqf(\mathbf{r},\,t)/c\hbar}$, where $f(\mathbf{r},t)$ is the function relating the two gauges. For the wavefunction, the gauge transformation corresponds to a phase change that varies from one point to another and is therefore not a global phase factor. However, the physical predictions obtained by using the wavefunctions ψ and $\tilde{\psi}$ are the same, since the operators that describe the physical quantities are also transformed when we change between the gauges (see Problem 9.5).

9.5. In Problem 9.4 it was shown that when we perform a gauge transformation

$$\begin{cases} \mathbf{A} \rightarrow \mathbf{A}' = \mathbf{A} + \nabla f \\ \phi \rightarrow \phi' = \phi - \dfrac{1}{c}\dfrac{\partial f}{\partial t} \end{cases} \qquad (9.5.1)$$

The wavefunction describing a particle of mass m and charge q transforms according to

$$\Psi(\mathbf{r},t) \rightarrow \Psi'(\mathbf{r},t) = e^{iqf(\mathbf{r},t)/c\hbar}\,\Psi(\mathbf{r},t) \qquad (9.5.2)$$

(a) Do the probability density and the probability current change when we pass from one gauge to another? (b) Suppose that at time t we want to measure a physical quantity Q. Does the probability of obtaining an eigenvalue q of Q depend on the gauge? (Assume for simplicity that q is nondegenerate.)

SOLUTION

(a) The probability density in the first gauge is

$$\rho(\mathbf{r},t) = \left|\Psi(\mathbf{r},t)\right|^2 = \Psi(\mathbf{r},t)\Psi^*(\mathbf{r},t) \qquad (9.5.3)$$

After the gauge transformation, and according to Eq. (9.5.2),

$$\rho'(\mathbf{r},t) = \left|\Psi'(\mathbf{r},t)\right|^2 = \Psi'(\mathbf{r},t)\Psi'^*(\mathbf{r},t) = e^{iqf(\mathbf{r},t)/c\hbar}\,\Psi(\mathbf{r},t)\,e^{-iqf(\mathbf{r},t)/c\hbar}\Psi^*(\mathbf{r},t) = \Psi(\mathbf{r},t)\Psi^*(\mathbf{r},t) \quad (9.5.4)$$

We see that the probability density is gauge-invariant. Now, the probability current density in the first gauge is

$$\mathbf{j} = \frac{1}{2m}\left\{\frac{\hbar}{i}\left(\Psi^*\nabla\Psi - \Psi\nabla\Psi^*\right) - \frac{2q}{c}\mathbf{A}\Psi^*\Psi\right\} \qquad (9.5.5)$$

When we perform the gauge transformation, Eq. (9.5.1), we have

$$\mathbf{j}' = \frac{1}{2m}\left\{\frac{\hbar}{i}[e^{-iqf(\mathbf{r},t)/c\hbar}\,\Psi^*\nabla(e^{iqf(\mathbf{r},t)/c\hbar}\,\Psi) - e^{iqf(\mathbf{r},t)/c\hbar}\Psi\nabla(e^{-iqf(\mathbf{r},t)/c\hbar}\,\Psi^*)]\right.$$

$$\left. -\frac{2q}{c}(\mathbf{A} + \nabla f)(e^{-iqf(\mathbf{r},t)/c\hbar}\,\Psi^*)(e^{iqf(\mathbf{r},t)/c\hbar}\,\Psi)\right\}$$

$$= \frac{1}{2m}\left\{\frac{\hbar}{i}\left[\frac{iq}{\hbar c}\Psi^*\nabla f\Psi + \Psi^*\nabla\Psi + \frac{iq}{\hbar c}\Psi\nabla f\Psi^* - \Psi\nabla\Psi^*\right] - \frac{2q}{c}(\mathbf{A} + \nabla f)\Psi^*\Psi\right\}$$

$$= \frac{1}{2m}\left\{\frac{\hbar}{i}\left[\Psi^*\nabla\Psi - \Psi\nabla\Psi^*\right] - \frac{2q}{c}\mathbf{A}\Psi^*\Psi\right\}$$

We see that the probability current density is gauge-invariant.

(b) Suppose that $\Phi(\mathbf{r}, t)$ is the eigenfunction of $\hat{Q}$ corresponding to the eigenvalue q:

$$\hat{Q}\Phi(\mathbf{r}, t) = q\Phi(\mathbf{r}, t) \tag{9.5.6}$$

According to the postulates of quantum mechanics (see Chap. 4), the probability of obtaining q when the system is in the state $\Psi(\mathbf{r}, t)$ is

$$P_q = \langle\phi|\Psi\rangle = \phi^*(\mathbf{r}, t)\Psi(\mathbf{r}, t) \tag{9.5.7}$$

When we make the gauge transformation, Eq. (9.5.1), the wavefunction $\phi(\mathbf{r}, t)$ will transform to

$$\phi(\mathbf{r}, t) \rightarrow \phi'(\mathbf{r}, t) = e^{iqf(\mathbf{r},t)/c\hbar}\phi(\mathbf{r}, t) \tag{9.5.8}$$

The probability of obtaining q will be determined according to Eqs. (9.5.2) and (9.5.9):

$$P_q' = \phi'^*(\mathbf{r}, t)\,\Psi'(\mathbf{r}, t) = e^{-iqf(\mathbf{r},t)/c\hbar}\,\phi^*(\mathbf{r}, t)e^{iqf(\mathbf{r},t)/c\hbar}\,\Psi(\mathbf{r}, t) = \phi^*(\mathbf{r}, t)\Psi(\mathbf{r}, t) = P_q \tag{9.5.9}$$

We can conclude that all the physical predictions do not depend on the gauge that has been chosen.

9.6. A one-dimensional harmonic oscillator consists of a particle with mass m and potential energy

$$V(x) = \frac{1}{2}m\omega^2x^2 \tag{9.6.1}$$

This particle has a charge q and is placed in a uniform electric field $\mathcal{E}$ parallel to the x axis, $\mathcal{E} = \mathcal{E}\mathbf{i}$. (a) Find a suitable potential field $\phi(x)$ corresponding to the electric field. (b) Write the Hamiltonian of the particle. (c) Perform a coordinate transformation $y = ax + b$ (a and b are constants), such that in the y coordinate the Hamiltonian is similar to that of a one-dimensional harmonic oscillator (with no charge). What are a and b? (d) Find the energy eigenvalues and eigenstates of the system.

SOLUTION

(a) We have $\mathcal{E} = \mathcal{E}\mathbf{i}$ and we seek $\phi(x, t)$ such that

$$\mathcal{E} = -\nabla\phi \tag{9.6.2}$$

Since $\mathcal{B} = 0$, we seek a gauge in which $\mathbf{A} = 0$. Integrating Eq. (9.6.2) we obtain $\phi(x) = -\mathcal{E}x + c$, where c is a constant of integration. Let us choose $c = 0$; then

$$\phi(x) = -\mathcal{E}x \tag{9.6.3}$$

(b) The total classical Hamiltonian is

$$H = \frac{p^2}{2m} + \frac{1}{2}m\omega^2x^2 - \mathcal{E}x \tag{9.6.4}$$

The first term on the right-hand side of Eq. (9.6.4) is the standard kinetic term, the second term is the harmonic oscillator potential energy, and the third term is the electrical potential energy.

(c) Write Eq. (9.6.4) in the following form:

$$H_y = \frac{p_y^2}{2m} + \frac{1}{2}m\omega_y^2 y^2 + H_0 \tag{9.6.5}$$

where H_0 is a constant and $y = ax + b$. Consider the kinetic term. We see that $p_y = p_x$, so $a = 1$. Now we can substitute $y = x + b$ into Eq. (9.6.5) and obtain

$$H_y = \frac{p_x^2}{2m} + \frac{1}{2}m\omega^2(x + b)^2 + H_0 = \frac{p_x^2}{2m} + \frac{1}{2}m\omega^2 x^2 + m\omega^2 bx + \frac{1}{2}m\omega^2 b^2 + H_0 \tag{9.6.6}$$

From Eqs. (9.6.4) and (9.6.6) we see that $H_x = H_y$ only if $b = -\varepsilon/m\omega^2$ and $H_0 = -\varepsilon^2/2m\omega^2$. To conclude, if we perform the coordinate transformation $y = x - \varepsilon/m\omega^2$, we get a one-dimensional harmonic oscillator with no charge, and the energy shifted by $-\varepsilon^2/2m\omega^2$.

(d) The energy eigenvalues of a one-dimensional harmonic oscillator are

$$E_n = \frac{1}{2}\hbar\omega\left(n + \frac{1}{2}\right) \tag{9.6.7}$$

corresponding to the eigenstate $\left|\psi_n\right\rangle$ We have a shifted harmonic oscillator; thus, the energy eigenvalues are now,

$$E_n = \frac{1}{2}\hbar\omega\left(n + \frac{1}{2}\right) - \frac{1}{2}\frac{\varepsilon^2}{m\omega^2} \tag{9.6.8}$$

Its eigenfunctions are

$$\psi_n(y) = \psi_n\left(x - \frac{\varepsilon}{m\omega^2}\right) \tag{9.6.9}$$

As a function of y, Eq. (9.6.9) expresses the standard one-dimensional harmonic oscillators' eigenfunctions. Note that as a function of x, however, those eigenfunctions are different.

9.7. Consider the constant magnetic field $\mathcal{B} = \mathcal{B}_0\mathbf{k}$. (a) Find the potential $\mathbf{A}$ corresponding to the symmetric gauge $\mathbf{A} = \frac{1}{2}\mathbf{r} \times \mathcal{B}$. (b) Find the potential $\mathbf{A}$ corresponding to a nonsymmetric gauge. (c) Compute the gauge function $f(\mathbf{r}, t)$ relating the two gauges used in parts (a) and (b).

SOLUTION

(a) In the symmetric gauge $\mathbf{A} = -\frac{1}{2}\mathbf{r} \times \mathcal{B}$ we get

$$\mathbf{A} = -\frac{1}{2}\begin{pmatrix} \mathbf{i} & \mathbf{j} & \mathbf{k} \\ x & y & z \\ 0 & 0 & \mathcal{B}_0 \end{pmatrix} = -\frac{1}{2}y\mathcal{B}_0\mathbf{i} + \frac{1}{2}x\mathcal{B}_0\mathbf{j} \tag{9.7.1}$$

so

$$\mathbf{A} = \frac{\mathcal{B}_0}{2}(-y, x, 0) \tag{9.7.2}$$

(b) We can use any other gauge and find a different $\mathbf{A}$. As an example, we can try to find $\mathbf{A}$ only in the x direction, $\mathbf{A} = \tilde{A}_x\mathbf{i}$. In that case,

$$\nabla \times \mathbf{A} = \begin{pmatrix} \mathbf{i} & \mathbf{j} & \mathbf{k} \\ \frac{\partial}{\partial x} & \frac{\partial}{\partial y} & \frac{\partial}{\partial z} \\ \tilde{A}_x & 0 & 0 \end{pmatrix} = +\left(\frac{\partial \tilde{A}_x}{\partial z}\right)\mathbf{j} - \left(\frac{\partial \tilde{A}_x}{\partial y}\right)\mathbf{k} = \mathcal{B}_0\mathbf{k} \tag{9.7.3}$$

By integrating Eq. (9.7.3) we obtain $\tilde{A}_x = -\mathcal{B}_0 y + c$. We can choose $c = 0$, so

$$\tilde{A}_x = -\mathcal{B}_0 y \qquad \tilde{A}_y = \tilde{A}_z = 0 \tag{9.7.4}$$

(c) We want to find the gauge function $f(\mathbf{r})$ such that $\mathbf{A} = \tilde{\mathbf{A}} + \nabla f$ (see Problem 9.2). From Eqs. (9.7.2) and (9.7.4), we find that

$$\begin{cases} \mathbf{A} = \dfrac{\mathcal{B}_0}{2}(-y, x, 0) \\[2mm] \tilde{\mathbf{A}} = \mathcal{B}_0(-y, 0, 0) \end{cases} \tag{9.7.5}$$

or, explicitly,

$$\begin{cases} A_x = -\dfrac{\mathcal{B}_0}{2}y = \tilde{A}_x + \partial_x f = -\mathcal{B}_0 y + \partial_x f \\[2mm] A_y = \dfrac{\mathcal{B}_0}{2}x = \tilde{A}y + \partial_y f = \partial_y f \end{cases} \tag{9.7.6}$$

Hence,

$$\frac{\partial f}{\partial x} = \frac{\mathcal{B}_0}{2}y \qquad \frac{\partial f}{\partial y} = \frac{\mathcal{B}_0}{2}x \tag{9.7.7}$$

By integrating Eq. (9.7.7) we obtain

$$f(x, y) = \frac{\mathcal{B}_0}{2}xy + \text{const.} \tag{9.7.8}$$

9.8. A particle with mass m and charge q is in a region of a constant magnetic field $\mathcal{B}$. Assume that $\mathcal{B}$ is in the $\mathbf{k}$ direction and use the Landau gauge; i.e., $\mathbf{A} = (-\mathcal{B}y, 0, 0)$. (a) What is the Hamiltonian of the particle? (b) Show that the Hamiltonian commutes with $\hat{p}_x$ and $\hat{p}_z$. (c) Work with the basis of the eigenstates of $\hat{p}_x$ and $\hat{p}_z$ and use a separation of variables to show that for the y component, the Schrödinger equation reduces to a Schrödinger equation of a harmonic oscillator (see Problem 9.6). (d) Find the eigenstates and eigenenergies of the Hamiltonian.

SOLUTION

(a) The classical Hamiltonian is

$$H = \frac{1}{2m}\left(\mathbf{p} - \frac{q}{c}\mathbf{A}\right)\cdot\left(\mathbf{p} - \frac{q}{c}\mathbf{A}\right) = \frac{1}{2m}\left(\mathbf{p} + \frac{q}{c}\mathcal{B}y\mathbf{i}\right)\cdot\left(\mathbf{p} + \frac{q}{c}\mathcal{B}y\mathbf{i}\right) \tag{9.8.1}$$

where $\mathbf{i}$ is a unit vector in the x direction. The Hamiltonian operator is therefore

$$\hat{H} = \frac{1}{2m}(\hat{p}_y^2 + \hat{p}_z^2) + \frac{1}{2m}\left(\hat{p}_x + \frac{q}{c}\mathcal{B}\hat{y}\right)^2 = \frac{1}{2m}\left[\hat{p}_x^2 + \hat{p}_y^2 + \hat{p}_z^2 + \frac{2q}{c}\mathcal{B}\hat{y}\hat{p}_x + \left(\frac{q}{c}\mathcal{B}\right)^2\hat{y}^2\right] \tag{9.8.2}$$

(b) To find the commutation relations between $\hat{H}$ and $\hat{p}_x$ or $\hat{p}_z$, we use the known relations

$$[\hat{p}_x, \hat{p}_y] = [\hat{p}_x, \hat{p}_z] = [\hat{p}_x, \hat{y}] = [\hat{p}_x, \hat{z}] = [\hat{p}_z, \hat{y}] = 0 \tag{9.8.3}$$

and obtain

$$[\hat{H}, \hat{p}_x] = \frac{1}{2m}\left([\hat{p}_x^2, \hat{p}_x] + \frac{2q\mathcal{B}}{c}\hat{y}[\hat{p}_x, \hat{p}_x]\right) \tag{9.8.4}$$

By definition, $[\hat{p}_x, \hat{p}_x] = [\hat{p}_z, \hat{p}_z] = 0$, so we easily find that $[\hat{H}, \hat{p}_x] = 0$, and also for $\hat{p}_z$

$$[\hat{H}, \hat{p}_z] = \frac{1}{2m}[\hat{p}_z^2, \hat{p}_z] = 0 \tag{9.8.5}$$

(c) Since $\hat{H}$ commutes with $\hat{p}_x$ and $\hat{p}_z$, we can find eigenstates of $\hat{H}$ that are also eigenstates of $\hat{p}_x$ and $\hat{p}_z$ (recall also that $[\hat{p}_x, \hat{p}_z] = 0$). We use a separation of variables; namely, $\psi(x, y, z) = \psi_x(x)\psi_y(y)\psi_z(z)$. For $\psi_x(x)$ and $\psi_z(z)$ we choose the eigenstates of $\hat{p}_x$ and $\hat{p}_z$, respectively:

$$\begin{cases} \psi_x(x) \equiv \psi_{p_x}(x) = e^{ip_x x/\hbar} \\ \psi_z(z) \equiv \psi_{p_z}(z) = e^{ip_z z/\hbar} \end{cases} \tag{9.8.6}$$

so

$$\psi(x, y, z) = e^{ip_x x/\hbar} e^{ip_z z/\hbar} \psi_y(y) \tag{9.8.7}$$

where p_x and p_z are now constant *numbers* (these are the eigenvalues). Using Eqs. (9.8.2) and (9.8.7) we get the Schrödinger equation:

$$\hat{H}\psi = \frac{1}{2m}\left[p_x^2 + p_z^2 + \hat{p}_y^2 + \frac{2q\mathcal{B}p_x}{c}\hat{y} + \left(\frac{q}{c}\mathcal{B}\right)^2 \hat{y}^2 \right]\psi(x, y, z) = E\psi(x, y, z) \tag{9.8.8}$$

Note that in Eq. (9.8.8), p_x and p_z are constant numbers and only $\hat{p}_y$ and $\hat{y}$ are operators. Let us denote $\frac{1}{2m}(p_x^2 + p_z^2) = a$; then Eq. (9.8.8) can be written as

$$\left[\frac{1}{2m}\hat{p}_y^2 + \left(\frac{q\mathcal{B}p_x}{mc}\right)\hat{y} + \frac{1}{2m}\left(\frac{q\mathcal{B}}{c}\right)^2 \hat{y}^2 \right]\psi(x, y, z) = (E - a)\psi(x, y, z) \tag{9.8.9}$$

We see now that the y component of the Schrödinger equation is similar to the Hamiltonian of Problem 9.6 [see, for example, Eq. (9.6.4)]. In order to show that the y component is identical to the Hamiltonian of a harmonic oscillator we make a transformation similar to the one in Problem 9.6; that is,

$$\begin{cases} \hat{y} \to \hat{\tilde{y}} = \hat{y} + \dfrac{cp_x}{q\mathcal{B}} \\ \hat{p}_y \to \hat{p}_{\tilde{y}} = \hat{p}_y \end{cases} \tag{9.8.10}$$

The Schrödinger equation, Eq. (9.8.9), then becomes

$$\left[\frac{1}{2m}\hat{p}_{\tilde{y}}^2 + \frac{1}{2m}\left(\frac{q\mathcal{B}}{c}\right)^2 \hat{\tilde{y}}^2 - \frac{p_x^2}{2m} \right]\psi = (E - a)\psi \tag{9.8.11}$$

or

$$\left[\frac{1}{2m}\hat{p}_{\tilde{y}}^2 + \frac{1}{2m}\left(\frac{q\mathcal{B}}{c}\right)^2 \hat{\tilde{y}}^2 \right]\psi = \left(E - \frac{p_z^2}{2m} \right)\psi \tag{9.8.12}$$

If we denote $\tilde{E} = E - p_z^2/2m$, Eq. (9.8.12) becomes

$$\left[\frac{1}{2m}\hat{p}_{\tilde{y}}^2 + \frac{1}{2}m\omega_B^2 \hat{\tilde{y}}^2 \right]\psi(x, \tilde{y}, z) = \tilde{E}\psi(x, \tilde{y}, z) \tag{9.8.13}$$

where $\omega_B^2 = \left(\dfrac{q\mathcal{B}}{cm}\right)^2$. We see that Eq. (9.8.13) is indeed a Schrödinger equation for a one-dimensional harmonic oscillator.

(d) Since Eq. (9.8.13) is the Schrödinger equation of a harmonic oscillator, we know its eigenvalues and eigenstates:

$$\tilde{E}_n = \hbar\omega_B\left(n + \frac{1}{2}\right) = \hbar\frac{q\mathcal{B}}{mc}\left(n + \frac{1}{2}\right) \tag{9.8.14}$$

and

$$\psi_{\tilde{y}}(\tilde{y}) = \left(\frac{m\omega_B}{\pi\hbar}\right)^{1/4} e^{-m\omega_B \tilde{y}^2/2\hbar} H_n(\tilde{y}) \tag{9.8.15}$$

where $H_n(x)$ are Hermite polynomials. The eigenvalues of the original Hamiltonian, Eq. (9.8.2), are E [see Eq. (9.8.8)]. Hence,

$$E_n = \tilde{E}_n + \frac{p_z^2}{2m} = \hbar \frac{qB}{mc}\left(n + \frac{1}{2}\right) + \frac{p_z^2}{2m} \qquad (9.8.16)$$

where the eigenfunctions $\psi_n(x, y, z)$ are

$$\psi_n(x, y, z) = \left(\frac{m\omega_B}{\pi\hbar}\right)^{1/4} e^{ip_x x/\hbar} e^{ip_z z/\hbar} \exp\left[-\frac{m\omega_B}{2\hbar}\left(y + \frac{cp_x}{qB}\right)^2\right] H_n\left(y + \frac{cp_x}{qB}\right) \qquad (9.8.17)$$

9.9. Solve Problem 9.8 for a particle of spin 1/2 (an electron, for example) and with a magnetic moment $\mu = \mu_s S$.

SOLUTION

(*a*) We add to the Hamiltonian, Eq. (9.8.1), the interaction energy between the spin and the magnetic field,

$$H = -\mu \cdot \mathcal{B} \qquad (9.9.1)$$

and obtain the total classical Hamiltonian:

$$H = \frac{1}{2m}\left(\mathbf{p} - \frac{q}{c}\mathbf{A}\right)^2 - \mu \cdot \mathcal{B} \qquad (9.9.2)$$

The magnetic field is $\mathcal{B} = \mathcal{B}\mathbf{k}$, and we use the gauge $\mathbf{A} = (-\mathcal{B}y, 0, 0)$ to obtain the Hamiltonian operator:

$$\hat{H} = \frac{1}{2m}\left[\hat{p}_x^2 + \hat{p}_z^2 + \hat{p}_y^2 + \frac{2q\mathcal{B}\hat{p}_x}{c}\hat{y} + \left(\frac{q\mathcal{B}}{c}\right)^2 \hat{y}^2\right] - \frac{\mu_s \mathcal{B}}{s}\hat{S}_z \qquad (9.9.3)$$

(*b*) One can easily see that the Hamiltonian, Eq. (9.9.3), commutes with $\hat{p}_x$ and $\hat{p}_z$. The only term that we need to check (after using the results of Problem 9.8) is $\frac{\mu_s \mathcal{B}}{s}\hat{S}_z$. Since the degrees of freedom of the spin are free from the spatial ones, we have $[\hat{\mathbf{p}}, \hat{\mathbf{S}}] = 0$. Specifically,

$$\left[\hat{p}_x, \frac{\mu_s \mathcal{B}}{s}\hat{S}_z\right] = \left[\hat{p}_z, \frac{\mu_s \mathcal{B}}{s}\hat{S}_z\right] = 0 \qquad (9.9.4)$$

(*c*) Including the spin states, we use the basis of the eigenstates of $\hat{p}_x$ and $\hat{p}_z$ as well as of $\hat{S}^2$ and $\hat{S}_z$; namely, our wavefunction is

$$\psi(x, y, z)\chi_{\text{spin}} = e^{ip_x x/\hbar} e^{ip_z z/\hbar} \psi_y(y)\chi(s = 1/2, S_z) \qquad (9.9.5)$$

where $\chi(s = 1/2, S_z)$ is the spin state of the electron that is an eigenstate of $\hat{S}^2$ and $\hat{S}_z$:

$$\hat{S}^2\chi(s = 1/2, S_z) = \hbar^2 s(s + 1)\chi(s = 1/2, \hat{S}_z) = \frac{4}{3}\hbar^2\chi(s = 1/2, S_z) \qquad (9.9.6)$$

$$\hat{S}_z\chi(s = 1/2, S_z) = \hbar S_z\chi(s = 1/2, S_z) = \left(\pm\frac{1}{2}\right)\hbar\chi(s = 1/2, S_z) \qquad (9.9.7)$$

We will represent the operator $\hat{\mathbf{S}}$ using the Pauli matrices $\hat{\mathbf{S}} = \frac{\hbar}{2}\hat{\sigma}$. The states $\chi\left(\frac{1}{2}, \pm\frac{1}{2}\right)$ can be written as

$$\chi\left(\tfrac{1}{2}, +\tfrac{1}{2}\right) = \begin{pmatrix} 1 \\ 0 \end{pmatrix} \qquad \chi\left(\tfrac{1}{2}, -\tfrac{1}{2}\right) = \begin{pmatrix} 0 \\ 1 \end{pmatrix} \qquad (9.9.8)$$

see Chap. 7.

(d) In order to find the eigenfunctions and eigenvalues, we follow Problem 9.8, part (d), and write the Schrödinger equation:

$$\left(\frac{1}{2m}\hat{p}_{\tilde{y}}^2 + \frac{1}{2}m\omega_B^2\tilde{y}^2 + \frac{1}{2m}\hat{p}_z^2 - \frac{\mu_s}{s}B\hat{S}_z\right)\psi(x,y,z)\chi_{spin} = E\psi(x,y,z)\chi_{spin} \tag{9.9.9}$$

where [following Problem 9.8, part (d); see Eqs. (9.8.10) and (9.8.13)]

$$\begin{cases} \hat{\tilde{y}} = \hat{y} + \dfrac{cp_x}{qB} \\ \omega_B = \dfrac{qB}{cm} \end{cases} \tag{9.9.10}$$

and p_z, $s = 1/2$, and $S_z = \pm 1/2$ are constants. Defining

$$\bar{E} = E - \frac{qB}{cm} + \frac{\mu_s}{s}BS_z \tag{9.9.11}$$

we obtain, from Eq. (9.9.9), a standard one-dimensional harmonic oscillator Schrödinger equation,

$$\left(\frac{1}{2m}\hat{p}_{\tilde{y}}^2 + \frac{1}{2}m\omega_B^2\hat{\tilde{y}}^2\right)\psi = \bar{E}\psi \tag{9.9.12}$$

with the eigenvalues $\bar{E} = \hbar\omega_B(n + 1/2)$ and the eigenfunctions $\psi(x,y,z)\chi_{spin}$, where $\psi(x,y,z)$ is as given in Eq. (9.8.17). Hence, the eigenvalues of our Schrödinger equation, Eq. (9.9.9), are

$$E = \hbar\frac{qB}{mc}\left(n + \frac{1}{2}\right) + \frac{p_z^2}{2m} - \frac{\mu_s}{s}BS_z \tag{9.9.13}$$

These eigenvalues are known as the *Landau levels*.

9.10. Consider the particle of Problem 9.8. (a) Assume that the particle is in a very large, but finite, box: $0 \le x \le L_x$, $-L_y \le y \le L_y$, and $0 \le z \le L_z$. Write the eigenfunctions for that case. (b) Find the number of states per unit area (in the xy plane).

SOLUTION

(a) Consider the Schrödinger equation

$$\hat{H}\psi(x,y,z) = E\psi(x,y,z) \tag{9.10.1}$$

where $\hat{H}$ is given by Eq. (9.8.2). We also have the boundary conditions

$$\text{I} \qquad \psi(x=0) = \psi(x=L_x) = 0 \tag{9.10.2}$$

$$\text{II} \qquad \psi(y=-L_y) = \psi(y=L_y) = 0 \tag{9.10.3}$$

$$\text{III} \qquad \psi(z=0) = \psi(z=L_z) = 0 \tag{9.10.4}$$

Using the separation of variables of Problem 9.8 and Eqs. (9.10.2) and (9.10.4), we replace Eq. (9.8.6) with

$$\begin{cases} \psi_x(x) = \dfrac{1}{\sqrt{2L_x}}\sin(p_x x) \\ \psi_z(z) = \dfrac{1}{\sqrt{2L_z}}\sin(p_z z) \end{cases} \tag{9.10.5}$$

where

$$\begin{cases} p_x = \dfrac{\pi}{L_x}\hbar n_x \qquad n_x = 0,1,2,\ldots \\ p_z = \dfrac{\pi}{L_x}\hbar n_z \qquad n_z = 0,1,2,\ldots \end{cases} \tag{9.10.6}$$

Assuming that L_y is very large such that $\frac{qB}{2\hbar c}L_y^2 \gg 1$, the y-part of the wavefunction, Eq. (9.8.15), will hardly be affected by the boundary condition Eq. (9.10.3), as is the case for the $\psi(\tilde{y})$ wavefunction. The eigenstates are therefore [see Eq. (9.8.17)]

$$\psi(x,y,z) = \left(\frac{m\omega_B}{\pi\hbar}\right)^{1/4}\frac{1}{2\sqrt{L_x L_z}}\sin(p_x x)\sin(p_z z)\exp\left[\frac{-m\omega_B}{2\hbar}\left(y+\frac{cp_x}{qB}\right)^2\right]H_n\left(y+\frac{cp_x}{qB}\right) \quad (9.10.7)$$

The eigenenergies are [see Eq. (9.8.16)]

$$E_{n_y n_z} = \hbar\frac{qB}{mc}\left(n_y+\frac{1}{2}\right)+\frac{1}{2m}\left(\frac{\pi\hbar}{L_z}\right)^2 n_z^2 \quad (9.10.8)$$

where we used $p_z = \pi\hbar n_z/L$ [see Eq. (9.10.6)]. Note that Eq. (9.10.8) does not depend on n_x, so we have a degeneracy.

(b) The number of states in the xy plane is the number of different possible n_x and n_y, such that the particle is inside the region $0 \le x \le L_x$, $-L_y \le y \le L_y$. We note that in the y direction we have a harmonic oscillator centered at $y_0 = -cp_x/qB$ [see Eqs. (9.8.10) and (9.8.11)]. Assuming that the deviations from the equilibrium point $y = y_0$ are small, we need only to demand that $-L_y \le y_0 \le L_y$. Hence,

$$-L_y \le -\frac{cp_x}{qB} \le L_y \quad (9.10.9)$$

Using Eq. (9.10.6) we get $-L_y \le -\frac{c}{qB}\left(\frac{\pi\hbar}{L_x}\right)n_x \le L_y$, or

$$-\left(\frac{qB}{\pi\hbar c}\right)L_x L_y \le n_x \le \left(\frac{qB}{\pi\hbar c}\right)L_x L_y \quad (9.10.10)$$

The number of different states in the region $0 \le x \le L_x$ and $-L_y \le y \le L_y$ is the number of different n_x in Eq. (9.10.10), namely,

$$n_x = \frac{qB}{\hbar c}L_x L_y \quad (9.10.11)$$

Including the two spin states for each n_x, we finally find the total number of states:

$$N = 2\frac{qB}{\hbar c}L_x L_y \quad (9.10.12)$$

Therefore, the number of states per unit area is

$$n = \frac{N}{\text{area}} = \frac{2\frac{qB}{\hbar c}L_x L_y}{2L_x L_y} = \frac{qB}{\hbar c} \quad (9.10.13)$$

9.11. Refer to Problem 9.10. In the case $p_x = 0$, show that the current $\mathbf{I}$ is indeed zero.

SOLUTION

Using the definition of the probability current density, see Eq. (9.3.11), we obtain the probability current:

$$\mathbf{J} = q\mathbf{j} = \frac{q}{2m}\left[\frac{\hbar}{i}\left(\psi^*\nabla\psi-\psi\nabla\psi^*\right)-\frac{2q}{c}\mathbf{A}\psi^*\psi\right] \quad (9.11.1)$$

Since ψ is real, $\psi^*\nabla\psi-\psi\nabla\psi^* = 0$, and

$$\mathbf{J} = -\frac{q^2}{2mc}\mathbf{A}\psi^*\psi \quad (9.11.2)$$

It was shown in Problem 9.5 that the probability current is gauge-invariant. We can choose, for example, the vector potential $\mathbf{A} = (-By,0,0)$ (see Problem 9.8). Hence,

$$\begin{cases}J_y = J_z = 0 \\ J_x = \frac{q^2}{2mc}By\,\psi^*\psi\end{cases} \quad (9.11.3)$$

Using Eq. (9.10.7) $p_x = 0$, we see that $\psi^*\psi$ is an *even* function of y. The current **I** is

$$\mathbf{I} = \int \mathbf{J}\, dx\, dy\, dz \tag{9.11.4}$$

We have $I_y = I_z = 0$, and

$$I_x = \frac{q^2 \mathcal{B}}{2mc} \int_{-L_y}^{L_y} y \left| \psi(y) \right|^2 dy \int_0^{L_x} \left| \psi_x(x) \right|^2 dx \int_0^{L_z} \left| \psi_z(z) \right|^2 dz \tag{9.11.5}$$

Since $\left| \psi(y) \right|^2$ is an even function (only) in the case where $p_x = 0$, we finally get $\int_{-L_y}^{L_y} \left| \psi(y) \right|^2 y\, dy = 0$ and $I_x = 0$. The classical motion of the particle is a circle and so the total current in the x or y directions is zero.

9.12. For the particle in Problem 9.10 and electric field $\mathcal{E} = \mathcal{E}\mathbf{j}$: (a) Find the eigenstates and eigenvalues of the particle. (b) If $p_x = 0$, show that $I_x \neq 0$ even though $\mathcal{E}$ is only in the y direction. What is the drift velocity?

SOLUTION

(a) We add to the Hamiltonian, Eq. (9.8.1), the potential energy:

$$H_{\text{electric}} = q\phi \tag{9.12.1}$$

where $\mathcal{E} = -\nabla\phi$. Since $\mathcal{E} = \mathcal{E}\mathbf{j}$, we have $\phi = -\mathcal{E}y$, and the total classical Hamiltonian is

$$H = \frac{1}{2m}\left(\mathbf{p} - \frac{q}{c}\mathbf{A} \right)^2 + q\phi = \frac{1}{2m}\left[p_x^2 + p_z^2 + p_y^2 + \frac{2q\mathcal{B}p_x}{c}y - 2mq\mathcal{E}y + \left(\frac{q\mathcal{B}}{c} \right)^2 y^2 \right] \tag{9.12.2}$$

Working in a coordinate representation, we get the Schrödinger equation:

$$\frac{1}{2m}\left[-\hbar^2\left(\frac{\partial^2}{\partial x^2} + \frac{\partial^2}{\partial y^2} + \frac{\partial^2}{\partial z^2} \right) + \frac{2q\mathcal{B}p_x}{c}y - 2mq\mathcal{E}y + \left(\frac{q\mathcal{B}}{c} \right)^2 y^2 \right] \psi(x,y,z) = E\psi(x,y,z) \tag{9.12.3}$$

where we use the fact that $\hat{H}_{\text{electric}}$ commutes with $\hat{p}_x$ and $\hat{p}_z$. The equation for $\psi(y)$ is

$$\frac{1}{2m}\left[\hbar^2\frac{\partial^2}{\partial y^2} + \left(\frac{2q\mathcal{B}p_x}{c} - 2m\mathcal{E}q \right)y + \left(\frac{q\mathcal{B}}{c} \right)^2 y^2 \right]\psi(y) = \varepsilon\psi(y) \tag{9.12.4}$$

where $\varepsilon = E - \dfrac{p_x^2}{2m} - \dfrac{p_z^2}{2m}$. Defining

$$\bar{y} = y + \frac{cp_x}{q\mathcal{B}} - \frac{v_D}{\omega_B} \tag{9.12.5}$$

where $v_D = \dfrac{c\mathcal{E}}{\mathcal{B}}$ and $\omega_B = \dfrac{q\mathcal{B}}{cm}$, and using Eq. (9.12.3), we get

$$\frac{1}{2m}\left(-\hbar^2\frac{\partial^2}{\partial\bar{y}^2} + \frac{1}{2}m\omega_B^2\,\bar{y}^2 \right)\psi(\bar{y}) = \bar{E}\psi(\bar{y}) \tag{9.12.6}$$

where

$$\bar{E} = E - \frac{p_z^2}{2m} + p_x v_D - \frac{1}{2}mv_D^2 \tag{9.12.7}$$

The eigenstates of Eq. (9.12.6) are the standard harmonic oscillator eigenfunctions, and the energy spectrum is

$$E_{n_x n_y n_z} = \bar{E}_{n_y} + \frac{p_z^2}{2m} - p_x v_D + \frac{1}{2} m v_D^2$$

$$= \hbar \omega_B \left(n_y + \frac{1}{2} \right) + \frac{1}{2m} \left(\frac{\pi^2 \hbar^2}{L_z^2} \right) n_z^2 - \frac{\pi \hbar v_D}{L_x} n_x + \frac{1}{2} m v_D^2 \tag{9.12.8}$$

Note that, unlike Eq. (9.10.8), Eq. (9.12.8) depends on n_x and the degeneracy is removed (due to the electric field).

(b) The current, Eq. (9.11.4), is $\mathbf{I} = \int \mathbf{J}\, dx\, dy\, dz$. Using Eq. (9.11.3) we have $I_y = I_z = 0$, and

$$I_x = \frac{q^2 \mathcal{B}}{2mc} \int_{-L_y}^{L_y} |\psi(y)|^2\, y\, dy \tag{9.12.9}$$

Notice that in contrast to Problem 9.11, here, even in the case where $p_x = 0$, the function $|\psi(y)|^2$ is not even since from Eq. (9.12.5) we can conclude that for $p_x = 0$,

$$\bar{y} = y - \frac{v_D}{\omega_B} \tag{9.12.10}$$

Note that $|\psi(\bar{y})|^2$ is even in $\bar{y}$ but *not* in y. If we make the coordinate transformation $y \to \bar{y}$ in Eq. (9.12.9) we obtain

$$I_x = \frac{q^2 \mathcal{B}}{2mc} \int_{-L_y + v_D/\omega_B}^{L_y - v_D/\omega_B} \left(\bar{y} + \frac{v_D}{\omega_B} \right) |\psi(\bar{y})|^2\, d\bar{y} \tag{9.12.11}$$

Now using $L_y \gg \dfrac{v_D}{\omega_B}$, we obtain

$$I_x \approx \frac{q^2 \mathcal{B}}{2mc} \int_{-\infty}^{\infty} \left(\bar{y} + \frac{v_D}{\omega_B} \right) |\psi(\bar{y})|^2\, d\bar{y} \tag{9.12.12}$$

The first term (linear with $\bar{y}$) will give zero since the integrand is antisymmetric. The second term will give, as we expected,

$$I_x = \frac{q^2 \mathcal{B}}{2mc} \frac{v_D}{\omega_B} \int_{-\infty}^{\infty} |\psi(\bar{y})|^2\, d\bar{y} = \frac{q^2 \mathcal{B}}{2mc} \frac{v_D}{\omega_B} = q v_D \tag{9.12.13}$$

where v_D is the *drift velocity* ($v_D = c\mathcal{E}/\mathcal{B}$).

9.13. Consider a spinless particle of mass m and charge q, subjected simultaneously to a scalar potential $V(\mathbf{r})$ and a magnetic field $\mathcal{B} = \mathcal{B}_0 \mathbf{k}$. Use the symmetric gauge $\mathbf{A} = -\frac{1}{2} \mathbf{r} \times \mathcal{B}$ and find the Hamiltonian of the particle. Write it as a sum of H_0, corresponding to the case of no magnetic field, and the additional term H_1.

SOLUTION

We have

$$H = \frac{1}{2m} \left(\mathbf{p} - \frac{q}{c} \mathbf{A} \right)^2 + V(\mathbf{r}) \tag{9.13.1}$$

Using Eq. (9.5), calculate

$$\left(\mathbf{p} - \frac{q}{c}\mathbf{A}\right)^2 = p^2 + \frac{q}{2c}[\mathbf{p}\cdot(\mathbf{r}\times\mathcal{B}) + (\mathbf{v}\times\mathcal{B})\cdot\mathbf{p}] + \frac{q^2}{4c^2}(\mathbf{r}\times\mathcal{B})^2$$

$$= p^2 + \frac{q\mathcal{B}_0}{2c}(-p_x y + p_y x - yp_x + xp_y) + \frac{q^2\mathcal{B}_0^2}{4c^2}(x^2 + y^2)$$

$$= p^2 + \frac{q\mathcal{B}_0}{c}(xp_y - yp_x) + \frac{q^2\mathcal{B}_0^2}{4c^2}(x^2 + y^2) = p^2 + \frac{q\mathcal{B}_0}{c}L_z + \frac{q^2\mathcal{B}_0^2}{4c^2}(x^2 + y^2) \quad (9.13.2)$$

Substituting Eq. (9.13.2) into Eq. (9.13.1), we obtain

$$H = \frac{1}{2m}p^2 + \frac{q\mathcal{B}_0}{2mc}L_z + \frac{q^2\mathcal{B}_0^2}{8mc^2}(x^2 + y^2) + V(\mathbf{r}) \quad (9.13.3)$$

We see that $H = H_0 + H_1$, where

$$H_0 = \frac{1}{2m}p^2 + V(\mathbf{r}) \quad (9.13.4)$$

and

$$H_1 = -\frac{\mu\mathcal{B}_0 L_z}{\hbar} + \frac{q^2\mathcal{B}_0^2}{8m}(x^2 + y^2) \quad (9.13.5)$$

and where μ denotes the *Bohr magneton*, $\mu = \dfrac{q\hbar}{2mc}$.

9.14. Polarized electrons, with a spin polarization (+) in the z direction, enter a region of constant magnetic field $\mathcal{B} = \mathcal{B}_0\mathbf{i}$. The electrons move in the y direction. After time T, the electrons reach a Stern–Gerlach apparatus in which the magnetic field is in the z direction. (a) Write the interaction Hamiltonian in the region of a constant magnetic field. (b) In a detector D we can detect only electrons with spin polarization (−) in the z direction. Find the values of $\mathcal{B}_0$ such that *all* the electrons will reach the detector D. (c) For the smallest value of $\mathcal{B}_0$ [found in part (b)], what percent of the electrons will reach D if the traveling time in the constant magnetic field region is $T/2$ (not T)?

SOLUTION

(a) The interaction between the electron and the magnetic field is due to the magnetic moment of the electron, $\boldsymbol{\mu}_e = \dfrac{2e}{m_e c}\mathbf{S}$, and the external magnetic field $\mathcal{B} = \mathcal{B}_0\mathbf{i}$. The interaction Hamiltonian is

$$H_{\text{int}} = \boldsymbol{\mu}_e \cdot \mathcal{B} = \frac{2e\mathcal{B}_0}{m_e c}\mathbf{S}\cdot\mathbf{i} = \frac{2e\mathcal{B}_0}{m_e c}S_x \quad (9.14.1)$$

We can use the two-vector representation of the $\pm z$ spin states (see Chap. 7),

$$\begin{cases} |+z\rangle \rightarrow \begin{pmatrix} 1 \\ 0 \end{pmatrix} \\[2mm] |-z\rangle \rightarrow \begin{pmatrix} 0 \\ 1 \end{pmatrix} \end{cases} \quad (9.14.2)$$

In this representation, the electron spin operator can be described by the Pauli matrices:

$$\hat{\mathbf{S}} = \frac{\hbar}{2}\hat{\sigma} \quad (9.14.3)$$

where

$$\hat{\sigma}_x = \begin{pmatrix} 0 & 1 \\ 1 & 0 \end{pmatrix} \qquad \hat{\sigma}_y = \begin{pmatrix} 0 & i \\ -i & 0 \end{pmatrix} \qquad \hat{\sigma}_z = \begin{pmatrix} 1 & 0 \\ 0 & 1 \end{pmatrix} \quad (9.14.4)$$

Using Eq. (9.14.4), we can write Eq. (9.14.1) as

$$\hat{H}_{\text{int}} = \frac{\hbar e \mathcal{B}_0}{m_e c} \begin{pmatrix} 0 & 1 \\ 1 & 0 \end{pmatrix} \tag{9.14.5}$$

(*b*) In order to find the state of the electrons at time *t* we need to solve the time-dependent Schrödinger equation:

$$i\hbar \frac{\partial |\psi\rangle}{\partial t} = \hat{H} |\psi\rangle \tag{9.14.6}$$

The state $|\psi\rangle$ can be written as

$$|\psi(t)\rangle = \alpha_+(t)|+z\rangle + \alpha_-(t)|-z\rangle \tag{9.14.7}$$

where $\alpha_+^2 + \alpha_-^2 = 1$, or in the two-vector representation,

$$|\psi(t)\rangle = \alpha_+(t)\begin{pmatrix} 1 \\ 0 \end{pmatrix} + \alpha_-(t)\begin{pmatrix} 0 \\ 1 \end{pmatrix} = \begin{pmatrix} \alpha_+(t) \\ \alpha_-(t) \end{pmatrix} \tag{9.14.8}$$

Using Eqs. (9.14.5) and (9.14.8), the Schrödinger equation, Eq. (9.14.6), becomes

$$i\hbar \frac{\partial}{\partial t} \begin{pmatrix} \alpha_+(t) \\ \alpha_-(t) \end{pmatrix} = \frac{\hbar e \mathcal{B}_0}{m_e c} \begin{pmatrix} 0 & 1 \\ 1 & 0 \end{pmatrix} \begin{pmatrix} \alpha_+(t) \\ \alpha_-(t) \end{pmatrix} = \frac{\hbar e \mathcal{B}_0}{m_e c} \begin{pmatrix} \alpha_+(t) \\ \alpha_-(t) \end{pmatrix} \tag{9.14.9}$$

Equation (9.14.9) is equivalent to the following two equations:

$$i \frac{d\alpha_+(t)}{dt} = \omega_0 \alpha_-(t) \tag{9.14.10}$$

$$i \frac{d\alpha_-(t)}{dt} = \omega_0 \alpha_+(t) \tag{9.14.11}$$

where $\omega_0 = e\mathcal{B}_0/m_e c$. Making another derivative of Eq. (9.14.11) we get

$$i \frac{d^2\alpha_-(t)}{dt^2} = \omega_0 \frac{d\alpha_+(t)}{dt} \tag{9.14.12}$$

From Eqs. (9.14.12) and (9.14.10) we obtain

$$\frac{d^2\alpha_-(t)}{dt^2} = -\omega_0^2 \alpha_-(t) \tag{9.14.13}$$

and similarly,

$$\frac{d^2\alpha_+(t)}{dt^2} = -\omega_0^2 \alpha_+(t) \tag{9.14.14}$$

The solutions of Eqs. (9.14.13) and (9.14.14) are

$$\begin{cases} \alpha_+(t) = a_+ \cos(\omega_0 t) + b_+ \sin(\omega_0 t) \\ \alpha_-(t) = a_- \cos(\omega_0 t) + b_- \sin(\omega_0 t) \end{cases} \tag{9.14.15}$$

where $a_\pm$ and $b_\pm$ are constants determined by the initial condition. The initial condition is

$$|\psi(t=0)\rangle = |+z\rangle = \begin{pmatrix} 1 \\ 0 \end{pmatrix} \tag{9.14.16}$$

So, $a_+ = 1$ and $a_- = 0$. From $\alpha_+^2 + \alpha_-^2 = 1$ we get $b_+ = 0$ and $b_- = 1$. Thus, the solutions of Eq. (9.14.15) are

$$\begin{cases} \alpha_+(t) = \cos(\omega_0 t) \\ \alpha_-(t) = \sin(\omega_0 t) \end{cases} \tag{9.14.17}$$

and the quantum state, Eq. (9.14.8), is

$$|\psi(t)\rangle = \begin{pmatrix} \cos(\omega_0 t) \\ \sin(\omega_0 t) \end{pmatrix} \tag{9.14.18}$$

After a time T, the state of the electrons is

$$|\psi(t)\rangle = \begin{pmatrix} \cos(\omega_0 T) \\ \sin(\omega_0 T) \end{pmatrix} \tag{9.14.19}$$

If we want *all* the electrons to reach the detector D, we must demand that

$$|\psi(T)\rangle = |-z\rangle = \begin{pmatrix} 0 \\ 1 \end{pmatrix} \tag{9.14.20}$$

since the detector D detects only electrons with polarization $-z$. From Eqs. (9.14.18) and (9.14.19) we obtain $|\cos(\omega_0 T)| = 0$ and $|\sin(\omega_0 T)| = 1$, or, equivalently,

$$\omega_0 T = \frac{\pi}{2} + \pi n \qquad n = 0, \pm 1, \pm 2, \ldots \tag{9.14.21}$$

Using $\omega_0 = e\mathcal{B}_0/m_e c$, we finally get

$$\mathcal{B}_0 = \frac{m_e c}{eT}\left(\frac{\pi}{2} + \pi n\right) \tag{9.14.22}$$

(c) The minimum positive value for $\mathcal{B}_0$ satisfying Eq. (9.14.21) is, for $n = 1$,

$$(\mathcal{B}_0)_{\min} = \frac{\pi m_e c}{2eT} \tag{9.14.23}$$

Assuming that $\mathcal{B}_0$ equals Eq. (9.14.22), the quantum state $|\psi(t)\rangle$ after time $T/2$ is

$$|\psi(T/2)\rangle = \begin{pmatrix} \cos(\omega_0 T/2) \\ \sin(\omega_0 T/2) \end{pmatrix} \tag{9.14.24}$$

Now, using Eq. (9.14.22), we have

$$\omega_0 = \frac{e(\mathcal{B}_0)_{\min}}{m_e c} = \frac{\pi}{2T} \tag{9.14.25}$$

Hence, from Eqs. (9.14.23) and (9.14.24),

$$|\psi(T/2)\rangle = \begin{pmatrix} \cos(\omega_0 T/2) \\ \sin(\omega_0 T/2) \end{pmatrix} = \frac{1}{\sqrt{2}}\begin{pmatrix} 1 \\ 1 \end{pmatrix} \tag{9.14.26}$$

The probability of finding the electron in the detector D is

$$P_D = |\langle -z|\psi(T/2)\rangle|^2 = \left|\frac{1}{\sqrt{2}}(0\ \ 1)\begin{pmatrix} 0 \\ 1 \end{pmatrix}\right|^2 = \frac{1}{2} \tag{9.14.27}$$

9.15. In this problem we examine how the energy levels of the hydrogen atom are modified in the presence of a static magnetic field; this effect is called the *Zeeman effect*. We shall ignore the effects of spin (the "normal" Zeeman effect). Suppose that the mass of the electron is m and its charge is q. (a) We denote by $\hat{H}_0$ the Hamiltonian of the electron in the hydrogen atom (without a magnetic field). Write the eigenstates of $\hat{H}_0$ that are also eigenstates of $\hat{L}^2$ and $\hat{L}_z$. What are the corresponding eigenvalues? (b) Suppose that the atom is placed in a uniform magnetic field B_0 along the **k** axis. Write the new Hamiltonian. Are the states of part (a) also eigenstates of the new Hamiltonian? How are the energy levels modified? Assume that the term $\frac{q^2 B^2}{8m}(x^2 + y^2)$ is negligible compared to $\frac{\mu_B}{\hbar}B_0\hat{L}_z$ (this can be shown by a detailed calculation).

SOLUTION

(*a*) The eigenstates of the Hamiltonian of the hydrogen atom can be written in the form

$$\phi_{nlm}(r, \theta, \varphi) = R_{nl}(r)Y_l^m(\theta, \varphi) \tag{9.15.1}$$

The number n determines the energy level, $E_n = -E_1/n^2$. The energy levels in a hydrogen atom are degenerate; for each n the number l can assume one of the values $l = 0, 1, 2, \ldots, n-1$, and m is an integer between $-l$ and l. The total degeneracy of the energy level E_n is n^2 (without spin). The wavefunction ϕ_{nlm} is an eigenfunction of $\hat{L}^2$ with an eigenvalue $l(l+1)\hbar^2$. It is also an eigenfunction of $\hat{L}_z$ with an eigenvalue $m\hbar$.

(*b*) According to Problem 9.13, the classical Hamiltonian is the sum of H_0 and

$$H_1 = -\frac{\mu}{\hbar}\mathcal{B}_0 L_z + \frac{q^2\mathcal{B}^2}{8m}(x^2 + y^2) \tag{9.15.2}$$

Now we assume (without a detailed proof) that the second term in Eq. (9.15.2) is negligible when compared to the first term. Since $\phi_{nlm}(\mathbf{r})$ is an eigenstate of $\hat{L}_z$, we have

$$(\hat{H}_0 + \hat{H}_1)\phi_{nlm}(\mathbf{r}) = \hat{H}_0\phi_{nlm}(\mathbf{r}) - \frac{\mu}{\hbar}\mathcal{B}_0\hat{L}_z\phi_{nlm}(\mathbf{r}) = (E_n - m\mu\mathcal{B}_0)\phi_{nlm}(\mathbf{r}) \tag{9.15.3}$$

We see that $\phi_{nlm}(\mathbf{r})$ are also eigenstates of the new Hamiltonian, but the energies are shifted by $m\mu\mathcal{B}_0$. Also, because of the presence of the magnetic field, the degeneracy is removed.

9.16. An electron is constrained to move on a one-dimensional ring of radius R, see Fig. 9.1. At the center of the ring there is a constant magnetic flux Φ in the z direction. (*a*) Find the vector potential $\mathbf{A}$ on the ring in the gauge in which it is independent of φ. (*b*) Write the Schrödinger equation for the constrained electron. (*c*) What are the general boundary conditions on the wavefunctions of the electron? (*d*) Find the eigenstates and eigenenergies of the electron. Use functions of the form $e^{ik\varphi}$.

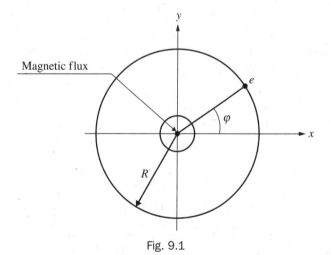

Fig. 9.1

SOLUTION

(*a*) The magnetic field is $\mathcal{B} = \mathcal{B}_\mathbf{k}$. The magnetic flux through the surface bounded by the ring is

$$\Phi = \int_{\substack{\text{inside} \\ \text{the ring}}} dx \int \mathcal{B} \cdot \mathbf{k}\, dy \tag{9.16.1}$$

We would like to find **A** on $r = R$, such that $\mathcal{B} = \nabla \times \mathbf{A}$ and **A** does not depend on ϕ. From Eq. (9.16.1) we obtain

$$\Phi = \iint_S (\nabla \times \mathbf{A}) \cdot \mathbf{k}\, dS \tag{9.16.2}$$

where S is the surface bounded inside the ring. Using Stokes's theorem we can write Eq. (9.16.2) as

$$\Phi = \oint_C \mathbf{A} \cdot d\mathbf{l} \tag{9.16.3}$$

where C is the boundary of S, which is the ring $\rho = R$, and $d\mathbf{l}$ is along the curve C. Now,

$$d\mathbf{l} = (R d\varphi)\, \boldsymbol{\varphi} \tag{9.16.4}$$

where $\boldsymbol{\varphi}$ is a unit vector tangential to the ring. From Eqs. (9.16.3) and (9.16.4) it follows that

$$\Phi = \int_0^{2\pi} A_\varphi R\, d\varphi \tag{9.16.5}$$

Using the gauge in which **A** does not depend on φ, we get, from Eq. (9.16.5), $\Phi = 2\pi R A_\varphi$. Finally,

$$\begin{cases} A_r = A_z = 0 \\ A_\varphi = \dfrac{\Phi}{2\pi R} \end{cases} \tag{9.16.6}$$

(b) Given the symmetry of the problem, it is more convenient to use cylindrical coordinates. To write the Schrödinger equation, we have to express the gradient ∇ in cylindrical coordinates as follows:

$$\nabla = \boldsymbol{\rho}\frac{\partial}{\partial \rho} + \boldsymbol{\varphi}\frac{1}{\rho}\frac{\partial}{\partial \varphi} + \mathbf{k}\frac{\partial}{\partial z} \tag{9.16.7}$$

where $\boldsymbol{\rho}$, $\boldsymbol{\varphi}$, and $\mathbf{k}$ are unit vectors in the ρ, φ, and z directions, respectively. Since the electron is constrained to move on the ring, φ, R, and z are all constant. Thus, the only nonvanishing part of ∇ in Eq. (9.16.7) is $\boldsymbol{\varphi}\dfrac{1}{\rho}\dfrac{\partial}{\partial \varphi}$. Applying Eqs. (9.16.6) and (9.16.7) on the ring we get

$$\hat{H} = \frac{1}{2m}\left(-i\hbar\nabla - \frac{e}{c}\mathbf{A}\right)^2 = \frac{1}{2m}\left(-i\hbar\frac{1}{R}\frac{\partial}{\partial\varphi} - \frac{e}{c}\frac{\Phi}{2\pi R}\right)^2 = \frac{1}{2mR^2}\left(-i\hbar\frac{\partial}{\partial\varphi} - \frac{e}{c}\frac{\Phi}{2\pi}\right)^2 \tag{9.16.8}$$

and the Schrödinger equation is

$$\frac{1}{2mR^2}\left(-i\hbar\frac{\partial}{\partial\varphi} - \frac{e}{c}\frac{\Phi}{2\pi}\right)^2 \psi(\varphi) = E\psi(\varphi) \tag{9.16.9}$$

(c) Since φ is defined over 2π, the general boundary condition for any function of φ determines that the function will be periodic in 2π; so, we have $|\psi(\varphi + 2\pi)| = |\psi(\varphi)|$ and similarly, for $\dfrac{\partial\psi}{\partial\varphi}$. We consider only absolute values—in quantum mechanics it is only $|\psi|^2$ that has real physical meaning.

(d) Check whether $\psi(\varphi) = \dfrac{1}{N}e^{ik\varphi}$ (k = constant) are solutions of Eq. (9.16.9). First, we find the normalization constant N:

$$R\int_0^{2\pi} |\psi(\varphi)|^2\, d\varphi = 2\pi R\frac{1}{N^2} = 1 \tag{9.16.10}$$

So, $N = \dfrac{1}{\sqrt{2\pi R}}$. Next, we use $\psi(\phi) = \dfrac{1}{N}e^{ik\varphi}$ in Eq. (9.16.9) and obtain

$$\frac{1}{2mR^2}\left[\hbar^2 k^2 - \hbar k\left(\frac{e\Phi}{c\pi}\right) + \left(\frac{e\Phi}{2\pi c}\right)^2\right] = E \tag{9.16.11}$$

or, equivalently,

$$\left(\hbar k - \frac{e\Phi}{2\pi c}\right)^2 = 2mR^2 E \tag{9.16.12}$$

We define $\Phi_0 \equiv \dfrac{c}{e\hbar}$ and write Eq. (9.16.12) as

$$\left(k - \frac{\Phi}{\Phi_0}\right)^2 = \frac{2mR^2}{\hbar^2}E \tag{9.16.13}$$

From the boundary condition and the wavefunction $\psi(\varphi) = \dfrac{1}{N}e^{ik\varphi}$, we have

$$2\pi k = 2\pi n \qquad n = 0, \pm 1, \pm 2, \ldots \tag{9.16.14}$$

From Eqs. (9.16.13) and (9.16.14) we get the eigenenergies:

$$E_n = \frac{\hbar^2}{2mR^2}\left(n - \Phi/\Phi_0\right)^2 \tag{9.16.15}$$

and the eigenstates:

$$\psi_n(\varphi) = \frac{1}{\sqrt{2\pi R}}e^{ik\varphi} \tag{9.16.16}$$

9.17. Refer to Problem 9.16, Eqs. (9.16.15) and (9.16.16). The magnetic field is zero on the ring (recall that the flux is *inside* the ring but not *on* the ring). (*a*) In classical mechanics, a particle (electron) constrained to move on the ring will not be affected by the magnetic flux. Is this also the case in quantum mechanics? Is the energy of the electron a function of the flux Φ? (*b*) Plot a graph describing the ground state of the electron as a function of Φ (or Φ/Φ_0). (*c*) The current on the ring can be defined by

$$I = c\frac{dH}{d\Phi} \tag{9.17.1}$$

where H is the Hamiltonian and Φ the flux. Write the current operator $\hat{I}$ in the coordinates representation. (*d*) Calculate the expectation value of $\hat{I}$ in state ψ_n. Find the relation between the energy and the current of the state ψ_n.

SOLUTION

(*a*) Using Eq. (9.16.15), we can easily see that the energy's eigenvalues for the electron depend on Φ; thus, in contrast to classical mechanics, in quantum mechanics a particle can be affected by a magnetic field even when the magnetic field is zero in the region in which the particle moves. This surprising phenomenon is known as the *Aharonov–Bohm effect*.

(*b*) The energy eigenvalues are

$$E_n = \frac{\hbar^2}{2mR^2}\left(n - \frac{\Phi}{\Phi_0}\right)^2 \tag{9.17.2}$$

The ground states depend on Φ (or Φ/Φ_0). For $-1/2 < \Phi/\Phi_0 < 1/2$, the minimum energy in Eq. (9.17.2) corresponds with $n = 0$ (Fig. 9.2). For $\Phi/\Phi_0 > 1/2$, the value $n = 0$ is no longer the minimum energy (the ground state). For $\dfrac{1}{2} < \Phi/\Phi_0 < \dfrac{3}{2}$, the minimum energy in Eq. (9.17.2) corresponds to $n = 1$. For $\dfrac{3}{2} < \Phi/\Phi_0 < \dfrac{5}{2}$, $\psi_{n=2}$ is the ground state, and so on. For $\dfrac{n-1}{2} < \Phi/\Phi_0 < \dfrac{n+1}{2}$ the ground state is ψ_n. So, the ground state is periodic in Φ/Φ_0 with period 1, as shown in Fig. 9.2.

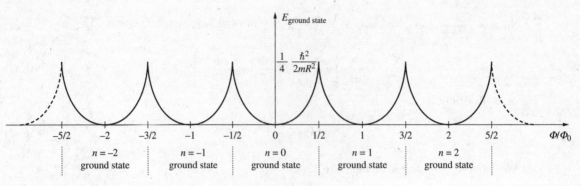

Fig. 9.2

(*c*) Using Eqs. (9.17.1) and (9.16.8) we have

$$\hat{I} = c\frac{\partial}{\partial \Phi}\left[\frac{1}{2mR^2}\left(-i\hbar\frac{\partial}{\partial \varphi} - \frac{e}{c}\frac{\Phi}{2\pi}\right)^2\right] = \frac{c}{mR^2}\left(-\frac{e}{2\pi c}\right)\left(-i\hbar\frac{\partial}{\partial \varphi} - \frac{e}{c}\frac{\Phi}{2\pi}\right)$$

$$= \frac{eh}{4\pi^2 mR^2}\left(i\frac{\partial}{\partial \varphi} - \frac{\Phi}{\Phi_0}\right) \tag{9.17.3}$$

(*d*) The expectation value of $\hat{I}$ is

$$|\hat{I}\rangle_{(n)} = \int_0^{2\pi} \psi_n^*(\varphi)[\hat{I}\psi_n(\varphi)]R\,d\varphi = \int_0^{2\pi} e^{-in\varphi}\left(\frac{eh}{4\pi^2 mR^2}\right)\left[\left(i\frac{\partial}{\partial \varphi} - \Phi/\Phi_0\right)e^{in\varphi}\right]R\,d\varphi$$

$$= \frac{eh}{2\pi mR}(n - \Phi/\Phi_0) = -\frac{eh}{mR}(n - \Phi/\Phi_0) \tag{9.17.4}$$

From Eqs. (9.17.2) and (9.17.4) we obtain

$$E_n = \frac{m}{2}\left(\frac{|\hat{I}\rangle_{(n)}}{e}\right)^2 \tag{9.17.5}$$

SUPPLEMENTARY PROBLEMS

9.18. Consider an electron in a region of a constant magnetic field of 1 gauss in the z direction. Assume that the electron is in a very large box, $0 \leq x \leq L_x$, $-L_y \leq y \leq L_y$, and $0 \leq z \leq L_z$. What is the number of state per unit area (in the xy plane)?

Ans. According to Eq. (9.10.11), $n = \dfrac{N}{\text{area}} \cong 80\dfrac{1}{\text{m}^2}$.

9.19. Solve Problem 9.8 using the symmetric gauge, $\mathbf{A} = \left(-\dfrac{\mathcal{B}}{2}y, \dfrac{\mathcal{B}}{2}x, 0\right)$. Show that the eigenvalues in Eq. (9.8.16) are the same (as they must be).

Ans. $H = \dfrac{1}{2m}\left[\left(p_x + \dfrac{q\mathcal{B}}{2c}y\right)^2 + \left(p_y - \dfrac{q\mathcal{B}}{2c}x\right)^2 + p_z^2\right]$.

9.20. Using Eq. (9.9.2), solve Problem 9.3 for a charged particle with spin and a magnetic moment μ_s.

Ans. (a) $\hat{H} = \dfrac{1}{2m}\left(-i\hbar\nabla - \dfrac{q}{c}\mathbf{A}\right)^2 - \mu_s \cdot \mathcal{B}$. (b) $\rho(\mathbf{r}_0) = \psi^*(\mathbf{r}_0)\psi(\mathbf{r}_0)$.

$$(c) \ \mathbf{j} = \frac{\hbar}{2mi}\left(\psi^*\nabla\psi - \psi\nabla\psi^*\right) - \frac{q}{mc}\mathbf{A}\psi^*\psi + \frac{\mu_s c}{s}\nabla\times(\psi^*\hat{\mathbf{S}}\psi). \qquad (9.20.1)$$

9.21. Conductivity is defined by

$$\sigma = \frac{i_{\text{tot}}}{V} \qquad (9.21.1)$$

where i_{tot} is the total current per unit length and V is the electric potential. Consider Problem 9.12. For this case, $\mathcal{E} = \mathcal{E}\mathbf{j}$, and $\phi = -\mathcal{E}y$, so $V = 2\mathcal{E}L_y$. The total current in the x direction is $(i_{\text{tot}})_x = Ni_x$, where N is the number of states in a complete Landau level, which is given in Eq. (9.10.12). Find σ for this case.

Ans. $\sigma = e^2/\hbar$.

9.22. Consider the following classical harmonic oscillator Hamiltonian:

$$H_0 = \frac{1}{2}(p_x^2 + p_z^2 + p_z^2) - \frac{1}{2}m\omega_0^2(x^2 + y^2) \qquad (9.22.1)$$

(a) Is it possible to find a basis of eigenstates that is common to $\hat{H}_0$ and $\hat{L}_z$? (b) Assume that the oscillator has a charge of q and is placed in a region of constant magnetic field $\mathcal{B} = \mathcal{B}_0\mathbf{k}$. Use the gauge $\mathbf{A} = -\dfrac{1}{2}\mathbf{r}\times\mathcal{B}$ and find the corresponding Hamiltonian of the system.

Ans. (a) Yes, since $[\hat{H}_0, \hat{L}_z] = 0$.

$$(b) \ \hat{H} = \frac{1}{2m}(\hat{p}_x^2 + \hat{p}_z^2 + \hat{p}_z^2) + \frac{1}{2m}\left[\left(\left(\frac{q\mathcal{B}_0}{2c}\right)^2 + \frac{1}{2}m^2\omega_0^2\right)\hat{x}^2 + \left(\left(\frac{q\mathcal{B}_0}{2c}\right)^2 + \frac{1}{2}m^2\omega_0^2\right)\hat{y}^2\right]$$

$$+ \frac{q\mathcal{B}_0}{2mc}(\hat{p}_x\hat{y} - \hat{p}_y\hat{x}).$$

9.23. Refer to Problem 9.22. (a) Is it possible to find a basis of eigenstates that is common to $\hat{L}_z$ and the Hamiltonian of Problem 9.22, part (b)? (b) Are the eigenstates of part (b) also the eigenstates of past (a)?

Ans. (a) Yes, since $[\hat{H}, \hat{L}_z] = 0$. (b) No, since $[\hat{H}, \hat{H}_0] \neq 0$.

9.24. Consider a hydrogen atom placed in a constant magnetic field of 10^4 gauss. Calculate the wavelengths corresponding to the three transitions between the levels $3d$ and $2p$.

Ans. $E_1 = \Delta E_{32}; E_2 = \Delta E_{32} + \dfrac{e\hbar}{2mc}\mathcal{B}; E_3 = \Delta E_{32} - \dfrac{e\hbar}{2mc}\mathcal{B}; \lambda_1 = 6500 \text{ Å}; \lambda_{2,3} = 6500 \pm 0.2 \text{ Å}.$

CHAPTER 10

Solution Methods in Quantum Mechanics—Part A

10.1 Time-Independent Perturbation Theory

The quantum mechanical study of a conservative physical system (whose Hamiltonian is not explicitly time-dependent) is based on the eigenvalue equation of the Hamiltonian operator. Some systems (e.g., the harmonic oscillator) are simple enough to be solved exactly. In general, the equation is not amenable to analytic solutions and an approximate solution is sought, usually using computer-based numerical methods.

In this section, we present the widely used *time-independent perturbation theory*. We use a method that is often encountered in physics: we study the primary factors that produce the main properties of the system, then we attempt to explain the secondary effects neglected in the first approximation.

Perturbation theory is appropriate when the Hamiltonian $\hat{H}$ of the system can be put in the form

$$\hat{H} = \hat{H}_0 + \lambda \hat{W} \tag{10.1}$$

where the eigenstates and eigenvalues of $\hat{H}_0$ are known and λ is a parameter. The operator $\lambda \hat{W}$ must be "much smaller" than $\hat{H}_0$; that is, the relation $\lambda \hat{W} \ll \hat{H}_0$, i.e., $\lambda \ll 1$, must hold and the matrix elements of $\hat{W}$ are comparable in magnitude to those of $\hat{H}_0$. More precisely, the matrix elements of $\hat{W}$ are of the same magnitude as the difference between the eigenvalues of $\hat{H}_0$.

The Unperturbed State

We assume that the unperturbed energies (that is, the eigenvalues of $\hat{H}_0$) form a discrete spectrum E_p^0, where p is an integral index. We denote the corresponding eigenstates by $|\phi_p^i\rangle$, where the additional index i distinguishes between the different linearly independent eigenvectors corresponding to the same eigenvalue in the case of a degenerate eigenvalue. We have

$$\hat{H}_0 |\phi_p^i\rangle = E_p^0 |\phi_p^i\rangle \tag{10.2}$$

where $|\phi_p^i\rangle$ form an orthonormal basis of the state space,

$$\begin{cases} \langle \phi_p^i | \phi_q^j \rangle = \delta_{pq} \delta_{ij} \\ \sum_p \sum_i |\phi_p^i\rangle \langle \phi_p^i| = \hat{I} \end{cases} \tag{10.3}$$

Possible Effects of the Perturbation

When the parameter λ is equal to zero, $\hat{H}(\lambda)$ is equal to the unperturbed Hamiltonian $\hat{H}_0$. The eigenvalues $E(\lambda)$ of $\hat{H}(\lambda)$ generally depend on λ. Figure 10.1 represents possible forms of the variation of energy levels with respect to λ.

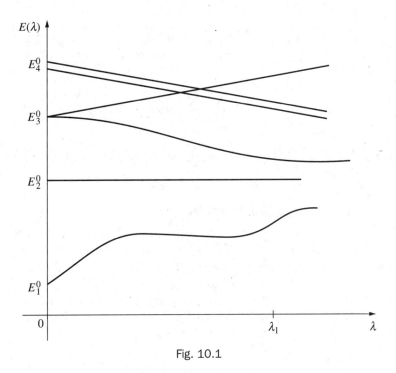

Fig. 10.1

In the case of a nondegenerate energy level, the perturbation may either affect the energy level (E_1^0 in Fig. 10.1) or not affect it (as in case of E_2^0). For a degenerate energy level, it is possible that the perturbation "splits" it into distinct energy levels, as in the case of E_3^0 in Fig. 10.1. We say then that the perturbation removes the degeneracy of the corresponding eigenvalue of $\hat{H}_0$. The perturbation may also leave the degeneracy of an energy level, as in the case of E_4^0 in Fig. 10.1.

Approximate Solution for the Eigenvalue Equation

We are looking for the eigenstates $|\psi(\lambda)\rangle$ and eigenvalues $E(\lambda)$ of the Hamiltonian $\hat{H}(\lambda)$:

$$\hat{H}(\lambda)|\psi(\lambda)\rangle = E(\lambda)|\psi(\lambda)\rangle \tag{10.4}$$

We shall assume that $E(\lambda)$ and $|\psi(\lambda)\rangle$ can be expanded in a power series of λ in the form

$$E(\lambda) = \varepsilon_0 + \lambda\varepsilon_1 + \cdots + \lambda^q\varepsilon_q \tag{10.5}$$

$$|\psi(\lambda)\rangle = |0\rangle + \lambda|1\rangle + \cdots + \lambda^q|q\rangle \tag{10.6}$$

When the parameter is equal to zero, we have the energy level and eigenstate of the unperturbed Hamiltonian. When $\lambda \ll 1$, each element in the series expansions, Eqs. (10.5) and (10.6), is much smaller (in general) then the previous one; in practice, it usually suffices to consider only the first few elements. The element containing λ is called the first-order correction, the one containing λ^2 is called the second-order correction, etc.

10.2   Perturbation of a Nondegenerate Level

Consider a particular nondegenerate eigenvalue E_n^0 of the unperturbed Hamiltonian, with eigenvector $|\phi_n\rangle$ (this eigenvector is unique to within a constant factor). We now give first- and second-order corrections for the energy level and corresponding eigenvector (the derivation is given in Problem 10.1).

$$E_n(\lambda) = E_n^0 + \lambda\langle\phi_n|\hat{W}|\phi_n\rangle + \lambda^2\sum_{p\neq n}\sum_i \frac{\left|\langle\phi_p^i|\hat{W}|\phi_n\rangle\right|^2}{E_n^0 - E_p^0} + O(\lambda^3) \tag{10.7}$$

$$|\psi_n(\lambda)\rangle = |\phi_n\rangle + \lambda \sum_{p \neq n} \sum_i \frac{\langle \phi_p^i | \hat{W} | \phi_p\rangle}{E_n^0 - E_p^0} |\phi_p^i\rangle + \lambda^2 \sum_{p \neq n} \sum_i \left[-\frac{\langle \phi_p^i | \hat{W} | \phi_p\rangle\langle \phi_p^i | \hat{W} | \phi_p\rangle}{(E_n^0 - E_p^0)^2} \right.$$

$$\left. + \sum_{q \neq n} \sum_j \frac{\langle \phi_p^i | \hat{W} | \phi_q^j\rangle\langle \phi_q^j | \hat{W} | \phi_n\rangle}{(E_n^0 - E_p^0)(E_n^0 - E_q^0)} \right] |\phi_p^i\rangle + O(\lambda^3) \quad (10.8)$$

Note that the first-order correction for the energy level is simply the mean value of the perturbation term $\lambda\hat{W}$ in the unperturbed state $|\phi_n\rangle$.

10.3   Perturbation of a Degenerate State

Assume that the level E_n^0 is g_n-fold degenerate. We present a method for calculating the first-order correction for the energies and the zero-order correction for the eigenstates. The derivation is given in Problem 10.8.

Arrange the numbers $\langle \phi_n^i | \hat{W} | \phi_n^{i'}\rangle$ in a $g_n \times g_n$ matrix (i is the row index and i' the column index). This matrix, which we denote $\hat{W}^{(n)}$, is "cut" out of the matrix that represents $\hat{W}$ in the $\{|\phi_p^i\rangle\}$ basis. Note that $\hat{W}^{(n)}$ is not identical to $\hat{W}$; it is an operator in the g_n-dimensional space corresponding to the energy level E_n^0.

The first-order corrections ε_1^j of the energy level E_n^0 are eigenvalues of the matrix $\hat{W}^{(n)}$. The zero-order eigenstates corresponding to E_n^0 are the eigenvectors of $\hat{W}^{(n)}$. Let $\varepsilon_1^j (j = 1, 2,\dots f_n^{(1)})$ be the roots of the characteristic equation of $\hat{W}^{(n)}$ (that is, the eigenvalues of $\hat{W}^{(n)}$). The degenerate energy level splits, to the first order, into $f_n^{(1)}$ distinct sublevels:

$$E_{n,k}(\lambda) = E_n^0 + \lambda\varepsilon_1^j \qquad j = 1, 2,\dots, f_n^{(1)} \leq g_n \qquad (10.9)$$

When $f_n^{(1)} = g_n$ we say that, to the first order, the perturbation W completely removes the degeneracy of the level E_n^0. When $f_n^{(1)} < g_n$ the degeneracy is only partially removed, or not at all removed if $f_n^{(1)} = 1$.

Suppose that a specific sublevel $E_{n,j}(\lambda) = E_n^0 + \lambda\varepsilon_1^j$ is q-fold degenerate, in the sense that there are q linearly independent eigenvectors of $W^{(n)}$ corresponding to it. We distinguish between two completely different situations:

1. Suppose that there is only one exact energy level $E(\lambda)$ that is equal to the first order to $E_{n,j}$. This energy is q-fold degenerate. [In Fig. 10.1 for example, the energy $E(\lambda)$ that approaches E_4^0 when $\lambda \to 0$ is twofold degenerate.] In this case, the zero-order eigenvector $|0\rangle$ of $\hat{H}(\lambda)$ cannot be completely specified, since the only condition is that this vector belongs to the q-dimensional eigensubspace of $\hat{H}(\lambda)$ corresponding to $E(\lambda)$. This situation often arises when the $\hat{H}_0$ and $\lambda\hat{W}$ possess common symmetry properties, implying an essential degeneracy of $\hat{H}(\lambda)$.

2. A second possibility arises when several different energies $E(\lambda)$ are equal, to the first order, to $E_{n,j}$. The difference between these energies appears in the calculation of the second order or higher. In this case, an eigenvector of $\hat{H}(\lambda)$ corresponding to one of these energies approaches an eigenvector of $E_{n,j}$ for $\lambda \to 0$; the inverse however, does not hold.

10.4   Time-Dependent Perturbation Theory

Consider a physical system with Hamiltonian $\hat{H}_0$. We assume the spectrum of $\hat{H}_0$ to be discrete and nondegenerate (the formulas can be generalized to other situations). We have

$$\hat{H}_0 |\phi_n\rangle = E_n |\phi_n\rangle \qquad (10.10)$$

Suppose that $\hat{H}_0$ is time-independent, but, at $t = 0$, a time-dependent perturbation is applied to the system

$$\hat{H}(t) = \hat{H}_0 + \lambda\hat{W}(t) \qquad (10.11)$$

where λ is a parameter, $\lambda \ll 1$, and $\hat{W}(t)$ is an operator of the same magnitude as $\hat{H}_0$, and is zero for $t < 0$. Suppose that the system is initially in the state $|\phi_i\rangle$, which is an eigenstate of $\hat{H}_0$ with eigenvalue E_i. We present an expression for calculating the first-order approximation of the probability $P_{if}(t)$ of finding the system in another eigenstate $|\phi_f\rangle$ of $\hat{H}_0$ at time t. The derivation of this expression is given in Problem 10.12.

$$P_{if}(t) = \frac{\lambda^2}{\hbar^2}\left|\int_0^t e^{i\omega_{fi}t'}\omega_{fi}(t')\,dt'\right|^2 \tag{10.12}$$

where ω_{if} is the *Bohr angular frequency*, defined by

$$\omega_{if} = \frac{E_i - E_f}{\hbar} \tag{10.13}$$

and $\omega_{if}(t)$ is the matrix element of $\hat{W}(t)$:

$$W_{fi}(t) = \langle \phi_f | \hat{W}(t) | \phi_i \rangle \tag{10.14}$$

Consider now the case of transition between a state $|\phi_i\rangle$ and a state $|\phi_f\rangle$ of energy E_f belonging to a continuous part of the spectrum of $\hat{H}_0$. In this case, the probability of transition at time t, $|\langle \phi_f | \psi(t)\rangle|^2$, is actually a probability density. That is, we must integrate the probability density over a range of final states in order to give a physical prediction.

The time-dependent perturbation theory can be applied to this situation. One very important result is *Fermi's golden rule*. This formula relates to the case of a constant perturbation. It can be demonstrated that, in this case, transitions can occur only between states of equal energies. The probability density P_{fi} of transition from $|\phi_i\rangle$ to $|\phi_f\rangle$ increases linearly with time, and

$$W_{fi} = \frac{dP_{fi}(t)}{dt} = \frac{2\pi}{\hbar}|\langle \psi_f | \hat{W}(t) | \psi_i\rangle|^2 \rho(E_f) \tag{10.15}$$

where $\rho(E_f)$ is the density of the final states.

SOLVED PROBLEMS

10.1. Derive the formulas for the first- and second-order energy corrections for a time-independent perturbation. Also, derive the first-order corrections to the eigenstates. Assume that there is no degeneracy.

SOLUTION

We write the Hamiltonian in the form $\hat{H} = \hat{H}_0 + \lambda\hat{W}$, where $\hat{H}_0$ is the Hamiltonian of the unperturbed system and $\hat{W}$ is the perturbation ($\lambda \ll 1$). We assume that the eigenstates $|\psi(\lambda)\rangle$ and the eigenenergies $E(\lambda)$ of the perturbed system can be expanded in a power series of λ:

$$|\psi(\lambda)\rangle = |0\rangle + \lambda|1\rangle + \cdots + \lambda^q|q\rangle \tag{10.1.1}$$

and

$$E(\lambda) = \varepsilon_0 + \lambda\varepsilon_1 + \cdots + \lambda^q\varepsilon_q \tag{10.1.2}$$

Substituting into the Schrödinger equation, we obtain

$$(\hat{H}_0 + \lambda\hat{W})\left[\sum_{q=0}^{\infty}\lambda^q|q\rangle\right] = \left[\sum_{q'=0}^{\infty}\lambda^{q'}\varepsilon_{q'}\right]\left[\sum_{q=0}^{\infty}\lambda^q|q\rangle\right] \tag{10.1.3}$$

Then, by equating the coefficients of successive powers of λ, we obtain

$$\hat{H}_0 \,|\, 0 \rangle = \varepsilon_0 \,|\, 0 \rangle \tag{10.1.4}$$

$$(\hat{H}_0 - \varepsilon_0) \,|\, 1 \rangle + (\hat{W} - \varepsilon_1) \,|\, 0 \rangle = 0 \tag{10.1.5}$$

and

$$(\hat{H}_0 - \varepsilon_0) \,|\, 2 \rangle + (\hat{W} - \varepsilon_1) \,|\, 1 \rangle - \varepsilon_2 \,|\, 0 \rangle = 0 \tag{10.1.6}$$

For the nth order we obtain

$$(\hat{H}_0 - \varepsilon_0) \,|\, n \rangle + (\hat{W} - \varepsilon_1) \,|\, n-1 \rangle - \varepsilon_2 \,|\, n-2 \rangle + \cdots - \varepsilon_n \,|\, 0 \rangle = 0 \tag{10.1.7}$$

Note that we are free to choose the norm and the phase of $|\psi(\lambda)\rangle$, so we require that $|\psi(\lambda)\rangle$ is normalized and that its phase is such that the inner product $\langle 0 \,|\, \psi(\lambda)\rangle$ is a real number. This implies that

$$\langle 0 \,|\, 0 \rangle = 1 \qquad \langle 0 \,|\, 1 \rangle = \langle 1 \,|\, 0 \rangle = 0 \qquad \langle 0 \,|\, 2 \rangle = \langle 2 \,|\, 0 \rangle = -\tfrac{1}{2}\langle 1 \,|\, 1 \rangle \tag{10.1.8}$$

For the nth order we obtain

$$\langle 0 \,|\, n \rangle = \langle n \,|\, 0 \rangle = -\tfrac{1}{2}(\langle n-1 \,|\, 1 \rangle + \langle n-2 \,|\, 2 \rangle + \cdots + \langle 2 \,|\, n-2 \rangle + \langle 1 \,|\, n-1 \rangle) \tag{10.1.9}$$

Note that when $\lambda \to 0$, we have $\varepsilon_0 = E_n^{(0)}$. Using Eq. (10.1.4), we conclude that $|\phi_n\rangle$ is proportional to $|0\rangle$; therefore, we choose $|\phi_n\rangle = |0\rangle$. Multiply Eq. (10.1.5) on the left by $\langle \phi_n |$:

$$\langle \phi_n \,|\, (\hat{H}_0 - \varepsilon_0) \,|\, 1 \rangle + \langle \phi_n \,|\, (\hat{W} - \varepsilon_1) \,|\, 0 \rangle = 0 \tag{10.1.10}$$

The first term in Eq. (10.1.10) is zero; therefore,

$$\varepsilon_1 = \langle \phi_n \,|\, \hat{W} \,|\, 0 \rangle = \langle \phi_n \,|\, \hat{W} \,|\, \phi_n \rangle \tag{10.1.11}$$

For the first order we have

$$E_n(\lambda) = E_n^{(0)} + \lambda \langle \phi_n \,|\, \hat{W} \,|\, \phi_n \rangle + O(\lambda^2) \tag{10.1.12}$$

We see that the first-order correction to the energy is simply equal to the mean value of the perturbation term $\hat{W}$ in the unperturbed state $|\phi_n\rangle$. Multiplying Eq. (10.1.5) by the basis vectors $\langle \phi_p |$ we obtain

$$\langle \phi_p \,|\, (\hat{H}_0 - E_n^{(0)}) \,|\, 1 \rangle + \langle \phi_p \,|\, (\hat{W} - \varepsilon_1) \,|\, \phi_n \rangle = 0 \qquad (p \neq n) \tag{10.1.13}$$

This leads to the equation

$$(E_p^{(0)} - E_n^{(0)}) \langle \phi_p \,|\, 1 \rangle + \langle \phi_p \,|\, \hat{W} \,|\, \phi_n \rangle = 0 \tag{10.1.14}$$

where we used the orthogonality of the basis vectors. Then,

$$\langle \phi_p \,|\, 1 \rangle = \frac{1}{E_p^{(0)} - E_n^{(0)}} \langle \phi_p \,|\, \hat{W} \,|\, \phi_n \rangle \qquad (p \neq n) \tag{10.1.15}$$

Since $\langle \phi_n \,|\, 1 \rangle = \langle 0 \,|\, 1 \rangle = 0$, we arrive at

$$|1\rangle = \sum_{p \neq n} \frac{\langle \phi_p \,|\, \hat{W} \,|\, \phi_n \rangle}{E_p^{(0)} - E_n^{(0)}} \,|\, \phi_p \rangle \tag{10.1.16}$$

Therefore, to the first order, the eigenvectors $|\phi_n(\lambda)\rangle$ of $\hat{H}$ that correspond to the unperturbed state $|\phi_n\rangle$ can be written as

$$|\psi_n(\lambda)\rangle = |\phi_n\rangle + \lambda \sum_{p \neq n} \frac{\langle \phi_p | \hat{W} | \phi_n \rangle}{E_n^{(0)} - E_p^{(0)}} |\phi_p\rangle + O(\lambda)^2 \qquad (10.1.17)$$

To obtain the second-order correction of the energy we multiply Eq. (10.1.6) by $\langle \phi_n |$:

$$\langle \phi_n | (\hat{H}_0 - E_n^{(0)}) | 2 \rangle + \langle \phi_n | (\hat{W} - \varepsilon_1) | 1 \rangle - \varepsilon_2 \langle \phi_n | \phi_n \rangle = 0 \qquad (10.1.18)$$

This leads to $\varepsilon_2 = \langle \phi_n | \hat{W} | 1 \rangle$. Substituting Eq. (10.1.16) for $|\psi(\lambda)\rangle$, we arrive at

$$\varepsilon_2 = \sum_{p \neq n} \frac{\langle \phi_p | \hat{W} | \phi_n \rangle}{E_n^{(0)} - E_p^{(0)}} \qquad (10.1.19)$$

Therefore, to the second order, the energy is given by

$$E_n(\lambda) = E_n^{(0)} + \lambda \langle \phi_n | \hat{W} | \phi_n \rangle + \lambda^2 \sum_{p \neq n} \frac{|\langle \phi_p | \hat{W} | \phi_n \rangle|^2}{E_n^{(0)} - E_p^{(0)}} + O(\lambda^3) \qquad (10.1.20)$$

10.2. Consider a particle in the two-dimensional, symmetrical, infinite potential well. The particle is subject to the perturbation $W = Cxy$, where C is a constant. (*a*) What are the eigenenergies and eigenfunctions of the unperturbed system? (*b*) Compute the first-order energy correction. (*c*) Find the wavefunction of the first excited level.

SOLUTION

(*a*) For the unperturbed system, the wavefunctions and eigenenergies are (see Chap. 3)

$$\psi_{n_1, n_2}^{(0)}(x, y) = \frac{2}{L} \sin\left(\frac{\pi n_1 x}{L}\right) \sin\left(\frac{\pi n_2 y}{L}\right) \qquad (10.2.1)$$

$$E_{n_1, n_2}^{(0)} = \frac{\pi^2 \hbar^2}{2mL^2} (n_1^2 + n_2^2) \qquad (10.2.2)$$

(*b*) The first-order correction to the energy is given by

$$\Delta E_{n_1, n_2}^{(1)} = \langle \psi_{n_1, n_2}^{(0)} | \hat{W} | \psi_{n_1, n_2}^{(0)} \rangle \qquad (10.2.3)$$

Thus,

$$\Delta E_{n_1, n_2}^{(1)} = \frac{4C}{L^2} \int_0^L x \sin\left(\frac{\pi n_1}{L} x\right)^2 dx \int_0^L y \sin\left(\frac{\pi n_1}{L}\right)^2 dy = \frac{L^2 C}{4} \qquad (10.2.4)$$

(*c*) In order to find the wavefunction of the first excited level, we compute the following matrix elements:

$$\langle \psi_{1,2}^{(0)} | \hat{W} | \psi_{1,2}^{(0)} \rangle = \langle \psi_{2,1}^{(0)} | \hat{W} | \psi_{2,1}^{(0)} \rangle = \frac{1}{4} L^2 C^2 \qquad (10.2.5)$$

and

$$\langle \psi_{1,2}^{(0)} | \hat{W} | \psi_{2,1}^{(0)} \rangle = \langle \psi_{2,1}^{(0)} | \hat{W} | \psi_{1,2}^{(0)} \rangle = \frac{256}{81\pi^4} L^2 C^2 \qquad (10.2.6)$$

Thus, the eigenvalue equation can be written as

$$L^2 C^2 \begin{pmatrix} \dfrac{1}{4} & \dfrac{256}{81\pi^4} \\ \dfrac{256}{81\pi^4} & \dfrac{1}{4} \end{pmatrix} \begin{pmatrix} u_1 \\ u_2 \end{pmatrix} = \lambda \begin{pmatrix} u_1 \\ u_2 \end{pmatrix} \qquad (10.2.7)$$

where $\lambda_{1,2} = \left(\dfrac{1}{4} \pm \dfrac{256}{81\pi^4}\right) L^2 C^2$ and $u_1 = \dfrac{1}{\sqrt{2}}, u_2 = \dfrac{1}{\sqrt{2}}$ or $u_1 = \dfrac{1}{\sqrt{2}}, u_2 = -\dfrac{1}{\sqrt{2}}$. Note that as the first excited level is twofold degenerate, there are two solutions for the wavefunctions:

$$\psi^{(1)} = \frac{1}{\sqrt{2}}(\psi^0_{1,2} + \psi^0_{2,1}) \qquad \psi^{(1)} = \frac{1}{\sqrt{2}}(\psi^{(0)}_{1,2} - \psi^{(0)}_{2,1}) \tag{10.2.8}$$

10.3. Consider a harmonic oscillator with a force constant k and a reduced mass m. The small perturbation $\hat{W} = a\hat{x}^3$ is applied to the oscillator. Compute the first-order correction to the wavefunctions and the first nonvanishing correction to the eigenenergies.

SOLUTION

The Hamiltonian of the system is given by

$$\hat{H} = \hat{H}_o + \hat{W} = -\frac{\hbar^2}{2m}\frac{d^2}{dx} + \frac{1}{2}k\hat{x}^2 + a\hat{x}^3 \tag{10.3.1}$$

The eigenenergies for the unperturbed Hamiltonian are $E^{(0)}_n = (n + 1/2)\hbar\omega$, and the eigenfunctions are given by

$$\phi^{(0)}_n(x) = \sqrt{\frac{1}{2^n n!}}\sqrt{\frac{\alpha}{\pi}}\, e^{-\alpha x^2/2}H_n(\sqrt{\alpha}x) \tag{10.3.2}$$

where $\alpha \equiv m\omega/\hbar$ and H_n are the Hermite polynomials. Note that when we compute the first-order correction $E^{(1)}_n$, we obtain an integral with an integrand of an odd function; the integral therefore vanishes and we have the result $E^{(1)}_n = \langle n|a\hat{x}^3|k\rangle = 0$. For the second-order correction we obtain

$$E^{(2)}_n = \sum_{k \neq n}\frac{|\langle n|\hat{W}|k\rangle|^2}{E^{(0)}_n - E^{(0)}_k} = \frac{|\langle n|a\hat{x}^3|n+3\rangle|^2}{E^{(0)}_n - E^{(0)}_{n+3}} + \frac{|\langle n|a\hat{x}^3|n+1\rangle|^2}{E^{(0)}_n - E^{(0)}_{n+1}} + \frac{|\langle n|a\hat{x}^3|n-1\rangle|^2}{E^{(0)}_n - E^{(0)}_{n-1}} + \frac{|\langle n|a\hat{x}^3|n-3\rangle|^2}{E^{(0)}_n - E^{(0)}_{n-3}}$$

$$\tag{10.3.3}$$

Note that this result can be obtained by using the relation $|\langle n|a\hat{x}^3|m\rangle|^2 = a\displaystyle\sum_k \langle n|\hat{x}^2|k\rangle\langle k|\hat{x}|m\rangle$. The required matrix elements are

$$\langle n|a\hat{x}^3|n+3\rangle = a\langle n|\hat{x}^2|n+2\rangle\langle n+2|\hat{x}|n+3\rangle = a\sqrt{\frac{(n+1)(n+2)(n+3)}{(2\alpha)^3}} \tag{10.3.4}$$

$$\langle n|a\hat{x}^3|n+1\rangle = a[\langle n|\hat{x}^2|n+2\rangle\langle n+2|\hat{x}|n+1\rangle + \langle n|\hat{x}^2|n\rangle\langle n|\hat{x}|n+1\rangle] = 3a\sqrt{\frac{(n+1)^3}{8\alpha^3}} \tag{10.3.5}$$

$$\langle n|a\hat{x}^3|n-1\rangle = a\langle n|\hat{x}^2|n-2\rangle\langle n-2|\hat{x}|n-1\rangle + \langle n|\hat{x}^2|n\rangle\langle n|\hat{x}|n-1\rangle = 3a\sqrt{\frac{n^3}{8\alpha^3}} \tag{10.3.6}$$

and

$$\langle n|a\hat{x}^3|n-3\rangle = a\langle n|\hat{x}^2|n-2\rangle\langle n-2|\hat{x}|n-3\rangle = a\sqrt{\frac{n(n-1)(n-2)}{8\alpha^3}} \tag{10.3.7}$$

Substituting into Eq. (10.3.3) yields

$$E^{(2)}_n = -\frac{15a^2}{4\hbar\omega\alpha^3}\left(n^2 + n + \frac{11}{30}\right) \tag{10.3.8}$$

The same matrix elements are required to calculate the first-order correction to the wavefunctions; hence, we obtain

$$\phi_n = \phi_n^{(0)} + \sum_{k \neq n} \frac{|\langle k | \hat{W} | n \rangle|^2}{E_n^{(0)} - E_k^0} \phi_k^0 + O(a^2) = \phi_n^{(0)} + \frac{a}{2\hbar\omega\alpha}\left[\frac{1}{3}\sqrt{\frac{n(n-1)(n-2)}{2\alpha}} \phi_{n-3}^{(0)} + O(a^2) \right.$$

$$\left. + 3n\sqrt{\frac{n}{2\alpha}} \phi_{n-1}^{(0)} - 3(n+1)\sqrt{\frac{n+1}{2\alpha}} \phi_{n+1}^{(0)} - \frac{1}{3}\sqrt{\frac{(n+1)(n+2)(n+3)}{2\alpha}} \phi_{n+3}^{(0)} \right] + O(a^2) \quad (10.3.9)$$

10.4. Consider a particle of mass m in a one-dimensional infinite potential well of width a:

$$V(x) = \begin{cases} 0 & 0 \leq x \leq a \\ \infty & \text{otherwise} \end{cases} \quad (10.4.1)$$

The particle is subject to perturbation of the form

$$W(x) = a\omega_0\delta(x - a/2) \quad (10.4.2)$$

where a is a real constant with dimension of energy. (a) Calculate the changes in the energy level of the particle in the first order of ω_0. (b) This problem can be solved without using perturbation theory; find the exact solution. Defining $k = \sqrt{2mE/\hbar^2}$, show that the possible levels of energy are given by one of the following equations:

$$\sin\left(\frac{ka}{2}\right) = 0 \quad \text{or} \quad \tan\left(\frac{ka}{2}\right) = -\frac{\hbar^2 k}{ma\omega_0} \quad (10.4.3)$$

How do these results depend on the absolute value and sign of ω_0? Show that for $\omega_0 \to 0$ one obtains the results of part (a).

SOLUTION

(a) For the unperturbed system the energy eigenvalues and eigenfunctions are given by

$$\psi_n^0(x) = \sqrt{\frac{2}{a}}\sin\left(\frac{\pi n x}{a}\right) \qquad E_n^{(0)} = \frac{\pi^2\hbar^2 n^2}{2ma^2} \quad (10.4.4)$$

The first-order corrections of the energy eigenvalues are given by

$$\Delta E_n^{(1)} = \langle \psi_n^{(0)} | \hat{W} | \psi_n^{(0)} \rangle = \frac{2}{a}\int_0^a \sin^2\left(\frac{\pi n x}{a}\right) a\omega_0 \, \delta\left(x - \frac{a}{2}\right) dx = \begin{cases} 2\omega_0 & n \text{ odd} \\ 0 & n \text{ even} \end{cases} \quad (10.4.5)$$

(b) Turning now to the exact solution, we divide the well potential into two regions: I and II, as shown in Fig. 10.2. The wavefunction for region I is $\psi_I(x) = A\sin(kx)$, and for region II, $\psi_{II}(x) = B\sin[k(a-x)]$.

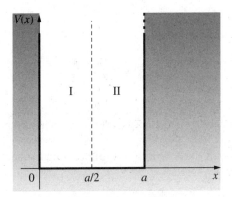

Fig. 10.2

From the boundary condition $\psi_I(x = a/2) = \psi_{II}(x = a/2)$ we have $A = B$. Using the normalization condition $\int_0^a |\psi(x)|^2 \, dx = 1$, we obtain $A = B = \sqrt{2\pi n/a^2}$. Hence, from the discontinuity relation between the derivatives $\psi'_I(x = a/2)$ and $\psi'_{II}(x = a/2)$, we obtain

$$\psi'_I(x = a/2) = \psi'_{II}(x = a/2) - \frac{2m}{\hbar^2} \lim_{\varepsilon \to 0} \int_{a/2-\varepsilon}^{a/2+\varepsilon} W(x) \sqrt{\frac{2}{a}} \sin(kx) \, dx$$

$$= \psi'_{II}(x = a/2) - \frac{2m}{\hbar^2} \sqrt{2a} \, \omega_0 \sin(ka/2) \tag{10.4.6}$$

Therefore, $k \cos(ka/2) = -k \cos(ka/2) - \frac{2ma\omega_0}{\hbar^2} \sin(ka/2)$, so

$$2k \cos(ka/2) = -\frac{2ma\omega_0}{\hbar^2} \sin(ka/2) \Rightarrow \tan(ka/2) = -\frac{\hbar^2 k}{ma\omega_0} \tag{10.4.7}$$

For $\sin(ka/2) = 0$, we obtain the unperturbed solution corresponding to $k = \pi n/2$, where n is an even number. As $\omega_0 \to 0$ we get $-\hbar^2/ma\omega_0 \to \pm\infty$, which, from Eq. (10.4.7), occurs when $ka/2 = \pi/2 + n\pi$, or $k = \pi n/a$ for odd n. We introduce $z \equiv -ka/2 + \pi n/2$, where n is an odd number. In this case, $\tan(ka/2) = \cot z$. Using the expansion of $\cot x$ in the vicinity of zero we can write

$$\cot z \approx \frac{1}{z} = \frac{1}{\pi n/2 - ka/2} = \tan\left(\frac{ka}{2}\right) = -\frac{\hbar^2 k}{ma\omega_0} \tag{10.4.8}$$

Note that the last equality comes from Eq. (10.4.7). Therefore,

$$k^2 - \left(\frac{\pi n}{a}\right)k - \frac{2m\omega_0}{\hbar^2} = 0 \tag{10.4.9}$$

and $k_{1,2} = \frac{1}{2}\left[\frac{\pi n}{a} \pm \sqrt{\left(\frac{\pi n}{a}\right)^2 + \frac{8m\omega_0}{\hbar^2}}\right]$. Using the expression

$$k = \frac{1}{2}\left(\frac{\pi n}{a} + \sqrt{\left(\frac{\pi n}{a}\right)^2 + \frac{8m\omega_0}{\hbar^2}}\right) \tag{10.4.10}$$

and the expansion $\sqrt{1+\varepsilon} = 1 + \frac{\varepsilon}{2} + \cdots (\varepsilon \ll 1)$ we obtain

$$k = \frac{1}{2}\left(\frac{\pi n}{a} + \frac{\pi n}{a}\sqrt{1 + \left(\frac{a}{\pi n}\right)^2 \frac{8m\omega_0}{\hbar^2}}\right) \approx \frac{\pi n}{a} + \frac{2m\omega_0}{\pi \hbar^2 n} \tag{10.4.11}$$

The energy eigenvalues are therefore

$$E_n = \frac{\hbar^2 k^2}{2m} \approx \frac{\hbar^2 \pi^2 n^2}{2ma^2} + 2\omega_0 \tag{10.4.12}$$

The first term on the right-hand side of Eq. (10.4.12) corresponds to the unperturbed energy eigenvalues, and the second term is the first-order correction that we obtained in part (a).

10.5. Consider a particle with mass m in a two-dimensional square box of length L. There is a weak potential in the box given by

$$V(x, y) = V_0 L^2 \delta(x - x_0) \, \delta(y - y_0) \tag{10.5.1}$$

(*a*) Evaluate the first-order correction to the energy of the ground state. (*b*) Write the expressions for the second-order correction to the energy, and the first-order correction to the wavefunction of the ground state. Explain how you would calculate the expressions for $(x_0, y_0) = (L/2, L/2)$. (*c*) Find an expression for the energy of the first excited state to the first order in V_0. What is the difference between the energy sublevels for $(x_0, y_0) = (L/4, L/4)$? (*d*) For the first excited state, find the points (x_0, y_0) defining a potential $V(x, y)$ that do not remove the degeneracy. Explain your result in terms of the symmetry of the problem.

SOLUTION

(*a*) The eigenfunctions and eigenenergies of the unperturbed state are (see Chap. 3)

$$\psi^{(0)}(x, y) = \frac{2}{L}\sin\left(\frac{\pi n}{L}x\right)\sin\left(\frac{\pi k}{L}y\right) \qquad E_{nk}^{(0)} = \frac{\pi^2\hbar^2}{2mL^2}(n^2 + k^2) \tag{10.5.2}$$

The ground state is nondegenerate, but since $E_{12}^{(0)} = E_{21}^{(0)}$, the first excited state is degenerate. For the ground state, the first-order correction of the energy is

$$E_{11}^{(1)} = \langle\psi_{11}^{(0)}|\hat{V}|\psi_{11}^{(0)}\rangle = \frac{4}{L^2}\int_0^L\int_0^L\sin^2\left(\frac{\pi x}{L}\right)\sin^2\left(\frac{\pi y}{L}\right)V_0L^2\delta(x-x_0)\delta(y-y_0)\,dx\,dy$$

$$= 4V_0\sin^2\left(\frac{\pi x_0}{L}\right)\sin^2\left(\frac{\pi y_0}{L}\right) \tag{10.5.3}$$

(*b*) For the second-order correction of the energy of the ground state we have

$$E_{11}^{(2)} = \sum_{\substack{n,k \\ (n,k)\neq(1,1)}} \frac{|\langle\psi_{nk}^{(0)}|\hat{V}|\psi_{11}^{(0)}\rangle|^2}{E_{11}^{(0)} - E_{n,k}^{(0)}}$$

$$= \sum_{\substack{n,k \\ (n,k)\neq(1,1)}} \frac{\left|\frac{4}{L^2}\iint\sin\left(\frac{\pi nx}{L}\right)\sin\left(\frac{\pi ky}{L}\right)V_0L^2\delta(x-x_0)\delta(y-y_0)\sin\left(\frac{\pi x}{L}\right)\sin\left(\frac{\pi y}{L}\right)dx\,dy\right|^2}{\frac{\pi^2\hbar^2}{2mL^2}(2 - n^2 - k^2)}$$

$$= \sum_{\substack{n,k \\ (n,k)\neq(1,1)}} \frac{\left[4V_0\sin\left(\frac{\pi nx_0}{L}\right)\sin\left(\frac{\pi ky_0}{L}\right)\sin\left(\frac{\pi x_0}{L}\right)\sin\left(\frac{\pi y_0}{L}\right)\right]^2}{\frac{\pi^2\hbar^2}{2mL^2}(2 - n^2 - k^2)} \tag{10.5.4}$$

When $(x_0, y_0) = (L/2, L/2)$ we obtain

$$E_{11}^{(2)} = \sum_{\substack{n,k \\ (n,k)\neq(1,1)}} \frac{16V_0^2\sin^2\left(\frac{\pi n}{2}\right)\sin^2\left(\frac{\pi k}{2}\right)}{\frac{\pi^2\hbar^2}{2mL^2}(2 - n^2 - k^2)}$$

$$= \frac{32V_0^2 2mL^2}{\pi^2\hbar^2}\left(\sum_{\substack{\text{odd }n,k \\ (n,k)\neq(1,1)}} \frac{1}{(2 - n^2 - k^2)}\right) \tag{10.5.5}$$

For the first-order correction of the ground state we have

$$|\psi_{11}^{(1)}\rangle = \sum_{\substack{n,k \\ (n,k) \neq (1,1)}} \frac{\langle \psi_{nk}^{(0)} | \hat{V} | \psi_{11}^{(0)} \rangle}{E_{11}^{(0)} - E_{nk}^{(0)}} |\psi_{nk}^{(0)}\rangle$$

$$= \sum_{\substack{n,k \\ (n,k) \neq (1,1)}} \frac{1}{\dfrac{\pi^2 \hbar^2}{2mL^2}(2 - n^2 - k^2)} \left[\iint \frac{4}{L^2} \sin\left(\frac{\pi x}{L}\right) \sin\left(\frac{\pi y}{L}\right) V_0 L^2 \, \delta(x - x_0)\delta(y - y_0) \right.$$

$$\left. \times \sin\left(\frac{n\pi x}{L}\right) \sin\left(\frac{\pi k y}{L}\right) dx\, dy \right] \frac{2}{L} \sin\left(\frac{\pi n x}{L}\right) \sin\left(\frac{\pi k y}{L}\right)$$

$$= \sum_{\substack{n,k \\ (n,k) \neq (1,1)}} \frac{4V_0 \sin\left(\dfrac{\pi x_0}{L}\right) \sin\left(\dfrac{\pi y_0}{L}\right) \sin\left(\dfrac{\pi n x_0}{L}\right) \sin\left(\dfrac{\pi k y_0}{L}\right)}{\dfrac{\pi^2 \hbar^2 (2 - n^2 - k^2)}{2mL^2}} \frac{2}{L} \sin\left(\frac{\pi n x}{L}\right) \sin\left(\frac{\pi k y}{L}\right) \quad (10.5.6)$$

We turn to the case where $x_0 = y_0 = L/2$. We substitute $n = 2p + 1$ and $k = 2q + 1$, and obtain

$$\psi_{11}^{(1)} = \sum_{p,q=0}^{\infty} \frac{4mLV_0}{\pi^2 \hbar^2 (p^2 + q^2 + p + q)} (-1)^{p+q} \sin\left[\frac{(2p+1)\pi x}{L}\right] \sin\left[\frac{(2q+1)\pi y}{L}\right] \quad (10.5.7)$$

(c) The first excited state is degenerate, $E_{12}^{(0)} = E_{21}^{(0)}$; according to Sec. 10.3, the secular equation will be

$$\begin{vmatrix} V_{12,12} - E_{12}^{(1)} & V_{12,12} \\ V_{21,12} & V_{21,21} - E_{12}^{(1)} \end{vmatrix} = 0 \quad (10.5.8)$$

Thus, we obtain

$$E_{12}^{(1)} = \frac{1}{2}\left[V_{12,12} + V_{21,21} \pm \sqrt{(V_{12,12} - V_{21,21})^2 + 4|V_{12,21}|^2} \right] \quad (10.5.9)$$

where $V_{nm} = \langle n | V(x,y) | m \rangle$ and

$$V_{nk,lm} = 4V_0 \sin\left(\frac{\pi n x_0}{L}\right) \sin\left(\frac{\pi k y_0}{L}\right) \sin\left(\frac{\pi l x_0}{L}\right) \sin\left(\frac{\pi m y}{L}\right) \quad (10.5.10)$$

For $x_0 = y_0 = L/4$ we obtain $V_{12,12} = V_{12,21} = V_{21,12} = V_{21,21} = 2V_0$, whereupon

$$E_{12}^{(1)} = \frac{1}{2}\left[2V_0 + 2V_0 \pm \sqrt{(2V_0 - 2V_0)^2 + 4(2V_0)^2} \right] = \begin{cases} 0 \\ 4V_0 \end{cases} \quad (10.5.11)$$

(d) The degeneracy will not be removed if

$$(V_{12,12} - V_{21,21})^2 + 4|V_{12,21}|^2 = 0 \quad (10.5.12)$$

Thus,

$$\left[\sin^2\left(\frac{\pi x_0}{L}\right) \sin^2\left(\frac{2\pi y_0}{L}\right) - \sin^2\left(\frac{2\pi x_0}{L}\right) \sin^2\left(\frac{\pi y_0}{L}\right) \right]^2$$

$$+ 4\sin^2\left(\frac{\pi x_0}{L}\right) \sin^2\left(\frac{2\pi x_0}{L}\right) \sin^2\left(\frac{\pi y_0}{L}\right) \sin^2\left(\frac{2\pi y_0}{L}\right) = 0$$

so

$$\sin^2\left(\frac{\pi x_0}{L}\right)\sin^2\left(\frac{2\pi y_0}{L}\right) + \sin^2\left(\frac{2\pi x_0}{L}\right)\sin^2\left(\frac{\pi y_0}{L}\right) = 0 \quad\Rightarrow\quad \sin\left(\frac{2\pi x_0}{L}\right) = \sin\left(\frac{2\pi y_0}{L}\right) = 0$$

$$(10.5.13)$$

Hence, each of the variables x_0 and y_0 can assume the values 0, L, and $L/2$; altogether we attain nine points in the two-dimensional box. These nine points are the only points where the symmetry of the system is not removed when the perturbation is applied.

10.6. Consider a particle of mass m subjected to the Hamiltonian

$$H = \begin{cases} \dfrac{p^2}{2m} + \dfrac{m\omega^2 r^2}{2} & 0 \le r \le a \\[2ex] \dfrac{p^2}{2m} & r > a \end{cases} \qquad (10.6.1)$$

where $r = \sqrt{x^2 + y^2}$. Use the second-order perturbation to find the corrections to the ground state energy.

SOLUTION

One can write the Hamiltonian in the following form:

$$H = \frac{p^2}{2m} + \frac{1}{2}m\omega^2 r^2 + V(r) = H_0 + V(r) \qquad (10.6.2)$$

where the perturbation is

$$V = \begin{cases} 0 & 0 \le r \le a \\ -m\omega^2 r^2/2 & r > a \end{cases} \qquad (10.6.3)$$

The wavefunction of $\hat{H}_0$ for the ground state is $\phi_{00}(r) = \sqrt{\dfrac{2}{\lambda^2}}\sqrt{r}\exp\left(-\dfrac{r^2}{2\lambda^2}\right)$, where $\lambda = \sqrt{\hbar/m\omega}$ and $E_0^{(0)} = \hbar\omega$. (In the function ϕ_{00} one of the zeros corresponds to an eigenfunction of the unperturbed Hamiltonian, and the other zero corresponds to the ground state.) For the first order in V we have

$$E_0 = \hbar\omega - \frac{2}{\lambda^2}\int_a^\infty \left(\frac{1}{2}m\omega^2 r^2\right)\exp\left(-\frac{r^2}{\lambda^2}\right)r\,dr = \hbar\omega - \frac{\hbar\omega}{2}\left[-\exp\left(\frac{r^2}{\lambda^2}\right)\left(1 + \frac{r^2}{\lambda^2}\right)\right]_a^\infty \qquad (10.6.4)$$

or $E_0 = \hbar\omega - \dfrac{\hbar\omega}{2}\left[1 + \dfrac{m\omega a^2}{\hbar}\right]\exp\left(-\dfrac{m\omega a^2}{\hbar}\right)$. This result is valid for $\hbar\omega \ll m\omega^2 a^2$. In the second order, the first state that contributes to the energy correction is $\phi_{10}(r)$ at energy $3\hbar\omega$, yielding the contribution

$$-\frac{1}{2\hbar\omega}\left(\int_a^\infty \phi_{10}(r)\left(-\frac{m\omega^2 r^2}{2}\right)\phi_{00}(r)\,r\,dr\right)^2 = -\frac{1}{2\hbar\omega}\left[-\frac{\hbar\omega}{2}\left\{\exp\left(-\frac{r^2}{\lambda^2}\right)\left(1 + \frac{r^2}{\lambda^2} + \frac{r^4}{\lambda^4}\right)\right\}\bigg|_a^\infty\right]^2$$

$$= -\frac{\hbar\omega}{8}\left[\exp\left(-\frac{m\omega a^2}{\hbar}\right)\left(1 + \frac{m\omega a^2}{\hbar} + \frac{m^2\omega^2 a^4}{\hbar^2}\right)\right]^2$$

$$(10.6.5)$$

Hence, we obtain

$$E_0 \cong \hbar\omega - \frac{\hbar\omega}{2}\left(1 + \frac{m\omega a^2}{\hbar}\right)\exp\left(-\frac{m\omega a^2}{\hbar}\right) - \frac{\hbar\omega}{8}\left(1 + \frac{m\omega a^2}{\hbar} + \frac{m^2\omega^2 a^4}{\hbar^2}\right)^2 \exp\left(-\frac{2m\omega a^2}{\hbar}\right) \quad (10.6.6)$$

Note that this analysis is incorrect only if $E > m\omega^2 a^2/2$.

10.7. Consider now a three-dimensional problem. In a given orthonormal basis, the Hamiltonian is represented by the matrix

$$\hat{H} = \begin{pmatrix} 1 & 0 & 0 \\ 0 & 3 & 0 \\ 0 & 0 & -2 \end{pmatrix} + \begin{pmatrix} 0 & C & 0 \\ C & 0 & 0 \\ 0 & 0 & C \end{pmatrix} \quad (10.7.1)$$

Here $\hat{H} = \hat{H}^0 + \hat{H}^1$ and C is a constant, $C \ll 1$. (*a*) Find the exact eigenvalues of $\hat{H}$. (*b*) Use the second-order perturbation to determine the eigenvalues. (*c*) Compare the results of parts (*a*) and (*b*).

SOLUTION

(*a*) The eigenvalues of $\hat{H}$ are the roots of the equation $\det(\hat{H} - \lambda\hat{I}) = 0$,

$$0 = \begin{vmatrix} 1-\lambda & C & 0 \\ C & 3-\lambda & 0 \\ 0 & 0 & C-2-\lambda \end{vmatrix} = (C-2-\lambda)\begin{vmatrix} 1-\lambda & C \\ C & 3-\lambda \end{vmatrix} = (C-2-\lambda)[\lambda^2 - 4\lambda + 3 - C^2] \quad (10.7.2)$$

Thus, $\lambda = C - 2, 2 \pm \sqrt{1+C^2}$.

(*b*) The second-order correction to the energy may be written as $E_n = E_n^{(0)} + E_n^{(1)} + E_n^{(2)}$, or

$$(\tilde{E})_i = (\hat{H}^0)_{ii} + (\hat{H}^1)_{ii} + \sum_{k \neq i} \frac{H^1_{ik} H^1_{ki}}{E_i^{(0)} - E_k^{(0)}} \quad (10.7.3)$$

It can be seen that $(\hat{H}^0)_{ii} = 1, 3,$ and -2. The first-order energy correction is given by $H^1_{11} = 0$, $H^1_{22} = 0$, and $H^1_{33} = C$. For the second correction we have

$$E_1^{(2)} = \frac{H^1_{12} H^1_{21}}{E_1^{(0)} - E_2^{(0)}} + \frac{H^1_{13} H^1_{31}}{E_1^{(0)} - E_3^{(0)}} = \frac{C^2}{-2} + \frac{0}{3} = -\frac{C^2}{2} \quad (10.7.4)$$

$$E_2^{(2)} = \frac{H^1_{21} H^1_{12}}{E_2^{(0)} - E_1^{(0)}} + \frac{H^1_{23} H^1_{32}}{E_2^{(0)} - E_3^{(0)}} = \frac{C^2}{3-1} + \frac{0 \cdot 0}{3} = \frac{C^2}{2} \quad (10.7.5)$$

and

$$E_3^{(2)} = \frac{H^1_{31} H^1_{13}}{E_3^{(0)} - E_1^{(0)}} + \frac{H^1_{32} H^1_{23}}{E_3^{(0)} - E_2^{(0)}} \quad (10.7.6)$$

Thus,

$$E_1 = 1 - \frac{C^2}{2} \quad (10.7.7)$$

$$E_2 = 3 + \frac{C^2}{2} \quad (10.7.8)$$

and

$$E_3 = -2 + C \quad (10.7.9)$$

(c) We expand $2 \pm \sqrt{1 + C^2}$ in a binomial series:

$$2 \pm \sqrt{1 + C^2} = 2 \pm \left(1 + \frac{1}{2}C^2 + \cdots\right) = 3 + \frac{1}{2}C^2, 1 - \frac{1}{2}C^2 \quad (C^2 \ll 1) \quad (10.7.10)$$

This gives the same result as the second-order corrections [Eqs. (10.7.7) and (10.7.8)].

10.8. Derive the first-order correction of a degenerate state according to perturbation theory (Sec. 10.3).

SOLUTION

We assume that the energy level E_p is g-fold degenerate, so we have g orthonormal vectors $|\phi_p^k\rangle$ such that

$$\hat{H}_0 |\phi_p^k\rangle = E_p |\phi_p^k\rangle \quad (10.8.1)$$

We add a perturbation $\lambda \hat{W}$ to the Hamiltonian $\hat{H}_0$, and we seek the possible energy levels ε corresponding to the first-order correction state $|0\rangle$:

$$[\hat{H}_0 + \lambda\hat{W}]|0\rangle = (E_p + \lambda\varepsilon)|0\rangle \quad (10.8.2)$$

We have

$$\langle \phi_p^k | \hat{W} | 0\rangle = \varepsilon \langle \phi_p^k | 0\rangle \quad (10.8.3)$$

Using the closure relation for the basis $\{|\phi_p^k\rangle\}$ we obtain

$$\sum_{p'}\sum_{k'} \langle \phi_p^k | \hat{W} | \phi_{p'}^{k'}\rangle\langle \phi_{p'}^{k'} | 0\rangle = \varepsilon \langle \phi_p^k | 0\rangle \quad (10.8.4)$$

Since $|0\rangle$ is an eigenvector of $\hat{H}_0$ with the eigenvalue E_p, it is orthogonal to every $|\phi_{p'}^{k'}\rangle$ for $p' \neq p$, so

$$\sum_{k' \neq 1}^{g} \langle \phi_p^k | \hat{W} | \phi_p^{k'}\rangle\langle \phi_p^{k'} | 0\rangle = \varepsilon \langle \phi_p^k | 0\rangle \quad (10.8.5)$$

We define the matrix $\{\hat{W}^p\}$ by

$$W_{ij}^p = \langle \phi_p^i | \hat{W} | \phi_p^j\rangle \quad (10.8.6)$$

Equation (10.8.5) is equivalent to the vector equation $W^p |0\rangle = \varepsilon |0\rangle$. Therefore, the possible values of ε are the solutions of

$$\det(\hat{W}^p - \lambda\hat{I}) = 0 \quad (10.8.7)$$

10.9. Consider an electron of mass m in a three dimensional box with energy $3\pi^2\hbar^2/ma^2$. A weak electric field in the z direction and of strength $\mathcal{E}$ is applied to the system; the perturbation is then $W = e\mathcal{E}z$. Compute the first-order correction to the electron's energy.

SOLUTION

A free electron in the three-dimensional box has energy $\pi^2\hbar^2 n^2/2ma^2$; and so $n_x^2 + n_y^2 + n_z^2 = 6$. Three vectors satisfy this condition:

$$(n_x, n_y, n_z) = (1, 1, 2) \quad (n_x, n_y, n_z) = (1, 2, 1) \quad (n_x, n_y, n_z) = (2, 1, 1) \quad (10.9.1)$$

The state is therefore threefold degenerate. The wavefunctions for these three possibilities are

$$\phi_{112} = \sqrt{\frac{8}{a^3}} \sin\left(\frac{\pi x}{a}\right)\sin\left(\frac{\pi y}{a}\right)\sin\left(\frac{2\pi z}{a}\right) \quad (10.9.2)$$

$$\phi_{121} = \sqrt{\frac{8}{a^3}} \sin\left(\frac{\pi x}{a}\right) \sin\left(\frac{2\pi y}{a}\right) \sin\left(\frac{\pi z}{a}\right) \tag{10.9.3}$$

and

$$\phi_{211} = \sqrt{\frac{8}{a^3}} \sin\left(\frac{2\pi x}{a}\right) \sin\left(\frac{\pi y}{a}\right) \sin\left(\frac{\pi z}{a}\right) \tag{10.9.4}$$

Note that $\langle 2, 1, 1 \,|\, \hat{z} \,|\, 2, 1, 1 \rangle = \langle 1, 2, 1 \,|\, \hat{z} \,|\, 1, 2, 1 \rangle = \langle 1, 1, 2 \,|\, \hat{z} \,|\, 1, 1, 2 \rangle$ and

$$\langle 2, 1, 1 \,|\, \hat{z} \,|\, 2, 1, 1 \rangle = \frac{8}{a^3} \int_0^a \sin^2\left(\frac{2\pi x}{a}\right) dx \int_0^a \sin^2\left(\frac{\pi y}{a}\right) dy \int_0^a z \sin^2\left(\frac{\pi z}{a}\right) dz$$

$$= \frac{2}{a} \int_0^a z \sin^2\left(\frac{\pi z}{a}\right) dz = \frac{a}{2} \tag{10.9.5}$$

It can be similarly shown that $\langle 2, 1, 1 \,|\, \hat{z} \,|\, 1, 2, 1 \rangle = \langle 2, 1, 1 \,|\, \hat{z} \,|\, 1, 1, 2 \rangle = \langle 1, 2, 1 \,|\, \hat{z} \,|\, 1, 1, 2 \rangle = 0$. Thus, all the off-diagonal matrix elements vanish and the energy is given by

$$E = \frac{3\pi^2 \hbar^2}{ma^2} + \frac{e\mathcal{E}a}{2} \tag{10.9.6}$$

10.10. Consider a hydrogen atom placed in a uniform static electric field $\mathcal{E}$ that points along the **k** direction. The term that corresponds to this interaction in the Hamiltonian is

$$W = -e\mathcal{E}z \tag{10.10.1}$$

Note that for the electric fields typically produced in a laboratory, the condition $\hat{W} \ll \hat{H}_0$ is satisfied. The appearance of the perturbation removes the degeneracy from some of the hydrogen states. This phenomenon is called the *Stark effect*. Calculate the Stark effect for $n = 2$ in a hydrogen atom.

SOLUTION

Before we explicitly calculate the matrix elements of the perturbation, we note that the perturbation has nonzero matrix elements only between states of opposite parity; as we are considering level $n = 2$, the relevant states are those with $l = 0$ and $l = 1$. Using symmetry, the m-values of the two states must be equal. Therefore,

$$\hat{W}_s = \begin{matrix} & 2s & 2p, m = 0 & 2p, m = 1 & 2p, m = -1 \\ & \begin{pmatrix} 0 & \langle 2s \,|\, \hat{W} \,|\, 2p, m = 0 \rangle & 0 & 0 \\ \langle 2p, m = 0 \,|\, \hat{W} \,|\, 2s \rangle & 0 & 0 & 0 \\ 0 & 0 & 0 & 0 \\ 0 & 0 & 0 & 0 \end{pmatrix} \end{matrix} \tag{10.10.2}$$

An explicit calculation gives $\langle 2p, m = 0 \,|\, \hat{W} \,|\, 2s \rangle = 3ea_0\mathcal{E}$, where a_0 is the Bohr radius. Note that the matrix element is linear in $\mathcal{E}$, so this correction is called the *linear Stark effect*. We transform to the basis that diagonalizes the perturbation; that basis is

$$\left\{ |2p, m = -1\rangle, |2p, m = 1\rangle, \frac{1}{\sqrt{2}}(|2s, m = 0\rangle + |2p, m = 0\rangle), \frac{1}{\sqrt{2}}(2s, |m = 0\rangle - |2p, m = 0\rangle) \right\} \tag{10.10.3}$$

Schematically, Fig. 10.3 depicts how the linear Stark effect removes some of the degeneracy of the $n = 2$ level.

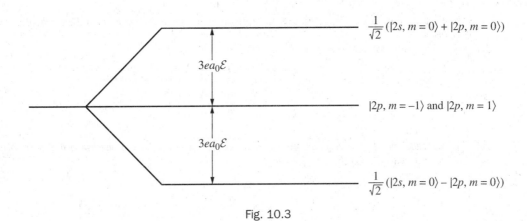

$$\frac{1}{\sqrt{2}}(|2s, m = 0\rangle + |2p, m = 0\rangle)$$

$3ea_0\mathcal{E}$

$|2p, m = -1\rangle$ and $|2p, m = 1\rangle$

$3ea_0\mathcal{E}$

$$\frac{1}{\sqrt{2}}(|2s, m = 0\rangle - |2p, m = 0\rangle)$$

Fig. 10.3

10.11. Consider a planar molecule consisting of four atoms: one atom is of type A and the three other atoms are of type B; see Fig. 10.4. An electron in the molecule can be found in the vicinity of each atom. If the electron is close to atom A, it has energy $E_1^{(0)}$; if it is close to any of the B atoms, it has energy $E_2^{(0)}$, where $E_1^{(0)} < E_2^{(0)}$. We denote the states by

$$|1\rangle \equiv (1000) \qquad |2\rangle \equiv (0100) \qquad |3\rangle \equiv (0010) \qquad |4\rangle \equiv (0001) \qquad (10.11.1)$$

(*a*) For the first approximation, the electron cannot move from one atom to another. Using the basis $\{|1\rangle, |2\rangle, |3\rangle, |4\rangle\}$, write the Hamiltonian $\hat{H}_0$ for this approximation. (*b*) For the case in which an electron can move from an atom B to atom A and back, but cannot move from one B to another, we denote by a the energy associated with the transition from atom A to an atom B, where $a \ll E_1$. Write the perturbation in this case. (*c*) Using perturbation theory, calculate the second-order correction to the energy of the state $|1\rangle$ and the first-order correction to the states $|2\rangle, |3\rangle$, and $|4\rangle$. (*d*) Calculate exactly the corrections to the energies of the states. Show that when $a \ll E_1$, one obtains the result of part (*c*).

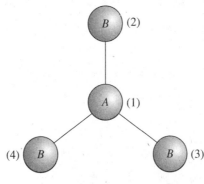

Fig. 10.4

SOLUTION

(*a*) In the basis $\{|1\rangle, |2\rangle, |3\rangle, |4\rangle\}$ the Hamiltonian $\hat{H}_0$ is represented by the following matrix:

$$\hat{H}_0 = \begin{pmatrix} E_1^{(0)} & 0 & 0 & 0 \\ 0 & E_2^{(0)} & 0 & 0 \\ 0 & 0 & E_2^{(0)} & 0 \\ 0 & 0 & 0 & E_2^{(0)} \end{pmatrix} \qquad (10.11.2)$$

(b) The perturbation matrix representing the transitions between the state $|1\rangle$ and each of the states $|2\rangle$, $|3\rangle$, or $|4\rangle$ is

$$\hat{W} = \begin{pmatrix} 0 & a & a & a \\ a & 0 & 0 & 0 \\ a & 0 & 0 & 0 \\ a & 0 & 0 & 0 \end{pmatrix} \tag{10.11.3}$$

(c) The energy level $E_1^{(0)}$ is nondegenerate. For the perturbation $\hat{W}$ the second-order correction is, in accordance with Eq. (10.6),

$$E_1^{(2)} = E_1^{(0)} + \langle 1 | \hat{W} | 1 \rangle - \sum_{i=2}^{4} \frac{|\langle i | \hat{W} | 1 \rangle|^2}{E_1^{(0)} - E_i^{(0)}} = E_1^{(0)} + \frac{3a^2}{E_1^{(0)} - E_2^{(0)}} \tag{10.11.4}$$

The energy level $E_2^{(0)}$ is threefold degenerate, so we need to use perturbation theory for a degenerate state. Since the matrix elements of $\hat{W}$ between the states $|2\rangle$, $|3\rangle$, and $|4\rangle$ are zero, the secular equation is

$$\det \begin{pmatrix} 0 - \varepsilon & 0 & 0 \\ 0 & 0 - \varepsilon & 0 \\ 0 & 0 & 0 - \varepsilon \end{pmatrix} = 0 \tag{10.11.5}$$

and therefore $-\varepsilon^2 = 0$, and the first-order correction to energy level $E_2^{(0)}$ is zero:

$$E_2^{(1)} = E_2^{(0)} \qquad E_3^{(1)} = E_2^{(0)} \qquad E_4^{(1)} = E_2^{(0)} \tag{10.11.6}$$

We see that, to the first order, the degeneracy is not removed.

(d) The total Hamiltonian is

$$\hat{H} = \begin{pmatrix} E_1^{(0)} & a & a & a \\ a & E_2^{(0)} & 0 & 0 \\ a & 0 & E_2^{(0)} & 0 \\ a & 0 & 0 & E_2^{(0)} \end{pmatrix} \tag{10.11.7}$$

To find the eigenenergies of $\hat{H}$, we must solve the quadratic equation $\det(\hat{H} - \lambda \hat{I}) = 0$. An explicit calculation gives

$$(E_1^{(0)} - \lambda)(E_2^{(0)} - \lambda)^3 - 3a^2(E_2^{(0)} - \lambda)^2 = 0 \tag{10.11.8}$$

or

$$(E_2^{(0)} - \lambda)^2[(E_1^{(0)} - \lambda)(E_2^{(0)} - \lambda) - 3a^2] = 0 \tag{10.11.9}$$

Thus, we obtain

$$\lambda_{1,2} = \frac{1}{2}\left[(E_1^{(0)} + E_2^{(0)}) \pm \sqrt{(E_1^{(0)} - E_2^{(0)})^2 + 12a^2}\right] \qquad \lambda_{3,4} = E_2^{(0)} \tag{10.11.10}$$

We see that the degeneracy level $E_2^{(0)}$ is not completely removed by the perturbation, but it is partly removed. For $a \ll E_1^{(0)}$ we have

$$\lambda_{1,2} = \frac{1}{2}\left[(E_1^{(0)} + E_2^{(0)}) \pm (E_1^{(0)} - E_2^{(0)})\sqrt{1 + \frac{12a^2}{(E_1^{(0)} - E_2^{(0)})^2}}\right]$$

$$\cong \frac{1}{2}\left[(E_1^{(0)} + E_2^{(0)}) \pm (E_1^{(0)} - E_2^{(0)})\left(1 + \frac{6a^2}{(E_1^{(0)} - E_2^{(0)})^2}\right)\right] \tag{10.11.11}$$

So,

$$\lambda_1 = E_1^{(0)} + \frac{3a^2}{E_1^{(0)} - E_2^{(0)}} \qquad \lambda_2 = E_2^{(0)} - \frac{3a^2}{E_1^{(0)} - E_2^{(0)}} \tag{10.11.12}$$

This is in accordance with the second-order correction for the $E_1^{(0)}$, see Eq. (10.11.4), and the first-order correction for the level $E_2^{(0)}$.

10.12. Derive the transition probability equation for the first-order, time-dependent perturbation theory.

SOLUTION

Let $c_n(t)$ be the components of the vector $|\psi(t)\rangle$ in the $\{|\phi_n\rangle\}$ basis:

$$|\psi(t)\rangle = \sum_n c_n(t)|\phi_n\rangle \qquad c_n(t) = \langle\phi_n|\psi(t)\rangle \tag{10.12.1}$$

We define $W_{nk} = \langle\phi_n|\hat{W}(t)|\phi_k\rangle$. The Schrödinger equation is

$$i\hbar\frac{d}{dt}|\psi(t)\rangle = [\hat{H}_0 + \lambda\hat{W}(t)]|\psi(t)\rangle \tag{10.12.2}$$

By multiplying Eq. (10.12.2) by $\langle\phi_n|$ and using Eq. (10.12.1) we obtain

$$i\hbar\frac{dc_n(t)}{dt} = E_n c_n(t) + \sum_k \lambda W_{nk}(t)c_k(t) \tag{10.12.3}$$

Using the Bohr angular frequency $\omega_{nk} = (E_n - E_k)/\hbar$ and the substitution $c_n(t) = a_n(t)e^{-iE_n t/\hbar}$, Eq. (10.12.3) becomes

$$i\hbar\frac{da_n(t)}{dt} = \lambda\sum_k e^{i\omega_{nk}t}W_{nk}(t)a_k(t) \tag{10.12.4}$$

We write $b_n(t)$ in the form of a power series expansion in λ:

$$a_n(t) = a_n^{(0)}(t) + \lambda a_n^{(1)}(t) + \lambda^2 a_n^{(2)}(t) + \cdots \tag{10.12.5}$$

We seek the solution to the first order in λ. For $t < 0$ we assume the system to be in the state $|\phi_i\rangle$, so according to Eq. (10.12.1) and the relation between $a_n(t)$ and $c_n(t)$ we have

$$a_n(t = 0) = \delta_{ni} \tag{10.12.6}$$

If we substitute Eq. (10.12.5) into Eq. (10.12.4) and equate the coefficient of λ^r on both sides of the equation, we obtain [by using Eq. (10.12.6)]

$$i\hbar\frac{db_n^{(1)}}{dt} = \sum_k e^{i\omega_{nk}t}W_{nk}(t)\delta_{ki} = e^{i\omega_{ni}t}W_{ni}(t) \tag{10.12.7}$$

Equation (10.7.7) can be integrated to obtain

$$a_n^{(1)}(t) = \frac{1}{i\hbar}\int_0^t e^{i\omega_{nk}t'}W_{nk}(t')\,dt' \tag{10.12.8}$$

Finally, the transition probability $P_{if}(t)$ between the states $|\phi_i\rangle$ and $|\phi_f\rangle$ is, according to Eq. (10.12.1), equal to $|c_f(t)|^2$. Note that $a_f(t)$ and $c_f(t)$ have the same modulus, and, to the first order,

$$a_f(t) \cong a_f^{(0)}(t) + \lambda a_f^{(1)}(t) \tag{10.12.9}$$

Since the transition is between two different stationary states, we have $b_f^{(0)}(t) = 0$, and consequently

$$P_{if}(t) = \lambda^2 \mid a_f^{(1)}(t) \mid^2 = \frac{\lambda^2}{\hbar^2}\left[\int_0^t e^{i\omega_{fi}t'} W_{fi}(t')\,dt'\right]^2 \tag{10.12.10}$$

where we used Eq. (10.12.8).

10.13. Consider a one-dimensional harmonic oscillator with angular frequency ω_0 and electric charge q. At time $t = 0$ the oscillator is in the ground state. An electric field is applied for time τ, so the perturbation is

$$W(t) = \begin{cases} -q\mathcal{E}x & 0 \le t \le \tau \\ 0 & \text{otherwise} \end{cases} \tag{10.13.1}$$

where $\mathcal{E}$ is a field strength and $\hat{x}$ is a position operator. (*a*) Using first-order perturbation theory, calculate the probability of transition to the state $n = 1$. (*b*) Using first-order perturbation theory, show that a transition to $n = 2$ is impossible.

SOLUTION

(*a*) We denote by P_{01} the probability of transition from the ground state to $n = 1$; then, according to the first-order time-dependent perturbation theory,

$$P_{01}^{(1)}(\tau) = \frac{1}{\hbar^2}\left[\int_0^\tau e^{i\omega_{10}t}\langle 1 \mid \hat{W} \mid 0\rangle\,dt\right]^2 = \left[\frac{1}{\hbar^2}\int_0^\tau e^{i\omega_{10}t}\,dt\int_{-\infty}^\infty \phi_1(x)(-q\mathcal{E}x)\phi_0(x)\,dx\right]^2 \tag{10.13.2}$$

where $\phi_0(x)$ and $\phi_1(x)$ are the energy eigenfunctions in the coordinate representation for $n = 0$ and $n = 1$, respectively. Using results for a harmonic oscillator we know that (see Chap. 5)

$$\phi_0(x) = \frac{1}{\pi^{1/4}\sqrt{x_0}}\exp\left[-\frac{1}{2}\left(\frac{x}{x_0}\right)^2\right] \qquad \phi_1(x) = \frac{1}{\pi^{1/4}x_0^{3/2}}\exp\left[-\frac{1}{2}\left(\frac{x}{x_0}\right)^2\right] \tag{10.13.3}$$

where $x_0 \equiv \sqrt{\dfrac{\hbar}{m\omega}}$. Substituting these into Eq. (10.13.2) we obtain

$$P_{01}^{(1)}(\tau) = \frac{1}{\hbar^2}\left[\int_0^\tau e^{i\omega_0 t}\left(-q\mathcal{E}\sqrt{\frac{\hbar}{2m\omega_0}}\right)dt\right]^2 = \frac{(q\mathcal{E})^2}{2m\hbar\omega_0}\left[\int_0^\tau e^{i\omega_{10}t}\,dt\right]^2$$

$$= \frac{(q\mathcal{E})^2}{2m\hbar\omega_0}\left[\frac{\sin(\omega_0\tau/2)}{\omega_0/2}\right]^2 \tag{10.13.4}$$

(*b*) To the first order, for the transition $n = 0 \to n = 2$, we can write

$$P_{02}^{(1)}(\tau) = \frac{1}{\hbar^2}\left[\int_0^\tau e^{i\omega_{20}t}\langle 2 \mid \hat{W} \mid 0\rangle\,dt\right]^2 \tag{10.13.5}$$

We have

$$\langle 2 \mid \hat{W} \mid 0\rangle = \langle 2 \mid (-q\mathcal{E}x)\mid 0\rangle = -q\mathcal{E}\sqrt{\frac{\hbar}{2m\omega}}\langle 2 \mid (a^\dagger + a)\mid 0\rangle = 0 \tag{10.13.6}$$

where we used the relation $x = \sqrt{\dfrac{\hbar}{2m\omega}}(a + a^\dagger)$ (see Chap. 5). Therefore, $P_{02}^{(1)}(\tau) = 0$.

10.14. Consider a one-dimensional harmonic oscillator embedded in a uniform electric field. The field can be considered as a small perturbation that depends on time according to

$$\mathcal{E}(t) = \frac{A}{\sqrt{\pi}\tau} \exp\left[-\left(\frac{t}{\tau}\right)^2\right] \qquad (10.14.1)$$

where A is a constant. If the oscillator was in the ground state until the field was turned on at $t = 0$, compute, in the first approximation, the probability of its excitation as a result of the action of the perturbation.

SOLUTION

Consider the total momentum p imparted to the oscillator by the field over the duration of the perturbation:

$$p = \int_{-\infty}^{\infty} e\mathcal{E}(t)\, dt = \frac{eA}{\sqrt{\pi}\tau} \int_{-\infty}^{\infty} e^{-(t/\tau)^2}\, dt = eA = \text{const.} \qquad (10.14.2)$$

We see that p does not depend on the time constant τ of the perturbation. This means that the areas under the curves of Fig. 10.5 are equal, for every τ.

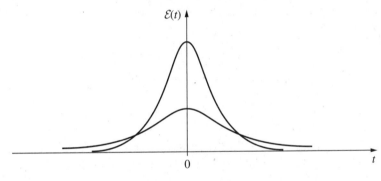

Fig. 10.5

The probability of a transition from the state n to the state k is given by

$$P_{nk} = \frac{1}{\hbar^2}\left[\int_{-\infty}^{\infty} V_{kn} e^{i\omega_{kn}t}\, dt\right]^2 \qquad (10.14.3)$$

where $V_{kn} = \int_{-\infty}^{\infty} \psi_k^{(0)*} V \psi_n^{(0)}\, dx$ is the matrix element of the perturbation and $\omega_{kn} = |E_k^{(0)} - E_n^{(0)}|/\hbar$. Let e, m, and ω denote the charge, mass, and natural frequency of the oscillator, respectively, where x denotes its deviation from its equilibrium position. In the case of a uniform field, the perturbation is given by

$$V(x, t) = -ex\mathcal{E}(t) \sim x \qquad (10.14.4)$$

The oscillator is the ground state ($n = 0$), so the nonvanishing elements of the perturbation matrix are

$$V_{01} = V_{10} = -\frac{p}{\sqrt{\pi}\tau}\sqrt{\frac{\hbar}{2m\omega}}\exp\left[-\left(\frac{t}{\tau}\right)^2\right] \qquad (10.14.5)$$

Thus, in the first approximation, a uniform field can produce a transition of the oscillator only to the first excited state. If we substitute Eq. (10.14.5) and $\omega_{kn} = \omega_{10} = |E_k^{(0)} - E_n^{(0)}|/\hbar = \omega$ into Eq. (10.14.3) we obtain

$$P_{01} = \frac{p^2}{2\pi\tau^2 m t \omega}\left[\int_{-\infty}^{\infty} \exp\left[i\omega t - \left(\frac{t}{\tau}\right)^2\right] dt\right]^2 \qquad (10.14.6)$$

Using the identity $\int_{-\infty}^{\infty} e^{i\beta x - \alpha x^2} dx = \sqrt{\frac{\pi}{\alpha}} e^{-\beta^2/4\alpha}$ we arrive at

$$P_{01} = \frac{p^2}{2m\hbar\omega} \exp\left[-\frac{1}{2}(\omega\tau)^2\right] \tag{10.14.7}$$

We conclude that for a given classically imparted momentum p, the probability of the excitation decreases with the increase of τ; so, for $\tau \gg 1/\omega$ this probability is extremely small. This is the case of a so-called *adiabatic perturbation*. On the contrary, for a rapid perturbation $\tau \ll 1/\omega$ the probability of excitation is constant. Note that in the limit $\tau \to 0$,

$$\lim_{\tau \to 0} \mathcal{E}(t) = A\delta(t) = \frac{p}{e}\delta(t) \tag{10.14.8}$$

and we have a *sudden perturbation*. In this case, the probability assumes the value

$$\lim_{\tau \to 0} P_{01} = \frac{p^2}{2m\hbar\omega} \tag{10.14.9}$$

which is equal to the ratio of the classically imparted energy $p^2/2m$ to the difference between the energy levels of the oscillator, $\hbar\omega$. The criterion for the applicability of perturbation theory is that the probability of excitation must be small compared to the probability that the oscillator will remain in the ground state:

$$P_{01} \ll (1 - P_{01}) \qquad \text{or} \qquad P_{01} \ll 1 \tag{10.14.10}$$

It is apparent from Eq. (10.14.7) that

$$\frac{p^2}{2m} = \frac{(eA)^2}{2m} \ll \hbar\omega \tag{10.14.11}$$

is a sufficient condition for Eq. (10.14.10). However, if the field's change is sufficiently adiabatic, that is, $\tau \gg 1/\omega$, then the condition of Eq. (10.14.11) is too rigorous and perturbation theory can be applied. (This is if $p^2/2m$ is of the order of $\hbar\omega$.)

10.15. Consider a linear oscillator in its ground state. Suppose that the equilibrium point begins to move slowly and uniformly at time $t = 0$, and that it stops at time $t = T$. Using the adiabatic approximation, find the probability that the oscillator will be excited. What is the validity of this approximation? (In an adiabatic approximation one assumes that the perturbation changes very slowly with time. It turns out that for adiabatic perturbation, the probability of excitation is very small.)

SOLUTION

The classical Hamiltonian of the oscillator at $t \geq 0$ has the form

$$H(t) = \frac{1}{2m}p^2 + \frac{1}{2}m\omega^2[x - a(t)]^2 \tag{10.15.1}$$

where $a(t)$, the position of the equilibrium point, is $v_0 t$ according to the given condition, with $v_0 =$ constant being the velocity of the equilibrium point. The instantaneous eigenfunctions of the Hamiltonian, Eq. (10.16.1), have the form

$$\psi_n = \left(\frac{m\omega}{\pi\hbar}\right)^{1/4} \frac{1}{\sqrt{2^n n!}} \exp\left[-\frac{m\omega}{2\hbar}(x - a(t))^2\right] H_n\left[-\sqrt{\frac{m\omega}{\hbar}}[x - a(t)]\right] \tag{10.15.2}$$

The matrix element of the operator $\frac{\partial \hat{H}}{\partial t} = -m\omega^2 v_0[x - a(t)]$ computed from these functions, is nonzero only for the transition $n = 0 \to n = 1$ (recall that the initial state is the ground state),

$$\left(\frac{\partial \hat{H}}{\partial t}\right)_{10} = -m\omega^2 v_0 \sqrt{\frac{\hbar}{2m\omega}} \tag{10.15.3}$$

Evidently, the spectrum of the energy levels of the oscillator does not change during the motion of the equilibrium point; i.e., all the ω are constant. The probability amplitude of the first excited state is obtained by substituting $\omega_{10} = \omega$, so

$$C_1(t) \approx -\frac{1}{i\hbar\omega^2} m\omega^2 v_0 \sqrt{\frac{\hbar}{2m\omega}} (e^{i\omega t} - 1) = iv_0 \sqrt{\frac{m}{2\hbar\omega}} (e^{i\omega t} - 1) \qquad (10.15.4)$$

Therefore, the probability that at time t the oscillator will be in the first excited state is

$$P_1(t) = |C_1(t)|^2 = \frac{mv_0^2}{\hbar\omega} (1 - \cos(\omega t)) \qquad (10.15.5)$$

Note that this probability oscillates with time. Thus, the probability of excitation for $t \geq T$ is

$$P_1(T) = \frac{mv_0^2}{\hbar\omega} (1 - \cos(\omega t)) \qquad (10.15.6)$$

For the adiabatic approximation to be valid, the inequality $P_1(T) \ll 1$ must hold for all t. This is equivalent to the condition

$$v_0 \ll \sqrt{\frac{\hbar\omega}{m}} \qquad (10.15.7)$$

10.16. Consider a hydrogen atom in its ground state at time $t = 0$. At the same time a uniform periodic electric field is applied to the atom. (*a*) Find the minimum frequency that the field needs in order to ionize the atom. (*b*) Using perturbation theory, find the probability of ionization per unit time. Assume that when the atom becomes ionized, its electron becomes free.

SOLUTION

(*a*) The equation for the transition probability per unit time from a state in a discrete spectrum to a state in a continuous spectrum, under the action of a periodic perturbation, has the form

$$dP_{n\nu} = \frac{2\pi}{\hbar} |V_{\nu n}|^2 \delta(E_\nu - E_n^{(0)} - \hbar\omega) d\nu \qquad (10.16.1)$$

where ω is the frequency of the periodic perturbation, n represents the set of quantum numbers that characterizes the states of the discrete spectrum, $d\nu$ is the corresponding infinitesimal energy interval of the continuous spectrum, $E_n^{(0)}$ is the unperturbed energy level in the discrete spectrum, E_ν is the unperturbed energy level in the continuous spectrum, and $V_{\nu n}$ is the matrix element of the perturbation operator for the considered transition. The perturbation operator has the form

$$\hat{W} = e(\mathcal{E}(t) \cdot \mathbf{r}) = e(\mathcal{E}_0 \cdot \mathbf{r}) \sin(\omega t) = \hat{V} \exp(-i\omega t) + \hat{V}^* \exp(i\omega t) \qquad (10.16.2)$$

where $\mathcal{E}(t)$ is the electric field, $|\mathcal{E}_0|$ its amplitude, and $\hat{V}$ is given by

$$\hat{V} = \frac{ie}{2} \mathcal{E}_0 \cdot \mathbf{r} \qquad (10.16.3)$$

Note that the δ-function in Eq. (10.16.1) assures that the transition takes place only when $E_\nu - E_n^{(0)} - \hbar\omega = 0$; therefore,

$$\omega_{min} = \frac{1}{\hbar} (E_\nu - E_n^{(0)})_{min} \qquad (10.16.4)$$

Since the hydrogen atom is in its ground state, we have

$$(E_\nu - E_n^{(0)})_{min} = \frac{me^4}{2\hbar^3} \qquad (10.16.5)$$

which gives us the minimum frequency of the electric field needed to ionize the atom.

(b) Consider the matrix element $V_{\nu n} = \int \psi_\nu^* \hat{V} \psi_n^{(0)} d^3 r$. For $\psi_n^{(0)}$ we take the ground-state wavefunction of the hydrogen atom:

$$\psi_n^{(0)} = \frac{1}{\sqrt{\pi a^3}} \exp\left(\frac{-r}{a}\right) \qquad \left(a = \frac{\hbar^2}{\mu e^2}\right) \tag{10.16.6}$$

For ψ_ν we approximate

$$\psi_\nu \approx \frac{1}{\sqrt{8\pi^3}} \exp(i\mathbf{k} \cdot \mathbf{r}) \tag{10.16.7}$$

where $\nu = \hbar k^2/4\pi m$. Note that $\psi_n^{(0)}$ is normalized to unity and ψ_ν is normalized to $\delta(\nu - \nu')$. Substituting all this into $V_{\nu n}$, we obtain

$$V_{\nu n} = \frac{ie}{2} \frac{1}{\sqrt{8\pi^3}} \frac{1}{\sqrt{\pi a^3}} \int \exp\left(-i\mathbf{k} \cdot \mathbf{r} - \frac{r}{a}\right) \mathcal{E}_0 \cdot \mathbf{r} \, d^3 r \tag{10.16.8}$$

To calculate the integral, we use the spherical coordinates (r, θ, φ). We assume that the wave or propagation vector $\mathbf{k}$ is directed along the polar axis, and denote the angle between $\mathbf{k}$ and $\mathcal{E}_0$ by χ. The scalar product $\mathcal{E}_0 \cdot \mathbf{r}$ is

$$\mathcal{E}_0 \cdot \mathbf{r} = \mathcal{E}_0 r [\cos \chi \cos \theta + \sin \chi \sin \theta \cos (\varphi - \varphi_0)] \tag{10.16.9}$$

where φ_0 is the corresponding coordinate of $\mathcal{E}_0$. Substituting Eq. (10.16.9) into Eq. (10.16.8) (denoting $z \equiv \cos \theta$) we obtain

$$V_{\nu n} = \frac{ie\mathcal{E}_0}{\pi\sqrt{(2a)^3}} \cos \chi \int_{-1}^{1} \left[\int_0^\infty \exp\left(-ikrz - \frac{r}{a}\right) r^3 dr \right] z \, dz = \frac{e\mathcal{E}_0 \cos \chi}{\pi\sqrt{(2a)^3}} \frac{16 a^5 k}{(1 + k^2 a^2)^3} \tag{10.16.10}$$

Let us now turn to $d\nu$:

$$d\nu = d^3\mathbf{k} = k^2 dk \, d\Omega_k = k^2 \frac{dk}{dE_\nu} d\Omega_k \, dE_\nu = \frac{mk}{\hbar^2} d\Omega_k dE_\nu \tag{10.16.11}$$

where we have used the relation $E_\nu = \hbar^2 k^2/2m$ and $d\Omega_k$ is an element of the solid angle with the axis along $\mathbf{k}$. Substituting Eqs. (10.16.10) and (10.16.11) into Eq. (10.16.1), we obtain

$$dP_{n\nu} \frac{|\mathcal{E}_0|^2 k^3 \cos^2 \chi}{(1 + k^2 a^2)^6} \times \delta(E_\nu - E_n^{(0)} - \hbar\omega) d\Omega_k \, dE_\nu \tag{10.16.12}$$

The probability of ionization when the electron makes a transition with a final wave vector $\mathbf{k}$ within the element $d\Omega_k$ is obtained by integrating Eq. (10.16.12) over dE_ν. Using the properties of δ-function in Eq. (10.16.12), we have to consider only the point where $E_\nu = E_n^{(0)} + \hbar\omega$; thus it follows that

$$k^2 = \frac{2mE_\nu}{\hbar^2} = \frac{2m(\omega - \omega_{min})}{\hbar} \tag{10.16.13}$$

and $1 + k^2 a^2 = \dfrac{\omega}{\omega_{min}}$. We now have

$$dP_k = \frac{64 a^3}{\pi\hbar} \left(\frac{\omega_{min}}{\omega}\right)^6 \left(\frac{\omega}{\omega_{min}} - 1\right)^{3/2} E_0 \cos^2\chi \, d\Omega_k \tag{10.16.14}$$

[The probability is denoted now by dP_k since Eq. (10.16.14) depends only on k.] We use the fact that $\cos^2\chi = 1/3$, and integrate Eq. (10.16.14) over the angles. We finally obtain the total probability of the atom ionization per unit time:

$$P = \frac{256}{3} \frac{a^3}{\hbar} \left(\frac{\omega_{min}}{\omega}\right)^6 \left(\frac{\omega}{\omega_0} - 1\right)^{3/2} E_0^2 \tag{10.16.15}$$

10.17. Consider a quantum system with two stationary eigenstates $|1\rangle$ and $|2\rangle$. The difference between their eigenvalues is given by $E_2 - E_1 = \hbar\omega_{21}$. At time $t = 0$, when the system is in state $|1\rangle$, a small perturbation that does not change in time and is equal to H' is applied. The following matrix elements are given:

$$\langle 1| \hat{H}' |1\rangle = 0 \qquad \langle 2| \hat{H}' |1\rangle = \hbar\omega_0 \qquad \langle 2| \hat{H}' |2\rangle = -\hbar\omega \qquad (10.17.1)$$

(*a*) Using the first-order time-dependent perturbation theory, calculate the probability of finding the system at time t in state $|1\rangle$, and the probability of finding it in state $|2\rangle$. (*b*) Solve the Schrödinger equation and find $|\psi(t)\rangle$. (*c*) What is the probability that at time t the system is in state $|2\rangle$? When is the approximation used in part (*a*) correct? At what time (for the first order) will the system have probability 1 in state $|2\rangle$?

SOLUTION

(*a*) From first-order time-dependent perturbation theory we have $P_{|1\rangle \to |2\rangle}$, and since there are only two eigenstates for the system, we obtain

$$P_{|1\rangle \to |1\rangle} = 1 - P_{|1\rangle \to |2\rangle} \qquad (10.17.2)$$

Using the formula $P_{if}^{(1)} = \dfrac{1}{\hbar^2}\left| \displaystyle\int_0^t e^{i\omega_{fi}t'} W_{fi}(t')\, dt' \right|^2$ we arrive at

$$P_{|1\rangle \to |2\rangle} \cong \frac{2}{\hbar^2}\left| \int_0^t e^{i\omega_{21}t'}\langle 2| \hat{H}' |1\rangle\, dt' \right|^2 = \frac{1}{\hbar^2}\hbar^2\omega_0^2\left| \int_0^t e^{i\omega_{21}t'}\, dt' \right|^2 = \omega_0^2\left| \frac{1}{i\omega_{21}}(e^{i\omega_{21}t} - 1) \right|^2$$

$$= \omega_0^2\left| \frac{e^{i\omega_{21}t/2}(e^{i\omega_{21}t/2} - e^{-i\omega_{21}t/2})}{i\omega_{21}} \right|^2 = \omega_0^2\left| \frac{e^{i\omega_{21}t/2}2i\sin(\omega_{21}t/2)}{i\omega_{21}} \right|^2$$

$$= \omega_0^2\left| e^{i\omega_{21}t/2} \right|^2\left| \frac{\sin(\omega_{21}t/2)}{\omega_{21}/2} \right|^2 = \omega_0^2\left| \frac{\sin(\omega_{21}t/2)}{\omega_{21}/2} \right|^2 \qquad (10.17.3)$$

Since $\omega_{21}t \ll 1$, $P_{|1\rangle \to |2\rangle} \cong \omega_0^2 t^2 \ll 1$ and thus $\omega_0 t \ll 1$. The two inequalities $\omega_{21}t \ll 1$ and $\omega_0 t \ll 1$ are the conditions for applicability of the first-order approximation. Consequently, $P_{|1\rangle \to |1\rangle} = 1 - P_{|1\rangle - |2\rangle} \cong 1$.

(*b*) **Method 1:** Diagonalization of the Hamiltonian $\hat{H} = \hat{H}_0 + \hat{H}'$.

First, we express the Hamiltonian explicitly in the basis of the eigenstates $|1\rangle$ and $|2\rangle$:

$$\hat{H} = \begin{pmatrix} E_1 & \hbar\omega_0 \\ \hbar\omega_0 & E_2 - \hbar\omega_{21} \end{pmatrix} = \begin{pmatrix} E_1 & \hbar\omega_0 \\ \hbar\omega_0 & E_1 \end{pmatrix} \qquad (10.17.4)$$

where we used the relation $E_2 - E_1 = \hbar\omega_2$. The eigenvalue equation is $\hat{H}v = \lambda v$, then $(E_1 - \lambda)^2 - (\hbar\omega_0)^2 = 0$ and $\lambda_{1,2} = E_1 \pm \hbar\hat{\omega}_0$. For two eigenvectors, v_1 and v_2, we obtain

$$v_1 = \frac{1}{\sqrt{2}}\begin{pmatrix} 1 \\ 1 \end{pmatrix} = \frac{1}{\sqrt{2}}(|1\rangle + |2\rangle) \qquad v_2 = \frac{1}{\sqrt{2}}\begin{pmatrix} 1 \\ -1 \end{pmatrix} = \frac{1}{\sqrt{2}}(|1\rangle - |2\rangle) \qquad (10.17.5)$$

So, for the state $|\psi(t)\rangle$ we have

$$|\psi(t)\rangle = a_1 e^{-i\lambda_1 t/\hbar}|v_1\rangle + a_2 e^{-i\lambda_2 t}|v_2\rangle \qquad (10.17.6)$$

Using the initial condition $|\psi(t = 0)\rangle = |1\rangle$ we get $a_1 = a_2 = 1/\sqrt{2}$, and eventually

$$|\psi(t)\rangle = \frac{1}{2}(e^{-i(E_1 + \hbar\omega_0)t/\hbar} + e^{-i(E_1 - \hbar\omega_0)t/\hbar})|1\rangle + \frac{1}{2}(e^{-i(E_1 + \hbar\omega_0)t/\hbar} - e^{-i(E_1 - \hbar\omega_0)t/\hbar})|2\rangle$$

$$= e^{-iE_1 t/\hbar}[\cos(\omega_0 t)|1\rangle - \sin(\omega_0 t)|2\rangle] \qquad (10.17.7)$$

Method 2: Explicit solution of the Schrödinger equation.
We write $|\psi(t)\rangle$ in the form

$$|\psi(t)\rangle = C_1(t)\, e^{-iE_1 t/\hbar}\, |1\rangle + C_2(t)\, e^{-iE_2 t/\hbar}\, |2\rangle \tag{10.17.8}$$

Substituting this into the Schrödinger equation $i\hbar \dfrac{\partial\,|\psi(t)\rangle}{\partial t} = (\hat{H}_0 + \hat{H}')\,|\psi(t)\rangle$, we obtain

$$i\hbar\left[\dot{C}_1(t)e^{-iE_1 t/\hbar} + \frac{iE_1}{\hbar}C_1(t)e^{-iE_1 t/\hbar}\right]|1\rangle + i\hbar\left[\dot{C}_2(t)e^{-iE_2 t/\hbar} - \frac{iE_2}{\hbar}C_2 t\, e^{-iE_1 t/\hbar}\right]|2\rangle$$

$$= (\hat{H}_0 + \hat{H}')[C_1(t)e^{-iE_1 t/\hbar}|1\rangle + C_2(t)e^{-iE_2 t/\hbar}|2\rangle] \tag{10.17.9}$$

Multiplying Eq. (10.17.9) by $\langle 1|$ yields

$$i\hbar\left[\dot{C}_1(t)e^{-iE_1 t/\hbar} - \frac{iE_1}{\hbar}C_1(t)e^{-iE_1 t/\hbar}\right] = C_1(t)e^{-iE_1 t/\hbar}(\langle 1|\hat{H}_0|1\rangle + \langle 1|\hat{H}'|1\rangle)$$

$$+ C_2(t)e^{-iE_2 t/\hbar}(\langle 1|\hat{H}_0|2\rangle + \langle 1|\hat{H}'|2\rangle)$$

$$= E_1 C_1(t)e^{-iE_1 t/\hbar} + C_2(t)\hbar\omega_0\, e^{-iE_2 t/\hbar} \tag{10.17.10}$$

which leads to

$$i\hbar\,\dot{C}_1(t) = e^{-i\omega_{21}t}C_2(t)\hbar\omega_0 \tag{10.17.11}$$

where $\omega_{21} = \dfrac{1}{\hbar}(E_2 - E_1)$. In the same way, multiplying Eq. (10.17.9) on the left by $\langle 2|$ results in

$$i\hbar\,\dot{C}_2(\psi) = C_1(t)e^{i\omega_{21}t}\hbar\omega_0 - C_2(t)\hbar\omega_{21} \tag{10.17.12}$$

Equations (10.17.11) and (10.17.12) give a system of differential equations with coefficients $C_1(t)$ and $C_2(t)$:

$$\begin{cases} i\hbar\,\dot{C}_1(t) = e^{-i\omega_{21}t}C_2(t)\hbar\omega_0 \\ i\hbar\,\dot{C}_2(t) = C_1(t)e^{i\omega_{21}t}\hbar\omega_0 - C_2(t)\hbar\omega_{21} \end{cases} \tag{10.17.13}$$

Extracting $C_2(t)$ from the first equation, $C_2(t) = \dfrac{i}{\omega_0}\dot{C}_1(t)e^{i\omega_{21}t}$, and differentiating:

$$\dot{C}_2(t) = \frac{i}{\omega_0}\left[\ddot{C}_1(t)e^{i\omega_{21}t} + i\omega_{21}\dot{C}_1(t)e^{i\omega_{21}t}\right] \tag{10.17.14}$$

Substituting these two expressions into the second equation in (10.17.13) we get

$$\ddot{C}_1(t) + \omega_0^2 C_1(t) = 0 \tag{10.17.15}$$

Using the initial condition $C_1(t = 0) = 0$, Eq. (10.17.15) gives $C_1(t) = \cos(\omega_0 t)$. Thus, we can calculate the coefficient $C_2(t)$ and find $C_2(t) = -i\sin(\omega_0 t)e^{i\omega_{21}t}$, so eventually,

$$|\psi(t)\rangle = e^{-iE_1 t/\hbar}[\cos(\omega_0 t)\,|1\rangle - i\sin(\omega_0 t)\,|2\rangle] \tag{10.17.16}$$

Note that the results of the two methods coincide.

(c) The probability of finding the system in state $|2\rangle$ is given by

$$P_{|1\rangle \to |2\rangle} = |\langle 2|\psi(t)\rangle|^2 = \sin^2(\omega_0 t) \tag{10.17.17}$$

Therefore, the approximation used in part (a) is correct when $\omega_0 t = 1$. The system will be in state $|2\rangle$ when $P = 0$ or $\omega_0 T = \pm\dfrac{\pi}{2} + \pi k$, $k \in N$. At times $T = \pm\dfrac{\pi}{2\omega_0} + \dfrac{\pi k}{\omega_0}$, $k \in N$, the system will be in state $|2\rangle$.

SUPPLEMENTARY PROBLEMS

10.18. Repeat Problem 10.3, using the raising and upper operators, $\hat{a}$ and $\hat{a}^\dagger$, respectively.

10.19. Consider a one-dimensional oscillator with a linear perturbation λx. For the ground state energy, compute the first two orders of the perturbation (use dimensionless units).

Ans. $E(\lambda) = 1 - \lambda^2/4$

10.20. A small perturbation, $W = ax^4$, is applied to a harmonic oscillator with force constant k and reduced mass m. Compute the first-order correction to the eigenenergies and first nonvanishing correction to the wavefunctions.

Ans. $E_n^{(1)} = \dfrac{3a}{2\alpha^2}\left(n^2 + n + \dfrac{1}{2}\right)$; $\phi_0 = \phi_0^{(0)} - \dfrac{3\sqrt{2}a}{4\hbar\omega\alpha^2}\phi_2^{(0)} + \cdots$

10.21. Consider the Hamiltonian $\hat{H} = \hat{H}_0 + \hat{V}(x, y)$, where $\hat{H}_0 = m\omega^2(\hat{x}^2 + \hat{y}^2)/2$ is the free Hamiltonian, and $\hat{V}(x, y) = \lambda m\omega^2 \hat{x}\hat{y}$ is a perturbation. (*a*) Find the exact ground state. (*b*) Using the second-order perturbation, calculate the ground state energy.

Ans.   (*a*) $\psi_0(x, y) = \sqrt{\dfrac{m\omega}{\pi\hbar}}(1 - \lambda^2)^{1/8} \exp\left(-\dfrac{m\omega(\sqrt{1-\lambda} + \sqrt{1+\lambda})x^2}{4\hbar}\right)$

$$\times \exp\left(-\frac{m\omega(\sqrt{1-\lambda} + \sqrt{1+\lambda})y^2}{4\hbar}\right)\exp\left(\frac{m\omega(\sqrt{1-\lambda} - \sqrt{1+\lambda})xy}{2\hbar}\right)$$

(*b*) $E_0^{(2)} = -\dfrac{\lambda^2\hbar\omega}{8}$, where the exact result is $E_0 = \dfrac{1}{2}\hbar\omega(\sqrt{1-\lambda} + \sqrt{1+\lambda}) \cong \hbar\omega - \dfrac{\lambda^2\hbar\omega}{8} + \cdots$

10.22. A particle with mass m and electric charge e moves in a one-dimensional harmonic potential, subjected to a weak electric field $\mathcal{E}$. (*a*) Calculate the corrections to the energy levels and to the eigenstates of the first nonvanishing order. (*b*) Calculate the electric dipole moment of the particle. (*c*) Solve parts (*a*) and (*b*) exactly, and compare the results to the approximate solutions.

Ans.   (*a*) $\Delta E = -\dfrac{(\mathcal{E}e)^2}{2m\omega^2}$; $|\psi_n\rangle = |\phi_n\rangle - \mathcal{E}e\sqrt{\dfrac{\hbar}{m\omega^3}}\left[\sqrt{\dfrac{n}{2}}\,|\phi_{n-1}\rangle - \sqrt{\dfrac{n+1}{2}}\,|\phi_{n+1}\rangle\right]$; (*b*) $P = \dfrac{\mathcal{E}e^2}{2m\omega^2}$

10.23. A plane rotator with electric dipole moment **d** and an inertia moment I is subject to a uniform electric field $\mathcal{E}$ that lies in the plane of rotation. Calculate the first nonvanishing corrections to the energy levels of the rotator. Consider the field $\mathcal{E}$ as a small perturbation. Hint: The perturbation is $W = -\mathbf{d} \cdot \mathcal{E}$.

Ans. $E_n = E_n^{(0)} + E_n^{(2)} = \dfrac{\hbar^2 n^2}{2I} + \dfrac{I(\mathcal{E}d)^2}{\hbar^2(4m^2 - 1)}$

10.24. Consider the classical Hamiltonian

$$H = \frac{P_1^2}{2m} + \frac{P_2^2}{2m} + \frac{1}{2}m\omega_0^2(x_1^2 + x_2^2) + V_{rel}(x_1 - x_2) \tag{10.24.1}$$

where $V_{rel}(x_1 - x_2) = \dfrac{1}{4}m\omega_1^2(x_1 - x_2)^2$. (*a*) Find the exact energy of this system. (*b*) Assuming that $W = V_{rel}(x_1 - x_2)$, use the second-order perturbation to compute the energy of the ground state.

Ans.   (*a*) $E_{Nn} = (N + 1/2)\hbar\omega_0 + (n + 1/2)\hbar\sqrt{\omega_0^2 + \omega_1^2}$ ($N, n = 0, 1, \ldots$), where

$$E_{00} = \frac{1}{2}\hbar\omega_0 + \frac{1}{2}\hbar\sqrt{\omega_0^2 + \omega_1^2} \cong \hbar\omega_0 + \frac{\hbar}{4}\frac{\omega_1^2}{\omega_0} - \frac{\hbar}{16}\frac{\omega_1^4}{\omega_0^3} + \cdots; \ (b)\ E_0 = \hbar\omega_0 + \frac{\hbar}{4}\frac{\omega_1^2}{\omega_0} - \frac{\hbar}{16}\frac{\omega_1^4}{\omega_0^3}$$

10.25. In the first approximation, compute the energy of the ground state of a two-electron atom or ion having a nuclear charge Z. Consider the interaction between the electrons as a small perturbation.

Ans. $E \approx E^{(0)} + E^{(1)} = -\left(Z^2 - \dfrac{5}{8}Z\right)\dfrac{me^4}{\hbar^2}$

10.26. Consider a quantum system that has an orthonormal basis of three unperturbed states. The perturbed Hamiltonian is represented by the matrix:

$$\hat{H} = \begin{pmatrix} E_1 & 0 & a \\ 0 & E_1 & b \\ a^* & b^* & E_2 \end{pmatrix}$$ (10.26.1)

where $E_2 > E_1$. Use a second-order nondegenerate perturbation to find the perturbed eigenvalues. Diagonalize the matrix and find the exact eigenvalues. Repeat using a second-order degenerate perturbation. Explain the inconsistencies arising from the different approaches.

Ans. Denote $|1\rangle = \begin{pmatrix} 1 \\ 0 \\ 0 \end{pmatrix}, |2\rangle = \begin{pmatrix} 0 \\ 1 \\ 0 \end{pmatrix}$, and $|3\rangle = \begin{pmatrix} 0 \\ 0 \\ 1 \end{pmatrix}$. Using a nondegenerate perturbation, $\Delta E^{(1)} = 0$,

$$\Delta E^{(2)}_{|1\rangle} = \frac{|a|^2}{E_2 - E_1} \qquad \Delta E^{(2)}_{|2\rangle} = \frac{|b|^2}{E_2 - E_1} \qquad \Delta E^{(2)}_{|3\rangle} = -\frac{|a|^2 + |b|^2}{E_2 - E_1}$$ (10.26.2)

The exact solution is

$$\Delta E_{|1\rangle} = 0 \qquad \Delta E_{|2\rangle} = \frac{|a|^2 + |b|^2}{E_2 - E_1} \qquad \Delta E_{|3\rangle} = -\frac{|a|^2 + |b|^2}{E_2 - E_1}$$ (10.26.3)

Using a degenerate perturbation, $\Delta E_{|1\rangle} = 0$; $\Delta E_{|2\rangle} = \dfrac{|a|^2 + |b|^2}{E_2 - E_1}$

10.27. Consider a molecule consisting of three atoms arranged on a line; see Fig. 10.6.

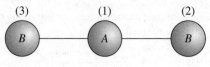

Fig. 10.6

If an electron is in the vicinity of atom A, its energy is E_1; if it is in the vicinity of either of the atoms B, its energy is E_2 ($E_1 < E_2$). (a) To the first approximation, assume that there is no transition of an electron between atoms. Find the Hamiltonian $\hat{H}_0$. (b) A small perturbation is applied and the electron can move from one atom to another. The energy associated with a transition is a, where $a \ll E_1$. To the first order, compute the corrections to the energies and eigenstates (for E_1 apply to the second order). (c) Suppose that at $t = 0$ the electron is near atom B. Using the approximation of part (b), calculate the probability that at $t > 0$ the electron will be in the vicinity of atom A. (d) Find the exact eigenenergies of the electron. (e) An electron can now move from an atom B to another atom B, and the energy associated with the transition is b, where $b \ll a$. Using perturbation theory, find the energies and eigenstates of $\hat{H}$ when the unperturbed Hamiltonian is $\hat{H}_0 + \hat{W}$, where $\hat{W}$ is the perturbation introduced in part (b).

Ans. (a) $\hat{H}_0 = \begin{pmatrix} E_1 & 0 & 0 \\ 0 & E_2 & 0 \\ 0 & 0 & E_2 \end{pmatrix}$; (b) $\hat{W} = \begin{pmatrix} 0 & a & a \\ a & 0 & 0 \\ a & 0 & 0 \end{pmatrix}$; $E_1 = E_1^{(0)} + \langle 1|\hat{W}|1\rangle + 2\dfrac{|\langle 2|\hat{W}|1\rangle|^2}{E_2 - E_1} = E_1^{(0)} + \dfrac{2a^2}{E_2 - E_1}$;

$$|\psi_1\rangle = |1\rangle - \frac{\langle 2|\hat{W}|1\rangle}{E_2 - E_1}|2\rangle - \frac{\langle 3|\hat{W}|1\rangle}{E_3 - E_1}|3\rangle = |1\rangle - \frac{a}{E_2 - E_1}(|2\rangle + |3\rangle) \text{ or } |\psi_1\rangle = \begin{pmatrix} 1 \\ -\dfrac{a}{E_2 - E_1} \\ -\dfrac{a}{E_2 - E_1} \end{pmatrix}. \text{ The}$$

states $|\psi_2\rangle$ and $|\psi_3\rangle$ are degenerate; therefore, to the first order, there are no corrections to the eigenstates.

(c) $P_{|2\rangle \to |1\rangle} = 0$; (d) $E_1 = E_3 = \frac{1}{2}\left(E_1^{(0)} + E_2^{(0)} \pm \sqrt{(E_1^{(0)} - E_2^{(0)})^2 - 8a^2}\right)$, $E_2 = E_2^{(0)}$; (e) $\tilde{E}_2 = E_2 - b$,

$$\tilde{E}_1 = \tilde{E}_3 = \frac{1}{2}\left(E_1 + E_2 + b \pm \sqrt{(E_1 - E_2 - b)^2 - 2a^2}\right)$$

10.28. In the first approximation, compute the shift in the energy level of the ground state of a hydrogen-like atom resulting from the fact that the nucleus is not a charge point. Regard the nucleus as a sphere of radius R throughout the volume of which the charge Ze is distributed evenly. Hint: The potential energy of an electron is the field of a nucleus that has an evenly distributed charge,

$$V(r) = \begin{cases} -\dfrac{Ze^2}{R}\left(\dfrac{3}{2} - \dfrac{1}{2}\dfrac{r^2}{R^2}\right) & \text{for } 0 \leq r \leq R \\[3mm] -\dfrac{Ze^2}{r} & \text{for } r \geq R \end{cases} \qquad (10.28.1)$$

Ans. $E_0 \approx E_0^{(0)} + E_0^{(1)} = E_0^{(0)}\left[1 - \dfrac{4}{5}\left(\dfrac{R}{a_0}\right)^2\right]$

10.29. Consider a harmonic oscillator described by

$$H = \frac{1}{2m} p_x^2 + \frac{1}{2} m\omega^2(t) x^2 \qquad (10.29.1)$$

where $\omega(t) = \omega_0 + \cos(at)\,\delta\omega$ and $\delta\omega \ll \omega_0$ (a is a constant). Assume that at $t = 0$ the system is in the ground state. Using perturbation theory, find the transition probability from the ground state to a final state f. You may use the result $\langle n | \hat{x}^2 | 0 \rangle = m\hbar\omega/\sqrt{2}$ for $n = 2$ and zero otherwise.

Ans. $P_{0 \to f}(t) \approx \dfrac{(\delta\omega)^2}{8\omega_0^2}\left[\dfrac{\sin(\omega_{fi} - a)t/2}{(\omega_{fi} - a)/2}\right](\sqrt{2}\,\delta_{a, 2\omega_0} + \delta_{a, 0})$

CHAPTER 11

Solution Methods in Quantum Mechanics—Part B

11.1 The Variational Method

The perturbation theory studied in Chap. 10 is not the only approximation method in quantum mechanics. In this section, we present another method applicable to conservative system. Consider a physical system with time-independent Hamiltonian $\hat{H}$. We assume for simplicity that the entire spectrum of $\hat{H}$ is discrete and nondegenerate:

$$(\hat{H} \mid \phi_n \rangle = E_n \mid \phi_n \rangle) \qquad n = 1,\ 2,\ 3,\dots \tag{11.1}$$

We denote by E_0 the smallest eigenvalue of $\hat{H}$ (that is, the smallest energy of the system). An arbitrary state $\mid \psi \rangle$ can be written in the form

$$\mid \psi \rangle = \sum_n c_n \mid \phi_n \rangle \tag{11.2}$$

Then

$$\langle \psi \mid \hat{H} \mid \psi \rangle = \sum_n \left| c_n \right|^2 E_n \geq E_0 \sum_n \left| c_n \right|^2 \tag{11.3}$$

On the other hand,

$$\langle \psi \mid \psi \rangle = \sum_n \left| c_n \right|^2 \tag{11.4}$$

Thus, we can conclude that for every ket,

$$\langle \hat{H} \rangle = \frac{\langle \psi \mid \hat{H} \mid \psi \rangle}{\langle \psi \mid \psi \rangle} \geq E_0 \tag{11.5}$$

Equation (11.5) is the basis of the *variational method*. A family of kets $\mid \psi\,(\alpha) \rangle$ called *trial kets,* is chosen. The mean value of $\hat{H}$ in the states $\mid \psi\,(\alpha) \rangle$ is calculated, and the expression $\langle \hat{H} \rangle(\alpha)$ is minimized with respect to the parameter α. The minimal value obtained is an approximation of the ground state energy E_0.

Equation (11.5) is actually a part of a more general result called the *Ritz theorem*: the mean value of the Hamiltonian $\hat{H}$ is stationary in the neighborhood of its discrete eigenvalues (see Problem 11.1).

The variational method can therefore be generalized and provide estimations for other energy levels besides the ground state. If the function $\langle \hat{H} \rangle(\alpha)$ obtained from the trial kets $\mid \psi\,(\alpha) \rangle$ has several extrema, they give approximate values of some of the energies E_n.

11.2 Semiclassical Approximation (The WKB Approximation)

Apart from the perturbation and variational methods described earlier, there is another method that is suitable for obtaining solutions to the one-dimensional Schrödinger equation. This is the so-called *semiclassical,* or *WKB approximation* (named after Wentzel, Kramers, and Brillouin). The WKB method can also be applied to three-dimensional problems if the potential is spherically symmetric and a radial differential equation can be separated.

The WKB method introduces an expansion in powers of $\hbar$ in which terms of order greater than $\hbar^2$ are neglected. Thus, one replaces the Schrödinger equation by its classical limit ($\hbar \to 0$). However, the method can be applied even in regions in which the classical interpretation is meaningless (regions inaccessible to classical particles).

Consider the Schrödinger equation in one dimension:

$$\frac{d^2\psi}{dx^2} + \frac{2m}{\hbar^2}[E - V(x)]\psi(x) = 0 \tag{11.6}$$

We consider only stationary states, and write the wavefunction in the form $\psi(x) = e^{iu(x)}$. We shall use the abbreviations

$$\begin{cases} k(x) = \dfrac{1}{\hbar}\sqrt{2m[E - V(x)]} & \text{for} \quad E > V(x) \\[2mm] k(x) = (-i)\chi(x) = \dfrac{-i}{\hbar}\sqrt{2m[V(x) - E]} & \text{for} \quad E < V(x) \end{cases} \tag{11.7}$$

Substituting $\psi(x)$ into Eq. (11.7) one finds that $u(x)$ satisfies the equation

$$i\frac{d^2u}{dx^2} - \left(\frac{du}{dx}\right)^2 + [k(x)]^2 = 0 \tag{11.8}$$

In the WKB approximation, we expand $u(x)$ in a power series of $\hbar$:

$$u(x) = u_0 + \frac{\hbar}{i}u_1 + \left(\frac{\hbar}{i}\right)^2 u_2 + \cdots \tag{11.9}$$

and we consider only u_0 and u_1. Then we obtain the approximate wavefunction according to the WKB method:

$$\psi(x) = \frac{C_1}{\sqrt{|k(x)|}}\exp\left\{i\int^x k(x')\,dx'\right\} + \frac{C_2}{\sqrt{|k(x)|}}\exp\left\{-i\int^x k(x')\,dx'\right\} \tag{11.10}$$

A region in which $E > V(x)$ is called a *classically allowed region* of motion, while a region in which $E < V(x)$ is called *classically inaccessible*. The points in the boundary between these two kinds of regions are called *turning points* [where $E = V(x)$].

Applicability Condition

The WKB approximation is based on the condition

$$\frac{1}{2}|k'(x)| \ll |k^2(x)| \tag{11.11}$$

This condition can be expressed in a number of equivalent forms. Using the de Broglie wavelength $\lambda = \dfrac{2\pi}{k}$ we can write Eq. (11.11) as

$$\frac{\lambda}{4\pi}\left|\frac{dk}{dx}\right| \ll k \tag{11.12}$$

Adjacent to the turning points, for which $k(x_0) = 0$, we have

$$k \approx \frac{dk}{dx}\bigg|_{x_0} (x - x_0)$$

(11.13)

Thus, the semiclassical approximation is applicable for a distance from the turning point satisfying the condition

$$|x - x_0| \gg \frac{\lambda}{4\pi}$$

(11.14)

The Connection Formulas

Consider a turning point. Assume that, except in its immediate neighborhood, the WKB approximation is applicable. The match between the WKB approximations on each side of the turning points depends on whether the classical region is to the left of the point (Fig. 11.1) or to the right of it (Fig. 11.2).

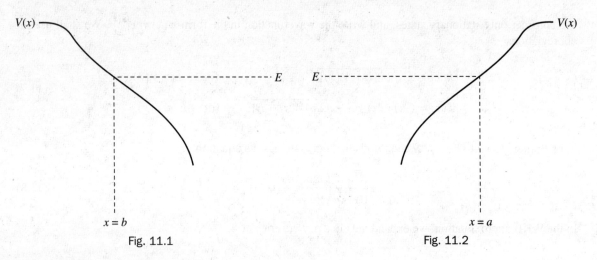

Fig. 11.1   Fig. 11.2

In the first case we have, $x > b$:

$$\psi_1(x) = \frac{A_1}{\sqrt{k}} \cos\left(\int_b^x k(x')\,dx' - B_1\pi \right)$$

(11.15)

while in the second case, for $x < a$,

$$\psi_2(x) = \frac{A_2}{k} \cos\left(\int_x^a k(x')\,dx' - B_2\pi \right)$$

(11.16)

Application to the Bound State

The WKB approximation can be applied to derive an equation for the energies of a bound state. Using the connection formulas in each side of the potential well one obtains (see Problem 11.13)

$$\int_a^b k(x)\,dx = \left(n + \frac{1}{2} \right)\pi \qquad n = 0, 1, 2, \ldots$$

(11.17)

which may be written

$$\oint p(x)\,dx = 2\pi\hbar\left(n + \frac{1}{2} \right) \qquad n = 0, 1, 2, \ldots$$

(11.18)

This equation is called the *Bohr-Sommerfeld quantization rule*.

Barrier Potential

If one considers a potential barrier of the form $V(x)$ between $x = a$ and $x = b$ and a particle with energy E, the transmission coefficient in the WKB approximation is given by

$$T \approx \exp\left[-\frac{2}{\hbar} \int_a^b \sqrt{2m[V(x) - E]}\, dx\right] \tag{11.19}$$

SOLVED PROBLEMS

11.1. We define $\langle \hat{H} \rangle$ by $\langle \hat{H} \rangle = \dfrac{\langle \psi | \hat{H} | \psi \rangle}{\langle \psi | \psi \rangle}$, where $|\psi\rangle$ is any vector in the state space. Show that $\langle \hat{H} \rangle$ is stationary (that is, $\delta \langle \hat{H} \rangle = 0$), if, and only if, $|\psi\rangle$ is an eigenvector of $\hat{H}$ with eigenvalue $\langle \hat{H} \rangle$.

SOLUTION

We write the equation $\langle \hat{H} \rangle = \langle \psi | \hat{H} | \psi \rangle / \langle \psi | \psi \rangle$ in the more convenient form $\langle \psi | \psi \rangle \langle \hat{H} \rangle = \langle \psi | \hat{H} | \psi \rangle$. Differentiating both sides gives

$$((\langle \delta\psi | \psi \rangle + \langle \psi | \delta\psi \rangle)\langle \hat{H} \rangle + \langle \psi | \psi \rangle \delta \langle \hat{H} \rangle = \langle \delta\psi | \hat{H} | \psi \rangle + \langle \psi | \hat{H} | \delta\psi \rangle \tag{11.1.1}$$

As $\langle \hat{H} \rangle$ is a scalar value, we may rewrite Eq. (11.1.1) as

$$\langle \psi | \psi \rangle \delta \langle \hat{H} \rangle = \langle \delta\psi | (\hat{H} - \langle \hat{H} \rangle) | \psi \rangle + \langle \psi | (\hat{H} - \langle \hat{H} \rangle) | \delta\psi \rangle \tag{11.1.2}$$

Defining $|\phi\rangle = (\hat{H} - \langle \hat{H} \rangle) | \psi \rangle$, we may reformulate Eq. (11.1.2) in the simpler form

$$\langle \psi | \psi \rangle \delta \langle \hat{H} \rangle = \langle \delta\psi | \phi \rangle + \langle \phi | \delta\psi \rangle \tag{11.1.3}$$

Equation (11.1.3) holds for any $|\delta\psi\rangle$, in particular for $|\delta\psi\rangle = |\phi\rangle \delta\lambda$, where $\delta\lambda$ is an infinitesimally small real number. Substituting into Eq. (11.1.3) we arrive at

$$\langle \psi | \psi \rangle \delta \langle \hat{H} \rangle = 2\delta\lambda \langle \phi | \phi \rangle \tag{11.1.4}$$

Now, if $\delta \langle \hat{H} \rangle = 0$, then according to Eq. (11.1.4) we must have $|\phi\rangle = 0$, so that $\hat{H} | \psi \rangle = \langle \hat{H} \rangle | \psi \rangle$, and we see that $|\psi\rangle$ is an eigenvector of $\hat{H}$ with eigenvalue $\langle \hat{H} \rangle$. On the other hand, if $\hat{H} | \psi \rangle = \langle \hat{H} \rangle | \psi \rangle$, then according to Eq. (11.1.4) we must have $\delta \langle \hat{H} \rangle = 0$, therefore $\langle \hat{H} \rangle$ is stationary.

11.2. Consider a one-dimensional harmonic oscillator:

$$\hat{H} = -\frac{\hbar^2}{2m}\frac{d^2}{dx^2} + \frac{1}{2}m\omega^2 x^2 \tag{11.2.1}$$

(a) For the one-parameter family of wavefunctions $\psi_\alpha(x) = e^{-\alpha x^2}$ ($\alpha > 0$), find a wavefunction that minimizes $\langle \hat{H} \rangle$. What is the value of $\langle \hat{H} \rangle_{min}$? (b) For another one-parameter family of wavefunctions $\psi_\beta(x) = xe^{-\beta x^2}$ ($\beta > 0$), find a wavefunction that minimizes $\langle \hat{H} \rangle$ and compute the value of $\langle \hat{H} \rangle_{min}$. (c) Repeat the same procedure for

$$\psi_\gamma(x) = \frac{1}{x^2 + \gamma} \qquad (\gamma > 0) \tag{11.2.2}$$

SOLUTION

(a) We begin by considering $\langle \hat{H} \rangle$:

$$\langle \hat{H} \rangle = \frac{\displaystyle\int_{-\infty}^{\infty} \psi_\alpha^*(x)\left[-\frac{\hbar^2}{2m}\frac{d^2}{dx^2} + \frac{1}{2}m\omega^2 x^2\right]\psi_\alpha(x)\, dx}{\displaystyle\int_{-\infty}^{\infty} \psi_\alpha^*(x)\psi_\alpha(x)\, dx} = \frac{\hbar^2}{2m}\alpha + \frac{1}{8}m\omega^2\frac{1}{\alpha} \tag{11.2.3}$$

We differentiate $\langle \hat{H} \rangle$ with respect to α:

$$\frac{d\langle \hat{H} \rangle}{d\alpha} = \frac{\hbar^2}{2m} - \frac{1}{8}m\omega^2 \frac{1}{\alpha^2} \tag{11.2.4}$$

From the condition $\left. \dfrac{d\langle \hat{H} \rangle}{d\alpha} \right|_{\alpha = \alpha_0} = 0$, we have $\dfrac{\hbar^2}{2m} - \dfrac{1}{8}m\omega^2 \dfrac{1}{\alpha_0^2} = 0$ and $\alpha_0 = \dfrac{m}{2}\dfrac{\omega}{\hbar}$; thus, α_0 gives the mini-

mum value of $\langle \hat{H} \rangle$ (as can be easily verified). The wavefunction that minimizes $\langle \hat{H} \rangle$ is $\psi_{\alpha_0}(x) = e^{-m\omega x^2/2\hbar}$, and

$$\langle \hat{H} \rangle_{\min} = \frac{\hbar^2}{2m}\alpha_0 + \frac{1}{8}m\omega^2 \frac{1}{\alpha_0} = \frac{1}{2}\hbar\omega \tag{11.2.5}$$

Thus, $\langle \hat{H} \rangle_{\min}$ coincides with the energy of the $n = 0$ level of a one-dimensional harmonic oscillator. Note that the family of functions we are studying coincides with the ground-state wavefunction of the harmonic oscillator.

(b) We proceed with the same method as in part (a):

$$\langle \hat{H} \rangle = \frac{\displaystyle\int_{-\infty}^{\infty} \psi_\beta^*(x)\left[-\frac{\hbar^2}{2m}\frac{d^2}{dx^2} + \frac{1}{2}m\omega^2 x^2\right]\psi_\beta(x)\,dx}{\displaystyle\int_{-\infty}^{\infty} \psi_\beta^*(x)\,\psi_\beta(x)\,dx} = \frac{3\hbar^2}{2m}\beta + \frac{3m\omega^2}{8}\frac{1}{\beta} \tag{11.2.6}$$

and

$$\frac{d\langle \hat{H} \rangle}{d\beta} = \frac{3\hbar^2}{2m} - \frac{3m\omega^2}{8}\frac{1}{\beta^2} = 0 \tag{11.2.7}$$

We obtain $\beta_0 = \dfrac{1}{2}\dfrac{m\omega}{\hbar}$ and $\psi_{\beta_0}(x) = xe^{-m\omega x^2/2\hbar}$; so, $\langle \hat{H} \rangle_{\min} = \dfrac{3}{2}\hbar\omega$. Thus, $\langle \hat{H} \rangle_{\min}$ equals the energy of the $n = 1$ level of the one-dimensional harmonic oscillator. (Try to explain this result.)

(c) Applying the procedure of parts (a) and (b), we obtain

$$\langle \hat{H} \rangle = \frac{\displaystyle\int_{-\infty}^{\infty} \psi_\gamma^*(x)\left[-\frac{\hbar^2}{2m}\frac{d^2}{dx^2} + \frac{1}{2}m\omega^2 x^2\right]\psi_\gamma(x)\,dx}{\displaystyle\int_{-\infty}^{\infty} \psi_\gamma^*(x)\,\psi_\gamma(x)\,dx} = \frac{\hbar^2}{2m}\frac{1}{\gamma} + \frac{1}{2}m\omega^2\gamma \tag{11.2.8}$$

and

$$\psi_{\gamma_0}(x) = \frac{1}{x^2 + \hbar^2/\sqrt{2}m\omega} \qquad \gamma_0 = \frac{1}{\sqrt{2}}\frac{\hbar}{m\omega} \tag{11.2.9}$$

hence, $\langle \hat{H} \rangle_{\min} = \sqrt{2}\dfrac{1}{2}\hbar\omega$. We see that $\langle \hat{H} \rangle_{\min}$ is equal to $\sqrt{2}$ times the ground-state energy.

11.3. (a) Using the variational method, estimate the ground-state energy of an atom of hydrogen. Choose as trial functions the spherically symmetrical functions $\phi_\alpha(r)$ whose r-dependence is given by

$$\phi_\alpha(r) = \begin{cases} C\left(1 - \dfrac{r}{\alpha}\right) & \text{for } r \leq \alpha \\ 0 & \text{for } r > \alpha \end{cases} \tag{11.3.1}$$

where C is a normalization constant and α is the variational parameter. (b) Find the extremum value of α. Compare this value with the Bohr radius a_0.

SOLUTION

(*a*) First we compute the normalization constant. This gives $C^2 = 15/\pi\alpha^3$. The kinetic energy is given by

$$\langle E_k \rangle = -\frac{2\pi\hbar^2}{2m} \int_0^\alpha r^2 \phi_\alpha(r) \left[\frac{1}{r} \frac{d^2(r\phi_\alpha)}{dr^2} \right] dr \tag{11.3.2}$$

Integration by parts gives

$$\langle E_k \rangle = -\frac{\pi\hbar^2}{m} \left(r\phi_\alpha(r) \frac{d(r\phi_\alpha)}{dr} \right) \Big|_0^\alpha + \frac{\pi\hbar^2}{m} \int_0^\alpha \left[\frac{d}{dr}(r\phi_\alpha(r)) \right]^2 dr \tag{11.3.3}$$

But since $(r\phi_\alpha(r))|_{r=0} = (r\phi_\alpha(r))|_{r=\alpha} = 0$, the first term vanishes and we have

$$\langle E_k \rangle = \frac{\pi\hbar^2}{m} \int_0^\alpha \left[\frac{d}{dr}(r\phi_\alpha(r)) \right]^2 dr = \frac{15\hbar^2}{2m} \alpha^{-3} \int_0^\alpha \left(1 - \frac{2r}{\alpha}\right)^2 dr$$

$$= \frac{15\hbar^2}{m} \alpha^{-3} \left[\alpha - 2\alpha + \frac{4}{3}\alpha \right] = \frac{5\hbar^2}{m} \frac{1}{\alpha^2} \tag{11.3.4}$$

The potential energy is

$$\langle V \rangle = 2\pi \int_0^\infty r^2 \phi_\alpha(r) V(r) \phi_\alpha(r)\, dr = 2\pi k e^2 \int_0^\alpha r\, |\phi_\alpha(r)|^2\, dr$$

$$= -30\, ke^2 \int_0^\alpha \left(r - \frac{2r^2}{\alpha} + \frac{r^3}{\alpha^2} \right) dr = -\frac{15ke^2}{6} \frac{1}{\alpha} \tag{11.3.5}$$

Thus, the total energy as a function of α is given by

$$\langle E(\alpha) \rangle = \langle E_k \rangle + \langle V \rangle = 5\left(\frac{\hbar^2}{m}\frac{1}{\alpha^2} - \frac{ke^2}{2}\frac{1}{\alpha} \right) \tag{11.3.6}$$

(*b*) The extremum condition $d\langle E \rangle/d\alpha = 0$ leads to

$$\frac{2\hbar^2}{m} \alpha_0^{-3} = \frac{1}{2} ke^2 \alpha_0^{-2} \Rightarrow \alpha_0 = \frac{4\hbar^2}{kme^2} \tag{11.3.7}$$

Note that the Bohr radius is $a_0 = \hbar^2/kme^2$; thus, $\alpha_0 = 4a_0$.

11.4. (*a*) Write the Schrödinger equation for the helium atom. What are the solutions for the ground state if one neglects the interaction between the two electrons? (*b*) Assume that the electrons perform an electric screening of each other and define Z as a variational parameter. Use the variation method to find $\langle \hat{H} \rangle$ and the screening charge.

SOLUTION

(*a*) We begin by considering the classical Hamiltonian of the helium atom:

$$H = \frac{p_1^2}{2m} + \frac{p_2^2}{2m} - Ze^2\left(\frac{1}{r_1} + \frac{1}{r_2}\right) + \frac{e^2}{r_{12}} \tag{11.4.1}$$

where $r_{12} = |r_1 - r_2|$. We transform the Hamiltonian to units in which $e = \hbar = m = 1$. In these units the Schrödinger equation becomes

$$\left[-\frac{1}{2}\nabla_1^2 - \frac{1}{2}\nabla_2^2 - Z\left(\frac{1}{r_1} + \frac{1}{r_2}\right) + \frac{1}{r_{12}} \right] \psi(r_1, r_2) = E\psi(r_1, r_2) \tag{11.4.2}$$

If one neglects the term e^2/r_{12} (the interaction term), the solutions are obtained by separation of variables:

$$\psi_0(r_1, r_2) = u_1(r_1) u_2(r_2) = \frac{Z^{3/2}}{\pi^{1/2}} e^{-Zr_1} \frac{Z^{3/2}}{\pi^{1/2}} e^{-Zr_2} = \frac{Z^3}{\pi} e^{-Z(r_1+r_2)} \qquad (11.4.3)$$

Note that the factors $\dfrac{Z^{3/2}}{\pi^{1/2}} e^{-Z\tau_1}$ and $\dfrac{Z^{3/2}}{\pi^{1/2}} e^{-Z\tau_2}$ are the ground-state functions of a hydrogen-like atom.

(b) In the presence of another electron, each of the electrons is influenced by a decreased charge from the nucleus. We define $Z_{\text{eff}} = Z - \sigma$, where σ is the screening charge. We choose the trial function to be

$$\psi_\sigma(r_1, r_2) = \frac{(Z - \sigma)^3}{\pi} \exp[-(Z - \sigma)(r_1 + r_2)] \qquad (11.4.4)$$

Since

$$\hat{H}\psi_\sigma = \left[-(Z - \sigma)^2 - \frac{\sigma}{r_1} - \frac{\sigma}{r_2} + \frac{1}{r_{12}} \right] \psi_\sigma \qquad (11.4.5)$$

then

$$\langle \hat{H} \rangle = \frac{\displaystyle\iint \psi_\sigma^* \hat{H} \psi_\sigma \, d^3r_1 \, d^3r_2}{\displaystyle\iint \psi_\sigma^* \psi_\sigma \, d^3r_1 \, d^3r_2} = \iint \left[-(Z - \sigma)^2 - \frac{\sigma}{r_1} - \frac{\sigma}{r_2} + \frac{1}{r_{12}} \right] \psi_\sigma^2 \, d^3r_1 \, d^3r_2$$

$$= -(Z - \sigma)^2 - 2\frac{(Z - \sigma)^3}{\pi} \int_0^\infty \frac{\sigma}{r} 4\pi r^2 e^{-(Z-\sigma)r} \, dr$$

$$+ \frac{(Z - \sigma)^6}{\pi^2} \iint \frac{e^{-2(Z-\sigma)(r_1+r_2)}}{r_{12}} \, d^3r_1 \, d^3r_2 \qquad (11.4.6)$$

or,

$$\langle \hat{H} \rangle = -(Z - \sigma)^2 - \frac{2(Z - \sigma)^3}{\pi} \frac{\pi\sigma}{(Z - \sigma)^2} + \frac{(Z - \sigma)^6}{\pi^2} \iint \frac{e^{-2(Z-\sigma)(r_1+r_2)}}{r_{12}} \, d^3r_1 \, d^3r_2 \qquad (11.4.7)$$

We solve the last integral using the expansion of $1/r_{12}$ by Legendre polynomials (see the Mathematical Appendix):

$$\frac{1}{r_{12}} = \begin{cases} \dfrac{1}{r_1} \displaystyle\sum_{n=0}^{\infty} \left(\dfrac{r_1}{r_2} \right)^n P_n(\cos\theta) & 0 \leq r_1 \leq r_2 \\[4mm] \dfrac{1}{r_1} \displaystyle\sum_{n=0}^{\infty} \left(\dfrac{r_2}{r_1} \right)^n P_n(\cos\theta) & r_2 \leq r_1 < \infty \end{cases} \qquad (11.4.8)$$

The only terms that contribute to the integral are the ones with $n = 0$ (since the exponent that enters the integral depends only on the values of r_1 and r_2, and not on the angle θ); thus,

$$\iint \frac{e^{-2(Z-\sigma)(r_1+r_2)}}{r_{12}} \, d^3r_1 \, d^3r_2 = \int e^{-2(Z-\sigma)r_2} \left[4\pi \left(\frac{1}{r_2} \int_0^{r_2} r_1^2 e^{-2(Z-\sigma)r_1} \, dr_1 + \int_{r_2}^{\infty} r_1 e^{-2(Z-\sigma)r_2} \, dr_1 \right) \right] d^3r_2$$

$$= \frac{5\pi^2}{8(Z - \sigma)^5} \qquad (11.4.9)$$

Thus, the expression for $\langle \hat{H} \rangle$ is

$$\langle \hat{H} \rangle = -(Z - \sigma)^2 - 2(Z - \sigma)\sigma + \frac{5}{8}(Z - \sigma) \qquad (11.4.10)$$

Using the condition $\dfrac{d\langle \hat{H} \rangle}{d\sigma} = 0$, we find $\sigma_0 = \dfrac{5}{16}$, and then $Z_{\text{eff}} = \dfrac{27}{16}e$.

11.5. Consider a one-dimensional attraction potential $V(x)$ such that $V(x) < 0$ for all x. Using the variational principle, show that such a potential has at least one bound state.

SOLUTION

For a particle moving in this potential we may choose the following trial wavefunction:

$$\psi = \sqrt[4]{\frac{2a}{\pi}} \exp(-ax^2) \qquad (11.5.1)$$

Note that the function is normalized to unity. Thus, for the ground-state energy we have

$$E_0 \leq \int_{-\infty}^{\infty} \psi^* \left(-\frac{\hbar^2}{2m}\frac{d^2}{dx^2} + V(x) \right) \psi \, dx \qquad (11.5.2)$$

Since $V(x) < 0$ for all x, it remains to prove that $E_0 < 0$. Substituting the trial function, we find

$$E_0 \leq \sqrt{\frac{2a}{\pi}} \int_{-\infty}^{\infty} \exp(-ax^2) \left(-\frac{\hbar^2}{2m}\frac{d^2}{dx^2} + V(x) \right) \exp(-ax^2)\, dx$$

$$= \sqrt{\frac{2a}{\pi}} \int_{-\infty}^{\infty} \left[\exp(-ax^2) \left(-\frac{\hbar^2}{2m}\frac{d^2}{dx^2} \right) \exp(-ax^2) + V(x)\exp(-2ax^2) \right] dx$$

$$= \sqrt{\frac{2a}{\pi}} \int_{-\infty}^{\infty} \left[\frac{a\hbar^2}{2m}[1 - 2ax^2]\exp(-2ax^2) + V(x)\exp(-2ax^2) \right] dx$$

$$= \frac{a\hbar^2}{2m} - \frac{a\hbar^2}{2m}\sqrt{\frac{2a}{\pi}} \int_{-\infty}^{\infty} 2ax^2 \exp(-2ax^2)\, dx + \sqrt{\frac{2a}{\pi}} \int_{-\infty}^{\infty} V(x)\exp(-2ax^2)\, dx \qquad (11.5.3)$$

We define

$$E_0' = \frac{a\hbar^2}{2m} + \sqrt{\frac{2a}{\pi}} \int_{-\infty}^{\infty} V(x)\exp(-2ax^2)\, dx \qquad (11.5.4)$$

Thus, since the integral $\sqrt{\dfrac{2a}{\pi}}\displaystyle\int_{-\infty}^{\infty} 2ax^2 \exp(-2ax^2)\, dx$ has a positive value, $E_0 < E_0'$. Consider now the minimum value of E_0':

$$\frac{\partial E_0'}{\partial a} = \frac{\hbar^2}{2m} + \sqrt{\frac{1}{2a\pi}} \int_{-\infty}^{\infty} V(x)\exp(-2ax^2)\, dx - \sqrt{\frac{2a}{\pi}} \int_{-\infty}^{\infty} 2x^2 V(x)\exp(-2ax^2)\, dx = 0 \qquad (11.5.5)$$

Combining Eqs. (11.5.4) and (11.5.5) we obtain

$$(E_0')_{\text{min}} = \sqrt{\frac{2a}{\pi}} \int_{-\infty}^{\infty} \exp(-2ax^2)(1 + 4ax^2)V(x)\, dx \qquad (11.5.6)$$

since $\exp(-2ax^2)$ and $(1 + 4ax^2)$ are positive functions and $V(x)$ is a negative function for all x, $(E_0')_{\text{min}} < 0$ and so is E_0.

11.6. Consider a particle in a one-dimensional potential $V(x) = \lambda x^4$. Using the variational method, find an approximate value for the energy of the ground state. Compare it to the exact value $E_0 = 1.06 \dfrac{\hbar^2}{2m} k^{1/3}$, where $k = 2m\lambda/\hbar^2$. Choose as a trial function $\psi = (2\alpha/\pi)^{1/4} e^{-\alpha x^2}$.

SOLUTION

First, note that the trial function $\psi(x) = (2\alpha/\pi)^{1/4} e^{-\alpha x^2}$ is normalized to unity; that is, $\displaystyle\int_{-\infty}^{\infty} |\psi|^2\, dx = 1$. The Hamiltonian is $\hat{H} = -\dfrac{\hbar^2}{2m}\dfrac{d^2}{dx^2} + \lambda x^4$; thus,

$$\langle \hat{H} \rangle = \frac{\displaystyle\int_{-\infty}^{\infty} \psi^*(x)\left(-\frac{\hbar^2}{2m}\frac{d^2}{dx^2} + \lambda x^4\right)\psi(x)\, dx}{\displaystyle\int_{-\infty}^{\infty} \psi^*(x)\psi(x)\, dx} \tag{11.6.1}$$

The denominator equals one as [$\psi(x)$ is normalized]; thus,

$$\langle \hat{H} \rangle = \int_{-\infty}^{\infty} \left(\frac{2\alpha}{\pi}\right)^{1/4} e^{-\alpha x^2}\left(-\frac{\hbar^2}{2m}\right)\frac{d^2}{dx^2}\left(\frac{2\alpha}{\pi}\right)^{1/4} e^{-\alpha x^2}\, dx + \int_{-\infty}^{\infty}\left(\frac{2\alpha}{\pi}\right)^{1/4} e^{-\alpha x^2}\lambda x^4\left(\frac{2\alpha}{\pi}\right)^{1/4} e^{-\alpha x^2}\, dx$$

$$= -\frac{\hbar^2}{2m}\sqrt{\frac{2\alpha}{\pi}}\int_{-\infty}^{\infty} e^{-2\alpha x^2}\, 2\alpha\,[2\alpha x^2 - 1]\, dx + \lambda\sqrt{\frac{2\alpha}{\pi}}\int_{-\infty}^{\infty} e^{-2\alpha x^2} x^4\, dx$$

$$= -\frac{\hbar^2}{2m}\sqrt{\frac{2\alpha}{\pi}}\, 4\alpha^2 \int_{-\infty}^{\infty} e^{-2\alpha x^2} x^2\, dx + \frac{\hbar^2}{2m}\sqrt{\frac{2\alpha}{\pi}}\, 2\alpha \int_{-\infty}^{\infty} e^{-2\alpha x^2}\, dx + \lambda\sqrt{\frac{2\alpha}{\pi}}\int_{-\infty}^{\infty} e^{-2\alpha x^2} x^4\, dx \tag{11.6.2}$$

The first integral is

$$I_1 \equiv -\frac{\hbar^2}{2m}\sqrt{\frac{2\alpha}{\pi}}\, 4\alpha^2 \int_{-\infty}^{\infty} e^{-2\alpha x^2} x^2\, dx = -\frac{\hbar^2}{2m}\sqrt{\frac{2\alpha}{\pi}}\, 4\alpha^2 \frac{1}{4\alpha}\sqrt{\frac{\pi}{2\alpha}} = -\frac{\hbar^2\alpha}{2m} \tag{11.6.3}$$

The second integral is

$$I_2 \equiv \frac{\hbar^2}{2m}\sqrt{\frac{2\alpha}{\pi}}\, 2\alpha \int_{-\infty}^{\infty} e^{-2\alpha x^2}\, dx = \frac{\hbar^2}{2m}\sqrt{\frac{2\alpha}{\pi}}\, 2\alpha\sqrt{\frac{\pi}{2\alpha}} = \frac{\hbar^2\alpha}{m} \tag{11.6.4}$$

and the third integral is

$$I_3 = \lambda\sqrt{\frac{2\alpha}{\pi}}\int_{-\infty}^{\infty} e^{-2\alpha x^2} x^4\, dx = \lambda\sqrt{\frac{2\alpha}{\pi}}\frac{3}{4(2\alpha)^2}\sqrt{\frac{\pi}{2\alpha}} = \frac{3\lambda}{16\alpha^2} \tag{11.6.5}$$

Substituting these integrals, we obtain

$$\langle \hat{H} \rangle = -\frac{\hbar^2\alpha}{2m} + \frac{\hbar^2\alpha}{m} + \frac{3\lambda}{16\alpha^2} = \frac{\hbar^2}{2m}\alpha + \frac{3}{16}\frac{\lambda}{\alpha^2} \tag{11.6.6}$$

Hence, $\dfrac{d\langle \hat{H}\rangle}{d\alpha} = \dfrac{\hbar^2}{2m} - \dfrac{3}{8}\dfrac{\lambda}{\alpha^3}$. Since $\dfrac{d\langle \hat{H}\rangle}{d\alpha}\bigg|_{\alpha=\alpha_0} = 0$, we obtain

$$\frac{\hbar^2}{2m} - \frac{3}{8}\frac{\lambda}{\alpha_0^3} = 0 \rightarrow \alpha_0 = \left(\frac{3m\lambda}{4\hbar^2}\right)^{1/3}$$

In terms of $k = 2m\lambda / \hbar^2$ we have $\alpha_0 = (3/8)^{1/3} k^{1/3}$. Substituting this value into Eq. (11.6.6), we obtain

$$\langle \hat{H} \rangle_{min} = \frac{3}{4} 3^{1/3} \frac{\hbar^2}{2m} k^{1/3} = 1.082 \frac{\hbar^2}{2m} k^{1/3} \qquad (11.6.7)$$

Comparing the last result to the exact value of E_0, we see that we have quite a good approximation. The error is approximately 2 percent.

11.7. Consider a particle moving in an arbitrary potential. Assuming that the potential $V(\mathbf{r})$ satisfies the semiclassical condition, estimate the number of discrete energy levels that the particle can occupy.

SOLUTION

The number of states that belong to a volume V in the phase space, and that correspond to a momentum in the range $0 \leq p \leq p_{max}$, and that correspond to particle coordinates in the volume dV equals $\frac{4}{3} \pi p_{max}^3 \frac{dV}{(2\pi\hbar)^3}$. For fixed $\mathbf{r}$, the particle may assume a momentum that satisfies the condition $E = p^2 / 2m + V(\mathbf{r}) \leq 0$. Thus, the maximal momentum is $p_{max} = \sqrt{-2mV(\mathbf{r})}$. Substituting p_{max}, we obtain the number of states in volume dV:

$$dN = \frac{4}{3} \pi [-2mV(\mathbf{r})]^{3/2} \frac{dV}{(2\pi\hbar)^3} \qquad (11.7.1)$$

So, the total number of states of the discrete spectrum is

$$N = \frac{\sqrt{2} m^{3/2}}{3\pi^2 \hbar^3} \int [-V(\mathbf{r})]^{3/2} d^3r \qquad (11.7.2)$$

The integration is carried over the region of space where $V(\mathbf{r}) < 0$. Note that the integral diverges if $V(\mathbf{r})$ decreases as r^{-n}, where $n < 2$.

11.8. (a) Find the condition for applicability of the WKB approximation to the case of the attracting Coulomb potential. (b) What are the implications of this condition for the Bohr model of the hydrogen atom?

SOLUTION

(a) We may write the applicability condition in the form

$$|dx| \gg \left| \frac{\hbar \, dp}{2p^2} \right| \qquad (11.8.1)$$

Omitting the factor 1/2, we obtain

$$\frac{\hbar}{p^2} \left| \frac{dp}{dx} \right| \ll 1 \qquad (11.8.2)$$

Note that

$$\frac{dp}{dx} = \frac{d}{dx} \sqrt{2m(E-V)} = -\frac{m}{p} \frac{dV}{dx} = \frac{mF}{p} \qquad (11.8.3)$$

where $F = -\dfrac{dV(x)}{dx}$ is the classical force. Substituting Eq. (11.8.3) into Eq. (11.8.2), we obtain the following condition:

$$\frac{m\hbar |F|}{p^3} \ll 1 \qquad (11.8.4)$$

For the attracting Coulomb field $F = -\alpha/r^2$, we can roughly estimate the momentum by writing

$$p \sim \sqrt{2m |V|} \sim \sqrt{\frac{m\alpha}{r}} \qquad (11.8.5)$$

Thus, Eq. (11.8.4) becomes $\dfrac{m\hbar(\alpha/r^2)}{m^{3/2}\alpha^{3/2}/r^{3/2}} = \dfrac{\hbar r^{-1/2}}{m^{1/2}\alpha^{1/2}} \ll 1$ and finally,

$$r \gg \frac{\hbar^2}{m\alpha} \tag{11.8.6}$$

(b) The Bohr radius of a hydrogen atom is given by $a_{Bohr} = \hbar^2/m\alpha$; thus, Eq. (11.8.6) becomes $r \gg a_{Bohr}$. For the Bohr model we know that the nth-level distance of an electron from a proton is given by $r_n = n^2 a_{Bohr}$, and so the WKB approximation is applicable for the levels $n \gg 1$.

11.9. Using the WKB approximation find the bounded states for a one-dimensional infinite potential well. Compare your results with the exact solution.

SOLUTION

Suppose that the boundaries of the potential well are at $x = \pm a$. At the boundaries the wavefunction has a value of zero. From Eqs. (11.15) and (11.16) we have

$$\begin{cases} 0 = \cos(-B_1\pi) \\ 0 = \cos(-B_2\pi) \end{cases} \tag{11.9.1}$$

and therefore, $B_1 = B_2 = 1/2$. Thus we get, according to Eq. (11.11),

$$\int_{-a}^{+a} k_n(x')\,dx' = 2ak_n = (n+1)\hbar\pi \tag{11.9.2}$$

We get

$$E_n = \frac{1}{2}\frac{\hbar^2 k_n^2}{m} = \frac{\pi^2\hbar^2(n+1)^2}{8ma^2} \tag{11.9.3}$$

Recall that the exact result is $E_n = \dfrac{\pi^2\hbar^2 n^2}{8ma^2}$.

11.10. Use a WKB approximation to obtain the energy levels of a linear harmonic oscillator.

SOLUTION

Consider the Bohr-Sommerfeld quantization rule:

$$\int_a^b p(x)\,dx = \hbar\pi(n+1/2) \qquad (n = 0, 1, 2, \ldots) \tag{11.10.1}$$

where $p(x) = \sqrt{2m[E - V(x)]}$ is the momentum of the oscillator, E is its energy, and $V(x)$ is its potential energy. Since $\oint p\,dx = 2\int_a^b p\,dx$ holds for a linear harmonic oscillator, we may write the Bohr–Sommerfeld quantization rule in the form of Eq. (11.10.1). For the harmonic oscillator we have $V = \frac{1}{2}m\omega^2 x^2$. The points a and b are the turning points that are determined by the condition $p(a) = p(b) = 0$ or $E - V = 0$; thus, $E - \frac{1}{2}m\omega^2 x^2 = 0$. So, we have

$$a = -\sqrt{\frac{2E}{m\omega^2}} \qquad b = \sqrt{\frac{2E}{m\omega^2}} \tag{11.10.2}$$

We introduce the new variable $z = x\sqrt{\dfrac{m\omega^2}{2E}}$, and obtain

$$\int_a^b p(x)\,dx = \frac{2E}{\omega}\int_{-1}^1 \sqrt{1 - z^2}\,dz = \frac{\pi E}{\omega} \tag{11.10.3}$$

Comparing this result to Eq. (11.10.1), we obtain

$$E_n = \hbar\omega\left(n + \frac{1}{2}\right)$$ (11.10.4)

Thus, in the case of the semiclassical approximation the result is identical to the exact solution.

11.11. Using the semiclassical approximation, calculate the transmission coefficient of a potential barrier

$$V(x) = \begin{cases} V_0\left(1 - \dfrac{x^2}{a^2}\right) & -a \leq x \leq a \\ 0 & \text{otherwise} \end{cases}$$ (11.11.1)

See Fig. 11.3.

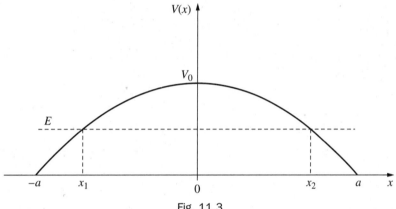

Fig. 11.3

SOLUTION

Let E be the energy of the particle and m its mass. The transmission coefficient in the semiclassical approximation is given by

$$T \approx \exp\left\{-\frac{2}{\hbar}\int_{x_1}^{x_2}\sqrt{2m\left[V(x) - E\right]}\,dx\right\}$$ (11.11.2)

where x_1 and x_2 are the turning points computed using the condition $V(x) = E$. Hence,

$$x_1 = -a\sqrt{1 - \frac{E}{V_0}} \qquad x_2 = +a\sqrt{1 - \frac{E}{V_0}}$$ (11.11.3)

Thus, Eq. (11.11.2) becomes

$$T \approx \exp\left\{-\frac{2}{\hbar}\int_{-a[1-(E/V_0)]^{1/2}}^{+a[1-(E/V_0)]^{1/2}}\sqrt{2m\left[V_0\left(1 - \frac{x^2}{a^2}\right) - E\right]}\,dx\right\}$$ (11.11.4)

Computing the integral gives

$$T \approx \exp\left[-\pi\sqrt{\frac{2m}{V_0}}\frac{a\left(V_0 - E\right)}{\hbar}\right]$$ (11.11.5)

Note that the expression of T is valid if the exponent in Eq. (11.11.5) is large; that is,

$$\pi\sqrt{\frac{2m}{V_0}}\frac{a\left(V_0 - E\right)}{\hbar} \gg 1$$ (11.11.6)

11.12. The limit $\hbar \to 0$ corresponds to the transition from quantum mechanics to classical mechanics. Assume that the wavefuncton can be written in the form $\psi(\mathbf{r}, t) = e^{iS(\mathbf{r},t)/\hbar}$, and that the system is in a stationary state, i.e., we can write $S(\mathbf{r}, t) = \sigma(\mathbf{r}) - Et$. Derive the following conditions for the applicability of the semiclassical approximation: (a) $(\nabla\sigma)^2 \gg \hbar|\nabla^2\sigma|$ and $p^2 \gg \hbar|\nabla \cdot \mathbf{p}|$; (b) in a particular case of one-dimensional motion, $\lambda \gg \left|\dfrac{\lambda\,d\lambda}{2\pi\,dx}\right|$, where λ is the wavelength according to the de Broglie relation $\lambda = h/p$. (c) $p^3 \gg m\hbar\left|\dfrac{dV}{dx}\right|$.

SOLUTION

(a) We begin by substituting the wavefunction $\Psi(\mathbf{r}, t) = e^{iS/\hbar}$ into the Schrödinger equation:

$$-\frac{\hbar^2}{2m}\nabla^2\Psi + V(\mathbf{r})\Psi = i\hbar\frac{\partial\Psi}{\partial t} \tag{11.12.1}$$

Hence,

$$\frac{1}{2m}(\nabla S \cdot \nabla S) - \frac{i\hbar}{2m}\nabla^2 S + V(\mathbf{r}) = -\frac{\partial S}{\partial t} \tag{11.12.2}$$

Using the assumption that the system is in a stationary state, we substitute $S(\mathbf{r}, t) = \sigma(\mathbf{r}) - Et$, and arrive at

$$\frac{1}{2m}(\nabla\sigma)^2 - \frac{i\hbar}{2m}\nabla^2\sigma + V(\mathbf{r}) = E \tag{11.12.3}$$

To achieve the transition from quantum mechanics to classical mechanics we must take the limit $\hbar \to 0$; then, the term $-\dfrac{i\hbar}{2m}\nabla^2\sigma$ in Eq. (11.12.3) can be neglected, and we obtain

$$\frac{1}{2m}(\nabla\sigma)^2 + V(\mathbf{r}) = E \tag{11.12.4}$$

This can be considered an equation of classical mechanics, provided that $\nabla\sigma_0 = \mathbf{p}$. However, the essence of the semiclassical approach is to arrive at equations that lead to classical mechanics equations, even for purely quantum systems where the transition $\hbar \to 0$ is not justified. Looking again at Eq. (11.12.3) we note that the transition from Eq. (11.12.3) to Eq. (11.12.4) can be achieved not only by taking the limit $\hbar \to 0$, but also by assuming that

$$(\nabla\sigma_0)^2 \gg \hbar|\nabla^2\sigma_0| \tag{11.12.5}$$

Therefore, Eq. (11.12.5) is a condition for the applicability of the semiclassical approximation. Equation (11.12.5) can be rewritten as $(\mathbf{p} = \nabla\sigma)$:

$$p^2 \gg \hbar|\nabla \cdot \mathbf{p}| \tag{11.12.6}$$

(b) In the case of one-dimensional motion, $\nabla \cdot \mathbf{p} = \dfrac{dp}{dx}$; using Eq. (11.12.6) we have

$$1 \gg \frac{\hbar|dp/dx|}{p^2} \tag{11.12.7}$$

Differentiating the de Broglie relation $\lambda = h/p$ with respect to x, we obtain

$$\left|\frac{d\lambda}{dx}\right| = \left|\frac{h\,dp}{p^2\,dx}\right| = \left|\frac{2\pi\hbar\,dp}{p^2\,dx}\right| \tag{11.12.8}$$

Then, according to Eq. (11.12.7), we have $\left|\dfrac{d\lambda}{2\pi\,dx}\right| \ll 1$, from which it follows that

$$\lambda \gg \left|\frac{\lambda\,d\lambda}{2\pi\,dx}\right| \tag{11.12.9}$$

The condition specified by Eq. (11.12.9) can be interpreted as follows: along the distance of $\lambda/2\pi$ the change in the wavelength must be much less than the wavelength itself.

(*c*) From classical mechanics we know that $p = \sqrt{2m(E-V)}$. Thus,

$$\frac{dp}{dx} = \frac{dp}{dV}\frac{dV}{dx} = -\frac{m}{\sqrt{2m(E-V)}}\frac{dV}{dx} = -\frac{m}{p}\frac{dV}{dx} \tag{11.12.10}$$

so $\left|\frac{dp}{dx}\right| = \frac{m}{p}\left|\frac{dV}{dx}\right|$. Substituting into Eq. (11.12.7), we obtain

$$p^3 \gg m\hbar\left|\frac{dV}{dx}\right| \tag{11.12.11}$$

11.13. Using the WKB approximation, derive the Bohr–Sommerfeld quantization rule.

SOLUTION

Consider a one-dimensional case where $E > [V(x)]_{\min}$ (see Fig. 11.4).

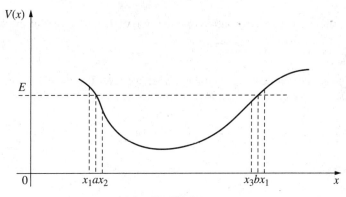

Fig. 11.4

For any value of E there are only two turning points $V(a) = V(b) = E$. The oscillating solution between two turning points is

$$\Psi_{\text{osc}} = \frac{C}{\sqrt{p}}\sin\left[\int_a^x k(x')\,dx' + \beta\right] \tag{11.13.1}$$

where C and β are constants. In small vicinities $x_1 \le a \le x_2$, $x_3 \le b \le x_4$; the WKB approximation is not applicable where the wavefunctions in these vicinities are given by

$$\Psi_a(x) = \begin{cases} \dfrac{A}{2\sqrt{|p|}}\exp\left\{-\displaystyle\int_x^a \chi(x')\,dx'\right\} & \text{at } x_1 \\[3mm] \dfrac{A}{\sqrt{p}}\sin\left\{\displaystyle\int_a^x k(x')\,dx'\right\} & \text{at } x_2 \end{cases} \tag{11.13.2}$$

and

$$\Psi_b(x) = \begin{cases} \dfrac{B}{2\sqrt{|p|}}\exp\left\{-\displaystyle\int_b^x \chi(x')\,dx'\right\} & \text{at } x_4 \\[3mm] \dfrac{B}{\sqrt{p}}\sin\left\{\displaystyle\int_x^b k(x')\,dx' + \frac{\pi}{4}\right\} & \text{at } x_3 \end{cases} \tag{11.13.3}$$

where $k(x) = \frac{1}{\hbar}\sqrt{2m[E-V(x)]}$ and $\chi(x) = \frac{1}{\hbar}\sqrt{2m[V(x)-E]}$. We require a smooth transition from the oscillating solution to the solutions in the vicinities of a and b and so the following conditions must be satisfied:

$$B = (-1)^{n+1}C \tag{11.13.4}$$

$$\int_b^a k(x')\,dx' = \pi n + \frac{\pi}{2} \tag{11.13.5}$$

where $n = 0, 1, 2, \ldots$. Recall that $p = \hbar k$ and introduces the loop integral

$$\oint p(x)\,dx = 2\int_a^b p(x)\,dx \tag{11.13.6}$$

This integral can be interpreted as integrating along the line from a to b and then back from b to a. Thus, substituting in Eq. (11.13.5), we arrive at

$$\left(\oint p(x)\,dx = 2\pi\hbar\left(n + \frac{1}{2}\right)\right) \qquad n = 0, 1, 2, \ldots \tag{11.13.7}$$

which is the Bohr–Sommerfeld quantization rule.

11.14. Use the semiclassical approximation in order to find the radial part of the wavefunction for a particle moving in a central potential field.

SOLUTION

From the theory of a particle in a central potential, we know that the radial part of the corresponding wavefunction can be written in the form $R(r) = u(r)/r$, where $u(r)$ satisfies the following equation:

$$\frac{du^2(r)}{dr^2} + \left[\frac{2m}{\hbar^2}(E - V(r)) - \frac{l(l+1)}{r^2}\right]u(r) = 0 \tag{11.14.1}$$

We will write $u(r)$ in the form

$$u(r) = C(r)\exp\left[i\left(\frac{S(r)}{\hbar}\right)\right] \tag{11.14.2}$$

where $C(r)$ and $S(r)$ are real functions. Substituting Eq. (11.14.2) into Eq. (11.14.1) we obtain

$$\frac{d^2C(r)}{dr^2}\exp\left[i\left(\frac{S}{\hbar}\right)\right] + \frac{i}{\hbar}\frac{dC(r)}{dr}\frac{dS(r)}{dr}\exp\left(\frac{iS}{\hbar}\right) + \frac{dC(r)}{dr}\exp\left(\frac{iS}{\hbar}\right)\left(\frac{i}{\hbar}\frac{dS(r)}{dr}\right)$$

$$+ C(r)\exp\left(\frac{iS}{\hbar}\right)\left(\frac{i}{\hbar}\frac{dS(r)}{dr}\right)^2 + C(r)\exp\left(\frac{iS}{\hbar}\right)\left(\frac{i}{\hbar}\frac{d^2S(r)}{dr^2}\right)$$

$$+ \left[\frac{2m}{\hbar^2}(E - V(r)) - \frac{l(l+1)}{r^2}\right]C(r)\exp\left(\frac{iS}{\hbar}\right) = 0 \tag{11.14.3}$$

Setting the real and imaginary parts of the left-hand side of Eq. (11.14.3) to zero we arrive at

$$2\frac{dC(r)}{dr}\frac{dS(r)}{dr} + C(r)\frac{d^2S(r)}{dr} = 0 \tag{11.14.4}$$

and

$$\left(\frac{dS(r)}{dr}\right)^2 - \frac{\hbar^2}{C(r)}\frac{d^2C(r)}{dr^2} = 2m[E - V(r)] - \frac{\hbar^2 l(l+1)}{r^2} \tag{11.14.5}$$

Integrating Eq. (11.14.4), we obtain $C(r) = (\text{const.}) \times \left(\frac{dS(r)}{dr}\right)^{-1/2}$. Since $\hbar^2$ is assumed to be a small quantity, we can solve Eq. (11.14.5) approximately. For small values of r, when the dominant term on the right-hand side of Eq. (11.14.5) is $\frac{\hbar^2 l(l+1)}{r^2}$, we have $\frac{dS(r)}{dr} \approx \frac{i\hbar\sqrt{l(l+1)}}{r}$ with $C(r) \sim \sqrt{r}$, and we arrive at the approximation

$$\frac{\hbar^2}{C(r)}\frac{d^2C(r)}{dr^2} \approx \frac{\hbar^2}{4r^2} \tag{11.14.6}$$

We now substitute Eq. (11.14.6) into Eq. (11.14.5) and thereby obtain a better approximation:

$$S(r) = \int \sqrt{2m[E - V(r)] - \frac{\hbar^2(l + 1/2)^2}{r^2}}\, dr \tag{11.14.7}$$

and

$$C(r) = \frac{\text{const.}}{\sqrt[4]{2m[E - V(r)] - \frac{\hbar^2(l + 1/2)^2}{r^2}}} \tag{11.14.8}$$

Substituting Eqs. (11.14.7) and (11.14.8) into Eq. (11.14.2) we obtain $u(r)$, and then $R(r) = u(r)/r$.

SUPPLEMENTARY PROBLEMS

11.15. Using the trial function $\psi = N \exp(-\alpha r^2)$, compute a variational upper limit for the ground state of a hydrogen atom and compare it to the exact value.

Ans. $\langle \hat{H} \rangle \approx -11.5$ eV. The exact value is -13.6 eV.

11.16. Using the variational method, compute the energy of the ground state of a hydrogen atom. Use the following trial functions: (a) $\psi_1 = A_1 e^{-br/a_0}$, (b) $\psi_1 = A_2 \left(b^2 + \frac{r^2}{a_0^2} \right)^{-1}$, and (c) $\psi_3 = A_3 \frac{r}{a_0} e^{-br/a_0}$, where a_0 is the Bohr radius. Compare your results with the exact result and discuss the causes for the differences. Hint: Compare the behavior of ψ_1, ψ_2, and ψ_3 with the true wavefunction.

Ans. (a) $b = 1$, $\langle \hat{H} \rangle_{\text{min}} = -\frac{e^2}{2a_0} = -E_H$; (b) $b = \frac{\pi}{4}$, $\langle \hat{H} \rangle_{\text{min}} = -0.81E_H$; (c) $b = \frac{3}{2}$, $\langle \hat{H} \rangle_{\text{min}} = -0.75E_H$;

where E_H is the energy of the ground state of a hydrogen atom.

11.17. Using variational calculus, give an estimate for the binding energy of the deuteron. Assume that the potential between a proton and a neutron is $V(r) = Ae^{-r/r_0}$, and use $\psi(r) = Ce^{-\beta r}$ as a trial function, where A and C are normalizaton constants and r_0 is a characteristic length of the potential.

Ans. $E = -2.1$ MeV.

11.18. Show that for motion in a central field, the condition for applicability of the WKB approximation is $l \gg 1$, where l is an angular momentum quantum number. Explain why the term "semiclassical approximation" is justified in this case.

Ans. Since an angular momentum equals $L = l\hbar$, we obtain relatively large values of an angular momentum, so L is "almost classical."

11.19. Consider the Hamiltonian of a nonharmonic oscillator $\hat{H} = -\frac{d^2}{dx^2} + x^2 + x^4$. Use the WKB approximation to find the ground state for $x \to \infty$.

Ans. $\psi \sim \frac{1}{x} \exp\left(\pm \frac{x^3}{3} \right)$ as $|x| \to \infty$

11.20. Use the WKB approximation to compute the transmission coefficient of an electron going through the potential barrier depicted in Fig. 11.5.

$$V(x) = \begin{cases} V_0 - \frac{1}{2}kx^2 & x^2 < 2V_0/k \\ 0 & \text{otherwise} \end{cases} \tag{11.20.1}$$

Ans. $T = \exp\left[-\frac{2}{\hbar} \int_{-\sqrt{2(V_0+E)/k}}^{\sqrt{2(V_0+E)/k}} \sqrt{2m\left(V_0 - \frac{1}{2}kx^2 - E \right)}\, dx \right]$

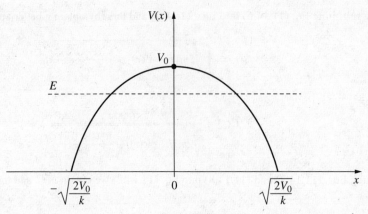

Fig. 11.5

11.21. Use the WKB approximation to find the transmission coefficient for the potential

$$V(x) = \begin{cases} 0 & x < 0 \\ V_0 - kx & x > 0 \end{cases} \tag{11.21.1}$$

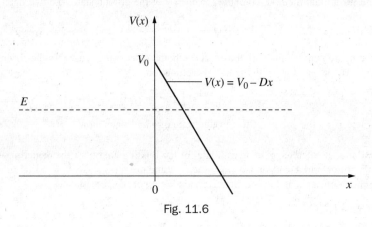

Fig. 11.6

where V_0 and k are constant.

Ans.   (a) $T = \exp\left[-\dfrac{2}{\hbar}\displaystyle\int_0^{(V_0-E)/k}\sqrt{2m(E - V_0 + kx)}\,dx\right] = \exp\left[-\dfrac{4\sqrt{2m}}{3\hbar k}(V_0 - E)^{3/2}\right]$

11.22. What is the probability of a particle with zero angular momentum escaping from a central potential

$$V(r) = \begin{cases} -V_0 & r < a \\ \dfrac{\alpha}{r} & r > a \end{cases} \tag{11.22.1}$$

Ans. $P = \exp\left[-\dfrac{2}{\hbar}\displaystyle\int_a^{\alpha/E}\sqrt{2m\left(\dfrac{\alpha}{r} - E\right)}\,dr\right] = \exp\left\{-\dfrac{2\alpha}{\hbar}\sqrt{\dfrac{2m}{E}}\left[\cos^{-1}\left(\sqrt{\dfrac{Ea}{\alpha}}\right) - \sqrt{\dfrac{Ea}{\alpha}\left(1 - \dfrac{Ea}{\alpha}\right)}\right]\right\}$

CHAPTER 12

Numerical Methods in Quantum Mechanics

12.1 Numerical Quadrature

The *numerical quadrature* of the definite integral of a function $f(x)$ between two limits a and b is accomplished by dividing the interval $[a, b]$ into N small intervals, between $N + 1$ points denoted by

$$a = x_0, x_1, \ldots, x_N = b \tag{12.1}$$

The points x_i are equally spaced using a constant step $h = (b - a)/N$:

$$x_i = x_0 + ih \qquad i = 0, 1, \ldots, N \tag{12.2}$$

The basic idea behind quadrature is to write the integrals as the sum of integrals over small intervals:

$$\int_a^b f(x)\,dx = \int_a^{a+h} f(x)\,dx + \int_{a+h}^{a+2h} f(x)\,dx + \cdots + \int_{b-h}^b f(x)\,dx \tag{12.3}$$

and in these small intervals, approximate $f(x)$ by a function that can be integrated exactly. We will demonstrate two methods of quadrature. The first method is called the *trapezoidal method;* it is based on the approximation of $f(x)$ to a linear function, as shown in Fig. 12.1.

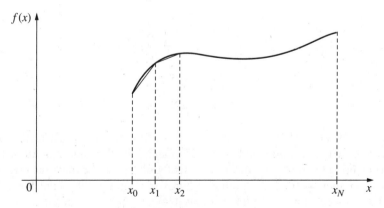

Fig. 12.1

In this case, the integral $\int_{x_i}^{x_{i+1}} f(x)\,dx = [f(x_{i+1}) + f(x_i)]\dfrac{h}{2}$, so if we denote $f(x_i) = f_i$, we obtain

$$\int_a^b f(x)\,dx \approx h\left[\frac{1}{2}f_0 + f_1 + f_2 + \cdots + f_{N-1} + \frac{1}{2}f_N\right] \tag{12.4}$$

The second method is called *Simpson's method*. It is based on the approximation of $f(x)$ via a second-degree polynomial at three points. In this case, the integral $\int_{x_i}^{x_{i+2}} f(x)\,dx \approx h\left[\dfrac{1}{3}f_i + \dfrac{4}{3}f_{i+1} + \dfrac{1}{3}f_{i+2}\right]$, so

$$\int_a^b f(x)\,dx = \int_a^{a+2h} f(x)\,dx + \int_{a+2h}^{a+4h} f(x)\,dx + \cdots$$

$$+ \int_{b-2h}^b f(x)\,dx \approx \frac{h}{3}[f_0 + 4f_1 + 2f_2 + 4f_3 + \cdots + f_N] \tag{12.5}$$

One should be aware of the fact that these methods are only an approximation of the exact integral. The approximation is improved as we consider larger N. In the trapezoidal method, the approximation error is proportional to $1/N^2$, while in Simpson's method, it is proportional to $1/N^4$; i.e., in general, the Simpson method is more accurate than the trapezoidal method.

12.2 Roots

In order to determine the roots of a function $f(x)$ we must solve the equation $f(x) = 0$. All numerical methods for finding roots depend on one or more initial guesses. In each algorithm, the root is approximated after a given number of iterations. Note that by initial guess we do not necessarily mean a close guess for the root, though the better the guess is, the faster the convergence will be (and less iterations will be needed). Thus, to obtain an efficient initial guess for a given root for the function $f(x)$, it is helpful to first plot the function.

    We describe three methods for finding roots. The first is called the *bisection method*. This method is useful when we know that the root is found in a specific interval, say, $[x_1, x_2]$, as shown in Fig. 12.2.

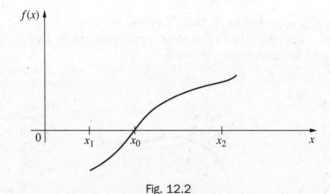

Fig. 12.2

We know that the signs of $f(x_1)$ and $f(x_2)$ are opposite. In the first iteration we evaluate $f(x)$ at the midpoint between x_1 and x_2; then we use the midpoint to replace the limit with the same sign. In each successive iteration, the interval containing the root gets smaller by a factor of $1/2$, so the maximal error in our estimation (if we assume that the midpoint is the root we are searching for) is simply half of the interval between the new limits x_1 and x_2. Thus, we need $n = \log_2(\varepsilon_0/\varepsilon)$ iterations to obtain the root with a maximal error of $\varepsilon/2$. Note that ε_0 is the initial interval, $\varepsilon_0 = |x_2 - x_1|$. The bisection method will always converge if the initial interval $[x_1, x_2]$ contains a root (or singularity points).

The second algorithm, the *Newton–Raphson method*, uses the derivative $f'(x)$ at an arbitrary point x. We begin with an initial guess x^1. Each new approximation for the root depends on the previous one:

$$x^{i+1} = x^i - \frac{f(x^i)}{f'(x^i)} \tag{12.6}$$

We stop when the value of $|x^{i+1} - x^i|$ is less than the tolerance we have selected. To understand how the method works, we write Eq. (12.6) in the form

$$f(x^i) + f'(x^i)(x^{i+1} - x^i) = 0 \tag{12.7}$$

Notice that the left-hand side of Eq. (12.7) is a linear extrapolation to the value of $f(x^{i+1})$, which should be zero.

The third method, called the *secant method*, is similar to the Newton–Raphson method. Here we do not evaluate the derivative but use the approximation,

$$f'(x^i) \approx \frac{f'(x^i) - f'(x^{i-1})}{x^i - x^{i-1}} \tag{12.8}$$

Hence we obtain

$$x^{i+1} = x^i - \frac{x^i - x^{i-1}}{f(x^i) - f(x^{i-1})} f(x^i) \tag{12.9}$$

12.3   Integration of Ordinary Differential Equations

Solving differential equations is of paramount importance in physics. Many key results are formulated in terms of differential equations. We introduce several methods for solving differential equations of the form

$$\frac{dy}{dx} = f(x, y) \tag{12.10}$$

The methods differ in their accuracy, and in the time it takes to obtain the required accuracy. One should decide which method to use according to these criteria. Note that higher-order differential equations such as

$$\frac{d^2y}{dx^2} = F(x, y) \tag{12.11}$$

can be written as

$$\frac{dz}{dx} = F(x, y) \qquad z = \frac{dy}{dx} \tag{12.12}$$

Thus, they can be solved using the same methods.

The first method, the *Euler method*, is the simplest and least accurate method. Write Eq. (12.10) approximately as a difference equation:

$$\frac{\Delta y}{\Delta x} = f(x, y) \tag{12.13}$$

or

$$\Delta y = f(x, y)\Delta x \tag{12.14}$$

Iterate the value of $y(x)$ from a starting point $y_0 = y(x_0)$ by

$$y_{n+1} = y_n + f(x_n, y_n)(x_{n+1} - x_n) \tag{12.15}$$

then set $\Delta x = x_{n+1} - x_n = h$ (constant); thus,

$$y_{n+1} = y_n + f(x_n, y_n)h \tag{12.16}$$

The point (x_{n+1}, y_{n+1}) depends only on the previous point (x_n, y_n). The accuracy of the iteration depends chiefly on the choice of h; a smaller h gives higher accuracy. The error in the approximation of y_{n+1} is proportional to h^2.

The second method, the *Runge–Kutta method,* is based on the Euler method using an approximation of $f(x, y)$ by a given order to the Taylor series expansion. The higher the order of the Taylor series (i.e., the higher the order of the Runge–Kutta method), the better the accuracy. Consider the second-order Runge–Kutta method:

$$y_{n+1} = y_n + k_2 \tag{12.17}$$

where

$$\begin{cases} k_1 = hf(x_n, y_n) \\ k_2 = hf(x_n + h/2, y_n + k_1/2) \end{cases} \tag{12.18}$$

with an error proportional to h^3. Similarly, the third order of the Runge–Kutta method is

$$y_{n+1} = y_n + \frac{1}{6}(k_1 + 4k_2 + k_3) \tag{12.19}$$

where

$$\begin{cases} k_1 = hf(x_n, y_n) \\ k_2 = hf(x_n + h/2, y_n + k_1/2) \\ k_3 = hf(x_n + h, y_n - k_1 + 2k_2) \end{cases} \tag{12.20}$$

with an error proportional to h^4. The fourth order of the Runge–Kutta method is

$$y_{n+1} = y_n + \frac{1}{6}(k_1 + 2k_2 + 2k_3 + k_4) \tag{12.21}$$

where

$$\begin{cases} k_1 = hf(x_n, y_n) \\ k_2 = hf(x_n + h/2, y_n + k_1/2) \\ k_3 = hf(x_n + h/2, y_n + k_2/2) \\ k_4 = hf(x_n + h, y_n + k_3) \end{cases} \tag{12.22}$$

with an error proportional to h^5, and so on.

The Schrödinger equation is a second-order differential equation. Thus, the methods described above need, as an initial condition, the value of the wavefunction and its derivative at a given point. Since the value of the derivative of the wavefunction is usually not given, we are left only with the value of the wavefunction at two points (the boundaries). We demonstrate here an algorithm to solve second-order differential equations with two boundary conditions—the *Numerov algorithm.*

Numerov's method is used to solve a differential equation of the form

$$\frac{d^2 y}{dx^2} + k^2(x)y = S(x) \tag{12.23}$$

We approximate the second derivative by the three-point difference formula:

$$\frac{y_{n+1} - 2y_n + y_{n-1}}{h^2} = y_n'' + \frac{h^2}{12} y_n'''' \tag{12.24}$$

where y_n'' and y_n'''' are the second and fourth derivatives at point x_n, respectively. Using Eq. (12.23) we arrive at

$$y_n'''' = \frac{d^2}{dx^2}[-k^2(x)y + S(x)]\bigg|_{x=x_n} \tag{12.25}$$

Denoting $k(x_n) = k_n$ and $S(x_n) = S_n$ yields

$$y_n'''' = -\frac{1}{h^2}\left[k_{n+1}^2 y_{n+1} - 2k_n^2 y_n + k_{n-1}^2 y_{n-1}\right] + \frac{1}{h^2}[S_{n+1} - 2S_n + S_{n-1}] \tag{12.26}$$

Substituting Eq. (12.26) into Eq. (12.23) we obtain

$$\left(1 + \frac{h^2}{12}k_{n+1}^2\right)y_{n+1} - 2\left(1 - \frac{5h^2}{12}k_n^2\right)y_n + \left(1 + \frac{h^2}{12}k_{n-1}^2\right)y_{n-1} = \frac{h^2}{12}(S_{n+1} + 10S_n + S_{n-1}) \tag{12.27}$$

where the error is proportional to h^6. This error can be shown to be better than that for the fourth order of the Runge–Kutta method.

Comment: All the following programs were written in standard FORTRAN 77 and were compiled on an IBM AIX RS/6000 workstation. The precision used was the default precision REAL *4.

SOLVED PROBLEMS

12.1. Write a FORTRAN subroutine:

```
Subroutine Simpson (FUNC, N, A, B, S)
INTEGER N
REAL FUNC (0:10000), A, B, S
```

This program computes the value of the integral of FUNC from A to B, using N iterations of the Simpson method. FUNC(0 : N) is an array of $N + 1$ values of the integral at $N + 1$ points separated by $h = (B - A)/N$. The value of the integral is updated in S.

SOLUTION

Consider the Simpson rule and note that

$$S = \frac{h}{3}[\text{FUNC}(0) + 4*\text{FUNC}(1) + 2*\text{FUNC}(2) + 4*\text{FUNC}(3) + \cdots + \text{FUNC}(N)] \tag{12.1.1}$$

The summation is slightly different for an odd and even N. One way to perform this summation is as follows:

```
S = FUNC(0) + FUNC(N)
Do loop i from 1 to N - 1
if i is even
S = S + 2*FUNC(i)
else
S = S + 4*FUNC(i)
end if
end do
S = S * (B - A)/(3*N)
```

This algorithm can be written in FORTRAN 77 as follows:

```
C** Subroutine to compute the value of a definite integral.
      Subroutine Simpson (func, n, a, b, s)
      integer n
      real func (0:1000) a, b, s
      s = 0
      s = func(0) + func(n)
      do 1 i=1, n-1

C** (1- mod(i, 2)) equals 0 if i even and equals 1 if i odd.
        s = s+2*2** (1- mod(i, 2))*func (i)
      1 continue
        s = s*(b-a)/(3*n)
      return
      end
```

12.2. Write a program to compute the integral

$$\int_a^b e^{x^2} dx \qquad\qquad (12.2.1)$$

using the Simpson method. The program should use as input the boundaries a, b, and N described in Sec. 12.1. Use different values of N for $a = 0$ and $b = 1$ to obtain an accuracy of 1×10^{-2}.

SOLUTION

Consider the following program:

```
      Program Problem 12.2
      integer n
      real func (0:1000), a, b, s
      real x, h

C** Get the boundaries of the interval.
        write (*,*)'Enter the interval bounds a and b:'
        read (*,*) a,b

C** Prepare file of results.
        open (unit=1, file='results.txt')
        write (1,*)'The value of the integral of the function exp (x**2)'
   10 format ('from', f4.2, 'to', f4.2)
        write (1, 10) a,b
        write (1,*)'N S The integral'

C** Get the number of points N.
    2 write (*,*)'Enter the number of points N (0<N<1001):'
        write (*,*)'Enter N<0 to stop'
        read (*,*) n
        if (n.gt.1000.or.n.lt.1) goto 3

C** The step value between points.
        h=(b-a)/n
C** Compute the value of the function on the N points.
        do 1 i=0, n
          x = a+h*float(i)
          func (i)=exp (x*x)
    1 continue

C** Compute the value of the integral.
        call Simpson (func, n, a, b, s)
```

```
C** Print results.
      write (1,*) n, s
      write (*,*) n, s
      goto 2
   3 stop
      end


C** Subroutine to compute the value of a definite integral.
      Subroutine Simpson (func, n, a, b, s)
      integer n
      real func (0:1000), a, b, s
      s=0.
      s=func(0) + func(n)
      do 1 i=1, n-1
C** (1-mod(i, 2)) equals 0 if i even and equals 1 if i odd.
      s=s+2*2** (1-mod(i,2)) *func(i)
   1 continue
      s=s* (b-a)/(3*n)
      return
      end
```

Running this program gives the following:

N	S The Integral	N	S The Integral
10	1.347725272	100	1.450347781
20	1.402942777	110	1.451459050
30	1.422343731	120	1.452386498
40	1.432232141	130	1.453171015
50	1.438225508	140	1.453844905
60	1.442246556	150	1.454429030
70	1.445130706	200	1.456477404
80	1.447300673	500	1.460176587
90	1.448992372	1000	1.461413145

Notice that we used the subroutine that we have written in Problem 12.1. Using subroutines makes the program easier to read, though it often slows the program.

The output results show the values of N and the corresponding values of S for $A = 0$ and $B = 1$. From these results we see that different N values correspond to different S values, though large values of N the value of S is more stable, i.e., the changes in its value are small. This is mostly true for well-behaved functions like the one we are dealing with in this problem.

12.3. Write two different FORTRAN programs to solve the equation $\cos x = x$. Consider an accuracy of five digits after the decimal point. Use the bisection method with $x_1 = 0$ and $x_2 = 1$, and the Newton–Raphson method with $x_1 = 1$.

SOLUTION

Consider the graph of the functions $y = \cos x$ and $y = x$ shown in Fig. 12.3.

The solution of $\cos x - x = 0$ is the value of x, where $y = \cos x$ and $y = x$ intersect. We conclude from Fig. 12.3 that this happens in the interval [0, 1]; hence, a good starting guess for the bisection method would be x1 = 0 and x2 = 1. For each iteration we will get a new value XM = (x1 + x2)/2, and we will compare it with the value of XM in the previous iteration XMOLD. If the difference between XM and XMOLD is consistently less than 1×10^{-5}, then we have an accuracy of five digits. Consider one way to write the program:

```
Program Problem 12.3-1
real x1, x2, xm, xmold
real toler, f1, f2, fm, f
integer iter

C** Initialize iterations number.
      iter=0
```

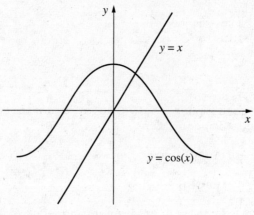

Fig. 12.3

```
C** Initial guesses.
      x1=0.
      x2=1.
      xm=(x1+x2)/2.
      xmold=x1

C** Maximal error in the approximation.
      toler=0.00001

C** If the new iteration does not give the same result of the previous
    iteration
C** within toler do the following:
      do while (abs (xm-xmold).gt.toler)
      iter=iter+1
C** Evaluate the f(x) at the different points.
      f1=f(x1)
      f2=f(x2)
      fm=f(xm)
      if ((fm*f1).lt.0) then

C** If the sign of f(xm) is similar to that of f(x2) then:
      x2=xm
      else

C** If the sign of f(xm) is similar to that of f(x1) then:
      x1=xm
      endif

C** Remember the result of the previous iteration.
      xmold=xm

C** new iteration:
      xm=(x1+x2)/2.
      end do

C** Print result.
      write (*,*) 'The zero of f(x) is:' ,xm
   10 format ('obtained after', i3, 'iterations.')
      write (*,10) iter
      stop
      end
```

```
C** Function for which we want to find the zero.
      real function f(x)
      real x
      f=cos(x)-x
      return
      end
```

This gives the result:

```
The zero of f(x) is 0.7390823364 obtained after 16 iterations.
```

Similarly, for the Newton–Raphson method we need only one starting guess x1, and we will use the same criterion for stopping the iterations. Recall that $x^{i+1} = x^i - f(x^i)/f'(x^i)$. If $f(x^i)/f'(x^i)$ is less than the tolerance, the iterations will stop.

```
      Program Problem 12.3-2
      real x1
      real f1, df1, toler
      integer iter

C** Initialize iterations.
      iter=0

C** Maximal error in the approximation.
      toler=0.00001

C** Initial guess.
      x1=1.

C** Evaluate the function f(x)=cos(x)-x and its derivative at x=x1:
      f1=cos(x1)-x1
      df1=-1.*sin(x1)-1.

C** If the new iteration does not give the same result of the previous
   iteration
C** within toler do the following:
      do while (abs(f1/df1).gt.toler)

C** New iteration.
      iter=iter+1

C** Evaluate the function f(x)=cos(x)-x and its derivative at x=x1:
      x1=x1-f1/df1
      f1=cos(x1)-x1
      df1=-1.*sin(x1)-1
      end do

C** Print result:
      write (*,*) 'The zero of f(x) is:' ,x1
   10 format ('obtained after', i3, 'iterations.')
      write (*,10) iter
      stop
      end
```

This gives the result:

```
The zero of f(x) is 0.7390851378 obtained after 3 iterations.
```

We see that both methods give the same result. The bisection method converged after 16 iterations. The Newton–Raphson method gave the result after only three iterations, confirming that this method converges faster than the bisection method. This is usually the case, though sometimes the Newton–Raphson method diverges, while the bisection method converges.

12.4. Find the lowest bound state energy for an electron moving under the potential

$$V(x) = \begin{cases} -V_0 & 0 \le z \le a \\ \infty & z < 0 \\ 0 & \text{otherwise} \end{cases} \tag{12.4.1}$$

where $a = 2 \text{ Å}$ and $V_0 = 10$ eV (see Fig. 12.4).

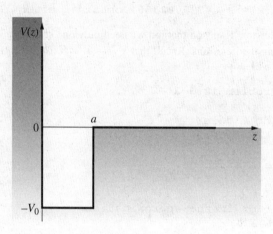

Fig. 12.4

SOLUTION

The Schrödinger equation for bound states, $-V_0 < E < 0$, is (see Chap. 3)

$$\psi = 0 \qquad \text{for } z < 0 \tag{12.4.2}$$

$$-\frac{\hbar^2}{2m}\frac{d^2\psi}{dz^2} - V_0\psi = E\psi \qquad \text{for } 0 \le z \le a \tag{12.4.3}$$

$$-\frac{\hbar^2}{2m}\frac{d^2\psi}{dz^2} = E\psi \qquad \text{for } a < z \tag{12.4.4}$$

Equation (12.4.3) yields $\dfrac{d^2\psi}{dz^2} = -\dfrac{2m}{\hbar^2}(E + V_0)\psi$ with $E + V_0 > 0$. Thus,

$$\psi(z) = A_1 \sin(k_1 z) + B_1 \cos(k_1 z) \qquad \text{for } 0 < z < a \tag{12.4.5}$$

where $k_1 = \sqrt{2m(E + V_0)/\hbar^2}$. Similarly, Eq. (12.4.4) yields $\dfrac{d^2\psi}{dz^2} = -\dfrac{2mE}{\hbar^2}\psi$. The solution is

$$\psi = A_2 e^{k_2 z} + B_2 e^{-k_2 z} \qquad \text{for } a < z \tag{12.4.6}$$

where $k_2 = \sqrt{-2mE/\hbar^2}$. The wavefunction should satisfy the boundary conditions $\psi(z \to -\infty) = 0$ and $\psi(z \to \infty) = 0$. The boundary condition $z \to -\infty$ is already satisfied, while the second boundary condition $z \to \infty$ is imposed by $A_2 = 0$. Now ψ must be continuous, so we must satisfy the conditions $B_1 = 0$ at $z = 0$ and

$$A_1 \sin(k_1 a) + B_1 \cos(k_1 a) = B_2 e^{-k_2 a} \qquad \text{(at } z = a) \tag{12.4.7}$$

This yields $A_1 \sin(k_1 a) = B_2 e^{-k_2 a}$. Similarly, ψ' must be continuous; hence,

$$A_1 k_1 \cos(k_1 a) = -B_2 k_2 e^{-k_2 a} \qquad \text{(at } z = a) \tag{12.4.8}$$

So, together we have

$$k_1 \cot(k_1 a) = -k_2 \tag{12.4.9}$$

Solving Eq. (12.4.9) gives the eigenenergy states for the electron. Note that minimal energy corresponds to minimal k_1 and k_2; thus, we should solve this equation numerically to find the minimal values of k_1 and k_2. To do this we write k_2 in terms of k_1:

$$k_1^2 = +\frac{2m}{\hbar^2}(E + V_0) \qquad k_2^2 = -\frac{2mE}{\hbar^2} \tag{12.4.10}$$

so, $2mV_0/\hbar^2 = k_1^2 + k_2^2$ or, $k_2 = \sqrt{\dfrac{2mV_0}{\hbar^2} - k_1^2}$. Thus, we obtain $-\cot(k_1 a) = \sqrt{2mV_0/\hbar^2 - k_1^2}/k_1$. Replacing $k_1 a$ by x we arrive at

$$-\cot x = \frac{\sqrt{2mV_0 a^2/\hbar^2 - x^2}}{x} \tag{12.4.11}$$

To find the minimal energy we draw a graph of $y_1 = -\cot x$ and $y_2 = \dfrac{\sqrt{2mV_0 a^2/\hbar^2 - x^2}}{x}$ and compute the value of x in the first intersection point between y_1 and y_2; see Fig. 12.5.

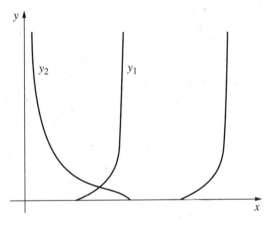

Fig. 12.5

The value of $2mV_0 a^2/\hbar^2$ is $10.498\,597$. We can use the program written in Problem 12.3 with the following function:

```
C** Function for which we want to find the zero.
      real function f(x)
      real x
      f=tan(x)+x/sqrt(10.49859654100631-x*x)
      return
      end
```

From Fig. 12.5 we see that the x value lies in the interval [2, 3]; so these will be our initial guesses in the program. Running the program with the appropriate change gives the following result:

```
The zero of f(x) is 2.336280823 obtained after 16 iterations.
```

This means that $k_1 a = \sqrt{2ma^2(E + V_0)/\hbar^2} = 2.336\,28$. Thus, the minimal energy eigenvalue is

$$E + V_0 = 5.2 \text{ eV} \tag{12.4.12}$$

12.5. Using the Numerov algorithm, write a program to solve the Schrödinger equation for an electron in a potential well:

$$V(x) = \begin{cases} 0 & 0 \le x \le a \\ \infty & \text{otherwise} \end{cases} \tag{12.5.1}$$

It is given that $a = 1$ Å. The program takes as input an initial guess for the energy value and gives as output the closest higher-energy eigenvalue. Compare your results to the analytical ones.

SOLUTION

The Schrödinger equation for this case is

$$\frac{d^2\psi}{dx^2} + \frac{2mE}{\hbar^2}\psi = 0 \tag{12.5.2}$$

Introducing the nondimensional variable $\xi = x/a$, we arrive at

$$\frac{d^2\psi}{d\zeta^2} + \frac{2ma^2E}{\hbar^2}\psi = 0 \tag{12.5.3}$$

This equation is of the form

$$\frac{d^2y}{dx^2} + k^2(x)y = S(x) \tag{12.5.4}$$

where $S(x) = 0$ and $k^2(x) = \text{const.} = 2mEa^2/\hbar^2$. In our program, we put in as an input the value of k and compute the initial value of $\psi(\zeta = 1) - (\texttt{psip})$. Then, using the Numerov method, we integrate the equation for k_i. We start from $\psi(0) = 0 - (\texttt{psim})$ and add to k an amount dk and integrate again. In each iteration we add dk until we get a value of $\texttt{psip}$ that has the opposite sign of the initial value of $\texttt{psip}$. At this point, we back up the value of k and jump in smaller steps dk than the value of 1×10^{-5}. We do this since we know that we passed over the value of k that we are trying to converge to. Running the following program with $k_i = 0$ gives the results shown at the end of the program. Note that we expect the convergence to correspond to the ground state, since it is the highest eigenvalue that is close to $E = 0$.

```
Program Problem 12.5
real k
real toler,psip,psiold

C** Get initial value of the wave number
    write (*,*) 'Enter the starting value of the wave number k:
    + (k<0 to stop)'
    read (*,*) k
    if (k.lt.0.) goto 20

C** Initial value of the step.
    dk=1.
    toler=1.E-05

C** Integrate the equation with initial value of k.
    call intgrt (k,psip)
    psiold=psip

C** Change the value of k.
  10 k=k+dk

C** integrate again with different values of k.
    call intgrt (k,psip)

C** If psip changes value backup (the secant method).
    if ((psip*psiold).lt.0) then
    k=k-dk
```

```
        dk=dk/2
        endif

C** If convergence is not achieved try again.
        if (abs (dk).gt.toler) goto 10
        write (*,*) ''
        write (*,*) ' The result is:'
        write (*,*) k

   20 stop
      end

C** Subroutine to integrate the Schrödinger equation using the Numerov
   method
        Subroutine intgrt (k,psip)
        real k,psia,psiz,h,const
        integer nstep

C** Number of steps
      nstep=100

C** Step value of normalized x.
      h=1.nstep

C** Left boundary condition.
        psim=0.
        psize=.01
        const=(k*h)**2/12.
        do 10 ix=1,nstep-1

C** Numerov method equation:
        psip=2* (1.-5. *const) *psiz -(1.+const)*psim
        psip=psip/(1+const)
        psim=psiz
        psiz=psip
   10 continue

C** The result achieved.
        write (*,*) 'The wave number:' ,k
        return
        end
```

Running the program with a starting value $k = 0.0$ yields the following:

```
The wave number:
   1.000000000   3.250000000   3.142578125   3.141601562
   2.000000000   3.187500000   3.141601562   3.141540527
   3.000000000   3.156250000   3.141113281   3.141601562
   4.000000000   3.140625000   3.141601562   3.141571045
   3.500000000   3.156250000   3.141357422   3.141601562
   3.250000000   3.148437500   3.141601562   3.141586304
   3.125000000   3.144531250   3.141479492   3.141601562
```

The result is 3.141586304.

Consider now the analytical solution. The eigenenergies are given by

$$E_n = \frac{\pi^2\hbar^2}{2ma^2}n^2$$ (12.5.5)

The ground state is $E_1 = \frac{\pi^2\hbar^2}{2ma^2}$, which corresponds to $k_1 = \sqrt{\frac{2ma^2}{\hbar^2}E_1} = \pi = 3.1415926\dots$

12.6. Consider the Schrödinger equation for potentials with radial symmetry $V(x, y, z) = V(r)$ and cylindrical symmetry $V(x, y) = V(\rho)$, and demonstrate how to solve these equations.

SOLUTION

For a problem with central potentials $V(r)$, the solution of the Schrödinger equation can be written as

$$\psi(\mathbf{r}) = \frac{R(r)}{r} Y_{lm}(\theta, \varphi) \tag{12.6.1}$$

where $Y_{lm}(\theta, \varphi)$ is the spherical harmonic, and $R(r)$ is a function of r satisfying the radial equation

$$\frac{d^2 R}{dr^2} + \frac{2M}{\hbar^2}\left[E - \frac{l(l+1)\hbar^2}{2Mr^2} - V(r) \right] R(r) = 0 \tag{12.6.2}$$

where E, l, and M are the eigenenergy, angular momentum, and mass, respectively. One can see that Eq. (12.6.2) is of the form of Eq. (12.23) with

$$S(r) = 0 \quad \text{and} \quad k^2(r) = \frac{2M}{\hbar^2}\left[E - \frac{l(l+1)\hbar^2}{2Mr^2} - V(r) \right] \tag{12.6.3}$$

This equation can be solved numerically using the Numerov alogrithm (see Problem 12.5). Similarly, for problems with a potential that has a cylindrical symmetry $V(\rho)$, the solution is of the form

$$\psi(\rho, \varphi, z) = \frac{R(\rho)}{\sqrt{\rho}} e^{im\varphi} e^{inz} \tag{12.6.4}$$

where m is the angular momentum in the z direction, n is an integer, and $R(\rho)$ is the solution of

$$\frac{d^2 R}{d\rho^2} + \frac{2M}{\hbar^2}\left[\frac{\hbar^2}{8M\rho^2} - \frac{\hbar^2(m^2 + n^2)}{2M} + E - V(\rho) \right] R(\rho) = 0 \tag{12.6.5}$$

where E and M are the energy eigenvalue and the mass, respectively. Also in this case it can be seen that this equation is of the form of Eq. (12.23) with

$$S(\rho) = 0 \quad \text{and} \quad k^2(\rho) = \frac{2M}{\hbar^2}\left[\frac{\hbar^2}{8M\rho^2} - \frac{\hbar^2(m^2 + n^2)}{2M} + E - V(r) \right] \tag{12.6.6}$$

Hence, this equation can also be solved with the Numerov method.

SUPPLEMENTARY PROBLEMS

12.7. Write a FORTRAN subroutine:

```
Subroutine Trapez (FUNC, N, A, B, S)
INTEGER N
REAL FUNC (0 : 1000), A, B, S
```

which computes the value of the integral of a function whose values are $N + 1$ points, given in the array FUNC in the interval $[A, B]$. The points are separated by $h = (B - A)/N$.

Ans.

```
C** Subroutine to compute the value of a definite integral.
    Subroutine Trapez (func,n,a,b,s)
    integer n
    real func(0:1000),a,b,s
    s=0.
    s=(func(0)+func(n))/2.
    do 1 i=1,n-1

C** (1-mod(i,2))equals 0 if i even and equals 1 if i odd
    s=s+func(i)
```

```
1 continue
  s=s*(b-a)/n
  return
  end
```

12.8. Solve numerically the integral obtained in Problem 5.3:

$$P_0 = 1 - \frac{2}{\sqrt{\pi}} \int_0^1 e^{-\eta^2} d\eta \qquad (12.8.1)$$

Use your preferred method.

Ans. Using the program from Problem 12.2, and changing the line `func(i) = exp (x*x)` into

$$\texttt{func(i) = 2/sqrt(a cos(-1.))*exp(-x*x)} \qquad (12.8.2)$$

we obtain $P_0 = 0.1578$. After calling the subroutine Simpson, we add the line

$$s = 1 - s \qquad (12.8.3)$$

12.9. Solve the equation $x^2 - 5 = 0$ with the initial guesses $x1 = 2$ and $x2 = 3$. Use the secant method

$$x^{i+1} = x^i - f(x^i) \frac{x^i - x^{i-1}}{f(x^i) - f(x^{i-1})} \qquad (12.9.1)$$

Obtain an accuracy of 1×10^{-5}.

Ans.

```
Program Problem 12.9
  real x1, x2, xtmp
  real f1, f2, toler
  integer iter
C** Initialize iterations' number.
    iter=0
C** Maximal error in the approximation.
    toler=0.00001
C ** Initial guesses.
    x1=2.
    x2=3.
C** Evaluate the function f(x)=x**2-5 at x=x1 and at x=x2:
    f1=x1*x1-5.
    f2=x2*x2-5.
C** If the new iteration does not give the same result of the previous
   iteration
C** within toler do the following:
    do while (abs x2-x1).gt.toler)
C** New iteration.
    iter=iter+1
    xtmp=x2-f2*(x2-x1)/(f2-f1)
    x1=x2
    x2=xtmp
C** Evaluate the function f(x)= x**2-5 at x=x1 and at x=x2:
    f1=x1*x1-5.
    f2=x2*x2-5.
    end do
C** Print result:
    write (*,*) 'The zero of f(x) is:',x1.
 10 format ('obtained after ',i3,' iterations.')
    write (*,10) iter
    stop
    end
```

CHAPTER 13

Identical Particles

13.1 Introduction

Suppose you have a basketball and your friend has a soccer ball with the same mass; you kick them toward each other, simultaneously, with the same velocity. Two things can happen: (*a*) The balls collide and each ball goes back to its owner. (*b*) The balls travel along parallel paths without touching and exchange hands. Since the balls have different shapes and colors you can tell which possibility occurred, (*a*) or (*b*). But if the balls were identical, you would not be able to tell what happened! When we consider identical quantum particles the situation gets even worse as we cannot even trace the exact trajectories of colliding particles. In this chapter we examine the special properties of a system composed of identical particles.

13.2 Permutations and Symmetries of Wavefunctions

Definition: We say that the particles of a system are *identical* (or indistinguishable) if no observer can detect any permutation of these particles.

The property of indistinguishability gives rise to symmetries in the system. Consider a system of n identical particles with the eigenvector $|\phi_i\rangle$ for the particle i ($i = 1, \ldots, n$). We denote the state of the system by a vector of eigenvectors $|\phi_1\rangle, |\phi_2\rangle, \ldots, |\phi_n\rangle$, keeping in mind that different ordering of the $|\phi_i\rangle$'s in two vectors corresponds to different vectors, e.g., if $n = 2$, $(|\phi_1\rangle, |\phi_2\rangle) \neq (|\phi_2\rangle, |\phi_1\rangle)$. If σ is a *permutation* on the letters $1, \ldots, n$, then it can be written as

$$\sigma = \begin{pmatrix} 1 & 2 & 3 & \cdots & n \\ \sigma(1) & \sigma(2) & \sigma(3) & \cdots & \sigma(n) \end{pmatrix} \tag{13.1}$$

meaning that the vector $1, 2, \ldots, n$ becomes $(|\sigma_1\rangle, |\sigma_2\rangle, \ldots, |\sigma_n\rangle)$ after the action of σ. Thus, σ permutes the eigenvectors:

$$\sigma(|\phi_1\rangle, \ldots, |\phi_n\rangle) = (|\phi_{\sigma(1)}\rangle, \ldots, |\phi_{\sigma(n)}\rangle) \tag{13.2}$$

One can see that σ acts as a linear operator. A permutation $\hat{\sigma}$ may be written as a product of *transpositions*, i.e., permutations that swap two letters. If the decomposition of $\hat{\sigma}$ consists of an even number of transpositions, then $\hat{\sigma}$ is called an even permutation, and we write $\text{sgn}(\hat{\sigma}) = 1$; if this number is odd, then $\hat{\sigma}$ is called an odd permutation denoted $\text{sgn}(\hat{\sigma}) = -1$. The vector $|u\rangle = |\phi_1\rangle, \ldots, |\phi_n\rangle$ is said to be symmetrical if $\hat{\sigma}|u\rangle = |u\rangle$ for an arbitrary permutation $\hat{\sigma}$. The same vector is said to be antisymmetric if $\hat{\sigma}|u\rangle = \text{sgn}(\hat{\sigma})|u\rangle$ for an arbitrary permutation $\hat{\sigma}$. We define two operators:

$$\hat{S} = \frac{1}{n!} \sum_{\sigma \text{ permutation}} \hat{\sigma} \tag{13.3}$$

and

$$\hat{A} = \frac{1}{n!} \sum_{\sigma \text{ permutation}} (\text{sgn}\,\hat{\sigma})\hat{\sigma} \tag{13.4}$$

$\hat{S}$ and $\hat{A}$ project the entire space of wavefunctions H on two subspaces: the space of symmetric wavefunctions a_S, and the space of antisymmetric wavefunctions a_A:

$$H_s = \hat{S}H \qquad H_A = \hat{A}H \tag{13.5}$$

and in addition $H = H_A \oplus H_S$; that is, every vector is a unique sum of a completely symmetrical vector and a completely antisymmetric vector. The verification is given in Problem 13.2.

An arbitrary antisymmetric wavefunction can be written $|u_A\rangle = \hat{A}|u\rangle$ for a wavefunction $|u\rangle = (|\phi_1\rangle, \ldots, |\phi_n\rangle)$. Hence, if $\{|\phi^{(j)}\rangle\}$ is a basis of the single-particle space of states, then a basis of the antisymmetric space of all n particles is given by applying $\hat{A}$ on a basis of the entire space, spanned by $|\phi^{j_1}\rangle, \ldots, |\phi^{j_n}\rangle$; thus,

$$|\alpha_{j_1, \ldots, j_n}\rangle = \hat{A}|(|\phi_1^{j_1}\rangle, |\phi_2^{j_2}\rangle, \ldots, |\phi_n^{j_n}\rangle) = \sum_{\sigma} \frac{1}{n!} (\text{sgn}\,\hat{\sigma})(|\phi_1^{j_{\sigma(1)}}\rangle, \ldots, |\phi^{j_{\sigma(n)}}\rangle)$$

or

$$|\alpha_{j_1, \ldots, j_n}\rangle = \frac{1}{n!} \begin{vmatrix} |\phi_1^{j_1}\rangle & |\phi_1^{j_2}\rangle & \cdots & |\phi_1^{j_n}\rangle \\ |\phi_2^{j_1}\rangle & |\phi_2^{j_2}\rangle & \cdots & |\phi_2^{j_n}\rangle \\ \vdots & & & \vdots \\ |\phi_n^{j_1}\rangle & |\phi_n^{j_2}\rangle & \cdots & |\phi_n^{j_n}\rangle \end{vmatrix} \tag{13.6}$$

is a basis of H_A. The last equality comes from the properties of the determinant. (Note that this is sometimes given as the definition of a determinant.) This determinant is known as the *Slater determinant* and is the solution for the Schrödinger equation for *noninteracting* fermions.

13.3 Bosons and Fermions

From experimental observations it seems there are two kinds of particles. The first kind consists of particles that have completely symmetrical wavefunctions; they are called *bosons*. The second kind consists of particles with completely antisymmetric wavefunctions; they are called *fermions*. There are no particles with mixed symmetry. The *Pauli exclusion principle* is a basic principle that is valid only for identical particles that are fermions. This principle states that two identical fermions cannot be in the same quantum state. An alternative formulation of this principle asserts that the probability of finding two identical fermions with the same quantum numbers is zero.

SOLVED PROBLEMS

13.1. (a) Compute the number of permutations on n letters. (b) Show that a product of two permutations is also a permutation.

SOLUTION

(a) The number of permutations equals the number of different orderings of n distinguished letters; the first letter has n places, the second letter has $n-1$ places, etc., and the nth letter has only one place. Hence, there are $n(n-1)(n-2)\cdots 1 = n!$ permutations.

(b) A permutation is a function $\hat{\sigma}$ from the set $\{1, \ldots, n\}$ to itself that is bijective, i.e., $\hat{\sigma}(i) \neq \hat{\sigma}(j)$ if $i \neq j$ and every i equals $\hat{\sigma}(j)$ for some j. A composition of two such functions is also a bijective function from $\{1, \ldots, n\}$ to itself, and hence a permutation.

13.2. Show that $\hat{S}$ and $\hat{A}$ are Hermitian operators.

SOLUTION

Let $\hat{\sigma}$ be any permutation, and denote $|u\rangle = (|\phi_1\rangle, \ldots, |\phi_n\rangle)$ and $|v\rangle = (|\theta_1\rangle, \ldots, |\theta_n\rangle)$; then

$$\langle v | \hat{\sigma} u \rangle = ((\langle\theta_1|, \ldots, \langle\theta_n|)(|\phi_{\sigma(1)}\rangle, \ldots, |\phi_{\sigma(n)}\rangle)) = \langle\theta_1|\phi_{\sigma(1)}\rangle\langle\theta_2|\phi_{\sigma(2)}\rangle \cdots \langle\theta_n|\phi_{\sigma(n)}\rangle$$

$$= \langle\theta_{\sigma^{-1}(1)}|\phi_1\rangle\langle\theta_{\sigma^{-1}(2)}|\phi_2\rangle \cdots \langle\theta_{\sigma^{-1}(n)}|\phi_n\rangle = \langle v\hat{\sigma}^{-1}|u\rangle \tag{13.2.1}$$

Hence, $\hat{\sigma}^\dagger = \hat{\sigma}^{-1}$ and therefore

$$\hat{S}^\dagger = \frac{1}{n!} \sum_{\sigma \text{ permutation}} \hat{\sigma}^\dagger = \frac{1}{n!} \sum_{\sigma \text{ permutation}} \hat{\sigma}^{-1} = \frac{1}{n!} \sum_{\sigma \text{ permutation}} \hat{\sigma} = \hat{S} \tag{13.2.2}$$

Also,

$$\hat{A}^\dagger = \frac{1}{n!} \sum_\sigma (\operatorname{sgn}\hat{\sigma})\hat{\sigma}^\dagger = \frac{1}{n!} \sum_\sigma (\operatorname{sgn}\hat{\sigma})\hat{\sigma}^{-1} = \frac{1}{n!} \sum_\sigma (\operatorname{sgn}\hat{\sigma}^{-1})\hat{\sigma}^{-1} = \frac{1}{n!} \sum_\sigma (\operatorname{sgn}\hat{\sigma})\hat{\sigma} = \hat{A} \tag{13.2.3}$$

13.3. Prove that $\hat{S}|u\rangle$ is a symmetric vector and $\hat{A}|u\rangle$ is an antisymmetric vector for an arbitrary $|u\rangle$.

SOLUTION

We prove that $\hat{S}|u\rangle$ is a symmetrical vector by showing that for an arbitrary permutation $\hat{\tau}, \hat{\tau}(\hat{S}|u\rangle) = \hat{S}|u\rangle$, so

$$\hat{\tau}\hat{S}|u\rangle = \hat{\tau}\frac{1}{n!} \sum_\sigma \hat{\sigma}|u\rangle = \frac{1}{n!} \sum_\sigma \hat{\tau}\hat{\sigma}|u\rangle = \frac{1}{n!} \sum_{\sigma'} \hat{\sigma}'|u\rangle = \hat{S}|u\rangle \tag{13.3.1}$$

Similarly,

$$\hat{\tau}\hat{A}|u\rangle = \hat{\tau}\frac{1}{n!} \sum_\sigma (\operatorname{sgn}\hat{\sigma})\hat{\sigma}|u\rangle = \frac{1}{n!} \sum_\sigma (\operatorname{sgn}\hat{\sigma})\hat{\sigma}\hat{\tau}|u\rangle$$

$$= (\operatorname{sgn}\hat{\tau})^{-1}\frac{1}{n!} \sum_\sigma (\operatorname{sgn}\hat{\sigma})(\operatorname{sgn}\hat{\tau})\hat{\sigma}\hat{\tau}|u\rangle = (\operatorname{sgn}\hat{\tau})\frac{1}{n!} \sum_\sigma (\operatorname{sgn}\hat{\sigma}\hat{\tau})\hat{\sigma}\hat{\tau}|u\rangle$$

$$= (\operatorname{sgn}\hat{\tau})\frac{1}{n!} \sum_{\sigma'} (\operatorname{sgn}\hat{\sigma}')\hat{\sigma}'|u\rangle = (\operatorname{sgn}\hat{\tau})\hat{A}|u\rangle \tag{13.3.2}$$

Note that the permutations form a *group*; thus every element has an inverse, and therefore

$$\sum \hat{\sigma} = \sum \hat{\sigma}^{-1} = \hat{\tau}\sum \hat{\sigma} \tag{13.3.3}$$

We used the fact that $\operatorname{sgn}(\sigma\tau) = (\operatorname{sgn}\sigma)(\operatorname{sgn}\tau)$, which can be verified.

13.4. Show that: (*a*) $\hat{S}^2 = \hat{S}$; (*b*) $\hat{A}^2 = \hat{A}$; (*c*) $\hat{A}\hat{S} = \hat{S}\hat{A} = 0$.

SOLUTION

(*a*) Using the results of Problem 13.3, we can write

$$\hat{S}^2 = \left(\frac{1}{n!} \sum_\sigma \hat{\sigma}\right)\hat{S} = \frac{1}{n!} \sum_\sigma \hat{\sigma}\hat{S} = \frac{1}{n!} \sum_\sigma \hat{\sigma}\hat{S} = \frac{1}{n!} \sum_\sigma \hat{S} = \frac{n!}{n!}\hat{S} = \hat{S} \tag{13.4.1}$$

(*b*) As in part (*a*) we have

$$\hat{A}^2 = \frac{1}{n!}\sum_{\sigma'}(\text{sgn}\,\hat{\sigma})\hat{\sigma}\hat{A} = \frac{1}{n!}\sum_{\sigma}(\text{sgn}\,\hat{\sigma})(\text{sgn}\,\hat{\sigma})\hat{A} = \frac{1}{n!}\sum_{\sigma}1\cdot\hat{A} = \hat{A} \qquad (13.4.2)$$

(*c*) By definition,

$$\hat{A}\hat{S} = \frac{1}{n!}\sum_{\sigma'}(\text{sgn}\,\hat{\sigma})\hat{\sigma}\hat{S} = \frac{1}{n!}\hat{S}\sum_{\sigma}\text{sgn}\,\hat{\sigma} = 0 \qquad (13.4.3)$$

and

$$\hat{S}\hat{A} = \frac{1}{n!}\sum_{\sigma}\hat{\sigma}\hat{A} = \frac{1}{n!}\hat{A}\sum_{\sigma}\text{sgn}\,\hat{\sigma} = 0 \qquad (13.4.4)$$

13.5. Use the symmetrization postulate for fermions to derive the Pauli exclusion principle.

SOLUTION

The symmetrization postulate for fermions states that the wavefunction of a system of n identical fermions is completely antisymmetric. Thus, it is a linear combination of vectors of the form $|\alpha_{j_1\ldots j_n}\rangle$. These normalized vectors can be written as

$$|\alpha_{j_1\ldots j_n}\rangle = \frac{1}{\sqrt{n!}}\begin{vmatrix} |\phi_1^{j_1}\rangle & |\phi_1^{j_2}\rangle & \cdots & |\phi_1^{j_n}\rangle \\ |\phi_2^{j_1}\rangle & |\phi_2^{j_2}\rangle & \cdots & |\phi_2^{j_n}\rangle \\ \vdots & & & \vdots \\ |\phi_n^{j_1}\rangle & |\phi_n^{j_2}\rangle & \cdots & |\phi_n^{j_n}\rangle \end{vmatrix} \qquad (13.5.1)$$

Hence, if *two* particles are in the same quantum state, two columns are the same, forcing the determinant to vanish; consequently, no nontrivial wavefunction exists in this case. This result proves the Pauli exclusion principle.

13.6. Show explicitly that Slater's determinant for two particles (fermions) is antisymmetric.

SOLUTION

The Slater determinant for two fermions is given by

$$|u(1,2)\rangle = \frac{1}{2!}\begin{vmatrix} |\phi_1^{j_1}\rangle & |\phi_1^{j_2}\rangle \\ |\phi_2^{j_1}\rangle & |\phi_2^{j_2}\rangle \end{vmatrix} = \frac{1}{2}(|\phi_1^{j_1}\rangle|\phi_2^{j_2}\rangle - |\phi_1^{j_2}\rangle|\phi_2^{j_1}\rangle) \qquad (13.6.1)$$

and

$$|u(2,1)\rangle = \frac{1}{2}(|\phi_2^{j_1}\rangle|\phi_1^{j_2}\rangle - |\phi_2^{j_2}\rangle|\phi_1^{j_1}\rangle) \qquad (13.6.2)$$

thus, $|u(2,1)\rangle = -|u(1,2)\rangle$.

13.7. Show that the Slater determinant is a zero-order approximation to the Schrödinger equation of a system of n identical fermions.

SOLUTION

Consider the Schrödinger equation $\hat{H}(1,2,\ldots,n)|\psi\rangle = E|\psi\rangle$. Neglecting the interactions between the particles, we write $\hat{H}_0(1,2,\ldots,n)$ for the zero-order approximation of $\hat{H}$:

$$\hat{H}_0(1,2,\ldots,n) = \hat{H}_0^s(1)\oplus\cdots\oplus\hat{H}_0^s(2) \qquad (13.7.1)$$

For every $\hat{H}_0^s(i)$ we have $\hat{H}_0^s(i)|\phi_i^j\rangle = E_i^j|\phi_i^j\rangle$, where i stands for particle number and j counts the different eigenvectors and eigenfunctions. Since the Slater determinant is a combination of different eigenfunctions such as $|\phi_1^{j_1}\rangle \cdots |\phi_n^{j_n}\rangle$ and since the particles do not interact, the function

$$|u_{1A}\rangle = \frac{1}{\sqrt{n!}} \begin{vmatrix} |\phi_1^{j_1}\rangle & |\phi_1^{j_2}\rangle & \cdots & |\phi_1^{j_n}\rangle \\ |\phi_2^{j_1}\rangle & |\phi_2^{j_2}\rangle & \cdots & |\phi_2^{j_n}\rangle \\ \vdots & & & \vdots \\ |\phi_n^{j_1}\rangle & |\phi_n^{j_2}\rangle & \cdots & |\phi_n^{j_n}\rangle \end{vmatrix}$$

(13.7.2)

is a solution to the equation $\hat{H}_0|\psi\rangle = E|\psi\rangle$.

13.8. Three imaginary "spinless" fermions are confined to a one-dimensional box of length L. The confinement potential is

$$V = \begin{cases} 0 & 0 \le x \le L \\ \infty & \text{otherwise} \end{cases}$$

(13.8.1)

We assume that there is no interaction between the fermions. *(a)* What is the ground state of the system? *(b)* Find the state of the system.

SOLUTION

(a) As shown in Chap. 3, the eigenstates of this system are

$$\psi_n = \sqrt{\frac{2}{L}}\sin\left(\frac{\pi n x}{L}\right) \qquad E_n = \frac{\pi^2\hbar^2 n^2}{2mL^2}$$

(13.8.2)

Since two fermions cannot occupy the same state, the three fermions are in distinct states, and since the system is in the ground state, the states will be ψ_1, ψ_2, and ψ_3 with a total energy $\dfrac{\pi^2\hbar^2}{2mL^2}(1^2 + 2^2 + 3^2)$. Schematically, the structure of the system is depicted in Fig. 13.1.

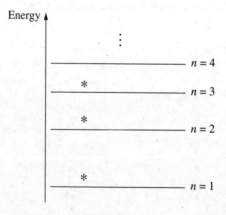

Fig. 13.1

(b) The antisymmetric state is given by

$$\psi = (\text{normalizing factor}) \times (\text{Slater determinant}) = \frac{1}{\sqrt{3!}} \begin{vmatrix} |\psi_1(x_1)\rangle & |\psi_2(x_1)\rangle & |\psi_3(x_1)\rangle \\ |\psi_1(x_2)\rangle & |\psi_2(x_2)\rangle & |\psi_3(x_2)\rangle \\ |\psi_1(x_3)\rangle & |\psi_2(x_3)\rangle & |\psi_3(x_3)\rangle \end{vmatrix}$$

(13.8.3)

13.9. Repeat Problem 13.8 for three electrons. Ignore the Coulomb interaction between the electrons.

SOLUTION

(*a*) An electron has spin 1/2; thus, the eigenstates and eigenvalues are

$$\psi_n^+ = \sqrt{\frac{2}{L}} \sin\left(\frac{n\pi x}{L}\right)\begin{pmatrix} 1 \\ 0 \end{pmatrix} \qquad \psi_n^- = \sqrt{\frac{2}{L}} \sin\left(\frac{n\pi x}{L}\right)\begin{pmatrix} 0 \\ 1 \end{pmatrix} \tag{13.9.1}$$

where $E_n = \pi^2\hbar^2 n^2/2mL^2$. The additional degree of freedom, namely, the spin, allows us to put two electrons in the first energy level, since this energy level corresponds now to two different eigenstates: spin up and spin down. Thus, there are two possible configurations for the ground state; they are depicted in Fig. 13.2.

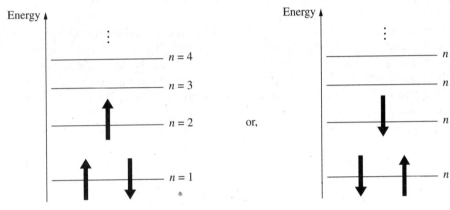

Fig. 13.2

(*b*) There are three basic functions for each diagram in Fig. 13.2. For the left diagram we have ψ_1^+, ψ_1^-, ψ_2^+ and for the right diagram we have ψ_1^+, ψ_1^-, ψ_2^-. Using the Slater determinant, we get

$$\Psi_{\text{left}} = \frac{1}{\sqrt{6}} \begin{vmatrix} |\psi_1^+(x_1)\rangle & |\psi_1^-(x_1)\rangle & |\psi_2^+(x_1)\rangle \\ |\psi_1^+(x_2)\rangle & |\psi_1^-(x_2)\rangle & |\psi_2^+(x_2)\rangle \\ |\psi_1^+(x_3)\rangle & |\psi_1^-(x_3)\rangle & |\psi_2^+(x_3)\rangle \end{vmatrix} \tag{13.9.2}$$

and

$$\Psi_{\text{right}} = \frac{1}{\sqrt{6}} \begin{vmatrix} |\psi_1^+(x_1)\rangle & |\psi_1^-(x_1)\rangle & |\psi_2^-(x_1)\rangle \\ |\psi_1^+(x_2)\rangle & |\psi_1^-(x_2)\rangle & |\psi_2^-(x_2)\rangle \\ |\psi_1^+(x_3)\rangle & |\psi_1^-(x_3)\rangle & |\psi_2^-(x_3)\rangle \end{vmatrix} \tag{13.9.3}$$

13.10. A system is composed of two fermions with spin 1/2. Find the "two-particle density function" and the "one-particle density function" if both electrons are in different normalized orthogonal states.

SOLUTION

Suppose that each of the electrons has a different spin $|\phi_1(\mathbf{r}); +\rangle$ and $|\phi_2(\mathbf{r}); -\rangle$, respectively. In this case the common wavefunction has the form

$$|\psi(1, 2, \mathbf{r}_1, \mathbf{r}_2)\rangle = |\phi_1(\mathbf{r}_1); +\rangle |\phi_2(\mathbf{r}_2); -\rangle - |\phi_1(\mathbf{r}_2); +\rangle |\phi_2(\mathbf{r}_1); -\rangle \tag{13.10.1}$$

So,

$$\rho_{\text{two par.}}(\mathbf{r}_1, \mathbf{r}_2) = \langle \psi | \psi \rangle = |\phi_1(\mathbf{r}_1)|^2 |\phi_2(\mathbf{r}_2)|^2 + |\phi_1(\mathbf{r}_2)|^2 |\phi_2(\mathbf{r}_1)|^2 \tag{13.10.2}$$

and

$$\rho_{\text{one par.}}(\mathbf{r}_1) = \int \rho_{\text{two par.}}(\mathbf{r}_1, \mathbf{r}_2)\, d^3 r_2 = |\phi_1(\mathbf{r}_1)|^2 + |\phi_2(\mathbf{r}_1)|^2 \tag{13.10.3}$$

If both electrons have spin $|+\rangle$, we obtain

$$|\psi(1, 2, \mathbf{r}_1, \mathbf{r}_2)\rangle = |\phi_1(\mathbf{r}_1); +\rangle\, |\phi_2(\mathbf{r}_2); +\rangle - |\phi_1(\mathbf{r}_2); +\rangle\, |\phi_2(\mathbf{r}_1); +\rangle \tag{13.10.4}$$

and

$$\rho_{\text{two par.}}(\mathbf{r}_1, \mathbf{r}_2) = |\phi_1(\mathbf{r}_1)|^2 |\phi_2(\mathbf{r}_2)|^2 - 2\phi_1(\mathbf{r}_1)\phi_2(\mathbf{r}_1)\phi_1(\mathbf{r}_2)\phi_2(\mathbf{r}_2) + |\phi_1(\mathbf{r}_2)|^2|\phi_2(\mathbf{r}_1)|^2 \tag{13.10.5}$$

13.11. A system contains two identical spinless particles. The one-particle states are spanned by an orthonormal system $\{|\phi_k\rangle\}$. Suppose that the particles' states are $|\phi_i\rangle$ and $|\phi_j\rangle$ ($i \neq j$). (a) Find the probability of finding the particles in the states $|\xi\rangle$ and $|\eta\rangle$ (not necessarily eigenstates). (b) What is the probability that one of them is in the state $|\xi\rangle$? (c) Suppose now that the particles are not identical and they are measured with an instrument that cannot distinguish between them. Answer parts (a) and (b) for this case.

SOLUTION

(a) The symmetric state of the system is given by

$$\Phi_1 = \frac{1}{\sqrt{2}}\left(|\phi_i^{(1)}\rangle\,|\phi_j^{(2)}\rangle + |\phi_j^{(1)}\rangle\,|\phi_i^{(2)}\rangle\right) \tag{13.11.1}$$

The new state is also symmetric; it is given by

$$\Phi_2 = \frac{1}{\sqrt{2}}\left(|\xi^{(1)}\rangle|\eta^{(2)}\rangle + |\xi^{(2)}\rangle|\eta^{(1)}\rangle\right) \tag{13.11.2}$$

Thus, the probability is

$$P_1 = |\langle\Phi_1|\Phi_2\rangle|^2 = |\langle\xi|\phi_i\rangle\langle\eta|\phi_j\rangle + \langle\eta|\phi_i\rangle\langle\xi|\phi_j\rangle|^2 \tag{13.11.3}$$

(b) Consider the symmetric state that corresponds to $|\xi\rangle$ and to the eigenstate $|\phi_k\rangle$:

$$|\Phi_{\xi,\phi_k}\rangle = \frac{1}{\sqrt{2}}\left(|\xi^{(1)}\rangle|\phi_k^{(2)}\rangle + |\phi_k^{(1)}\rangle|\xi\rangle\right) \tag{13.11.4}$$

In order to find the probability of one particle being in the state $|\xi\rangle$, we multiply $|\Phi_{\xi,\phi_k}\rangle$ on the left-hand side with $\langle\Phi_1|$ (the original state) and sum over all k:

$$P_2 = \sum_k |\langle\Phi_1|\Phi_{\xi,\phi_k}\rangle|^2 = \sum_k |\langle\phi_i|\xi\rangle\langle\phi_j|\phi_k\rangle + \langle\phi_j|\xi\rangle\langle\phi_i|\phi_k\rangle|^2$$

$$= \sum_k |\langle\phi_i|\xi\rangle\delta_{jk} + \langle\phi_i|\xi\rangle\delta_{ik}|^2 = |\langle\phi_i|\xi\rangle|^2 + |\langle\phi_j|\xi\rangle|^2 \tag{13.11.5}$$

(c) The state of the system is now $|\Phi_1\rangle$. Hence, by multiplying with the final state $\langle\xi^{(1)}|\langle\eta^{(2)}| + \langle\xi^{(2)}|\langle\eta^{(1)}|$ we obtain

$$P_3 = |\langle\xi^{(1)}|\eta^{(2)}|\Phi_1\rangle|^2 + |\langle\xi^{(2)}|\eta^{(1)}|\Phi_1\rangle|^2 = |\langle\xi|\phi_i\rangle\langle\eta|\phi_j\rangle + \langle\xi|\phi_j\rangle\langle\eta|\phi_i\rangle|^2 = P_1 \tag{13.11.6}$$

and

$$P_3 = \sum_k |\langle \xi^{(1)} | \phi_k^{(2)} | \Phi_1 \rangle|^2 = \sum_{k'} |\langle \phi_{k'}^{(1)} | \xi^{(2)} | \Phi_1 \rangle|^2 = P_2 \tag{13.11.7}$$

13.12. Suppose that a domain D contains n identical particles, and outside D there are additional identical particles such that the interaction between particles not in the same domain is negligible. Show that in region D it is enough to do antisymmetrization of the n particles in D without considering the rest of the identical particles. In your answer, refer only to the case of $n = 2$ fermions. (The result for bosons is the same.)

SOLUTION

Let $|\chi\rangle$ and $|\phi\rangle$ be physical antisymmetric states of the D-particles. Those functions vanish outside D. Neglecting the other identical particles, the probability of getting an eigenvalue of $|\chi\rangle$ when the system is at state $|\phi\rangle$ is $\omega = |\langle \chi | \phi \rangle|^2$. We now show that the same result is obtained when we do not neglect the other $N - 2$ fermions.

Let $\{|\theta_i\rangle\}$ be a complete set of orthonormal physical (antisymmetric) vectors of the $N - 2$ particles outside of D; that is, $|\theta_i\rangle$ vanishes in D. Define F as a permutation between two particles in D or between two particles not in D. Also, define G as a permutation between particles from D and particles not in D. There are $2!(N - 2)!$ permutations of the F-kind, and $N! - 2!(N - 2)!$ permutations of the G-kind. The total physical state of the system must be antisymmetric for all N particles. In the basis $|\chi\theta_i\rangle$,

$$|X\rangle_{\text{phy}} = C\hat{A} |\chi\theta_i\rangle \tag{13.12.1}$$

$\hat{A}$ is the antisymmetrization operator where C is a normalization constant, which we now compute:

$$\langle \chi'\theta' | \hat{A} | \chi\theta \rangle = \frac{1}{N!} \sum_\sigma \text{sgn } \sigma \langle \chi'\theta' | \hat{A} | \chi\theta \rangle$$

$$= \frac{1}{N!} \left(\sum_F \text{sgn } F \langle \chi'\theta' | F | \chi\theta \rangle + \sum_G \text{sgn } G \langle \chi'\theta' | G | \chi\theta \rangle \right) \tag{13.12.2}$$

By the definitions of $|\chi\rangle$ and $|\theta\rangle$, the second term vanishes; so,

$$\langle \chi'\theta' | \hat{A} | \chi\theta \rangle = \frac{1}{N!} \sum_F (\text{sgn } F)^2 \langle \chi'\theta' | \chi\theta \rangle = \frac{2!(N-2)!}{N!} \langle \chi'\theta' | \chi\theta \rangle \tag{13.12.3}$$

Thus $C = \sqrt{\dfrac{N!}{2!(N-2)!}}$. The probability of getting an eigenvalue of $|\chi\rangle$ for the two fermions when the $(N-2)$-state is $|\psi\rangle$ and the D-state is $|\phi\rangle$ will be

$$P = \sum_i {}_{\text{phy}}\langle X_i | X \rangle_{\text{phy}} = \sum_i |\langle \chi\theta_i | \hat{A}^\dagger CCA | \phi\psi \rangle|^2 = C^4 \sum_i |\langle \chi\theta_i | \hat{A}^2 | \phi\psi \rangle|^2 = C^4 \sum_i |\langle \chi\theta_i | \hat{A} | \phi\psi \rangle|^2$$

$$= C^4 \sum_i |C^{-2} \langle \chi\theta_i | \phi\psi \rangle|^2 = \sum_i |\langle \chi\theta_i | \phi\psi \rangle|^2 = \langle \chi | \phi \rangle^2 \sum_i |\langle \theta_i | \psi \rangle|^2 = |\langle \chi | \phi \rangle|^2 \tag{13.12.4}$$

SUPPLEMENTARY PROBLEMS

13.13. Prove that the Pauli exclusion principle does not hold for bosons.

13.14. Show explicitly that the Slater determinant for three fermions is antisymmetric.

13.15. Show that any function on the real line is a sum of symmetric and antisymmetric functions.

Ans. $f(x) = \dfrac{f(x) + f(-x)}{2} + \dfrac{f(x) - f(-x)}{2}$

13.16. What happens to the Slater determinant if there is a linear dependency between $|\phi^{j_1}\rangle \cdots |\phi^{j_n}\rangle$?

Ans. It vanishes.

13.17. Three particles are confined within the potential

$$V(x, y) = \begin{cases} 0 & 0 \le x \le a \text{ and } 0 \le y \le b \\ \infty & \text{otherwise} \end{cases} \qquad (13.17.1)$$

Find the ground state of the system when the particles are bosons.

Ans. $|\psi_0(\mathbf{r}_1, \mathbf{r}_2, \mathbf{r}_3)\rangle = |\phi_{1,1}(\mathbf{r}_1)\phi_{1,1}(\mathbf{r}_2)\phi_{1,1}(\mathbf{r}_3)\rangle$, where $\phi_{n_x,n_y}(x, y) = \sqrt{\dfrac{4}{ab}} \sin\left(\dfrac{n_x\pi x}{a}\right)\sin\left(\dfrac{n_y\pi y}{b}\right)$.

13.18. Refer to Problem 13.14 and find the ground state of the system when the particles are "spinless" fermions. (That is, use Pauli's exclusion principle, but neglect the additional degree of spin.)

Ans. $|\psi_0(\mathbf{r}_1, \mathbf{r}_2, \mathbf{r}_3)\rangle = \dfrac{1}{\sqrt{3!}} \begin{vmatrix} |\phi_{11}(\mathbf{r}_1)\rangle & |\phi_{12}(\mathbf{r}_1)\rangle & |\phi_{21}(\mathbf{r}_1)\rangle \\ |\phi_{11}(\mathbf{r}_2)\rangle & |\phi_{12}(\mathbf{r}_2)\rangle & |\phi_{21}(\mathbf{r}_2)\rangle \\ |\phi_{11}(\mathbf{r}_3)\rangle & |\phi_{12}(\mathbf{r}_3)\rangle & |\phi_{21}(\mathbf{r}_3)\rangle \end{vmatrix}$

13.19. Solve Problems 13.14 and 13.15 without neglecting the spin.

Ans. $|\psi_0(\mathbf{r}_1, \mathbf{r}_2, \mathbf{r}_3)\rangle = \dfrac{1}{\sqrt{3!}} \begin{vmatrix} |\phi_{11}^+(\mathbf{r}_1)\rangle & |\phi_{11}^-(\mathbf{r}_1)\rangle & |\phi_{12}^-(\mathbf{r}_1)\rangle \\ |\phi_{11}^+(\mathbf{r}_2)\rangle & |\phi_{11}^-(\mathbf{r}_2)\rangle & |\phi_{12}^-(\mathbf{r}_2)\rangle \\ |\phi_{11}^+(\mathbf{r}_3)\rangle & |\phi_{11}^-(\mathbf{r}_3)\rangle & |\phi_{12}^-(\mathbf{r}_3)\rangle \end{vmatrix}$ and, three additional states by substituting

$\phi_{12}^+, \phi_{21}^-,$ and ϕ_{21}^+ for ϕ_{12}^-.

13.20. Solve Problem 13.10 for two bosons.

Ans. $|\Phi(1, 2, \mathbf{r}_1, \mathbf{r}_2)\rangle = |\phi_1(\mathbf{r}_1); S_1\rangle|\phi_2(\mathbf{r}_2); S_2\rangle + |\phi_1(\mathbf{r}_2); S_1\rangle|\phi_2(\mathbf{r}_1); S_2\rangle$

$\rho_{\text{two par.}}(\mathbf{r}_1, \mathbf{r}_2) = \begin{cases} |\phi_1(\mathbf{r}_1)|^2 |\phi_2(\mathbf{r}_2)|^2 + |\phi_1(\mathbf{r}_2)|^2 |\phi_2(\mathbf{r}_1)|^2 & S_1 \ne S_2 \\ |\phi_1(\mathbf{r}_1)\phi_2(\mathbf{r}_2) + \phi_1(\mathbf{r}_2)\phi_2(\mathbf{r}_1)|^2 & S_1 = S_2 \end{cases}$

$\rho_{\text{one par.}}(\mathbf{r}_1) = \displaystyle\int \rho_{\text{two par.}}(\mathbf{r}_1, \mathbf{r}_2) d^3r_2 = |\phi_1(\mathbf{r}_1)|^2 + |\phi_2(\mathbf{r}_1)|^2$

CHAPTER 14

Addition of Angular Momenta

14.1 Introduction

Consider two angular momenta $\hat{\mathbf{j}}_1$ and $\hat{\mathbf{j}}_2$. These momenta can be angular momenta relating to two different particles or angular momenta relating to one particle (angular momentum and spin). These two momenta act in different state spaces, and all their components commute with one another. The individual eigenstates of $\hat{\mathbf{j}}_1$ and $\hat{\mathbf{j}}_2$ will be denoted, as usual, by $|j_1 m_1\rangle$ and $|j_2 m_2\rangle$, so that (see Chap. 6)

$$\begin{cases} \hat{\mathbf{j}}_1^2 |j_1 m_1\rangle = \hbar^2 j_1(j_1 + 1)|j_1 m_1\rangle \\ \hat{j}_{1z}|j_1 m_1\rangle = \hbar m_1|j_1 m_1\rangle \end{cases} \tag{14.1}$$

and similarly for $\hat{\mathbf{j}}_2$. The state space of the compound system is obtained by taking the direct product (tensor product) of the individual state space of the two angular momenta:

$$|j_1 m_1\rangle \otimes |j_2 m_2\rangle = |j_1 j_2; m_1 m_2\rangle \equiv |m_1 m_2\rangle \tag{14.2}$$

For fixed j_1 and j_2, m_1 and m_2 have the values

$$\begin{cases} m_1 = -j_1, -j_1 + 1, \ldots, j_1 \\ m_2 = -j_2, -j_2 + 1, \ldots, j_2 \end{cases} \tag{14.3}$$

where the set of numbers $\{j_1, m_1\}$ and $\{j_2, m_2\}$ are either integers or half-integers. The state space of the compound system is $(2j_1 + 1)(2j_2 + 1)$-dimensional space. The states $|m_1 m_2\rangle$ are, according to their construction, eigenstates of the operators $\{\hat{\mathbf{j}}_1^2, \hat{\mathbf{j}}_2^2, \hat{j}_{1z}, \hat{j}_{2z}\}$.

14.2 $\{\hat{\mathbf{j}}_1^2, \hat{\mathbf{j}}_2^2, \hat{\mathbf{J}}^2, \hat{J}_z\}$ Basis

In the absence of interaction between $\hat{\mathbf{j}}_1$ and $\hat{\mathbf{j}}_2$, the operators $\hat{\mathbf{j}}_1$ and $\hat{\mathbf{j}}_2$ commute with the Hamiltonian, and thus, $|j_1 m_1\rangle$ and $|j_2 m_2\rangle$ are also eigenstates of the system. However, if $\hat{\mathbf{j}}_1$ and $\hat{\mathbf{j}}_2$ interact with

$$\hat{H} = \hat{H}_0 + \alpha \hat{\mathbf{j}}_1 \cdot \hat{\mathbf{j}}_2 \qquad \text{(where } \alpha \text{ is a coupling constant)} \tag{14.4}$$

then $\hat{\mathbf{j}}_1$ and $\hat{\mathbf{j}}_2$ are not conserved, but $\hat{\mathbf{J}} = \hat{\mathbf{j}}_1 + \hat{\mathbf{j}}_2$ is conserved. Thus, it is better to transform to an eigenstate basis of the operators $\{\hat{\mathbf{j}}_1^2, \hat{\mathbf{j}}_2^2, \hat{\mathbf{J}}^2, \hat{J}_z\}$. The eigenstates in this basis will be denoted by $|j_1 j_2 JM\rangle \equiv |JM\rangle$, and satisfy

$$\begin{cases} \hat{\mathbf{J}}^2|JM\rangle = \hbar^2 J(J + 1)|JM\rangle \\ \hat{J}_z|JM\rangle = \hbar M|JM\rangle \end{cases} \tag{14.5}$$

In this case,

$$J = |j_1 - j_2|, |j_1 - j_2| + 1, \ldots, j_1 + j_2 \tag{14.6}$$

and for each value of J,

$$M = -J, -J+1, \ldots, J \tag{14.7}$$

Note that

$$\hat{\mathbf{j}}_1^2 |JM\rangle = \hbar^2 j_1(j_1+1)|JM\rangle \tag{14.8}$$

Therefore, using the identity

$$2\hat{\mathbf{j}}_1 \cdot \hat{\mathbf{j}}_2 = \hat{\mathbf{J}}^2 - \hat{\mathbf{j}}_1^2 - \hat{\mathbf{j}}_2^2 \tag{14.9}$$

we have

$$\hat{\mathbf{j}}_1 \cdot \hat{\mathbf{j}}_2 |JM\rangle = \frac{\hbar^2}{2}[J(J+1) - j_1(j_1+1) - j_2(j_2+1)]|JM\rangle \tag{14.10}$$

As a result, $|JM\rangle$ are also eigenstates of the operators $\hat{\mathbf{j}}_1 \cdot \hat{\mathbf{j}}_2$. In a commonly employed terminology, one refers to $|JM\rangle$ as an eigenstate in the *coupled representation* and to $|m_1 m_2\rangle$ as an eigenstate in the *uncoupled representation*.

14.3 Clebsch–Gordan Coefficients

The two sets of orthonormal states $|m_1 m_2\rangle$ and $|JM\rangle$ are related by a unitary transformation; that is, we can write the eigenstates $|JM\rangle$ in terms of $|m_1 m_2\rangle$ by

$$|JM\rangle = \sum_{m_1,m_2} \langle m_1 m_2 | JM\rangle |m_1 m_2\rangle \tag{14.11}$$

where $\langle m_1 m_2 | JM\rangle$ are the *Clebsch–Gordan coefficients*. It is possible to obtain a general expression for the Clebsch–Gordan coefficients. However, it is often simpler to construct the coefficients for particular cases. They can be calculated by successive applications of the *step operators* $\hat{J}_\pm = \hat{J}_x \pm i\hat{J}_y$ on the vectors $|JM\rangle$, using the following relations:

$$\begin{cases} \hat{J}_\pm |JM\rangle = \hbar\sqrt{J(J+1) - M(M\pm 1)}\,|J, M\pm 1\rangle \\ \hat{J}_{1\pm} |m_1 m_2\rangle = \hbar\sqrt{J_1(J_1+1) - m_1(m_1+1)}\,|m_1\pm 1, m_2\rangle \end{cases} \tag{14.12}$$

together with the *phase condition*,

$$|J = J_1 + J_2, M = \pm(j_1+j_2)\rangle = |m_1 = \pm j_1, m_2 = \pm j_2\rangle \tag{14.13}$$

Some properties of the Clebsch–Gordan coefficients are given below:

$$\langle m_1 m_2 | JM\rangle = 0 \quad \text{unless} \quad M = m_1 + m_2 \tag{14.14}$$

$$\langle m_1 m_2 | JM\rangle \text{ is real} \tag{14.15}$$

$$\sum_{m_1=-j_1}^{j_1} \sum_{m_2=-j_2}^{j_2} \langle JM | m_1 m_2\rangle \langle m_1 m_2 | J'M'\rangle = \delta_{JJ'}, \delta_{MM'} \tag{14.16}$$

$$\sum_{J=|j_1-j_2|}^{j_1+j_2} \sum_{M=-J}^{J} \langle m_1 m_2 | JM \rangle \langle JM | m_1' m_2' \rangle = \delta_{m_1 m_1'} \delta_{m_2 m_2'} \tag{14.17}$$

$$\sqrt{J(J+1) - M(M \pm 1)} \langle m_1 m_2 | J, M+1 \rangle = \sqrt{j_1(j_1+1) - m_1(m_1 \mp 1)} | m_1 \mp 1, m_2 | JM \rangle$$
$$+ \sqrt{j_2(j_2+1) - m_2(m_2 \mp 1)} \langle m_1, m_2 - 1 | JM \rangle \tag{14.18}$$

$$\langle m_2 m_1 | JM \rangle = (-1)^{j_1+j_2-J} \langle m_1 m_2 | JM \rangle \tag{14.19}$$

$$\langle -m_1, -m_2 | J, -M \rangle = (-1)^{j_1+j_2-J} \langle m_1 m_2 | JM \rangle \tag{14.20}$$

SOLVED PROBLEMS

14.1. Consider two angular momenta of magnitudes j_1 and j_2. The total angular momentum of this system is then $\hat{\mathbf{J}} = \hat{\mathbf{J}}_1 + \hat{\mathbf{J}}_2$, where $\hat{\mathbf{J}}_1$ and $\hat{\mathbf{J}}_2$ are commuting operators. Let $|m_1 m_2\rangle$ be the common eigenstates of the observables $\{\hat{\mathbf{J}}_1^2, \hat{\mathbf{J}}_2^2, \hat{J}_{1z}, \hat{J}_{2z}\}$. Let $|JM\rangle$ be the common eigenstates of $\{\hat{\mathbf{J}}_1^2, \hat{\mathbf{J}}_2^2, \hat{\mathbf{J}}^2, \hat{J}_z\}$. (*a*) Find all possible values for m_1 and m_2. (*b*) Find the possible values for J and M. (*c*) Show that the state space of the compound system has dimensionality

$$\sum_{J=|j_1-j_2|}^{j_1+j_2} (2J+1) = (2j_1+1)(2j_2+1) \tag{14.1.1}$$

where j_1 and j_2 are fixed quantum numbers.

SOLUTION

(*a*) Let us denote by $|j_1 m_1\rangle$ the eigenvectors common to the observables $\{\hat{\mathbf{J}}_1^2, \hat{J}_{1z}\}$, of respective eigenvalues $\hbar j_1(j_1+1)$ and $\hbar m_1$. Similarly, let $|J_2 m_2\rangle$ be the eigenvectors common to $\{\hat{\mathbf{J}}_2^2, \hat{J}_{2z}\}$. The state space of the compound system is obtained by taking the tensor product of individual state spaces of the two angular momenta. Thus,

$$|j_1 m_1\rangle \otimes |j_2 m_2\rangle = |j_1, j_2; m_1, m_2\rangle \equiv |m_1 m_2\rangle \tag{14.1.2}$$

where j_1 and j_2 are fixed quantum numbers. The possible values of $|m_1 m_2\rangle$ are given by

$$\begin{cases} m_1 = -j_1, \ -j_1+1, \ldots, j_1 \\ m_2 = -j_2, \ -j_2+1, \ldots, j_2 \end{cases} \tag{14.1.3}$$

where the set of numbers $\{j_1, m_1\}$ and $\{j_2, m_2\}$ are either integers or half-integers. The dimension of the state space of the compound system is $(2j_1+1)(2j_2+1)$ (according to the number of independent eigenstates for basis $|m_1 m_2\rangle$).

(*b*) The state space of the system is a direct sum of orthogonal subspaces of definite total angular momentum J. Thus,

$$|JM\rangle = \sum_{m_1, m_2} \langle m_1 m_2 | JM \rangle | m_1 m_2 \rangle \tag{14.1.4}$$

where $\langle m_1 m_2 | JM \rangle \propto \delta_{M, m_1 + m_2}$ are Clebsch–Gordan coefficients. Assuming that $j_1 \geq j_2$, we have

$$J = j_1 - j_2, j_1 - j_2 + 1, \ldots, j_1 + j_2 \tag{14.1.5}$$

Consequently, the possible values of M for each value of J are

$$M = -J, -J + 1, \ldots, J \tag{14.1.6}$$

Clearly, each value of J in Eq. (14.1.4) corresponds to a subspace of dimension $(2J + 1)$ of definite total angular momentum.

(c) Consider the left side of Eq. (14.1.1). Using me results of part (b) and setting $J = j_1 - j_2 + i$, we find

$$\sum_{J = |j_1 - j_2|}^{j_1 + j_2} (2J + 1) = \sum_{i=0}^{2j_2} [2(j_1 - j_2 + i) + 1]$$

$$= \frac{1}{2}[(2j_1 - 2j_2 - 1) + (2j_1 + 2j_2 + 1)](2j_2 + 1)$$

$$= (2j_1 + 1)(2j_2 + 1) \tag{14.1.7}$$

14.2. Two angular momenta of respective magnitudes j_1 and j_2 and total angular momentum $\hat{\mathbf{J}} = \hat{\mathbf{j}}_1 + \hat{\mathbf{j}}_2$, are described by the basis $|m_1 m_2\rangle \equiv |j_1 m_1\rangle \otimes |j_2 m_2\rangle$. By construction, the states $|m_1 m_2\rangle$ are eigenstates of $\{\hat{\mathbf{j}}_1^2, \hat{\mathbf{j}}_2^2, \hat{J}_{1z}, \hat{J}_{2z}\}$ and $\hat{J}_z = \hat{J}_{1z} + \hat{J}_{2z}$. (a) Find all the eigenvalues of the operator $\hat{J}_z$ and their degree of degeneracy. (b) Consider the states

$$\begin{cases} |\psi_+\rangle = |m_1 = j_1, m_2 = j_2\rangle \\ |\psi_-\rangle = |m_2 = -j_1, m_2 = -j_2\rangle \end{cases} \tag{14.2.1}$$

for which m_1 and m_2 both assume either maximal or minimal values. Show that the states $|\psi_+\rangle$ and $|\psi_-\rangle|$ are eigenstates of $\hat{\mathbf{J}}^2$ (as well as of $\hat{J}_z$) and find the corresponding eigenvalues.

SOLUTION

(a) The basis states $|m_1 m_2\rangle$ satisfy

$$\begin{cases} \hat{\mathbf{j}}_1^2 |m_1 m_2\rangle = \hbar^2 j_1(j_1 + 1)|m_1 m_2\rangle \\ \hat{\mathbf{j}}_2^2 |m_1 m_2\rangle = \hbar^2 j_2(j_2 + 1)|m_1 m_2\rangle \end{cases} \tag{14.2.2}$$

where j_1 and j_2 are fixed quantum numbers and

$$\begin{cases} \hat{J}_{1z} |m_1 m_2\rangle = \hbar m_1 |m_1 m_2\rangle & m_1 = -j_1, -j_1 + 1, \ldots, j_1 \\ \hat{J}_{2z} |m_1 m_2\rangle = \hbar m_2 |m_1 m_2\rangle & m_2 = -j_2, -j_2 + 1, \ldots, j_2 \end{cases} \tag{14.2.3}$$

where m_1 and m_2 are either integers or half-integers. Using Eq. (14.2.2), we immediately find

$$\hat{J}_z |m_1 m_2\rangle = (\hat{J}_{1z} + \hat{J}_{2z})|m_1 m_2\rangle = \hbar(m_1 + m_2)|m_1 m_2\rangle \equiv \hbar M |m_1 m_2\rangle \tag{14.2.4}$$

Consequently, the eigenvalues of J_z are $\hbar M$, where the quantum number $M = m_1 + m_2$ takes the values

$$M = -(j_1 + j_2), -(j_1 + j_2) + 1, \ldots, j_1 + j_2 \tag{14.2.5}$$

The degree of degeneracy $g(M)$ of these values has the following properties:

1. The value $M = M_{max} = (j_1 + j_2)$ is not degenerate:

$$g(j_1 + j_2) = 1 \tag{14.2.6}$$

2. The degree of degeneracy is increased by 1 as M decreases by 1 until a maximum degeneracy is reached for the value $M = j_1 - j_2$. The degeneracy remains constant as long as $|M| \leq j_1 - j_2$ and is equal to

$$g(M) = 2j_2 + 1 \qquad -(j_1 - j_2) \leq M \leq j_1 - j_2 \tag{14.2.7}$$

3. For $M < -(j_1 - j_2)$, $g(M)$ decreases by 1 as M decreases by 1. The value $M = M_{min} = -(j_1 + j_2)$ is not degenerate. Generally, $g(M)$ is an even function of M:

$$g(-M) = g(M) \tag{14.2.8}$$

(b) From Eqs. (14.2.7) and (14.2.8), the states $|\psi_\pm\rangle$ are eigenvectors of $\hat{J}_z$, with respective nondegenerate eigenvalues $\lambda_\pm = \pm\hbar(j_1 + j_2)$. Since the operators $\hat{J}_z$ and $\hat{\mathbf{J}}^2$ commute, we have

$$\hat{J}_z \hat{\mathbf{J}}^2 |\psi_\pm\rangle = \hat{\mathbf{J}}^2 (\hat{J}_z |\psi_\pm\rangle) = \lambda_\pm (\hat{\mathbf{J}}^2 |\psi_\pm\rangle) \tag{14.2.9}$$

Consequently, the vectors $|\tilde{\psi}_\pm\rangle \equiv \hat{\mathbf{J}}^2 |\psi_\pm\rangle$ are also eigenvectors of $\hat{J}_z$ with the same eigenvalues $\lambda_\pm$. However, due to the nondegeneracy of λ_+ (or λ_-), the eigenvectors $|\tilde{\psi}_+\rangle$ must be proportional to $|\psi_+\rangle$ (and similarly, $|\tilde{\psi}_-\rangle$ is proportional to $|\psi_-\rangle$). Therefore, $\hat{\mathbf{J}}^2 |\psi_\pm\rangle \propto |\psi_\pm\rangle$, so that $|\psi_+\rangle$ and $|\psi_-\rangle$ are eigenvectors of $\hat{\mathbf{J}}^2$ as well as of $\hat{J}_z$. Indeed, since $|\psi_\pm\rangle$ both correspond to the extreme possible values of m_1 and m_2,

$$(\hat{J}_{1+}\hat{J}_{2-} + \hat{J}_{1-}\hat{J}_{2+})|m_1 = j_1, \quad m_2 = j_2\rangle = (\hat{J}_{1+}\hat{J}_{2-} + \hat{J}_{1-}\hat{J}_{2+})|m_1 = -j_1, \quad m_2 = -j_2\rangle \equiv 0 \tag{14.2.10}$$

and

$$\begin{cases} (\hat{J}_{1z}\hat{J}_{2z})|m_1 = j_1, \quad m_2 = j_2\rangle = j_1 j_2 |m_1 = j_1, \quad m_2 = j_2\rangle \\ (\hat{J}_{1z}\hat{J}_{2z})|m_1 = -j_1, \quad m_2 = -j_2\rangle = j_1 j_2 |m_1 = -j_1, \quad m_2 = -j_2\rangle \end{cases} \tag{14.2.11}$$

Therefore,

$$\hat{\mathbf{J}}^2 |\psi_\pm\rangle = (\hat{\mathbf{J}}_1^2 + \hat{\mathbf{J}}_2^2 + 2\hat{J}_{1z}\hat{J}_{2z} + \hat{J}_{1+}\hat{J}_{2-} + \hat{J}_{1-}\hat{J}_{2+})|\psi_\pm\rangle$$

$$= \hbar^2 [j_1(j_1 + 1) + j_2(j_2 + 1) + 2j_1 j_2]|\psi_\pm\rangle$$

$$= \hbar^2 [(j_1 + j_2) + (j_1 + j_2 + 1)]|\psi_\pm\rangle \tag{14.2.12}$$

Thus, $|\psi_+\rangle$ and $|\psi_-\rangle$ both correspond to the same eigenvalue of $\hat{\mathbf{J}}^2$ given by $\hbar^2 J(J + 1) = \hbar^2 (j_1 + j_2) \times (j_1 + j_2 + 1)$.

14.3. Consider two angular momenta, both of magnitude J. Let $\hat{\mathbf{J}} = \hat{\mathbf{J}}_1 + \hat{\mathbf{J}}_2$ be the total angular momentum and $\hat{P}$ the interchange operator defined by $\hat{P}|m_1 m_2\rangle = |m_2 m_1\rangle$. (a) Find the eigenvalues of $\hat{P}$. (b) Show that $\hat{P}$ commutes with $\hat{\mathbf{J}}$; i.e., $[\hat{P}, \hat{\mathbf{J}}] = 0$ (and $[\hat{P}, \hat{\mathbf{J}}^2] = 0$). (c). Obtain the simultaneous eigenvalues of $\hat{\mathbf{J}}^2$ and $\hat{P}$.

SOLUTION

(a) Let us denote by $|\psi\rangle$ an eigenvector of $\hat{P}$ with an eigenvalue λ; namely, $\hat{P}|\psi\rangle = \lambda|\psi\rangle$. Therefore,

$$(\hat{P})^2 |\psi\rangle = \hat{P}\hat{P}|\psi\rangle = \lambda^2 |\psi\rangle \tag{14.3.1}$$

Expanding $|\psi\rangle$ in the (complete) $|m_1 m_2\rangle$ basis, we have

$$|\psi\rangle = \sum_{m_1, m_2} \langle m_1 m_2 |\psi\rangle |m_1 m_2\rangle \tag{14.3.2}$$

However, by the definition of $\hat{P}$, $(\hat{P})^2|m_1m_2\rangle = |m_1m_2\rangle$, and then

$$(\hat{P})^2|\psi\rangle = \sum_{m_1,m_2}\langle m_1m_2|\psi\rangle((\hat{P})^2|m_1m_2\rangle) = |\psi\rangle \tag{14.3.3}$$

Comparing Eqs. (14.3.1) and (14.3.3) we find that $\lambda^2 = 1$ and, as a result, the eigenvalues of $\hat{P}$ must be $\lambda = \pm 1$.

(b) The action of the operator $\hat{\mathbf{J}} = \hat{\mathbf{J}}_1 + \hat{\mathbf{J}}_2$ on the basis states

$$|m_1m_2\rangle = |j_1m_1, j_2m_2\rangle \equiv |j_1m_1\rangle \otimes |j_2m_2\rangle \tag{14.3.4}$$

can be written as

$$(\hat{\mathbf{J}}_1 + \hat{\mathbf{J}}_2)|m_1m_2\rangle = (\hat{\mathbf{J}}_1|j_1m_1\rangle) \otimes |j_2m_2\rangle + |j_1m_1\rangle \otimes (\hat{\mathbf{J}}_2|j_2m_2\rangle) \tag{14.3.5}$$

Therefore,

$$\hat{P}\hat{\mathbf{J}}|m_1m_2\rangle = |j_2m_2\rangle \otimes (\hat{\mathbf{J}}_2|j_1m_1\rangle) + (\hat{\mathbf{J}}_1|j_2m_2\rangle) \otimes |j_1m_1\rangle \tag{14.3.6}$$

Similarly [using Eq. (14.3.5) with the interchange $m_1 \leftrightarrow m_2$],

$$\hat{\mathbf{J}}\hat{P}|m_1m_2\rangle = \hat{\mathbf{J}}|m_2m_1\rangle = (\hat{\mathbf{J}}_1|j_2m_2\rangle) \otimes |j_1m_1\rangle + |j_2m_2\rangle \otimes (\hat{\mathbf{J}}_2|j_1m_1\rangle) \tag{14.3.7}$$

Clearly, the last two expressions, Eqs. (14.3.7) and (14.3.6), coincide. Hence,

$$[\hat{P}, \hat{\mathbf{J}}] = 0 \quad \rightarrow \quad [\hat{P}, \hat{\mathbf{J}}^2] = 0 \tag{14.3.8}$$

(c) The results of part (b) imply that the $|JM\rangle$ basis vector can be taken as simultaneous eigenvectors of the set $\{\hat{\mathbf{J}}_1^2, \hat{\mathbf{J}}_2^2, \hat{\mathbf{J}}^2, \hat{J}_z; \hat{P}\}$. This means that $|JM\rangle$ states have definite parity ± 1 under the operator interchange $\hat{P}$. Indeed, using Eq. (14.3.2) together with the symmetry property of the Clebsch–Gordan coefficients,

$$\langle m_2m_1|JM\rangle = (-1)^{j_1+j_2-J}\langle m_2m_1|JM\rangle \tag{14.3.9}$$

we find

$$\hat{P}|JM\rangle = \sum_{m_1,m_2}\langle m_1m_2|JM\rangle(\hat{P}|m_1m_2\rangle) = \sum_{m_1,m_2}\langle m_1m_2|JM\rangle|m_2m_1\rangle$$

$$= \sum_{m_1,m_2}\langle m_2m_1|JM\rangle|m_1m_2\rangle \tag{14.3.10}$$

where in the last line we interchanged the order of the summation index. Therefore,

$$\hat{P}|JM\rangle = (-1)^{j_1+j_2-J}\sum_{m_1,m_2}\langle m_1m_2|JM\rangle|m_1m_2\rangle = (-1)^{j_1+j_2-J}|JM\rangle \tag{14.3.11}$$

In particular, for $j_1 = j_2 = j$, the number J assumes the values $J = 0, 1, \ldots, 2j$, and then

$$\hat{P}|JM\rangle = (-1)^{2j-J}|JM\rangle \tag{14.3.12}$$

14.4. A system of two independent spin 1/2 particles whose orbital motion can be neglected is described by the basis $|S_1 = \frac{1}{2}m_1\rangle \otimes |S_2 = \frac{1}{2}, m_2\rangle \equiv |m_1m_2\rangle$, where $|m_1m_2\rangle$ are common eigenstates of $\hat{S}_1^2, \hat{S}_2^2, \hat{S}_{1z}, \hat{S}_{2z}$. Consider the total spin operator $\hat{\mathbf{S}} = \hat{\mathbf{S}}_1' + \hat{\mathbf{S}}_2$, with components $\hat{\mathbf{S}} = (\hat{S}_x, \hat{S}_y, \hat{S}_z)$ and magnitude $\hat{\mathbf{S}}^2 = |\hat{\mathbf{S}}_1 + \hat{\mathbf{S}}_2|^2$. (a) Apply the operators $\hat{S}_\pm = \hat{S}_x \pm i\hat{S}_y$ and $\hat{S}_z$ on states $|m_1m_2\rangle$ and calculate the results. (b) As in part (a), apply $\hat{S}^2 = \hat{S}_1^2 + \hat{S}_2^2 + 2\hat{S}_{1z}\hat{S}_{2z} + \hat{S}_{1+}\hat{S}_{2-} + \hat{S}_{1-}\hat{S}_{2+}$ on $|m_1 m_2\rangle$ and calculate the results. (c) Construct the states $|sm_s\rangle$, which are eigenstates of $\hat{S}_1^2, \hat{S}_2^2, \hat{S}^2$, and $\hat{S}_z$, as linear combinations of $|m_1 m_2\rangle$. Find the corresponding eigenvalues and verify that $\hat{S}^2|sm_s\rangle = \hbar^2 s(s+1)|sm_s\rangle$ and $\hat{S}_z|sm_s\rangle = \hbar m_s|sm_s\rangle$. (d) Discuss the symmetry properties of the $|sm_s\rangle$ under the interchange of the particles $\hat{P}|m_1 m_2\rangle = |m_2 m_1\rangle$.

SOLUTION

(a) To calculate the action of $\hat{S} = \hat{S}_1 + \hat{S}_2$, on the states $|m_1 m_2\rangle$, we introduce the following notations:

$$|m_1 = \pm\tfrac{1}{2}, m_2 = \pm\tfrac{1}{2}\rangle = \{|++\rangle, |+-\rangle, |-+\rangle, |--\rangle\}$$

So,

$$\begin{cases} \hat{S}_1 |m_1 m_2\rangle = \dfrac{\hbar}{2}(\hat{\sigma}_1 \otimes \hat{I}_2)\,|m_1 m_2\rangle = \dfrac{\hbar}{2}(\sigma|m_1\rangle)\,|m_2\rangle \\[3mm] \hat{S}_2 |m_1 m_2\rangle = \dfrac{\hbar}{2}(\hat{I}_1 \otimes \hat{\sigma}_2)\,|m_1 m_2\rangle = \dfrac{\hbar}{2}|m_1\rangle(\sigma|m_2\rangle) \end{cases} \qquad (14.4.1)$$

Here, $\hat{I}_{1,2}$ and $\hat{\sigma}_{1,2} = (\hat{\sigma}_x, \hat{\sigma}_y, \hat{\sigma}_z)_{1,2}$ denote single-spin operators, which are represented by the 2×2 unit matrix and the three Pauli matrices (respectively) and satisfy

$$\begin{array}{llll} \hat{\sigma}_z |+\rangle = |+\rangle & \hat{\sigma}_z |-\rangle = -|-\rangle & \hat{\sigma}_+ |-\rangle = 2\,|+\rangle & \hat{\sigma}_- |+\rangle = 2\,|-\rangle \\[2mm] \hat{\sigma}_+ |+\rangle = 0 & \hat{\sigma}_- |-\rangle = 0 & (\hat{\sigma}_\pm \equiv \hat{\sigma}_x \pm i\hat{\sigma}_y, \quad \hat{\sigma}^2 = 3\hat{I}) \end{array} \qquad (14.4.2)$$

The total spin operator, $\hat{S} = \hat{S}_1 + \hat{S}_2$, takes the form $\hat{S} = \dfrac{\hbar}{2}(\hat{\sigma}_1 \otimes \hat{I}_2 + \hat{I}_1 \otimes \hat{\sigma}_2)$ and consequently,

$$\begin{cases} \hat{S}_z = \dfrac{\hbar}{2}(\hat{\sigma}_{1z} \otimes \hat{I}_2 + \hat{I}_1 \otimes \hat{\sigma}_{2z}) & (14.4.3) \\[4mm] \hat{S}_\pm = \dfrac{\hbar}{2}(\hat{\sigma}_{1\pm} \otimes \hat{I}_2 + \hat{I}_1 \otimes \hat{\sigma}_{2\pm}) & (14.4.4) \end{cases}$$

Therefore, using Eqs. (14.4.3) and (14.4.4),

$$\begin{cases} \hat{S}_z |++\rangle = \hbar|++\rangle \\[2mm] \hat{S}_z |+-\rangle = \hat{S}_z |-+\rangle = 0 \\[2mm] \hat{S}_z |--\rangle = -\hbar|--\rangle \end{cases} \qquad (14.4.5)$$

Similarly, using Eqs. (14.4.4) and (14.4.2),

$$\begin{cases} \hat{S}_+ |--\rangle = \hat{S}_- |++\rangle = \hbar(|+-\rangle + |-+\rangle) \\[2mm] \hat{S}_+ |+-\rangle = \hat{S}_+ |-+\rangle = \hbar\,|++\rangle \\[2mm] \hat{S}_- |+-\rangle = \hat{S}_- |-+\rangle = \hbar\,|--\rangle \\[2mm] \hat{S}_+ |++\rangle = \hat{S}_- |--\rangle = 0 \end{cases} \qquad (14.4.6)$$

(b) In the notations of part (a) the operator $\mathbf{S}^2 = |\hat{S}_1 + \hat{S}_2|^2$ equals

$$\hat{S}^2 = \dfrac{\hbar^2}{4}(6 + 2\hat{\sigma}_{1z} \otimes \hat{\sigma}_{2z} + \hat{\sigma}_{1+} \otimes \hat{\sigma}_{2-} + \hat{\sigma}_{1-} \otimes \hat{\sigma}_{2+}) \qquad (14.4.7)$$

where the identities $\hat{S}_{1x}\hat{S}_{2x} + \hat{S}_{1y}\hat{S}_{2y} = \frac{1}{2}(\hat{S}_{1+}\hat{S}_{2-} + \hat{S}_{1-}\hat{S}_{2+})$ and $\hat{\sigma}^2 = (3)\hat{I}$ have been used. Therefore, from Eqs. (14.4.2) and (14.4.7) we get

$$\begin{cases} \hat{\mathbf{S}}^2|{++}\rangle = \dfrac{\hbar^2}{4}(6+2)|{++}\rangle = 2\hbar^2|{++}\rangle \\[2mm] \hat{\mathbf{S}}^2|{+-}\rangle = \dfrac{\hbar^2}{4}[(6-2)|{+-}\rangle + 4\,|{-+}\rangle] = \hbar^2(|{+-}\rangle + |{-+}\rangle) \\[2mm] \hat{\mathbf{S}}^2|{-+}\rangle = S^2\,|{+-}\rangle \\[2mm] \hat{\mathbf{S}}^2|{--}\rangle = \dfrac{\hbar^2}{4}(6-2)|{--}\rangle = 2\hbar^2|{--}\rangle \end{cases} \tag{14.4.8}$$

(c) By direct inspection of Eqs. (14.4.5) and (14.4.8) and in accordance with the results of Problem 14.2, we find

$$\begin{aligned} \hat{\mathbf{S}}^2|{++}\rangle = 2\hbar^2|{++}\rangle \qquad & \hat{S}_z|{++}\rangle = \hbar\,|{++}\rangle \\[2mm] \hat{\mathbf{S}}^2|{--}\rangle = 2\hbar^2|{--}\rangle \qquad & \hat{S}_z|{--}\rangle = -\hbar\,|{--}\rangle \end{aligned} \tag{14.4.9}$$

Moreover,

$$\begin{cases} \hat{\mathbf{S}}^2(|{+-}\rangle + |{-+}\rangle) = 2\hbar^2(|{+-}\rangle + |{-+}\rangle) \\[2mm] \hat{\mathbf{S}}^2(|{+-}\rangle - |{-+}\rangle) = 0 \end{cases} \tag{14.4.10}$$

and

$$\hat{S}_z(|{+-}\rangle + |{-+}\rangle) = \hat{S}_z(|{+-}\rangle - |{-+}\rangle) = 0 \tag{14.4.11}$$

Therefore, up to the unimportant global phase we obtain

$$\left.\begin{aligned} |s=1, m_s=1\rangle &= |{++}\rangle \\[2mm] |s=1, m_s=0\rangle &= \frac{1}{\sqrt{2}}(|{+-}\rangle + |{-+}\rangle) \\[2mm] |s=1, m_s=-1\rangle &= |{--}\rangle \end{aligned}\right\} \quad \begin{array}{c} s=1 \\ \text{triplet} \end{array} \tag{14.4.12}$$

$$\left.\begin{aligned} |s=0, m_s=0\rangle = \frac{1}{\sqrt{2}}(|{+-}\rangle - |{-+}\rangle) \end{aligned}\right\} \quad \begin{array}{c} s=0 \\ \text{singlet} \end{array}$$

where the states $\{|sm_s\rangle\}$ are orthonormal and they all satisfy

$$\begin{aligned} \hat{\mathbf{S}}^2|sm_s\rangle &= \hbar^2 s(s+1)|sm_s\rangle & s &= 1, 0 \\[2mm] \hat{S}_z|sm_s\rangle &= \hbar m_s|sm_s\rangle & m_s &= 1, 0, -1 \end{aligned} \tag{14.4.13}$$

(d) The symmetry properties of applying the interchange $m_1 \leftrightarrow m_2$ to the $|sm_s\rangle$ states follow from the expressions in Eq. (14.4.1). By direct observation of these equations we can see that the $s=1$ (triplet) states are not affected by the interchange operation, whereas the $S=0$ (singlet) state changes its sign. That is,

$$\begin{cases} \hat{P}(\text{triplet}) = \text{triplet} \\[2mm] \hat{P}(\text{singlet}) = -\text{singlet} \end{cases} \tag{14.4.14}$$

where $\hat{P}|m_1m_2\rangle \equiv |m_2m_1\rangle$ is the interchange operator.

Note: The expressions of Eq. (14.4.14) are in accordance with Eq. (14.3.13), where one only needs to replace $2j \to 1$ and $J \to s = 0, 1$.

14.5. Let $\hat{\mathbf{S}} = \hat{\mathbf{S}}_1 + \hat{\mathbf{S}}_2$ be the total angular momentum of two spin 1/2 particles ($s_1 = s_2 = 1/2$). Calculate the Clebsch–Gordan coefficients $\langle m_1 m_2 | s m_s \rangle$ by successive applications of $\hat{S}_\pm = \hat{S}_x \pm i\hat{S}_y$ on the vectors $|s m_s \rangle$. Work separately in the two subspaces $s = 1$ and $s = 0$.

SOLUTION

In order to find the Clebsch–Gordan coefficients for the addition of spin $s_1 = s_2 = 1/2$, we shall use the following relations [see Eqs. (14.12) in Sec. 14.3]:

$$\hat{S}_\pm | s m_s \rangle = \hbar \sqrt{s(s+1) - m_s(m_s \pm 1)} \, | s, m_s \pm 1 \rangle$$

$$\begin{cases} \hat{S}_{1\pm} | m_1 m_2 \rangle = \hbar \sqrt{s_1(s_1+1) - m_1(m_1 \pm 1)} \, | m_1 \pm 1, m_2 \rangle \\ \hat{S}_{2\pm} | m_1 m_2 \rangle = \hbar \sqrt{s_2(s_2+1) - m_2(m_2 \pm 1)} \, | m_1, m_2 \pm 1 \rangle \end{cases} \tag{14.5.1}$$

We shall also use the phase condition

$$| s = s_1 + s_2, m_s = \pm(s_1 + s_2) \rangle = | m_1 = \pm s_1, m_2 = \pm s_2 \rangle \tag{14.5.2}$$

Note: The states $| s = s_1 + s_2, m_s = \pm(s_1 + s_2) \rangle$ are eigenstates of $\hat{\mathbf{S}}^2$ and $\hat{S}_z$, with nondegenerate eigenvalues $\lambda_\pm = \pm\hbar \, (s_1 + s_2)$, respectively (see Prob. 14.2). Therefore,

$$| s = s_1 + s_2, m_s = \pm(s_1 + s_2) \rangle = e^{i\phi} | m_1 = \pm s_1, m_2 = \pm s_2 \rangle$$

and the phase ϕ may be chosen as $\phi = 0$.

For subspace $s = 1$: From Eq. (14.5.2) we immediately have

$$| 1, 1 \rangle = \left| \tfrac{1}{2}, \tfrac{1}{2} \right\rangle = | + + \rangle \tag{14.5.3}$$

Then, operating with $\hat{S}_- = \hat{S}_{1-} + \hat{S}_{2-}$ on both sides of Eq. (14.5.3) and using Eq. (14.5.1), we obtain

$$\begin{cases} \hat{S}_- | 1, 1 \rangle = \hbar \sqrt{1(1+1) - 1(1-1)} \, | 1, 0 \rangle = \hbar\sqrt{2} \, | 1, 0 \rangle \\ \hat{S}_- | 1, 1 \rangle = (\hat{S}_{1-} + \hat{S}_{2-}) \left| \tfrac{1}{2}, \tfrac{1}{2} \right\rangle = \hbar\sqrt{1} \left| -\tfrac{1}{2}, \tfrac{1}{2} \right\rangle + \hbar\sqrt{1} \left| \tfrac{1}{2}, -\tfrac{1}{2} \right\rangle \end{cases} \tag{14.5.4}$$

Thus,

$$| 1, 0 \rangle = \frac{1}{\sqrt{2}} \left(\left| \tfrac{1}{2}, -\tfrac{1}{2} \right\rangle + \left| -\tfrac{1}{2}, \tfrac{1}{2} \right\rangle \right) = \frac{1}{\sqrt{2}} (| + - \rangle + | - + \rangle) \tag{14.5.5}$$

Similarly, operating with $\hat{S}_-$ once again on the state $| 1, 0 \rangle$, we find

$$\begin{cases} \hat{S}_- | 1, 0 \rangle = \hbar \sqrt{1(1+1) - 0(0-1)} \, | 1, -1 \rangle = \hbar\sqrt{2} \, | 1, -1 \rangle \\ \hat{S}_- | 1, 0 \rangle = \frac{1}{\sqrt{2}} \hat{S}_{1-} \left(\left| \tfrac{1}{2}, -\tfrac{1}{2} \right\rangle + \left| -\tfrac{1}{2}, \tfrac{1}{2} \right\rangle \right) + \frac{1}{\sqrt{2}} \hat{S}_{2-} \left(\left| \tfrac{1}{2}, -\tfrac{1}{2} \right\rangle + \left| -\tfrac{1}{2}, \tfrac{1}{2} \right\rangle \right) \\ \quad = \frac{\hbar}{\sqrt{2}} \left(\left| -\tfrac{1}{2}, -\tfrac{1}{2} \right\rangle + \left| -\tfrac{1}{2}, -\tfrac{1}{2} \right\rangle \right) = \frac{2}{\sqrt{2}} \left| -\tfrac{1}{2}, -\tfrac{1}{2} \right\rangle \end{cases} \tag{14.5.6}$$

Therefore, in accordance with the condition in Eq. (14.5.2),

$$| 1, -1 \rangle = \left| -\tfrac{1}{2}, -\tfrac{1}{2} \right\rangle = | - - \rangle \tag{14.5.7}$$

For subspace $s = 0$: Since $m_s = m_1 + m_2$ (in this case $m_s = 0$), we have

$$|0, 0\rangle = \alpha\left|\frac{1}{2}, -\frac{1}{2}\right\rangle + \beta\left|-\frac{1}{2}, \frac{1}{2}\right\rangle \tag{14.5.8}$$

Next, due to the orthonormality of $|s m_s\rangle$ basis we get

$$\langle 1, 0 | 0, 0\rangle = 0 \quad \rightarrow \quad \frac{1}{\sqrt{2}}(\alpha + \beta) = 0 \quad \rightarrow \quad \beta = -\alpha$$

$$\langle 0, 0 | 0, 0\rangle = 1 \quad \rightarrow \quad |\alpha|^2 + |\beta|^2 = 1 \quad \rightarrow \quad 2|\alpha|^2 = 1 \quad \rightarrow \quad \alpha = 1/\sqrt{2}$$

Therefore,

$$|0, 0\rangle = \frac{1}{\sqrt{2}}\left(\left|\frac{1}{2}, -\frac{1}{2}\right\rangle - \left|-\frac{1}{2}, \frac{1}{2}\right\rangle\right) \tag{14.5.9}$$

14.6. Let $\hat{\mathbf{S}} = \hat{\mathbf{S}}_1 + \hat{\mathbf{S}}_2$ be the total angular momentum of two spin 1 particles. (a) Represent the vectors $|s m_s\rangle$ as linear combinations of $|s_1 m_1\rangle \otimes |s_2 m_2\rangle \equiv |m_1\rangle |m_2\rangle$ in the subspace $s = 2$. (b) Repeat part (a), working in the subspace $s = 1$. (c) Repeat part (a), working in the subspace $s = 0$.

SOLUTION

(a) For $s = 2$, $m_s = 2$ ($m_s = m_1 + m_2$), we immediately have

$$|2, 2\rangle = |1\rangle |1\rangle \tag{14.6.1}$$

Applying $\hat{S}_- = \hat{S}_{1-} + \hat{S}_{2-}$ to both sides of Eq. (14.6.1) we find

$$\begin{cases} \hat{S}_-|2, 2\rangle = \hbar\sqrt{2(2+1) - 2(2-1)}\,|2, 1\rangle \\ \hat{S}_-|1\rangle|1\rangle = \hbar\sqrt{1(1+1)}(|0\rangle|1\rangle + |1\rangle|0\rangle) \end{cases} \tag{14.6.2}$$

Thus,

$$|2, 1\rangle = \frac{1}{\sqrt{2}}(|0\rangle|1\rangle + |1\rangle|0\rangle) \tag{14.6.3}$$

Applying $\hat{S}_- = \hat{S}_{1-} + \hat{S}_{2-}$ once more to both sides of Eq. (14.6.3), we obtain

$$\begin{cases} \hat{S}_-|2, 1\rangle = \hbar\sqrt{2(2+1)}\,|2, 0\rangle \\ \frac{1}{\sqrt{2}}\hat{S}_-(|0\rangle|1\rangle + |1\rangle|0\rangle) = \frac{\hbar}{\sqrt{2}}[\sqrt{2}(|-1\rangle|1\rangle + |0\rangle|0\rangle + |0\rangle|0\rangle + |1\rangle|-1\rangle)] \end{cases} \tag{14.6.4}$$

Hence,

$$|2, 0\rangle = \frac{1}{\sqrt{6}}[|-1\rangle|1\rangle + 2|0\rangle|0\rangle + |1\rangle|-1\rangle] \tag{14.6.5}$$

Similarly, we obtain

$$|2, -1\rangle = \frac{1}{\sqrt{2}}(|0\rangle|-1\rangle + |-1\rangle|0\rangle) \tag{14.6.6}$$

and finally,

$$|2, -2\rangle = |-1\rangle|-1\rangle \tag{14.6.7}$$

Note: One can, obviously, take Eq. (14.6.7) as a starting point and calculate the state $|2, -1\rangle$ "up the ladder" with the help of the operator $\hat{S}_+ = \hat{S}_{+1} + \hat{S}_{+2}$.

(b) For $S = 1$, the state $|1, 1\rangle$ can be written as

$$|1, 1\rangle = \alpha |1\rangle |0\rangle + \beta |0\rangle |1\rangle \tag{14.6.8}$$

where the constants α and β are determined by orthonormality. Thus,

$$\langle 2, 1 | 1, 1\rangle = 0 \rightarrow \frac{1}{\sqrt{2}} (\alpha + \beta) = 0 \rightarrow \beta = -\alpha$$
$$\langle 1, 1 | 1, 1\rangle = 1 \rightarrow |\alpha|^2 + |\beta|^2 = 1 \rightarrow 2 |\alpha|^2 = 1 \tag{14.6.9}$$

which leads to

$$|1, 1\rangle = \frac{1}{\sqrt{2}} (|1\rangle |0\rangle - |0\rangle |1\rangle) \tag{14.6.10}$$

Now,

$$\begin{cases} \hat{S}_- |1, 1\rangle = \hbar \sqrt{1(1+1)} |1, 0\rangle \\ \frac{1}{\sqrt{2}} \hat{S}_- (|1\rangle |0\rangle + |0\rangle |1\rangle) = \frac{\hbar}{\sqrt{2}} \sqrt{2} (|0\rangle |0\rangle + |1\rangle |-1\rangle - |0\rangle |0\rangle - |-1\rangle |1\rangle) \end{cases} \tag{14.6.11}$$

so that

$$|1, 0\rangle = \frac{1}{\sqrt{2}} (|1\rangle |-1\rangle - |-1\rangle |1\rangle) \tag{14.6.12}$$

Repeating the process once again, we obtain

$$|1, -1\rangle = \frac{1}{\sqrt{2}} (|-1\rangle |0\rangle - |0\rangle |-1\rangle) \tag{14.6.13}$$

(c) The subspace $s = 0$ contains only one state that can be written as

$$|0\rangle |0\rangle = \gamma |1\rangle |-1\rangle + \delta |-1\rangle |1\rangle + \rho |0\rangle |0\rangle \tag{14.6.14}$$

where γ, δ, and ρ are arrived at from orthonormality conditions:

$$\left. \begin{cases} \langle 2, 0 | 0, 0\rangle = 0 \\ \langle 1, 0 | 0, 0\rangle = 0 \\ \langle 0, 0 | 0, 0\rangle = 1 \end{cases} \right\} \Rightarrow \gamma = \frac{1}{\sqrt{3}}, \quad \delta = -\frac{1}{\sqrt{3}}, \quad \rho = \frac{1}{\sqrt{3}} \tag{14.6.15}$$

Therefore,

$$|0, 0\rangle = \frac{1}{\sqrt{3}} (|1\rangle |-1\rangle - |0\rangle |0\rangle + |-1\rangle |1\rangle) \tag{14.6.16}$$

Note: The states $s = 0, 2$ are symmetric under the exchange of particles, whereas in $s = 1$ they are antisymmetric.

14.7. A system of two angular momenta, of respective magnitudes $j_1 = 1$ and $j_2 = 2$, is described by the basis $|j_1 = 1, m_1\rangle \otimes |j_2 = \frac{1}{2}, m_2\rangle$. The system is in a state $|JM\rangle$, where $\hat{\mathbf{J}}$ is the total angular momentum and M is the z component of $\hat{\mathbf{J}}$. Consider, in particular, the states $(a) |J = \frac{3}{2}, M = \frac{3}{2}\rangle$ and $(b) |J = \frac{1}{2}, M = \frac{1}{2}\rangle$. For each state calculate the probability of measuring each pair of possible values (m_1, m_2), and find the expectation values of $\hat{J}_{1z}$ and $\hat{J}_{2z}$. (c) Calculate the expectation value of $\hat{J}_y$ in the state $|J = \frac{1}{2}, M = \frac{1}{2}\rangle$.

SOLUTION

(a) The possible values for (m_1, m_2) are

$$\begin{cases} j_1 = 1 & \rightarrow \quad m_1 = 1, 0, -1 \\ j_2 = \frac{1}{2} & \rightarrow \quad m_2 = \frac{1}{2}, -\frac{1}{2} \end{cases} \tag{14.7.1}$$

The possible values of $|JM\rangle$ are then

$$\begin{cases} J = \frac{3}{2} & \to \quad M = \frac{3}{2}, \frac{1}{2}, -\frac{1}{2}, -\frac{3}{2} \\ J = \frac{1}{2} & \to \quad M = \frac{1}{2}, -\frac{1}{2} \end{cases} \tag{14.7.2}$$

In particular, for $|J = \frac{3}{2}, M = \frac{3}{2}\rangle$ we have

$$\left| J = \tfrac{3}{2}, M = \tfrac{3}{2} \right\rangle = \left| j_1 = 1, m_1 = 1 \right\rangle \left| j_2 = \tfrac{1}{2}, m_2 = \tfrac{1}{2} \right\rangle \tag{14.7.3}$$

Therefore,

$$\begin{cases} \text{prob}\left(m_1 = 1, m_2 = \frac{1}{2} \right) = \left| \left\langle m_1 = 1, m_2 = 1/2 \middle| J = \tfrac{3}{2}, M = \tfrac{3}{2} \right\rangle \right|^2 = 1 \\ \text{prob}\left(m_1 \neq 1 \quad \text{or} \quad m_2 \neq \frac{1}{2} \right) = 0 \end{cases} \tag{14.7.4}$$

The expectation values of $\hat{J}_{1z}$ and $\hat{J}_{2z}$ are given by

$$\langle JM | \hat{J}_{1z} | JM \rangle = \hbar m_1$$
$$\langle JM | \hat{J}_{2z} | JM \rangle = \hbar m_2 \tag{14.7.5}$$

Hence, for $m_1 = 1, m_2 = \dfrac{1}{2}$, we find

$$\langle \hat{J}_{1z} \rangle = \hbar, \qquad \langle \hat{J}_{2z} \rangle = \hbar/2 \tag{14.7.6}$$

(b) First, let us write the state $|J = \frac{1}{2}, M = \frac{1}{2}\rangle$ as a linear combination of $|m_1 m_2\rangle$ states. Starting from Eq. (14.7.3) we find

$$\begin{cases} \hat{J}_- \left| J = \tfrac{3}{2}, M = \tfrac{3}{2} \right\rangle = \hbar \sqrt{\frac{3}{2}\left(\frac{3}{2}+1\right) - \frac{3}{2}\left(\frac{3}{2}-1\right)} \left| J = \tfrac{3}{2}, M = \tfrac{1}{2} \right\rangle \\ \hat{J}_- \left| m_1 = 1, m_2 = \tfrac{1}{2} \right\rangle = \hbar\sqrt{1(1+1)} \left| m_1 = 0, m_2 = \tfrac{1}{2} \right\rangle + \hbar \sqrt{\frac{1}{2}\left(\frac{1}{2}+1\right) + \frac{1}{2}\cdot\frac{1}{2}} \left| m_1 = 1, m_2 = -\tfrac{1}{2} \right\rangle \end{cases} \tag{14.7.7}$$

Thus,

$$\left| J = \tfrac{3}{2}, M = \tfrac{1}{2} \right\rangle = \sqrt{\frac{2}{3}} \left| m_1 = 0, m_2 = \tfrac{1}{2} \right\rangle + \sqrt{\frac{1}{3}} \left| m_1 = 1, m_2 = -\tfrac{1}{2} \right\rangle \tag{14.7.8}$$

Consequently, due to orthogonality,

$$\left| J = \tfrac{1}{2}, M = \tfrac{1}{2} \right\rangle = \sqrt{\frac{1}{3}} \left| m_1 = 0, m_2 = \tfrac{1}{2} \right\rangle - \sqrt{\frac{2}{3}} \left| m_1 = 1, m_2 = -\tfrac{1}{2} \right\rangle \tag{14.7.9}$$

Hence,

$$\begin{cases} \text{prob}\left(m_1 = 0, m_2 = \tfrac{1}{2} \right) = \left| \left\langle m_1 = 0, m_2 = \tfrac{1}{2} \middle| J = \tfrac{1}{2}, M = \tfrac{1}{2} \right\rangle \right|^2 = \tfrac{1}{3} \\ \text{prob}\left(m_1 = 1, m_2 = -\tfrac{1}{2} \right) = \left| \left\langle m_1 = 1, m_2 = -\tfrac{1}{2} \middle| J = \tfrac{1}{2}, M = \tfrac{1}{2} \right\rangle \right|^2 = \tfrac{2}{3} \end{cases} \tag{14.7.10}$$

where for all the other pairs $P(m_1, m_2) = 0$. The expectation values of $\hat{J}_{1z}$ and $\hat{J}_{2z}$ in the state $|J = \frac{1}{2}, M = \frac{1}{2}\rangle$ are given by Eqs. (14.7.5) and (14.7.10). Indeed, substituting Eq. (14.7.9) into Eq. (14.7.5), we obtain

$$\begin{cases} \langle \hat{J}_{1z}\rangle = \frac{1}{3}(m_1 = 0)\hbar + \frac{2}{3}(m_1 = 1)\hbar = \frac{2}{3}\hbar \\ \langle \hat{J}_{2z}\rangle = \frac{1}{3}(m_2 = \frac{1}{2})\hbar + \frac{2}{3}(m_2 = -\frac{1}{2})\hbar = -\frac{1}{6}\hbar \end{cases} \tag{14.7.11}$$

(c) The operator $\hat{J}_y$ can be written as

$$\hat{J}_y = \frac{1}{2i}(\hat{J}_+ - \hat{J}_-) \tag{14.7.12}$$

Therefore,

$$\langle JM|\hat{J}_y|JM\rangle = \frac{\hbar}{2i}\langle JM|(\sqrt{J(J+1) - M(M+1)}\,|J, M+1\rangle + \sqrt{JJ+1 - MM-1}\,|J, M-1\rangle = 0 \tag{14.7.13}$$

Alternatively, for $|J = \frac{1}{2}, M = \frac{1}{2}\rangle$ we can choose the well-known spin 1/2 representation (see Chap. 7):

$$\left|J = \frac{1}{2}, M\,\frac{1}{2}\right\rangle = \begin{pmatrix} 1 \\ 0 \end{pmatrix} \quad \left|J = \frac{1}{2}, M = -\frac{1}{2}\right\rangle = \begin{pmatrix} 0 \\ 1 \end{pmatrix} \quad J_y = \frac{\hbar}{2}\begin{pmatrix} 0 & -i \\ i & 0 \end{pmatrix} \tag{14.7.14}$$

This leads to the following expression:

$$\langle \hat{J}_y\rangle = (1 \quad 0)\frac{\hbar}{2}\begin{pmatrix} 0 & -i \\ i & 0 \end{pmatrix}\begin{pmatrix} 1 \\ 0 \end{pmatrix} = 0 \tag{14.7.15}$$

which coincides with Eq. (14.7.13).

14.8. Consider a system of two spin 1/2 particles whose orbital variables are ignored. The Hamiltonian of the system is $\hat{H} = \varepsilon_1\hat{\sigma}_{1z} + \varepsilon_2\hat{\sigma}_{2z}$, where ε_1 and ε_2 are real constants, and $\hat{\sigma}_{1z}$, $\hat{\sigma}_{2z}$ are the projections of the spins $\hat{\mathbf{S}}_1 = \frac{\hbar}{2}\hat{\sigma}_1$ and $\hat{\mathbf{S}}_2 = \frac{\hbar}{2}\hat{\sigma}_2$ of the two particles onto the z axis. (a) The initial state of the system, at $t = 0$, is $|\psi(0)\rangle = \frac{1}{\sqrt{2}}(|+-\rangle + |-+\rangle)$. $\hat{S}^2 = (\hat{\mathbf{S}}_1 + \hat{\mathbf{S}}_2)^2$ is measured at time t. What are the values that can be arrived at and what are their probabilities? (b) If the initial state of the system is arbitrary, what Bohr frequencies might appear in the evolution of $\langle \hat{S}^2\rangle$? (c) Answer parts (a) and (b) for $\hat{S}_x = \hat{S}_{1x} + \hat{S}_{2x}$.

SOLUTION

(a) The eigenstates of $\hat{S}^2 = (\hat{\mathbf{S}}_1 + \hat{\mathbf{S}}_2)^2$ (and $\hat{S}_z$) are the $|sm_s\rangle$ states, where $s = 1, 0$ correspond to the triplet and singlet states, respectively. The results of the measurement of $\hat{S}^2$ are, therefore,

$$\begin{cases} s = 1 \rightarrow 2\hbar^2 \\ s = 0 \rightarrow 0 \end{cases} \tag{14.8.1}$$

However, the states $|sm_s\rangle$ are *not* eigenstates of the Hamiltonian and consequently the probabilities, prob $(s = 1)$ and prob $(s = 0)$, are changed as a function of time. The stationary states of the system are

$$\left|m_1 = \pm\frac{1}{2}, m_2 = \pm\frac{1}{2}\right\rangle = \{|++\rangle, |+-\rangle, |-+\rangle, |--\rangle\} \tag{14.8.2}$$

and its energy levels are given by

$$\hat{H}|-\rangle = (\varepsilon_1\hat{\sigma}_{1z} + \varepsilon_2\hat{\sigma}_{2z})|-\rangle = (\pm\varepsilon_1 \pm \varepsilon_2)|-\rangle \tag{14.8.3}$$

Therefore, taking into account the initial state of the system,

$$|\psi(0)\rangle = \frac{1}{\sqrt{2}}(|+-\rangle + |-+\rangle) = |s = 1, m_s = 0\rangle \tag{14.8.4}$$

we find

$$|\psi(t)\rangle = \frac{1}{\sqrt{2}}\left\{\exp-i\varepsilon_1 - \varepsilon_2 t/\hbar \,|+-\rangle + \exp i\varepsilon_1 - \varepsilon_2 t/\hbar \,|-+\rangle\right\} \tag{14.8.5}$$

Now, writing the states of Eq. (14.8.5) in the form

$$\begin{cases}|+-\rangle = \dfrac{1}{\sqrt{2}}(|1,0\rangle + |0,0\rangle)\\[2mm] |-+\rangle = \dfrac{1}{\sqrt{2}}(|1,0\rangle - |0,0\rangle)\end{cases} \tag{14.8.6}$$

and substituting Eq. (14.8.6) into Eq. (14.8.5) yields

$$|\psi(t)\rangle = \cos\frac{(\varepsilon_1-\varepsilon_2)t}{\hbar}|1,0\rangle - i\sin\frac{(\varepsilon_1-\varepsilon_2)t}{\hbar}|0,0\rangle \tag{14.8.7}$$

Hence, the probabilities prob $(s=1)$ and prob $(s=0)$ are

$$\begin{cases}\text{prob }(s=1) = \left|\displaystyle\sum_{m_s=1,0,-1}\langle s=1,m_s|\psi(t)\rangle\right|^2 = \cos^2\frac{(\varepsilon_1-\varepsilon_2)t}{\hbar} & (14.8.8)\\[4mm] \text{prob }(s=0) = \left|\langle s=0,m_s=0|\psi(t)\rangle\right|^2 = \sin^2\frac{(\varepsilon_1-\varepsilon_2)t}{\hbar} & (14.8.9)\end{cases}$$

Moreover, the expectation value of $\hat{\mathbf{S}}^2$ is

$$\langle\psi(t)|\hat{\mathbf{S}}^2|\psi(t)\rangle = 2\hbar^2\cdot\text{prob }(s=1)+0\cdot\text{prob }(s=0)$$

$$= 2\hbar^2\cos^2[(\varepsilon_1-\varepsilon_2)t/\hbar] = \hbar^2[1+\cos(\omega_B t)] \tag{14.8.10}$$

where $\omega_B = 2(\varepsilon_1-\varepsilon_2)t/\hbar$ is the Bohr frequency. Note that Eqs. (14.8.6) and (14.8.7) contain linear combination of the $|sm_s\rangle$ states with $m_s=0$. Indeed, from Eqs. (14.8.3) and (14.8.4) we find that the operator $\hat{S}_z = \hat{S}_{1z}+\hat{S}_{2z}$ commutes with the Hamiltonian and $\hat{S}_z|\psi(0)\rangle = 0$. Thus,

$$|\psi(t)\rangle = C_1(t)|1,0\rangle + C_2(t)|0,0\rangle \tag{14.8.11}$$

where $C_1(t)$ and $C_2(t)$ are time-dependent (complex) coefficients. As a result, we also have

$$\begin{cases}\text{prob }(s=1) = \left|\langle s=1,m_s=0|\psi(t)\rangle\right|^2 = |C_1(t)|^2\\[2mm] \text{prob }(s=0) = \left|\langle s=0,m_s=0|\psi(t)\rangle\right|^2 = |C_2(t)|^2\end{cases} \tag{14.8.12}$$

where the sum in Eq. (14.8.8) is reduced to a single term ($m_s=0$).

(b) We consider an arbitrary initial state of the form

$$|\psi(0)\rangle = \alpha|++\rangle + \beta|+-\rangle + \gamma|-+\rangle + \delta|--\rangle \tag{14.8.13}$$

where α, β, γ, and δ are complex constants. In this case, the evolution of $|\psi(t)\rangle$ is given by

$$|\psi(t)\rangle = \alpha e^{-i(\varepsilon_1+\varepsilon_2)t/\hbar}|++\rangle + \beta e^{-i(\varepsilon_1-\varepsilon_2)t/\hbar}|+-\rangle + \gamma e^{i(\varepsilon_1-\varepsilon_2)t/\hbar}|-+\rangle + \delta e^{i(\varepsilon_1+\varepsilon_2)t/\hbar}|--\rangle \tag{14.8.14}$$

Using Eq. (14.8.6), we then find

$$\psi(t) = \alpha e^{-i(\varepsilon_1+\varepsilon_2)t/\hbar}|1,1\rangle + \delta e^{i(\varepsilon_1+\varepsilon_2)t/\hbar}|1,-1\rangle$$

$$+\frac{1}{\sqrt{2}}(\beta e^{-i(\varepsilon_1-\varepsilon_2)t/\hbar} + \gamma e^{i(\varepsilon_1-\varepsilon_2)t/\hbar})|1,0\rangle$$

$$+\frac{1}{\sqrt{2}}(\beta e^{-i(\varepsilon_1-\varepsilon_2)t/\hbar} - \gamma e^{i(\varepsilon_1-\varepsilon_2)t/\hbar})|0,0\rangle \tag{14.8.15}$$

Therefore, the expectation value of $\mathbf{S}^2$ is

$$\langle \psi(t)|\hat{\mathbf{S}}^2|\psi(t)\rangle = 2\hbar^2 \left\{ |\alpha|^2 + |\delta|^2 + \frac{1}{2}(|\beta|^2 + |\gamma|^2) + \text{Re}\,[\beta * \gamma e^{2i(\varepsilon_1 - \varepsilon_2)t/\hbar}] \right\} \qquad (14.8.16)$$

Clearly, $\langle \hat{\mathbf{S}}^2\rangle$ is characterized by a single Bohr frequency that is identical to the one from part (a) and equals $\omega_B = 2(\varepsilon_1 - \varepsilon_2)/\hbar$.

Note: For $\alpha = \delta = 0$ and $\beta = \gamma = \sqrt{2}$, Eq. (14.8.16) is reduced to

$$\langle \psi(t)|\hat{\mathbf{S}}^2|\psi(t)\rangle = \hbar^2 \left[1 + \cos\left(\frac{2(\varepsilon_1 - \varepsilon_2)}{\hbar} t \right) \right] \qquad (14.8.17)$$

which coincides with Eq. (14.8.10).

(c) To find the expectation value $\hat{S}_x$, we return to Eq. (14.8.14) and calculate the ket $(\hat{S}_{1x} + \hat{S}_{2x})|\psi(t)\rangle$. This gives

$$\hat{S}_x|\psi(t)\rangle = \frac{\hbar}{2}\{[\alpha e^{-i(\varepsilon_1 + \varepsilon_2)t/\hbar} + \delta e^{i(\varepsilon_1 + \varepsilon_2)t/\hbar}](|+-\rangle + |-+\rangle)$$

$$+ [\beta e^{-i(\varepsilon_1 - \varepsilon_2)t/\hbar} + \gamma e^{i(\varepsilon_1 - \varepsilon_2)t/\hbar}](|++\rangle + |--\rangle)\} \qquad (14.8.18)$$

Therefore,

$$\langle \psi(t)|\hat{S}_x|\psi(t)\rangle = \frac{\hbar}{2}\{\alpha * \beta e^{2i\varepsilon_2 t/\hbar} + \alpha * \gamma e^{2i\varepsilon_1 t/\hbar} + \delta * \beta e^{-2i\varepsilon_1 t/\hbar} + \delta * \gamma e^{-2i\varepsilon_2 t/\hbar}$$

$$+ \beta\alpha * e^{-2i\varepsilon_2 t/\hbar} + \beta * \delta e^{2i\varepsilon_1 t/\hbar} + \gamma * \alpha e^{-2i\varepsilon_1 t/\hbar} + \gamma * \delta e^{2it\varepsilon_2/\hbar}\}$$

$$= \hbar\,\text{Re}\{(\alpha * \beta + \gamma * \delta)e^{2i\varepsilon_2 t/\hbar} + (\alpha * \gamma + \beta * \delta)e^{2i\varepsilon_2 t/\hbar}\} \qquad (14.8.19)$$

In this case, the Bohr frequencies that appear in the evolution of $\langle \hat{S}_x\rangle$ are $\omega_{B1} = 2\varepsilon_1/\hbar$ and $\omega_{B2} = 2\varepsilon_2/\hbar$.

14.9. The total angular momentum of a spin 1/2 particle is $\mathbf{J} = \mathbf{L} + \mathbf{S}$, where $\mathbf{L}$ is the orbital momentum and $\mathbf{S}$ is the spin (l is an integer, $s = 1/2$). Let $|l, m_l\rangle \otimes |s = 1/2, m_s\rangle \equiv |m_l, m_s\rangle$ be the eigenstates of $\{\hat{\mathbf{L}}^2, \hat{\mathbf{S}}^2, \hat{L}_z, \hat{S}_z\}$ and $|JM\rangle$ the eigenstates of $\{\hat{\mathbf{J}}^2, \hat{J}_z\}$. Find the Clebsch–Gordan coefficients $\langle m_l, m_s|JM\rangle$ by successive applications of $\hat{J}_\pm = \hat{L}_\pm + \hat{S}_\pm$ to the vectors $|JM\rangle$. Work separately in the two subspaces $J = l + 1/2$ and $J = l - 1/2$.

SOLUTION

First we notice that if $l = 0$ the vectors $|m_l = 0, m_s = \pm 1/2\rangle$ are eigenstates of $\{\hat{\mathbf{J}}^2, \hat{J}_z\}$. In this case $J = s = 1/2$ and $M = m_s = \pm 1/2$. Therefore,

$$|J = 1/2, M = 1/2\rangle = |m_l = 0, m_s = \pm 1/2\rangle \equiv |m = 0, \pm\rangle \qquad (14.9.1)$$

The only nonzero Clebsch–Gordan coefficients are then $\langle 0, +|\frac{1}{2}, \frac{1}{2}\rangle = \langle 0, -|\frac{1}{2}, -\frac{1}{2}\rangle = 1$. On the other hand, for $l \neq 0$, there are two possibilities:

$$\begin{cases} J = l + \dfrac{1}{2} \quad M = l + \dfrac{1}{2}, l - \dfrac{1}{2}, \ldots, -\left(l + \dfrac{1}{2}\right) \\[3mm] J = l - \dfrac{1}{2} \quad M = l - \dfrac{1}{2}, l - \dfrac{3}{2}, \ldots, -\left(l - \dfrac{1}{2}\right) \end{cases} \qquad (14.9.2)$$

In this case ($l \neq 0$), we will consider the subspaces $J = l + \dfrac{1}{2}$ and $J = l - \dfrac{1}{2}$ separately, and show that

$$\begin{cases} |J = l + \dfrac{1}{2}, M\rangle = \dfrac{1}{\sqrt{2l+1}}\left[\sqrt{l + M + \dfrac{1}{2}}\,|m = M - \dfrac{1}{2}, +\rangle + \sqrt{l - M + \dfrac{1}{2}}\,|m = M + \dfrac{1}{2}, -\rangle \right] & (14.9.3) \\[5mm] |J = l - \dfrac{1}{2}, M\rangle = \dfrac{1}{\sqrt{2l+1}}\left[\sqrt{l + M + \dfrac{1}{2}}\,|m = M + \dfrac{1}{2}, -\rangle + \sqrt{l - M + \dfrac{1}{2}}\,|m = M - \dfrac{1}{2}, +\rangle \right] & (14.9.4) \end{cases}$$

where $|m_l, m_s\rangle \equiv |m, \pm\rangle$ and $M = m_l + m_s = m \pm \frac{1}{2}$.

For $J = l + \frac{1}{2}$: The subspace $J = l + \frac{1}{2}$ contains a multiple of $2l + 1$ independent eigenfunctions. As usual (see Problem 13.2), the maximal eigenvalue, $M_{max} = l + \frac{1}{2}$ is nondegenerate. Therefore,

$$\left|J = l + \frac{1}{2}, M = l + \frac{1}{2}\right\rangle = |m = l, +\rangle \tag{14.9.5}$$

Now, applying the operator $\hat{J}_- = \hat{L}_- + \hat{S}_-$ to Eq. (14.9.5), we get

$$\begin{cases} \hat{J}_-\left|l + \frac{1}{2}, l + \frac{1}{2}\right\rangle = \hbar\sqrt{(J + M)(J - M + 1)}\left|l + \frac{1}{2}, l - \frac{1}{2}\right\rangle = \hbar\sqrt{2l + 1}\left|l + \frac{1}{2}, l - \frac{1}{2}\right\rangle \\ \hat{J}_-|l, +\rangle = (\hat{L}_- + \hat{S}_-)|l, +\rangle = \hbar(\sqrt{2l}\,|l - 1, +\rangle + |l, -\rangle) \end{cases} \tag{14.9.6}$$

Thus, in accordance with Eq. (14.9.3)

$$\left|J = l + \frac{1}{2}, M = l - \frac{1}{2}\right\rangle = \frac{1}{\sqrt{2l + 1}}[\sqrt{2l}\,|l - 1, +\rangle + |l, -\rangle] \tag{14.9.7}$$

Expression (14.9.7) can be generalized by recurrence. In general,

$$\hat{J}_-\left|l + \frac{1}{2}, M\right\rangle = \hbar\sqrt{\left(l + M + \frac{1}{2}\right)\left(l - M + \frac{3}{2}\right)}\left|l + \frac{1}{2}, M - 1\right\rangle$$

$$\begin{cases} \hat{J}_-\left|M - \frac{1}{2}, +\right\rangle = \hbar\sqrt{\left(l + M + \frac{1}{2}\right)\left(l - M + \frac{3}{2}\right)}\left|M - \frac{3}{2}, +\right\rangle + \hbar\left|M - \frac{1}{2}, -\right\rangle \\ \hat{J}_-\left|M + \frac{1}{2}, -\right\rangle = \hbar\sqrt{\left(l + M + \frac{1}{2}\right)\left(l - M + \frac{3}{2}\right)}\left|M - \frac{1}{2}, -\right\rangle \end{cases} \tag{14.9.8}$$

Therefore, the application of $\hat{J}_- = \hat{L}_- + \hat{S}_-$ to both sides of Eq. (14.9.3) leads to

$$\left|l + \frac{1}{2}, M - 1\right\rangle = \frac{1}{\sqrt{2l + 1}}\left\{ \frac{\sqrt{\left(l + M + \frac{1}{2}\right)\left(l + M - \frac{1}{2}\right)\left(l - M + \frac{3}{2}\right)}}{\sqrt{\left(l + M + \frac{1}{2}\right)\left(l - M + \frac{3}{2}\right)}}\left|M - \frac{3}{2}, +\right\rangle \right.$$

$$\left. + \frac{\sqrt{l + M + \frac{1}{2}}\left(1 + l - M\frac{1}{2}\right)}{\sqrt{\left(l + M + \frac{1}{2}\right)\left(l - M + \frac{3}{2}\right)}}\left|M - \frac{1}{2}, -\right\rangle \right\}$$

$$= \frac{1}{\sqrt{2l + 1}}\left[\sqrt{l + M - \frac{1}{2}}\left|M - \frac{3}{2}, +\right\rangle + \sqrt{l - M + \frac{3}{2}}\left|M - \frac{1}{2}, -\right\rangle\right] \tag{14.9.9}$$

Indeed, the resulting expression in Eq. (14.9.9) is identical to Eq. (14.9.3), where M is changed to $M - 1$. For $J = l - \frac{1}{2}$: The state $\left|J = l - \frac{1}{2}, M = l - \frac{1}{2}\right\rangle$ is a linear combination of $|l, -\rangle$ and $|l - 1, +\rangle$. Note that this is the only possible way to obtain $m_l + m_s = l - \frac{1}{2}$, as in Eq. (14.9.7). Thus,

$$\left|J = l - \frac{1}{2}, M = l - \frac{1}{2}\right\rangle = \alpha|l - 1, +\rangle + \beta|l, -\rangle \tag{14.9.10}$$

This state must be orthogonal to Eq. (14.9.7). Therefore,

$$\alpha = \frac{\sqrt{2l}}{\sqrt{2l+1}} \qquad \beta = -\frac{1}{\sqrt{2l+1}}$$

Namely,

$$\left|J = l-\frac{1}{2}, M = l-\frac{1}{2}\right\rangle = \frac{1}{\sqrt{2l+1}}[\sqrt{2l}\,|l,-\rangle - |l-1,+\rangle] \tag{14.9.11}$$

Now, we can apply $\hat{J}_- = \hat{L}_- + \hat{S}_-$ to Eq. (14.9.11) and find all the other coefficients. A calculation similar to that of $J = l + 1/2$ yields

$$\left|l-\frac{1}{2}, M-1\right\rangle = \frac{1}{\sqrt{2l+1}}\left[\sqrt{l+M-\frac{1}{2}}\left|M-\frac{1}{2},-\right\rangle + \sqrt{l-M-\frac{1}{2}}\left|M-\frac{3}{2},+\right\rangle\right] \tag{14.9.12}$$

The last expression is identical to Eq. (14.9.4), where M is changed into $M-1$.

14.10. Two spin 1/2 particles (who orbital variables are ignored) are described by an unperturbed Hamiltonian $\hat{H}_0 = -A(\hat{\sigma}_{1z} + \hat{\sigma}_{2z})$. We add the perturbation $\hat{H}_1 = \varepsilon(\hat{\sigma}_{1x}\hat{\sigma}_{2x} + \hat{\sigma}_{1y}\hat{\sigma}_{2y})$, where $\hat{\sigma} = (\hat{\sigma}_x, \hat{\sigma}_y, \hat{\sigma}_z)$ are Pauli matrices, and $\varepsilon \ll A$ are positive constants. (a) Find the eigenvalues and eigenfunctions of $\hat{H}_0$. (b) Calculate (exactly) the energy levels and the corresponding eigenfunctions of the total Hamiltonian $\hat{H}_0 + \hat{H}_1$. (c) Using the perturbation theory, calculate the first-order corrections to the energy levels of $\hat{H}_0$. Compare them to the exact results of part (b).

SOLUTION

(a) The two spin 1/2 particles are described by the standard basis $|m_1 = \pm\frac{1}{2}, m_2 = \pm\frac{1}{2}\rangle = \{|++\rangle, |+-\rangle, |-+\rangle, |--\rangle\}$. Since $\hat{H}_0 = -\frac{2}{\hbar}A(\hat{S}_{1z} + \hat{S}_{2z})$, we find

$$\begin{cases} \hat{H}_0|++\rangle = -2A|++\rangle \\ \hat{H}_0|+-\rangle = \hat{H}_0|-+\rangle = 0 \\ \hat{H}_0|--\rangle = 2A|--\rangle \end{cases} \tag{14.10.1}$$

Thus, the eigenvalues of $\hat{H}_0$ are $-2A$, 0, and $2A$.

(b) The total Hamiltonian $\hat{H}_0 + \hat{H}_1$ can be written as

$$\hat{H} = -A(\hat{\sigma}_{1z} + \hat{\sigma}_{2z}) + \frac{\varepsilon}{2}[(\hat{\sigma}_1 + \hat{\sigma}_2)^2 - \hat{\sigma}_1^2 - \hat{\sigma}_2^2 - 2\hat{\sigma}_{1z}\hat{\sigma}_{2z}] \tag{14.10.2}$$

Clearly, $\hat{H}$ commutes with the operators $\{\hat{S}_1^2, \hat{S}_2^2, \hat{S}^2, \hat{S}_z\}$, where $\hat{S} = \hat{S}_1 + \hat{S}_2$ is the total spin of the particles. Therefore, the eigenstates of the total Hamiltonian are the following triplet and singlet states:

$$\begin{cases} |1,1\rangle = |++\rangle \\ |1,0\rangle = \frac{1}{\sqrt{2}}(|+-\rangle + |-+\rangle) \\ |1,-1\rangle = |--\rangle \end{cases} \tag{14.10.3}$$

$$|0,0\rangle = \frac{1}{\sqrt{2}}(|+-\rangle - |-+\rangle)$$

The corresponding energy levels are, then,

$$\begin{cases} \hat{H}|1,1\rangle = (-2A + 4\varepsilon - 3\varepsilon - \varepsilon)\,|1,1\rangle = -2A\,|1,1\rangle \\[2mm] \hat{H}|1,0\rangle = (0 + 4\varepsilon - 3\varepsilon + \varepsilon)\,|1,0\rangle = 2\varepsilon\,|1,0\rangle \\[2mm] \hat{H}|1,-1\rangle = (2A + 4\varepsilon - 3\varepsilon - \varepsilon)\,|1,-1\rangle = 2A\,|1,-1\rangle \end{cases} \tag{14.10.4}$$

and

$$\hat{H}|0,0\rangle = (0 + 0 - 3\varepsilon + \varepsilon)\,|0,0\rangle = -2\varepsilon\,|0,0\rangle \tag{14.10.5}$$

(c) The matrix elements of $\hat{H}_1 = \dfrac{\varepsilon}{2}(\hat{\sigma}_{1+}\hat{\sigma}_{2-} + \hat{\sigma}_{1-}\hat{\sigma}_{2+})$ in the unperturbed basis $\{|++\rangle, |+-\rangle, |-+\rangle, |--\rangle\}$ are given by the following matrix:

$$\begin{array}{c} \quad\quad |++\rangle \quad |+-\rangle \quad |-+\rangle \quad |--\rangle \\ \begin{array}{c} |++\rangle \\ |+-\rangle \\ |-+\rangle \\ |--\rangle \end{array} \begin{pmatrix} 0 & 0 & 0 & 0 \\ 0 & 0 & 2\varepsilon & 0 \\ 0 & 2\varepsilon & 0 & 0 \\ 0 & 0 & 0 & 0 \end{pmatrix} \end{array} \tag{14.10.6}$$

The unperturbed energy levels are $\varepsilon_1 = -2A$, $\varepsilon_2 = \varepsilon_3 = 0$, and $\varepsilon_4 = 2A$. Therefore,

$$\begin{cases} \Delta\varepsilon_1 = \langle ++|\hat{H}_1|++\rangle = 0 \\[2mm] \Delta\varepsilon_4 = \langle --|\hat{H}_1|--\rangle = 0 \end{cases} \tag{14.10.7}$$

where ε_1 and ε_4 are the nondegenerate energy levels. As for the degenerate zero eigenvalue, we consider the determinant

$$\det(\hat{H}_1 - \lambda\hat{I}) = \begin{vmatrix} -\lambda & 2\varepsilon \\ 2\varepsilon & -\lambda \end{vmatrix} = \lambda^2 - 4\varepsilon^2 \tag{14.10.8}$$

Thus,

$$\Delta\varepsilon_{2,3} = \pm 2\varepsilon \tag{14.10.9}$$

Equations (14.10.7) and (14.10.9) lead to

$$\begin{cases} E_1 = \varepsilon_1 + \Delta\varepsilon_1 = -2A \\[2mm] E_{2,3} = \varepsilon_{2,3} + \Delta\varepsilon_{2,3} = \pm 2\varepsilon \\[2mm] E_4 = \varepsilon_4 + \Delta\varepsilon_4 = 2A \end{cases} \tag{14.10.10}$$

which agrees with the exact result of part (b).

14.11. The motion of an electron in a central field of force is described by a Hamiltonian of the form $\hat{H} = \hat{H}_0 + \hat{H}_{so}$, where $\hat{H}_0 = \dfrac{\hat{\mathbf{p}}^2}{2m} + \hat{V}(r)$ and $\hat{H}_{so} = \zeta(r)\hat{\mathbf{L}}\cdot\hat{\mathbf{S}}$. The spin-orbit coupling leads to energy differences between levels with the same values of $\hat{\mathbf{L}}^2$ and $\hat{\mathbf{S}}^2$ but different values of $\hat{J}^2$, where $\mathbf{J} = \mathbf{L} + \mathbf{S}$. (a) Show that $[\hat{H}, \hat{\mathbf{L}}^2] = [\hat{H}, \hat{\mathbf{S}}] = 0$ but $[\hat{H}, \hat{L}_z] \neq 0$ and $[\hat{H}, \hat{S}_z] \neq 0$. (b) Show that $[\hat{H}, \hat{\mathbf{J}}^2] = [\hat{H}, \hat{J}_z] = 0$. (c) Consider the stationary states of H that are also eigenstates of the observables $\{\hat{\mathbf{L}}^2, \hat{\mathbf{S}}^2, \hat{\mathbf{J}}^2, \hat{J}_z\}$. Express the angular part of these eigenfunctions in terms of spherical harmonics and two-component spinors. (d) Let the eigenfunctions of part (c) be characterized by the quantum numbers l, J, and M (which are related to the eigenvalues of $\hat{\mathbf{L}}^2$, $\hat{\mathbf{J}}^2$, and $\hat{J}_z$, respectively). Determine the possible values of $\hat{L}_z$ and $\hat{S}_z$ and find their probabilities and average values.

SOLUTION

(*a*) The Hamiltonian $\hat{H}_0$ commutes with all the components of $\hat{\mathbf{L}}$ and $\hat{\mathbf{S}}$, and the operator $\hat{\mathbf{L}}$ acts only on the angular variables (θ, φ) (see Chap. 6). Therefore,

$$[\hat{H}, \hat{\mathbf{L}}^2] = [\hat{H}_0 + \zeta(r)\hat{\mathbf{L}}\cdot\hat{\mathbf{S}}, \hat{\mathbf{L}}^2] = \zeta(r)[\hat{\mathbf{L}}\cdot\hat{\mathbf{S}}, \hat{\mathbf{L}}^2] \qquad (14.11.1)$$

In addition, $[\hat{S}_i, \hat{L}_j] = 0$ and $[\hat{L}_i, \hat{\mathbf{L}}^2] = 0$ for all the components $i, j = x, y, z = 1, 2, 3$. Thus,

$$[\hat{H}, \hat{\mathbf{L}}^2] = \zeta(r)\sum_{i=1}^{3}([\hat{L}_i, \hat{\mathbf{L}}^2]\hat{S}_i + \hat{L}_i[\hat{S}_i, \hat{\mathbf{L}}^2]) = 0 \qquad (14.11.2)$$

Similarly, by changing the roles of $\hat{\mathbf{L}}$ and $\hat{\mathbf{S}}$ in Eq. (14.11.2), we obtain

$$[\hat{H}, \hat{\mathbf{S}}^2] = \zeta(r)\sum_{L=1}^{3}([\hat{L}_i, \hat{\mathbf{S}}^2]\hat{S}_i + \hat{L}_i[\hat{S}_i, \hat{\mathbf{S}}^2]) = 0 \qquad (14.11.3)$$

Furthermore, using the relations $[\hat{L}_i, \hat{L}_j] = i\hbar\varepsilon_{ijk}L_k$, we obtain

$$[\hat{H}, \hat{L}_z] = [\hat{H}_0 + \zeta(r)\hat{\mathbf{L}}\cdot\hat{\mathbf{S}}, \hat{L}_z] = \zeta(r)[\hat{L}_x\hat{S}_x + \hat{L}_y\hat{S}_y + \hat{L}_z\hat{S}_z, \hat{L}_z]$$

$$= \zeta(r)[\hat{L}_x, \hat{L}_z]\hat{S}_x + \zeta(r)[\hat{L}_y\hat{L}_z]\hat{S}_y = i\hbar\zeta(r)(-\hat{L}_y\hat{S}_x + \hat{L}_x\hat{S}_y) \neq 0 \qquad (14.11.4)$$

and finally,

$$[\hat{H}, \hat{S}_z] = \zeta(r)\hat{L}_x[\hat{S}_x, \hat{S}_z] + \zeta(r)\hat{L}_y[\hat{S}_y, \hat{S}_z] = i\hbar\zeta(r)(-\hat{L}_x\hat{S}_y + \hat{L}_y\hat{S}_x) \neq 0 \qquad (14.11.5)$$

(*b*) From Eqs. *(14.11.4)* and *(14.11.5)*, we immediately find

$$[\hat{H}, \hat{J}_z] = [\hat{H}, \hat{L}_z + \hat{S}_z] = 0 \qquad (14.11.6)$$

Moreover,

$$[\hat{H}, \hat{\mathbf{J}}^2] = [\hat{H}, (\hat{\mathbf{L}} + \hat{\mathbf{S}})^2] = [\hat{H}, \hat{\mathbf{L}}^2 + \hat{\mathbf{S}}^2 + 2\hat{\mathbf{L}}\cdot\hat{\mathbf{S}}] = 2[\hat{H}, \hat{\mathbf{L}}\cdot\hat{\mathbf{S}}]$$

$$= 2[\hat{H}_0 + \zeta(r)\hat{\mathbf{L}}\cdot\hat{\mathbf{S}}, \hat{\mathbf{L}}\cdot\hat{\mathbf{S}}] = [\hat{H}_0, \hat{\mathbf{L}}\cdot\hat{\mathbf{S}}] + 2\zeta(r)[\hat{\mathbf{L}}\cdot\hat{\mathbf{S}}, \hat{\mathbf{L}}\cdot\hat{\mathbf{S}}] = 0 \qquad (14.11.7)$$

(*c*) The results of parts (*a*) and (*b*) imply that one can find the basis of states $|nl, s, J, M\rangle = R_{nl}(r)|JM\rangle$, which is made up of the simultaneous eigenfunctions of the mutually commuting observables $\{\hat{H}, \hat{\mathbf{L}}^2, \hat{\mathbf{S}}^2, \hat{\mathbf{J}}^2, \hat{J}_z\}$. The angular part of these eigenfunctions, $|JM\rangle$, had already been worked out in Problem 14.10, where we found the following expressions:

$$\begin{cases} |J = l + \dfrac{1}{2}, M\rangle = \dfrac{1}{\sqrt{2l+1}}\left[\sqrt{l + M + \dfrac{1}{2}}\,|M - \dfrac{1}{2}, +\rangle - \sqrt{l - M + \dfrac{1}{2}}\,|M + \dfrac{1}{2}, -\rangle\right] \\[2em] |J = l - \dfrac{1}{2}, M\rangle = \dfrac{1}{\sqrt{2l+1}}\left[\sqrt{l + M + \dfrac{1}{2}}\,|M + \dfrac{1}{2}, -\rangle - \sqrt{l - M + \dfrac{1}{2}}\,|M - \dfrac{1}{2}, +\rangle\right] \end{cases} \qquad (14.11.8)$$

The states $|M \pm \dfrac{1}{2}, \pm\rangle \equiv |M, \pm\rangle$ on the right side of Eq. (14.11.8) denote the product-basis eigenstates $|lm\rangle \otimes |s = 1/2, \pm\rangle$ for an electron of an orbital angular momentum l and spin $s = 1/2$. In the coordinate representation, $\langle \mathbf{r}, (r, \theta, \varphi)|lm\rangle = Y_l^m(\theta, \varphi)$, where $Y_l^m(\theta, \varphi)$ are the spherical harmonic functions (see Chap. 6). Therefore,

$$\begin{cases} |J = l + \dfrac{1}{2}, M\rangle = \sqrt{\dfrac{l + M + \dfrac{1}{2}}{2l+1}}\, Y_l^{M-1/2}(\theta, \varphi)|+\rangle + \sqrt{\dfrac{l - M + \dfrac{1}{2}}{2l+1}}\, Y_l^{M+1/2}(\theta, \varphi)|-\rangle \\[2em] |J = l + \dfrac{1}{2}, M\rangle = \sqrt{\dfrac{l + M + \dfrac{1}{2}}{2l+1}}\, Y_l^{M+1/2}(\theta, \varphi)|-\rangle + \sqrt{\dfrac{l - M + \dfrac{1}{2}}{2l+1}}\, Y_l^{M-1/2}(\theta, \varphi)|+\rangle \end{cases} \qquad (14.11.9)$$

where $-J \le M \le J$. By construction, the angular wavefunctions in Eq. (14.11.8) or Eq. (14.11.9) satisfy

$$\begin{cases} \hat{\mathbf{J}}^2 |JM\rangle = \hbar^2 J(J+1)|JM\rangle \\ \hat{J}_z |JM\rangle = \hbar M|JM\rangle \end{cases}$$

$$\begin{cases} \hat{\mathbf{L}}^2 |JM\rangle = \hbar^2 l(l+1)|JM\rangle \\ \hat{\mathbf{S}}^2 |JM\rangle = \hbar^2 (3/4)|JM\rangle \end{cases} \tag{14.11.10}$$

Consequently,

$$\hat{\mathbf{L}} \cdot \hat{\mathbf{S}} |JM\rangle = \frac{1}{2}(\hat{\mathbf{J}}^2 - \hat{\mathbf{L}}^2 - \hat{\mathbf{S}}^2)|JM\rangle = \frac{\hbar^2}{2}[j(j+1) - l(l+1) - 3/4]|JM\rangle \tag{14.11.11}$$

(d) The operator $\hat{L}_z$ can assume the values $\hbar m$, where m is an integer and $-l \le m \le l$. The operator $\hat{S}_z$ can assume the values $\pm\hbar/2$, where $\pm$ corresponds to up/down spin states. The probabilities of these values are determined by the Clebsch–Gordan coefficients of Eq. (14.11.8), and depend on the state of the system.

In the state $|J = l + \frac{1}{2}, M\rangle$, we find

$$\begin{cases} \text{prob}\left(m = M - \frac{1}{2}, +\right) = \dfrac{l + M + 1/2}{2l + 1} \\ \text{prob}\left(m = M + \frac{1}{2}, -\right) = \dfrac{l - M + 1/2}{2l + 1} \end{cases} \tag{14.11.12}$$

Where $|M| \le l + 1/2$. If $M = l + 1/2$, then prob $(m = l, +) = 1$, and all the other combinations have zero probability. The expectation value of L_z is

$$|\hat{L}_z\rangle = \langle l + \tfrac{1}{2}, M|\hat{L}_z|l + \tfrac{1}{2}, M\rangle = \text{prob}\left(m = M - \frac{1}{2}\right)\hbar\left(M - \frac{1}{2}\right)$$

$$+ \text{prob}\left(m = M + \frac{1}{2}\right)\hbar\left(M + \frac{1}{2}\right)$$

$$= \frac{\hbar}{2l+1}\left[\left(l + M + \frac{1}{2}\right)\left(M - \frac{1}{2}\right) + \left(l - M + \frac{1}{2}\right)\left(M + \frac{1}{2}\right)\right]$$

$$= \hbar l\,\frac{2M}{2l+1} \tag{14.11.13}$$

Similarly, the average value of $\hat{S}_z$ is

$$\langle \hat{S}_z\rangle = \langle l + \tfrac{1}{2}, M|\hat{S}_z|l + \tfrac{1}{2}, M\rangle = \frac{\hbar}{2l+1}\left[\left(l + M + \frac{1}{2}\right)\cdot\frac{1}{2} + \left(l - M + \frac{1}{2}\right)\left(-\frac{1}{2}\right)\right]$$

$$= \frac{\hbar}{2}\,\frac{2M}{2l+1} \tag{14.11.14}$$

In the state $|J = l - \frac{1}{2}, M\rangle$, we find

$$\begin{cases} \text{prob}\left(m = M - \frac{1}{2}, -\right) = \dfrac{l + M + 1/2}{2l + 1} \\ \text{prob}\left(m = M - \frac{1}{2}, +\right) = \dfrac{l - M + 1/2}{2l + 1} \end{cases} \tag{14.11.15}$$

where $|m| \leq l - (1/2)$. Therefore, the expectation values of L_z and S_z in this state are,

$$\begin{cases} \langle \hat{L}_z \rangle = \langle l - \frac{1}{2}, M | \hat{L}_z | l - \frac{1}{2}, M \rangle = \hbar M \\[2mm] \langle \hat{S}_z \rangle = \langle l - \frac{1}{2}, M | \hat{S}_z | l - \frac{1}{2}, M \rangle = -\frac{\hbar}{2} \frac{2M}{2l+1} \end{cases} \tag{14.11.16}$$

14.12. The spin-orbit interaction for the electron in a hydrogen-like atom is given by $\hat{H}_{so} = \zeta(r)\hat{\mathbf{L}} \cdot \hat{\mathbf{S}}$, where $\zeta(r) = \dfrac{1}{2m_e^2 c^2} \left(\dfrac{1}{r} \dfrac{dV(r)}{dr} \right)$ and $V(r) = -Ze^2/r$. (a) Derive an equation for the energy levels of such atoms in terms of the quantum numbers l and J. (b) Show that the spin-orbit correction to the unperturbed energy levels is proportional to Z^4.

SOLUTION

(a) The complete Hamiltonian of our problem is $\hat{H} = \hat{H}_0 + \hat{H}_{so}$, where

$$\hat{H}_0 = \frac{\mathbf{P}^2}{2m_e} + \hat{V}(r) = \frac{\hbar^2}{2m_e} \frac{1}{r} \frac{\partial^2}{\partial r^2} r + \frac{1}{2m_e r^2} \hat{\mathbf{L}}^2(\theta, \varphi) + \hat{V}(r) \tag{14.12.1}$$

and $\hat{H}_{so}$ is treated as a small perturbation. For convenience, we take the unperturbed wavefunctions of $\hat{H}_0$ to be the simultaneous eigenfunctions of $\{\hat{\mathbf{L}}^2, \hat{\mathbf{S}}^2, \hat{\mathbf{J}}^2, \hat{J}_z\}$, where $\hat{\mathbf{J}} \equiv \hat{\mathbf{L}} + \hat{\mathbf{S}}$. Thus,

$$\hat{H}_0 R_{nl}^0(r) | JM \rangle = E_{nl}^0 R_{nl}^0(r) | JM \rangle \tag{14.12.2}$$

where $R_{nl}^0(r)$ are the radial wavefunctions of $\hat{H}_0$, and E_{nl}^0 are the corresponding energy levels (see Chap. 8). The kets $| JM \rangle$ in Eq. (14.12.2) represent the angular part of the wavefunctions of $\hat{H}_0$, including the spin states. In this representation [see Eqs. (14.11.7), (14.11.8), and (14.11.10)], and for $l \neq 0$, we have

$$\hat{H}_0 R_{nl}^0(r) | JM \rangle = \frac{\hbar^2 \zeta(r)}{2} R_{nl}^0(r) [J(J+1) - l(l+1) - 3/4] | JM \rangle \tag{14.12.3}$$

where $J = l \pm 1/2$ and $|M| \leq J$. Expression (14.12.3) shows that the perturbation $\hat{H}_{so}$ is already diagonal in the subspace $\{n, l = J \pm 1/2\}$, which corresponds to a degenerate energy level E_{nl}^0. Using the first-order perturbation theory we therefore find

$$E(n, l, J) = E_{nl}^0 + \langle nl, JM | \hat{H}_{so} | nl, JM \rangle \tag{14.12.4}$$

where $\langle r | nl \rangle \equiv R_{nl}^0(r)$. Defining the integral over the radial functions to be

$$\zeta_{nl} \equiv \langle nl | \zeta(r) | nl \rangle = \int r^2 R_{nl}^{0*}(r) \zeta(r) R_{nl}^0(r) \, dr \tag{14.12.5}$$

and using Eq. (14.12.3) we obtain

$$E(n, l, J) = E_{nl}^0 + \frac{\hbar^2}{2} \zeta_{nl} [J(J+1) - l(l+1) - 3/4] \tag{14.12.6}$$

Since $J = l \pm 1/2$, we can distinguish between two cases:

$$E(n, l, J) = \begin{cases} E_{nl}^0 + \zeta_{nl} \hbar^2 l/2 & J = l + 1/2 \\[2mm] E_{nl}^0 + \zeta_{nl} \hbar^2 (l+1)/2 & J = l - 1/2 \end{cases} \tag{14.12.7}$$

Each of these energy levels is $(2J + 1)$ degenerate. The degeneracy can be removed by a magnetic field (see Problem 14.13).

(b) The first-order energy correction due to spin-orbit interaction is proportional to the radial integral ξ_{nl}. For $l \neq 0$, we have

$$\xi_{nl} = \langle nl | \frac{1}{2m_e^2 c^2} \left(\frac{1}{r} \frac{dV}{dr} \right) | nl \rangle = \frac{1}{2m_e^2 c^2} \langle nl | \frac{1}{r} \frac{dV}{dr} \left(-\frac{Ze^2}{r} \right) | nl \rangle$$

$$= \frac{Ze^2}{2m_e^2 c^2} \langle nl | r^{-3} | nl \rangle = \frac{Z\alpha^2 \hbar^2}{2m_e^2 e^2} \langle nl | r^{-3} | nl \rangle \tag{14.12.8}$$

A detailed calculation of $\langle r^{-3} \rangle_{nl}$ yields (see Chap. 8)

$$\langle nl | r^{-3} | nl \rangle = \left(\frac{1}{a_B n} \right)^3 \frac{1}{l(l + 1/2)(l + 1)} \tag{14.12.9}$$

where $a_B = \hbar^2/Ze^2 m_e$ is the Bohr radius. Therefore,

$$\zeta_{nl} = \frac{(Ze)^4 m_e}{2\hbar^4} \frac{\alpha^2}{n^3} \frac{1}{l(l + 1/2)(l + 1)} \tag{14.12.10}$$

14.13. A hydrogen-like atom is placed in a weak magnetic field $\mathcal{B} = \mathcal{B}\mathbf{k}$, where the interaction is described by the *Zeeman Hamiltonian*, $\hat{H}' = \mu_B \mathcal{B}(\hat{L}_z + 2\hat{S}_z)/\hbar$. (a) Assume that in the absence of $\mathcal{B}$, the wavefunctions of the atom are eigenfunctions of $\hat{\mathbf{L}}^2$, $\hat{\mathbf{S}}^2$, $\hat{\mathbf{J}}^2$, and $\hat{J}_z$, where $\hat{\mathbf{J}} = \hat{\mathbf{L}} + \hat{\mathbf{S}}$. Use the first-order perturbation theory to calculate the energy splittings due to the magnetic field. (b) The electron of such an atom is excited to a p-state. How many components does each of the levels split into when a weak magnetic field is applied?

SOLUTION

(a) The perturbing Zeeman Hamiltonian can be written in the following form:

$$\hat{H}' = \frac{\mu_B \mathcal{B}(\hat{L}_z + 2\hat{S}_z)}{\hbar} = \frac{\mu_B \mathcal{B}(\hat{J}_z + \hat{S}_z)}{\hbar} \tag{14.13.1}$$

where μ_B is the *Bohr magneton*. The energy levels, $E = E(n, l, J) + \Delta E$, of the complete Hamiltonian $\hat{H} = \hat{H}_0 + \hat{H}_{so} + \hat{H}'$ are then given by

$$\Delta E = \mu_B \mathcal{B} \langle J = l \pm \frac{1}{2}, M | (\hat{J}_z + \hat{S}_z) | J = l \pm \frac{1}{2}, M \rangle = \mu_B \mathcal{B} \left[M + \langle J = l \pm \frac{1}{2}, M | \hat{S}_z | J = l \pm \frac{1}{2}, M \rangle \right]$$

$$\tag{14.13.2}$$

The matrix element of S_z was already calculated in Prob. 14.11. Combining the appropriate results from Eqs. (14.11.12) and (14.11.14), we find

$$\langle J = l \pm \frac{1}{2}, M | \hat{S}_z | J = l \pm \frac{1}{2}, M \rangle = \pm \frac{\hbar M}{2l + 1} \tag{14.13.3}$$

Hence,

$$\Delta E = \mu_B \mathcal{B} \left[1 \pm \frac{1}{2l + 1} \right] \tag{14.13.4}$$

(b) In the absence of a magnetic field there are two degenerate energy levels, which are specified by the quantum numbers ($l = 1$, $J = 1/2$), respectively [see Eq. (14.12.7)]. When the magnetic field B is applied, the degeneracy is removed. The $J = 3/2$ level is split into four components since $M = -3/2, -1/2,$

+1/2, +3/2. Similarly, the $J = 1/2$ level is split into two components corresponding to $M = -1/2, +1/2$. The energy changes are given by Eq. (14.13.4).Thus,

$$\Delta E\,(l,\,J) = g\,(l,\,J)\mu_B \mathcal{B} M \tag{14.13.5}$$

$$g(l,\,J) = \left[1 \pm \frac{1}{(2l+1)}\right] \tag{14.13.6}$$

where g is the *Landé factor*. In particular, $g\,(1,\,3/2) = 4/3$, and $g\,(1,\,1/2) = 2/3$.

SUPPLEMENTARY PROBLEMS

14.14. Show that the Clebsch–Gordan coefficients satisfy the following recurrence relations:

$$\sqrt{J(J+1) - M(M \pm 1)}\,\langle m_1 m_2 | J, M+1\rangle = \sqrt{j_1(j_1+1) - m_1(m_1 \mp 1)}\,\langle m_1 \mp 1, m_2 | JM\rangle$$

$$+ \sqrt{j_2(j_2+1) - m_2(m_2 \mp 1)}\,\langle m_1, m_2 - 1 | JM\rangle \tag{14.14.1}$$

14.15. Consider a deuterium atom composed of a nucleus of spin $I = 1$ and an electron. The electronic angular momentum is $\mathbf{J} = \mathbf{L} + \mathbf{S}$, where $\mathbf{L}$ is the orbital angular momentum of the electron and $\mathbf{S}$ is its spin. The total angular momentum of the atom is $\hat{\mathbf{F}} = \hat{\mathbf{J}} + \hat{\mathbf{I}}$, where $\hat{\mathbf{I}}$ is the nuclear spin. The eigenvalues of $\hat{\mathbf{J}}^2$ and $\hat{\mathbf{F}}^2$ are $J(J+1)\,\hbar^2$ and $F(F+1)$, respectively. (a) What are the possible values of the quantum numbers J and F for a deuterium atom in the $1s$ ground state? (b) Answer the same question in the $2p$ excited state. (c) What are the possible values of the quantum numbers J and F for a hydrogen atom in the $2p$ level? The hydrogen atom's nucleus is a pr oton of spin $I = 1/2$.

Ans. (a) $J = 1/2$, $F = 1/2$, $3/2$

(b) if $J = 1/2$, $F = 1/2$, $3/2$;   if $J = 3/2$, $F = 1/2$, $3/2$, $5/2$

(c) if $J = 1/2$, $F = 0$, 1;   if $J = 3/2$, $F = 1$, 2

14.16. Let $\hat{\mathbf{S}} = \hat{\mathbf{S}}_1 + \hat{\mathbf{S}}_2 + \hat{\mathbf{S}}_3$ be the total spin of three independent spin 1/2 particles, and let $|m_1 m_2 m_3\rangle$ be the common eigenstates of $\hat{S}_{1z}$, $\hat{S}_{2z}$, and $\hat{S}_{3z}$ (there are $2^3 = 8$ states), (a) What are the possible values of the total spin? (b) Find a basis of eigenstates common to $\hat{S}^2$ and $\hat{S}_z$, in terms of the $|m_1 m_2 m_3\rangle$. Hint: First consider the addition of two spins, then add the results to the third spin. (c) Do the operators $\hat{S}^2$ and $\hat{S}_z$ form a complete basis?

Ans.

(a) $1/2$, $3/2$

(b) $\left|\frac{1}{2},\frac{1}{2}\right\rangle = \frac{1}{\sqrt{2}}\left(|+-+\rangle - |-++\rangle\right) = \sqrt{\frac{2}{3}}\,|++-\rangle - \sqrt{\frac{1}{6}}\left(|+-+\rangle + |-++\rangle\right),$

$\left|\frac{1}{2},-\frac{1}{2}\right\rangle = \frac{1}{\sqrt{2}}\left(|+--\rangle - |-+-\rangle\right) = \sqrt{\frac{1}{6}}\left(|+--\rangle + |-+-\rangle\right) - \sqrt{\frac{2}{3}}\,|--+\rangle, \left|\frac{3}{2},\frac{3}{2}\right\rangle = |+++\rangle,$

$\left|\frac{3}{2},\frac{1}{2}\right\rangle = \frac{1}{\sqrt{3}}\left(|++-\rangle + |+-+\rangle + |-++\rangle\right), \left|\frac{3}{2},-\frac{1}{2}\right\rangle = \frac{1}{\sqrt{3}}\left(|+--\rangle + |-+-\rangle + |--+\rangle\right), \left|\frac{3}{2},-\frac{3}{2}\right\rangle = |---\rangle$

(c) No, since the states $\left|\frac{1}{2}, \pm\frac{1}{2}\right\rangle$ do not have a unique decomposition in $|m_1 m_2 m_3\rangle$ basis.

CHAPTER 15

Scattering Theory

15.1 Cross Section

Consider the typical scattering problem depicted in Fig. 15.1.

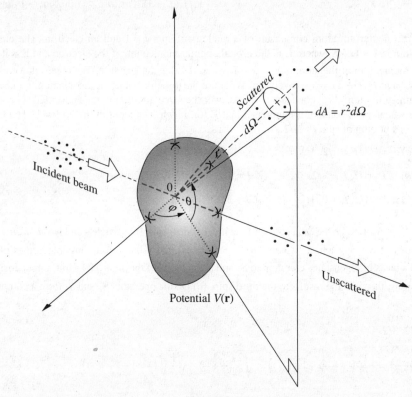

Fig. 15.1

A beam of particles scatters from the potential $V(\mathbf{r})$ with coordinate origin at point O. We define the *differential cross section* $d\sigma/d\Omega$ as the ratio of the number of scattered particles $dn(\theta, \varphi)$ per unit time within the solid angle $d\Omega$ divided by the incident particle flux F:

$$\frac{d\sigma}{d\Omega} = \frac{dn(\theta, \varphi)}{F\,d\Omega} \tag{15.1}$$

where $d\sigma/d\Omega$ has the dimensions of a surface. We assume:

1. Any interaction between the scattered particles themselves is neglected.
2. Multiple scattering processes are neglected. A multiple scattering process is a process in which a scattered particle can be scattered multiple times in the same target range.
3. The incident beam width is much larger than a typical range of the scattering potential, so that the particle will have a well-defined momentum.

The *total cross section* is obtained by integrating over $d\Omega$:

$$\sigma_T = \int \frac{d\sigma}{d\Omega} d\Omega \tag{15.2}$$

When the scattering is from a potential, say, $V(\mathbf{r})$, the differential cross section is the same in the Lab and center-of-mass (CM) frames:

$$\left(\frac{d\sigma}{d\Omega}\right)^{\text{Lab}} = \left(\frac{d\sigma}{d\Omega}\right)^{\text{CM}} \tag{15.3}$$

However, if we consider electric scattering of particle 1 from particle 2, then the differential cross section in the two frames will be different, and is given by

$$\left(\frac{d\sigma}{d\Omega}\right)^{\text{Lab}} = \frac{(1 + \gamma^2 + 2\gamma\cos\theta)^{3/2}}{|1 + \gamma\cos\theta|} \left(\frac{d\sigma}{d\Omega}\right)^{\text{CM}} \tag{15.4}$$

where θ is the scattering angle in the CM frame and $\gamma = m_1/m_2$.

15.2 Stationary Scattering States

Consider a scattering problem relating to particles with mass μ (in this section we use the reduced mass μ and not the standard mass m) and well-defined momentum $\mathbf{p} = \hbar\mathbf{k}$, which scatters from a *time-independent potential* $V = V(\mathbf{r})$. The Hamiltonian of the system is

$$\hat{H} = \hat{H}_0 + \hat{V}(\mathbf{r}) \tag{15.5}$$

where $\hat{H}_0$ is the free Hamiltonian, $\hat{H}_0 = \hbar^2 k^2/2\mu$. The wavefunction for a scattered particle with energy $E > 0$ is obtained by solving the stationary Schrödinger equation:

$$[\nabla^2 + k^2 - \hat{U}(\mathbf{r})]\phi(\mathbf{r}) = 0 \tag{15.6}$$

where

$$k = \sqrt{\frac{2\mu E}{\hbar^2}} \qquad \hat{U}(\mathbf{r}) = \frac{2\mu}{\hbar^2}\hat{V}(\mathbf{r}) \tag{15.7}$$

For a collision between two particles, $\hat{V}(\mathbf{r})$ is the interaction potential between them ($\mathbf{r} = \mathbf{r}_1 - \mathbf{r}_2$), and E is the kinetic energy associated with the particle of reduced mass μ in the CM frame.

For a potential $V(\mathbf{r})$ of shorter range than the *Coulomb potential* [$rV(\mathbf{r}) \to 0$ where $r \to \infty$], the solution of the Schrödinger equation can be written as a composition of an incident plane wave and a spherical wave of amplitude $f(\theta, \varphi)$:

$$\phi(r)_{r\to\infty} \to e^{ikz} + f(\theta, \varphi)\frac{e^{ikr}}{r} \tag{15.8}$$

The *scattering amplitude* is given by

$$f_k(\theta, \varphi) = -\frac{1}{4\pi} \int e^{-i\mathbf{k}_f \cdot \mathbf{r}'} U(\mathbf{r}') \phi(\mathbf{r}') d^3 r' \qquad \left(k_f = \frac{\mathbf{k} \cdot \mathbf{r}}{r} \right) \qquad (15.9)$$

The amplitude $f_k(\theta, \varphi)$ depends on the potential and the scattering angles θ and φ. This quantity is directly related to the differential cross section

$$\frac{d\sigma(\theta, \varphi)}{d\Omega} = |f_k(\theta, \varphi)|^2 \qquad (15.10)$$

15.3   Born Approximation

The Born approximation is obtained by treating the potential $U(\mathbf{r})$ as a small perturbation. Equation (15.9) then gives

$$f_k^B(\theta, \varphi) = -\frac{1}{4\pi} \int e^{-i\mathbf{q} \cdot \mathbf{r}'} U(\mathbf{r}') \phi(\mathbf{r}') d^3 r' \qquad (15.11)$$

where $\mathbf{q} = \mathbf{k}_f - \mathbf{k}_i$ and $k_{f,i}$ are the final and initial momentum, respectively. Note that in the Born approximations the scattering amplitude f_k^B is proportional to the Fourier transform of the potential $U(\mathbf{r})$ with respect to $\mathbf{q}$. If the potential has spherical symmetry, $U(\mathbf{r}) = U(r)$; Eq. (15.11) is simplified by taking $\mathbf{q}$ as the polar axis and integrating over $d\Omega'$. For this case, we obtain

$$f_k^B(\theta) = -\frac{2\mu}{\hbar^2 q} \int_0^\infty \sin(qr) r V(r) dr \qquad (15.12)$$

where $q = 2k \sin(\theta/2)$ is the *momentum transfer* and $k = |\mathbf{k}_f| = |\mathbf{k}_i|$; see Fig. 15.2

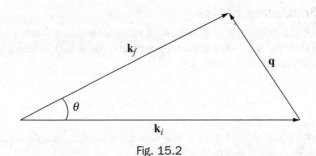

Fig. 15.2

The Born approximation is valid when either of the two following conditions holds:

$$1. \quad \bar{V} \ll \frac{\hbar^2}{\mu a^2} \qquad ka \lesssim 1$$

$$(15.13)$$

$$2. \quad \bar{V} \ll \left[\frac{\hbar^2}{\mu a^2} \right] ka \qquad ka \gg 1$$

where a is the range of the potential and $\bar{V}$ is the "averaged" potential defined by

$$\bar{V} = \frac{1}{4\pi a^2} \int \frac{\bar{V}(r)}{r} d^3 r \qquad (15.14)$$

The second condition shows that the Born approximation is always applicable for sufficiently fast (high-energy) particles. This condition is weaker than the first one; hence, if the potential can be regarded as a perturbation at low energies, it can always be so regarded at high energies, whereas the converse is not necessarily true.

15.4   Partial Wave Expansions

Consider a potential with spherical symmetry, $V(\mathbf{r}) = V(r)$. In this case, the stationary wavefunction $\phi_k(r, \theta)$ and the scattering amplitude $f_k(\theta)$ can be expanded in terms of Legendre polynomials $P_l(\cos\theta)$:

$$\phi_k(r, \theta) = \sum_{l=0}^{\infty} A_l \frac{\chi_l(r) P_l(\cos\theta)}{r} \tag{15.15}$$

and

$$f_k(\theta) = \sum_{l=0}^{\infty} (2l + 1) f_l P_l(\cos\theta) \tag{15.16}$$

where the coefficients A_l, f_l, and the functions $\chi_l(r)$ are to be determined. $\chi_l(r)$ satisfies the radial Schrödinger equation,

$$\left[\frac{d^2}{dr^2} + k^2 - U(r) - \frac{l(l+1)}{r^2} \right] \chi_l(r) = 0 \tag{15.17}$$

where the boundary conditions are $\chi_l(0) = 0$. In the asymptotic region $r \to \infty$,

$$\chi_l(r)_{r\to\infty} \sim [A_l j_l(kr) + B_l n_l(kr)] r = \frac{1}{k} C_l \sin\left(kr - \frac{\pi l}{2} + \delta_l \right) \tag{15.18}$$

where j_l and n_l are the spherical Bessel and Neumann functions, respectively. The parameter δ_l is called the *phase shift*, since it determines the difference in phase between this solution and the solution of the free radial Schrödinger equation:

$$\chi_l^0(r)_{r\to\infty} \sim \frac{1}{k} C_l \sin\left(kr - \frac{\pi l}{2} \right) \tag{15.19}$$

Similarly, we can expand the plane waves in terms of the Legendre polynomials:

$$e^{ikz} = e^{ikr\cos\theta} = \sum_{l=0}^{\infty} i^l (2l + 1) j_l(kr) P_l(\cos\theta) \tag{15.20}$$

Now, substituting the expansions of e^{ikz}, $f_k(\theta)$, and $\phi_k(r, \theta)$ in Eq. (15.15) we obtain $A_l = (2l + 1) i^l e^{i\delta_l}$, and

$$f_k(\theta) = \frac{1}{2ik} \sum_{l=0}^{\infty} (2l + 1)(e^{2i\delta_l} - 1) P_l(\cos\theta) \tag{15.21}$$

Thus, the differential cross section is given by

$$\frac{d\sigma}{d\Omega} = \frac{1}{k^2} \left| \sum_{l=0}^{\infty} (2l + 1) e^{i\delta_l} \sin\delta_l P_l(\cos\theta) \right|^2 \tag{15.22}$$

and total cross section is

$$\sigma_T = 2\pi \int_0^\pi |f(\theta)|^2 \sin\theta\, d\theta = \frac{4\pi}{k^2} \sum_{l=0}^{\infty} (2l + 1) \sin^2\delta_l \tag{15.23}$$

From Eqs. (15.21) and (15.23) we verify directly that

$$\sigma_T = \frac{4\pi}{k} \text{Im}(f_k(0)) \tag{15.24}$$

The last result is called the *optical theorem*. The phase shifts δ_l are completely determined by the asymptotic form of the radial function $\chi_l(r)$. Expansion of Eq. (15.23) is particularly useful for a short-range potential that vanishes outside the region $r < a$. In this case, the partial waves that satisfy the condition $l(l+1) > ka$ may be neglected. Moreover, since the radial wavefunction $R_l(r) = \chi_l(r)/r$ and its derivative are continuous at the boundary $r = a$, we have

$$\tan \delta_l = \frac{kj_l{}'(ka) - \gamma_l j_l(ka)}{kn_l{}'(ka) - \gamma_l n_l(ka)} \tag{15.25}$$

where γ_l is the *logarithmic derivative*, defined as

$$\gamma_l = \frac{1}{R_l}\frac{dR_l}{dr}\bigg|_{r=a^-} \qquad \left[R_l(r) = \frac{1}{r}\chi_l(r)\right] \tag{15.26}$$

For sufficiently weak potential for which the Born approximation holds, all the phase shifts are small and are given by

$$\sin \delta_l \approx \delta_l = -\frac{2\mu}{\hbar^2}\int V(r) j_l^2(kr)\, dr \tag{15.27}$$

15.5   Scattering of Identical Particles

The case where two identical particles collide requires special consideration. If the total spin of the system is even, the differential cross section is

$$\frac{d\sigma}{d\Omega} = |f(\theta) + f(\pi - \theta)|^2 \tag{15.28}$$

while if the total spin is odd, the differential cross section is

$$\frac{d\sigma}{d\Omega} = |f(\theta) - f(\pi - \theta)|^2 \tag{15.29}$$

For example, if $s = 1/2$, the spin wavefunction can be in singlet (total spin is zero) or triplet (total spin is one) states.

For an unpolarized beam of particles with spin s, the system can be in $(2s + 1)^2$ spin states that are distributed with equal probabilities. From the total number of possibilities, $(2s + 1)$ spin states are antisymmetric. Therefore, the differential cross section is

$$\frac{d\sigma}{d\Omega} = |f(\theta)|^2 + |f(\pi - \theta)|^2 + \frac{(-1)^{2s}}{2s+1} 2\mathrm{Re}[f(\theta)f^*(\pi - \theta)] \tag{15.30}$$

SOLVED PROBLEMS

15.1. A particle of mass μ and momentum $\mathbf{p} = \hbar\mathbf{k}$ is scattered by the potential $V(\mathbf{r}) = \dfrac{e^{-r/a}}{r}V_0 a$, where V_0 and $a > 0$ are real constants (*Yukawa potential*). (*a*) Using the Born approximation, calculate the differential cross section. (*b*) Obtain the total cross section.

SOLUTION

(*a*) The range of the Yukawa potential is characterized by the distance a. We assume that $V_0 a^2 \ll \hbar^2/\mu$, so that the Born approximation is valid for all the values of ka [see Eq. (15.13)]. The scattering amplitude is then given by

$$f(\theta, \varphi) = -\frac{1}{4\pi}\frac{2\mu V_0 a}{\hbar^2}\int e^{-i\mathbf{q}\cdot\mathbf{r}}\frac{e^{-r/r_0}}{r}\, d^3r \tag{15.1.1}$$

Since the potential has spherical symmetry $V(\mathbf{r}) = V(r)$, we can carry out the integration using the relation

$$\int r^2 e^{-i\mathbf{q}\cdot\mathbf{r}} V(r)\, dr\, d\Omega = \frac{4\pi}{q}\int_0^\infty \sin(qr)\, V(r)\, r\, dr \tag{15.1.2}$$

where $r = |\mathbf{r}|$ and $d\Omega = \sin\theta\, d\theta\, d\varphi$. Therefore,

$$f(\theta) = -\frac{2\mu V_0 a}{\hbar^2 k}\int_0^\infty r\sin(kr)\, e^{-r/a}\, dr = -\frac{2\mu V_0 a^3}{\hbar^2}\frac{1}{1+q^2 a^2} = -\frac{2\mu V_0 a^3}{\hbar^2}\frac{1}{1+[2ka\sin(\theta/2)]^2} \tag{15.1.3}$$

Finally, the differential cross section $\dfrac{d\sigma}{d\Omega} = |f(\theta)|^2$ is

$$\frac{d\sigma(\theta)}{d\Omega} = \frac{4\mu^2 V_0^2 a^6}{\hbar^4}\frac{1}{[1+4k^2 a^2\sin^2(\theta/2)]^2} \tag{15.1.4}$$

Note that due to the spherical asymmetry the cross section does not depend on the azimuthal angle.

(b) The total scattering cross section is obtained by integration:

$$\sigma = \int \frac{d\sigma(\theta)}{d\Omega}\, d\Omega = \frac{4\mu^2 V_0^2 a^6}{\hbar^4}\frac{4\pi}{1+4k^2 a^2} \tag{15.1.5}$$

Note that the infinite range limit ($a \to \infty$, $V_0 \to 0$, and $V_0 a = Z_1 Z_2 e^2 = $ constant) of the Yukawa potential corresponds to the Coulomb interaction between two ions of charges $Z_1 e$ and $Z_2 e$. At this point, Eq. (15.14) is reduced to the well-known *Rutherford formula*,

$$\frac{d\sigma}{d\Omega} = \frac{4\mu^2}{\hbar^4}\frac{Z_1^2 Z_2^2 e^4}{16k^4\sin^4(\theta/2)} = \frac{Z_1^2 Z_2^2 e^4}{16E^2\sin^4(\theta/2)} \tag{15.1.6}$$

where $E = (\hbar^2 k^2)/2\mu$ is the kinetic energy of the particles in the CM frame and μ is their reduced mass.

15.2. Using the Born approximation, calculate the differential cross section $d\sigma/d\Omega$ for a central Gaussian potential of the form $V(\mathbf{r}) = \dfrac{V_0}{\sqrt{4\pi}}e^{-r^2/4a^2}$. Compare your result with the differential cross section for the Yukawa potential $V(\mathbf{r}) = \dfrac{V_0 a}{r}e^{-r/a}$.

SOLUTION

For the Gaussian potential, in the Born approximation we have

$$f(\theta) = -\frac{2\mu}{\hbar^2 q}\int_0^\infty \sin(qr)\, V(r)\, r\, dr = \frac{2\mu V_0}{\hbar^2 q\sqrt{4\pi}}\frac{\partial}{\partial q}\int_0^\infty \cos(qr)\, e^{-r^2/4a^2}\, dr$$

$$= \frac{2\mu V_0}{\sqrt{4\pi}\hbar^2 q}\frac{\partial}{\partial q}\frac{\sqrt{4\pi}}{2}a e^{-q^2 a^2} = -\frac{2\mu V_0 a^3 q}{\hbar^2 q}e^{-q^2 a^2} \tag{15.2.1}$$

where $q = 2k\sin(\theta/2)$. Therefore,

$$\left(\frac{d\sigma}{d\Omega}\right)_{\text{Gaussian}} = \frac{4\mu^2 V_0^2 a^6}{\hbar^4}e^{-2q^2 a^2} \tag{15.2.2}$$

For the Yukawa potential, we found in Problem 15.1 that

$$\left(\frac{d\sigma}{d\Omega}\right)_{\text{Yukawa}} = \frac{4\mu^2 V_0^2 a^6}{\hbar^4}\frac{1}{\left[1+q^2 a^2\right]^2} \tag{15.2.3}$$

The differential cross section of Eqs. (15.2.2) and (15.2.3) are plotted in Fig. 15.3 (in a^2 units). Note that for $qa \ll 1$, both cross sections coincide and are given by

$$\frac{d\sigma}{d\Omega} \approx \frac{4\mu^2 V_0^2 a^6}{\hbar^4}(1-2q^2 a^2) \tag{15.2.4}$$

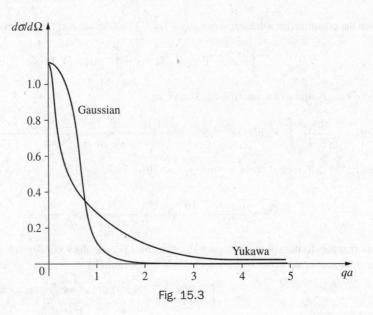

Fig. 15.3

Thus, for a small momentum transfer (i.e., large distance) the specific form of the short-range scattering potential is not important. On the other hand, for a large momentum transfer, the Gaussian cross section decreases more rapidly as compared to the Yukawa cross section. This is expected since for short distances the Gaussian potential is much weaker than the Yukawa potential.

15.3. Show that if the scattering potential has a translation invariance property, $V(\mathbf{r} + \mathbf{R}) = V(\mathbf{r})$, where $\mathbf{R}$ is a constant vector, then the Born approximation scattering vanishes unless $\mathbf{q} \cdot \mathbf{R} = 2\pi n$, where n is an integer.

SOLUTION

The translation symmetry of the potential, $V(\mathbf{r}) = V(\mathbf{r} + \mathbf{R})$, implies

$$\int e^{-i\mathbf{q}\cdot\mathbf{r}} V(\mathbf{r}) \, d^3r = \int e^{-i\mathbf{q}\cdot\mathbf{r}} V(\mathbf{r} + \mathbf{R}) \, d^3r \tag{15.3.1}$$

By changing variables $\mathbf{r} \to \mathbf{r} + \mathbf{R}$ on the right-hand side of Eq. (15.3.1) we obtain

$$\int e^{-i\mathbf{q}\cdot\mathbf{r}} V(\mathbf{r}) \, d^3r = \int e^{-i\mathbf{q}\cdot\mathbf{r}'+i\mathbf{q}\cdot\mathbf{R}} V(\mathbf{r}') \, d^3r' \tag{15.3.2}$$

Therefore,

$$\int e^{-i\mathbf{q}\cdot\mathbf{R}} V(\mathbf{r}) \, [1 - e^{i\mathbf{q}\cdot\mathbf{R}}] \, d^3r = 0 \tag{15.3.3}$$

Equation (15.3.3) holds when either of the following two conditions is satisfied

$$\int e^{-i\mathbf{q}\cdot\mathbf{r}} V(\mathbf{r}) \, d^3r = 0 \qquad \text{(arbitrary } \mathbf{q}) \tag{15.3.4}$$

$$e^{i\mathbf{q}\cdot\mathbf{R}} = 1 \to \mathbf{q}\cdot\mathbf{R} = 2\pi n \qquad \text{(}n \text{ is an integer)} \tag{15.3.5}$$

The Born scattering amplitude $f^B(\mathbf{q})$ is proportional to the Fourier transform of the potential $V(\mathbf{r})$. We therefore conclude that $f^B(\mathbf{q})$ vanishes identically, unless the condition of Eq. (15.3.5) is satisfied. Normally,

$$f^B(\mathbf{q}) = \sum_{\mathbf{k}} f_{\mathbf{q}} \delta_{\mathbf{q},\mathbf{k}} \qquad (\mathbf{k}\cdot\mathbf{R} = 2\pi n) \tag{15.3.6}$$

Note that the translation symmetry of the scattering potential corresponds to the scattering form of a lattice. For any vector $\mathbf{R}$ of the lattice, the set of vectors $\mathbf{k}$ that satisfy $\mathbf{k}\cdot\mathbf{R} = 2\pi n$ constitutes the reciprocal lattice.

Therefore, as a result of the conditions of Eq. (15.3.5), the scattering amplitude vanishes unless the momentum transfer **q** is equal to some vector of the reciprocal lattice. This is precisely the Bragg–von Laue scattering condition.

15.4. Using the Born approximation, express the differential cross section for nonrelativistic scattering of an electron from a spherical symmetric charge distribution $\rho(r)$ as the product of the cross section for a point charge q (Rutherford scattering) and the square of a form factor $F(k)$, where k is the momentum transfer. Evaluate $F(k)$ explicitly for uniform charge distribution of radius R and for a Gaussian charge distribution.

SOLUTION

In the Born approximation, the differential cross section is given by

$$\frac{d\sigma(\theta)}{d\Omega} = \frac{\mu^2}{4\pi^2\hbar^4}\left[\int e^{-i\mathbf{k}\cdot\mathbf{r}}V(\mathbf{r})\,d^3r\right]^2 \tag{15.4.1}$$

where μ denotes the nonrelativistic electron mass and **k** is the transferred momentum. By definition, the potential of the electron due to a symmetric charge distribution $V(\mathbf{r}) = V(r)$ can be written as the convolution integral:

$$V(\mathbf{r}) = -\int \frac{e\rho(\mathbf{r}')}{|\mathbf{r}-\mathbf{r}'|}d^3r' = \left(-\frac{eq}{r}\right)\left(\frac{\rho(r)}{q}\right) \tag{15.4.2}$$

The first term of the right-hand side of Eq. (15.4.2) corresponds to the Coulomb interaction, and leads, after regularization (see Problem 15.1), to the Rutherford cross section. Therefore,

$$\frac{d\sigma(\theta)}{d\Omega} = \left(\frac{d\sigma}{d\Omega}\right)_{Rutherford}\underbrace{\left[\frac{1}{q}\int e^{-i\mathbf{k}\cdot\mathbf{r}}\rho(r)\,d^3r\right]^2}_{F(k)} \tag{15.4.3}$$

For a uniform charge distribution of radius R we have

$$\rho(r) = \begin{cases} \dfrac{3q}{4\pi R^3} & r < R \\ 0 & r > 0 \end{cases} \tag{15.4.4}$$

Thus, we obtain

$$F(k) = \left[\frac{4\pi}{k}\left(\frac{3}{4\pi}\frac{1}{R^3}\right)\int_0^R r\sin(kr)\,dr\right]^2 = \left[\frac{3}{R^3k^2}\left(\frac{\sin(kr)}{k}-r\cos(kr)\right)\right]^2 \tag{15.4.5}$$

Similarly, for a Gaussian distribution $\rho(r) = \dfrac{q}{\pi^{3/2}R^3}e^{-r^2/R^2}$:

$$F(k) = \left[\frac{4\pi}{k}\frac{1}{\pi^{3/2}R^3}\int_0^\infty r\sin(kr)e^{-r^2/R^2}\,dr\right]^2 = \left[\frac{1}{4\pi}e^{-\frac{r^2k^2}{4}}\right]^2 \tag{15.4.6}$$

15.5. Consider scattering from a spherical symmetric potential. The solution of the Schrödinger equation is given by the expansion $\phi(r,\theta) = \sum_{l=0}^\infty R_l(r)P_l(\cos\theta)$, where $R(r)$ is the solution of the radial wave equation and $P_l(\cos\theta)$ is the Legendre polynomial of order l. In the limit $r \to \infty$ the asymptotic form of the wavefunction is

$$\phi(r,\theta)_{r\to\infty} \sim e^{ikz} + \frac{1}{r}f(\theta)e^{ikr} \tag{15.5.1}$$

where $f(\theta)$ is the scattering amplitude. Similarly, the asymptotic form of $R(r)$ is

$$R(r)_{r\to\infty} \sim A_l \frac{\sin\left(kr - \frac{\pi}{2}l + \delta_l\right)}{kr} \tag{15.5.2}$$

where δ_l are phase shifts. (a) Use Eqs. (15.5.1) and (15.5.2) to obtain the Legendre expansion of $f(\theta)$. (b) Show that the total cross section is given by

$$\sigma_T = \frac{4\pi}{k^2} \sum_{l=0}^{\infty} (2l+1)\sin^2\delta_l \tag{15.5.3}$$

SOLUTION

(a) The asymptotic form of the wavefunction is given in Eqs. (15.5.1) and (15.5.2):

$$\phi(r,\theta)_{r\to\infty} \sim \sum_{l=0}^{\infty} A_l \frac{\sin\left(kr - \frac{\pi}{2}l + \delta_l\right)}{kr} P_l(\cos\theta) = e^{ikz} + \frac{1}{r}f(\theta)e^{ikr} \tag{15.5.4}$$

Using the Legendre expansion of e^{ikz},

$$e^{ikz} = e^{ikr\cos\theta} = \sum_{l=0}^{\infty} (2l+1)i^l j_l(kr) P_l(\cos\theta) \tag{15.5.5}$$

we find that

$$\sum_{l=0}^{\infty} A_l \frac{\sin\left(kr - \frac{\pi}{2}l + \delta_l\right)}{kr} P_l(\cos\theta) = \sum_{l=0}^{\infty}\left[(2l+1)i^l \frac{\sin\left(kr - \frac{\pi}{2}l + \delta_l\right)}{kr} + \frac{1}{r}f_l(\theta)e^{ikr}\right]P_l(\cos\theta) \tag{15.5.6}$$

where $f(\theta) = \sum_{l=0}^{\infty} f_l P_l(\cos\theta)$. Now we write $\sin x = \frac{e^{ix} - e^{-ix}}{2i}$, and obtain

$$A_l e^{i\left(kr - \pi\frac{l}{2} + \delta_l\right)} - (2l+1)i^l e^{i\left(kr - \pi\frac{l}{2}\right)} = 2ikf_l e^{ikr} \tag{15.5.7}$$

$$A_l e^{-ikr - \pi\frac{l}{2} + \delta_l} - 2l + 1i^l e^{-ikr - \pi\frac{l}{2}} = 0 \tag{15.5.8}$$

Therefore, from Eq. (15.5.8) we obtain $A_l = (2l+1)i^l e^{i\delta_l}$ and then, by substituting back into Eq. (15.5.8),

$$f(\theta) = (2ik)^{-1}\sum_{l=0}^{\infty} (2l+1)(e^{2i\delta_l} - 1)P_l(\cos\theta) \tag{15.5.9}$$

(b) The total cross section is

$$\sigma = \int |f(\theta)|^2 d\Omega = 2\pi \int_{-1}^{1} \frac{d(\cos\theta)}{4k^2}\left|\sum_{l=0}^{\infty}(2l+1)(e^{2i\delta_l} - 1)P_l(\cos\theta)\right|^2$$

$$= \frac{\pi}{2k^2}\int_{-1}^{1} d(\cos\theta)\sum_{l,l'=0}^{\infty}(2l'+1)(2l+1)(e^{2i\delta_l} - 1)(e^{2i\delta_l} - 1)P_{l'}(\cos\theta)P_l(\cos\theta) \tag{15.5.10}$$

Now, $\int_{-1}^{1} d(\cos\theta) P_{l'}(\cos\theta) P_l(\cos\theta) = \frac{2}{(2l+1)}\delta_{ll'}$. Therefore,

$$\sigma_T = \frac{\pi}{k^2}\sum_{l=0}^{\infty}(2l+1)(2 - e^{2i\delta_l} - e^{-2i\delta_l}) = \frac{4\pi}{k^2}\sum_{l=0}^{\infty}(2l+1)\sin^2\delta_l \tag{15.5.11}$$

15.6. Consider the *hard sphere potential* of the form

$$V(r) = \begin{cases} 0 & r > r_0 \\ \infty & r < r_0 \end{cases}$$

where $k_0 r_0 \ll 1$. (a) Assume only s-wave scattering and calculate $\delta_0(k)$, $f(k)$, $d\sigma/d\Omega$, and σ_T. (b) Write the radial Schrödinger equation for $l = 1$, and show that the solution for the p-wave scattering is of the form

$$\chi_{k1}(r) = A\left[\frac{\sin(kr)}{kr} - \cos(kr) + a\left(\frac{\cos(kr)}{kr} + \sin(kr)\right)\right]$$

where A and a are constants. (c) Determine $\delta_1(k)$ from the condition imposed on $\chi_{k1}(r_0)$. (d) Show that in the limit $k \to 0$, $\delta_1(k) \sim (k_0 r_0)^3$ and $\delta_1(k) \ll \delta_0(k)$.

SOLUTION

(a) The radial Schrödinger equation for $r > r_0$ is

$$\left[\frac{d^2}{dr^2} + k^2 - \frac{l(l+1)}{r^2}\right]\chi_{kl}(r) = 0 \qquad (\text{for } r > 0) \tag{15.6.1}$$

which due to the infinitely repelling potential must be constrained by the condition $\chi_{kl}(r_0) = 0$. Therefore, the s-wave general solution is,

$$\chi_{k0}(r) = \begin{cases} C_0 \sin k(r - r_0) & r > r_0 \\ 0 & r < r_0 \end{cases} \tag{15.6.2}$$

The phase shift $\delta_0(k)$ is, by definition, given by the asymptotic form of the equation; namely, $\delta_0(k) = -kr_0$. Thus, in the *s-wave approximation*,

$$\begin{cases} f_k(\theta) = k^{-1}e^{-ikr_0}\sin(kr_0) \approx r_0 e^{-ikr_0} \\ \frac{d\sigma}{d\Omega} = k^{-2}\sin^2(kr_0) \approx r_0^2 \\ \sigma_T = \frac{4\pi}{k^2}\sin^2(kr_0) \approx 4\pi r_0^2 \end{cases} \tag{15.6.3}$$

(b) From Eq. (15.6.1), the p-wave radial equation is

$$\left[\frac{d^2}{dr^2} + k^2 - \frac{2}{r^2}\right]\chi_{k1}(r) = 0 \tag{15.6.4}$$

The general solution is given by [see Eq. (15.18) in Sec. 15.4]

$$\chi_{k1}(r) = c_1 r j_1(kr) + d_1 r n_1(kr) \tag{15.6.5}$$

where $j_1(kr)$ and $n_1(kr)$ are the spherical Bessel functions:

$$j_1(x) = \frac{\sin x}{x^2} - \frac{\cos x}{x} \qquad n_1(x) = -\frac{\cos x}{x^2} - \frac{\sin x}{x} \tag{15.6.6}$$

For $A = c_1/k$, $Aa = -d_1/k$ we obtain

$$\chi_{k1}(r) = A\left[\frac{\sin(kr)}{kr} - \cos(kr) + a\left(\frac{\cos(kr)}{kr} + \sin(kr)\right)\right] \tag{15.6.7}$$

where A and a are both r-independent constants.

(c) From Eq. (15.6.7) and the condition $\chi_{k1}(r_0) = 0$, we find

$$a = \frac{\cos(kr_0) - \dfrac{\sin(kr_0)}{kr_0}}{\dfrac{\cos(kr_0)}{kr_0} + \sin(kr_0)} \tag{15.6.8}$$

Furthermore, the asymptotic form of $\chi_{k1}(r)$ is

$$\chi_{k1}(r)_{r\to\infty} \sim A[-\cos(kr) + a\sin(kr)] = C_1 \sin\left(kr - \frac{\pi}{2} + \delta_1\right)$$

$$= C_1\left[\sin\left(kr - \frac{\pi}{2}\right)\cos\delta_1 + \cos\left(kr - \frac{\pi}{2}\right)\sin\delta_1\right]$$

$$= C_1 \cos\delta_1[-\cos(kr) + \sin(kr)\tan\delta_1] \tag{15.6.9}$$

Identifying in Eq. (15.6.9), $A = c_1\cos\delta_1$ and $a = \tan\delta_1$, and using Eq. (15.6.8) we obtain

$$\tan\delta_1(k) = \frac{\cos(kr_0) - \dfrac{\sin(kr_0)}{kr_0}}{\dfrac{\cos(kr_0)}{kr_0} + \sin(kr_0)} \tag{15.6.10}$$

(d) In the limit $kr_0 \ll 1$ we have

$$\sin(kr_0) \approx kr_0 + \frac{(kr_0)^3}{6} \qquad \cos(kr_0) \approx 1 - \frac{(kr_0)^2}{2} \tag{15.6.11}$$

and Eq. (15.6.10) takes the form

$$\tan\delta_1(k) \approx \frac{1}{3}(kr_0)^3 \Rightarrow \delta_1(k) = -\frac{1}{3}(kr_0)^3 \tag{15.6.12}$$

15.7. A (point) particle is scattered by a second particle with a rigid core; that is, the scattering potential is $V(r) = 0$ for $r > a$ and $V(r) = \infty$ for $r < a$. The energy of the scattered particle satisfies $ka = 1$. (a) Find the expression for δ_l. Complete Table 15.1 (express δ_l in radians).

Table 15.1

	$\tan\delta_l$	δ_l	$\sin\delta_l$
$l = 0$			
$l = 1$			
$l = 2$			

(b) Calculate the differential cross section $d\sigma/d\Omega$ for angles 0 and π, taking into account only the waves $l = 0$ and $l = 1$. (c) Calculate the total cross section σ_T taking into account only the waves $l = 0$ and $l = 1$. (d) What is the accuracy of part (c)?

SOLUTION

(a) The phase shifts for a rigid sphere are given by the equation

$$\tan\delta_l = \frac{j_l(ka)}{n_l(ka)} \tag{15.7.1}$$

Using the known expressions of the spherical Bessel functions (see the Mathematical Appendix)

$$j_0(x) = \frac{\sin x}{x} \qquad\qquad n_0(x) = -\frac{\cos x}{x}$$

$$j_1(x) = \frac{\sin x}{x^2} - \frac{\cos x}{x} \qquad\qquad n_1(x) = -\frac{\cos x}{x^2} - \frac{\sin x}{x} \qquad (15.7.2)$$

$$j_2(x) = \left(\frac{3}{x^2} - \frac{1}{x}\right)\sin x - \frac{3\cos x}{x^2} \qquad n_2(x) = -\left(\frac{3}{x^2} - \frac{1}{x}\right)\cos x - \frac{3\sin x}{x^2}$$

and substituting $x = ka = 1$, we find $\tan \delta_0 = -1.56$, $\tan \delta_1 = -0.22$, and $\tan \delta_2 = -0.02$. Therefore,

Table 15.2

	$\tan \delta_l$	δ_l	$\sin \delta_l$
$l = 0$	−1.56	−1.00	−0.84
$l = 1$	−0.22	−0.22	−0.22
$l = 2$	−0.02	−0.02	−0.02

(b) The differential cross section is given by

$$\frac{d\sigma}{d\Omega} = \frac{1}{k^2}\left|\sum_{l=0}^{\infty}(2l+1)e^{i\delta_l}\sin\delta_l\,P_l(\cos\theta)\right|^2 \qquad (15.7.3)$$

For $l = 0, 1$ and $k = a^{-1}$,

$$\frac{d\sigma}{d\Omega} = a^2\left|\sin\delta_0 e^{i\delta_0} + 3\sin\delta_1 e^{i\delta_1}\cos\theta\right|^2$$

$$= a^2[\sin^2\delta_0 + 6\sin\delta_0\sin\delta_1\cos(\delta_0-\delta_1)\cos\theta + 9\sin^2\delta_1\cos^2\theta] \qquad (15.7.4)$$

Substituting $\theta = 0, \pi$, we obtain

$$\left.\frac{d\sigma}{d\Omega}\right|_{0,\pi} = a^2\left|\sin^2\delta_0 \pm 6\sin\delta_0\sin\delta_1\cos(\delta_0-\delta_1)+9\sin^2\delta_1\right| \qquad (15.7.5)$$

with δ_1 and δ_0 given in Table 15.2.

(c) The total cross section is given by

$$\sigma_T = \frac{4\pi}{k^2}\sum_{l=0}^{\infty}(2l+1)\sin^2\delta_l \qquad (15.7.6)$$

For $l = 0, 1$ and $k = a^{-1}$,

$$\sigma_T = 4\pi a^2[\sin^2\delta_0 + 3\sin^2\delta_1] \approx 0.854\pi a^2 \qquad (15.7.7)$$

(d) A rough estimate on the accuracy of the result in part (c) is given by calculating the additional term $l = 2$:

$$\sigma_T \approx (0.85 + 0.002)\,4\pi a^2 \qquad (15.7.8)$$

15.8. Consider the potential of a square well of depth V_0:

$$V(r) = \begin{cases} -V_0 & r < a \\ 0 & r > a \end{cases} \qquad (15.8.1)$$

Set $k = \sqrt{2mE/\hbar^2}$, $k_0 = \sqrt{2mV_0/\hbar^2}$, and $K^2 = k^2 + k_0^2$. (a) Calculate the phase shifts δ_0 and δ_1 for low-energy scattering ($ka \ll 1$). (b) Find the condition for *resonance scattering* of the s-waves and p-waves. (c) Calculate the total cross section for *"off-resonance"* scattering at low energies ($ka \ll 1$ and $\delta_1 \ll \delta_0 \ll 1$).

SOLUTION

(a) We begin from the radial part of the Schrödinger equation:

$$\begin{cases} \left[\dfrac{d^2}{dr^2} + K^2 - \dfrac{l(l+1)}{r^2}\right]\chi_l^{(1)}(r) = 0 & \text{(for } r > a) \\[4mm] \left[\dfrac{d^2}{dr^2} + k^2 - \dfrac{l(l+1)}{r^2}\right]\chi_l^{(2)}(r) = 0 & \text{(for } r > a) \end{cases}$$

(15.8.2)

where $\chi_l^{(1)}$ and $\chi_l^{(2)}$ denote the solutions at $r < a$ and $r > a$, respectively. The general form of $\chi_l^{(1)}$ and $\chi_l^{(2)}$ is given by

$$\chi_l^{(1)} = A_l\, rj_l(Kr) + B_l\, rn_l(Kr)$$

$$\chi_l^{(2)} = C_l\, rj_l(kr) + D_l\, rn_l(kr)$$

(15.8.3)

where j_l and n_l are the spherical Bessel functions, and A_l, B_l, C_l, and D_l are constants. In particular,

$$\begin{cases} j_0(x) = \dfrac{\sin x}{x} & n_0(x) = -\dfrac{\cos x}{x} \\[4mm] j_1(x) = \dfrac{\sin x}{x^2} - \dfrac{\cos x}{x} & n_1(x) = -\dfrac{\cos x}{x^2} - \dfrac{\sin x}{x} \end{cases}$$

(15.8.4)

Actually, since the radial wavefunction $R_l(r) = \chi_l(r)/r$ must be regular at the origin ($r = 0$), we can set $B_l = 0$ in Eq. (15.8.3). Hence, in the interior region ($r < a$), we have

$$R_l(r) = A_l j_l(Kr)$$

(15.8.5)

The phase shifts δ_l can now be determined by calculating the logarithmic derivative of $R_l(r)$ [see Sec. 15.4 Eqs. (15.25) and (15.26)]:

$$\tan\delta_l = \frac{kj_l'(ka) - \gamma_l j_l(ka)}{kn_l'(ka) - \gamma_l n_l(ka)}$$

(15.8.6)

where $\gamma_l = \left(\dfrac{1}{R_l}\dfrac{dR_l}{dr}\right)\bigg|_{r=a^-}$. Substituting Eq. (15.8.5) for $R_l(r)$ into Eq. (15.8.6) and using Eq. (15.8.4), we find

$$\begin{cases} \gamma_0 = K\cot(Ka) - \dfrac{1}{a} & (l = 0) \\[4mm] \gamma_1 = \dfrac{K^2 a}{1 - Ka\cot(Ka)} - \dfrac{2}{a} & (l = 1) \end{cases}$$

(15.8.7)

so that, for $l = 0$,

$$\tan\delta_0 = \frac{k\left(\dfrac{ka\cos(ka) - \sin(ka)}{(ka)^2}\right) - \gamma_0\dfrac{\sin(ka)}{ka}}{k\left(\dfrac{ka\sin(ka) + \cos(ka)}{(ka)^2}\right) + \gamma_0\dfrac{\cos(ka)}{ka}}$$

(15.8.8)

In the limit $ka \to 0$, Eq. (15.8.8) reduces to

$$\tan\delta_0 \approx -\frac{\gamma_0 ka^2}{1 + \gamma_0 a} \qquad ka \ll 1$$

(15.8.9)

and similarly,

$$\tan \delta_1 \approx -\frac{(ka)^3}{3}\frac{1 - \gamma_1 a}{2 + \gamma_1 a} \qquad ka \gg 1 \qquad\qquad (15.8.10)$$

where γ_0 and γ_1 are given by Eq. (15.8.7). Note that unless $\gamma_0 a = -1$ or $\gamma_1 a = -2$, both δ_0 and δ_1 vanish as $k \to 0$ and $\delta_0 \ll \delta_1 \ll 1$.

(b) Resonance scattering occurs when a particular phase shift becomes exponentially large. Resonance scattering of s-waves ($ka \ll 1$, $l = 0$) is found by using Eqs. (15.8.7) and (15.8.9). Thus, $1 + \gamma_0 a = 0 \Rightarrow Ka \cot(ka) = 0$ and the resonance condition is

$$Ka = (2n + 1)\frac{\pi}{2} \qquad (n = 1, 2, \ldots) \qquad\qquad (15.8.11)$$

Similarly, resonance scattering of p-waves ($ka \ll 1$, $l = 1$) is $2 + \gamma_1 a = 0 \Rightarrow Ka \cot(ka) = \pm\infty$ and the resonance condition is

$$Ka = n\pi \qquad (n = 1, 2, \ldots) \qquad\qquad (15.8.12)$$

(c) The total cross section is given by

$$\sigma_T = \frac{4\pi}{k^2}\sum_{l=0}^{\infty}(2l + 1)\sin^2 \delta_l \qquad\qquad (15.8.13)$$

Recall that unless $\gamma_0 a = -1$ or $\gamma_1 a = -2$ [see Eqs. (15.8.9) and (15.8.10)] both δ_0 and δ_1 vanish as $k \to 0$. However, as a consequence of the $1/k^2$ factor in Eq. (15.8.3), only the $l = 0$ partial wave gives a finite contribution to the cross section. Thus, for off-resonance scattering ($Ka \ll 1$, $\delta_0 \ll \delta_1 \ll 1$)

$$\sigma_T \approx \frac{4\pi}{k^2}\sin^2 \delta_0 = \frac{4\pi\gamma_0^2 a^4}{(1 + \gamma_0 a)^2} = 4\pi a^2\left(1 - \frac{\tan(Ka)}{Ka}\right)^2 \qquad\qquad (15.8.14)$$

where $K = \sqrt{k_0^2 + k^2} \ne (2n + 1)\frac{\pi}{2a}$.

15.9. Refer to the potential in Problem 15.8. (a) Find the differential cross section $d\sigma/d\Omega$ for s-wave resonance scattering ($ka \ll 1$, $l = 0$). (b) Find $d\sigma/d\Omega$ for p-wave resonance scattering ($ka \ll 1$, $l = 1$).

SOLUTION

(a) From Problem 15.8, we have

$$\begin{cases} \tan \delta_0 = -\dfrac{\gamma_0 ka^2}{1 + \gamma_0 a} \\[2mm] \gamma_0 a = Ka \cot(Ka) - 1 \end{cases} \qquad\qquad (15.9.1)$$

where $K = \sqrt{k_0^2 + k^2} = k_0\left(1 + \dfrac{k^2}{k_0^2}\right)^{1/2} \approx k_0\left(1 + \dfrac{k^2}{2k_0^2}\right)$. Near the resonance, $1 - r_0 a \approx 0$ and δ_0 is not necessarily small. However, using Eq. (15.9.1) and the identity $\sin \delta_0 = 1/(1 + \cot^2 \delta_0)$,

$$\sin^2 \delta_0 = \frac{(ka)^2(\gamma_0 a)^2}{(ka)^2(\gamma_0 a)^2 + (1 + \gamma_0 a)^2} \qquad\qquad (15.9.2)$$

Furthermore, if $ka \ll 1$, we can expand $\gamma_0(K)$ in a Taylor series about $K = k_0$:

$$\gamma_0(K) = \gamma_0\big|_{K=k_0} + \frac{\partial \gamma}{\partial K}\bigg|_{K=k_0}(K - k_0) + \cdots \qquad\qquad (15.9.3)$$

where $K - k_0 = \dfrac{1}{2}\left(\dfrac{k}{k_0}\right)^2$. Using Eq. (15.9.1) we then find that in the leading terms of Ka, $\gamma_0 = \alpha_0 + \beta_0 k^2$, with

$$\begin{cases} \alpha_0 = k_0 \cot(k_0 a) - \dfrac{1}{a} \\ \beta_0 = \dfrac{1}{2k_0}\left[\cot(k_0 a) - \dfrac{k_0 a}{\sin^2(k_0 a)}\right] \approx -\dfrac{a}{2} \end{cases} \tag{15.9.4}$$

Hence,

$$1 + \gamma_0 a \approx 1 + \alpha_0 a + \beta_0 a k^2 = k_0 a \cot(k_0 a) - \dfrac{(ka)^2}{2} \tag{15.9.5}$$

Finally, substituting Eq. (15.9.5) back into Eq. (15.9.2) we obtain

$$\dfrac{d\sigma}{d\Omega} = \dfrac{a^2}{k^2 a^2 + \left[\xi_0 - \dfrac{(ka^2)}{2}\right]^2} \qquad (l = 0) \tag{15.9.6}$$

where $ka \ll 1$ and $\xi_0 = k_0 a \cot(k_0 a)$. Recall that near the resonance $|\xi_0| \le 1$, $d\sigma/d\Omega$ for $\xi_0 = 1$ and $l = 0$ as is shown in Fig. 15.4 (in a^2 units).

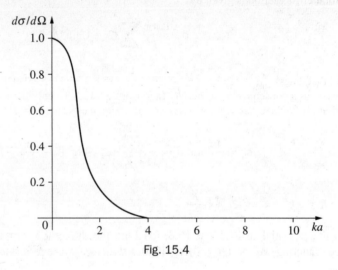

Fig. 15.4

(b) From Problem 15.8 we have

$$\begin{cases} \tan\delta_1 = \dfrac{(ka)^3}{3}\dfrac{1 - \gamma_1 a}{2 + \gamma_1 a} \\ \gamma_1 a = \dfrac{K^2 a^2}{1 - Ka\cot(Ka)} - 2 \end{cases} \tag{15.9.7}$$

In this case we find

$$\sin^2\delta_1 = \dfrac{1}{1 + \left[\dfrac{2 + \gamma_1 a}{1 - \gamma_1 a}\right]^2 \dfrac{9}{(ka)^6}} \tag{15.9.8}$$

where $1 - \gamma_1 a \approx 3$. Repeating the calculations in part (b), we have

$$K = k_0 + \dfrac{1}{2}\left(\dfrac{k}{k_0}\right)^2 \qquad \gamma_1(K) \approx \alpha_1 + \beta_1 k^2 \tag{15.9.9}$$

where near the resonance, the coefficients α_1 and β_1 are

$$\begin{cases} \alpha_1 = -k_0 \tan(k_0 a) - \dfrac{2}{a} \\ \beta_1 = -\dfrac{a}{2} \end{cases} \tag{15.9.10}$$

Hence,

$$2 + \gamma_1 a = 2 + \alpha_1 a + \beta_1 a k^2 = -ka \tan(k_0 a) - \frac{(ka)^2}{2} \equiv \xi_1 - \frac{(ka)^2}{2} \qquad (15.9.11)$$

where $ka \ll 1$ and $|\xi_1| \leq 1$. The contribution of p-wave resonance scattering is

$$\frac{d\sigma}{d\Omega} = \frac{9}{k^2} \cos^2 \theta \sin^2 \delta_1 \qquad (15.9.12)$$

Therefore, substituting Eq. (15.9.8) into Eq. (15.9.12) with the help of Eq. (15.9.11),

$$\frac{d\sigma}{d\Omega} = \frac{9k^4 a^6 \cos^2 \theta}{(ka)^6 + \left[\xi_1 - \frac{(ka)^2}{2} \right]^2} \qquad (l = 1) \qquad (15.9.13)$$

15.10. Using the Born approximation, calculate the phase shifts δ_1 for scattering in a centrally symmetric field.

SOLUTION

The scattering amplitude for a central field in the Born approximation is given by

$$f^B(\theta) = -\frac{1}{k} \int_0^\infty r \sin(kr) U(r) \, dr \qquad (15.10.1)$$

This approximation is valid for a sufficiently weak potential when all the phase shifts $\delta_l \ll 1$. The expression of $f(\theta)$ in terms of δ_l is

$$f^B(\theta) = \frac{1}{k} \sum_{l=0}^\infty (2l+1) e^{i\delta_l} \sin \delta_l \, P_l(\cos \theta) \qquad (15.10.2)$$

which reduces to

$$f^B(\theta) \approx \frac{1}{k} \sum_{l=0}^\infty (2l+1) \delta_l \, P_l(\cos \theta) \qquad (15.10.3)$$

Multiplying Eq. (15.10.3) by $P_l (\cos \theta)$ and integrating (using the orthogonality relations of Legendre polynomials) we find $\int_{-1}^1 f^B(\theta) P_l(\cos \theta) \, d(\cos \theta) \approx +\frac{2\delta_l}{k}$. Therefore, by comparing with Eq. (15.10.1)

$$+\frac{2\delta_l}{k} = -\frac{1}{k} \int_0^\infty r \sin(kr) U(r) \, dr \int_{-1}^1 P_l(\cos \theta) \, d(\cos \theta) = -\int_0^\infty r^2 U(r) \, dr \int_{-1}^1 \frac{\sin(kr)}{kr} P_l(\cos \theta) \, d(\cos \theta)$$

$$= -\int_0^\infty 2 j_l^2(kr) r^2 U(r) \, dr \qquad (15.10.4)$$

Namely, if all the phase shifts are small, one has

$$\delta_l^B = -k \int_0^\infty r^2 U(r) \, j_l^2(kr) \, dr \qquad (15.10.5)$$

Using the relations $U = 2\mu V/\hbar^2$ and $j_l(r) = \left(\frac{\pi}{2r} \right)^{1/2} J_{l+1/2}(r)$ leads finally to

$$\delta_l^B = -\frac{\pi \mu k}{\hbar^2} \int_0^\infty r V(r) [J_{l+1/2}(kr)]^2 \, dr \qquad (15.10.6)$$

15.11. For the potential $V(r) = V_0 R \delta(r - R)$: (a) Calculate using the Born approximation, the quantities $f(\theta)$ and $d\sigma/d\Omega$. Specify the limits of validity of your calculation for both high- and low-energy scattering, respectively. (b) Calculate the phase shifts δ_l for all the partial waves in the approximation that correspond to the Born approximation. (c) Find the condition for which s-wave scattering is dominant. Obtain the differential cross section for this case and compare with the result from part (a).

SOLUTION

(a) The scattering amplitude in the Born approximation is given by

$$f^B(\theta) = -\frac{1}{4\pi}\frac{2\mu}{\hbar^2}\int e^{i\mathbf{q}\cdot\mathbf{r}}V(\mathbf{r})\,d^3r \tag{15.11.1}$$

where μ is the mass of the particle and $\mathbf{q} = \mathbf{k}_f + \mathbf{k}_i$ is its momentum transfer. For a spherical symmetric potential, the angular integration can always be performed and Eq. (15.11.1) reduces to

$$f^B(\theta) = -\frac{2\mu}{q\hbar^2}\int_0^\infty r\sin(qr)V(r)\,dr \tag{15.11.2}$$

Substituting in Eq. (15.11.2) the potential $V(r) = V_0 R\delta(r - R)$

$$f^B(\theta) = -\frac{2\mu V_0 R^2}{q\hbar^2}\sin(qR) \tag{15.11.3}$$

where $q = 2k\sin(\theta/2)$ and $k = \sqrt{2\mu E/\hbar^2}$. Therefore,

$$\frac{d\sigma}{d\Omega} = |f^B(\theta)|^2 = \frac{4\mu^2 V_0^2 R^4}{\hbar^4 q^2}\sin^2(qR) \tag{15.11.4}$$

The Born approximation is applicable in cases where the scattering potential can be considered as a perturbation, namely, under the condition

$$\left|\int_0^\infty (e^{2ikr} - 1)V(r)\,dr\right| \ll \frac{\hbar k}{\mu} \tag{15.11.5}$$

In our problem, this condition of validity can be written as

$$\left|\int_0^\infty e^{ikr}\sin(kr)V(r)\,dr\right| = V_0 R\sin(kR) \ll \frac{\hbar^2 k}{2\mu} \tag{15.11.6}$$

We can now distinguish between two limiting cases that depend on the value of kR:

$$\frac{2\mu V_0 R}{\hbar^2 k} = \frac{2V_0 R}{\hbar v} \ll 1 \qquad \text{(high energies)} \tag{15.11.7}$$

$$\frac{2\mu V_0 R}{\hbar^2} \ll 1 \qquad \text{(low energies, } kR \ll 1) \tag{15.11.8}$$

We note that the first condition (kR arbitrary) is less restrictive than the second one ($kr \ll 1$). Equation (15.11.7) indicates that the Born approximation is applicable for scattering at sufficiently high energies. Equation (15.11.8) shows, on the other hand, that if $kR \ll 1$, then the Born approximation is valid for all velocities $v = \hbar k/\mu$ (in both cases one must, of course, consider scattering from a relatively weak and short-ranged potential). We can also verify, from Eqs. (15.11.4) and (15.11.5), that in the low-energy limit ($qR \to 0$), the Born scattering cross section is completely isotropic.

(b) Recall (Problem 15.10) that the Born approximation corresponds to the case where all the phase shifts are relatively small ($\delta_l \approx \sin\delta_l \leq 1$). Thus, we obtain

$$\delta_l = -\frac{\pi\mu}{\hbar^2}\int_0^\infty rV(r)[J_{l+1/2}(kr)]^2\,dr = -\frac{\pi\mu R^2 V_0}{\hbar^2}[J_{l+1/2}(kR)]^2 \tag{15.11.9}$$

Note that using the asymptotic Bessel function expressions

$$J_{l+1/2}(x)_{x\to\infty} \to \sqrt{\frac{2}{\pi x}}\sin(x - \pi l/2) \tag{15.11.10}$$

$$J_{l+1/2}(x)_{x\to 0} \to \sqrt{\frac{2}{\pi}}\frac{x^{l+1/2}}{(2l + 1)!!} \tag{15.11.11}$$

we can recover the conditions shown in Eqs. (15.11.7) and (15.11.8) of part (*a*). Substituting expression (15.11.11) into Eq. (15.11.9), we find that for arbitrary value of kR,

$$|\delta_l| < \frac{\pi\mu R^2 V_0}{\hbar^2}\frac{2}{\pi kR} \ll 1 \tag{15.11.12}$$

Thus, the condition $|\delta_l| \ll 1$ for all coincides with Eq. (15.11.8). Similarly, substituting expression (15.11.11) into Eq. (15.11.9) for small value $kR \ll 1$,

$$\delta_l \approx \frac{\pi\mu R^2 V_0}{\hbar^2}\frac{2}{\pi}\frac{(kR)^{2l+1}}{[(2l+1)!!]^2} \tag{15.11.13}$$

Hence, the condition $\delta_0 \gg \delta_l$ coincides with Eq. (15.11.8).

(*c*) From Eq. (15.11.13) we find that if $kR \ll 1$ then $\delta_0 \gg \delta_l$. This result is in agreement with the general analysis of partial wave expansion, which states that for a finite-range potential the main contribution to the scattering amplitude comes from values of $l < kR$, where R is the range of the potential. Using Eq. (15.11.13) for *s*-wave scattering ($l = 0$) we obtain

$$\delta_0 \approx \sin\delta_0 \approx -\frac{2\mu R^3 V_0 k}{\hbar^2} \tag{15.11.14}$$

Thus, the leading term of the differential cross section is

$$\frac{d\sigma}{d\Omega} = \frac{1}{k^2}\left|e^{i\delta_0}\sin\delta_0\right|^2 = \frac{4\mu^2 R^6 V_0^2}{\hbar^2} \tag{15.11.15}$$

As expected from the previous discussion, Eqs. (15.11.4) and (15.11.14) coincide in the limit $qR \to 0$. In this case, both the *s*-wave approximation and the Born approximation lead to a differential cross section that depends neither on the angle of scattering nor on the energy of the incident particle.

15.12. A particle of mass μ is scattered from a spherical repelling potential of radius R:

$$V(r) = \begin{cases} V_0 & r \le R \\ 0 & r \ge R \end{cases}$$

(*a*) Using the Born approximation, calculate the total cross section in the limit of low energies.
(*b*) Repeat the calculation of σ_T by using the partial wave expansion, and considering only the *s*-wave contribution.

SOLUTION

(*a*) The scattering amplitude in the Born approximation is

$$f_k^B(\theta) = -\frac{1}{4\pi}\frac{2\mu V_0}{\hbar^2}\frac{4\pi}{q}\int_0^\infty \sin(qr)\,r\,dr = -\frac{2\mu V_0}{\hbar^2 q}\left[\frac{\sin(qR)}{q^2} - \frac{R\cos(qR)}{q}\right] \tag{15.12.1}$$

This leads in the limit $qR \to 0$ to the isotropic cross section:

$$\frac{d\sigma^B}{d\Omega} = |f_k^B(\theta)|^2 = \frac{4\mu^2 V_0^2 R^6}{9\hbar^4} \tag{15.12.2}$$

so that the total cross section is given by

$$\sigma_T^B = \int\frac{d\sigma^B}{d\Omega}\,d\Omega = \frac{16\pi\mu^2 V_0^2 R^6}{9\hbar^4} \tag{15.12.3}$$

(*b*) In the limit $E \to 0$ it is sufficient to consider only *s*-wave scattering. In order to determine the phase shift δ_0 we examine the radial Schrödinger equation for $\chi_0(r)$:

$$\begin{cases} \left[\dfrac{d^2}{dr^2} + \dfrac{2\mu E}{\hbar^2}\right]\chi_0^1(r) = 0 & \Rightarrow\quad \chi_0^1(r) = A\sin(kr + \delta_0) & r > R \\[2mm] \left[\dfrac{d^2}{dr^2} + \dfrac{2\mu}{\hbar^2}(E - V_0)\right]\chi_0^2(r) = 0 & \Rightarrow\quad \chi_0^2(r) = B\sinh\left(kr\sqrt{(V_0/E)-1}\right) & r \le R \end{cases} \tag{15.12.4}$$

where $k = (2\mu E/\hbar^2)^{1/2}$ and $V_0 \gg E$. These solutions satisfy the boundary conditions

$$\chi_0^1(R) = \chi_0^2(R) \qquad \chi_0'^{(1)}(R) = \chi_0'^{(2)}(R) \tag{15.12.5}$$

Namely,

$$\begin{cases} A \sinh(kR + \delta_0) = B \sinh(KR) \\ A \cos(kR + \delta_0) = B \cosh(KR) \end{cases} \tag{15.12.6}$$

where $K = k([V_0/E] - 1)^{1/2} \approx k(V_0/E)^{1/2}$, and thus

$$\tan(KR + \delta_0) \approx (E/V_0)^{1/2} \tanh(KR) \tag{15.12.7}$$

and since $kR \ll 1$,

$$\begin{cases} \delta_0 = (E/V_0)^{1/2} \tanh(KR) - kR \\ f_0(\theta) = \dfrac{1}{k} e^{i\delta_0} \sin\delta_0 \end{cases} \tag{15.12.8}$$

Finally, the total cross section is given by

$$\sigma_T^0 \approx \frac{4\pi}{k^2}\sin^2\delta_0 \approx \frac{4\pi}{k^2}\delta_0^2 = 4\pi R^2\left[1 - \frac{\tanh(KR)}{KR}\right]^2 \tag{15.12.9}$$

Note that Eqs. (15.12.3) and (15.12.9) coincide only in the limit of a very short-range potential ($kR \ll 1$). Note also that although both methods lead to isotropic differential cross sections, the Born approximation involves a violation of the *optical theorem*.

15.13. Particles are scattered from the potential $V(r) = g/r^2$, where g is a positive constant. (*a*) Write the radial wave equations and give their regular solutions. (*b*) Prove that the phase shifts are given by

$$\delta_l = \frac{\pi}{2}\left[l + \frac{1}{2} - \sqrt{\left(l + \frac{1}{2}\right)^2 + \frac{2\mu g}{\hbar^2}}\right] \tag{15.13.1}$$

(*c*) Find the energy dependence of the cross section for a fixed scattering angle, (*d*) Find δ_l for $2\mu g/\hbar^2 \ll 1$ and show that the differential cross section is

$$\frac{d\sigma}{d\theta} = \frac{\pi^3}{2\hbar^2}\frac{g^2\mu}{E}\cot\left(\frac{\theta}{2}\right) \tag{15.13.2}$$

where E is the energy of the scattered particle. (*e*) For the same potential, calculate the differential cross section in the Born approximation and compare it with the above result.

SOLUTION

(*a*) The radial wave equation is

$$\left[\frac{d^2}{dr^2} + k^2 - U(r) - \frac{l(l+1)}{r^2}\right]\chi_{kl}(r) = 0 \tag{15.13.3}$$

with $k = \sqrt{2\mu E/\hbar^2}$, $U = 2\mu g/\hbar^2 r^2$, and $\phi_l = R(r)Y_l^m = \chi_{kl}(r)Y_l^m$. Substituting the given potential we get

$$\left(\frac{d^2}{dr^2} + k^2 - \frac{1}{r^2}\left[\frac{2\mu g}{\hbar^2} + l(l+1)\right]\right)\chi_{kl}(r) = 0 \tag{15.13.4}$$

For $g = 0$, the solution of Eq. (15.13.4) is given by a free spherical wave:

$$\chi_{kl}^0(r) = \sqrt{\frac{2k^2 r^2}{\pi}}\, j_l(kr)_{r\to\infty} \sim \frac{\sin(kr - \pi l/2)}{kr} \tag{15.13.5}$$

Therefore, the asymptotic solution for $R(r) = \chi_{kl}/r$ is

$$R_{kl}(r) \sim \frac{\sin(kr + \pi l/2 + \delta_l)}{kr} = \frac{\sin(kr - \pi\tilde{l}/2)}{kr} \tag{15.13.6}$$

where $\tilde{l}$ is given by the relation

$$\tilde{l}(\tilde{l}+1) = l(l+1) + \frac{2\mu g}{\hbar^2} \tag{15.13.7}$$

(b) By comparing the two sides of Eq. (15.13.6), we obtain

$$\delta_l = (l - \tilde{l})\frac{\pi}{2} \tag{15.13.8}$$

where $\tilde{l}$ is found by solving the quadratic equation (15.13.7):

$$\tilde{l} = -\frac{1}{2} \pm \frac{1}{2}\sqrt{1 + 4\left[l(l+1) + \frac{2\mu g}{\hbar^2}\right]} = -\frac{1}{2} \pm \sqrt{\frac{1}{4} + l(l+1) + \frac{2\mu g}{\hbar^2}}$$

$$= -\frac{1}{2} \pm \sqrt{\left(l + \frac{1}{2}\right)^2 + \frac{2\mu g}{\hbar^2}} \qquad \text{sign } (+) \rightarrow \tilde{l} > 0 \tag{15.13.9}$$

Finally, substituting Eq. (15.3.8) into Eq. (15.13.7) leads to Eq. (15.13.1).

(c) The cross section is given by

$$\frac{d\sigma}{d\Omega} = \frac{1}{k^2}\left|\sum_{l=0}^{\infty} (2l+1) e^{i\delta_l} \sin\delta_l \, P_l(\cos\theta)\right|^2 \tag{15.13.10}$$

Since the δ_l are not dependent on k (in our particular case), we have

$$\frac{d\sigma}{d\Omega} \propto \frac{1}{k^2} \propto \frac{1}{E}\bigg|_{\theta=\text{const.}} \tag{15.13.11}$$

(d) For $2\mu g/\hbar^2 \ll 1$, using Eq. (15.13.1) we obtain

$$\delta_l = \frac{\pi}{2}l + \frac{1}{2} - \left(l + \frac{1}{2}\right)\left[1 + \frac{2\mu g}{\hbar^2\left(l+\frac{1}{2}\right)^2}\right]^{1/2}$$

$$\approx \frac{\pi}{2}l + \frac{1}{2} - \left(l + \frac{1}{2}\right)\left[1 + \frac{\mu g}{\hbar^2\left(l+\frac{1}{2}\right)^2}\right] = -\frac{\pi}{2}\frac{\mu g}{\hbar^2\left(l+\frac{1}{2}\right)} \ll 1 \tag{15.13.12}$$

Thus, substituting into Eq. (15.13.10),

$$\frac{d\sigma}{d\Omega} = \frac{1}{k^2}\left|\sum_{l=0}^{\infty} (2l+1)\frac{\pi}{2}\frac{\mu g}{\hbar^2(l+1/2)} P_l(\cos\theta)\right|^2$$

$$= \frac{1}{k^2}\left|\sum_{l=0}^{\infty} \frac{\pi\mu g}{\hbar^2} P_l(\cos\theta)\right|^2 = \frac{\pi^2\mu^2 g^2}{\hbar^4 k^2}\left|\sum_{l=0}^{\infty} P_l(\cos\theta)\right|^2 \tag{15.13.13}$$

In order to sum the series, we will use the generating function of $P_l(x)$:

$$\sum_{l=0}^{\infty} P_l(x)t^l = \frac{1}{\sqrt{1-2tx+t^2}} \Rightarrow \sum_{l=0}^{\infty} P_l(\cos\theta) = \frac{1}{2\sin(\theta/2)} \tag{15.13.14}$$

Therefore,

$$\frac{d\sigma}{d\Omega} = \frac{\pi^2 \mu^2 g^2}{4\hbar^4 k^2 \sin^2(\theta/2)} = \frac{\pi^2 \mu g^2}{8\hbar^2 E} \frac{1}{\sin^2(\theta/2)} \qquad (15.13.15)$$

Finally, using $d\Omega = \sin\theta \, d\theta \, d\varphi$, we get

$$\frac{d\sigma}{d\theta} = \frac{\pi^3 \mu g^2}{4\hbar^2 E} \frac{\sin\theta}{\sin^2(\theta/2)} = \frac{\pi^3 \mu g^2}{2\hbar^2 E} \frac{\sin\theta}{1 - \cos\theta} \qquad (15.13.16)$$

This result coincides with Eq. (15.13.2).

(*e*) In the Born approximation, the scattering amplitude is

$$f_k(\theta, \varphi) = -\frac{1}{4\pi} \int e^{-i\mathbf{q}\cdot\mathbf{r}'} U(\mathbf{r}') \, d^3 r' = -\frac{2\mu g}{4\pi\hbar^2} \int \frac{1}{r^2} e^{-i\mathbf{q}\cdot\mathbf{r}'} d^3 r' = -\frac{2\mu g}{\hbar^2} \int_\theta^\infty \frac{\sin(qr)}{qr} dr$$

$$= -\frac{\pi \mu g}{\hbar^2 q^2} \qquad [q = 2k\sin(\theta/2)] \qquad (15.13.17)$$

Therefore,

$$\frac{d\sigma}{d\Omega} = |f_k(\theta, \varphi)|^2 = \frac{\pi^2 \mu^2 g^2}{4\hbar^4 k^2} \frac{1}{\sin^2(\theta/2)} \qquad (15.13.18)$$

which coincides with Eq. (15.13.15). This result is expected since all the phase shifts are small [see Sec. 15.4, Eq. (15.27)].

15.14. Calculate the total cross section for scattering from a completely absorbing sphere of radius $a\,(ka \gg 1)$.

SOLUTION

The problem of scattering in the presence of absorbing can be treated phenomenologically by introducing the *complex scattering potential*: $V(r) \rightarrow V_R - iV_I\,(V_I \geq 0)$. Then, one ends up with complex phase shifts $\delta_l = \xi_l + i\eta_l$, such that $|s_l| \equiv |e^{i2\delta_l}| \leq 1$, where $|s_l| = 0$ correspond to the case of complete absorption. (Note that the equality $|s_l| = 1$ is satisfied for real phase shifts, i.e., nonabsorbing media.) By introducing complex phase shifts one then finds that the total cross section consists of two parts, $\sigma_T = \sigma_{el} + \sigma_{abs}$, which are given as

$$\sigma_{el} = \frac{\pi}{k^2} \sum_{l=0}^{\infty} (2l + l) \, |1 - s_l|^2 \qquad (15.14.1)$$

and

$$\sigma_{abs} = \frac{\pi}{k^2} \sum_{l=0}^{\infty} (2l + l)(1 - |s_l|^2)^2 \qquad (15.14.2)$$

Recall that for a potential of finite range a, if

$$l(l + 1) > (ka)^2 \Rightarrow \delta_l = 0 \rightarrow s_l = 1 \qquad (15.14.3)$$

Hence, in our problem we have

$$\begin{cases} s_l = 0 & l(l + 1) < (ka)^2 \\ s_l = 1 & l(l + 1) > (ka)^2 \end{cases} \qquad (15.14.4)$$

Setting $L(L + 1) = (ka)^2$ and substituting s_l of Eq. (15.14.3) back into Eq. (15.14.1) yields

$$\sigma_{el} = \sigma_{abs} = \frac{\pi}{k^2} \sum_{l=0}^{L} (2l + 1) = \frac{\pi}{k^2} L(L + 1) = \frac{\pi}{k^2} (ka)^2 = \pi a^2 \qquad (15.14.5)$$

Therefore,

$$\sigma_T = 2\pi a^2 \qquad (15.14.6)$$

Note that this result is two times larger than the classical result. However, it is half the result of scattering from a hard sphere.

15.15. Two ions of He^+ are scattered from each other. The nuclear spin of the ions is zero. The interaction between the ions is Coulombic. (*a*) Write the scattering amplitude in the frame of the center of mass. (*b*) Find the differential cross section if the total spin is zero (singlet). (*c*) Repeat part (*b*), with total spin of one (triplet). (*d*) What is the differential cross section for a system of unpolarized ions?

SOLUTION

(*a*) The scattering amplitude for Coulombic interactions (see Problem 15.19) is

$$f(\theta) = \frac{n}{2k\sin^2(\theta/2)}e^{-in\ln(\sin^2(\theta/2))+i\pi+2i\eta_0} \qquad (15.15.1)$$

where $\eta_0 \equiv \arg\Gamma(1+in)$ and $n \equiv \mu Z'Z\dfrac{e^2}{\hbar^2 k}$. Here, $\mu = m_{He}/2$ is the reduced mass, $k = \sqrt{2\mu E/\hbar^2}$, and $Z = Z' = 1$.

(*b*) The nuclear spin is zero. Thus, the ions are identical fermions (each has spin 1/2 contributed by its electron). If the total spin is zero, the system is in an antisymmetric spin state, and hence the orbital wavefunction must be symmetric

$$\left(\frac{d\sigma}{d\Omega}\right)^{s=0} = |f(\theta) + f(\pi-\theta)|^2 = \frac{n^2}{4k^2}\left|\frac{e^{-2in\ln(\sin(\theta/2))}}{\sin^2(\theta/2)} + \frac{e^{-2in\ln(\cos(\theta/2))}}{\cos^2(\theta/2)}\right|^2$$

$$= \frac{n^2}{4k^2}\left[\frac{1}{\sin^4(\theta/2)} + \frac{1}{\cos^4(\theta/2)} + \frac{2\cos[n\ln\tan^2(\theta/2)]}{\sin^2(\theta/2)\cos^2(\theta/2)}\right] \qquad (15.15.2)$$

(*c*) This is the same as in part (*b*), but now the system is in a symmetric spin state (triplet). Hence, the orbital wavefunction must be antisymmetric:

$$\left(\frac{d\sigma}{d\Omega}\right)^{s=1} = |f(\theta) - f(\pi-\theta)|^2 = \frac{n^2}{4k^2}\left[\frac{1}{\sin^4(\theta/2)} + \frac{1}{\cos^4(\theta/2)} - \frac{2\cos[n\ln\tan^2(\theta/2)]}{\sin^2(\theta/2)\cos^2(\theta/2)}\right] \qquad (15.15.3)$$

(*d*) For an unpolarized ion beam, the probability of having total spin $s = 0$ is 1/4, and the probability of total spin $s = 1$ is 3/4. Therefore,

$$\frac{d\sigma}{d\Omega} = \frac{1}{4}\left(\frac{d\sigma}{d\Omega}\right)^{s=0} + \frac{3}{4}\left(\frac{d\sigma}{d\Omega}\right)^{s=1} \qquad (15.15.4)$$

Substituting the results from Eqs. (15.15.2) and (15.15.3) leads to

$$\frac{d\sigma}{d\Omega} = \frac{n^2}{4k^2}\left[\frac{1}{\sin^4(\theta/2)} + \frac{1}{\cos^4(\theta/2)} - \frac{\cos[n\ln\tan^2(\theta/2)]}{\sin^2(\theta/2)\cos^2(\theta/2)}\right] \qquad (15.15.5)$$

Note: In the limit of low energies $n \gg 1$, Eq. (15.15.5) differs from the classical result. However, the term oscillates rapidly so averaging over very small angles destroys the interference.

15.16. The interaction potential of two identical particles of spin 1/2 is

$$\hat{V}(r) = V(r)[(3)\hat{I} + \hat{\sigma}_1 \cdot \hat{\sigma}_2]$$

where $\hat{\sigma}_i$ are Pauli matrices and $\hat{I}$ is the unit operator (see Chap. 7) in the spin space. $V(r)$ is given by

$$V(r) = \begin{cases} -\dfrac{\hbar^2}{4\mu r^2} & r < R \\ 0 & r > R \end{cases} \qquad \left(\mu = \frac{m}{2}\right)$$

(a) What is the result of applying the spin operator $[3\hat{I} + \hat{\sigma}_1 \cdot \hat{\sigma}_2]$ on the singlet state and on the triplet state? (b) Two such particles are scattered on each other at low energies, $kR \gg 1$ ($k = \sqrt{(2\mu E/\hbar^2)}$). What is the dominant phase shift that contributes to the scattering amplitude (and the cross section) if the total spin of the system is $s = 0$? (c) For the conditions in part (b), what is the dominant phase shift if $s = 1$? (d) Calculate the phase shift of part (b) in the limit $kR \ll 1$. Find the cross section. (e) Calculate the phase shift of part (c) in the limit $kR \ll 1$. Find the cross section. (f) Find the cross section for an unpolarized beam.

SOLUTION

(a) The total spin of the system is $\hat{\mathbf{S}} = \hbar\hat{\sigma}/2$, where $\hat{\sigma} = \hat{\sigma}_1 + \hat{\sigma}_2$. Hence,

$$\hat{\sigma}^2 = \hat{\sigma}_1^2 + \hat{\sigma}_2^2 + 2\hat{\sigma}_1 \cdot \hat{\sigma}_2 \tag{15.16.1}$$

From the properties of Pauli matrices,

$$\hat{\sigma}_1^2 = \hat{\sigma}_1 \cdot \hat{\sigma}_1 = \hat{\sigma}_{1x}^2 + \hat{\sigma}_{1y}^2 + \hat{\sigma}_{1z}^2 = 3\hat{I} \tag{15.16.2}$$

and similarly, $\hat{\sigma}_2^2 = \hat{\sigma}_2 \cdot \hat{\sigma}_2 = 3\hat{I}$. In the singlet state $\sigma^2|singlet\rangle = 0$; therefore, using Eq. (15.16.1) we find

$$(\hat{\sigma}_1 \cdot \hat{\sigma}_2)|singlet\rangle = \frac{1}{2}(0 - 3 - 3)\hat{I}|singlet\rangle = -3\hat{I}|singlet\rangle \tag{15.16.3}$$

In the triplet state $\sigma^2|triplet\rangle = 8|triplet\rangle$; hence, similar to the previous calculation,

$$(\hat{\sigma}_1 \cdot \hat{\sigma}_2)|triplet\rangle = \frac{1}{2}(8 - 3 - 3)\hat{I}|triplet\rangle = \hat{I}|triplet\rangle \tag{15.16.4}$$

Finally, for the operator $[3\hat{I} + \hat{\sigma}_1 \cdot \hat{\sigma}_2]$, we obtain

$$[3\hat{I} + \hat{\sigma}_1 \cdot \hat{\sigma}_2]|singlet\rangle = (3 - 3)|singlet\rangle = 0$$

$$[3\hat{I} + \hat{\sigma}_1 \cdot \hat{\sigma}_2]|triplet\rangle = (3 + 1)|triplet\rangle = 4|triplet\rangle \tag{15.16.5}$$

(b) For total spin $s = 0$ the system is in the antisymmetric singlet state. Since the total wavefunction must be antisymmetric (fermions), the orbital wavefunction is symmetric. In general, only even partial waves contribute to a symmetric orbital wavefunction. In our case $\hat{V} = 0$ so all the phase shifts vanish.

(c) For total spin $s = 1$, the system is in one of the three triplet states. The spin wavefunction is symmetric and the orbital wavefunction must be antisymmetric. Thus, only odd partial waves contribute, and for $kR \ll 1$ the dominant phase shift is δ_1.

(d) Let us consider explicitly the phase shift δ_0 for the $s = 0$ state. The radial wavefunction $R_{kl}(r) = \chi_{kl}(r)/r$ is found by solving

$$\left[\frac{d^2}{dr^2} - \frac{l(l+1)}{r^2} - \frac{2\mu}{\hbar^2}\hat{V} + k^2\right]\chi_{kl}(r) = 0 \tag{15.16.6}$$

The solution $R_{k0}(r)$ is found by setting $\hat{V} = 0$ and $l = 0$ in Eq. (15.16.8). Therefore,

$$R_{k0}(r) = \frac{\sin(kr)}{kr} = j_0(kr) \tag{15.16.7}$$

The logarithmic derivative γ_0 is then

$$\gamma_0 = \frac{1}{R_0}\frac{dR_0}{dr}\bigg|_{r=R} = k\cot(kR) - \frac{1}{R} = -\frac{kj_1(kR)}{j_0(kR)} \tag{15.16.8}$$

where $j_0'(x) = -j_1(x)$ has been used. Since $\hat{V} = 0$ we expect that all phase shifts vanish. In particular,

$$\tan\delta_0 = \frac{kj_0'(kR) - \gamma_0 j_0(kR)}{kn_0'(kR) - \gamma_0 n_0(kR)} = \frac{-kj_1(kR) - kj_1(kR)}{kn_0'(kR) - \gamma_0 n_0(kR)} = 0 \tag{15.16.9}$$

and $(\hat{\sigma})^{s=0} = 0$.

(*e*) The dominant contribution for states $s = 1$ comes from δ_1. Substituting $l = 1$ and $\hat{V} = 4V(r) = \hbar^2/\mu r^2$ [see Eqs. (15.16.2) and (15.16.5)] back into Eq. (15.16.6), we have

$$\left[\frac{d^2}{dr^2} - \frac{2}{r^2} + \frac{2\mu}{\hbar^2} \frac{\hbar^2}{\mu r^2} + k^2 \right] \chi_{k1}(r) = 0 \qquad (15.16.10)$$

Therefore, $R_{k1}(r) = R_{k0}(r) = j_0(kr)$ and $\gamma_1 = \gamma_0$. The phase shift δ_1 is now given by

$$\tan \delta_1 = \frac{k j_1'(kR) - \gamma_1 j_1(kR)}{k n_1'(kR) - \gamma_1 n_1(kR)} \qquad (15.16.11)$$

In the limit $kR \to 0$, we have

$$j_0(x) \approx 1 - \frac{x^2}{3!} \qquad j_1(x) = \frac{x}{3} \qquad n_1(x) \approx -\frac{1 + x^2/2}{x^2} \qquad j_1'(x) = \frac{1}{3} \qquad n_1'(x) \approx +\frac{2}{x^3} \qquad (15.16.12)$$

Substituting $\gamma_1 R \approx -(kR)^2/3$ in Eq. (15.16.11), we find $\tan \delta_1 \approx \frac{1}{6}(kR)^3 \ll 1$. The scattering amplitude for δ_1 is

$$f(\theta) = \frac{3}{k} e^{i\delta_1} \sin \delta_1 P_1(\cos \theta) \qquad (15.16.13)$$

After antisymmetrization, we obtain

$$\left(\frac{d\sigma}{d\Omega} \right)^{s=1} = |f(\theta) + f(\pi - \theta)|^2 = |2f(\theta)|^2 = \frac{36}{k^2} \sin^2 \delta_1 \cos^2 \theta \qquad (15.16.14)$$

Finally, substituting $\sin \delta_1 = \tan \delta_1$ gives

$$\left(\frac{d\sigma}{d\Omega} \right)^{s=1} = R^2 (kR)^4 \qquad (15.16.15)$$

(*f*) The cross section for an unpolarized beam is

$$\frac{d\sigma}{d\Omega} = \frac{1}{4} \left(\frac{d\sigma}{d\Omega} \right)^{s=0} + \frac{3}{4} \left(\frac{d\sigma}{d\Omega} \right)^{s=1} = \frac{3}{4} R^2 (kR)^4 \qquad (15.16.16)$$

15.17. Consider the scattering of two identical spinless particles of mass m. The interaction potential depends on the distance r between the particles and is given by

$$V(r) = \begin{cases} -\dfrac{h}{16m} \left(\dfrac{1}{R} + \dfrac{1}{a} \right)^2 & r < R \\ 0 & r > R \end{cases} \qquad (15.17.1)$$

where $R \ll a$ are constants. (*a*) Find the phase shift $\delta_0(k)$ in the low-energy limit,

$$kR \ll \frac{R}{a} \ll 1 \qquad k = \sqrt{\frac{2\mu E}{\hbar^2}} \qquad (15.17.2)$$

where E is the energy in the center-of-mass frame, and μ is the reduced mass. (*b*) Calculate the total cross section. (*c*) Repeat your calculation for scattering of two identical spin 1/2 fermions that are polarized in the singlet state. (*d*) Calculate [in the approximation of parts (*b*) and (*c*)] the total cross section for unpolarized spin 1/2 fermions.

SOLUTION

(*a*) The reduced mass of the two identical particles of mass m is $\mu = m/2$. Setting

$$V(r) = \begin{cases} -\dfrac{\pi^2 \hbar^2}{8\mu} \left(\dfrac{1}{R} + \dfrac{1}{a} \right)^2 \equiv -V_0 & r < a \\ 0 & r > R \end{cases} \qquad (15.17.3)$$

and defining the constants

$$K = \sqrt{\frac{2\mu(E+V_0)}{\hbar^2}} = \sqrt{k^2 + \frac{1}{4}\pi^2\left(\frac{1}{R}+\frac{1}{a}\right)^2} \qquad k_0 \equiv \frac{\pi}{2}\left(\frac{1}{R}+\frac{1}{a}\right) \tag{15.17.4}$$

we have (see Problem 15.8)

$$\tan\delta_0 = -\frac{\gamma_0 kR^2}{1+\gamma_0 R} \qquad (kR \ll 1) \tag{15.17.5}$$

where γ_0 is given by $\gamma_0 = K\cot(KR) - \frac{1}{R}$. Thus, substituting γ_0 into Eq. (15.17.5) we find

$$\tan\delta_0(k) = -KR + \frac{k}{K}\tan(KR) \tag{15.17.6}$$

In the limit of Eq. (15.17.2), $K \to k_0$. Hence,

$$KR \to k_0R \approx \frac{\pi}{2}\left(1+\frac{R}{a}\right) \qquad \frac{k}{K} \approx \frac{2kR}{\pi}\left(1-\frac{R}{a}\right) \qquad \tan(KR) \approx \tan\left[\frac{\pi}{2}\left(1+\frac{R}{a}\right)\right] \approx -\frac{a}{R} \tag{15.17.7}$$

Therefore, keeping the leading terms of orders kR and R/a in Eq. (15.17.6), we find

$$\tan\delta_0 \approx -kR\left[1+\frac{2}{\pi}\frac{a}{R}-\frac{2}{\pi}\right] \tag{15.17.8}$$

which in the limit $R/a \ll 1$ leads to $\tan\delta_0 = -\frac{2ka}{\pi} \ll 1$.

(b) The scattering amplitude in the s-wave approximation is

$$f_0(\theta) = \frac{1}{k}e^{i\delta_0}\sin\delta_0 \tag{15.17.9}$$

For identical spinless particles, the amplitude must be symmetrical and therefore the differential cross section is

$$\frac{d\sigma_0}{d\Omega} = |f_0(\theta)+f_0(\pi-\theta)|^2 = \frac{4}{k^2}\sin^2\delta_0 \tag{15.17.10}$$

Thus, substituting δ_0 in $\tan\delta_0 = -(2ka)/\pi$ and integrating over $d\Omega$ we obtain

$$\sigma_0 = \frac{64}{\pi}a^2 \tag{15.17.11}$$

(c) For identical fermions in the singlet spin state the orbital wavefunction must be symmetric. Therefore, the result of part (b) remains unchanged:

$$(\sigma_0)^{s=0} = \frac{64}{\pi}a^2 \tag{15.17.12}$$

(d) For unpolarized spin 1/2 particles, the probability of total spin 0 is 1/4 and the probability of spin 1 is 3/4. Therefore,

$$\sigma_0 = \frac{1}{4}(\sigma_0)^{s=0} + \frac{3}{4}(\sigma_0)^{s=1} \tag{15.17.13}$$

However, due to antisymmetrization of the orbital wavefunction in the triplet state, δ_0 does not contribute and $(\sigma_0)^{s=1} = 0$; hence,

$$\sigma_0 = \frac{1}{4}(\sigma_0)^{s=0} = \frac{16}{\pi}a^2 \tag{15.17.14}$$

15.18. A particle of mass m_1 and speed v_1 is scattered inelastically by a particle of mass m_2 at rest in the Lab frame, where $m_2 > m_1$ (Fig. 15.5), resulting in two particles of mass m_3 and m_4, $m_1 + m_2 = m_3 + m_4$. Assume that in this process, an amount of energy Q is converted from the rest energy of $m_1 + m_2$ into kinetic energy of $m_3 + m_4$. (a) Find the relations between the scattering angles of m_3 in CM (θ) and Lab (θ_0). (b) Find the relation between the differential cross section $d\sigma(\theta)/d\Omega$ and $d\sigma(\theta_0)/d\Omega$ in the CM and Lab frames, respectively.

Lab frame

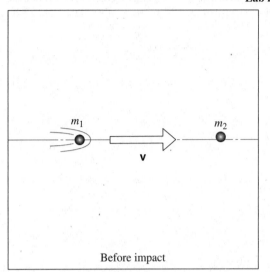

Before impact

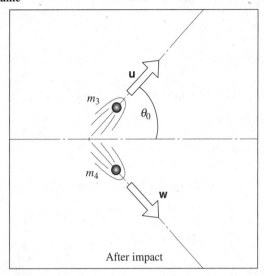

After impact

CM frame

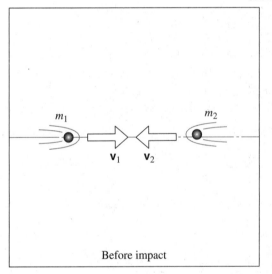

Before impact

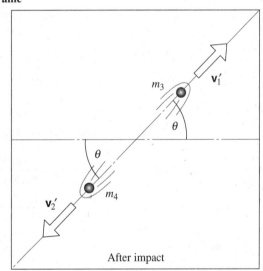

After impact

Fig. 15.5

SOLUTION

(*a*) From conservation of momentum and the definition of CM we obtain

$$
\begin{cases}
m_1 v_1 = m_2 v_2 \\
m_3 v_1' = m_4 v_2'
\end{cases}
\tag{15.18.1}
$$

Similarly, from conservation of energy in the CM frame,

$$
\begin{cases}
E = \dfrac{1}{2} m_1 v_1^2 + \dfrac{1}{2} m_2 v_2^2 \\
E + Q = \dfrac{1}{2} m_3 v_1'^2 + \dfrac{1}{2} m_4 v_2'^2
\end{cases}
\tag{15.18.2}
$$

where E is the initial kinetic energy in the CM frame, and Q is the kinetic energy gain from the collision. Taking $v_1 = v - V$ and $v_2 = -V$, where V is the velocity of the CM frame relative to the Lab, we find that

$$V = \frac{m_1}{m_1 + m_2} v \qquad v_1 = \frac{m_2}{m_1 + m_2} v \tag{15.18.3}$$

Therefore, in the center-of-mass frame where the total momentum is zero, $u \cos\theta_0 = v_1' \cos\theta + V$, $u \sin\theta_0 = v_1' \sin\theta$. Hence

$$\tan\theta_0 = \frac{\sin\theta}{\cos\theta + V/v_1'} \equiv \frac{\sin\theta}{\cos\theta + \gamma} \tag{15.18.4}$$

where $\gamma = V/v_1'$.

(b) From Eqs. (15.18.1) and (15.18.2), we have

$$v_2 = \frac{m_1}{m_2} v_1' \qquad v_2' = \frac{m_3}{m_4} v_1' \tag{15.18.5}$$

$$\frac{E}{E+Q} = \frac{m_1 m_4}{m_3 m_2} \left(\frac{m_1 + m_2}{m_3 + m_4} \right) \frac{v_1^2}{v_1'^2} = \frac{m_1 m_4}{(m_1 + m_2)^2 m_3} \frac{v^2}{v_1^2} \tag{15.18.6}$$

Therefore,

$$\gamma^2 = \frac{v^2}{v_1'^2} = \frac{m_1 m_3}{m_2 m_4} \frac{E}{E+Q} \tag{15.18.7}$$

The relation between the cross section is found from the condition

$$\left(\frac{d\sigma}{d\Omega} \right)^{\text{Lab}} \sin\theta_0 \, d\theta_0 \, d\varphi_0 = \left(\frac{d\sigma}{d\Omega} \right)^{\text{CM}} \sin\theta \, d\theta \, d\varphi \tag{15.18.8}$$

However, $\varphi^{\text{CM}} = \varphi^{\text{Lab}}$ and from Eq. (15.18.4) we have

$$\begin{cases} \cos^2\theta_0 = \dfrac{(\cos\theta + \gamma)^2}{1 + 2\gamma\cos\theta + \gamma^2} \\[2mm] \sin\theta_0 \, d\theta_0 (1 + 2\gamma\cos\theta + \gamma^2)^{3/2} = |1 + \gamma\cos\theta| \sin\theta \, d\theta \end{cases} \tag{15.18.9}$$

Hence,

$$\left(\frac{d\sigma_0}{d\Omega} \right)^{\text{Lab}} = \frac{(1 + 2\gamma\cos\theta + \gamma^2)^{3/2}}{|1 + \gamma\cos\theta|} \left(\frac{d\sigma}{d\Omega} \right)^{\text{CM}} \tag{15.18.10}$$

15.19. (a) Write the Schrödinger equation for a system of two charged particles with charges Ze and $Z'e$ that interact by Coulombic interaction (use parabolic coordinates). (b) Write the solution in the form

$$u(\xi, \eta) = e^{ikz} v(\xi, \eta) \tag{15.19.1}$$

Show that the asymptotic solution of $v(\xi, \eta)$ for an outgoing wave in the limit $r \to \infty$ does not depend on the coordinate η. (c) Express $v(\xi)$ in terms of the confluent hypergeometric function and find the asymptotic solution that is regular at the origin. (d) Find the differential cross section and show that it coincides with the Rutherford formula.

SOLUTION

(a) The Schrödinger equation in the CM frame is

$$\left[-\frac{\hbar^2}{2\mu} \nabla^2 + \frac{ZZ'e^2}{r} \right] u(r) = Eu(r) \tag{15.19.2}$$

where $E = \hbar^2 k^2 / 2\mu$ and μ is the reduced mass. In parabolic coordinates,

$$\begin{cases} \xi = r(1 - \cos\theta) = r - z \\ \eta = r(1 + \cos\theta) = r + z \\ \varphi = \varphi \end{cases} \qquad \begin{cases} x = \sqrt{\xi\eta}\,\cos\varphi \\ y = \sqrt{\xi\eta}\,\sin\varphi \\ z = \dfrac{1}{2}(\eta - \xi) \end{cases} \qquad (15.19.3)$$

The Laplacian is given by

$$\nabla^2 = \frac{4}{\xi + \eta}\left[\frac{\partial}{\partial\xi}\left(\xi\frac{\partial}{\partial\xi}\right) + \frac{\partial}{\partial\eta}\left(\eta\frac{\partial}{\partial\eta}\right)\right] + \frac{\partial^2}{\partial\varphi^2} \qquad (15.19.4)$$

and Eq. (15.19.2) is written in the following form:

$$\left\{\frac{4}{\xi + \eta}\left[\frac{\partial}{\partial\xi}\left(\xi\frac{\partial}{\partial\xi}\right) + \frac{\partial}{\partial\eta}\left(\eta\frac{\partial}{\partial\eta}\right) - \frac{\mu Z Z' e^2}{h^2}\right] + \frac{\partial^2}{\partial\varphi^2} + k^2\right\} u(r) = 0 \qquad (15.19.5)$$

(b) From the azimuthal symmetry of the solution we have $u = u(\xi, \eta)$. In the limit $r \to \infty$ the outgoing wave is of the form $r^{-1}e^{ikr}$. Therefore,

$$u(\xi, \eta) = e^{ikz}v(r - z, r + z)_{r \to \infty} \to e^{ikz}v(r - z) = e^{ikz}v(\xi) \qquad (15.19.6)$$

Equation (15.19.6) leads to a separation of variables in the form

$$u(\xi, \eta) = e^{ikz}v(\xi) = e^{ik\eta/2}e^{-ik\xi/2}v(\xi) \qquad (15.19.7)$$

(c) Substituting Eq. (15.19.7) into Eq. (15.19.5), the Schrödinger equation is reduced to an equation for $v(\xi)$:

$$\xi\frac{d^2v}{d\xi^2} + (1 - ik\xi)\frac{dv}{d\xi} - nkv = 0 \qquad \left(n \equiv \frac{\mu Z Z' e^2}{\hbar^2 k}\right) \qquad (15.19.8)$$

This equation is of the form

$$z\frac{d^2F}{dz^2} + (b - z)\frac{dF}{dz} - aF = 0 \qquad (15.19.9)$$

and its solution is the confluent hypergeometric function $F(a, b, z)$, where $z = ik\xi$, $a = -in$, and $b = 1$:

$$v(\xi) = AF(-in, 1, ik\xi) \qquad (15.19.10)$$

The asymptotic solution of $F(a, b, z)$, which is regular at the origin, behaves like

$$F_{z \to \infty} \to \Gamma(b)\left[\frac{i(-z)^{-a}}{\Gamma(b - a)}\left(1 + \frac{a(a - b)}{z}\right) - \frac{ie^z z^{a-b}}{\Gamma(a)}\left(1 + \frac{(1 - a)(b - a)}{z}\right) + \cdots\right] \qquad (15.19.11)$$

Substituting $z = ik\xi$, $a = -in$, and $b = 1$, we find

$$v(\xi)_{\xi \to \infty} \to A\frac{e^{n\pi/2}}{\Gamma(1 + in)}\left[e^{n\ln k\xi} + f_c(\theta)\frac{1}{r}e^{i(k\xi - n\ln 2kr)}\right] \qquad (15.19.12)$$

where

$$f_c(\theta) = \frac{\Gamma(1 + in)}{i\Gamma(-in)}\frac{e^{in\ln\sin^2(\theta/2)}}{2k\sin^2(\theta/2)} \qquad (15.19.13)$$

Therefore,

$$u_{r \to \infty} \to \frac{Ae^{n\pi/2}}{\Gamma(1 + in)} \left[e^{i[kz + n \ln k(r-z)]} + f_c(\theta) \frac{1}{r} e^{i[kr - n \ln 2kr]} \right]$$ (15.19.14)

(*d*) Note that *u* is not of the form

$$u_{r \to \infty} \to e^{ikz} + f(\theta) \frac{e^{ikr}}{r}$$ (15.19.15)

The reason is that the Coulombic potential does not decrease rapidly enough. However, we can generalize the result and find the cross section by

$$\frac{d\sigma}{d\Omega} = |f(\theta)|^2 = \frac{n}{4k^2 \sin^2(\theta/2)}$$ (15.19.16)

This is the famous Rutherford formula.

15.20. The scattering amplitude for neutron-proton scattering is given by

$$f(\theta) = \langle \xi_f | (A + B\hat{\sigma}^P \cdot \hat{\sigma}^N) | \xi_i \rangle$$ (15.20.1)

where *A* and *B* are "constants," $\hat{\sigma}$ are Pauli matrices, and $\{|\xi_i\rangle, |\xi_f\rangle\}$ are the initial and final spin states of the system $|\xi\rangle_{i,f} = \{|+_p +_N\rangle, |+_p -_N\rangle, |-_p +_N\rangle, |-_p +_N\rangle\}$. (*a*) Calculate the scattering amplitude for each of the 16 possibilities. (*b*) Find the differential cross section for scattering of $|+\rangle_N \to |+\rangle_N$ and $|+\rangle_N \to |-\rangle_N$ when the spin of the emergent proton is not measured by the detector. (*c*) Find the cross section for scattering in the states $|singlet\rangle \to |singlet\rangle$, $|triplet\rangle \to |triplet\rangle$, $|singlet\rangle \to |triplet\rangle$.

SOLUTION

(*a*) The operator $\hat{\sigma}^P \cdot \hat{\sigma}^N = \hat{\sigma}_x^P \hat{\sigma}_x^N + \hat{\sigma}_y^P \hat{\sigma}_y^N + \hat{\sigma}_z^P \hat{\sigma}_z^N$ operates separately on the proton and neutron states. For example:

$$\langle + |_p \langle + |_N (A + B\hat{\sigma}^P \cdot \hat{\sigma}^N) |+\rangle_p |+\rangle_N = A + B(\langle + |_p \hat{\sigma}_x |+\rangle_p \langle + |_N \hat{\sigma}_x |+\rangle_N$$

$$+ \langle + |_p \hat{\sigma}_y |+\rangle_p \langle + |_N \hat{\sigma}_y |+\rangle_N + \langle + |_N \hat{\sigma}_z |+\rangle_N \langle + |_p \hat{\sigma}_z |+\rangle_p)$$ (15.20.2)

Using the results $\hat{\sigma}_x |+\rangle = |-\rangle$, $\hat{\sigma}_y |+\rangle = i |-\rangle$, $\hat{\sigma}_z |+\rangle = |+\rangle$, and the orthogonality of the spin states $\langle + |-\rangle = 0$, we obtain

$$\langle + |_p \langle + |_N (A + B\hat{\sigma}^P \cdot \hat{\sigma}^N) |+\rangle_p |+\rangle_N = A + B$$ (15.20.3)

Similarly,

$$\langle + |_p \langle + |_N (A + B\hat{\sigma}^P \cdot \hat{\sigma}^N) |+\rangle_p |-\rangle_N = B[\langle + | \hat{\sigma}_x |+\rangle \langle + | \hat{\sigma}_x |-\rangle + \langle + | \hat{\sigma}_y |+\rangle \langle + | \hat{\sigma}_y |-\rangle + \langle + | \hat{\sigma}_z |+\rangle \langle + | \hat{\sigma}_z |-\rangle] = 0$$

(15.20.4)

All the 16 possible scattering processes are then summarized in Table 15.3.

(*b*) We consider the case where the incident proton is in a general spin state $\alpha |+\rangle_p + \beta |-\rangle_p (|\alpha|^2 + |\beta|^2 = 1)$. Since the state of the emergent proton is not measured (and different components do not interfere),

$$\left(\frac{d\sigma}{d\Omega} \right)_{|+\rangle_N \to |+\rangle_N} = |f_+|^2 + |f_-|^2$$ (15.20.5)

Table 15.3

	$\langle+\|_p \langle+\|_N$	$\langle-\|_p \langle+\|_N$	$\langle+\|_p \langle-\|_N$	$\langle-\|_p \langle-\|_N$
$\langle+\|_p \langle+\|_N$	$A + B$	0	0	0
$\langle-\|_p \langle+\|_N$	0	$A - B$	$2B$	0
$\langle+\|_p \langle-\|_N$	0	$2B$	$A - B$	0
$\langle-\|_p \langle-\|_N$	0	0	0	$A + B$

where $f_\pm$ is the amplitude for having a proton in $|\pm\rangle_p$ final states, respectively. Using Table 15.3 for the entries that correspond to the process $|+\rangle_N \rightarrow |-\rangle_N$ we find

$$\begin{pmatrix} f_+ \\ f_- \end{pmatrix} = \begin{pmatrix} A + B & 0 \\ 0 & A - B \end{pmatrix}\begin{pmatrix} \alpha \\ \beta \end{pmatrix} \equiv \hat{M}\begin{pmatrix} \alpha \\ \beta \end{pmatrix} \tag{15.20.6}$$

Therefore,

$$\left(\frac{d\sigma}{d\Omega}\right)_{|+\rangle_N \rightarrow |+\rangle_N} = (\alpha^* \beta^*)\hat{M}^\dagger \hat{M}\begin{pmatrix} \alpha \\ \beta \end{pmatrix} = (\alpha^* \beta^*)\begin{pmatrix} |A + B|^2 & 0 \\ 0 & |A - B|^2 \end{pmatrix}\begin{pmatrix} \alpha \\ \beta \end{pmatrix}$$

$$= |\alpha|^2|A + B|^2 + |\beta|^2|A - B|^2$$

We assume now that the incident protons are not polarized. This means that we have equal probabilities of $1/2$ of finding a proton in $|+\rangle_p$ or $|-\rangle_p$ initial states. Therefore, substituting $\alpha = 1$, $\beta = 0$, and $\alpha = 0$, $\beta = 1$ into Eq. (15.20.7) we obtain

$$\left(\frac{d\sigma}{d\Omega}\right)_{|+\rangle_N \rightarrow |+\rangle_N} = \frac{1}{2}(|A + B|^2 + |A - B|^2) = |A|^2 + |B|^2 \tag{15.20.7}$$

Note that this result can be written as

$$\left(\frac{d\sigma}{d\Omega}\right)_{|+\rangle_N \rightarrow |+\rangle_N} = \frac{1}{2}Tr\,(\hat{M}^\dagger \hat{M}) \tag{15.20.8}$$

which is valid for the case of unpolarized particles of spin $1/2$. In order to use Eq. (15.20.9) for the process $|+\rangle_N \rightarrow |-\rangle_N$, we replace the matrix $\hat{M}$ of Eq. (15.20.6) by

$$\begin{pmatrix} f_+ \\ f_- \end{pmatrix} = \begin{pmatrix} 0 & 2B \\ 0 & 0 \end{pmatrix}\begin{pmatrix} \alpha \\ \beta \end{pmatrix} \equiv \hat{M}\begin{pmatrix} \alpha \\ \beta \end{pmatrix} \tag{15.20.9}$$

This immediately gives us

$$\left(\frac{d\sigma}{d\Omega}\right)_{|+\rangle_N \rightarrow |-\rangle_N} = \frac{1}{2}(0 + 4|B|^2) = 2|B|^2 \tag{15.20.10}$$

(*c*) Consider the system in a singlet state where the total spin is zero:

$$|singlet\rangle = \frac{1}{\sqrt{2}}(|+\rangle_p|-\rangle_N - |-\rangle_p|+\rangle_N) \tag{15.20.11}$$

Therefore, the scattering amplitude is

$$f_{|singlet\rangle \rightarrow |singlet\rangle} = \frac{1}{2}(f_{|+-\rangle \rightarrow |+-\rangle} - f_{|+-\rangle \rightarrow |-+\rangle} - f_{|-+\rangle \rightarrow |+-\rangle} + f_{|-+\rangle \rightarrow |-+\rangle})$$

$$= \frac{1}{2}[A - B - 2B - 2B + (A - B)] = A - 3B \tag{15.20.12}$$

Indeed, a great deal of algebra can be saved by noting the singlet state and the triplet states are eigenstates of the operator $\hat{\sigma}_N \cdot \hat{\sigma}_p$ with eigenvalues -3 and 1, respectively:

$$(\hat{\sigma}_N \cdot \hat{\sigma}_p)|singlet\rangle = -3|singlet\rangle$$

$$(\hat{\sigma}_N \cdot \hat{\sigma}_p)|triplet\rangle = |triplet\rangle \tag{15.20.13}$$

Thus, the scattering amplitudes are

$$f(singlet \rightarrow singlet) = \langle singlet|(A + B\hat{\sigma}_N \cdot \hat{\sigma}_p)|singlet\rangle = A - 3B$$

$$f(triplet \rightarrow triplet) = \langle triplet|(A + B\hat{\sigma}_N \cdot \hat{\sigma}_p)|triplet\rangle = A + B \tag{15.20.14}$$

$$f(singlet \rightarrow triplet) = \langle triplet|(A + B\hat{\sigma}_N \cdot \hat{\sigma}_p)|singlet\rangle = 0$$

The cross sections are therefore

$$\left(\frac{d\sigma}{d\Omega}\right)_{singlet \rightarrow singlet} = |A - 3B|^2$$

$$\left(\frac{d\sigma}{d\Omega}\right)_{triplet \rightarrow triplet} = |A + B|^2 \tag{15.20.15}$$

15.21. Consider the time-independent Schrödinger equation in one dimension with $V(x) = 0$ only in the finite region $|x| < x_0$. (a) Show that for any solution of the Schrödinger equation $\phi(x)$, the probability current is a constant that does not depend on the position x. (b) The asymptotic form of the wavefunction $\phi(x)$ can be written as

$$\begin{cases} \phi_L(x) = Ae^{ikx} + Be^{-ikx} & x \ll -x_0 \\ \phi_R(x) = Ce^{ikx} + De^{-ikx} & x \gg -x_0 \end{cases} \tag{15.21.1}$$

where A, B, C, and D are complex constants that are related by the scattering matrix $\hat{S}$:

$$\begin{pmatrix} B \\ C \end{pmatrix} = \hat{S}\begin{pmatrix} A \\ D \end{pmatrix}$$

Show that $\hat{S}$ is a unitary matrix.

SOLUTION

(a) The time-independent Schrödinger equation is

$$-\frac{\hbar^2}{2m}\nabla^2\phi + (V - E)\phi = 0 \tag{15.21.2}$$

Since V and E are real, any solution ϕ satisfies the conjugate equation as well:

$$-\frac{\hbar^2}{2m}\nabla^2\phi^* + (V - E)\phi^* = 0$$

Multiplying these equations by ϕ^* and ϕ, respectively, and then subtracting the resulting expressions, leads to

$$\phi^*\left(-\frac{\hbar^2}{2m}\nabla^2\phi + (V - E)\phi\right) - \left(-\frac{\hbar^2}{2m}\nabla^2\phi^* + (V - E)\phi^*\right)\phi = -\frac{\hbar^2}{2m}(\phi^*\nabla^2\phi - (\nabla^2\phi^*)\phi) = 0 \tag{15.21.3}$$

Thus,

$$-i\frac{\hbar^2}{2m}\nabla\cdot[\phi^*\nabla\phi-(\nabla\phi^*)\phi]=-i\hbar\nabla\cdot\hat{\mathbf{J}}=0 \tag{15.21.4}$$

Namely,

$$\frac{dJ(x)}{dx}=0 \quad\text{where}\quad J(x)=\frac{\hbar}{2im}\left[\phi^*\frac{d\phi}{dx}-\phi\frac{d\phi^*}{dx}\right] \tag{15.21.5}$$

(b) In the previous section we showed that the probability current $J(x)$ is conserved and does not depend on x for any solution $\phi(x)$ of the Schrödinger equation. For large negative values of x we have

$$\frac{2im}{\hbar}J_L=(A^*e^{-ikx}+B^*e^{ikx})(ikAe^{ikx}-ikBe^{-ikx})-(Ae^{ikx}+Be^{-ikx})(-ikA^*e^{-ikx}+ikB^*e^{ikx})$$

$$=2ik(|A|^2-|B|^2) \tag{15.21.6}$$

Therefore,

$$J_L=\frac{\hbar k}{m}(|A|^2-|B|^2) \tag{15.21.7}$$

Similarly, for large positive values of x,

$$J_R=\frac{\hbar k}{m}(|C|^2-|D|^2) \tag{15.21.8}$$

Now, from current conservation, $J_L=J_R$, and

$$|A|^2-|B|^2=|C|^2-|D|^2 \Rightarrow |B|^2+|C|^2=|A|^2+|D|^2 \tag{15.21.9}$$

from which it follows that the scattering matrix is unitary, that is,

$$\hat{S}^\dagger\hat{S}=\hat{I} \tag{15.21.10}$$

SUPPLEMENTARY PROBLEMS

15.22. A particle with mass m_1 is scattered elastically by a particle of mass m_2 at rest in the Lab frame. (a) Find the relation between the scattering angle of m_2 in the Lab frame and the scattering angle in the CM frame. Show that in the Lab frame the particle m_2 will always recoil in the front half of the sphere. (b) Find the relation between the scattering angle of m_1 in the Lab and CM frames. (c) What is the range of possible angles for scattering of particle m_1 in the Lab frame for the following conditions: i. $m_1/m_2<1$; ii. $m_1/m_2=1$; iii. $(m_1/m_2)>1$.

Ans. (a) $\tan\theta_2=\dfrac{\sin\theta}{1-\cos\theta}\left(0\le\theta<\pi\to\tan\theta_2\ge0\to0\le\theta_2\le\dfrac{\pi}{2}\right)$

(b) $\tan\theta_1=\dfrac{\sin\theta}{\cos\theta+\gamma}\left(\gamma=\dfrac{m_1}{m_2}\right)$

(c) i. $\gamma<1\to0\le\theta_1\le\pi$; ii. $\gamma=1\to\theta_1=\dfrac{\pi}{2}\to0\le\theta_1\le\dfrac{\pi}{2}$

iii. $\gamma>1\to0\le\theta_1\le\theta_1^{\max}=\sin^{-1}(1/\gamma)$

15.23. A particle of mass m_1 is elastically scattered by a particle of a mass m_2 at rest in the Lab frame. (a) Consider particle m_1. Find the relation between the differential cross section in the center of the mass frame, $d\sigma(\theta,\varphi)/d\Omega$, and the differential cross section in the Lab frame, $d\sigma_0(\theta_0,\varphi_0)/d\Omega$. (b) Assume $m_1=m_2$. Find the differential cross section for scattering m_1 in the Lab frame, if it is given that the cross section in the center-of-mass frame is symmetrical. (c) Calculate the total cross section for part (b). Show explicitly that the total cross section is not dependent on the related frame.

Ans. (a) $\dfrac{d\sigma_0}{d\Omega}=\dfrac{(1+\gamma^2+2\gamma\cos\theta)^{3/2}}{|1+\gamma\cos\theta|}\dfrac{d\sigma}{d\Omega};\quad\left(\gamma=\dfrac{m_1}{m_2}\right)$

(b) $\dfrac{d\sigma_0}{d\Omega} = 4\cos\theta_0 \dfrac{d\sigma}{d\Omega}$ $\left(0 < \theta_0 \le \dfrac{\pi}{2}, 0 < \varphi_0 \le 2\pi\right)$

(c) $\sigma_0 = \displaystyle\int \dfrac{d\sigma_0}{d\Omega_0} d\Omega_0 = \dfrac{4\sigma}{4\pi} \int_0^{\pi/2} \cos\theta_0 \sin\theta_0\, d\theta_0 \int_0^{2\pi} d\varphi_0 = \sigma$

15.24. Assuming azimuthal symmetry, find the relation between the scattering amplitude and the differential cross section.

Ans. $d\sigma/d\Omega = |f_k(\theta)|^2$.

15.25. Using Fermi's golden rule calculate the probability density (per unit time) of the transition of a particle (mass m and energy E) from initial state $|p_i\rangle$ to final state $|p_f\rangle$. Show that the cross section $d\sigma/d\Omega = W(p_i, p_f)/J_i$, where W is the transition probability density and J_i, the probability current density $J_i = \left(\dfrac{1}{2\pi\hbar}\right)^3 \sqrt{\dfrac{3E_i}{m}}$, coincides with the Born approximation.

15.26. Consider the potential $V = -V_0$ for $r \le a$ and $V = 0$ for $r > a$. Show that the s-bound states ($l = 0, E < 0$) satisfy the quantization condition: $\tan(Ka) = -K/k$, where

$$K^2 = (k_0^2 + k^2) \qquad k_0 = \left(\dfrac{2\mu V_0}{\hbar^2}\right)^{1/2} \qquad k = \left(\dfrac{2\mu E}{\hbar^2}\right)^{1/2}$$

15.27. Building on Problem 15.26, show that the phase shift for s-wave scattering states ($l = 0, E = 0$) is $\delta_0 = \xi(k) - kr_0$, where $\tan Ka = +(K/k)\tan[\xi(k)]$.

15.28. Find the condition for resonance scattering at low energies ($ka \ll 1$), and demonstrate that for near resonance
$$\dfrac{d\sigma}{d\Omega} \approx \dfrac{1}{k^2 + k_0^2 \cot^2(k_0 a)}.$$

15.29. Given the potential well $V(r) = -V_0$ for $r < R$ and $V(r) = 0$ for $r > R$, (a) show that for $q = 2k\sin(\theta/2)$ the scattering amplitude $f(\theta)$ is

$$f(\theta) = \dfrac{\mu V_0}{\hbar^2}\dfrac{2}{q}\left(\dfrac{\sin(Rq)}{q^2} - \dfrac{R\cos(Rq)}{q}\right) \qquad (15.29.1)$$

(b) Show that the differential cross section in the limit $Rq \ll 1$ is a constant that is not dependent on k or θ. (c) Consider the potential $V(\mathbf{r}) = B\delta(\mathbf{r})$. Use the Born approximation to find the differential cross section. Calculate the constant B so that the results from parts (b) and (c) coincide.

Ans. (c) $\dfrac{d\sigma}{d\Omega} = \dfrac{\mu^2 B^2}{4\pi^2\hbar^4}$; $B = \dfrac{4\pi}{3}V_0 R^3$

15.30. For the potential $V = -V_0$ for $r \le a$ and $V = 0$ for $r > a$, find the conditions for $\delta_0 = \pi$.

Ans. $ka \ll 1$ and $\tan(ka) = ka$; $k \equiv \sqrt{2mV_0/\hbar^2}$

15.31. Derive the optical theorem $\sigma_{total} = 4\pi Im f_k(0)/k$. Hint: Use the partial wave expansion of $f(\theta)$ and

$$\sigma_{el} = \dfrac{\pi}{k^2}\sum_{l=0}^{\infty}(2l+1)|e^{2i\delta_l} - 1|^2 \qquad \sigma_{abs} = \dfrac{\pi}{k^2}\sum_{l=0}^{\infty}(2l+1)(1 - |e^{2i\delta_l}|)^2$$

15.32. Consider scattering of two identical spinless particles of mass m. The energy of the scattered particle is $E_0 = \hbar^2 k^2/2m$, whereas the target particle is at rest. The interaction potential between the particles is $V(r) = V_0/r^2$, where r is the relative coordinate. (a) Find the phase shifts δ_l. (b) Write the differential cross section $d\sigma(\theta)/d\Omega$ in the center-of-mass frame. (c) Obtain $d\sigma_0(\theta_0)/d\Omega$ in the Lab frame, where the target particle is initially at rest.

Ans. (a) $\delta_l = \dfrac{\pi}{2}\left[l - \dfrac{1}{2}\left(-1 + \sqrt{1 + 4\left[l(l+1) + \dfrac{2\mu V_0}{\hbar^2}\right]}\right)\right]$

(b) $\dfrac{d\sigma}{d\Omega} = \dfrac{16}{k^2}\left[\displaystyle\sum_{L=0}^{\infty}(4L+1)e^{i\delta_{2L}}\sin\delta_{2L}\,P_{2L}(\cos\theta)\right]^2$; (c) $\dfrac{d\sigma(\theta_0)}{d\Omega} = 4\cos\theta_0\,\dfrac{d\sigma(2\theta)}{d\Omega}$

15.33. (a) Calculate, in Born approximation, the scattering amplitude of a particle with mass μ from a spherical well potential with radius a and depth V_0; calculate the boundary of a spherical well "point" when $a \to 0$ and $V_0 \to \infty$ with $V_0 a^3 = C$ for a given constant C. (b) A neutron is scattered by a neutron. The neutron mass is m, and we assume that the potential between the two neutrons satisfies the conditions given in part (a). Calculate the scattering amplitude and the differential cross section (in the center-of-mass frame) when the neutron pair is in singlet state and in triplet state.

Ans. (a) $f(\theta) = \dfrac{3\mu C}{\hbar^2}\left[\dfrac{\sin(qa) - qa\cos(qa)}{(qa)^3}\right]$; $q = 2k\sin(\theta/2)$; $\mu = \dfrac{m}{2}$; $f(\theta)_{qa\to0} \to \dfrac{2\mu C}{3\hbar^2}$

(b) singlet: $f_s(\theta) = f(\theta) + f(\pi - \theta) = \dfrac{2}{3}\dfrac{mC}{\hbar^2}$; $\left(\dfrac{d\sigma}{d\Omega}\right)^{s=0} = \dfrac{4}{9}\dfrac{m^2 C^2}{\hbar^4}$

triplet: $f_A(\theta) = f(\theta) - f(\pi - \theta) = 0$; $\left(\dfrac{d\sigma}{d\Omega}\right)^{s=1} = 0$

15.34. Consider elastic scattering of two helium atoms in their ground state. Assume that we can describe them as impenetrable spheres, each of radius a. Designate by σ_{43}, σ_{33}, and σ_{44} the total cross section of (He^4, He^3), (He^3, He^3) and (He^4, He^4), respectively. (a) Using partial waves expansions, derive the three differential cross sections. (b) Prove that for $ka \ll 1$, the relations $\sigma_{43}:\sigma_{33}:\sigma_{44} = 1:1:4$ hold.

Ans. (a) $\tan\delta_l = \dfrac{j_l(ka)}{n_l(ka)}$ for $ka \ll 1 \to -\dfrac{(ka)^{2l+1}}{(2l+1)[(2l-1)!!]^2}$; $f_l \equiv \dfrac{2l+1}{k}e^{i\delta_l}\sin\delta_l$

$\dfrac{d\sigma_{43}}{d\Omega} = \left[\displaystyle\sum_{l=0}^{\infty}f_l P_l(\cos\theta)\right]^2$; $\dfrac{d\sigma_{33}}{d\Omega} = \left[\displaystyle\sum_{l=0,\,even}^{\infty}f_l P_l(\cos\theta)\right]^2 + 3\left[\displaystyle\sum_{l=1,\,odd}^{\infty}f_l P_l(\cos\theta)\right]^2$;

$\dfrac{d\sigma_{44}}{d\Omega} = 4\left[\displaystyle\sum_{l=0}^{\infty}f_l P_l(\cos\theta)\right]^2$

(b) $\sigma_{43} = 4\pi a^2$; $\sigma_{33} = 2\pi a^2[2 + 3(ka)^4]$; $\sigma_{44} = 16\pi a^2$

CHAPTER 16

Semiclassical Treatment of Radiation

16.1   The Interaction of Radiation with Atomic Systems

The classical Hamiltonian of a particle with mass m, charge e, and spin $\mathbf{S}$ in an external electromagnetic field is given by

$$H = \frac{1}{2m}\left(\mathbf{p} - \frac{e}{c}\mathbf{A}\right)^2 + V(\mathbf{r}) + e\phi - \frac{e}{mc}\mathbf{S}\cdot\mathcal{B} \tag{16.1}$$

where $\mathbf{A}$ is the vector potential, ϕ is the scalar potential, and $\mathcal{B} = \nabla \times \mathbf{A}$ is the magnetic field. It is possible to choose a gauge for which H will be simpler. The gauge generally employed in problems dealing with radiation is the *Coulomb gauge*. This gauge is also called the *radiation gauge* or the *transversal gauge*. In this gauge one chooses

$$\nabla\cdot\mathbf{A} = 0 \qquad \phi = 0 \tag{16.2}$$

Thus, the Hamiltonian obtained in this gauge is

$$\hat{H} = \left[\frac{\hat{\mathbf{p}}^2}{2m} + \hat{V}(\mathbf{r})\right] + \left[-\frac{e}{mc}\mathbf{A}\cdot\hat{\mathbf{p}} + \frac{e^2}{2mc^2}\mathbf{A}^2 - \frac{e}{mc}\hat{\mathbf{S}}\cdot\mathcal{B}\right] \tag{16.3}$$

with $\hat{H}_0$ as the unperturbed Hamiltonian (in the absence of an external field) and $\hat{H}'(t)$ as the perturbation Hamiltonian

$$\hat{H} = \hat{H}_0 + \hat{H}'$$

For a semiclassical treatment of the radiation we assume that the term A^2 is very small and negligible (see Problem 16.2). In this case,

$$\hat{H}'(t) = -\frac{e}{mc}\mathbf{A}\cdot\hat{\mathbf{p}} - \frac{e}{mc}\hat{\mathbf{S}}\cdot\mathcal{B} \tag{16.4}$$

This limit is called the *low intensity limit*.

16.2   Time-Dependent Perturbation Theory

In the low-intensity limit, $\hat{H}'(t)$ can be treated as a small time-dependent perturbation. If the system is initially in the state $|i\rangle$ and the perturbation is turned on at $t = 0$, the first-order amplitude for finding the system in the state $|f\rangle$ at time t is given by

$$a_{fi}^{(1)}(t) = \frac{1}{i\hbar}\int_0^t e^{i\omega_{fi}t'}\langle f|\hat{H}'(t')|i\rangle\,dt' \tag{16.5}$$

where $\hbar\omega_{fi} = E_f - E_i$. In a semiclassical treatment one usually assumes that the electromagnetic field $\mathbf{A}$ is described by a plane wave:

$$\mathbf{A}(\mathbf{r}, t) = 2|A_0|\boldsymbol{\varepsilon}\cos(\mathbf{k}\cdot\mathbf{r} - \omega t + \theta) = A_0\boldsymbol{\varepsilon}\exp[i(\mathbf{k}\cdot\mathbf{r} - \omega t)] + A_0^*\boldsymbol{\varepsilon}\exp[-i(\mathbf{k}\cdot\mathbf{r} - \omega t)] \quad (16.6)$$

where $A_0 = |A_0|e^{i\theta}$ is a complex number, $\boldsymbol{\varepsilon}$ is a unit vector in the direction of polarization, $\mathbf{k}$ is the wave or propagation vector, and $\boldsymbol{\varepsilon}\cdot\mathbf{k} = 0$ (transversal gauge). Therefore,

$$a_{fi}^{(1)}(t) = -\frac{e^{i(\omega_{fi}-\omega)t} - 1}{\omega_{fi} - \omega}\frac{T_{fi}^+}{\hbar} - \frac{e^{i(\omega_{fi}+\omega)t} - 1}{\omega_{fi} + \omega}\frac{T_{fi}^G}{\hbar} \quad (16.7)$$

where

$$\begin{cases} T_{fi}^+ \equiv -\dfrac{e}{mc}\langle f|e^{i\mathbf{k}\cdot\mathbf{r}}lA_0[\boldsymbol{\varepsilon}\cdot\hat{\mathbf{p}} + i\hat{\mathbf{S}}\cdot(\mathbf{k}\times\boldsymbol{\varepsilon})]|i\rangle \\[1.5em] T_{fi}^G \equiv -\dfrac{e}{mc}\langle f|e^{-i\mathbf{k}\cdot\mathbf{r}}A_0^*[\boldsymbol{\varepsilon}\cdot\hat{\mathbf{p}} - i\hat{\mathbf{S}}\cdot(\mathbf{k}\times\boldsymbol{\varepsilon})]|i\rangle \end{cases} \quad (16.8)$$

See Problem 16.4.

16.3   Transition Rate

Consider the transition amplitude $a_{fi}^{(1)}(t)$. A resonant transition is obtained when the frequency of the external radiation field is close to one of the characteristic frequencies of the unperturbed system, i.e., $\omega \approx \pm f_i$. In this case, one can neglect the interference term in Eq. (16.7) and distinguish between resonant absorption ($\omega_{fi} > 0$) and resonant emission ($\omega_{fi} < 0$). The transition probability is then given by

$$P_{fi} \cong \frac{|T_{fi}^+|}{\hbar^2}\left(\frac{\sin[(\omega_{fi} - \omega)t/2]}{(\omega_{fi} - \omega)/2}\right)^2 \qquad \omega_{fi} > 0 \quad (16.9)$$

(see Problem 16.4) and for induced emission:

$$P_{fi} \cong \frac{|T_{fi}^-|}{\hbar^2}\left(\frac{\sin[(\omega_{fi} - \omega)t/2]}{(\omega_{fi} + \omega)/2}\right)^2 \qquad \omega_{fi} < 0 \quad (16.10)$$

For a strictly monochromatic field, these transition probabilities depend strongly on the difference $\omega - |\omega_{fi}|$, and lead to a nonstationary transition rate. A transition probability that is linear in time (constant transition rate) is obtained if one considers the transition from an initial state $|i\rangle$ to a continuum of final states $|f\rangle$. In this case, the transition rate is obtained by using a *Fermi golden rule*:

$$W_{fi}^{\pm} = \frac{dP^{\pm}(t)}{dt} = \frac{2\pi}{\hbar}|\langle f|\hat{T}^{\pm}|i\rangle|^2\rho(E_f = E_i \pm \hbar\omega) \quad (16.11)$$

where $\rho(E_f)$ is the density of the final states. Similarly, when the radiation field is not monochromatic, but rather contains a spectrum of frequencies $u(\omega)$, the transition rate is

$$W_{fi} = \frac{4\pi^2 e^2}{m^2\hbar^2}\frac{u(\omega_{fi})}{\omega_{fi}^2}\langle f|e^{\pm i\mathbf{k}\cdot\mathbf{r}}[\boldsymbol{\varepsilon}\cdot\hat{\mathbf{p}} \pm i\hat{\mathbf{S}}\cdot(\mathbf{k}\times\boldsymbol{\varepsilon})]|i\rangle|^2 \quad (16.12)$$

where $|i\rangle$ and $|f\rangle$ are the initial and final (discrete) states, and the plus/minus signs correspond to absorption and induced emission, respectively.

16.4 Multipole Transitions

In the long wavelength approximation, $e^{\pm i\mathbf{k}\cdot\mathbf{r}} \approx 1 + i\mathbf{k}\cdot\mathbf{r} \cdots$ so $T_{fi}^{\pm}$ is given by the following multipole expansion:

$$T_{fi}^{\pm} \approx im\omega_{fi}\langle f|\,\boldsymbol{\varepsilon}\cdot\hat{\mathbf{r}}\,|i\rangle + \frac{i}{2}\langle f|\,(\hat{\mathbf{L}} + 2\hat{\mathbf{S}})\cdot(\mathbf{k}\times\boldsymbol{\varepsilon})|i\rangle - \frac{m\omega_{fi}}{2}\langle f|(\mathbf{k}\cdot\hat{\mathbf{r}})(\boldsymbol{\varepsilon}\cdot\hat{\mathbf{r}})|i\rangle \tag{16.13}$$

The first term in Eq. (16.13) corresponds to an *electric-dipole transition*. The second term corresponds to a *magnetic-dipole transition*, and the third term corresponds to an *electric-quadrupole transition*. Usually, the transition rate is dominated by the electric–dipole term; in this case the transition rate is

$$W_{fi} = \frac{4\pi^2 e^2}{\hbar^2} u(\omega_{fi})\,|\langle f|\,\boldsymbol{\varepsilon}\cdot\hat{\mathbf{r}}\,|i\rangle|^2 \tag{16.14}$$

However, for particular states $|i\rangle$ and $|f\rangle$, $\langle f|\,\boldsymbol{\varepsilon}\cdot\hat{\mathbf{r}}\,|i\rangle$ may vanish. This state is called the *forbidden transition*. Note that for an isotropic external radiation field, the polarization vector $\boldsymbol{\varepsilon}$ is randomly oriented. Averaging the components of the unit vector $\boldsymbol{\varepsilon}$ over all angles gives

$$W_{fi} = \frac{4\pi^2 e^2}{3\hbar^2} u(\omega_{fi})\,|\langle f|\,\hat{\mathbf{r}}\,|i\rangle|^2 \equiv B_{fi}u(u_{fi}) \tag{16.15}$$

B_{fi} are known as the *Einstein coefficients for absorption and induced emission.*

16.5 Spontaneous Emission

An excited atomic system can also emit radiation in the absence of an external radiation field. The transition rate for a spontaneous transition, in the dipole approximation, is given by

$$W_{fi}^{\text{spon}} = \frac{4}{3}\frac{e^2}{\hbar}\frac{\omega_{fi}^3}{c^3}\,|\langle f|\,\hat{\mathbf{r}}\,|i\rangle|^2 \equiv A_{fi} \tag{16.16}$$

where A_{fi} is the *Einstein coefficient for spontaneous emission.*

SOLVED PROBLEMS

16.1. The motion of a charged particle in an external electromagnetic field is described by the classical Hamiltonian

$$H = \frac{1}{2m}\left(\mathbf{p} - \frac{e}{c}\mathbf{A}\right)^2 + V(\mathbf{r}) + e\phi \tag{16.1.1}$$

where $\mathbf{A}(r, t)$ and $\phi(r, t)$ are the electromagnetic potentials, e is the charge, and c is the speed of light. Show that the time-dependent Schrödinger equation $i\hbar\dfrac{\partial\psi}{\partial t} = \hat{H}\psi$ is invariant under the following gauge transformation:

$$\begin{cases} \mathbf{A} \to \mathbf{A}' = \mathbf{A} + \nabla\chi(\mathbf{r}, t) \\[2mm] \phi \to \phi' = \phi - \dfrac{1}{c}\dfrac{\partial\chi}{\partial t} \\[2mm] \psi \to \psi' = e^{ie\chi(r,t)/\hbar c}\psi \end{cases} \tag{16.1.2}$$

SOLUTION

Under the gauge transformation of Eq. (16.1.2), the Schrödinger equation $i\hbar \dfrac{\partial \psi'}{\partial t} = \hat{H}'\psi'$, takes the form

$$i\hbar \frac{\partial}{\partial t}(\hat{T}\psi) = \left[\frac{1}{2m}\left(\hat{\mathbf{p}} - \frac{e}{c}\mathbf{A}'\right)^2 + \hat{V}(\mathbf{r}) + e\phi'(r,t)\right]\hat{T}\psi$$

$$= \left[\frac{1}{2m}\left(\hat{\mathbf{p}} - \frac{e}{c}\mathbf{A} - \frac{e}{c}\nabla\chi\right)^2 + \hat{V}(\mathbf{r}) + e\phi - \frac{e}{c}\frac{\partial\chi}{\partial t}\right]\hat{T}\psi \qquad (16.1.3)$$

However,

$$\frac{\partial\psi'}{\partial t} = \frac{\partial}{\partial t}(\hat{T}\psi) = \hat{T}\left(\frac{\partial\psi}{\partial t} + \frac{ie}{\hbar c}\psi\frac{\partial\chi}{\partial t}\right) \qquad (16.1.4)$$

and

$$\hat{\mathbf{p}}(\hat{T}\psi) = -i\hbar\nabla(T\psi) = \hat{T}\left(\hat{\mathbf{p}}\psi + \frac{e}{c}\psi\nabla\chi\right) \qquad (16.1.5)$$

Therefore, the right-hand side of Eq. (16.1.3) equals

$$\frac{1}{2m}\left(\hat{\mathbf{p}} - \frac{e}{c}\mathbf{A} - \frac{e}{c}\nabla\chi\right)\cdot\hat{T}\left(\hat{\mathbf{p}} - \frac{e}{c}\mathbf{A}\right)\psi + \hat{T}\left[\hat{V}(\mathbf{r}) + e\phi - \frac{e}{c}\frac{\partial\chi}{\partial t}\right]\psi$$

$$= \hat{T}\left\{\frac{1}{2m}\left(\hat{\mathbf{p}} - \frac{e}{c}\mathbf{A}\right)^2 + \hat{V}(\mathbf{r}) + e\phi - \frac{e}{c}\frac{\partial\chi}{\partial t}\right\}\psi \qquad (16.1.6)$$

and consequently, expression (16.1.3) reduces to

$$\hat{T}\left(i\hbar\frac{\partial}{\partial t} - \frac{e}{c}\frac{\partial\chi}{\partial t}\right)\psi = \hat{T}\left(\hat{H} - \frac{\partial\chi}{\partial t}\right)\psi \qquad (16.1.7)$$

Multiplying Eq. (16.1.7) on the left by $\hat{T}^\dagger$ we obtain $i\hbar\dfrac{\partial\psi}{\partial t} = \hat{H}\psi$, which is the Schrödinger equation in the original gauge.

16.2. An atomic electron with mass m, charge e, and spin $\mathbf{S}$ interacts with an external radiation field described by the vector potential $\mathbf{A}(r,t)$. The Hamiltonian of the system is

$$\hat{H} = \hat{H}_0 + \hat{H}'(t) \qquad (16.2.1)$$

where $\hat{H}_0 = \hat{p}^2/2m + \hat{V}(\mathbf{r})$ is the "atomic" Hamiltonian, and $\hat{H}'(t)$ is the time-dependent remaining interaction. (*a*) Show that the interaction Hamiltonian can be written as

$$\hat{H}'(t) = -\frac{e}{mc}\mathbf{A}\cdot\hat{\mathbf{p}} + \frac{e^2}{2mc^2}\mathbf{A}^2 - \frac{e}{mc}\hat{\mathbf{S}}\cdot\mathcal{B} \qquad (16.2.2)$$

where $\nabla\cdot\mathbf{A} = 0$, $\phi = 0$, and $\mathcal{B} = \nabla\times\mathbf{A}$. (*b*) Consider the low-intensity limit and estimate the relative magnitudes of the various interaction terms.

SOLUTION

(*a*) The Hamiltonian of the electron in an external electromagnetic field is

$$\hat{H} = \frac{1}{2m}\left(\hat{\mathbf{p}} - \frac{e}{c}\mathbf{A}\right)^2 + V(\mathbf{r}) + e\phi - \frac{e}{mc}\hat{\mathbf{S}}\cdot\mathcal{B} \qquad (16.2.3)$$

where $V(\mathbf{r})$ is the binding potential of the nucleus, $(\phi, \mathbf{A})$ are the scalar and vector electromagnetic potentials, and $\mathcal{B} = \nabla \times \mathbf{A}$ is the magnetic field. Equation (16.2.3) leads to

$$\hat{H} = \frac{\hat{\mathbf{p}}^2}{2m} - \frac{e}{2mc}(\hat{\mathbf{p}} \cdot \mathbf{A} + \mathbf{A} \cdot \hat{\mathbf{p}}) + \frac{e^2}{2mc^2}\mathbf{A}^2 + V(\mathbf{r}) + e\phi - \frac{e}{mc}\hat{\mathbf{S}} \cdot \mathcal{B}$$

$$= \hat{H}_0 + e\phi - \frac{e}{2mc}(\hat{\mathbf{p}} \cdot \mathbf{A} + \mathbf{A} \cdot \hat{\mathbf{p}}) + \frac{e^2}{2mc^2}\mathbf{A}^2 - \frac{e}{mc}\hat{\mathbf{S}} \cdot \mathcal{B} \tag{16.2.4}$$

This expression is further simplified if we choose the gauge $\nabla \cdot \mathbf{A} = 0$ and $\phi = 0$ (the transversal gauge). Taking into account that $\hat{\mathbf{p}} = -i\hbar\nabla$, and operating with $(\hat{\mathbf{p}} \cdot \mathbf{A})$ on an arbitrary function $\psi(\mathbf{r})$, we find

$$(\hat{\mathbf{p}} \cdot \mathbf{A})\psi(\mathbf{r}) = -i\hbar \sum_{\alpha=1}^{3} \frac{\partial}{\partial x^\alpha} A_\alpha(\mathbf{r})\psi(\mathbf{r}) = -i\hbar \sum_{\alpha}^{3} \left[\left(\frac{\partial}{\partial x^\alpha} A_\alpha \right)\psi + A_\alpha \frac{\partial}{\partial x^\alpha} \psi \right]$$

$$= -i\hbar(\nabla \cdot \mathbf{A})\psi + \mathbf{A} \cdot \hat{\mathbf{p}}\psi = \mathbf{A} \cdot \hat{\mathbf{p}}\psi(\mathbf{r}) \tag{16.2.5}$$

Therefore,

$$\hat{H} = \hat{H}_0 + \hat{H}'(t) = \hat{H}_0 - \frac{e}{mc}\mathbf{A} \cdot \hat{\mathbf{p}} + \frac{e^2}{2mc^2}\mathbf{A}^2 - \frac{e}{mc}\hat{\mathbf{S}} \cdot \mathcal{B} \tag{16.2.6}$$

where $\hat{H}_0$ is the unperturbed "atomic" Hamiltonian and $\hat{H}'(t)$ is the time-dependent interaction.

(b) Consider, for example, a hydrogen-like atom interacting with a monochromatic radiation field of angular frequency $\omega = ck$. In this case, the magnitude of each term in Eq. (16.2.6) can be approximated by its root-mean-square value in a given unperturbed stationary state of $\hat{H}_0$. Let us define the following root-mean-square values:

$$\begin{cases} A \equiv \sqrt{\langle\psi|\hat{\mathbf{A}} \cdot \hat{\mathbf{A}}|\psi\rangle} \\ p \equiv \sqrt{\langle\psi|\hat{\mathbf{p}} \cdot \hat{\mathbf{p}}|\psi\rangle} \end{cases} \tag{16.2.7}$$

and examine the relative magnitudes of the three interaction terms of Eq. (16.2.6):

$$\begin{cases} \hat{H}_1' = -\frac{e}{mc}\mathbf{A}(\mathbf{r}, t) \cdot \hat{\mathbf{p}} \\ \hat{H}_2' = \frac{e^2}{2mc^2}\mathbf{A}^2(\mathbf{r}, t) \\ \hat{H}_s' = -\frac{e}{mc}\hat{\mathbf{S}} \cdot \mathcal{B}(\mathbf{r}, t) \end{cases} \tag{16.2.8}$$

where $|\psi\rangle$ is an eigenstate of $\hat{H}_0$ for which $A \neq 0$ and $p \neq 0$. Consider, first the ratio $\hat{H}_2'/\hat{H}_1'$:

$$\frac{\hat{H}_2'}{\hat{H}_1'} \approx \frac{e^2 A^2}{eAcp} \approx \frac{eAp/mc}{p^2/m} \approx \frac{H_1'}{\hat{H}_0} \tag{16.2.9}$$

In the low-intensity limit $\hat{H}_1'/\hat{H}_0'$ is a small perturbation. Consequently, the ratio $\hat{H}_2'/\hat{H}_1'$ is also small. Note that in the high-intensity limit, where the radiation is of the order of the atomic field, $\hat{H}_2'$ can become as large as $\hat{H}_1'$. Consider now the ratio $\hat{H}_s'/\hat{H}_1'$. Since $\mathcal{B} = \nabla \times \mathbf{A} \approx kA$, we obtain

$$\frac{\hat{H}_s'}{\hat{H}_1'} \approx \frac{\hbar B}{Ap} \approx \frac{\hbar kA}{Ap} \approx \frac{\hbar}{p\lambda} \tag{16.2.10}$$

Due to the uncertainty relation, $\hbar/p$ is of the order of the Bohr radius (for hydrogen, $a_0 = 0.5$ Å) and for optical sources $\lambda \cong 5000$ Å. Therefore $\hat{H}_s'/\hat{H}_1' \approx 10^{-4} \ll 1$.

Note: The results of Eqs. (16.2.9) and (16.2.10) suggest that $\hat{H}_2'$ and $\hat{H}_s'$ can be neglected in the low-intensity limit. This conclusion does not hold in the following situations:

1. *Forbidden transitions* where the dipole matrix element of $\hat{H}_1'$ vanishes and $\hat{H}_1'$ is reduced to the same order of magnitude as $\hat{H}_s'$.
2. *Strictly forbidden transitions* where the matrix element of $\hat{H}_1'$ vanishes identically.

16.3. A monochromatic radiation field of angular frequency $\omega = ck$ is described by the following vector potential:

$$\mathbf{A}(\mathbf{r}, t) = 2\,|\mathbf{A}_0|\cos(\mathbf{k}\cdot\mathbf{r} - \omega t + \theta)$$

$$= \mathbf{A}_0 \exp[i(\mathbf{k}\cdot\mathbf{r} - \omega t)] + \mathbf{A}_0^* \exp[-i(\mathbf{k}\cdot\mathbf{r} - \omega t)] \qquad (16.3.1)$$

where $\mathbf{A}_0 = |\mathbf{A}_0|\,e^{i\theta}$ is the complex polarization vector, $\mathbf{k}$ is the wave vector, and $\mathbf{A}_0\cdot\mathbf{k} = 0$. (a) Calculate the electric field $\mathcal{E}(\mathbf{r}, t)$ and the magnetic field $\mathcal{B}(\mathbf{r}, t)$ associated with the potential $\mathbf{A}(\mathbf{r}, t)$. (b) Find the Poynting vector $\mathcal{S} = \dfrac{c}{4\pi}\mathcal{E}\times\mathcal{B}$, and verify the relation

$$u = \frac{I}{c} = \frac{\omega^2}{2\pi c^2}\,|\mathbf{A}_0|^2 \qquad (16.3.2)$$

where I is the irradiance of the radiation and u is the energy density.

SOLUTION

(a) The electric field $\mathcal{E} = -\dfrac{1}{c}\dfrac{\partial \mathbf{A}}{\partial t}$ is given by

$$\mathcal{E}(\mathbf{r}, t) = \frac{i\omega}{c}\mathbf{A}_0 \exp[i(\mathbf{k}\cdot\mathbf{r} - \omega t)] - \frac{i\omega}{c}\mathbf{A}_0^* \exp[-i(\mathbf{k}\cdot\mathbf{r} - \omega t)]$$

$$= ik\mathbf{A}_0 \exp[i(\mathbf{k}\cdot\mathbf{r} - \omega t)] - ik\mathbf{A}_0^* \exp[-i(\mathbf{k}\cdot\mathbf{r} - \omega t)]$$

$$= -2k|\mathbf{A}_0|\sin(\mathbf{k}\cdot\mathbf{r} - \omega t + \theta) \qquad (16.3.3)$$

The magnetic field $\mathcal{B} = \nabla\times\mathbf{A}$ is given by

$$\mathcal{B}(\mathbf{r}, t) = i\mathbf{k}\times\mathbf{A}_0 \exp[i(\mathbf{k}\cdot\mathbf{r} - \omega t)] - i\mathbf{k}\times\mathbf{A}_0^* \exp[-i(\mathbf{k}\cdot\mathbf{r} - \omega t)]$$

$$= -2\mathbf{k}\times|\mathbf{A}_0|\sin(\mathbf{k}\cdot\mathbf{r} - \omega t + \theta) \qquad (16.3.4)$$

(b) The intensity of the radiation field is found by averaging the Poynting vector $\mathcal{S} = \dfrac{c}{4\pi}\mathcal{E}\times\mathcal{B}$ over time. Using Eqs. (16.3.3) and (16.3.4) we find

$$\mathcal{S} = \frac{c}{\pi}k|\mathbf{A}_0|\times(\mathbf{k}\times|\mathbf{A}_0|)\sin^2(\mathbf{k}\cdot\mathbf{r} - \omega t + \theta)$$

$$= \frac{\omega}{\pi}\sin^2(\mathbf{k}\cdot\mathbf{r} - \omega t + \theta)|\mathbf{A}_0|^2\,\mathbf{k} \qquad (16.3.5)$$

Thus, after averaging $\mathcal{S}(\mathbf{r}, t)$ over one oscillation period,

$$I = |\overline{\mathcal{S}}| = \frac{\omega^2}{\pi c}|\mathbf{A}_0|^2\,\overline{\sin^2(\mathbf{k}\cdot\mathbf{r} - \omega t + \theta)} = \frac{\omega^2}{2\pi c}|\mathbf{A}_0|^2 \qquad (16.3.6)$$

where $\overline{\sin^2(\mathbf{k}\cdot\mathbf{r} - \omega t + \theta)} = 1/2$. Similarly, the mean energy density averaged over time is

$$u = \frac{1}{4\pi}\overline{(\mathcal{E}^2 + \mathcal{B}^2)} = \frac{1}{2\pi}[k^2|\mathbf{A}_0|^2 + (\mathbf{k}\times\mathbf{A}_0)\cdot(\mathbf{k}\times\mathbf{A}_0^*)] = \frac{\omega^2}{2\pi c^2}|\mathbf{A}_0|^2 \qquad (16.3.7)$$

Indeed, from Eqs. (16.3.6) and (16.3.7) we recover Eq. (16.3.2):

$$u = \frac{I}{c} = \frac{\omega^2}{2\pi c^2} |\mathbf{A}_0|^2 \qquad (16.3.8)$$

where $|\mathbf{A}_0|^2 = \mathbf{A}_0 \mathbf{A}_0^*$.

Note: Following from the definition of the Poynting vector as the energy density flux of the radiation, the irradiance I is the energy per unit area per unit time, which propagates along the $\mathbf{k}$ direction. This quantity can also be associated with the number of *photons* (i.e., the number of *quanta* or photons with energy $\hbar\omega$), which propagate along the $\mathbf{k}$ direction. Using Eq. (16.3.6), we find that the flux of photons (i.e., the number of photons per unit area per unit time) is given by

$$F \equiv \frac{I}{\hbar\omega} = \frac{\omega}{2\pi\hbar c} |\mathbf{A}_0|^2 \qquad (16.3.9)$$

16.4. An atomic electron of mass m, charge $e = -|e|$, and spin $\hat{\mathbf{S}}$ interacts with a monochromatic radiation field of angular frequency $\omega = ck$. The Hamiltonian of the system is

$$\hat{H} = \hat{H}_0 + \hat{H}'(t) = \hat{H}_0 - \frac{e}{mc}\mathbf{A}\cdot\hat{\mathbf{p}} - \frac{e}{mc}(\nabla \times \mathbf{A})\cdot\hat{\mathbf{S}} \qquad (16.4.1)$$

where $\hat{H}'(t)$ is a small perturbation (the low-intensity limit). The vector potential $\mathbf{A}(\mathbf{r}, t)$ is given by the following plane wave:

$$\mathbf{A}(\mathbf{r}, t) = 2|A_0|\boldsymbol{\varepsilon}\cos(\mathbf{k}\cdot\mathbf{r} - \omega t + \theta)$$

$$= A_0\boldsymbol{\varepsilon}\exp[i(\mathbf{k}\cdot\mathbf{r} - \omega t)] + A_0^*\boldsymbol{\varepsilon}\exp[-i(\mathbf{k}\cdot\mathbf{r} - \omega t)] \qquad (16.4.2)$$

where $A_0 = |A_0|e^{i\theta}$ is a complex number, $\boldsymbol{\varepsilon}$ is a unit vector in the direction of polarization, $\mathbf{k}$ is the wave vector, and $\boldsymbol{\varepsilon}\cdot\mathbf{k} = 0$ (transversal gauge). Let $|i\rangle$ and $|f\rangle$ be two eigenstates of the unperturbed Hamiltonian $\hat{H}_0$, which correspond to the energy levels E_i and E_f, respectively ($E_i \neq E_f$). Assuming that the perturbation $\hat{H}(t)$ is turned on at $t = 0$, calculate the probability $P_{fi}(t)$ for resonant transition $|i\rangle \to |f\rangle$.

SOLUTION

We consider the Hamiltonian in Eq. (16.4.1), and treat $\hat{H}'(t)$ as a small time-dependent perturbation. If the system is initially in the state $|i\rangle$ and the perturbation is turned on at $t = 0$, the first-order amplitude for finding the system in state $|f\rangle$ at $t > 0$ is given by

$$a_{fi}^{(1)}(t) = \frac{1}{i\hbar}\int_0^t e^{\omega_{fi}it'}\langle f|\hat{H}'(t')|i\rangle\,dt' = \frac{ie}{mc\hbar}\int_0^t e^{i\omega_{fi}t'}\langle f|\mathbf{A}(\mathbf{r}, t)\cdot\hat{\mathbf{p}} + \hat{\mathbf{S}}\cdot[\nabla \times \mathbf{A}(\mathbf{r}, t)]|i\rangle\,dt' \qquad (16.4.3)$$

with $\hbar\omega_{fi} \equiv E_f - E_i$ (see Chap. 10). Substituting $\mathbf{A}(\mathbf{r}, t)$ from Eq. (16.4.2), and integrating over dt' we obtain

$$a_{fi}^{(1)}(t) = \frac{ie}{mc\hbar}\int_0^t \left\{ e^{i(\omega_{fi} - \omega)t'}\langle f|A_0 e^{i\mathbf{k}\cdot\mathbf{r}}[\boldsymbol{\varepsilon}\cdot\hat{\mathbf{p}} + i\hat{\mathbf{S}}\cdot(\mathbf{k}\times\boldsymbol{\varepsilon})]|i\rangle \right.$$

$$\left. + e^{i(\omega_{fi} + \omega)t'}\langle f|A_0^* e^{-i\mathbf{k}\cdot\mathbf{r}}[\boldsymbol{\varepsilon}\cdot\hat{\mathbf{p}} - i\hat{\mathbf{S}}\cdot(\mathbf{k}\times\boldsymbol{\varepsilon})]|i\rangle \right\}dt' \qquad (16.4.4)$$

Therefore,

$$a_{fi}^{(1)}(t) = -\frac{e^{i(\omega_{fi} - \omega)t} - 1}{\omega_{fi} - \omega}\frac{T_{fi}^+}{\hbar} - \frac{e^{i(\omega_{fi} + \omega)t} - 1}{\omega_{fi} + \omega}\frac{T_{fi}^-}{\hbar} \qquad (16.4.5)$$

where we define

$$\begin{cases} T_{fi}^+ \equiv -\dfrac{e}{mc}\langle f|e^{i\mathbf{k}\cdot\mathbf{r}}A_0[\boldsymbol{\varepsilon}\cdot\hat{\mathbf{p}} + i\hat{\mathbf{S}}\cdot(\mathbf{k}\times\boldsymbol{\varepsilon})]|i\rangle \\[2mm] T_{fi}^- \equiv -\dfrac{e}{mc}\langle f|e^{-i\mathbf{k}\cdot\mathbf{r}}A_0^*[\boldsymbol{\varepsilon}\cdot\hat{\mathbf{p}} - i\hat{\mathbf{S}}\cdot(\mathbf{k}\times\boldsymbol{\varepsilon})]|i\rangle \end{cases} \qquad (16.4.6)$$

Equation (16.4.5) contains time-factors of the form (see Fig. 16.1)

$$\frac{e^{i(\omega_{fi}\pm\omega)t}-1}{\omega_{fi}\pm\omega}=ie^{i(\omega_{fi}\pm\omega)/2}\frac{\sin[(\omega_{fi}\pm\omega)t/2]}{(\omega_{fi}+\omega)/2}\tag{16.4.7}$$

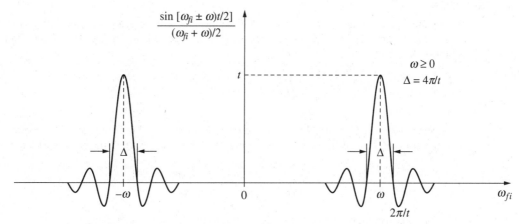

Fig. 16.1

Consequently, the transition probability $P_{fi}(t)=|a_{fi}^{(1)}(t)|^2$ is appreciable only if $|\omega-\omega_{fi}|<4\pi/t\equiv\Delta$ (or if $|\omega+\omega_{fi}|<\Delta$). In this case, and for $\Delta\ll2|\omega_{fi}|$, one can neglect the interference term of $P_{fi}(t)$ and distinguish between two resonant transitions:

Absorption ($\omega_{fi}>0$):

$$P_{fi}(t)\cong\frac{|T_{fi}^+|^2}{\hbar^2}\left(\frac{\sin[(\omega_{fi}-\omega)t/2]}{(\omega_{fi}-\omega)/2}\right)^2\tag{16.4.8}$$

Induced emission ($\omega_{fi}<0$):

$$P_{fi}(t)\cong\frac{|T_{fi}^-|^2}{\hbar^2}\left(\frac{\sin[(\omega_{fi}+\omega)t/2]}{(\omega_{fi}+\omega)/2}\right)^2\tag{16.4.9}$$

Note: It is worthwhile to emphasize that the resonance approximations in Eqs. (16.4.8) and (16.4.9) are only valid under two conditions:

1. $P_{fi}(t)\ll1$ (applicability of first-order perturbation theory).

2. $\dfrac{2\pi}{t}\ll|\omega_{fi}|\approx\omega$ (no interference term in $P_{fi}(t)$).

These conditions are compatible if

$$|T_{fi}^\pm|\ll\hbar\omega_{fi}$$

16.5. A bounded spinless particle of mass m and charge e interacts with a nonmonochromatic field of radiation that covers a spread of incoherent frequencies in the range $\omega\pm\delta\omega/2$. The particle is described by the Hamiltonian $\hat{H}_0=\hat{p}^2/2m+\hat{V}(\mathbf{r})$ and the irradiance of the radiation is given by $I=cu(\omega)\delta\omega$, where $u(\omega)$ is the energy density per unit angular frequency (see Problem 16.3). Consider the transition probability $P_{fi}(t)$, where $|i\rangle$ and $|f\rangle$ are two eigenstates of the unperturbed Hamiltonian $\hat{H}_0$. (a) Show that the transition rates, for absorption and for induced emission, are given by

$$W_{fi}^{abs}=\frac{4\pi^2e^2}{m^2\hbar^2}\frac{u(\omega_{fi})}{\omega_{fi}^2}|\langle f|e^{+i\mathbf{k}\cdot\mathbf{r}}\boldsymbol{\varepsilon}\cdot\hat{\mathbf{p}}|i\rangle|^2\qquad\text{for }E_f>E_i\tag{16.5.1}$$

$$W_{if}^{ind}=\frac{4\pi^2e^2}{m^2\hbar^2}\frac{u(\omega_{if})}{\omega_{fi}^2}|\langle f|e^{-i\mathbf{k}\cdot\mathbf{r}}\boldsymbol{\varepsilon}\cdot\hat{\mathbf{p}}|i\rangle|^2\qquad\text{for }E_f>E_i\tag{16.5.2}$$

where $\hbar\omega_{fi} \equiv E_f - E_i$, and $|\mathbf{k}| = |\omega_{fi}|/c$. (b) Assume that $E_f > E_i$, and verify the principle of detailed balance:

$$W_{fi}^{abs} = W_{if}^{ind} \tag{16.5.3}$$

SOLUTION

(a) We assume that the radiation covers a spread of frequencies with no phase relation between different frequency components. Treating each frequency component separately and using the results of Problem 16.4 we obtain

$$\delta P_{fi}^{\pm}(t) = \frac{e^2 |A_0|^2}{m^2 c^2 \hbar^2} \left| \langle f | e^{\pm i\mathbf{k}\cdot\mathbf{r}} \boldsymbol{\varepsilon} \cdot \hat{\mathbf{p}} | i \rangle \right|^2 \left(\frac{\sin\left[(\omega_{fi} \pm \omega)t/2\right]}{(\omega_{fi} \pm \omega)/2} \right)^2 \tag{16.5.4}$$

where the plus/minus signs of $\delta P_{fi}^{\pm}(t)$ correspond to absorption and induced emission, respectively. The total transition $P_{fi}^{\pm}(t)$ is then found by replacing $|A_0|^2$ in Eq. (16.5.4) by the relation in Eq. (16.3.2):

$$|A_0|^2 = \frac{2\pi c^2 I}{\omega^2} = \frac{2\pi c^2 u(\omega)\,\delta\omega}{\omega^2} \tag{16.5.5}$$

and summing over all the incoherent frequencies in the range $\omega \pm \delta\omega$. Thus,

$$P_{fi}^{\pm}(t) = \frac{2\pi e^2}{m^2 \hbar^2} \sum_{\delta\omega} \frac{u(\omega_{if})\,\delta\omega}{\omega^2} \left| \langle f | e^{\pm i\mathbf{k}\cdot\mathbf{r}} \boldsymbol{\varepsilon} \cdot \hat{\mathbf{p}} | i \rangle \right|^2 \left(\frac{\sin\left[(\omega_{fi} \pm \omega)t/2\right]}{(\omega_{fi} \pm \omega)/2} \right)^2 \tag{16.5.6}$$

where $|\mathbf{k}| = \omega/c$. The time factor in Eq. (16.5.6) has a sharp peak at $\omega = \pm\omega_{fi}$. Therefore, we can replace the summation over $\delta\omega$ by an integral and extend the limits of integration to $\pm\infty$. This gives

$$P_{fi}^{\pm}(t) = \frac{2\pi e^2}{m^2 \hbar^2} \int_{-\infty}^{\infty} \frac{u(\omega)}{\omega^2} \left| \langle f | e^{\pm i\mathbf{k}\cdot\mathbf{r}} \boldsymbol{\varepsilon} \cdot \hat{\mathbf{p}} | i \rangle \right|^2 \left(\frac{\sin\left[(\omega_{fi} \pm \omega)t/2\right]}{(\omega_{fi} \pm \omega)/2} \right)^2 d\omega \tag{16.5.7}$$

The last term in Eq. (16.5.7) can now be replaced by $\pi t \delta\left[(\omega_{fi} \pm \omega)/2\right]$. Hence,

$$P_{fi}^{\pm}(t) = \frac{4\pi^2 e^2 t}{m^2 \hbar^2} \int_{-\infty}^{\infty} \frac{u(\omega)}{\omega^2} \left| \langle f | e^{\pm i\mathbf{k}\cdot\mathbf{r}} \boldsymbol{\varepsilon} \cdot \hat{\mathbf{p}} | i \rangle \right|^2 \delta(\omega_{fi} \pm \omega)\,d\omega \tag{16.5.8}$$

Finally, the transition rates, $W_{fi}^{\pm}(t) \equiv dP_{fi}^{\pm}(t)/dt$, are given by

$$W_{fi}^{abs} = \frac{dP_{fi}^{+}(t)}{dt} = \frac{4\pi^2 e^2}{m^2 \hbar^2} \frac{u(\omega_{fi})}{\omega_{fi}^2} \left| \langle f | e^{+i\mathbf{k}\cdot\mathbf{r}} \boldsymbol{\varepsilon} \cdot \hat{\mathbf{p}} | i \rangle \right|^2 \qquad \text{for } \omega_{fi} > 0 \tag{16.5.9}$$

$$W_{if}^{ind} = \frac{dP_{fi}^{-}(t)}{dt} = \frac{4\pi^2 e^2}{m^2 \hbar^2} \frac{u(\omega_{if})}{\omega_{fi}^2} \left| \langle f | e^{-i\mathbf{k}\cdot\mathbf{r}} \boldsymbol{\varepsilon} \cdot \hat{\mathbf{p}} | i \rangle \right|^2 \qquad \text{for } \omega_{fi} < 0 \tag{16.5.10}$$

where $\hbar\omega_{fi} \equiv E_f - E_i$ and $|\mathbf{k}| = |\omega_{fi}|/c$.

(b) We consider the transitions $|i\rangle \leftrightarrow |f\rangle$, where $E_f > E_i$. Using expressions (16.5.1) and (16.5.2),

$$W_{fi}^{abs} = \frac{4\pi^2 e^2}{m^2 \hbar^2} \frac{u(\omega_{fi})}{\omega_{fi}^2} \left| \langle f | e^{i\mathbf{k}\cdot\mathbf{r}} \boldsymbol{\varepsilon} \cdot \hat{\mathbf{p}} | i \rangle \right|^2 \tag{16.5.11}$$

$$W_{if}^{ind} = \frac{4\pi^2 e^2}{m^2 \hbar^2} \frac{u(\omega_{fi})}{\omega_{fi}^2} \left| \langle i | e^{-i\mathbf{k}\cdot\mathbf{r}} \boldsymbol{\varepsilon} \cdot \hat{\mathbf{p}} | f \rangle \right|^2 \tag{16.5.12}$$

The matrix element in Eq. (16.5.12) can now be written as

$$\langle i|e^{-i\mathbf{k}\cdot\mathbf{r}}\boldsymbol{\varepsilon}\cdot\hat{\mathbf{p}}|f\rangle = \langle f|[(e^{-i\mathbf{k}\cdot\mathbf{r}})(\boldsymbol{\varepsilon}\cdot\hat{\mathbf{p}})]^{\dagger}|i\rangle^{*} = \langle f|(\boldsymbol{\varepsilon}\cdot\hat{\mathbf{p}})(e^{-i\mathbf{k}\cdot\mathbf{r}})^{\dagger}|i\rangle \tag{16.5.13}$$

where $\dagger$ denotes the Hermitian conjugate operator. However, $\mathbf{k}\cdot\boldsymbol{\varepsilon} = 0$ and consequently $[\boldsymbol{\varepsilon}\cdot\hat{\mathbf{p}}, e^{\pm i\mathbf{k}\cdot\mathbf{r}}] = 0$. Hence,

$$\langle f|(\boldsymbol{\varepsilon}\cdot\hat{\mathbf{p}})(e^{-i\mathbf{k}\cdot\mathbf{r}})^{\dagger}|i\rangle^{*} = \langle f|\boldsymbol{\varepsilon}\cdot\hat{\mathbf{p}}\,e^{i\mathbf{k}\cdot\mathbf{r}}|i\rangle^{*} = \langle f|e^{i\mathbf{k}\cdot\mathbf{r}}\boldsymbol{\varepsilon}\cdot\hat{\mathbf{p}}|i\rangle^{*} \tag{16.5.14}$$

where $[e^{\pm i\mathbf{k}\cdot\mathbf{r}}]^{\dagger} = e^{\pm i\mathbf{k}\cdot\mathbf{r}}$ has been used. Finally, we obtain

$$\langle i|e^{-i\mathbf{k}\cdot\mathbf{r}}\boldsymbol{\varepsilon}\cdot\hat{\mathbf{p}}|f\rangle = \langle f|e^{i\mathbf{k}\cdot\mathbf{r}}\boldsymbol{\varepsilon}\cdot\hat{\mathbf{p}}|i\rangle^{*} \tag{16.5.15}$$

Therefore, $W_{fi}^{abs} = W_{if}^{ind}$.

16.6. Consider the matrix element $T_{fi}^{\pm} \equiv \langle f|e^{i\mathbf{k}\cdot\mathbf{r}}[\boldsymbol{\varepsilon}\cdot\hat{\mathbf{p}} + i\hat{\mathbf{S}}\cdot(\mathbf{k}\times\boldsymbol{\varepsilon})]|i\rangle$, for a one-electron system in a linearly polarized radiation field. Prove that in the long wavelength approximation, $T_{fi}^{\pm}$ is given by the following multipole expansion:

$$T_{fi}^{\pm} \approx im\omega_{fi}\langle f|\boldsymbol{\varepsilon}\cdot\mathbf{r}|i\rangle + \frac{i}{2}\langle f|(\hat{\mathbf{L}} + 2\hat{\mathbf{S}})\cdot(\mathbf{k}\times\boldsymbol{\varepsilon})|i\rangle - \frac{m\omega_{fi}}{2}\langle f|(\mathbf{k}\cdot\hat{\mathbf{r}})(\boldsymbol{\varepsilon}\cdot\hat{\mathbf{r}})|i\rangle \tag{16.6.1}$$

where $\boldsymbol{\varepsilon}$ is the unit polarization vector, $\mathbf{k}$ is the wave or propagation vector, and $\mathbf{L} = \mathbf{r}\times\mathbf{p}$ is the orbital angular momentum. The three terms in Eq. (16.6.1) correspond to electric-dipole, magnetic-dipole, and electric-quadrupole transitions.

SOLUTION

In the long wavelength limit, $\exp(i\mathbf{k}\cdot\mathbf{r}) = 1 + i\mathbf{k}\cdot\mathbf{r} + \cdots$. Therefore,

$$T_{fi}^{\pm} \approx \langle f|\boldsymbol{\varepsilon}\cdot\hat{\mathbf{p}}|i\rangle + i\langle f|\hat{\mathbf{S}}\cdot(\mathbf{k}\times\boldsymbol{\varepsilon})|i\rangle + i\langle f|(\mathbf{k}\cdot\mathbf{r})(\boldsymbol{\varepsilon}\cdot\hat{\mathbf{p}})|i\rangle \tag{16.6.2}$$

However, $\mathbf{k}\cdot\boldsymbol{\varepsilon} = 0$, so that $\mathbf{k}\cdot\mathbf{r}$ and $\boldsymbol{\varepsilon}\cdot\hat{\mathbf{p}}$ are commuting operators that satisfy the relation

$$(\mathbf{r}\times\hat{\mathbf{p}})\cdot(\mathbf{k}\times\boldsymbol{\varepsilon}) = (\mathbf{k}\cdot\mathbf{r})(\boldsymbol{\varepsilon}\cdot\hat{\mathbf{p}}) - (\boldsymbol{\varepsilon}\cdot\mathbf{r})(\mathbf{k}\cdot\hat{\mathbf{p}})$$

Thus,

$$2(\mathbf{k}\cdot\mathbf{r})(\boldsymbol{\varepsilon}\cdot\hat{\mathbf{p}}) = \hat{\mathbf{L}}\cdot(\mathbf{k}\times\boldsymbol{\varepsilon}) + (\mathbf{k}\cdot\mathbf{r})(\boldsymbol{\varepsilon}\cdot\hat{\mathbf{p}}) + (\boldsymbol{\varepsilon}\cdot\mathbf{r})(\mathbf{k}\cdot\hat{\mathbf{p}}) \tag{16.6.3}$$

where $\mathbf{L} = \mathbf{r}\times\mathbf{p}$. Substituting Eq. (16.6.3) in Eq. (16.6.2) gives

$$T_{fi}^{\pm} \approx \langle f|\boldsymbol{\varepsilon}\cdot\hat{\mathbf{p}}|i\rangle + \frac{i}{2}\langle f|(\hat{\mathbf{L}} + 2\hat{\mathbf{S}})\cdot(\mathbf{k}\times\boldsymbol{\varepsilon})|i\rangle + \frac{i}{2}\langle f|(\mathbf{k}\cdot\mathbf{r})(\boldsymbol{\varepsilon}\cdot\hat{\mathbf{p}}) + (\mathbf{k}\cdot\hat{\mathbf{p}})(\boldsymbol{\varepsilon}\cdot\mathbf{r})|i\rangle \tag{16.6.4}$$

Therefore, in order to obtain Eq. (16.6.1) we only have to verify the following matrix identities:

$$\begin{cases} \langle f|\boldsymbol{\varepsilon}\cdot\hat{\mathbf{p}}|i\rangle = im\omega_{fi}\langle f|(\boldsymbol{\varepsilon}\cdot\mathbf{r})|i\rangle \\ \langle f|(\mathbf{k}\cdot\mathbf{r})(\boldsymbol{\varepsilon}\cdot\hat{\mathbf{p}}) + (\boldsymbol{\varepsilon}\cdot\mathbf{r})(\mathbf{k}\cdot\hat{\mathbf{p}})|i\rangle = im\omega_{fi}\langle f|(\mathbf{k}\cdot\mathbf{r})(\boldsymbol{\varepsilon}\cdot\hat{\mathbf{r}})|i\rangle \end{cases} \tag{16.6.5}$$

To that end, we recall that $|i\rangle$ and $|f\rangle$ are eigenstates of $\hat{H}_0 = \hat{\mathbf{p}}^2/2m + \hat{V}(\mathbf{r})$ and choose our coordinate system so that the vector $\boldsymbol{\varepsilon}$ is on the z axis and the vector $\mathbf{k}$ is on the y axis. In this case,

$$[\boldsymbol{\varepsilon}\cdot\hat{\mathbf{r}}, \hat{H}_0] = [\hat{z}, \hat{H}_0] = \frac{1}{2m}[\hat{z}, \hat{\mathbf{p}}^2] = \frac{i\hbar}{m}p_z \tag{16.6.6}$$

and

$$[\mathbf{k} \cdot \hat{\mathbf{r}}, \hat{H}_0] = [\hat{y}\hat{z}, \hat{H}_0] = \frac{i\hbar}{m}(\hat{y}\hat{p}_z + \hat{p}_y\hat{z}) \tag{16.6.7}$$

Furthermore,

$$\langle f | [\hat{z}, \hat{H}_0] | i \rangle = (E_i - E_f) \langle f | \hat{z} | i \rangle = -\hbar\omega_{fi}\langle f | \hat{z} | i \rangle \tag{16.6.8}$$

$$\langle f | [\hat{y}\hat{z}, \hat{H}_0] | i \rangle = (E_i - E_f) \langle f | \hat{y}\hat{z} | i \rangle = -\hbar\omega_{fi}\langle f | \hat{y}\hat{z} | i \rangle \tag{16.6.9}$$

Hence,

$$\begin{cases} \langle f | \hat{p}_z | i \rangle = im\omega_{fi}\langle f | \hat{z} | i \rangle \\ \langle f | (\hat{y}\hat{p}_z + \hat{p}_y\hat{z}) | i \rangle = im\omega_{fi}\langle f | \hat{y}\hat{z} | i \rangle \end{cases} \tag{16.6.10}$$

which, for $\boldsymbol{\varepsilon} = \mathbf{k}$ and $\mathbf{k} = k\mathbf{j}$, coincide with expressions (16.6.5).

16.7. Find the selection rules for emission and absorption of (*a*) electric-dipole radiation, (*b*) magnetic-dipole radiation, and (*c*) electric-quadrupole radiation, by an electron in a central potential.

SOLUTION

(*a*) *Electric-dipole transitions:* To obtain the selection rules for electric-dipole transitions we consider matrix elements of the form $\langle f | \hat{x} | i \rangle$, $\langle f | \hat{y} | i \rangle$, and $\langle f | \hat{z} | i \rangle$ where $| i \rangle$ and $| f \rangle$ are eigenstates of an electron moving in a central potential. The unperturbed wavefunction is then given by

$$\begin{cases} | i \rangle \equiv | n_i, l_i, m_i \rangle \rightarrow \psi_{n_i l_i m_i} = R_{n_i l_i} Y_{l_i}^{m_i}(\theta, \varphi) \\ | f \rangle \equiv | n_f, l_f, m_f \rangle \rightarrow \psi_{n_f l_f m_f} = R_{n_f l_f} Y_{l_f}^{m_f}(\theta, \varphi) \end{cases} \tag{16.7.1}$$

where $Y_l^m(\theta, \varphi)$ are the spherical harmonic functions. In this representation,

$$\begin{cases} x \pm iy = r \sin\theta e^{\pm i\varphi} = \mp\sqrt{\dfrac{8\pi}{3}}\, r Y_1^{\pm 1}(\theta, \varphi) \\ z = r\cos\theta = \sqrt{\dfrac{4\pi}{3}}\, r Y_1^0(\theta) \end{cases} \tag{16.7.2}$$

Therefore, the matrix element $\langle f | z | i \rangle$ is proportional to the angular integral

$$\int \left(Y_{l_f}^{m_f}\right)^*(\theta, \varphi) Y_1^0(\theta) Y_{l_i}^{m_i}(\theta, \varphi) \, d\Omega \tag{16.7.3}$$

which is different from zero only if $\Delta l = l_f - l_i = \pm 1$ and $\Delta m = m_f - m_i = 0$. Similarly, the matrix elements $\langle f | x | i \rangle$ and $\langle f | y | i \rangle$ are proportional to linear combinations of the form

$$\int \left(Y_{l_f}^{m_f}\right)^*(\theta, \varphi) Y_1^{\pm 1}(\theta) Y_{l_i}^{m_i}(\theta, \varphi) \, d\Omega \tag{16.7.4}$$

which are different from zero only if $\Delta l = \pm 1$ and $\Delta m = \pm 1$. Grouping these results together we finally obtain

$$\begin{cases} \Delta l = l_f - l_i = \pm 1 \\ \Delta m = m_f - m_i = 0, \pm 1 \end{cases} \tag{16.7.5}$$

(b) Magnetic-dipole transitions: The selection rules for magnetic-dipole transitions are found from matrix elements of the form $\langle f | \hat{L}_x | i \rangle$, $\langle f | \hat{L}_y | i \rangle$, and $\langle f | \hat{L}_z | i \rangle$. From the general properties of angular momentum (see Chap. 6) we immediately find

$$\langle f | (\hat{L}_x + i\hat{L}_y) | i \rangle = \langle n_f, l_f, m_f | \hat{L}_+ | n_i, l_i, m_i \rangle \sim \delta_{l_f l_i} \delta_{m_f, m_i+1} \tag{16.7.6}$$

$$\langle f | (\hat{L}_x - i\hat{L}_y) | i \rangle = \langle n_f, l_f, m_f | \hat{L}_- | n_i, l_i, m_i \rangle \sim \delta_{l_f l_i} \delta_{m_f, m_i-1} \tag{16.7.7}$$

$$\langle f | \hat{L}_z | i \rangle = \langle n_f, l_f, m_f | \hat{L}_z | n_i, l_i, m_i \rangle \sim \hbar m_i \delta_{l_f l_i} \delta_{m_f m_i} \tag{16.7.8}$$

Therefore, the magnetic-dipole matrix elements vanish identically unless

$$\begin{cases} \Delta l = l_f - l_i = 0 \\ \Delta m = m_f - m_i = 0, \pm 1 \end{cases} \tag{16.7.9}$$

Note: In the presence of spin, one also obtains $\Delta m_s = m_{s_f} - m_{s_i} = 0, \pm 1$. However, this selection rule is trivially satisfied by spin 1/2 particles.

(c) Electric-quadrupole transitions: For electric-dipole radiation, we have to calculate matrix elements of the products xz, yz, and zx. We note, for example, that yz can be expressed as a linear combination of $r^2 Y_2^1(\theta, \varphi)$ and $r^2 Y_2^{-1}(\theta, \varphi)$. Therefore, the matrix element $\langle f | \hat{yz} | i \rangle$ contains angular integrations of the form

$$\int \left(Y_{l_f}^{m_f} \right)^* (\theta, \varphi) Y_2^{\pm 1}(\theta) Y_{l_i}^{m_i}(\theta, \varphi) d\Omega \tag{16.7.10}$$

These integrals are different from zero only if $\Delta l = 0, \pm 2$ (excluding the case $l_f = l_i = 0$) and $\Delta m = \pm 1$. The last condition becomes $\Delta m = \pm 2, \pm 1, 0$ if one considers arbitrary polarizations. The electric-quadrupole selection rules are then found to be

$$\begin{cases} \Delta l = l_f - l_i = 0, \pm 2 \\ \Delta m = m_f - m_i = 0, \pm 1, \pm 2 \end{cases} \tag{16.7.11}$$

where the case of $l_f = l_i = 0$ is excluded.

Notes: (1) The electric-dipole interaction is an odd operator, which connects only states of different parities. Since the parity of $|nlm\rangle$ is given by $(-1)^l$, Δl must be odd in accordance with Eq. (16.7.5). (2) The magnetic-dipole and electric-quadrupole interactions are even operators that connect only states of the same parity. This is, again, compatible with Eq. (16.7.9) and Eq. (16.7.11). (3) The magnetic-dipole and electric-quadrupole transitions are never in competition with the electric-dipole transition. (4) For $\Delta l = 0$ and $\Delta m = 0, \pm 1$, there is a contribution from both the magnetic-dipole and the electric-quadrupole interactions. However, for $\Delta l = 2$ we have pure quadrupole transition.

16.8. An isotropic three-dimensional harmonic oscillator of mass m, angular frequency ω_0, and charge e is placed in a linearly polarized field of radiation. Calculate the probability per unit time for resonant transitions of frequency $\omega_{fi} = \omega_0$ and $\omega_{fi} = \pm 2\omega_0$.

SOLUTION

Let us choose a coordinate system such that the unit vector **ε** is on the z axis and the vector **k** is on the y axis. The transition rate, for absorption (and for induced emission), is then given by

$$W_{fi} = \frac{4\pi^2 e^2}{m^2 \hbar^2} \frac{u(\omega_{fi})}{\omega_{fi}^2} | \langle n_x^f, n_y^f, n_z^f | e^{+iky} \hat{p}_z | n_x^i, n_y^i, n_z^i \rangle |^2 \tag{16.8.1}$$

where $|n_x, n_y, n_z\rangle$ and $E_{n_x n_y n_z} = \hbar\omega_0(n_x + n_y + n_z + 3/2)$ are the eigenstates and eigenvalues of the unperturbed harmonic oscillator. Using the results of Chap. 5, we find

$$\begin{cases} \hat{p}_z \,|\, n_x, n_y, n_z\rangle = i\sqrt{\dfrac{m\hbar\omega_0}{2}} \left(\sqrt{n_z + 1}\, | n_x, n_y, n_z + 1\rangle - \sqrt{n_z}\, | n_x, n_y, n_z - 1\rangle \right) \\[3mm] ky \,|\, n_x, n_y, n_z\rangle = k\sqrt{\dfrac{\hbar}{2m\omega_0}} \left(\sqrt{n_y + 1}\, | n_x, n_y + 1, n_z\rangle - \sqrt{n_y}\, | n_x, n_y - 1, n_z\rangle \right) \end{cases} \tag{16.8.2}$$

Therefore,

$$\langle n_x^f, n_y^f, n_z^f \,|\, e^{+iky}\hat{p}_z \,|\, n_x^i, n_y^i, n_z^i \rangle = \langle n_x^f | n_x^i \rangle \langle n_y^f | (1 + ky + \cdots) | n_y^i \rangle \langle n_z^f | \hat{p}_z | n_y^i \rangle \tag{16.8.3}$$

where the higher terms of order $\hbar\omega_0/mc^2 \ll 1$ have been neglected. Note that these terms are important only for high-order transitions in which $\omega_{fi} = 3\omega_0, 4\omega_0, \ldots$. Expression (16.8.3) is different from zero only if

$$\Delta n_x = 0, \qquad \Delta n_y = 0, \pm 1, \qquad \text{and} \qquad \Delta n_z = \pm 1 \tag{16.8.4}$$

In particular, there is no competition between the electric-dipole ($\Delta n_y = 0$) and the electric-quadrupole transitions ($\Delta n_y = \pm 1$). The energy difference for each transition is $\omega_{fi} = \omega_0(\Delta n_x + \Delta n_y + \Delta n_z)$. Thus,

$$\langle n_x^f, n_y^f, n_z^f \,|\, e^{+iky}\hat{p}_z \,|\, n_x^i, n_y^i, n_z^i \rangle = \begin{cases} i\sqrt{\dfrac{m\hbar\omega_0}{2}} \sqrt{n_z^i + 1} & \text{for } \omega_{fi} = \omega_0 \\[3mm] i\sqrt{\dfrac{\hbar k}{2}} \sqrt{n_z^i + 1}\sqrt{n_y^i + 1} & \text{for } \omega_{fi} = 2\omega_0 \end{cases} \tag{16.8.5}$$

Finally, substituting Eq. (16.8.5) in Eq. (16.8.1) and using the relation $k = \omega_{fi}/c$, we obtain

$$W_{fi} = 2\pi^2 e^2 \times \begin{cases} \dfrac{u(\omega_0)}{m\hbar\omega_0} (n_z^i + 1) & \text{for } \omega_{fi} = \omega_0 \\[3mm] \dfrac{u(\omega_0)}{m^2 c^2} (n_z^i + 1)(n_y^i + 1) & \text{for } \omega_{fi} = 2\omega_0 \end{cases} \tag{16.8.6}$$

Note that for the same incident intensity, $W(2\omega_0)/W(\omega_0) \sim \hbar\omega_0/mc^2$.

16.9. A two-level system with eigenvalues $E_2 > E_1$ is in thermodynamic equilibrium with a heat reservoir at absolute temperature T. The system undergoes the following transitions: (i) absorption $1 \rightarrow 2$, (ii) induced emission $2 \rightarrow 1$, and (iii) spontaneous emission $2 \rightarrow 1$. The transition rates for each of these processes are given by

$$\begin{cases} W_{21}^{\text{abs}} = P_1 B_{21} u(\omega_{21}) \\[3mm] W_{12}^{\text{ind}} = P_2 B_{12} u(\omega_{21}) \\[3mm] W_{12}^{\text{spon}} = P_2 A_{12} \end{cases} \tag{16.9.1}$$

where $u(\omega_{21})$ is the energy distribution of the radiation field, P_j is the probability of finding the system in level j of degeneracy $g_j (j = 1, 2)$, and A_{12} and B_{12} are the Einstein coefficients for spontaneous and induced emission, respectively. (*a*) Calculate the probabilities P_1 and P_2 under equilibrium conditions. (*b*) Use Eq. (16.9.1) together with Planck's formula for *blackbody radiation* to show that

$$\begin{cases} g_1 B_{21} = g_2 B_{12} \\[3mm] A_{12} = \dfrac{\hbar\omega_{21}^3}{\pi^2 c^3} B_{12} \end{cases} \tag{16.9.2}$$

SOLUTION

(*a*) Under thermal equilibrium at absolute temperature T, the probability of finding a system in one of its stationary states $|i\rangle$ with an eigenvalue ε_i is proportional to the Boltzman factor $e^{-\varepsilon_i/kT}$. In this problem, ε_i assumes the values $\varepsilon_i = E_1, E_2$ with respective degeneracies $g_i = g_1, g_2$ (a two-level system). Therefore,

$$\begin{cases} P_1 = Cg_1 e^{-E_1/kT} \\ P_2 = Cg_2 e^{-E_2/kT} \end{cases} \tag{16.9.3}$$

where C is the normalization constant. Since $P_1 + P_2 = 1$, we immediately find that

$$C^{-1} = g_1 e^{-E_1/kT} + g_2 e^{-E_2/kT} \tag{16.9.4}$$

Since $E_2 - E_1 = \hbar\omega_{21}$, we have

$$\frac{P_1}{P_2} = \frac{g_1}{g_2} e^{\hbar\omega_{21}/kT} \tag{16.9.5}$$

(*b*) Suppose that a larger number of systems, such as in part (*a*), form a closed cavity that is kept in equilibrium with its own thermal radiation at constant temperature T. In this case,

$$W_{21}^{\text{abs}} = W_{12}^{\text{ind}} + W_{12}^{\text{spon}} \tag{16.9.6}$$

Therefore, from Eq. (16.9.1), we obtain

$$P_1 B_{21} u(\omega_{21}) = P_2 B_{12} u(\omega_{21}) + P_2 A_{12} \tag{16.9.7}$$

or equivalently, by using Eq. (16.9.5),

$$[g_1 e^{\hbar\omega_{21}/kT} B_{21} - g_2 B_{12}] u(\omega_{21}) = g_2 A_{12} \tag{16.9.8}$$

The thermal radiation inside the cavity is distributed according to Planck's formula:

$$u(\omega) = \frac{\hbar\omega^3}{\pi^2 c^3 (e^{\hbar\omega/kT} - 1)} \tag{16.9.9}$$

Therefore, Eq. (16.9.8) takes the form

$$g_1 B_{21} \left(e^{\hbar\omega_{21}/kT} - \frac{g_2 B_{12}}{g_1 B_{21}} \right) \frac{\hbar\omega_{21}^3}{\pi^2 c^3} = g_2 A_{12} (e^{\hbar\omega_{21}/kT} - 1) \tag{16.9.10}$$

Hence,

$$\begin{cases} g_1 B_{21} = g_2 B_{12} \\ A_{12} = \dfrac{\hbar\omega_{21}^3}{\pi^2 c^3} B_{12} \end{cases} \tag{16.9.11}$$

16.10. Calculate the Einstein coefficients, A_{1s2p}, B_{1s2p}, and B_{2p1s}, for an electron moving in a central potential. Recall that $1s = (n = 1, l = 0)$ and $2p = (n = 2, l = 1)$.

SOLUTION

Let us first consider the probability per unit time for the transition $1s \to 2p$ (absorption). Since the states $2p$ are degenerate with respect to the magnetic quantum number, we have

$$W_{2p1s} = \frac{4\pi^2 e^2}{3\hbar^2} u(\omega_{21}) \sum_{m'=-1}^{1} |\langle 21m' | \hat{\mathbf{r}} | 100 \rangle|^2 \equiv B_{2p1s} u(\omega_{21}) \tag{16.10.1}$$

However,

$$\sum_{m'} |\langle n', l+1, m' | \hat{\mathbf{r}} | nlm \rangle|^2 = (l+1) |\langle n', l+1 | \hat{r} | nl \rangle|^2 \tag{16.10.2}$$

and

$$\sum_{m'} |\langle (n', l-1, m') | \hat{\mathbf{r}} | nlm \rangle|^2 = l |\langle n', l-1 | \hat{r} | nl \rangle|^2 \tag{16.10.3}$$

Therefore, substituting $l = 0$ in Eq. (16.10.3) and using Eq. (16.10.1), we obtain

$$B_{2p1s} = \frac{4\pi^2 e^2}{3\hbar^2} |\langle 21 | \hat{r} | 10 \rangle|^2 \tag{16.10.4}$$

where $\langle 21 | \hat{r} | 10 \rangle = \displaystyle\int_0^\infty R_{21}^*(r) r^3 R_{10}(r) dr$ is the radial integral. The coefficients for the transition $2p \to 1s$ (emission) are found by setting $g_{1s} = 1$ and $g_{2p} = 3$ in Eq. (16.9.11). This gives

$$\begin{cases} B_{1s2p} = \dfrac{4\pi^2 e^2}{9\hbar^2} |\langle 10 | \hat{r} | 21 \rangle|^2 \\[4mm] A_{1s2p} = \dfrac{4\omega_{21}^3 e^2}{9\hbar c^3} |\langle 10 | \hat{r} | 21 \rangle|^2 \end{cases} \tag{16.10.5}$$

16.11. Find the probability per unit time of spontaneous transition for a hydrogen atom in the first excited state.

SOLUTION

The probability per unit time for the transition $2p \to 1s$ (emission) is given by

$$W_{1s2p} = u(\omega_{21}) B_{1s2p} + A_{1s2p} \tag{16.11.1}$$

Thus, using Eq. (16.10.5), we obtain

$$W_{1s2p} = \frac{4\pi^2 e^2}{3\hbar^2} \left[u(\omega_{21}) + \frac{\hbar\omega_{21}^3}{\pi^2 c^3} \right] |\langle 100 | \hat{\mathbf{r}} | 21m' \rangle|^2 \tag{16.11.2}$$

where $|21m'\rangle$ is one of the three $2p$ states. In particular, for the hydrogen atom in the first excited level,

$$|\langle 100 | \hat{\mathbf{r}} | 21m' \rangle|^2 = \frac{1}{3} |\langle 10 | \hat{\mathbf{r}} | 21 \rangle|^2 = \frac{5}{9} a_0^2 \tag{16.11.3}$$

where $a_0 = \hbar^2/me^2$ is the Bohr radius. Therefore,

$$A_{1s2p} = \frac{20}{27} \frac{e^2 \omega_{21}^3}{\hbar c^3} a_0^2 = \frac{20}{27} \alpha \frac{\omega_{21}^3}{c^2} a_0^2 = \frac{20}{27} \frac{\omega_{21}^3}{c^4} \frac{\hbar^2}{m^2 \alpha} \tag{16.11.4}$$

where $\alpha = e^2/\hbar c \approx 1/137$ is the *fine structure constant*. However,

$$\hbar\omega_{21} = \frac{3}{4} \frac{e^2}{2a_0} = \frac{3}{4} \frac{\alpha^2 mc^2}{2} \tag{16.11.5}$$

Hence,

$$A_{1s2p} = \frac{20}{8^3} \alpha^5 \frac{mc^2}{\hbar} = \frac{5}{48} \alpha^3 \omega_{21} \approx 6.25 \times 10^{-8} \text{ sec}^{-1} \tag{16.11.6}$$

Expression (16.11.6) leads to a radiative lifetime of the order 1.5×10^{-9} sec.

16.12. A linear harmonic oscillator of mass m, angular frequency ω_0, and charge e is excited by a nonresonant radiation field of the form

$$A(\mathbf{r}, t) = \begin{cases} 2A_0 \mathbf{k} \cos(ky - \omega t) & t > 0 \\ 0 & t \leq 0 \end{cases} \qquad (16.12.1)$$

where $\omega \neq \omega_0$. Let $|n\rangle$ and $E_n = \hbar\omega_0(n + 1/2)$ be the eigenstates and the eigenvalues of the oscillator, and let $|\psi(t)\rangle$ be its time-dependent state vector in the presence of radiation. (*a*) Use first-order perturbation theory to find an expression for $|\psi(t)\rangle$. Assume that initially $|\psi(t = 0)\rangle = |0\rangle$. (*b*) Calculate the induced dipole moment that is proportional to the amplitude of the external electric field.

SOLUTION

(*a*) The time-dependent state vector can be written as

$$|\psi(t)\rangle = e^{-iE_0 t/\hbar} |0\rangle + \sum_{n \neq 0} a_n(t) e^{-iE_0 t/\hbar} |n\rangle \qquad (16.12.2)$$

where $a_n(t) = 0$ for $t < 0$. Using first-order perturbation theory (see Chap. 10) for $\hat{H}(t) = -\dfrac{e}{mc} A(\mathbf{r}, t) \cdot \hat{\mathbf{p}}$, we find

$$a_n^{(1)}(t) = \frac{1}{i\hbar} \int_0^t e^{i\omega_{n0} t'} \langle n | \hat{H}'(t') | 0 \rangle \, dt' = \frac{ie}{mc\hbar} \int_0^t e^{i\omega_{n0} t'} 2A_0 \cos(ky - \omega t) \langle n | p_z | 0 \rangle \, dt' \qquad (16.12.3)$$

Therefore (see Problem 16.4),

$$a_n^{(1)}(t) = -\frac{e^{i(\omega_{n0} - \omega)t} - 1}{\omega_{n0} - \omega} \frac{T_{n0}^+}{\hbar} - \frac{e^{i(\omega_{n0} + \omega)t} - 1}{\omega_{n0} + \omega} \frac{T_{n0}^-}{\hbar} \qquad (16.12.4)$$

where

$$\begin{cases} T_{n0}^+ \equiv -\dfrac{e}{mc} \langle n | A_0 e^{iky} \hat{p}_z | 0 \rangle = -\dfrac{ie\omega_{n0}}{e} A_0 e^{iky} \langle n | e\hat{z} | 0 \rangle \\[3mm] T_{n0}^- \equiv -\dfrac{e}{mc} \langle n | A_0 e^{-iky} \hat{p}_z | 0 \rangle = -\dfrac{ie\omega_{n0}}{e} A_0 e^{-iky} \langle n | e\hat{z} | 0 \rangle \end{cases} \qquad (16.12.5)$$

Finally, multiplying the ket $|\psi(t)\rangle$ by a global phase factor $e^{iE_0 t/\hbar}$, we obtain

$$|\tilde{\psi}(t)\rangle = |\psi(t)\rangle e^{iE_0 t/\hbar} = |0\rangle + \sum_{n \neq 0} b_n(t) |n\rangle \qquad (16.12.6)$$

where the coefficients $b_n(t) \equiv a_n(t) e^{-i\omega_{n0}}$ are given by Eq. (16.12.4):

$$b_n(t) = -\frac{e^{-i\omega t} - e^{-i\omega_{n0} t}}{\omega_{n0} - \omega} \frac{T_{n0}^+}{\hbar} - \frac{e^{i\omega t} - e^{-i\omega_{n0} t}}{\omega_{n0} + \omega} \frac{T_{n0}^-}{\hbar} \qquad (16.12.7)$$

(*b*) The induced dipole moment is given by $\langle D(t) \rangle = \langle \tilde{\psi}(t) | e\hat{z} | \tilde{\psi}(t) \rangle$. Thus, up to the first order in A_0, we find

$$\langle D(t) \rangle = \langle 0 | ez | 0 \rangle + \sum_{n \neq 0} b_n(t) \langle 0 | e\hat{z} | n \rangle + \sum_{n \neq 0} b_n^*(t) \langle 0 | e\hat{z} | n \rangle \qquad (16.12.8)$$

Next, we substitute the coefficients $b_n(t)$ from Eq. (16.12.7) and neglect all the terms that oscillate at frequencies $\pm\omega_{n0}$. (These terms disappear in the limit $t \to \infty$ due to the finite lifetimes of all the excited states.) This gives

$$\langle D(t) \rangle = \langle 0 | e\hat{z} | 0 \rangle - \frac{2}{\hbar} \, \text{Re} \left\{ \sum_{n \neq 0} \left[\frac{T_{n0}^+ \langle 0 | e\hat{z} | n \rangle e^{-i\omega t}}{\omega_{n0} - \omega} + \frac{T_{n0}^- \langle 0 | e\hat{z} | n \rangle e^{i\omega t}}{\omega_{n0} + \omega} \right] \right\} \qquad (16.12.9)$$

namely,

$$\langle D(t) \rangle = \langle 0 | e\hat{z} | 0 \rangle - \frac{2A_0}{\hbar c} \sum_{n \neq 0} |\langle 0 | e\hat{z} | n \rangle|^2 \omega_{n0} \, \text{Im} \left[\frac{e^{-i(ky-\omega t)}}{\omega_{n0} - \omega} + \frac{e^{-i(ky-\omega t)}}{\omega_{n0} + \omega} \right] \qquad (16.12.10)$$

Finally, since $\mathcal{E} = -\dfrac{1}{c}\dfrac{\partial \mathbf{A}}{\partial t} = -2A_0 k\, \mathbf{k}\sin(ky - \omega t)$, we obtain

$$\langle D(t) \rangle = \langle 0 | e\hat{z} | 0 \rangle + \frac{2\mathcal{E}_z}{\hbar} \sum_{n \neq 0} \frac{|\langle 0 | e\hat{z} | n \rangle|^2}{\omega_{n0}^2 - \omega^2} \omega_{n0} \qquad (16.12.11)$$

In particular, for the linear harmonic oscillator, expression (16.12.11) is reduced to the classical formula; i.e.,

$$\langle D(t) \rangle = \frac{e^2}{m(\omega_0^2 - \omega^2)} \mathcal{E}_z \qquad (16.12.12)$$

SUPPLEMENTARY PROBLEMS

16.13. Refer to Problem 16.4 and find the transition rate W_{fi} (probability per unit time) for the transition from the initial state $|i\rangle$ to a continuum of final states of energies $E_f \pm dE_f/2$ (Fermi's golden rule).

Ans. $W_{fi} = \dfrac{dP_{fi}(t)}{dt} = \dfrac{2\pi}{\hbar} |\langle f | \hat{T}^+ | i \rangle|^2 \rho(E_f = E_i + \hbar\omega)$, where $\rho(E_f) \equiv dN_f/dE_f$ is the density of final states and T_{fi}^+ is given in Eq. (16.4.6).

16.14. Find the transition rate for absorption and for induced emission of electric-dipole radiation by a one-electron system in an isotropic radiation field. Hint: The transition rate is found by averaging the electric-dipole matrix element over all possible directions of polarization.

Ans. $W_{fi} = \dfrac{4\pi^2 e^2}{3\hbar^2} u(\omega_{fi}) |\langle f | \hat{\mathbf{r}} | i \rangle|^2$, where $|\langle f | \hat{\mathbf{r}} | i \rangle|^2 \equiv \langle f | \hat{\mathbf{r}} | i \rangle \cdot \langle f | \hat{\mathbf{r}} | i \rangle^*$

16.15. The oscillator strength of a transition $|k\rangle \to |n\rangle$ is defined as

$$f_{nk} = f_{nk}^x + f_{nk}^y + f_{nk}^z \equiv (2m\omega_{nk}/\hbar) |\langle n | \hat{\mathbf{r}} | k \rangle|^2 \qquad (16.15.1)$$

where $|n\rangle$ and $|k\rangle$ are eigenstates of $\hat{H}_0 = \dfrac{\hat{\mathbf{p}}^2}{2m} + \hat{V}(r)$. Show that f_{nk} satisfies the sum rule $\displaystyle\sum_n f_{nk} = 3$.

16.16. In the presence of a spin-orbit interaction, find the selection rules for emission and absorption of (*a*) electric-dipole radiation, (*b*) magnetic-dipole radiation, and (*c*) electric-quadrupole radiation. Note that the selection rules can be obtained by expanding the stationary states $|ls; JM_J\rangle$ in terms of $|lm\rangle \otimes |sm_s\rangle$, where $\mathbf{J} = \mathbf{L} + \mathbf{S}$.

Ans. (*a*) Electric-dipole transitions: $\Delta l = \pm 1$; $\Delta J = 0, \pm 1$; $\Delta M_J = 0, \pm 1$

(*b*) Magnetic-dipole transitions: $\Delta l = 0$; $\Delta J = 0, \pm 1$; $\Delta M_J = 0, \pm 1$

(*c*) Electric-quadrupole transitions: $\Delta l = 0, \pm 2$; $\Delta J = 0, \pm 1, \pm 2$; $\Delta M_J = 0, \pm 1, \pm 2$

Mathematical Appendix

A.1 Fourier Series and Fourier Transform

If $f(x)$ is a periodic function with a fundamental period L, then it can be expanded in a Fourier series:

$$f(x) = \sum_{n=-\infty}^{\infty} a_n e^{ik_n x} \tag{A.1}$$

where $k_n = 2\pi n/L$. The coefficients a_n of the series are given by

$$a_n = \frac{1}{L} \int_0^L f(x) e^{-ik_n x} dx \tag{A.2}$$

The Fourier transform of a function $f(x)$ is defined as

$$F(k) = F[f(x)] = \frac{1}{\sqrt{2\pi}} \int_{-\infty}^{\infty} f(x) e^{-ikx} dx \tag{A.3}$$

while the inverse Fourier transform is

$$f(x) = \frac{1}{\sqrt{2\pi}} \int_{-\infty}^{\infty} F(k) e^{ikx} dk \tag{A.4}$$

Notice that in quantum mechanics we define the transformations slightly differently, as follows:

$$\Psi(k) = F[\psi(x)] = \frac{1}{\sqrt{2\pi\hbar}} \int_{-\infty}^{\infty} \psi(x) e^{-ipx/\hbar} dx \tag{A.5}$$

and

$$\psi(x) = \frac{1}{\sqrt{2\pi\hbar}} \int_{-\infty}^{\infty} \Psi(k) e^{ipx/\hbar} dk \tag{A.6}$$

Two formulas of Fourier transform theory are especially relevant.

Identity of norms:
$$\int_{-\infty}^{\infty} |f(x)|^2 dx = \int_{-\infty}^{\infty} |F(k)|^2 dk \tag{A.7}$$

Parseval's theorem:
$$\int_{-\infty}^{\infty} f(x) g^*(x) dx = \int_{-\infty}^{\infty} F(k) G^*(k) dk \tag{A.8}$$

A.2   The Dirac δ-Function

The Dirac δ-function is defined by the relation

$$\int_{-\infty}^{\infty} f(x)\delta(x - x_0)\,dx = f(x_0) \tag{A.9}$$

Some important and useful properties of the δ-function are given below:

$$\delta(-x) = \delta(x) \tag{A.10}$$

$$\delta(cx) = \frac{1}{c}\delta(x) \quad \text{for} \quad c > 0 \tag{A.11}$$

$$x\delta(x - x_0) = x_0\delta(x - x_0) \tag{A.12}$$

Note that $x\delta(x) = 0$. Also,

$$f(x)\delta(x - x_0) = f(x_0)\delta(x - x_0) \tag{A.13}$$

$$\delta(x^2 - c^2) = \frac{1}{2c}[\delta(x - c) + \delta(x + c)] \quad \text{for } c > 0 \tag{A.14}$$

$$\delta[f(x)] = \sum_i \frac{1}{f'(x_i)}\delta(x - x_i) \tag{A.15}$$

where x_i are simple zeros of the function $f(x)$.

$$\int_{-\infty}^{\infty} \delta(x - x_1)\delta(x - x_2)\,dx = \delta(x_1 - x_2) \tag{A.16}$$

We define $\delta'(x)$ by the relation

$$\int_{-\infty}^{\infty} f(x)\delta'(x)\,dx = -f'(0) \tag{A.17}$$

Some properties that are connected to $\delta'(x)$ are given below:

$$\delta'(-x) = -\delta'(x) \tag{A.18}$$

$$\delta^{(n)}(-x) = (-1)^n \delta^{(n)}(x) \tag{A.19}$$

$$x\delta^{(n)}(x) = -n\delta^{(n-1)}(x) \tag{A.20}$$

$$\int_{-\infty}^{\infty} f(x)\delta^n(x)\,dx = (-1)^n f^{(n)}(0) \tag{A.21}$$

The δ-function in three-dimensional space is defined by

$$\int f(\mathbf{r})\delta(\mathbf{r} - \mathbf{r}_0)\,dx\,dy\,dz = f(\mathbf{r}_0) \tag{A.22}$$

where $\delta(\mathbf{r} - \mathbf{r}_0) = \delta(x - x_0)\delta(y - y_0)\delta(z - z_0)$. In spherical coordinates (r, θ, φ) we have

$$\delta(\mathbf{r} - \mathbf{r}_0) = \frac{1}{r^2 \sin\theta}\delta(r - r_0)\delta(\theta - \theta_0)\delta(\varphi - \varphi_0)$$

$$= \frac{1}{r^2}\delta(r - r_0)\delta(\cos\theta - \cos\theta_0)\delta(\varphi - \varphi_0) \qquad (A.23)$$

The integral representation of the δ-function is obtained by using the definition of Fourier transform [see Sec. A.1], so that

$$\delta(x - x_0) = \frac{1}{2\pi}\int_{-\infty}^{\infty} e^{ik(x-x_0)}\,dx \qquad (A.24)$$

The *step function* $\theta(x)$ (also called the *Heaviside function*) is defined as

$$\theta(x) = \begin{cases} 1 & \text{for} \quad x > 0 \\ 0 & \text{for} \quad x < 0 \end{cases} \qquad (A.25)$$

The relation between $\delta(x)$ and $\theta(x)$ is

$$\delta(x) = \frac{d\theta(x)}{dx} \qquad (A.26)$$

Finally, we mention an important relation for $\delta(\mathbf{r})$:

$$\nabla^2\left(\frac{1}{r}\right) = -4\pi\delta(\mathbf{r}) \qquad (A.27)$$

A.3   Hermite Polynomials

The *Hermite polynomials* $H_n(x)$ are defined by the relation

$$H_n(x) = (-1)^n e^{x^2}\left(\frac{d^n}{dx^n}e^{-x^2}\right) \qquad n = 0, 1, 2, \ldots \qquad (A.28)$$

The $H_n(x)$ are the solutions to the *differential equation*

$$\frac{d^2 H_n(x)}{dx^2} - 2x\frac{dH_n(x)}{dx} + 2nH_n(x) = 0 \qquad (A.29)$$

The *orthogonality relation* for $H_n(x)$ is

$$\int_{-\infty}^{\infty} e^{-x^2} H_m(x)H_n(x)\,dx = \sqrt{\pi}\,2^n n!\,\delta_{mn} \qquad (A.30)$$

Two important *recurrence relations* for $H_n(x)$ are

$$\frac{dH_n(x)}{dx} = 2nH_n(x) \qquad H_{n+1}(x) = 2xH_n(x) - 2nH_{n-1}(x)$$

The first few Hermite polynomials are given below:

$$H_0(x) = 1 \qquad\qquad H_1(x) = 2x \qquad\qquad H_2(x) = 4x^2 - 2$$
$$H_3(x) = 8x^3 - 12x \qquad H_4(x) = 16x^4 - 48x^2 + 12$$

A.4   Legendre Polynomials

Legendre polynomials $P_l(x)$ are given by *Rodrigue's formula*,

$$P_l(x) = \frac{(-1)^l}{2^n n!} \frac{d^l}{dx^l}(x^2 - 1)^l \tag{A.31}$$

The first few Legendre polynomials are given below:

$$P_0(x) = 1 \qquad\qquad P_1(x) = x \qquad\qquad P_2(x) = \frac{1}{2}(3x^2 - 1)$$

$$P_3(x) = \frac{1}{2}(5x^3 - 3x) \qquad P_4(x) = \frac{1}{8}(35x^4 - 30x^2 + 3)$$

In terms of $\cos\theta$ the first few Legendre polynomials are

$$P_0(\cos\theta) = 1 \qquad\qquad P_1(\cos\theta) = \cos\theta$$

$$P_2(\cos\theta) = \frac{1}{4}(1 + 3\cos 2\theta) \qquad P_3(\cos\theta) = \frac{1}{8}(3\cos\theta + 5\cos 3\theta)$$

The orthogonality relation of the Legendre polynomials is

$$\int_{-1}^{1} P_l(x)P_{l'}(x)\,dx = \frac{2}{2l+1}\delta_{ll'} \tag{A.32}$$

A.5   Associated Legendre Functions

Associated Legendre functions $P_l^m(x)$ are defined as

$$P_l^m(x) = \sqrt{(1-x^2)^m}\,\frac{d^m}{dx^m}P_l(x) \qquad \text{for } -1 \le x \le 1 \tag{A.33}$$

where $m \ge 0$. $P_l(x)$ are the Legendre polynomials. Note that

$$P_l^0(x) = P_l(x) \qquad P_l^m(x) = 0 \quad \text{for} \quad m > l \tag{A.34}$$

The differential equation that $P_l^m(x)$ satisfies is

$$\left[(1-x^2)\frac{d^2}{dx^2} - 2x\frac{d}{dx} + \left(l(l+1) - \frac{m^2}{1-x^2}\right)\right]P_l^m(x) = 0 \tag{A.35}$$

The first few associated Legendre functions are given below:

$$P_1^1(x) = \sqrt{1-x^2} \qquad\qquad P_2^1(x) = 3x\sqrt{1-x^2} \qquad P_2^2(x) = 3(1-x^2)$$

$$P_3^1(x) = \frac{3}{2}(5x^2-1)\sqrt{1-x^2} \qquad P_3^2(x) = 15x(1-x^2) \qquad P_3^3(x) = 15\sqrt{(1-x^2)^3}$$

The orthogonality relation of the associated Legendre functions is

$$\int_{-1}^{1} P_l^m(x)P_{l'}^m(x)\,dx = \int_0^\pi P_l^m(\cos\theta)P_{l'}^m(\cos\theta)\sin\theta\,d\theta = \frac{2}{2l+1}\frac{(l+m)!}{(l-m)!}\delta_{ll'} \tag{A.36}$$

A.6 Spherical Harmonics

The spherical harmonics are defined as

$$Y_l^m(\theta, \varphi) = (-1)^m \sqrt{\frac{2l+1}{4\pi}\frac{(l-m)!}{(l+m)!}}\, P_l^m(\cos\theta)\, e^{im\varphi} \quad \text{for} \quad m \geq 0 \tag{A.37}$$

and

$$Y_l^{-m}(\theta, \varphi) = (-1)^m [Y_l^m(\theta, \varphi)]^* \tag{A.38}$$

The differential equation that Y_l^m satisfies is

$$\left[\frac{1}{\sin\theta}\frac{\partial}{\partial\theta}\left(\sin\theta\frac{\partial}{\partial\theta}\right) + \frac{1}{\sin^2\theta}\frac{\partial^2}{\partial\varphi^2} + l(l+1)\right]Y_l^m(\theta, \varphi) = 0 \tag{A.39}$$

The Y_l^m have well-defined parity given as follows:

$$Y_l^m(\pi - \theta, \pi + \varphi) = (-1)^l Y_l^m(\theta, \varphi) \tag{A.40}$$

The orthonormalization relation of Y_l^m is written as

$$\int_0^{2\pi} d\varphi \int_0^{\pi} [Y_{l'}^{m'}(\theta, \varphi)]^* Y_l^m(\theta, \varphi)\sin\theta\, d\theta = \delta_{l'l}\delta_{m'm} \tag{A.41}$$

and the closure relation

$$\sum_{l=0}^{\infty}\sum_{m=-l}^{l} Y_l^m(\theta, \varphi)[Y_l^m(\theta', \varphi')]^* = \delta(\cos\theta - \cos\theta')\delta(\varphi - \varphi') = \frac{1}{\sin\theta}\delta(\theta - \theta')\delta(\varphi - \varphi') \tag{A.42}$$

Some important recurrence relations are given below:

$$e^{i\varphi}\left(\frac{\partial}{\partial\theta} - m\cot\theta\right)Y_l^m(\theta, \varphi) = \sqrt{l(l+1) - m(m+1)}\, Y_l^{m+1}(\theta, \varphi) \tag{A.43}$$

$$e^{-i\varphi}\left(-\frac{\partial}{\partial\theta} - m\cot\theta\right)Y_l^m(\theta, \varphi) = \sqrt{l(l+1) - m(m-1)}\, Y_l^{m-1}(\theta, \varphi) \tag{A.44}$$

$$Y_l^m(\theta, \varphi)\cos\theta = \sqrt{\frac{(l+1+m)(l+1-m)}{(2l+1)(2l+3)}}\, Y_{l+1}^m + \sqrt{\frac{(l+m)(l-m)}{(2l+1)(2l-1)}}\, Y_{l-1}^m \tag{A.45}$$

The first few Y_l^m are given below:

$$Y_0^0 = \frac{1}{\sqrt{4\pi}}$$

$$Y_1^0 = \sqrt{\frac{3}{4\pi}}\cos\theta \qquad Y_1^1 = -\sqrt{\frac{3}{8\pi}}\sin\theta\, e^{i\varphi}$$

$$Y_2^0 = \sqrt{\frac{5}{16\pi}}(3\cos^2\theta - 1) \qquad Y_2^1 = -\sqrt{\frac{15}{8\pi}}\sin\theta\cos\theta\, e^{i\varphi} \qquad Y_2^2 = \sqrt{\frac{15}{32\pi}}\sin^2\theta\, e^{2i\varphi}$$

$$Y_3^0 = \sqrt{\frac{7}{16\pi}}(5\cos^3\theta - 3\cos\theta) \qquad Y_3^1 = -\sqrt{\frac{21}{64\pi}}\sin\theta(5\cos^2\theta - 1)e^{i\varphi}$$

$$Y_3^2 = \sqrt{\frac{105}{32\pi}}\sin^2\theta\cos\theta\, e^{2i\varphi} \qquad Y_3^3 = -\sqrt{\frac{35}{64\pi}}\sin^3\theta\, e^{3i\varphi}$$

An important result for spherical harmonics is

$$P_l(\cos\alpha) = \frac{4\pi}{2l+1} \sum_{m=-l}^{l} (-1)^m Y_l^m(\theta_1, \varphi_1) Y_l^m(\theta_2, \varphi_2) \tag{A.46}$$

where α is the angle between the directions (θ_1, φ_1) and (θ_2, φ_2). This result is known as the *spherical harmonics addition theorem*.

A.7   Associated Laguerre Polynomials

First we shall deal with the Laguerre polynomials given by *Rodrigue's formula*,

$$L_l(x) = e^x \frac{d^l}{dx^l}(x^l e^{-x}) \tag{A.47}$$

The associated Laguerre polynomials are defined as

$$L_l^m(x) = \frac{d^m}{dx^m} L_l(x) \tag{A.48}$$

where l and m are nonnegative integers. Note that

$$L_l^0(x) = L_l(x) \qquad L_l^0(x) = 0 \quad \text{for} \quad m > 1 \tag{A.49}$$

The first few associated Laguerre polynomials are given below:

$$L_1^1(x) = -1 \qquad\qquad L_2^1(x) = 2x - 4 \qquad\qquad L_2^2(x) = 2$$
$$L_3^1(x) = -3x^2 + 18x - 18 \qquad L_3^2(x) = -6x + 18 \qquad L_3^3(x) = -6$$

The orthogonality relation of the associated Laguerre polynomials is

$$\int_0^\infty x^m e^{-x} L_l^m(x) L_{l'}^m(x)\, dx = \frac{(l!)^3}{(l-m)!}\delta_{ll'} \tag{A.50}$$

A.8   Spherical Bessel Functions

Bessel's differential equation is given as

$$\left[x^2 \frac{d^2}{dx^2} + x \frac{d}{dx} + (x^2 - l^2) \right] J_l(x) = 0 \tag{A.51}$$

where $l \geq 0$. The solutions to this equation are called *Bessel functions* of order l. $J_l(x)$ are given by the series expansion

$$J_l(x) = \frac{x^l}{2^l \Gamma(l+1)} \left[1 - \frac{x^2}{2(2l+2)} + \frac{x^4}{2\cdot 4(2l+2)(2l+4)} \right] = \sum_{R=0}^{\infty} \frac{(-1)^k (x/2)^{l+2k}}{n!\,\Gamma(l+k+1)} \tag{A.52}$$

If $l = 0, 1, 2, \ldots$, then $J_{-l}(x) = -1^l J_l(x)$. If $l \neq 0, 1, 2, \ldots$, then $J_l(x)$ and $J_{-l}(x)$ are linearly independent. In this case, $J_l(x)$ is bounded at $x = 0$, while $J_{-l}(x)$ is the unbounded Bessel function of the second kind. $N_l(x)$ (also called *Neumann functions*) are defined by

$$N_l(x) = \frac{J_l(x)\cos(l\pi) - J_{-l}(x)}{\sin(l\pi)} \qquad (l \neq 0, 1, 2, \ldots) \tag{A.53}$$

These functions are unbounded at $x = 0$. The general solution of Eq. (A.51) is

$$\begin{cases} y(x) = AJ_l(x) + BJ_{-l}(x) & l \neq 0, 1, 2, \ldots \\ y(x) = AJ_l(x) + BN_l(x) & \text{all } l \end{cases} \tag{A.54}$$

where A and B are arbitrary constants. Spherical Bessel functions are related to Bessel functions according to

$$j_l(x) = \sqrt{\frac{\pi}{2x}} J_{l+1/2}(x) \tag{A.55}$$

Also, the Neumann spherical functions are related to the Neumann function $N_l(x)$ by

$$n_l(x) = \sqrt{\frac{\pi}{2x}} N_{l+1/2}(x) \tag{A.56}$$

The functions $j_l(x)$ and $n_l(x)$ are given explicitly as

$$j_l(x) = (-x)^l \left(\frac{1}{x} \frac{d}{dx} \right)^l \left(\frac{\sin x}{x} \right) \tag{A.57}$$

$$n_l(x) = -(-x)^l \left(\frac{1}{x} \frac{d}{dx} \right)^l \left(\frac{\cos x}{x} \right) \tag{A.58}$$

The first few $j_l(x)$ and $n_l(x)$ are given below:

$$j_0(x) = \frac{\sin x}{x} \qquad\qquad\qquad n_0(x) = -\frac{\cos x}{x}$$

$$j_1(x) = \frac{\sin x}{x^2} - \frac{\cos x}{x} \qquad\qquad n_1(x) = -\frac{\cos x}{x^2} - \frac{\sin x}{x}$$

$$j_2(x) = \left(\frac{3}{x^3} - \frac{1}{x} \right) \sin x - \frac{3}{x^2} \cos x \qquad n_2(x) = -\left(\frac{3}{x^3} - \frac{1}{x} \right) \cos x - \frac{3}{x^2} \sin x$$

The asymptotic behavior of the $j_l(x)$ and $n_l(x)$ as $x \to \infty$ and $x \to 0$ is given by

$$\begin{cases} j_l(x)_{x \to 0} \to \dfrac{x^l}{(2l+1)!!} \\ \\ n_l(x)_{x \to 0} \to -\dfrac{(2l-1)!!}{x^{l+1}} \end{cases} \tag{A.59}$$

$$\begin{cases} j_l(x)_{x \to \infty} \to \dfrac{1}{x} \sin\left(x - \dfrac{\pi l}{2} \right) \\ \\ n_l(x)_{x \to \infty} \to -\dfrac{1}{x} \cos\left(x - \dfrac{\pi l}{2} \right) \end{cases} \tag{A.60}$$

where $(2l + 1)!! = 1 \cdot 3 \cdot 5 \cdots (2l - 1)(2l + 1)$.

Index